DATABASE PROCESSING

EDITION

DATABASE PROCESSING
Fundamentals, Design, and Implementation

David M. Kroenke

Prentice-Hall International, Inc.

© 1995, 1992, 1988, 1983, and 1977 by Prentice-Hall, Inc.
A Simon & Schuster Company
Englewood Cliffs, New Jersey 07632

Printed in the United States of America
10   9   8   7   6   5   4   3   2   1

ISBN 0-13-320128-7

Prentice-Hall International (UK) Limited, *London*
Prentice-Hall of Australia Pty. Limited, *Sydney*
Prentice-Hall Canada Inc., *Toronto*
Prentice-Hall Hispanoamericana, S.A., *Mexico*
Prentice-Hall of India Private Limited, *New Delhi*
Prentice-Hall of Japan, Inc., *Tokyo*
Simon & Schuster Asia Pte. Ltd., *Singapore*
Editora Prentice-Hall do Brasil, Ltda., *Rio de Janeiro*
Prentice-Hall, Inc., *Englewood Cliffs, New Jersey*

Contents

Chapter **6**: Database Design Using
Entity-Relationship Models 157

Chapter **7**: Database Design with
Semantic Object Models 182

Chapter **8**: Database Application Design 209

PART

Database Implementation with the
Relational Model 241

Chapter **9**: Foundations of Relational Implementation 243

PART

Database Implementation with Hierarchical and Network Data Models 371

Administration 445

PART

Chapter 15: Data Administration and Database Administration 447

Distributed Processing 479

PART

Chapter 16: Client Server and Related Applications 481

Preface

The years since the fourth edition of this text was published have been exciting ones in the database community. Three important trends have emerged that are making database products more powerful and database technology more accessible.

First, during this time, personal computer DBMS products have become more powerful and easier to use, and their price has decreased substantially. Products such as Microsoft's Access and Borland's Paradox for Windows not only provide the power of a true relational DBMS on a PC, but also include facilities for developing GUI-based forms, reports, and menus. In addition, these products include languages that take the first steps toward object-oriented programming for the business-oriented person. All of this capability is provided to the user for about $100, one-fifth the price of the personal DBMS products that were for sale when the fourth edition of the text was published.

Second, new modeling methodologies and tools, especially those based on object-oriented thinking, have become available. Two studies in the past year have shown semantic object modeling to be far superior to older techniques, such as the entity-relationship approach. A controlled study done at the University of North Texas[1] compared entity-relationship modeling (using IEF™) with semantic object modeling (with SALSA™) and found that the subjects using semantic object modeling were able to create better models, faster, and with greater satisfaction than subjects using entity-relationship modeling. A second study performed at Auburn University[2] found that students who had no prior database knowledge or experience could, after three hours of instruction, successfully use semantic object modeling and the SALSA tool. In fact, these students were able to outperform, as measured in quality, speed, and satisfaction, graduates of a 45-hour database class who were using more traditional technologies.

Semantic objects make database modeling more understandable to the student and enable students to be far more productive. Using this approach and SALSA, I

---

[1] Lee Pelley, "Comparing Semantic Object Modeling Using SALSA with Entity-Relationship Modeling Using IEF," University of North Texas Information Sciences Research Center, 1993.

[2] Tom Marshall, "Using SALSA and the Semantic Object Model," Auburn University Report, 1993.

have been able to raise substantially the level of discourse of modeling topics in my introductory database course.

In light of this trend, the coverage of semantic object modeling has been improved in this edition. Moreover, an arrangement has been made with Wall Data to include the SALSA data modeling tool with every copy of this text, at no additional charge to the student. See the SALSA discussion that follows this preface for more information.

The trend toward object-oriented modeling will not, of course, become evident overnight. Students will still find many companies that continue to use E-R modeling, especially as part of corporate-standard CASE tools. Consequently, the more traditional materials still need to be taught. Thus, this edition maintains extensive coverage of the E-R model in both Chapters 3 and 6.

The third important trend in the past several years has been the emergence of client server processing in general and client server database processing in particular. For many reasons, companies have begun to download and even offload databases from the enterprise mainframe to a server database. This has been done both to gain better economies of scale due to downsizing and to give the users better access to (often replicated) database data. In light of this trend, the client server topic has been given increased attention in Chapter 16 of this edition.

OUTLINE OF TEXT

This text is divided into seven parts. Part I concerns fundamental concepts. Chapter 1 introduces database processing and discusses its nature, advantages, disadvantages, and history. It presents examples of database applications at various scales of use. Chapter 2 discusses the components and functions of database applications. This chapter is important not only because it shows the student what we have to work with, but also because it describes, in broad scope, the relationships of users, databases, and database applications.

Part II addresses database modeling. Chapter 3 presents a brief overview of the database development process. Then it describes the entity-relationship model and applies that model to two examples. Chapter 4 continues data modeling with a description of the semantic object model and an illustration of its use. Chapter 4 is in close agreement with the symbols and terminology used by the SALSA product, and it should be very easy for students to use that tool in conjunction with this chapter.

Part III discusses and illustrates database design. Chapter 5 formally introduces the relational model and explains normalization theory. This text uses the relational model in two ways. In Chapter 5, we consider this model as a design tool. We use it to express logical (or DBMS-independent) designs. Later, in Chapters 11 and 12, we consider the implementation of databases using DBMS products based on the relational model.

Chapters 6 and 7 apply the concepts from Chapters 4, 5, and 6 to teach students how to perform database design. Chapter 6 shows how to transform data models expressed in terms of the entity-relationship model into relational DBMS-independent database designs. Chapter 7 then illustrates the transformation of semantic object models into similar designs. Chapter 8 concludes the design part with a discussion of database application design. Menu, form, and report design are discussed in the context of semantic objects.

The next two parts consider database implementation. Part IV describes and illustrates database implementation using the relational model. Chapter 9 presents an overview of the role of the relational model in database implementation and presents important relational algebra commands. Chapter 10 presents SQL. These two chapters set the stage for Chapters 11 and 12.

Chapter 11 shows the implementation of a personal computer database and applications using Microsoft Access. This presents a small-scale case project that can be readily assimilated by the student. Chapter 12 then illustrates the implementation of a larger, enterprise-oriented database using DB2. This particular DBMS was chosen for two reasons. First, as a mainframe DBMS, it raises important implementation issues that microcomputer DBMS products do not raise. Second, DB2 is popular and students are likely to encounter it in their careers.

Nonrelational implementation is considered in Part V. Chapter 13 describes the nature and characteristics of transaction processing and develops an example of a transaction-oriented database design that is then implemented using DL/I—a hierarchical data model that has seen wide use in industry as the basis of IMS/DB. Chapter 14 presents the network model and defines the fundamental concepts of the CODASYL DBTG model.

Although these topics may seem too dated to be included in a database text in 1995, they are still important for some audiences. The graduates of many programs go on to work in MIS departments that have legacy systems using both DL/I and DBMS products based on the CODASYL model. This material is important for those students.

Data and database administration are the subjects discussed in Part VI, which consists of only Chapter 15. Data administration is defined as an organization-wide function, whereas database administration is defined as specific to the management of a particular database and its applications. The discussion of database administration includes the management of concurrent processing, security, and backup and recovery.

Part VII, the last part of this text, addresses client server and distributed processing. Chapter 16 presents distributed application processing and describes the fundamentals of resource sharing and client server architectures on local area networks. Chapter 17 concludes the text with a discussion of the major issues in true distributed database processing. Chapter 16 is pragmatic and concerns what is being done today. Chapter 17 is theoretical and concerns issues that need to be solved for the future.

ACKNOWLEDGMENTS

I wish to thank P. J. Boardman, my editor, who has been the sponsor of this text over a very rocky period for college publishing. I appreciate P. J.'s support and clear and honest direction during this period. I'd also like to thank the reviewers of this text:

Ahmed Zaki, *College of William and Mary*
Douglas Bock, *Southern Illinois University at Edwardsville*
Barbara Beccue, *Illinois State University*

Martha Myers, *Kennesaw State College*
Mike Johnson, *Microsoft*

My sincere thanks to the Wall Data Corporation, especially Jim Simpson, CEO, and John Wall, executive vice president, for their willingness to provide the readers of this text with a free copy of SALSA. To protect this agreement, please note that the license agreement of this copy stipulates that it can only be used by the purchaser of this text and only for educational purposes. See the SALSA discussion that follows for information about purchasing a license to use this software for other purposes.

Finally, I would like to thank all of the developers of SALSA, with whom I have spent many enjoyable hours. I am especially grateful to Don Gray, Chris Olds, Lee Eggebrotten, Matt Gordon, Manooch Mehr, Cathy Stanford, Kenji Kawai, Danny Rosenthal, Julia Cai, and Catherine Weatbrook.

D.M.K.

Using SALSA™

Database Processing, fifth edition, contains a copy of a schema generation tool named SALSA.[3] You can use SALSA to develop and validate data models using semantic objects (see Chapters 4 and 7) and to generate schemas for the following DBMS products: Microsoft Access, Versions 1.0 and 1.1; Borland's Paradox for Windows, Version 4.5; and those that use standard SQL schema definition as expressed in the 92-ANSI SQL language syntax.

SALSA is a complete Windows 3.1 product, comparable to any commercial schema generation product. SALSA is owned and licensed by the Wall Data Corporation. Wall Data has most generously produced this copy at its own expense and made it available to Prentice Hall at no charge. Wall Data grants you, the purchaser of this text, the right to use this product for educational purposes only. See the license agreement in the SALSA help text for more information. To protect the publisher's agreement with Wall Data, please respect this license agreement. If you wish to use SALSA for any commercial purpose, contact Wall Data at (206) 442-1460.

SYSTEM REQUIREMENTS

SALSA requires a personal computer running Windows 3.1. Although Wall Data states that the minimum system requirements for SALSA is a 386 personal computer with 8 megabytes of memory of RAM, I think SALSA can be run successfully on a 386 with 4 megabytes.

SALSA does not require a mouse, but it is much easier and more fun to run if you have one. Also, a color monitor is not necessary, but SALSA is color-enhanced (meaning that it does make use of color) and your task will be easier if you have a color monitor.

---

[3]   SALSA is a trademark of the Wall Data Corporation. For brevity, the ™ will be omitted in this discussion.

USING SALSA

SALSA requires 3 megabytes of available disk storage. To install it, first start Windows 3.1. Then insert the SALSA disk in the a: drive, and from the Program Manager, Select File, Run. Type a:\setup in the dialog box and click OK. SALSA will install itself on your computer and create a SALSA group program window.

The best way to gain a quick introduction to SALSA is to click the question mark icon labeled *Try This!* When you do this, a program will start SALSA and bring up a set of intructions in a separate window. If you follow these instructions, you will be introduced to the basic SALSA modeling procedures. For more instruction, open the help and select tutorials. These will give you a more in-depth introduction to SALSA.

The SALSA interface is very similar to the symbols and nomenclature used in this text. In particular, if you read Chapter 4, you should be able to use SALSA without problem. There is, however, considerably more functionality in SALSA than is covered in this text. See the SALSA tutorials for more information.

DATABASE PROCESSING

Introduction

Part I provides a broad overview of the subject of database processing. By way of introduction, Chapter 1 describes three applications that typify the wide range of databases in use today, as well as the benefits and evolution of database technology. Chapter 2 introduces the components of a database system and of the DBMS (a program that creates and processes the database). Chapter 2 also presents an overview of the development of database applications.

The goal of these two chapters is to explain the purposes of databases and database applications and to introduce important technology. That is, Part I sets the stage for the discussion of data modeling that begins in Chapter 3.

INTRODUCTION TO DATABASE PROCESSING

The skills needed to design and develop a database and its related applications are in great demand, and many challenging, fulfilling, and well-paying positions are available. The reason is that almost every business person needs the benefits of database technology, but very few know how to use that technology and few want to learn. Hence, there is a high demand for people who can serve as liaisons between business users and database technology. The goal of this book is to teach you the knowledge and skills you will need to provide that service.

THREE DATABASE EXAMPLES

To understand the role of database technology in business, consider the following three examples.

Mary Richards House Painting

Mary Richards is a professional house painter who owns and operates a small company consisting of herself, another professional painter, and, when needed, part-time painters. Mary has been in business for ten years and has earned a reputation as a high-quality painter who works for a reasonable (neither cheap nor excessive) rate. Mary gets most of her work through repeat business from customers who hire her to paint their houses and also from their word-of-mouth referrals. In addition, Mary gets some work from building contractors and professional interior designers.

Customers remember Mary far better than she remembers them. Indeed, sometimes she is embarrassed when a customer calls and says something like, "Hi Mary, this is John Maples. You painted my house three years ago." Mary knows she is supposed to remember the caller and the work she did for him, but since she paints more than fifty houses a year, it usually is difficult for her to do so. This situation becomes worse when the customer says something like, "My neighbor liked the job you did on our house and would like something similar done to her house."

In order to help her memory and to keep better track of her business records, Mary had a consultant develop a database and database application that she uses on her personal computer. The database stores records regarding customers, jobs, and sources, in the form of tables, as shown in the example in Figure 1-1.

It is the job of a program called a database management system (DBMS) to store and retrieve the data in these tables. Unfortunately, when such data is in the form of tables, it is not very useful to Mary. Rather, she would like to know how customers

FIGURE 1-1

Example Tables of Data

Microsoft Access — Example Tables of Data

Table: CUSTOMER

CUSTOMER_ID	CustomerName	Area	Number	Street	City	State	Zip	SOURCE_ID
1	Wu, Jason	303	555-0089	123 E. Elm	Denver	CO	80210	3
2	Maples, Marilyn	303	773-0333	2518 S. Link Lane	Boulder	CO	80210	4
3	Jackson, Chris	303	774-9988	4700 Lafayette St	Denver	CO	80220	3

Table: JOB

JOB_ID	JobDate	Description	AmountBilled	AmountPaid	CUSTOMER_ID
1	3/3/93	Paint Exterior in white	$1,750.00	$1,750.00	1
2	7/7/93	Paint dining room & kitchen	$778.00	$778.00	1
3	10/15/93	Prep and paint upstairs baths	$550.00	$550.00	1
4	4/3/93	Prep & paint exterior	$2,750.00	$1,875.00	2
5	7/7/93	Paint garage	$550.00	$550.00	3

Record: 1

Table: SOURCE

SOURCE_ID	Name	AreaCode	Number
2	Valley Designs	303	549-8876
3	Aspen Construction	303	776-8899
4	Mary Engers Design	303	767-7783

Record: 1

Datasheet View

and jobs and referrals relate to one another, for example, what jobs she has done for a particular customer or what customers have been referred by a particular person.

To provide this capability, Mary's consultant created a database application that processes data entry forms and produces reports. Consider the example in Figure 1-2. Here, Mary keys into the form a customer's name or telephone number. The database application then retrieves the appropriate data from the DBMS and displays it in a format like that shown in Figure 1-3. From this Mary can determine which jobs she has done for that customer.

Consider again the data in Figure 1-1, and notice that the rows in the tables cross-reference and are linked to one another. Each JOB contains the Customer_ID of the CUSTOMER who purchased that JOB, and each CUSTOMER contains the Source_ID of the person who referred that customer. These references are used to produce the forms like that shown in Figure 1-3. Other uses of the database include recording bid estimates, tracking referral sources, and producing mailing labels for the direct sales literature that Mary sends out from time to time.

As you can imagine, Mary is unlikely to know how to design the tables in Figure

FIGURE 1-2

Form for Finding a Customer

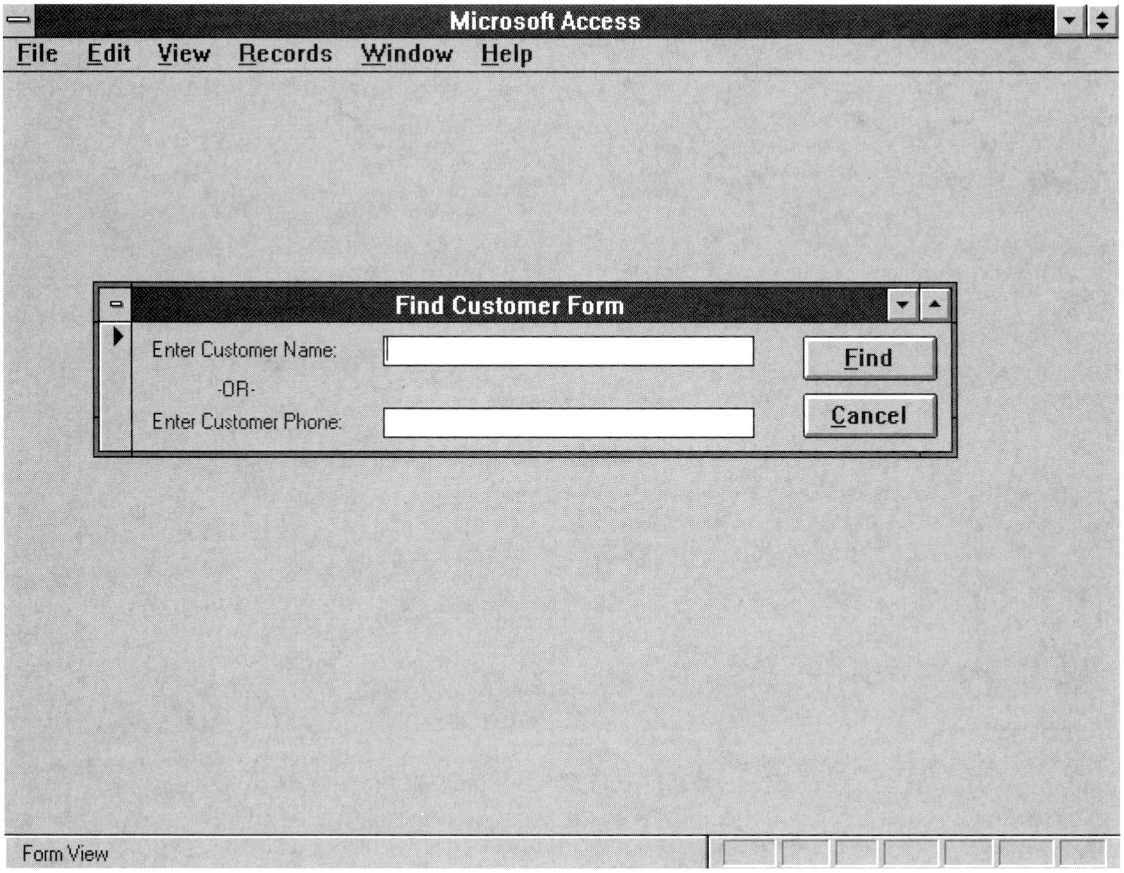

1-1, how to use a DBMS to create those tables, and how to develop the application to create the form in Figure 1-3. But by the time you have finished this course, you should know how to use database technology to combine the data in the tables in Figures 1-1 to create the form in Figure 1-3. You should also know how to design and manipulate tables to create forms and reports of far greater complexity.

■ SeaView Yacht Sales

Databases can be considerably more complicated than the one that Mary Richards uses. Consider, for example, the case of SeaView Yacht Sales. SeaView sells and leases medium-to-large sailboats. It has two full-time partners, four salespeople, and an office administrator. SeaView maintains its own marina where it keeps most of the boats that it has for sale. Its salespeople also cooperate with personnel from other brokerages to sell boats that are not part of its own inventory.

SeaView maintains a database to keep track of its customers and their purchasing interests, its boats for sale, and other data of interest to the salespeople. The

FIGURE 1-3

Example Data Entry Form for Mary Richards House Painting

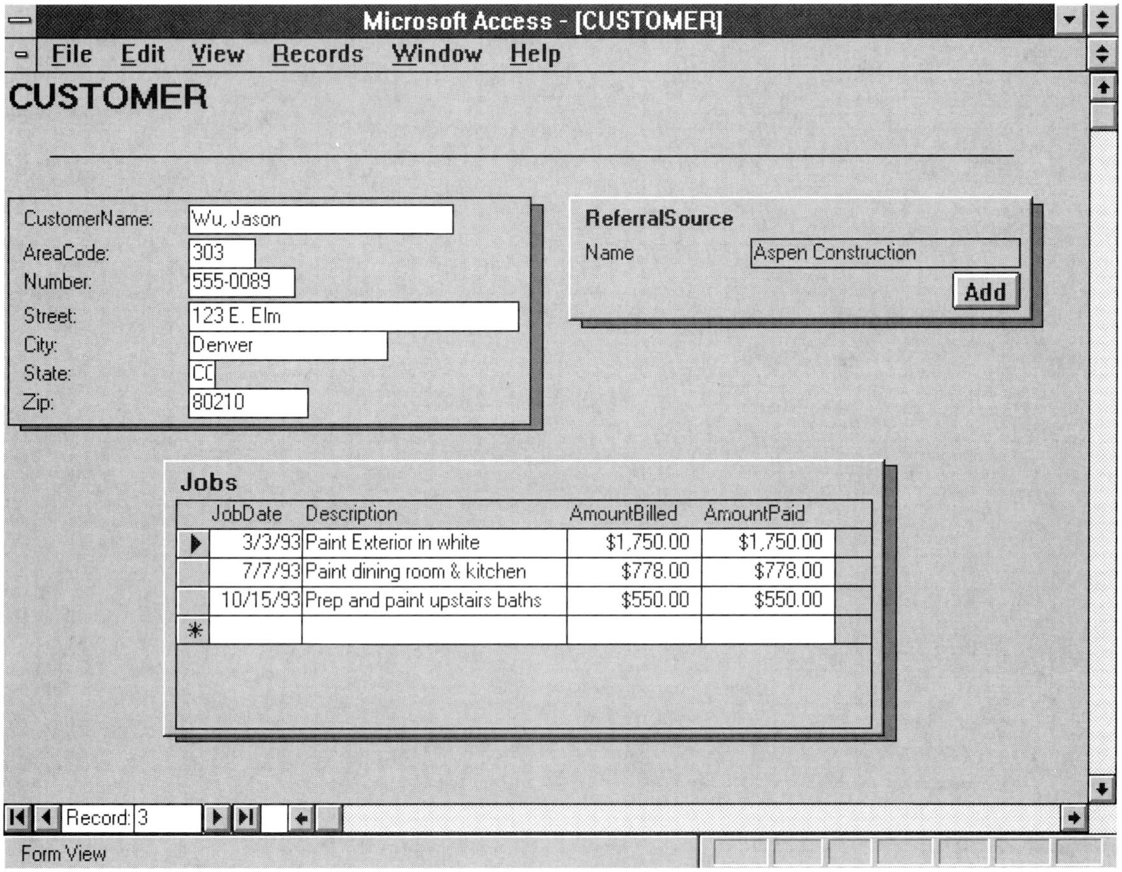

database is shared by all of the personnel in the office and is located on a local area network server (see Figure 1-4).

Figure 1-5 shows two forms that SeaView's salespeople use. Part (a) shows data concerning a particular type of sailboat, including those customers who are interested in purchasing that type and the boats of that type that are for sale. Part (b) contains data on a particular customer, including the types of boats that that person might want to buy. It also lists the boats (if any) that that customer owns.

The database required to support the forms shown in Figure 1-5 is more complicated than that used by Mary Richards, as it contains seven different tables, as shown in Figure 1-6, which are used to create these forms. These tables reference one another in the same way that the tables in Figure 1-1 do. Each row in the CUSTOMER table, for example, contains the number of the SALESPERSON assigned to that CUSTOMER. In fact, the table named CUSTOMER_BOAT_TYPE_INT contains only references and is used to keep track of which customers are interested in which types of boat designs. The database application obtains data from such tables and combines it to create the forms and reports that SeaView needs.

■ State Licensing and Vehicle Registration Bureau

Now consider an even larger application of database technology. This example is of a state licensing and auto registration bureau. It has fifty-two centers that conduct drivers' tests and issue and renew drivers' licenses and also thirty-seven offices that sell vehicle registrations.

The personnel in these offices access a database to perform their jobs. Before issuing or renewing a driver's license, that person's records in the database are checked for traffic violations, accidents, or arrests. This data is used to determine whether the license can be renewed and, if so, whether it should carry any limita-

FIGURE 1-4

Local Area Network with Database Server
Used by SeaView Yacht Sales

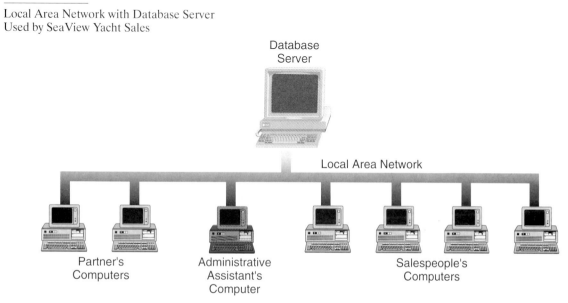

FIGURE 1-5

Two Forms Used by SeaView Yacht Sales:
(a) Boat Type Form and (b) Customer Form

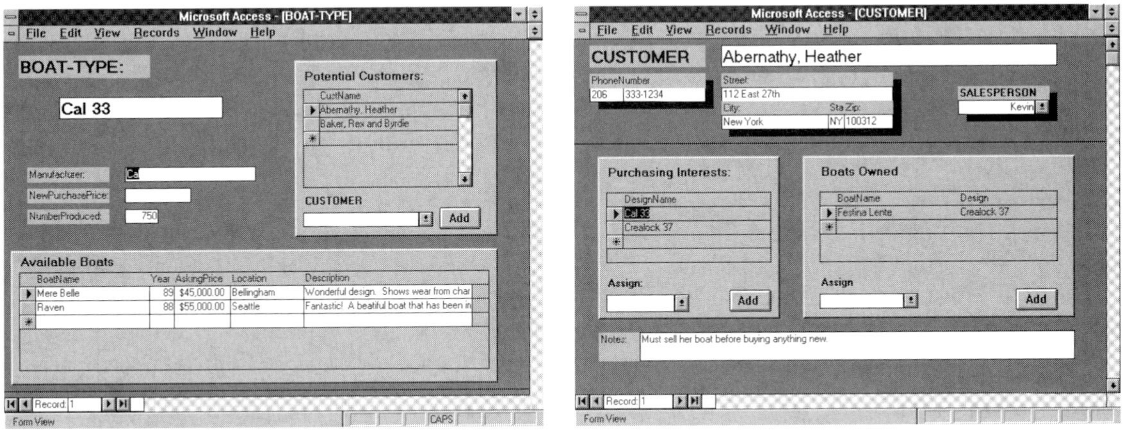

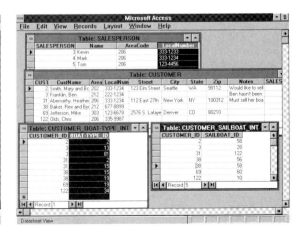

tions. Similarly, personnel in the auto registration department access the database to determine whether an auto has been registered before and, if so, to whom and whether there are any outstanding matters that should prohibit the registration.

This database has hundreds of users, including not only the license and registration personnel but also the people in the state department of revenue and in law enforcement. Not surprisingly, the database is large and complex, with more than forty different tables of data, several of which contain hundreds of thousands of rows of data.

■ Comparison of Database Applications

These three examples represent a sampling of the uses of database technology. Hundreds of thousands of databases are like the one used by Mary Richards House

FIGURE 1-6

Tables in the SeaView Database

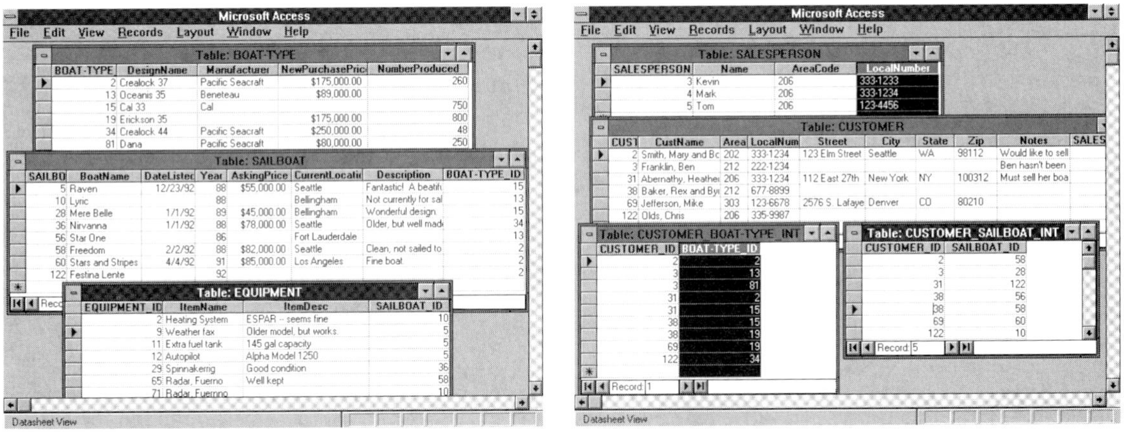

FIGURE 1-7

Characteristics of Different Types of Databases

Type	Example	Typical Number of Users	Typical Size of Database
Personal	Mary Richards House Painting	1	<10 Megabytes
Work Group	SeaView Yacht Sales	<25	<100 Megabytes
Organizational	Licensing and Registration	Hundreds	>1 Trillion Bytes

Painting, single-user databases with a relatively small amount of data—say less than ten megabytes. The forms and reports for these are generally simple and straightforward.

Other databases are like the one used by SeaView; they have more than one user but usually fewer than twenty or thirty users all together. They contain a moderate amount of data, say, fifty or a hundred megabytes. The forms and reports need to be complex enough to support several different business functions.

The largest databases are like those in the auto registration case, which have hundreds of users and trillions of bytes of data. Many different applications are in use, each application having its own forms and reports. The characteristics of these types of databases are summarized in Figure 1-7.

When you finish this book, you should be able to design and create a database and database application like those used by Mary Richards and SeaView. You will probably not be able to create one as large and complicated as the vehicle registration database, but you will be able to serve as an effective member of a team that does design and create such a database.

THE RELATIONSHIP OF APPLICATION PROGRAMS AND THE DBMS

All of the preceding examples and, indeed, all database applications have the general structure shown in Figure 1-8: The user interacts with a database application, which in turn interfaces with the DBMS, which accesses the database data.

At one time, the boundary between the application program and the DBMS was clearly defined. Applications were written in third-generation languages like COBOL, and those applications called on the DBMS for data management services. In fact, this still is done, most frequently on large mainframe databases.

The features and functions of many DBMS products, however, have grown to the point that today, the DBMS itself can process sizable portions of the application. For example, most DBMS products contain report writers and form generators that can be integrated into an application. This fact is important to us for two reasons.

FIGURE 1-8

Relationship Between a Database Application and a DBMS

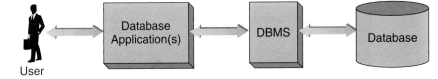

First, although the bulk of this text considers the design and development of databases, we will often refer to the design and development of the database application. After all, no user wants just a database. Instead, users want forms, reports, and queries that are based on their data. They could not care less about the database itself.

Second, from time to time you will note an overlap between the material discussed in this class and that in your systems development class, because developing effective database applications requires many of the skills that you have learned or will learn in your systems development class. Likewise, most systems development classes today also include the design of databases. The difference between the two courses is one of emphasis. Here, our emphasis is on the design and construction of the database. In a systems class, the emphasis is on the development of information systems—most of which use database technology.

File-processing Systems

The best way to understand the general nature and characteristics of databases today is to look at the characteristics of systems that predated the use of database technology. These systems reveal the problems that database technology has solved.

The first business information systems stored groups of records in separate files and were called **file-processing systems.** Figure 1-9, for example, depicts two file-

FIGURE 1-9

Two File-processing Systems

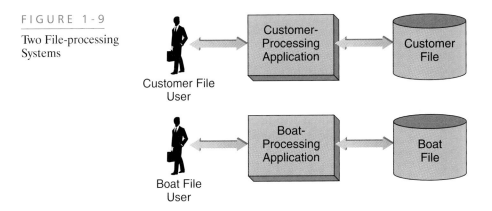

processing systems that SeaView Yachts could use. One system processes CUS-TOMER data, and the other one processes BOAT data.

Although file-processing systems are a great improvement over manual record-keeping systems, they have important limitations:

* Data is separated and isolated.
* Data is often duplicated.
* Application programs are dependent on file formats.
* Files are often incompatible with one another.
* It is difficult to represent data in the way that the users view it.

Separated and Isolated Data

The salespeople at SeaView need to relate their customers to the boats that they are interested in buying. For the system in Figure 1-9, the data needs to be extracted somehow from CUSTOMER and BOAT files and combined into a single file. With file processing, this is difficult. First, systems analysts and computer programmers must determine which parts of each of the files are needed; then they must decide how the files are related to one another; and finally they must coordinate the processing of the files so that the correct data is extracted. Coordinating two files is difficult enough, but imagine the task of coordinating ten or more of them!

Data Duplication

In the SeaView example, a customer's name, address, and other data may be stored many times. That is, the data is stored once for CUSTOMER and again for each BOAT that a CUSTOMER owns. Although this duplicate data wastes file space, that is not the most serious problem; rather, the most serious problem with duplicated data concerns **data integrity**.

A collection of data has integrity if the data are logically consistent, that is, if they mesh together logically. Poor data integrity can often be seen in file-processing systems. For example, if a customer changes his or her name or address, then all those files containing that data must be updated, but the danger is that all of the files might *not* be updated, causing discrepancies among them.

Data integrity problems are serious. If data items differ, they will produce inconsistent results. For example, if a report from one application disagrees with a report from another application, who will be able to tell which one is correct? When results are inconsistent, the credibility of the stored data, and even the MIS function itself, comes into question.

Application Program Dependency

With file processing, application programs depend on the file formats. Usually in file-processing systems the physical formats of files and records are part of the application code. In COBOL, for example, file formats are written in the DATA DIVISION. The problem with this arrangement is that when changes are made in the file formats, the application programs also must be changed.

For example, if the customer record is modified to expand the zip-code field from five to nine digits, all programs using that customer record must be modified, even if they do not use the zip-code field. Because there might be twenty programs that process the customer file, such a change means that a programmer has to identify all the affected programs, modify them, and then retest them—all time-consuming and error-prone tasks. Also, requiring programmers to modify programs that do not use the field whose format has changed is a waste of money.

Incompatible Files

One of the consequences of program data dependency is that file formats depend on the language or product used to generate them. Thus the format of a file processed by a COBOL program is different from the format of a file processed by a BASIC program, which is different still from the format of a file processed by a C program.

As a result, files cannot be readily combined or compared. Suppose, for example, FILE-A contains CUSTOMER data that includes CustomerNumber and FILE-B contains BOAT data that also includes CustomerNumber. Suppose an application requires that we combine records that have matching Customers. If FILE-A were processed by a COBOL program and FILE-B were processed by a C program, we would need to convert both files to a common structure before we could combine the records. This would be time-consuming and, sometimes, difficult. Such problems grow worse as the number of files to be combined increases.

The Difficulty of Representing Data the Way the Users View It

It is difficult to represent file-processing data in a form that seems natural to users. Users want to see CUSTOMER data in a format like that in Figure 1-5(b). But in order to show the data in this way, several different files need to be extracted, combined, and presented together. This difficulty arises because with file processing, relationships among records are not readily represented or processed. Since a file-processing system cannot quickly determine which CUSTOMERs want to purchase which BOATs, producing a form showing CUSTOMER preferences is quite difficult.

Database-processing Systems

Database technology was developed largely to overcome the limitations of file-processing systems. To understand how, compare the file-processing system in Figure 1-9 with the database system in Figure 1-8. File-processing programs directly access files of stored data. In contrast, database-processing programs call the DBMS to access the stored data. This difference is significant because it makes the application-programming job easier; that is, application programmers do not have to be concerned with the ways in which data is physically stored. Rather, they are free to concentrate on matters important to the user instead of matters important to the computer system.

■ Integrated Data

In a database system, all the application data is stored in a single facility called the **database**. An application program can ask the DBMS to access customer data or sales data or both. If both are needed, the application programmer specifies only how the data is to be combined, and the DBMS performs the necessary operations to do it. Thus the programmer is not responsible for writing programs to coordinate the files, as must be done for the system in Figure 1-9.

■ Less Duplication of Data

With database processing, the duplication of data is minimal. For example, in Sea-View's database, the customer's number, name, and address are stored only once. Whenever this data is needed, the DBMS can retrieve it, and when it is modified, only one update is necessary. Because data is stored in only one place, data integrity problems are less common—there is less opportunity for discrepancies among multiple copies of the same data item.

■ Program/Data Independence

Database processing reduces the dependency of programs on file formats. All record formats are stored in the database itself (along with the data), and they are accessed by the DBMS, not by application programs. Unlike file-processing programs, database application programs need not include the format of all the files and records they process. Instead, application programs must contain only a definition (the length and data type) of each of the data items they need from the database. The DBMS maps the data items into records and handles other similar transformations, an operation called **program/data independence**.

Program/data independence minimizes the impact of data format changes on application programs. Format changes are input to the DBMS, which in turn updates the data it maintains concerning the structure of the database. For the most part, application programs are unaware that the format has changed. This also means that whenever data items are added, changed, or deleted from the database, only those programs that use these particular data items have to be modified. For applications consisting of dozens of programs, this can be a considerable savings of time.

■ Easier Representation of the Users' View of Data

As you will discover throughout this text, database technology makes it possible to represent, in a straightforward fashion, the objects found in the user's world. The forms in Figure 1-5 can readily be produced from a database because the relationships among the records of data are stored in it.

DEFINITION OF A DATABASE

The term *database* suffers from many different interpretations. It has been used to refer to everything from a collection of index cards to the volumes and volumes of data that a government collects about its citizens. In this text, we use this term with a specific meaning: *A database is a self-describing collection of integrated records.* It is important to understand each part of this definition.

■ A Database Is Self-describing

A database is self-describing: It contains, in addition to the user's source data, a description of its own structure. This description is called a **data dictionary** (or **data directory**, or **metadata**). It is the data dictionary that makes program/data independence possible.

In this sense, a database is similar to a library, which is a self-describing collection of books. In addition to the books, the library contains a card catalog describing them. In the same way, the data dictionary (which is part of the database, just as the card catalog is part of the library) describes the data contained in the database.

Why is this self-describing characteristic of a database so important? First, it promotes program/data independence. That is, it makes it possible to determine the structure and content of the database by examining the database itself. We do not need to guess what the database contains, nor do we need to maintain external documentation of the file and record formats (as is done in file-processing systems).

Second, if we change the structure of the data in the database (such as adding new data items to an existing record), we enter only that change in the data dictionary. Few, if any, programs will need to be changed. In most cases, only those programs that process the altered data items must be changed.

If you are familiar with COBOL, you know that the structure of the data for file-processing programs is described in the DATA DIVISION. Compared with database processing, this practice is inefficient. It is like putting a copy of your library's card catalog in the home or office of every library user. Then when the library buys a new book, the card catalog has to be changed in dozens or hundreds of places!

You may have learned in your COBOL or other programming courses that it is good practice to store the files' structure in a copy library and extract this structure from the library when the files are compiled. A similar strategy is used with databases. The structure of the database is extracted from the database and loaded into the program before the program is compiled.

■ A Database Is a Collection of Integrated Records

The standard hierarchy of data is as follows: Bits are aggregated into bytes or characters; characters are aggregated into fields; fields are aggregated into records; and records are aggregated into files (see Figure 1-10[a]). It is tempting to follow the pattern of that statement and say that files are aggregated into databases. Although this statement is true, it does not go far enough.

A database includes **files** of user data and more. As we mentioned earlier, a database contains a description of itself in **metadata**. In addition, a database includes **indexes** that are used to represent relationships among the data and also to improve the performance of database applications. Finally, the database often contains data about the applications that use the database. The structure of a data entry form, or a report, is sometimes part of the database. This last category of data we

FIGURE 1-10

Hierarchy of Data Elements: (a) Hierarchy of Data Elements in File Processing
and (b) Hierarchy of Data Elements in Database Processing

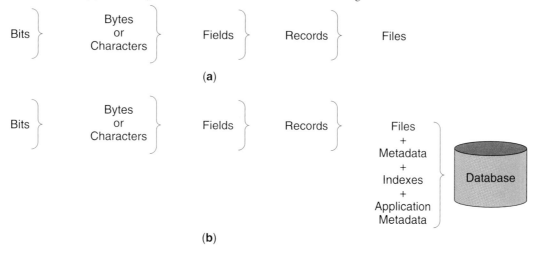

(a)

(b)

call **application metadata**. Thus a database contains the four types of data shown in
Figure 1-10(b): files of user data, metadata, indexes, and application metadata.

A Database Is a Model of a Model

A database is a model. It is tempting to say that a database is a model of reality or of
some portion of reality as it relates to a business. This, however, is not true. A database does not model reality or some portion thereof. Instead, a database is a model
of the *user's model*. For example, Mary Richards's database is a model of the way in
which Mary Richards views her business. As she sees it, her business has customers,
jobs, and referrals. Her database, therefore, contains representations of facts concerning those entities. The names and addresses of customers, the dates and descriptions of her jobs, and the names of her referral sources all are measurements that
are important to her view of her business.

Databases vary in their level of detail. Some are simple and crude. A list of customers and the amounts they owe are an approximate representation of Mary's
mental model. A more detailed representation includes jobs, referrals, and the trips
made for each job. And a very detailed representation contains the amount and type
of paint used on each job, the number of paintbrushes required, and the hours of
labor on specific job tasks such as taping, painting woodwork, painting walls,
cleanup, and the like.

The degree of detail that should be incorporated into a database depends on the
information desired. Clearly, the more information that is wanted, the more detail
the database must have. Deciding on the appropriate amount of detail is an important part of the job of designing a database. As you will discover, the principal criterion is the level of detail that exists in the minds of the users.

Businesses change. People come and go. Products are introduced and phased
out. Money is earned and spent. As these changes occur, the data that represents

the business also must be altered. If not, the data will become outdated and inaccurately represent the business.

Transactions are representations of events. When events take place, the transactions for the events must be processed against the database. To do this, someone (a data entry clerk, a salesperson, or a teller, for example) activates a transaction-processing program and enters the transaction data. The program then calls on the DBMS to alter the database. Transaction-processing programs usually produce displays or print responses such as order confirmations or receipts.

A SHORT HISTORY OF DATABASE PROCESSING

Database processing was originally used in major corporations and large organizations as the basis of large transaction-processing systems. An example is the licensing and vehicle registration example considered earlier. Later, as microcomputers gained popularity, database technology migrated to micros and was used for single-user, personal database applications like that described for Mary Richards. Next, as micros were connected together in work groups, database technology moved to the work-group setting, in client server applications. Finally, attempts are being made today to integrate all of these different databases into unified and consistent distributed databases.

■ The Organizational Context

The initial application of database technology was to resolve problems with the file-processing systems discussed earlier in this chapter. In the mid-1960s, large corporations were producing data at phenomenal rates in file-processing systems, but the data was becoming difficult to manage, and new systems were becoming increasingly difficult to develop. Furthermore, management wanted to be able to relate the data in one file system to that in another.

The limitations of file processing prevented the easy integration of data. Database technology, however, held out the promise of a solution to these problems, and so large companies began to develop organizational databases. Companies centralized their operational data, such as orders, inventory, and accounting data, in these databases. The applications were primarily organizationwide, transaction-processing systems.

At first, when the technology was new, database applications were difficult to develop, and there were many failures. Even those applications that were successful were slow and unreliable: The computer hardware could not handle the volume of transactions quickly; the developers had not yet discovered more efficient ways to store and retrieve data; and the programmers were still new at accessing databases, and sometimes their programs did not work correctly.

Companies found another disadvantage of database processing: vulnerability. If a file-processing system fails, only that particular application will be out of commission. But if the database fails, all of its dependent applications will be out of commission.

Gradually the situation improved. Hardware and software engineers learned how to build systems powerful enough to support many concurrent users and fast enough to keep up with the daily workload of transactions. New ways of controlling, protecting, and backing up the database were devised. Standard procedures for database processing evolved, and programmers learned how to write more efficient and more maintainable code. By the mid-1970s, databases could efficiently and reliably process organizational applications. With many of the early problems resolved, management turned its attention to finding new uses for this new huge pool of organizational data.

Managers knew that somehow all of that data could provide information for both tactical (short-term) and strategic (long-term) decision making. To do this, however, the users had to access the data themselves, as they could not be expected to wait weeks or months for programmers to "get the information out of the computer."

Unfortunately, most of the applications had to be carried out in procedural languages such as COBOL and PL/I, but the users did not have the time or resources to become professional programmers. Besides, they were interested only in getting the answers to their questions, not in learning COBOL or navigating through a database to extract just the right bytes of data. It seemed that users and computers were existing in two different worlds. And yet all that data was there waiting to be put to even more good uses, a situation that set the stage for the next major development in database processing: the relational model.

■ The Relational Model

In 1970, E. F. Codd published a landmark paper[1] in which he applied concepts from a branch of mathematics called relational algebra to the problem of storing large amounts of data. Codd's paper started a movement in the database community that in a few years led to the definition of the **relational database model**. This model is a particular way of structuring and processing a database, and we discuss it at length in Chapters 5 and 9 through 12.

BENEFITS OF THE RELATIONAL MODEL

The advantage of the relational model is that data is stored, at least conceptually, in a way that users can readily understand. Data is stored as tables, and relationships among rows of tables are visible in the data. This approach, unlike that of earlier database models, enables users to obtain information from databases without the assistance of MIS professionals.

Recall that databases store not only data but also the relationships among them. Consider, for example, the production of a student transcript. Figure 1-11 shows the basic data required to construct a student transcript: data regarding the students and data regarding the courses the students have completed. But to construct a transcript, we must have both the data and the relationships among the data values—in this case, the relationships between particular students and courses.

DBMS products vary in the way they represent such data relationships. Early DBMS products stored the relationships in systems data such as indexes, which

---

[1] E. F. Codd, "A Relational Model of Data for Large Shared Databanks," *Communications of the ACM*, June 1970, pp. 377–387.

effectively hid the relationships from anyone who did not have some knowledge of the data structures. Although programmers and other MIS professionals learned how to use these structures in order to navigate through the database, the typical end user did not know what they were and did not want to find out. Thus, users were dependent on information systems professionals to write programs to get their information. This always took time and often was frustrating.

The relational model changed this. One of the keystones of the relational model is storing relationships in user-visible data. In Figure 1-11 the relationship between students and courses is stored in the Student_ID field found in the COURSE record. We can retrieve a course record and, by examining its contents, determine which students took that course. We can also process the data in the other direction: Given a Student_ID number, a relational DBMS can determine which courses he or she has completed. The examples of data in Figures 1-1 and 1-6 also show the use of IDs to represent relationships among rows.

When using the relational model, the user must specify only which records he or she wants to process (for example, all the course records for student 100 or the names of all the students who completed course BD100). The DBMS will figure out how to navigate through the database.

Relational database management systems can be used for most applications, including the transaction processing of organizational databases. But one type of application has found the relational model to be particularly useful, namely, the decision-support system (DSS). Decision-support applications typically address unstructured problems and involve much ad hoc, or unpredictable, processing. As one executive put it, "I know I'm doing DSS when I don't know the second question to ask until I see the answer to the first question." DSS users usually are higher-level managers (or assistants to such people) who are willing and able to learn relational

FIGURE 1-11

Example of Relationships Stored in Data

Student_ID	StudentName	Phone
100	Jones, Mary	323-0098
200	Parks, Franklin	232-9987
300	Thomas, Martha	887-4484

Student Data

Course Number	Course Name	Semester	Grade	Student_ID
BD100	Intro MIS	F	A	100
BA402	Accting Seminar	S	C	200
BF315	Mgmt Principles	S	B	200
BD100	Intro MIS	F	C	300
BD200	Database	S	B	300
BA150	Intro to Accting	F	B	100
MA102	Intro Calculus	F	B	100
CS100	Intro Comp Sci	F	A	300

Course Data

DBMS tools to accomplish their goals. Because the products based on the relational model are generally easy to use, relational databases are often the heart of a DSS.

RESISTANCE TO THE RELATIONAL MODEL

Initially the relational model encountered a good deal of resistance. Relational database systems require more computer resources, and so at first they were much slower than the systems based on earlier database models. Although they were easier to use, the slow response time was often unacceptable. To some extent, relational DBMS products were impractical until the 1980s when faster computer hardware was developed and the price–performance ratio of computers fell dramatically.

The relational model also seemed foreign to many programmers, who were accustomed to writing programs in which they processed data one record at a time. But relational DBMS products process data most naturally an entire table at a time. Accordingly, programmers had to learn a new way to think about data processing.

Finally, relational systems are designed to enable a layperson to process a database with limited assistance from an MIS professional. Although there is no doubt that relational processing more closely resembles the user's world than do processing databases based on other models, relational DBMS products are still foreign to many users.

So even though the relational model had many advantages, it did not gain true popularity until computers became more powerful. In particular, as microcomputers entered the scene, more and more CPU cycles could be devoted to a single user. Such power was a boon to relational DBMS products and set the stage for the next major database development.

Microcomputer DBMS Products

In 1979, a small company called Ashton-Tate introduced a microcomputer product, dBase II (pronounced "d base two"), and called it a relational DBMS. In an exceedingly successful promotional tactic, Ashton-Tate distributed—nearly free of charge—more than 100,000 copies of its product to purchasers of the then-new Osborne microcomputers. Many of the people who bought these computers were pioneers in the microcomputer industry. They began to invent microcomputer applications using dBase, and the number of dBase applications grew quickly. As a result, Ashton-Tate became one of the first major corporations in the microcomputer industry. Later, Ashton-Tate was purchased by Borland, which now sells the dBase line of products.

The success of this product, however, confused and confounded the subject of database processing. The problem was this: According to the definition prevalent in the late 1970s, dBase II was neither a DBMS nor relational (though it was marketed as both). In fact, it was a programming language with generalized file-processing (not database-processing) capabilities. The systems that were developed with dBase II appeared much more like those in Figure 1-9 than the ones in Figure 1-8. The million or so users of dBase II thought they were using a relational DBMS, when in fact, they were not.

Thus the terms *database management system* and *relational database* were used loosely at the start of the microcomputer boom. Most of the people who were processing a microcomputer database were really managing files, and so they were not receiving the benefits of database processing, although they did not realize it. Today, the situation has changed as the microcomputer marketplace has become more mature and sophisticated. dBase III Plus is truly a *DBMS* (we define DBMS in the next chapter), and dBase IV is truly a *relational* DBMS.[2]

Although dBase did pioneer the application of database technology on microcomputers, at the same time, other vendors began to move their products from the mainframe to the microcomputer. Oracle, Focus, and Ingres are three examples of DBMS products that were ported down to microcomputers. They are truly DBMS programs, and most would agree that they are truly relational as well. In addition, other vendors developed new relational DBMS products especially for micros. Paradox, Revelation, MDBS, Helix, and a number of other products fall into this category.

One impact of the move of database technology to the micro was the dramatic improvement in DBMS user interfaces. Users of microcomputer systems are generally not MIS professionals, and they will not put up with the clumsy and awkward user interfaces common on mainframe DBMS products. Thus as DBMS products were devised for micros, user interfaces had to be simplified and made easier to use. This was possible because micro DBMS products operate on dedicated computers and because more computer power was available to process the user interface. Today, DBMS products provide rich and robust user interfaces using graphical user interfaces such as Microsoft Windows. Two such products are Microsoft's Access and Borland's Paradox for Windows.[3]

The combination of microcomputers, the relational model, and vastly improved user interfaces enabled database technology to move from an organizational context to a personal-computing context. When this occurred, the number of sites that used database technology exploded. In 1980 there were about ten thousand sites using DBMS products in the United States; today there are well over five million such sites!

■ Client Server Database Applications

In the middle to late 1980s, end users began to connect their separated microcomputers using a new type of computer communications capability called **local area networks (LANs)**. These networks enabled computers to send data to one another at previously unimaginable rates. The first applications of this technology shared peripherals, such as large-capacity fast disks, expensive printers and plotters, and facilitated intercomputer communication via electronic mail. In time, however, end users wanted to share their databases as well, which led to the development of multiuser database applications on local area networks.

---

[2]   To some extent, this confusion still exists: Some people who are processing separated files say (and think) that they are processing a database.

[3]   Microsoft Access™ is a trademark of the Microsoft Corporation. Paradox for Windows™ is a trademark of the Borland Coporation. For convenience, in this book, these products will be referred to simply as Access and Paradox for Windows.

The LAN-based multiuser architecture is considerably different from the multiuser architecture used on mainframe and minicomputer databases. With a mainframe or minicomputer, only one CPU is involved in database application processing, but with LAN systems, many CPUs can be simultaneously involved. Because this situation was both advantageous (greater performance) and more problematic (coordinating the actions of independent CPUs), it led to a new style of multiuser database processing called the **client server database architecture**.

This client server architecture is the basis for most work-group database processing today. Although minicomputers can be used in a work-group setting, this is seldom done—mainly for reasons of cost. Thus, the client server architecture has become quite important, and we address this architecture in detail in Chapter 16.

Distributed Database Processing

Organizational database applications address the problems of file processing and allow more integrated processing of organizational data. Personal and work-group database systems bring database technology even closer to the user by allowing him or her access to locally managed databases. **Distributed databases** combine these types of database processing by allowing personal, work-group, and organizational databases to be combined into integrated but distributed systems. As such, they offer even more flexible data access and processing but unfortunately pose many problems, as yet unsolved.

The essence of distributed databases is that all of the organization's data is spread over many computers—micros, LAN servers, and mainframes—that communicate with one another as they process the database. The goals of distributed database systems are to make it appear to each user that he or she is the only user of the organization's data and to provide the same consistency, accuracy, and timeliness that he or she would have if no one else were using the distributed database.

Among the more pressing problems with distributed databases are those of security and control. Enabling so many users to access the database (there can be hundreds of concurrent users) and controlling what they do to that distributed database are complicated tasks.

Coordinating and synchronizing the data can be difficult. If one user group downloads and updates part of the database and then transmits the changed data back to the mainframe, how does the system prevent, in the meantime, another user from attempting to use the version of the data it finds on the mainframe? Imagine this problem involving dozens of files and hundreds of users using scores of pieces of computer equipment.

In fact, as Chapters 16 and 17 point out, the concept of a distributed database actually blurs the definition of a database. Supposedly a database is a centralized, controlled collection of data and relationships. But if we fragment it and copy it onto many different computers, we have altered the original database concept.

Whereas the transitions from organizational to personal to work-group database processing were relatively easy, the difficulties facing the database designers and engineers of the distributed DBMS are monumental. Chapters 16 and 17 discuss what they are and the current attempts to overcome them.

OBJECT-ORIENTED DBMS (ODBMS)

In the late 1980s a new style of programming called *object-oriented programming* (OOP) began to be used, which has a substantially different orientation from that of traditional programming, as is explained in Chapter 4. In brief, the data structures processed with OOP are considerably more complex than those processed with traditional languages. These data structures also are difficult to store in existing relational DBMS products. As a consequence, a new category of DBMS products called *object-oriented database systems* is evolving to store and process OOP data structures.

For a variety of reasons, OOP is seldom used for business information systems. First, it is difficult to use and it is very expensive to develop OOP applications. Second, most organizations have millions or billions of bytes of data already organized in relational databases, and they are unwilling to bear the cost and risk required to convert those databases to an OODBMS format. Finally, most OODBMS have been developed to support engineering applications, and so they do not have features and functions that are appropriate or readily adaptable to business information applications.

Consequently, for the foreseeable future, OODBMS are likely to occupy a minor niche in commercial information systems applications. Although Chapter 4 does describe OOP and OODBMS in more detail, only a small portion of the material in this text addresses this technology. Instead, the bulk of the discussion concerns technologies that you are likely to use in the first five years of your career.

■ Warning: Spreadsheets Are NOT Databases

Before concluding this chapter, it is important to clear up a misconception about the term *database*. Most of the popular spreadsheet products such as Lotus 1-2-3, Excel, and Quatro Pro contain features and functions that have been labeled *database*, but they are using the term very loosely, in a manner that is incompatible with the way in which it is used in this text.

A spreadsheet has only a small portion of the functionality that we expect from a database and a database management system. To illustrate, consider Figure 1-12, which shows a spreadsheet containing data about Mary Richards House Painting's customers and jobs. Observe that each row of the spreadsheet contains all of the data about a customer, along with all of the data about a job. If we were to add the referrals, then the data about each referral would have to be added to each of these rows.

Again, look at Figure 1-12 and consider what must be done if a customer changes addresses. Every row for that customer must be updated. Compare Figure 1-12 with the database representation of this data in Figure 1-1. There is little duplication of data (the values of Customer_ID and Source_ID). When a customer changes address, only the appropriate row in the CUSTOMER table must be altered.

There are many other important limitations in spreadsheet "databases." Do not be misled. The database technology that you will learn in this book is far more robust than that in used in spreadsheets.

FIGURE 1-12

Spreadsheet Representation of Database Data

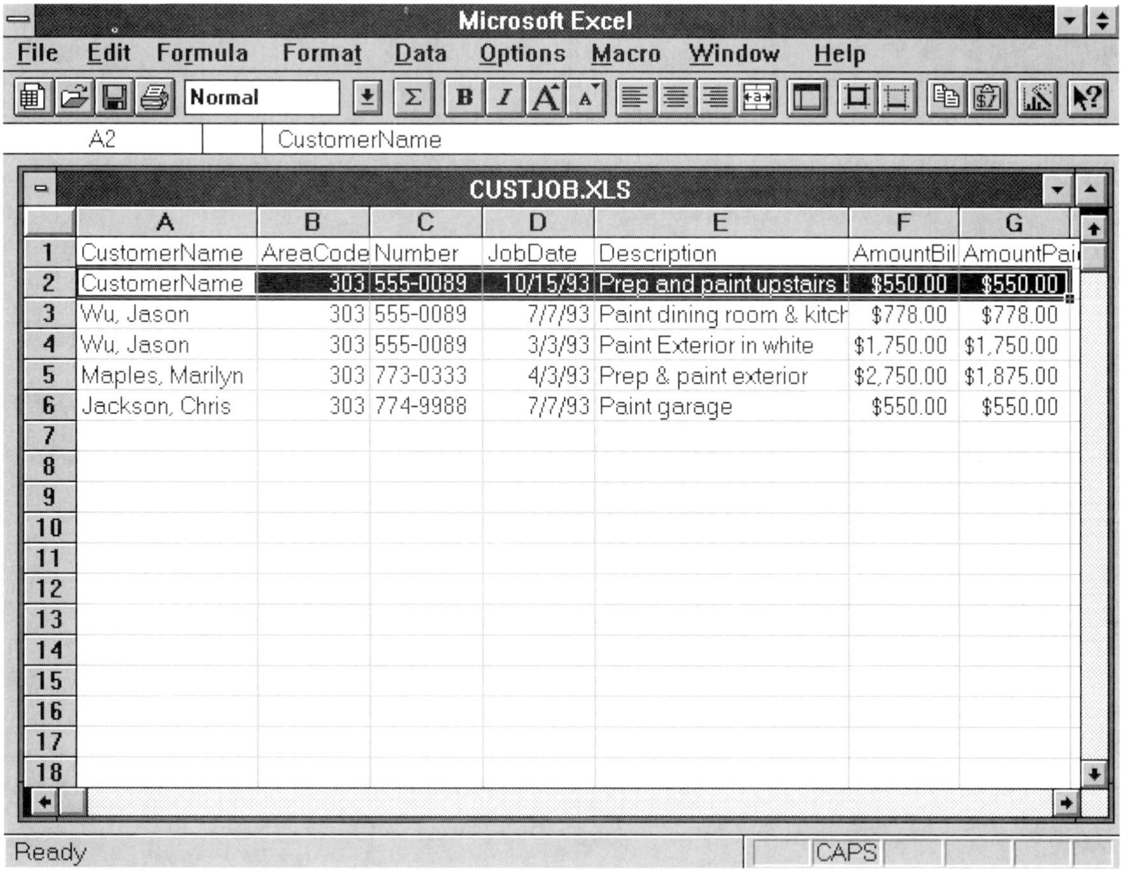

	A	B	C	D	E	F	G
1	CustomerName	AreaCode	Number	JobDate	Description	AmountBil	AmountPai
2	CustomerName		303	555-0089	10/15/93	Prep and paint upstairs	$550.00	$550.00
3	Wu, Jason	303	555-0089	7/7/93	Paint dining room & kitch	$778.00	$778.00
4	Wu, Jason	303	555-0089	3/3/93	Paint Exterior in white	$1,750.00	$1,750.00
5	Maples, Marilyn	303	773-0333	4/3/93	Prep & paint exterior	$2,750.00	$1,875.00
6	Jackson, Chris	303	774-9988	7/7/93	Paint garage	$550.00	$550.00

SUMMARY

Database processing is one of the most important courses in the information systems curriculum. Almost all business people need the benefits of database technology, but few know how to use it themselves. Thus there is a great demand for people who can serve as a liaison between the technology and the business users.

Database technology is used in a variety of applications. Some serve only a single user on a single computer; others are used by work groups of twenty or thirty people on a local area network; and still others are used by hundreds of users and involve trillions of bytes of data.

The components of a database application are the database, the database management systems (DBMS), and the application programs. Sometimes the application programs are entirely separate from the DBMS; other times substantial portions of the application are provided by features and functions of the DBMS.

File-processing systems store data in separate files, each of which contains a different type of data. File-processing systems have several limitations. With separated files, it is difficult to combine data stored in separate files, as the data is often duplicated among files, leading to data integrity problems. Application programs are dependent on file formats, causing maintenance problems when the formats change and the files become incompatible, requiring file conversions. And it is difficult to represent data from the users' viewpoint.

Database-processing systems were developed to overcome these limitations. In the database environment, the database management system is the interface between application programs and the database. The data is integrated, and its duplication is reduced. Only the DBMS is affected by changes in the physical formats of stored data. And if data items are changed, added, or deleted, few application programs will require maintenance. With database technology, it is easier to represent objects in the users' environment.

A database is a self-describing collection of integrated records. It is self-describing because it contains a description of itself in a data dictionary. A data dictionary is also known as a data directory or metadata. A database is a collection of integrated records because the relationships among the records are stored in the database. This arrangement enables the DBMS to construct even complicated objects by combining data based on the stored relationships. Relationships are often stored in overhead data. Thus the three parts of a database are the application data, the data dictionary, and the overhead data.

Database technology developed in several stages. Early databases focused on the transaction processing of organizational data. Then, the relational model, together with the microcomputer, led to the use of personal database applications. With the advent of local area networks, departments began to implement work-group client server databases. Today, efforts are under way to integrate all of these different types of databases into distributed databases.

GROUP I QUESTIONS

1.1   Why is database processing an important subject?

1.2   Describe the nature and characteristics of a single user database application used by an individual like Mary Richards.

1.3   Describe the nature and characteristics of a database application used by a work group like SeaView Yacht Sales.

1.4   Describe the nature and characteristics of a database application used by a state's licensing and vehicle registration bureau.

1.5   Explain the nature and function of each of the components of Figure 1-8.

1.6   How is the relationship between application programs and the DBMS changing over time?

1.7   List the limitations of file-processing systems as described in this chapter.

1.8   Explain how database technology overcomes the limitations you listed in your answer to Question 7.

1.9   Define the term *database*.

1.10   What is metadata? What are indexes? What is application metadata?

1.11   Explain why a database is a model. Describe the difference between a model of reality and a model of a user's model of reality. Why is this difference important?

1.12   Give an example, other than one in this chapter, of a personal database application.

1.13   Give an example, other than one in this chapter, of a work-group database application.

1.14   Give an example, other than one in this chapter, of a large-enterprise database application.

1.15   What were some of the weaknesses of early organizational database applications?

1.16   What is the primary advantage of the relational model?

1.17   Why was the relational model initially resisted?

1.18   Summarize the events in the development of microcomputer DBMS products.

1.19   What was the major factor that gave rise to work-group database applications?

1.20   How does the client-server architecture differ from mainframe or minicomputer multiuser architectures?

1.21   Explain the general nature of distributed processing. What are some of the difficult problems to be faced?

GROUP II QUESTIONS

1.22   Should a database course be required for an information systems major? Give reasons to support your answer. (It might be interesting to save your reasons and review them at the end of the course.)

1.23   Interview a salesperson at a local computer store. Ask for information on microcomputer database management systems. Does the store distinguish between file management systems and database management systems? If so, what are the differences? Does the store distinguish between relational and nonrelational DBMS products. If so, what are the differences?

1.24   Interview people who use a database application. What business functions are served? What information is produced? What objects are involved? Is this application a personal, work-group, or organizational application?

CHAPTER

COMPONENTS OF A DATABASE SYSTEM

This chapter presents a broad overview of the components of database systems and the relationships among them, which will help place into perspective the detailed descriptions of the technology in following chapters.

THE DATABASE

Figure 2-1 shows the main components of a database system. The **database** is processed by the **DBMS**, which is used by both developers and **users**, who can use the DBMS either directly or indirectly via **application programs**. We discuss the database in this section and the DBMS and applications in subsequent sections.

As described in Chapter 1, a database contains four main elements: user data, metadata, indexes, and application metadata.

■ User Data

Today, most databases represent user data as relations. We formally define the term *relation* in Chapter 5. For now, consider a relation to be a table of data. The columns of the table contain fields or attributes, and the rows of the table contain records for particular entities in the business environment.

FIGURE 2-1

Components of Database Systems

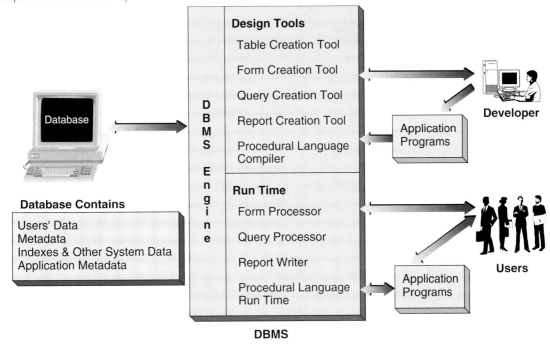

DBMS

Not all relations are equally desirable; some relations are better structured than others. Chapter 5 describes a process called *normalization* that is used to create well-structured relations. To get an idea of the difference between poorly structured and well-structured relations, consider the relation R1 (StudentName, StudentPhone, AdviserName, AdviserPhone) with the following data:

StudentName	StudentPhone	AdviserName	AdviserPhone
Baker, Rex	232-8897	Parks	236-0098
Charles, Mary	232-0099	Parks	236-0098
Johnson, Beth	232-4487	Jones	236-0110
Scott, Glenn	232-4444	Parks	236-0098
Zylog, Frita	232-5588	Jones	236-0110

The problem with this relation is that it has data concerning two different topics, students and advisers. A relation structured in this way presents a number of problems when it is updated. For example, if adviser Parks changes his or her telephone number, three rows of data must be changed. For this reason, the data would be better represented by the two relations R2(StudentName, StudentPhone, AdviserName) with data

StudentName	StudentPhone	AdviserName
Baker, Rex	232-8897	Parks
Charles, Mary	232-0099	Parks
Johnson, Beth	232-4487	Jones
Scott, Glenn	232-4444	Parks
Zylog, Frita	232-5588	Jones

and R3(AdviserName, AdviserPhone) with data

AdviserName	AdviserPhone
Parks	236-0098
Jones	236-0110

Now if an adviser changes his or her phone, only one row of R3 has to be changed. Of course, to produce a report that shows the names of students along with their adviser's phone numbers, the rows of these two tables will need to be combined. It turns out, however, that it is far better to store the relations separately and combine them when producing a report than to store them as one combined table.

FIGURE 2-2

Examples of Metadata

SysTables Table

Table Name	Number of Columns	Primary Key
Student	4	Student Number
Adviser	3	AdviserName
Course	3	ReferenceNumber
Enrollment	3	{StudentNumber, ReferenceNumber}

SysColumns Table

Column Name	Table Name	Data Type	Length*
StudentNumber	Student	Integer	4
FirstName	Student	Text	20
LastName	Student	Text	30
Major	Student	Text	10
Name	Adviser	Text	25
Phone	Adviser	Text	12
Department	Adviser	Text	15
ReferenceNumber	Course	Integer	4
Title	Course	Text	10
NumberHours	Course	Decimal	4
StudentNumber	Enrollment	Integer	4
ReferenceNumber	Enrollment	Integer	4
Grade	Enrollment	Text	2

* Lengths are stated in bytes, which are the same as characters of text data.

◼ Metadata

As defined in Chapter 1, a database is self-describing, which means that it contains a description of its structure as part of itself. This description of the structure is called **metadata.** Since DBMS products are designed to store and manipulate tables, most products store the metadata in the form of tables, sometimes called system tables.

Figure 2-2 shows an example of metadata stored in two system tables. The first stores a list of tables that are in the database, indicating how many columns are in each table and what column(s) is the primary key. This key is the unique identifier of a row. The second table stores a list of columns in each table and the data type and length of each column. Although these two tables are typical of system tables, others are used to store lists of indexes, keys, rules, and other portions of the database structure.

Storing metadata in tables is not only efficient for the DBMS; it is also convenient for users because they can use the same query tools for metadata as they do for user data. Thus, once a user learns how to use the DBMS's query facility to query a user table, he or she can use that same facility to query system tables. Later in this book we discuss a language called SQL that is used to query and update tables, for both metadata and user data.

As an example of how you might use SQL for this purpose, suppose that you have developed a database with fifteen tables and two hundred columns. You remember that several of the columns have the data type *currency*, but you cannot remember which ones. By using SQL, you can access the SysColumns Table to find out which columns have that data type.

◼ Indexes

A third type of database data improves the performance and accessibility of the database. This data, which is sometimes called **overhead data**, consists principally of indexes, although other types of data structures, such as linked lists, are sometimes used (see the appendix for a discussion of indexes and linked lists).

Figure 2-3 shows a table of student data and two indexes. To demonstrate the necessity of having these indexes, suppose that the data is stored on disk in ascending order of StudentNumber and that the user wants to print a report of student data sorted by LastName. To do this, all of the data could be extracted from the source table and sorted, but for all but the simplest examples, this would be a time-consuming process.

Alternatively, an index like the LastName index in Figure 2-3 could be created. The entries in this index are sorted by value of LastName, and so the entries of the index can be read and used to access the student data in sorted order. Suppose further that student data must also be printed in order of student major. Again, the data could be extracted from the source table and sorted, or an index like the Major index could be constructed and used as just described.

Indexes are used not only for sorting but also for quick access to data. For example, a user wants to access only those students that have the value 'Info Systems' for Major. Without an index, the entire source table must be searched. But with the index, the index entry can be found and used to find all of the qualifying rows. Although indexes are not needed for a table with as few rows as the STUDENT

FIGURE 2-3

Examples of Database Indexes

Example STUDENT Table

Student Number	FirstName	LastName	Major
100	James	Baker	Accounting
200	Mary	Abernathy	Info Systems
300	Beth	Jackson	Accounting
400	Eldridge	Johnson	Finance
500	Chris	Tufte	Accounting
600	John	Smathers	Info Systems
700	Michael	Johnson	Accounting

LastName Index

LastName	StudentNumber
Abernathy	200
Baker	100
Jackson	300
Johnson	400, 700
Smathers	600
Tufte	500

Major Index

Major	StudentNumber
Accounting	100, 300, 500, 700
Info Systems	200, 600
Marketing	400

table in Figure 2-3, consider a table that has ten thousand or twenty thousand rows of data. In that case, sorting or searching the entire table would be very slow.

Indexes are indeed helpful for sorting and searching operations, but at a cost. Every time a row in the STUDENT table is updated, the indexes must also be updated. This is not necessarily bad; it just means that indexes are not free and so should be reserved for cases in which they are truly needed.

▪ Application Metadata

The fourth and final type of data that is stored in the database is **application metadata**, which is used to store the structure and format of user forms, reports, queries, and other application components. Not all DBMS support application components, and of those that do, not all store the structure of those components as application metadata in the database. However, most of the modern DBMS products do store such data. In general, neither the database developers nor the users access the application metadata directly. Instead, they use tools in the DBMS to process it.

THE DBMS

DBMS products vary considerably in the features and functions that they provide. The first such products were developed for use on mainframes in the late 1960s, and they had very primitive features. Since then, DBMS products have been continually enhanced and improved not only to process database data better but also to incorporate features that facilitate the creation of database applications.

In this chapter we use Microsoft Access to illustrate the capabilities of DBMS products, because it provides features and functions that typify the characteristics of a modern DBMS. Microsoft Access is not, however, the only such DBMS, and our selecting it is not meant to be an endorsement of it over other, similar products, such as Borland's Paradox for Windows.

As shown in Figure 2-1, the features and functions of a DBMS can be divided into three subsystems: the design tools subsystem, the run-time subsystem, and the DBMS engine.

■ The Design Tools Subsystem

The design tools subsystem has a set of tools to facilitate the design and creation of the database and its applications. It typically includes tools for creating tables, forms, queries, and reports. DBMS products also provide programming languages and interfaces to programming languages. For example, Access has two languages, a macro language that does not require in-depth programming knowledge and a version of BASIC called Access Basic. When using the form, query, and report design tools, these languages can be used to develop application features and functions that extend beyond those currently available.

■ Run-time Subsystem[1]

The run-time subsystem processes the application components that are developed using the design tools. For example, Access has a run-time facility that materializes forms and connects form elements with table data. For example, a form has been defined that includes a text box to display the value of StudentNumber of the STUDENT table. During execution, when the form is opened, the form run-time processor extracts the value of StudentNumber from the current STUDENT row and displays it in the form. All of this is automatic; neither the user nor the developer need do anything once the form is created. Other run-time processors answer queries and print reports. In addition, there is a run-time component that processes application program requests for reading and writing database data.

---

[1] Do not confuse the term *run-time subsystem* with the term *run-time product*. Some vendors use the term *run-time product* to refer to a product that includes the run-time and DBMS engine components but not the design tools subsystem. Such a product can be used to process an application that has already been developed. The purpose of run-time products is to reduce the cost of the application to the end user. Normally, the run-time product is much less expensive (sometimes even free) than the full DBMS product. Hence, only the developer buys the full product that includes the design tools subsystem; the end users buy only the run-time product.

Although not shown in Figure 2-1, DBMS products must also provide an application program interface for standard languages such as COBOL, C, and ANSI BASIC. Some type of subprogram call library or a similar facility enables programs written in standard languages to read table data, to add and update data, and even to define new tables and queries.

■ The DBMS Engine

The third component of the DBMS is the DBMS engine, which is the intermediary between the design tools and run-time subsystems and the data itself. The DBMS engine receives requests from the other two components—stated in terms of tables, rows, and columns—and translates those requests into commands to the operating system to read and write data on physical media.

The DBMS engine is also involved with transaction management, locking, and backup and recovery. As we show in Chapter 16, actions against the database often must be made as a complete unit. When processing an order, for example, changes in the CUSTOMER, ORDER, and INVENTORY tables should be made as a group: Either all of them should be made, or none of them should be made. The DBMS engine helps coordinate the activities to ensure that either all of the group or none of the group is applied.

CREATING THE DATABASE

A *database schema* defines a database's structure, its tables, relationships, domains, and business rules. A database schema is a design, the foundation on which the database and the applications are built.

■ An Example of a Schema

To illustrate a schema and why it is important, consider an example. Highline College is a small liberal arts college in the Midwest. Its student activities department sponsors intramural athletic leagues, but it has a problem keeping track of the athletic equipment that has been checked out to various team captains.

TABLES

To address this problem, the department created a database consisting of the following two tables:[2]

CAPTAIN (CaptainName, Phone, Street, City, State, Zip)

and

ITEM (Quantity, Description, Date-Out, Date-In)

where the table names are shown outside the parentheses and the column names are shown inside the parentheses.

---

[2] As we show in Chapters 3 through 6, the most important and difficult task in database development is designing the table structure. By starting this example with the tables already defined, we have thus skipped a major portion of this task.

Neither CaptainName nor Description is necessarily a unique name, as two captains could just as easily be named 'Mary Smith' and there certainly are many items called 'Soccer Balls.' In order to make sure that each row can be identified (the importance of this will be made more clear in later chapters), we add two columns to these tables, as follows:

CAPTAIN (CAPTAIN_ID, CaptainName, Phone, Street, City, State, Zip)
ITEM (ITEM_ID, Quantity, Description, Date-Out, Date-In)

RELATIONSHIPS

The relationship between these two tables is as follows: One row of CAPTAIN relates to many rows of ITEM, but a row of ITEM relates to one, and only one, row of CAPTAIN. The general notation for a relationship like this is **1:N** and is pronounced "one to N" or "one to many." The term 1:N means that one row of the first table is related to many rows of the second.

For the tables shown here, there is no way to tell which row of CAPTAIN relates to which rows of ITEM. Therefore, to show that relationship, we add CAPTAIN_ID to ITEM. The complete structure of the two tables is as follows:

CAPTAIN (CAPTAIN_ID, CaptainName, Phone, Street, City, State, Zip)
ITEM (ITEM_ID, Quantity, Description, Date-Out, Date-In, CAPTAIN_ID)

With this structure, it is easy to determine which captain has checked out a given ITEM. For example, to find out who has checked out item 1234, we examine the row for item 1234 and find the value of CAPTAIN_ID stored in that row. We can then use that value to determine the name and phone number of that captain.

DOMAINS[3]

A domain is a set of values that a column may have. We must specify a domain for each column of each table. Consider the domains for the columns of ITEM. Suppose that both ITEM_ID and Quantity have the domain of integer numbers, that Description is text of length 25, that both Date-Out and Date-In have the domain of date, and that Captain_ID also has the domain of integer numbers. In addition to the physical format, we also need to decide whether any of the domains are to be unique to the table. For our example, we want ITEM_ID to be unique and so must specify its domain in that way. Since a captain may have more than one ITEM checked out, CAPTAIN_ID is not unique to the ITEM table.

The domains of the columns of CAPTAIN also must be specified. CAPTAIN_ID is integer, and all the rest of the columns are text of different lengths. CAPTAIN_ID must be unique to the CAPTAIN table.

BUSINESS RULES

The last element of a database schema is business rules, which are restrictions on the business's activities that need to be reflected in the database and database applications. The following are examples of business rules for Highline College:

---

[3]   This discussion is simplified considerably so as to focus on the components of a database system. A more complete discussion of domains appears in Chapter 4.

1. In order to check out any equipment, a captain must have a local phone number.
2. No captain may have more than seven soccer balls checked out at any one time.
3. Captains must return all equipment within five days after the end of each semester.
4. No captain may check out more equipment if he or she has any overdue.

Business rules are an important part of the schema because they specify the constraints on allowed data values that must be enforced no matter how the data changes reach the DBMS engine. Regardless of whether the request for an invalid data change comes from the user of a form, a query/update request, or an application program, the DBMS should reject it.

Unfortunately, DBMS products today offer only limited enforcement of business rules, and so most such rules must be enforced by the application programs and procedures carried out by the user. This situation is changing, however, and DBMS products are being developed to enforce business rules.

FIGURE 2-4

Creating a Table with Microsoft Access

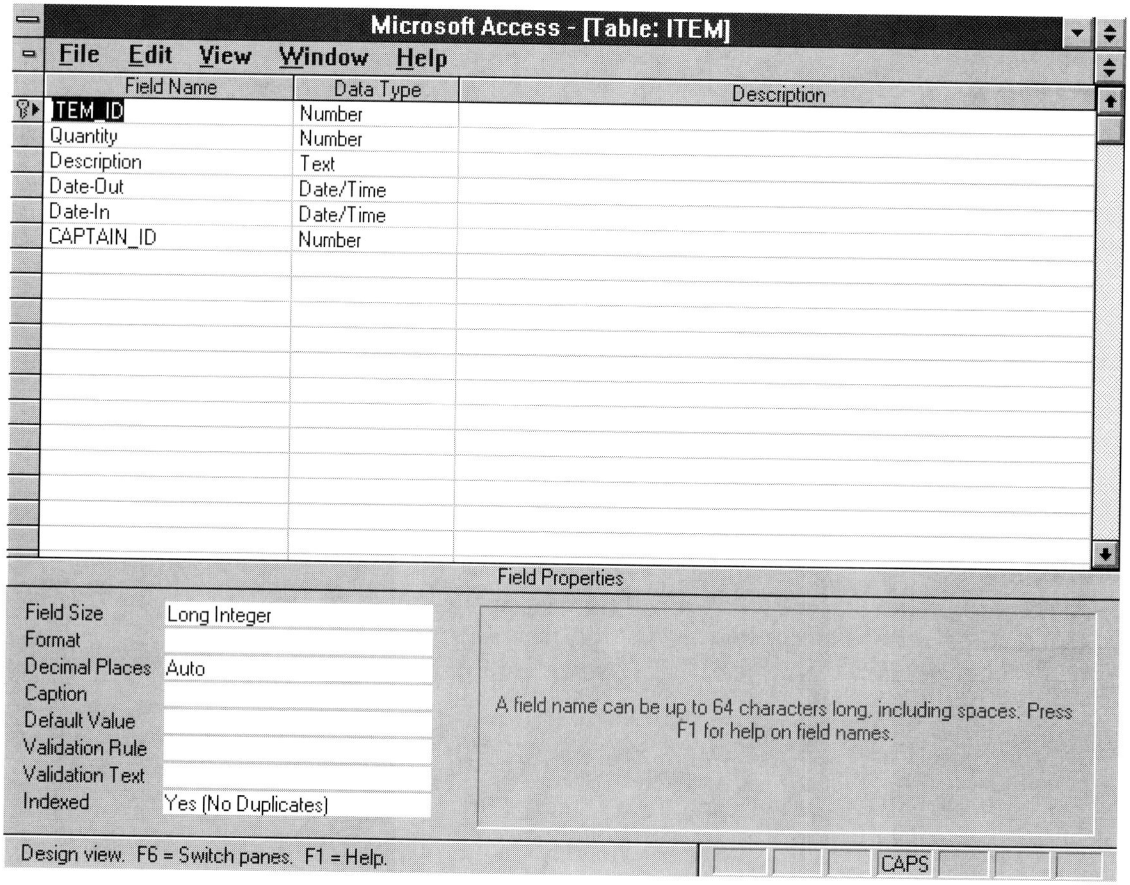

Creating Tables

Once the schema has been designed, the next step is creating the database tables using the DBMS's table creation tools. Figure 2-4 shows the form used with Microsoft Access to create the ITEM table. Each table column name is typed in the Field Name form column, and the data type of the column is specified in the Data Type column. Additional data about the column—such as text length, field format, caption, and other data—is specified in the entry fields in the lower left-hand column of the form.

In Figure 2-4, the focus is on the ITEM_ID column. Observe that the indexed property at the bottom of the form has been set to Yes (No Duplicates), which means that an index of unique values is to be created for the ITEM_ID column. To complete the table definition, the CAPTAIN table is created in a similar way.

Representing Relationships

The relationship between CAPTAIN and ITEM is 1:N, which we represent in the schema by placing the key of CAPTAIN in ITEM. In Figure 2-4, we place CAPTAIN_ID in the ITEM table. A column like CAPTAIN_ID in the ITEM table is sometimes called a **foreign key** because it is the key of a table that is foreign to the table in which it resides. When creating forms, queries, and reports, the DBMS can provide more services and help to the developer if it knows that CAPTAIN_ID in ITEM is a foreign key of CAPTAIN.

DBMS products vary in the way that they declare this status. With Microsoft Access, the declaration is made by defining the relationship, as shown in Figure 2-5.[4] CAPTAIN_ID of the primary table (CAPTAIN) is set equal to CAPTAIN_ID of the related table (ITEM).

One of the advantages of declaring a relationship to the DBMS is that whenever columns from the two tables are placed in a form, query, or report, the DBMS will know how to relate the rows of the tables. Although this can be declared each time for each form, query, or report, declaring it once saves time and reduces the chance of errors. Once the tables, columns, and relationships have been defined, the next step is to build the application components.

COMPONENTS OF APPLICATIONS

A database application consists of forms, queries, reports, menus, and application programs. As shown in Figure 2-1, the forms, queries, and reports can be defined using tools supplied with the DBMS. Application programs must be written in either a language that is part of the DBMS or a standardized language and connected to the database through the DBMS.

[4]   The lower portion of this form contains a check box labeled Enforce Referential Integrity. Ignore this section for now. Referential integrity is discussed at length in both Chapter 8 and Chapter 11.

FIGURE 2-5

Declaring a Relationship with Microsoft Access

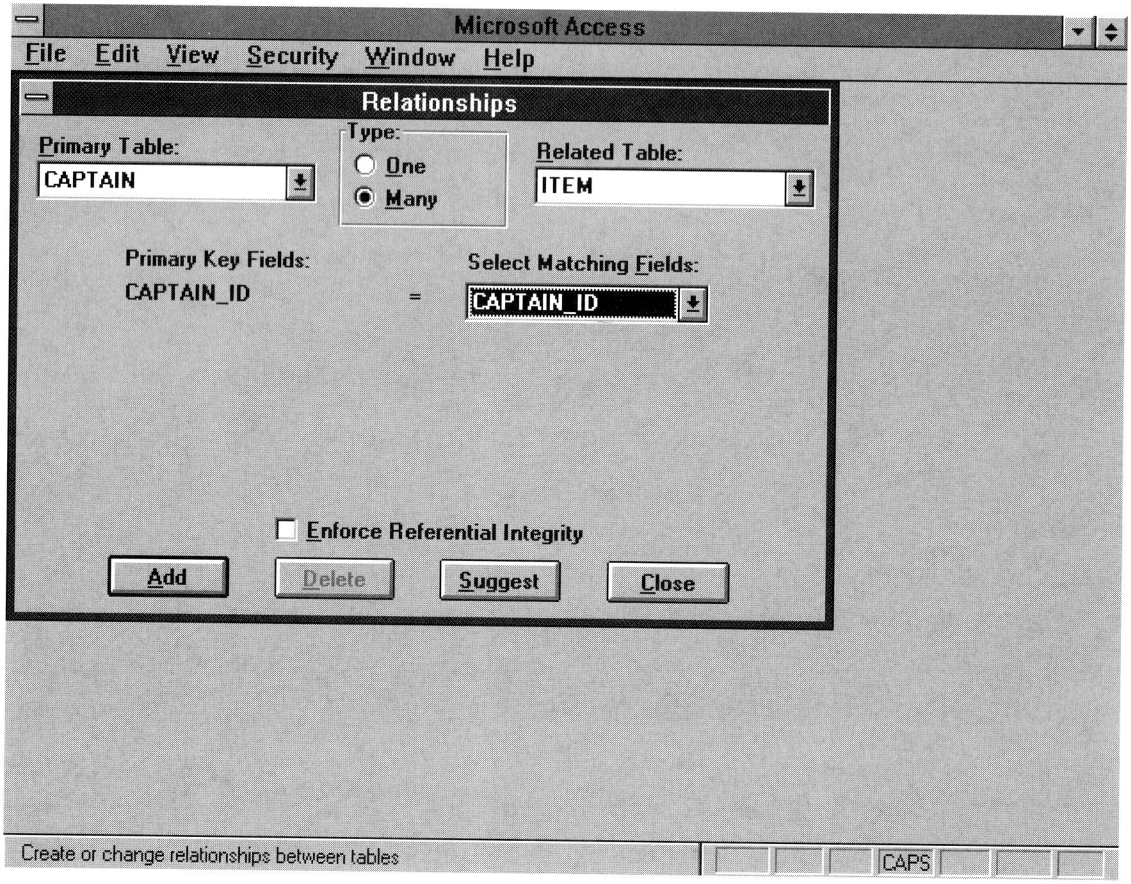

Forms

Figure 2-6 shows a data entry form that is used at Highline College to enter both captain and item checkout data. The user enters the captain data at the top of the form and the item checkout data in a grid below the captain data.

The form shown in Figure 2-6 was developed using the Access form generation tool. Figure 2-7 shows how this tool was used to locate the first text box, the one that contains the CaptainName column. Using the form tool, a text box was drawn on a blank form. The left-hand box is the box label, which is 'CaptainName:' The right-hand text box is used to hold values of the CaptainName column.

Once the box is drawn, its properties are set in the property sheet (the window shown on the right-hand side of the figure labeled 'Text Box'). Note that the property Control Source has been set to CaptainName. This informs Access that the values entered into this text box should be stored in the CaptainName column of the

FIGURE 2-6

Highline College Data Entry

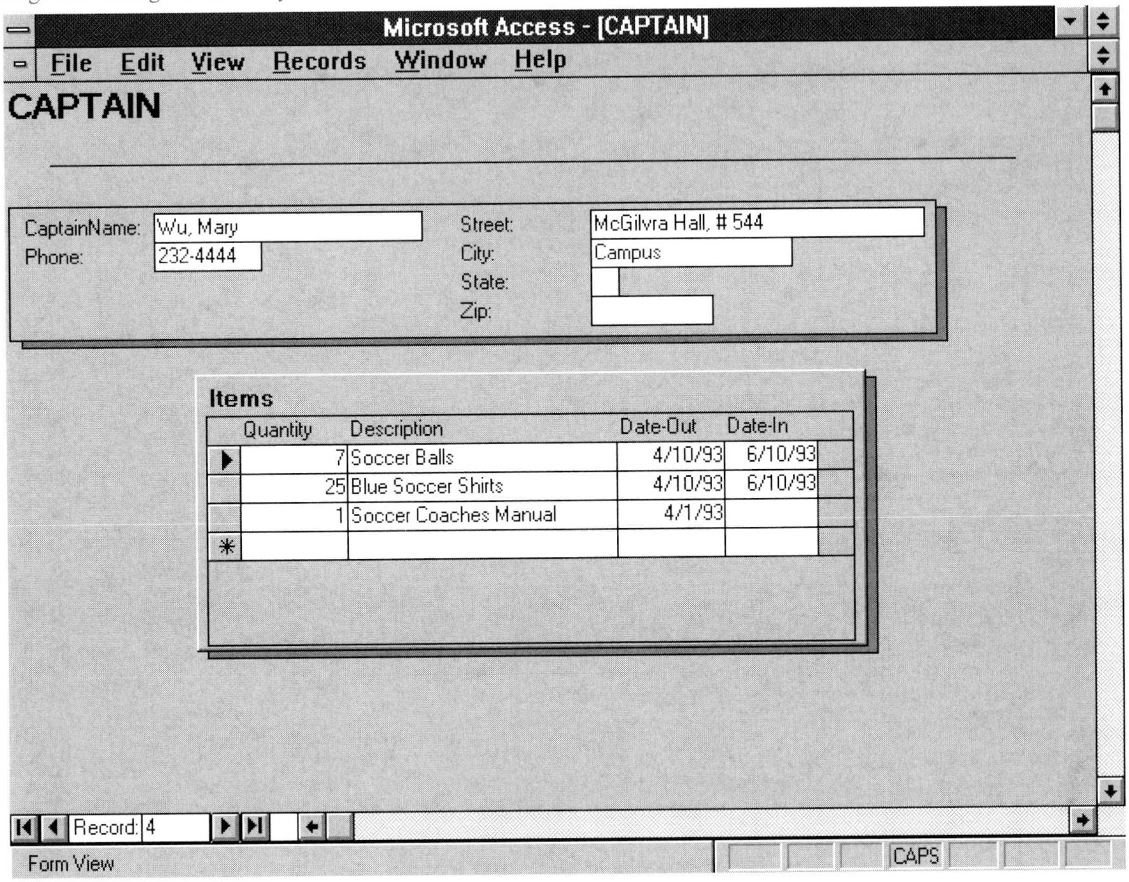

```
┌──────────────────────────────────────────────────────────────────────────┐
│                    Microsoft Access - [CAPTAIN]                            │
├──────────────────────────────────────────────────────────────────────────┤
│  File   Edit   View   Records   Window   Help                              │
│ CAPTAIN                                                                    │
│                                                                            │
│  CaptainName:  Wu, Mary                  Street:   McGilvra Hall, # 544     │
│  Phone:        232-4444                  City:     Campus                   │
│                                          State:                            │
│                                          Zip:                              │
│                                                                            │
│             Items                                                          │
│                 Quantity   Description            Date-Out   Date-In       │
│             ▶         7  Soccer Balls              4/10/93   6/10/93        │
│                      25  Blue Soccer Shirts        4/10/93   6/10/93        │
│                       1  Soccer Coaches Manual     4/1/93                   │
│             *                                                              │
│                                                                            │
│  ┃◀ ◀ Record: 4  ▶ ▶┃  ◀                                                   │
│  Form View                                              CAPS               │
└──────────────────────────────────────────────────────────────────────────┘
```

CAPTAIN table. Then when the form is used to display existing data, the value of CaptainName is taken from the table and displayed in this text box.

You may be wondering how Access knows to use the CAPTAIN table. Before the situation shown in Figure 2-7, the user set the source property of the form equal to CAPTAIN, thereby telling Access to base the form on the columns of the CAPTAIN table.

In this application, neither CAPTAIN_ID nor ITEM_ID is visible in the form in Figure 2-6. Such IDs are hidden from the user. Whenever the user creates a new CAPTAIN by opening a blank form, an application program in the background assigns a value for CAPTAIN_ID. Similarly, whenever the user clicks on the ITEM grid to create a new row in the grid, the background application creates a new value of ITEM_ID, and it also assigns the current value of CAPTAIN_ID to the new ITEM row.

Why are these IDs hidden? The reason is that they have no meaning to the users. Highline does not assign IDs to captains or to particular items that are checked out.

FIGURE 2-7

Creating a Form with Microsoft Access

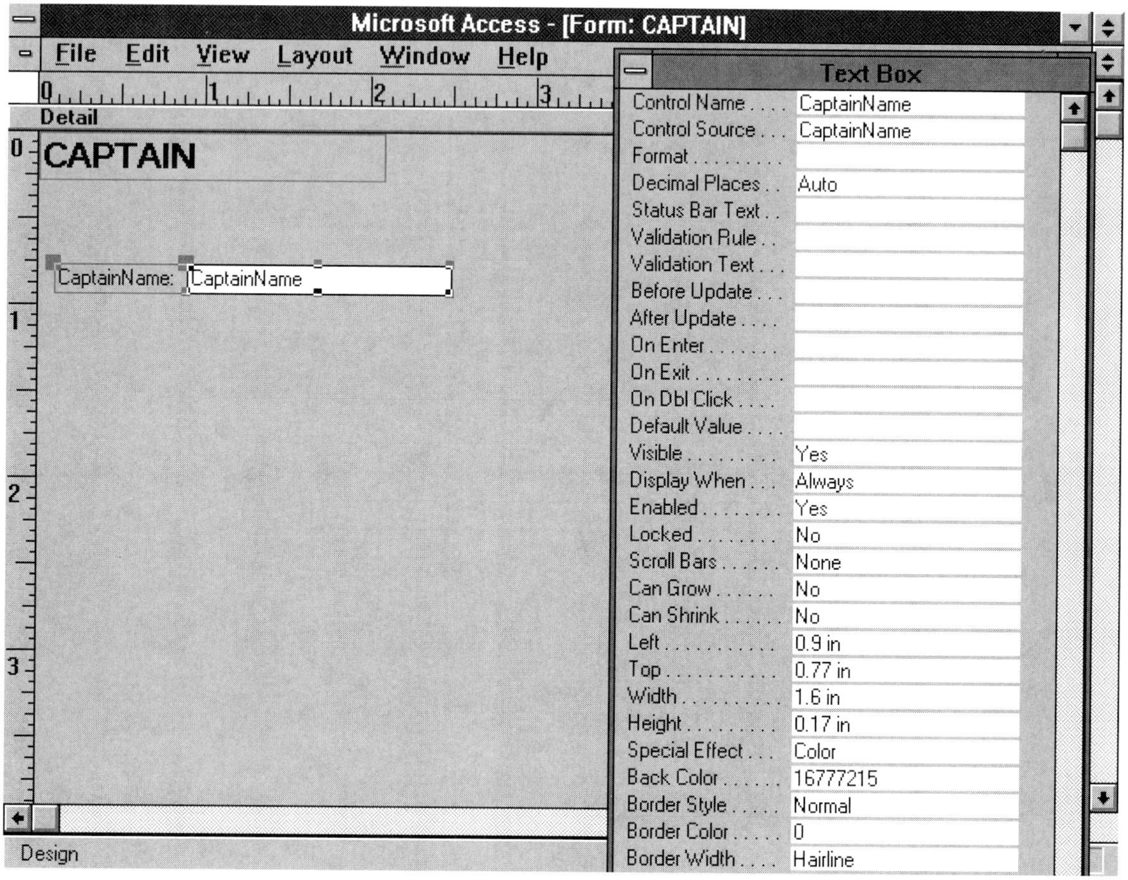

If they did, then these IDs would be used and would be made visible. Instead, these IDs have been created only so that each row of each table will be uniquely identifiable to Access. Since these IDs have no meaning to the user, they are hidden and are called **surrogate keys.**

■ Queries

From time to time, users want to query the data to answer questions or to identify problems or particular situations. For example, suppose that at the start of the fall semester, 1993, one of the users wants to know whether any equipment that was checked out before September 1, 1993, has not yet been checked back in. If it has not, the user wants to know the name of the captain, his or her phone number, and the quantity and description of the items checked out.

There are a number of ways that such a query can be expressed. One is to use the data access language SQL, which is explained in Chapter 8. Another way is to use

FIGURE 2-8

Creating a Query with Microsoft Access

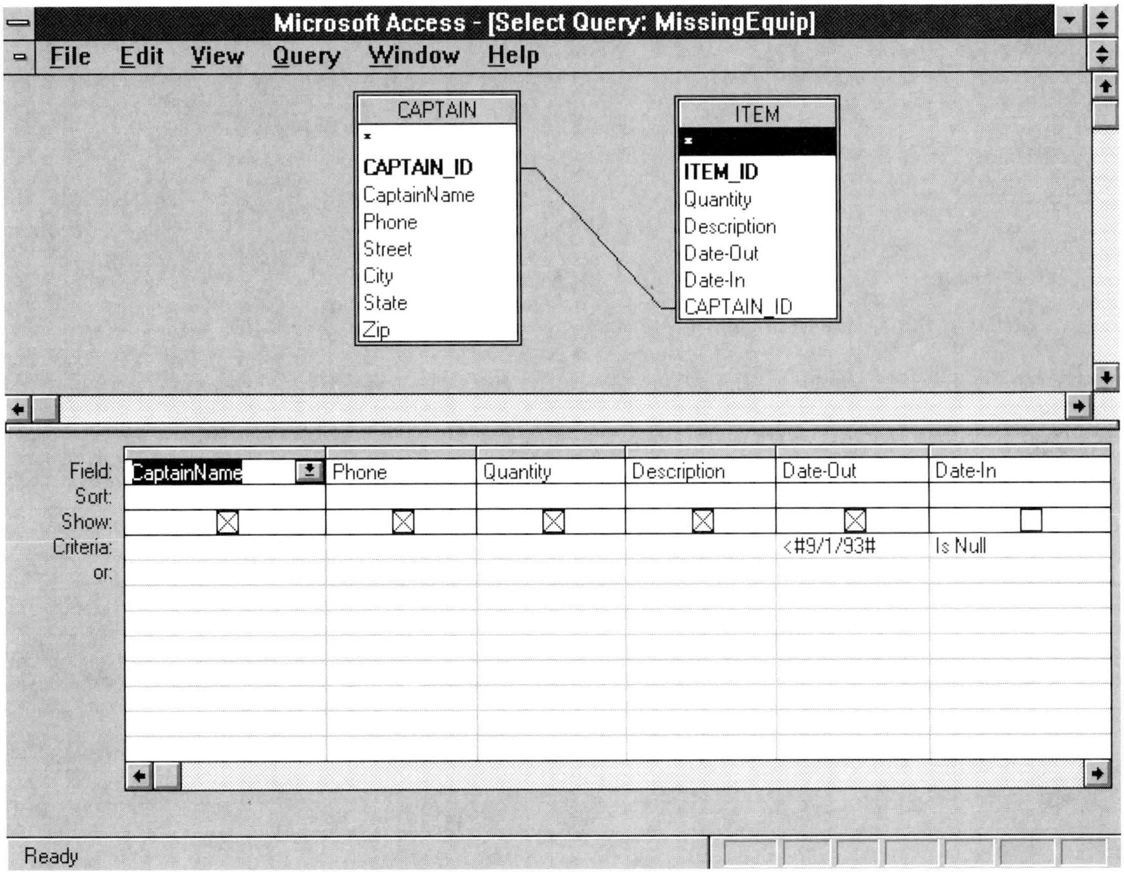

query by example (QBE). Figure 2-8 shows the creation of this query using QBE in Microsoft Access.

To create a query, the user places into the query window the names of the tables that are to be queried. This has already been done in the upper section of the form shown in Figure 2-8. Since the relationship between CAPTAIN and ITEM has already been defined for Access (in Figure 2-5), Access knows that the two tables are linked by CAPTAIN_ID, as shown by the line drawn between CAPTAIN_ID in the two table boxes in Figure 2-8.

Next the query creator indicates which columns of data are to be returned by the query. With Access, this is done by dragging and dropping the names of the columns from the table boxes into the grid in the bottom half of the form. In Figure 2-8, the columns CaptainName, Phone, Quantity, Description, Date-Out, and Date-In have been placed into the query. Then the query criteria are specified in the row labeled Criteria. These criteria are that data must be before (<) 9/1/93. (In Access, dates are surrounded by pound signs [#].) Also, the value of Date-In is to be equal to Null,

FIGURE 2-9

Example Result of Query in Figure 2-8

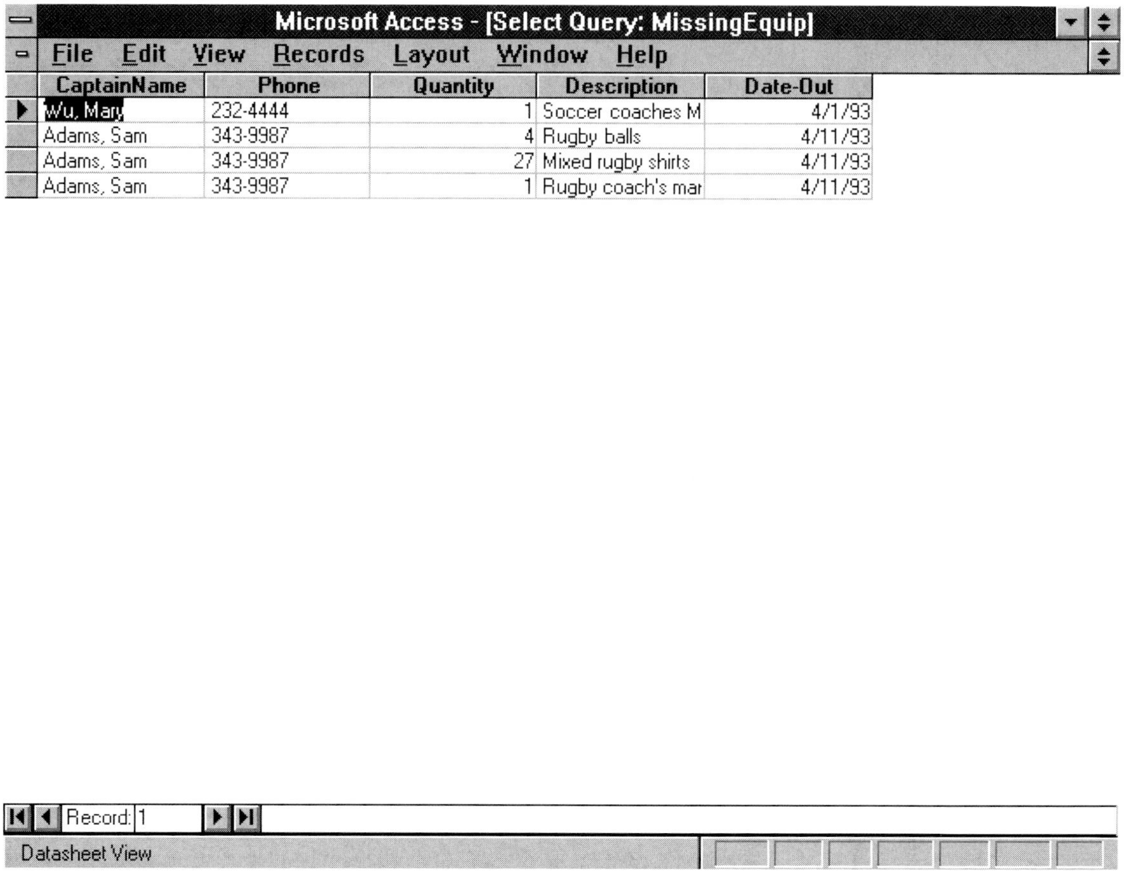

CaptainName	Phone	Quantity	Description	Date-Out
Wu, Mary	232-4444	1	Soccer coaches M	4/1/93
Adams, Sam	343-9987	4	Rugby balls	4/11/93
Adams, Sam	343-9987	27	Mixed rugby shirts	4/11/93
Adams, Sam	343-9987	1	Rugby coach's mar	4/11/93

which means that no value for Date-In has been specified. Finally, the Date-In Show check box is clicked off, which means that Date-In will not be shown in the resulting query. There is no reason to show this column, since all of the values are null. The result of this query for sample data is shown in Figure 2-9. Note that all of the equipment shown was checked out before 9/1/93, as was required in the query definition.

With Access and most other DBMS products, queries can be saved as part of the application, so that they can be rerun as necessary. In addition, queries can be parameterized, meaning that they can be constructed so as to accept criteria values at the time they are run. For example, the query in Figure 2-8 can be parameterized so that the user enters the value of Date-Out when the query is run. Any items that were checked out before that date but that have not yet been checked back in will be shown.

■ Reports

A report is a formatted display of database data, an example of which is shown in Figure 2-10. This report, which is shown as it would be displayed on a computer

FIGURE 2-10

Highline College Example Report

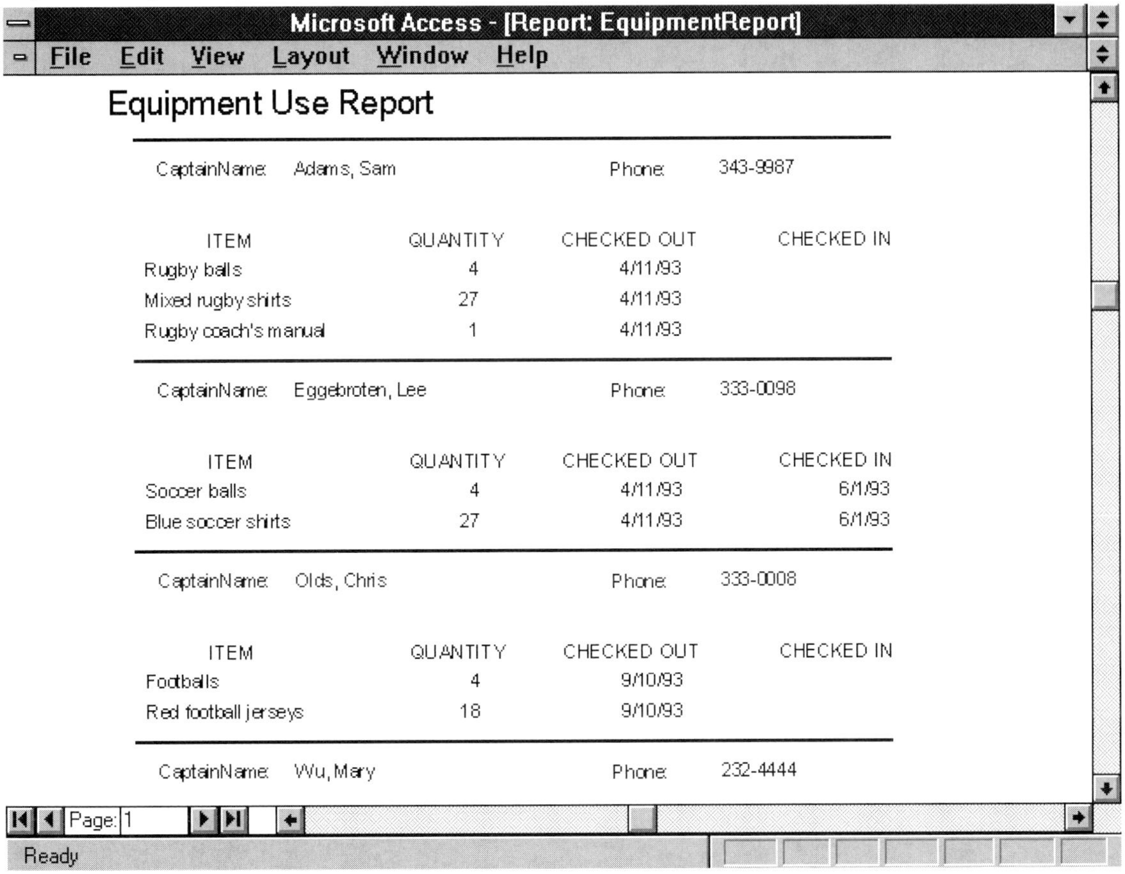

Equipment Use Report

| CaptainName: | Adams, Sam | | Phone: | 343-9987 |

ITEM	QUANTITY	CHECKED OUT	CHECKED IN
Rugby balls	4	4/11/93	
Mixed rugby shirts	27	4/11/93	
Rugby coach's manual	1	4/11/93	

| CaptainName: | Eggebroten, Lee | | Phone: | 333-0098 |

ITEM	QUANTITY	CHECKED OUT	CHECKED IN
Soccer balls	4	4/11/93	6/1/93
Blue soccer shirts	27	4/11/93	6/1/93

| CaptainName: | Olds, Chris | | Phone: | 333-0008 |

ITEM	QUANTITY	CHECKED OUT	CHECKED IN
Footballs	4	9/10/93	
Red football jerseys	18	9/10/93	

| CaptainName: | Wu, Mary | | Phone: | 232-4444 |

Page: 1

Ready

screen, contains a section for each team captain and a list of the items checked out by that captain in the section. For example, the items checked out by captain 'Adams, Sam' are shown in the first section of the report.

Developing a report is similar to developing a data entry form, although in some ways it is easier because a report can be thought of as a write-only form. In other ways, constructing a report is more difficult because reports often have a more complicated structure than forms do.

Figure 2-11 shows the display of the Access report definition tool that was used to create the report in Figure 2-10. The text 'Equipment Use Report' has been typed in the section labeled Page Header, an action that causes Access to print 'Equipment Use Report' at the top of each page of the report. Next a section has been defined by creating the CaptainName Header. Two fields have been entered in this header, one for CaptainName and another for Phone, and the column labels have been placed in this header. Defining such a section causes Access to create the captain groups shown in Figure 2-10 and to have them printed in sorted order by CaptainName. Finally, the columns that are to be shown in each captain section are

FIGURE 2-11

Developing a Report with Microsoft Access

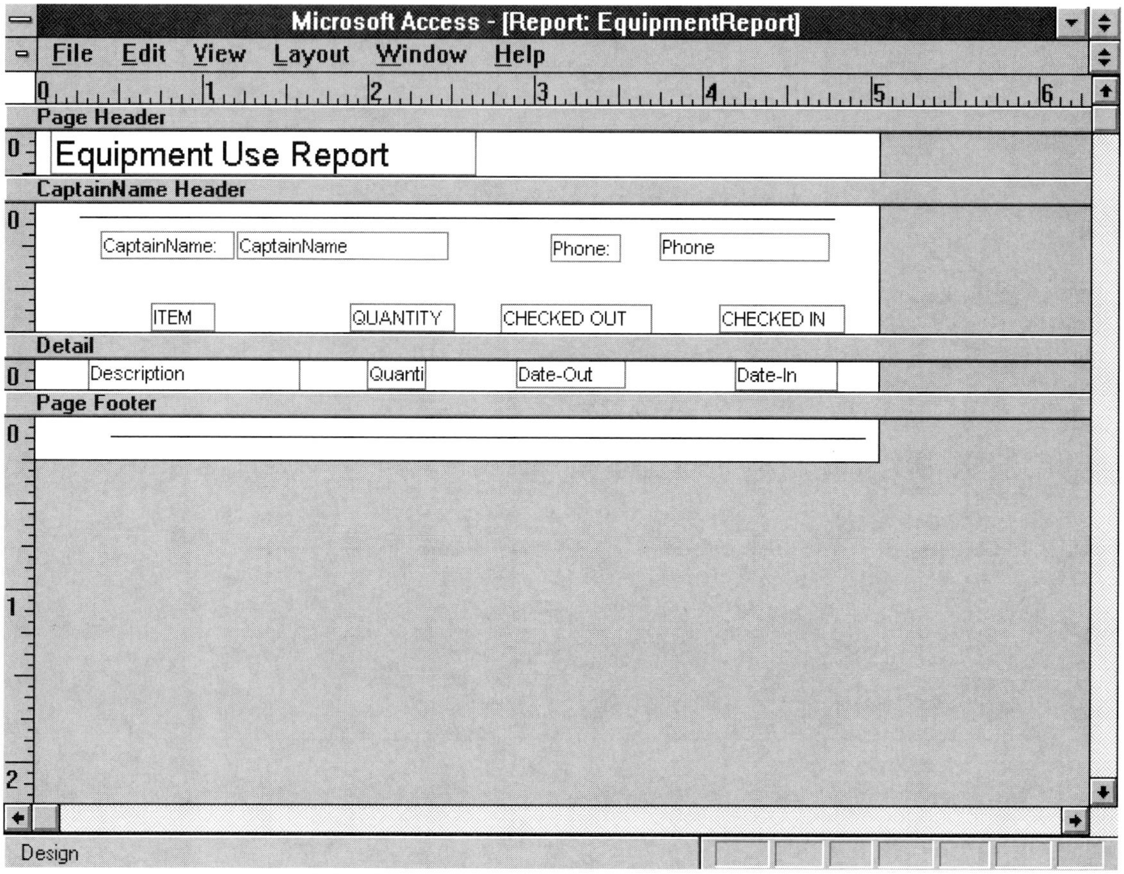

placed in the Detail section. In Figure 2-11, the Description, Quantity, Date-Out, and Date-In columns are to be displayed.

In general, reports can have many sections. In a more complex example, say course/student enrollment, a report could be sorted by COLLEGE, by DEPART-MENT, by COURSE, and by STUDENT. In this case the report would have three sections and a detail line for each STUDENT.

■ Menus

Menus are used to organize the application components so as to make them more accessible to the end user. Figure 2-12 shows an example menu for the Highline application. The line across the top of the form presents the highest-level options: File, Forms, Queries, Reports and Help. The underlined letters represent keyboard shortcut keys. If the user types <Alt> plus the underlined letter, the submenu choices will be displayed.

FIGURE 2-12

Example Menu

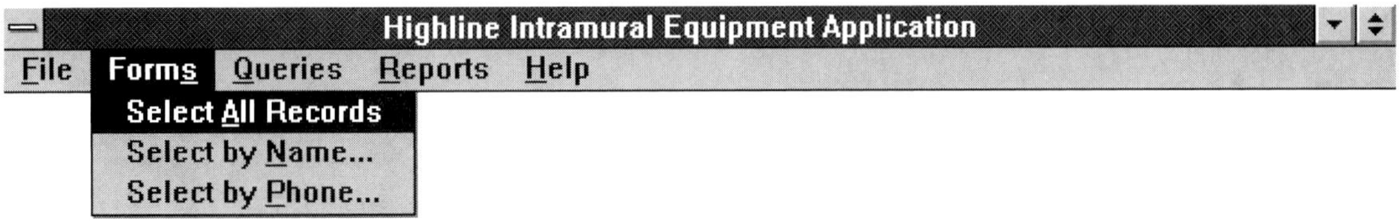

In Figure 2-12, the user has keyed <Alt> plus the letter *R*. The submenu choices are Select All Records, Select by Name, and Select by Phone. Again, keyboard shortcut keys can be used to select one of these items by typing <Alt> and the underlined letter of the choice. In Windows, the ellipsis (. . .) after a menu item means that a dialogue box (a subform) will be displayed to obtain additional information from the user. Menus make the application more accessible to the user by showing what options are available and helping the users select those actions they want performed.

■ Application Programs

The final component of a database application is application programs. As we mentioned earlier, such programs can be written in a language that is specific to the DBMS or in a standard language that interfaces with the DBMS through a predefined program interface. Here we use the version of BASIC included with Microsoft Access.

Consider the problem of assigning IDs to new rows of data. Whenever the user creates a new record via a form, Access generates an Insert event. The application programmer can trap or intercept the processing of this event by naming a function to be called when a row is inserted. Figure 2-13 illustrates this for the CAPTAIN form. (For reasons not important to our discussion, the CAPTAIN form is named *AppForm_CAPTAIN* in this figure.) The properties of the form are in the window labeled Form. The fourth property, *On Insert*, is used to declare the name of the routine that is to be called when a new row is to be inserted throught the form. Here this property is set to call the function GetNextID. It passes the name of the current form and a number that the application uses to identify the CAPTAIN table.

Figure 2-14 shows two Access Basic functions. It is not necessary to understand the details of them; indeed, there is more in them than we can or need to discuss at this point. Instead, look at the two functions to get a general idea of how an application program references a database.

The Highline application contains a table called WTableList that keeps data about all of the tables in the database. This table is metadata created by the application. One of the columns in this table is named MaxID. When a table is opened, the value of this column is read from the database and entered into an array named *ObjectID*. The position of the tables in this array depends on their table number. CAPTAIN has been allocated table 1 and so occupies the first position in the array.

When GetNext ID is called, the first line of code checks to see whether ObjectID (TableNum) equals zero. If so, the table is not yet open, and so the function

FIGURE 2-13

Design View of Captain Form

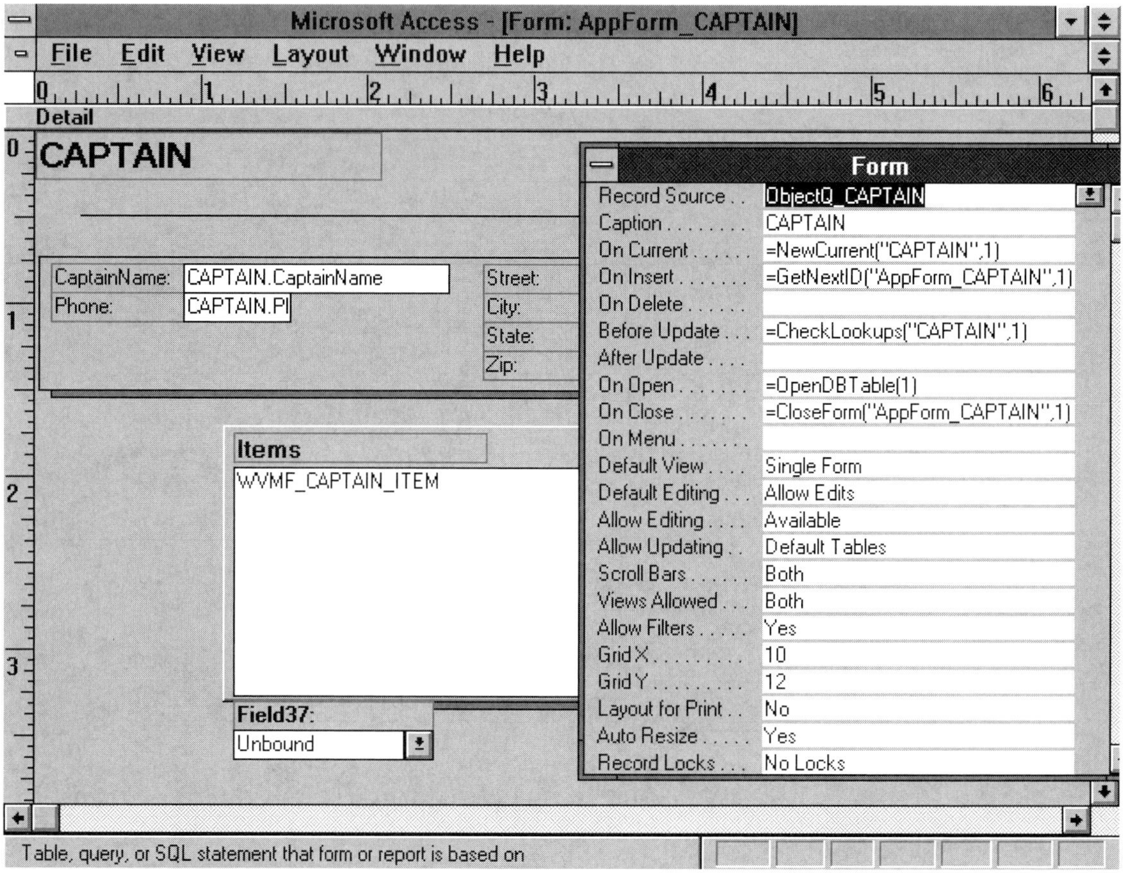

OpenDBTable is called to open it. If ObjectID(TableNum) is not zero, then one is added to the value in this array, and the new value is placed in the form. The third statement is peculiar to Access Basic and simply is used to set the value of the text box named Text1 to the value of ObjectID(TableNum). Since Text1 has been bound to the column named CAPTAIN_ID, this statement causes the new ID to be entered into that column.

If OpenDBTable is called, then the table named WTableList is opened, and the row for table TableNum is found with the statement

TableTable.Seek "=", TableNum

Then ObjectID(TableNum) is set to the value of the column MaxID, by means of the statement

ObjectID(TableNum) = TableTable!MaxID.

Not shown in Figure 2-14 is a third function that is called when the form is closed. At that time, the current value of the array ObjectID is written out to the column MaxID in the WTableList table.

FIGURE 2-14

Access BASIC Example

```
Function GetNextID (FormName As String, TableNum As Long)
'ObjectID is an array common to all run time routines
'it is filled when the table is first opened

Dim T as Variant

    If ObjectID(TableNum) = 0 Then T = OpenDBTable(TableNum)
    ObjectID(TableNum) = ObjectID(TableNum) + 1
    Forms(FormName).Text1 = ObjectID(TableNum)

End Function

Function OpenDBTable (TableNum As Long)
'ObjectID is an array common to all run time routines
'DB is type Database and is common
'TableTable is type Table and is common

  If ObjectID(TableNum) <> 0 Then Exit Function

    Set DB = CurrentDB()                         'establish DB variable
    Set TableTable = DB.OpenTable("WTableList")  'open table of tables
    TableTable.Index = "PrimaryKey"              'set up seek

    TableTable.Seek "=", TableNum                'find row for this table
    If TableTable.NoMatch = –1 Then
        Call ProcessError(TNumProblem)           'process error
        Exit Function
    End If

    ObjectID(TableNum) = TableTable!MaxID        'fill entry in ObjectID
    TableTable.Close

End Function
```

Again, do not be alarmed if you do not understand the syntax of these statements. They are peculiar to Microsoft Access and not important to us at this point. Your objective here should be to get a general idea of how the forms, tables, and application programs interact to create the application.

DEVELOPING DATABASES

Volumes and volumes have been written on the development of information systems in general and on the development of database applications in particular. Therefore, we do not need to discuss here systems development processes in any depth, but we will conclude this chapter with an overview of the processes used to develop databases and database applications.

■ General Strategies

A database is a model of the users' model of their business activities. Therefore, in order to build an effective database and related applications, the development team must become thoroughly familiar with the users' model. To do this, they build a data model that identifies the things to be stored in the database and defines their structure and the relationships among them. This familiarity must be obtained early in the development process, by interviewing the users and building a statement of requirements. Most such statements include the use of **prototypes**, which are sample databases and applications that represent various aspects of the system to be created.

There are two general strategies for developing a database: top-down and bottom-up. **Top-down development** proceeds from the general to the specific. It begins with a study of the strategic goals of the organization, the means by which those goals can be accomplished, the information requirements that must be satisfied to reach those goals, and the systems necessary to provide that information. From such a study, an abstract data model is constructed.

Using this high-level model, the development team progressively works downward toward more and more detailed descriptions and models. Intermediate-level models also are expanded with more detail until the particular databases and related applications can be identified. One or more of these applications is then selected for development. Over time, the entire high-level data model is transformed into lower-level models, and all of the indicated systems, databases, and applications are created.

Bottom-up development operates in the reverse order of abstraction, by beginning with the need to develop a specific system. The means of selecting the first system varies from organization to organization. In some organizations, a steering committee chooses the application; in others, the users may choose it themselves; and in still others, the loudest voice in the executive office wins out.

By whatever means, a particular system is selected for development. The development team then obtains statements of requirements by considering the outputs and inputs of any existing computer-based systems, by analyzing the forms and reports for existing manual systems, and by interviewing the users to find out their need for new reports, forms, queries, and other requirements. From all of this, the team develops the information system. If the system involves a database, the team uses the requirement specifications to build a data model, and from the model, it designs and implements the database. When this system is finished, other projects are started in order to build additional information systems.

Proponents of the top-down approach claim that it is superior to the bottom-up approach because the data models (and subsequent systems) are constructed with a global perspective. They believe that such systems have better interfaces to one another, are more consistent, and require far less rework and modification.

Proponents of the bottom-up approach claim that it is superior to top-down because it is faster and less risky. They assert that top-down modeling results in many studies that are difficult to complete and that the planning process often ends in analysis paralysis. Although bottom-up modeling does not necessarily produce the best set of systems, it does produce useful systems quickly. The benefits of these systems begin accruing much faster than with top-down modeling, and they can more than compensate for any rework or modification that will need to be done to adjust the system to a global perspective.

This text explains the tools and techniques that can be used with either style of systems development. For example, although both entity-relationship modeling (Chapter 3) and semantic object modeling (Chapter 4) work with either top-down or bottom-up development, the entity-relationship approach is particularly effective with top-down development, and the semantic object approach is particularly effective with bottom-up development.

■ Data Modeling

As we stated, the most important goal of the requirements phase is creating a model of the users' data. Whether this is done in top-down or bottom-up fashion, it involves interviewing users, documenting requirements, and, from those requirements, building the data model and prototypes. Such a model identifies what is to be stored in the database and defines their structure and the relationships among them.

For example, consider Figure 2-15(a), a list of orders made by a salesperson during a specific period of time. For this report to be produced by a database application, the database must contain the data shown, and so the database developers need to examine the report and work backward to the data that must be stored in the database. In this case, there must be data concerning salespeople (name and region) and data concerning orders (company, order date, and amount).

Database development is complicated by the fact that there is not just one requirement but many and that the requirements usually overlap. The report in Figure 2-15(b) is also about salespeople, but instead of orders, it lists commission checks. From this report, we can surmise that there are different types of orders and that each type has a different commission rate.

The orders implied by the report in Figure 2-15(b) somehow relate to the orders listed in Figure 2-15(a), but how they do so is not entirely clear. The development team must determine this relationship by inference from reports and forms, from interviews with users, from the team's knowledge of the subject matter, and from other sources.

DATA MODELING AS INFERENCING

When the users say they need forms and reports with specific data and structures, their statement implies a model that the users have of the things in their world. The users may not, however, be able to describe exactly what that model is. If a developer were to ask the typical user, "What is the structure of the data model in your brain regarding salespeople?" the user would, at best, look quizzical, because most users do not think in that way.

Instead, the developers must infer, from the users' statements about forms and reports, the structure and relationships of the things to be stored in the database. The developers then record these inferences in a data model that is transformed into a database design, and that design is implemented using a DBMS. Applications are then constructed that produce the reports and forms for the users.

Building a data model is thus a process of inference. Reports and forms are like shadows projected on a wall. The users can describe the shadows, but they cannot describe the shapes that give rise to the shadows. Therefore the developers must infer, work backward, and reverse-engineer the structures and relationships of those shapes from the shadows.

FIGURE 2-15

Examples of Two Related Reports: (a) Sample SALES Report and (b) Sample
COMMISSION Report

Salesperson Order List
14-Jun-94

Name	Region	CompanyName	OrderDate	Amount
Kevin Dougherty	**Western**			
		Cabo Controls	9/12/94	$2,349.88
				$2,349.88
Mary B. Wu	**Western**			
		Ajax Electric	9/17/94	$23,445.00
		American Maxell	9/24/94	$17,339.44
				$40,784.44
			Grand Total:	**$43,134.32**

(a)

Salesperson Commission Check Report
14-Jun-94

Name	LocalNumber	CheckDate	CType	CAmount
Kevin Dougherty	**232-9988**			
		9/30/94	XZ	$487.38
				$487.38
Mary B. Wu	**232-9987**			
		9/30/94	C	$237.44
		9/30/94	A	$1,785.39
				$2,022.83
			Grand Total:	**$2,510.21**

(b)

This inferencing process is, unfortunately, more art than science. It is possible to learn the tools and techniques for data modeling; in fact, such tools and techniques are the subject of the next two chapters, and using those tools and techniques is an art that requires experience guided by intuition.

The quality of the model is important. If the documented data model accurately reflects the data model in the users' minds, there is an excellent chance that the resulting reports will be close to the users' needs. But if the documented data model inaccurately reflects this data model, it is unlikely that the report to be produced will be close to what the users really want.

MODELING IN MULTIUSER SYSTEMS

The data modeling process becomes even more complicated for multiuser work-group and organizational databases, because their many users envision many different data models. Occasionally these data models are inconsistent, although sometimes the inconsistencies can be resolved. For example, they may differ only in wording. That is, the users may be employing the same term for different things or different terms for the same things.

Sometimes, however, the differences cannot be reconciled. In such cases, the database developer must document the differences and help the users resolve them, and this usually means that some people have to change the way they view their world.

An even greater challenge is presented by large systems in which no single user has a model of the complete structure. Each user understands some of the work group's or organization's data model, but no single user understands all of it. In such cases, the database becomes the logical union of the pieces of the work group's or organization's model, and the developers must document that logical union in the data model. And this can be quite difficult.

CONFUSION ABOUT THE TERM *MODEL*

The next two chapters present two alternative tools for building data models: the entity-relationship model and the semantic object model. Both models are structures for describing and documenting users' data requirements. To avoid confusion, note the different uses of the term *model.* The development team analyzes the requirements and builds a *users' data model* or a *requirements data model.* This model is a representation of the structure and relationships of what needs to be in the database to support the users' requirements. To create the users' data model, the development team uses tools called entity-relationship and the semantic object data models, which consist of language and diagramming standards for representing the users' data model. Their role in database development is similar to that of flowcharting and pseudocode in programming.

SUMMARY

The components of a database system are the database, the DBMS, and application programs, which are used by both developers and users. A database contains data, metadata, indexes, and application metadata. Most databases today represent data as relations or tables, although not all relations are equally desirable. Undesirable relations can be improved through a process called normalization. Metadata is often stored in special tables called system tables.

A DBMS's features and functions can be grouped into three subsystems. The design tools subsystem defines the database and the structure of applications or application components. The functions of the run-time subsystem are to materialize the forms, reports, and queries by reading or writing database data. The DBMS engine is the intermediary between the other two subsystems and the operating system. It receives requests stated in terms of tables and rows and columns and translates those requests into read and write requests.

A schema is a description of the structure of a database and includes descriptions of tables, relationships, domains, and business rules. The rows of one table can be related to the rows of other tables. This chapter illustrated a 1:N relationship between table rows; there are other relationship types as well, as we will discuss in the next chapter.

A domain is a set of values that a column may have. We must specify a domain for each column of each table.

Finally, business rules are restrictions on the business's activities that must be reflected in the database and database applications.

The facilities of the DBMS are used to create table structures, to define relationships, and to create forms, reports, queries, and menus. DBMS products also include facilities for interacting with application programs written in either DBMS-specific languages or standard languages like COBOL.

Since a database is a model of the users' model of the business, database development begins by learning and recording this model. Sometimes it is expressed in prototypes of the application or application components to be constructed.

The two general styles of development are top-down development, which proceeds from the general to the specific, and bottom-up development, which proceeds from the specific to the general. With top-down, applications are developed with a global perspective; with bottom-up, applications are developed more quickly. Sometimes a combination of the two approaches is used.

Data models are constructed by a process that involves inferencing from users' statements. Forms, reports, and queries are gathered, and the developers work backward to infer the structures that the users envision. This is necessary because most users cannot describe their data models directly. Data modeling can be especially difficult and challenging in multiuser applications, in which the users' view may contradict one another and no single user can visualize the entire view of the business activity.

The term *data model* is used in two ways, to refer to a model of the users' view of their data and to refer to the tools used to define the users' view of their data.

GROUP I QUESTIONS

2.1 Name the major components of a database system, and briefly explain the function of each.

2.2 Give an example, other than the one in this chapter, of a relation that is likely to have problems when it is updated. Use relation R1 as an example.

2.3 Transpose the relation in your answer to Question 2 into two or more relations that do not have update problems. Use relations R2 and R3 as examples.

2.4 Explain the roles of metadata and system tables.

2.5 What is the function of indexes? When are they desirable, and what is their cost?

2.6 What is the function of application metadata? How does it differ from metadata?

2.7 Explain the features and functions of the definition tools subsystem of a DBMS.

2.8   Describe the features and functions of a DBMS's run-time subsystem.

2.9   Explain the features and functions of the DBMS engine.

2.10   What is a database schema? List its components.

2.11   How are relationships represented in a relational database design? Give an example of two tables with a 1:N relationship, and explain how the relationship is expressed in the data.

2.12   What is a domain, and why is it important?

2.13   What are business rules? Give an example of possible business rules for the relations in your answer to Question 11.

2.14   What is a foreign key? Which column(s) in your answer to Question 11 is a foreign key?

2.15   Explain the purpose of forms, reports, queries, and menus.

2.16   What two types of application program languages do most DBMS products contain?

2.17   What is the first important task in developing a database and related applications?

2.18   What is the role of a prototype?

2.19   Describe top-down development. What are its advantages and disadvantages?

2.20   Describe bottom-up development. What are its advantages and disadvantages?

2.21   Explain the two different meanings of the term *data model.*

GROUP II QUESTIONS

2.22   Implement a database with the relations CAPTAIN and ITEM in any DBMS to which you can gain access. Use one of the DBMS products facilities to enter data into each of these relations. Create and process a query to use the DBMS's facility to process a query that identifies those items checked out before September 1, 1993, that have not yet been checked back in. Print the name of the captain, his or her phone number, and the quantity and description of any such items.

2.23   Interview a professional database application developer, and find out the process that this person uses to develop databases. Is this top-down development, bottom-up development, or some other strategy? How does this developer build data models and with what tools? What are the biggest problems usually encountered in developing a database?

2.24   Consider the statement "A database is a model of the users' model of reality." How does it differ from "A database is a model of reality"? Suppose two developers disagree about a data model, and one of them asserts, "My model is a better representation of reality." What does this person really mean? What differences are likely to result when a developer believes the first statement more than the second statement?

Data Modeling

Data modeling is the process of creating a representation of the users' view of the data. It is the most important task in the development of effective database applications. If the data model incorrectly represents the users' view of the data, they will find the applications difficult to use, incomplete, and very frustrating. Data modeling is the basis for all subsequent work in the development of databases and their applications.

Part II describes two different data modeling tools: Chapter 3 considers the entity relationship model, which was introduced in 1976 and has a considerable following among CASE vendors and others. Chapter 4 describes the semantic object model, which was introduced in 1988. As the newer model, it has a smaller following but is generally considered to be richer and easier to use than the E-R model. It is the basis of SALSA™, a data modeling tool licensed by Wall Data, Inc.

CHAPTER

THE ENTITY-RELATIONSHIP MODEL

This chapter describes and illustrates the use of the first of two data models we will study in this text. This model, the entity-relationship model, is used to interpret, specify, and document requirements for database-processing systems. Because it provides constructs for showing the overall structures of the users' data requirements, it is especially useful for top-down database design.

In the next chapter, we consider a second important data model, the semantic object model. It also can be used to document requirements for databases, but it is closer to the users and permits the specification of more details. It is especially useful for bottom-up database design.

These two models provide a language for expressing the users' data model, or the structure of data and data relationships in the users' work environment. With programming, one learns pseudocode, or flowcharting, to express program logic; so, too, with database design, one learns data models to express data structure.

DEFINING THE ENTITY-RELATIONSHIP MODEL

The **entity-relationship model (E-R model)** was introduced by Peter Chen in 1976.[1] In his paper, Chen set out the foundation of the model, which has since been

---

[1] P. P. Chen, "The Entity-Relationship Model—Towards a Unified View of the Data," *ACM Transactions on Database Systems*, January 1976, pp. 9–36.

extended and modified by Chen and many others.[2] In addition, the E-R model has been made part of a number of CASE tools, which also have modified it. Today, there is no single, standardized E-R model but, instead, a set of common constructs from which most of the E-R variants are composed. This chapter describes these common constructs and shows how they are used. Be aware, however, that during your career you may encounter variants of the approach presented here. In addition, the symbols used to express the E-R model differ considerably. Those used here are typical and popular, but they are by no means the only acceptable symbols that can be used.

Entities

An entity is something that can be identified in the users' work environment, something important to the users of the system that is to be built. Examples of entities are EMPLOYEE John Doe, CUSTOMER 12345, SALES-ORDER 1000, SALESPERSON Jane Smith, and PRODUCT A4200. Entities are grouped into **entity classes**, or collections of entities of the same type. In this text, entity classes are printed in capital letters. Thus the name EMPLOYEE is the name of a class of employee entities.

You should be able to distinguish between an entity class and an instance of an entity: An entity class is the general form or description of a thing, such as a CUSTOMER, whereas an instance of an entity class is the representation of a particular entity, such as CUSTOMER 12345. The terms *entity* and *entity class* are often used interchangeably. There are usually many instances of an entity in an entity class. For example, within the class CUSTOMER, there are many instances—one for each customer represented in the database.

Attributes

Entities have **attributes** or, as they are sometimes called, **properties**, which describe the entity's characteristics. Examples of attributes are EmployeeName, DateOfHire, and JobSkillCode. In this text, attributes are printed in both uppercase and lowercase letters. The E-R model assumes that all instances of a given entity class have the same attributes.

As defined in the original E-R model, attributes can be single or multiple valued, or they can be composite. For example, in CUSTOMER, the composite attribute Address can be defined as the group {Street, City, State, Zip}. Some implementations of the E-R model, however, do not allow multivalued or composite attributes.

Identifiers

Entity instances have names that identify them. For example, EMPLOYEE instances have SocialSecurityNumber; CUSTOMERs have CustomerNumber or CustomerName; and SALES-ORDERs have OrderNumber. The identifier of an

---

[2] T. J. Teory, D. Yand, and J. P. Fry, "A Logical Design Methodology for Relational Databases Using the Extended Entity-Relationship Model," *ACM Computing Surveys*, June 1986, pp. 197–222.

FIGURE 3-1

CUSTOMER: An Example
of an Entity

CUSTOMER
entity contains:
  CustNumber
  CustName
  Address
  City
  State
  Zip
  ContactName
  PhoneNumber

Two instances of CUSTOMER:

12345	67890
Ajax Manufacturing	Jefferson Dance Club
123 Elm St	345-10th Avenue
Memphis	Boston
TN	MA
32455	01234
P. Schwartz	Frita Bellingsley
223-5567	210-8896

entity instance is one or more of its attributes. An identifier may be either unique or not unique. If it is unique, its value will identify one, and only one, entity instance. But if it is not unique, the value will identify a set of instances. In the latter case (such as CustomerName of CUSTOMER), additional data, such as an address or telephone number, must be considered in order to find a unique instance. Figure 3-1 shows an entity and two instances of it.

■ Relationships

Entities can be associated with one another in **relationships**. The E-R model contains both relationship classes and relationship instances. Relationship classes are associations among entity classes, and relationship instances are associations among entity instances. Relationships can have attributes.

As defined in the original E-R model, a relationship can include many entities; the number of entities in a relationship is the **degree** of the relationship. In Figure 3-2(a), the SP-ORDER relationship is of degree 2 because each instance of the relationship involves two entity instances: a SALESPERSON entity instance and an ORDER entity instance.[3] In Figure 3-2(b), the PARENT relationship is of degree 3, since each instance involves three entities: MOTHER, FATHER, and CHILD.

Although the E-R model allows relationships of any degree, most applications of the model involve only relationships of degree 2. Such relationships are sometimes called **binary relationships**.

---

[3] For brevity, we sometimes drop the word *instance* when the context makes it clear that an instance rather than an entity class is involved.

FIGURE 3-2

Relationships of Different
Degrees: (a) Example
Relationship of Degree 2 and
(b) Example Relationship of
Degree 3

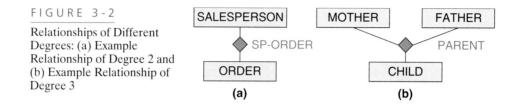

(a) (b)

THREE TYPES OF BINARY RELATIONSHIPS

Figure 3-3 shows the three types of binary relationships. In a 1:1 (read "one-to-one") relationship, a single-entity instance of one type is related to a single-entity instance of another type. In Figure 3-3(a), the AUTO-ASSIGNMENT relationship associates a single EMPLOYEE with a single AUTO. According to this diagram, no employee has more than one automobile assigned, and no automobile is assigned to more than one employee.

Figure 3-3(b) shows the second type of relationship, 1:N (read "one to N" or "one to many"). In this relationship, called a DORM-OCCUPANT relationship, a single instance of DORMITORY relates to many instances of STUDENT. According to this sketch, a dormitory has many students, but a student has only one dormitory.

The positions of the 1 and the N are significant. The 1 is close to the line connecting DORMITORY, which means that the 1 refers to the DORMITORY side of the relationship, and the N is close to the line connecting STUDENT, which means that the N refers to the STUDENT side of the relationship. If the 1 and N were reversed and the relationship were written N:1, a DORMITORY would have one

FIGURE 3-3

Three Types of Binary Relationships: (a)
1:1 Binary Relationship, (b) 1:N Binary
Relationship, (c) N:M Binary Relationship,
and (d) Relationship Representation with
Crow's Feet

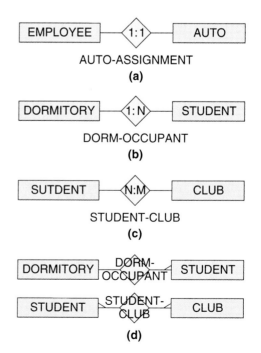

STUDENT, and a STUDENT would have many DORMITORIES. This is not, of course, the case.

Figure 3-3(c) shows the third type of binary relationship, N:M (read "N to M" or "many to many"). This relationship is named STUDENT-CLUB, and it relates instances of STUDENT to instances of CLUB. A student can join more than one club, and a club can have many students as members.

The numbers inside the relationship diamond show the maximum number of entities that can occur on one side of the relationship. Such constraints are sometimes called the relationship's **maximum cardinality**. The relationship in Figure 3-3(b), for example, is said to have a maximum cardinality of 1:N. But the cardinalities are not restricted to the values shown here. It is possible, for example, for the maximum cardinality to be other than 1 and N. The relationship between BASKETBALL-TEAM and PLAYER, for example, could have a maximum cardinality of 5.

Relationships of the types shown in Figure 3-3 are sometimes called **HAS-A relationships**. This term is used because an entity *has a* relationship with another entity. For example, an EMPLOYEE has an AUTO; a STUDENT has a DORMITORY; and a CLUB has STUDENTs.

ENTITY-RELATIONSHIP DIAGRAMS

The sketches in Figure 3-3 are called **entity-relationship** or **E-R diagrams**. Such diagrams are standardized, but only loosely. According to this standard, entity classes are shown by rectangles; relationships are shown by diamonds; and the maximum cardinality of the relationship is shown inside the diamond.[4] The name of the entity is shown inside the rectangle, and the name of the relationship is shown near the diamond.

Although in some E-R diagrams the name of the relationship is shown inside the diamond, this can make the diagram look awkward, since the diamonds may have to be large and out of scale in order to include the relationship name. To avoid this, relationship names are sometimes written over the diamond. When the name is placed inside or on top of the diamond, the relationship cardinality is shown by placing crow's feet on the lines connecting to the entity(ies) on the many side of the relationship. Figure 3-3(d) shows the DORM-OCCUPANT and STUDENT-CLUB relationships with such crow's feet.

As we stated, the maximum cardinality indicates the maximum number of entities that can be involved in a relationship. The diagrams do not indicate the minimum. For example, Figure 3-3(b) shows that a student is related, at maximum, to one dormitory, but it does not show whether a student *must be* related to a dormitory instance.

A number of different ways are used to show **minimum cardinality**. One way, illustrated in Figure 3-4, is to place a hash mark across the relationship line to indicate that an entity must exist in the relationship and to place an oval across the rela-

---

[4] The graphical symbols that originated with the model (which are the symbols described here) are not the best ones for displaying a model in a GUI system such as the Macintosh or Microsoft Windows. In fact, the E-R model was developed long before any GUI system was popular. Consequently, as vendors developed GUI CASE tools, they chose to invent new symbols for presenting their designs. The result is that an E-R CASE tool may use symbols different from these. This kind of problem is common in the information systems industry: Standards are often "extended" as technology evolves.

FIGURE 3-4

Relationship with Minimum Cardinality
Shown

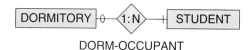

DORM-OCCUPANT

tionship line to indicate that there may or may not be an entity in the relationship. Accordingly, Figure 3-4 shows that a DORMITORY must have a relationship with at least one STUDENT but that a STUDENT is not required to have a relationship with a DORMITORY. The complete relationship restrictions are that a DORMITORY has a minimum cardinality of one and a maximum cardinality of many STUDENT entities. A STUDENT has a minimum cardinality of zero and a maximum cardinality of one DORMITORY entities.

A relationship may exist among entities of the same class. For example, the relationship ROOMS-WITH could be defined on the entity STUDENT. Figure 3-5(a) shows such a relationship, and Figure 3-5(b) shows instances of entities that conform to this relationship. Relationships among entities of a single class are sometimes called **recursive relationships**.

ATTRIBUTES IN ENTITY-RELATIONSHIP DIAGRAMS

In some versions of E-R diagrams, the attributes are shown in ellipses and are connected to the entity or relationship to which they belong. Figure 3-6(a) shows the DORMITORY and STUDENT entities and the DORM-OCCUPANT relationship with the attributes. As shown, DORMITORY has DormName, Location, and NumberOfRooms attributes, and STUDENT has Student, StudentName, and StudentYear attributes. The relationship DORM-OCCUPANT has the attribute Rent, which shows the amount of rent paid by a particular student in a particular dorm.

Listing too many attributes on the E-R diagram may make it cluttered and difficult to interpret. In these cases, entity attributes are listed separately, as shown in Figure 3-6(b). Many CASE tools show such attributes in pop-up GUI windows.

FIGURE 3-5

Recursive Relationship

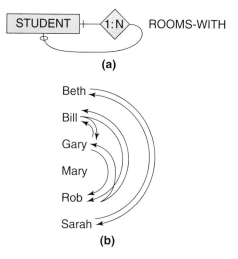

(a)

(b)

FIGURE 3-6

Showing Properties in Entity-Relationship Diagrams: (a) Entity-Relationship Diagram with Properties Shown and (b) Entity-Relationship Diagram with Properties Listed Separately

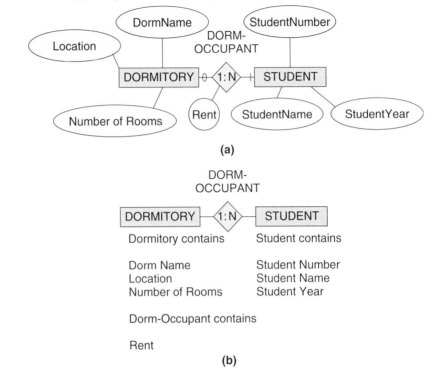

(a)

DORM-
OCCUPANT

DORMITORY ⟨1:N⟩ STUDENT

Dormitory contains   Student contains

Dorm Name   Student Number
Location   Student Name
Number of Rooms   Student Year

Dorm-Occupant contains

Rent

(b)

■ Weak Entities

The entity-relationship model defines a special type of entity called a **weak entity**. Such entities are those whose presence in the database depends on the presence of another entity. An example of such a relationship is that between employees and their dependents. In Figure 3-7(a), the entity DEPENDENT depends on the presence of the entity EMPLOYEE. This means that DEPENDENT data can be stored in the database only if the DEPENDENT has a relationship with an EMPLOYEE entity.

As shown in this figure, weak entities are signified by rounding the corners of the entity rectangle. In addition, the relationship on which the entity depends for its

FIGURE 3-7

Weak Entities: (a) Example of a Weak Entity and (b) ID-dependent Entity

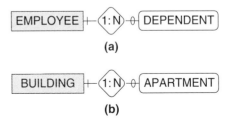

existence is shown in a diamond with rounded corners. Alternatively, in some E-R diagrams (not shown here), weak entities are depicted by using a double line for the boundary of the weak entity rectangle and double diamonds for the relationship on which the entity depends.

The E-R model includes a special type of weak entity called an **ID-dependent entity**. To understand it, compare the relationship among the entities in Figure 3-7(b) with that among the entities in Figure 3-7(a). In Figure 3-7(b), an APARTMENT is logically dependent on a BUILDING; that is, an APARTMENT cannot exist if there is no BUILDING to contain it.

Although both DEPENDENT and APARTMENT are shown as weak entities, there is an important difference between them. A dependent person can physically exist even if no employee claims that person as a dependent. That is, this person's logical existence does not depend on the existence of someone who claims him or her as a dependent. For APARTMENT, however, no entity instance can exist without a BUILDING, because the very existence of an APARTMENT requires the existence of a BUILDING. Thus ID-dependent entities are logically dependent on some other entity.

One way to identify an ID-dependent entity is to examine its identifier. Such entities always have an identifier with two or more attributes. Furthermore, the identifier of an ID-dependent entity includes the identifier of the entity on which it logically depends. For example, the identifier of APARTMENT is {BuildingName, ApartmentNumber}, and the identifier of BUILDING is BuildingName. Hence, the identifier of APARTMENT includes the identifier of BUILDING.

ID-dependent entities are common. Another example is the entity VERSION in the relationship PRODUCT : VERSION, where PRODUCT is a software product and VERSION is a release of that software product. The identifier of PRODUCT is ProductName, and the identifier of VERSION is {ProductName, ReleaseNumber}. A third example is EDITION in the relationship TEXTBOOK : EDITION. The identifier of TEXTBOOK is ISBN, and the identifier of EDITION is {ISBN, EditionNumber}.

■ Subtype Entities[5]

Some entities contain optional sets of attributes. Consider, for example, CLIENT, with attributes ClientNumber, ClientName, and AmountDue. Suppose that a CLIENT can be an individual, a partnership, or a corporation and that additional data is to be stored depending on the type. Assume that this additional data is as follows:

INDIVIDUAL-CLIENT:

Address, SocialSecurityNumber

PARTNERSHIP-CLIENT:

ManagingPartnerName, Address, TaxIdentificationNumber

CORPORATE-CLIENT:

ContactPerson, Phone, TaxIdentificationNumber

---

[5] Subtypes were added to the E-R model after the publication of Chen's initial paper, and they are part of what is called the *extended E-R model*.

One possibility is to allocate all of these attributes to the entity CLIENT, as shown in Figure 3-8(a). In this case, some of the attributes are not applicable. ManagingPartnerName has no meaning for an individual or corporate client, and so it cannot have a value.

A closer-fitting model would instead define three subtype entities, as shown in Figure 3-8(b). Here the INDIVIDUAL-CLIENT, PARTNERSHIP-CLIENT, and CORPORATE-CLIENT entities are shown as **subtypes** of CLIENT. CLIENT, in

FIGURE 3-8

Subtype Entities: (a) CLIENT Without Subtype Entities, (b) CLIENT with Subtype Entities, and (c) Nonexclusive Subtypes with Optional Supertype

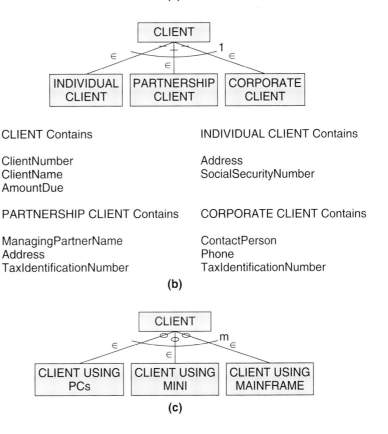

Client Contains

ClientNumber
ClientName
AmountDue
Address
SocialSecurityNumber
ManagingPartnerName
TaxIdentificationNumber
ContactPerson
Phone

(a)

CLIENT Contains

ClientNumber
ClientName
AmountDue

PARTNERSHIP CLIENT Contains

ManagingPartnerName
Address
TaxIdentificationNumber

INDIVIDUAL CLIENT Contains

Address
SocialSecurityNumber

CORPORATE CLIENT Contains

ContactPerson
Phone
TaxIdentificationNumber

(b)

(c)

turn, is a **supertype** of the INDIVIDUAL-CLIENT, PARTNERSHIP-CLIENT, and CORPORATE-CLIENT entities.

The ∈ next to the relationship lines indicates that INDIVIDUAL-CLIENT, PARTNERSHIP-CLIENT, and CORPORATE-CLIENT are subtypes of CLIENT. Each subtype entity must belong to the supertype CLIENT. The curved line with a 1 next to it indicates that a CLIENT entity must belong to one, and only one, subtype. It means that the subtypes are exclusive and that one of them is required.

Subtypes are not always mutually exclusive, however, nor are they always required. Figure 3-8(c) shows the CLIENT-USING subtypes within CLIENT. The m indicates that CLIENT may belong from zero to many CLIENT-USING subtypes. Structures such as this are sometimes called **generalization hierarchies** because CLIENT is a generalization of the three subtypes. Sometimes, too, this relationship type is called an **IS-A relationship**, since, in Figure 3-8(b), INDIVIDUAL-CLIENT *is a* CLIENT, just as PARTNERSHIP-CLIENT and CORPORATE-CLIENT also are CLIENTs.

A way to verify that the term *IS-A* is appropriate is to consider the identifier of all four of these entities. They all have the same identifier, ClientNumber, and so they all have the same name and hence all refer to the same entity. Contrast this situation with the HAS-A relationships shown in Figure 3-3.

Generalization hierarchies have a special characteristic called **inheritance**, which means that the entities in subtypes inherit attributes of the supertype entity class. PARTNERSHIP-CLIENT, for example, inherits ClientName and AmountDue from CLIENT. Again, for inheritance to be appropriate, both of these entity classes must have the same identifier.

Figure 3-9 is an example E-R diagram that contains all of the elements of the E-R model that we have been discussing. It shows the entities and relationships for

FIGURE 3-9

Example Entity-Relationship Diagram

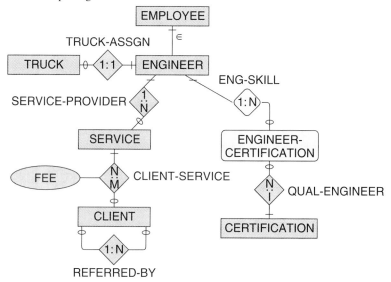

an engineering consulting company that analyzes the construction and condition of houses and other buildings and facilities.

There is an entity class for the company's employees. Because some EMPLOY-EEs are ENGINEERs, there is a subtype relationship between EMPLOYEE and ENGINEER. Every ENGINEER must be an EMPLOYEE; ENGINEER has a 1:1 relationship to TRUCK; and each TRUCK must be assigned to an ENGINEER, but not all ENGINEERs have a TRUCK.

ENGINEERs provide SERVICEs to CLIENTs. An ENGINEER can provide from zero to many services, but a given SERVICE must be provided by an ENGI-NEER and can be provided by only that ENGINEER. CLIENTs have many SER-VICEs, and a SERVICE can be requested by many CLIENTs. A CLIENT must have purchased at least one SERVICE, but SERVICE need not have any CLIENTs. The CLIENT–SERVICE relationship has an attribute Fee, which shows the amount that a particular client paid for a particular service. (Other attributes of entities and relationships are not shown in this diagram.)

Sometimes CLIENTs refer one another, which is indicated by the recursive rela-tionship REFERRED-BY. A given CLIENT can refer one or more other CLIENTs. A CLIENT may or may not have been referred by another client, and a CLIENT may be referred by only one CLIENT.

The ENGINEER-CERTIFICATION entity shows that a given engineer has completed the education and testing required to earn a particular certificate. An ENGINEER may have earned certifications. ENGINEER-CERTIFICATION's existence is dependent on ENGINEER through the relationship ENG-SKILL. CERTIFICATION is the entity that describes a particular certification.

■ Documentation of Business Rules

Chapter 2 defined a database schema as consisting of tables, relationships, domains, and business rules. We can obtain or infer the first three of these from an E-R model, but we cannot obtain business rules from the model. Thus these rules are sometimes added to the E-R model during the data modeling stage.

The E-R model is developed from an analysis of requirements obtained from users. During this analysis, business rules often are brought up, and indeed, most systems analysts make it a point to ask about them.

Consider the entities TRUCK and ENGINEER in Figure 3-9. Does the business have rules concerning who is assigned a TRUCK? If there are not enough TRUCKs for one to be assigned to every ENGINEER, what rules determine who gets a TRUCK? It might be that the database application is to assign trucks based on which ENGINEER has the most number of SERVICEs scheduled during some period of time, the most number of SERVICEs out of the office, or some other rule.

Another example concerns the allocation of ENGINEERs to SERVICEs. There probably are rules concerning the type of ENGINEERING-CERTIFICATION that an ENGINEER must have in order to be assigned to particular types of SERVICE. To inspect an apartment building, for example, the ENGINEER may need to be licensed as a professional ENGINEER. Even if there is no law that dictates this rule, it may be the policy of the company to enforce it.

Business rules may or may not be enforced by the DBMS or by the application program. Sometimes business rules are written in manual procedures that the users of the database application are to follow. At this point, the way in which the rules are to be enforced is not important. What is important is to document these rules so that they become part of the system's requirements.

■ The Entity-Relationship Model and CASE Tools

Developing a data model using the entity-relationship model has become easier in recent years, because the tools for building E-R diagrams are included in many popular CASE products. Products such as IEW, IEF, DEFT, Design/1, and others have drawing and diagramming facilities to create E-R diagrams. Such products also integrate entities with the database relations that represent them, which can facilitate the administration, management, and maintenance of the database.

We do not assume the use of a CASE tool for the discussions in this text. But if your university has such a tool, by all means use it to create E-R diagrams for exercises you are assigned. The E-R diagrams created using these tools are generally more visually pleasing, and they are far easier to change and adapt.

EXAMPLES

The best way to gain proficiency with any modeling tool is to study examples and to use the tool to make your own models. The remainder of this chapter presents three case applications to help you with the first task. The questions at the end are for the second task.

Example 1: The Jefferson Dance Club

The Jefferson Dance Club teaches social dancing and offers both private and group lessons. Jefferson charges $45 per hour per student (or couple) for a private lesson and $6 per hour per student for a group lesson. Private lessons are offered throughout the day, from noon until 10 P.M., six days a week. Group lessons are offered in the evenings.

Jefferson employs two types of instructor: full-time salaried instructors and part-time teachers. The full-time instructors are paid a fixed amount per week, and the part-time instructors are paid either a set amount for an evening or a set amount for teaching a particular class.

In addition to the lessons, Jefferson sponsors two weekly social dances featuring recorded music. The admission charge is $5 per person. The Friday night dance is the more popular and averages around eighty people; the Sunday night dance attracts about thirty attendees. The purpose of the dances is to give the students a place in which to practice their skills. No food or drinks are served.

Jefferson would like to develop an information system to keep track of students and the classes they have taken. Jefferson's managers would also like to know how many and which types of lessons each teacher has taught and to be able to compute the average cost per lesson for each of their instructors.

■ Entities

The best way to begin an entity-relationship model is to determine potential entities. Entities are usually represented by nouns (places, persons, concepts, events, equipment, and so on) in documents or interviews. A search of the previous example for important nouns that relate to the information system reveals the following list:

- Private lesson
- Group lesson
- Teacher
- Full-time teacher
- Part-time teacher
- Dance
- Customer

Clearly, the nouns *private lesson* and *group lesson* have something in common, as do the nouns *teacher, full-time teacher,* and *part-time teacher.* One solution is to define an entity LESSON, with subtypes PRIVATE-LESSON and GROUP-LESSON, and another entity TEACHER, with subtypes FULL-TIME-TEACHER and PART-TIME-TEACHER. Additional entities are DANCE and CUSTOMER.

As stated in Chapter 2, data modeling is as much art as it is science. The solution just described is one of several feasible solutions. A second solution is to eliminate LESSON and TEACHER from the list in the preceding paragraph and to eliminate all subtypes. A third solution is to eliminate LESSON (since lesson was never mentioned by itself as a noun) but to keep TEACHER and its subtypes. Here we choose the third case because it seems to be the best fit for the data we have. Thus the list of entities is PRIVATE-LESSON, GROUP-LESSON, TEACHER, FULL-TIME-TEACHER, PART-TIME-TEACHER, DANCE, and CUSTOMER.

Choosing among these alternatives requires analyzing the requirements and considering the design implications of each of them. Sometimes it helps to consider the attributes of the entities. If, for example, the entity LESSON has no attributes other than its identifier, then it is not required.

■ Relationships

To begin, TEACHER has two subtype entities, FULL-TIME-TEACHER and PART-TIME-TEACHER. A given teacher must be one or the other, as the subtypes are mutually exclusive.

Consider next the relationships between TEACHER and PRIVATE-LESSON and GROUP-LESSON. A TEACHER can teach many PRIVATE-LESSONs, and normally a PRIVATE-LESSON is taught by a single teacher. However, further discussion with Jefferson's management reveals that for advanced dancers, especially those preparing for competitions, sometimes two teachers are involved in a private lesson. Therefore the relationship between TEACHER and PRIVATE-LESSON must be many to many. Assume, however, that only one teacher is involved in a group lesson. The relationships just described are shown in Figure 3-10.

FIGURE 3-10

Initial E-R Diagram for
the Jefferson Dance Club

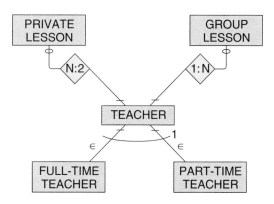

CUSTOMERs can take either PRIVATE-LESSONs or GROUP-LESSONs. Sometimes a lesson is taken by a single individual and sometimes by a couple. There are two ways in which this situation can be modeled. An entity COUPLE can be defined as having a one-to-two relationship with CUSTOMER, or either CUSTOMER or COUPLE can have a relationship with PRIVATE-LESSON. We assume that couples do not take group lessons or that if they do, it is not important to store that fact in the database. This alternative is shown in Figure 3-11(a).

PRIVATE-LESSON's existence is dependent on CUSTOMER or COUPLE. That is, a lesson cannot exist unless it is given to either a CUSTOMER or a COUPLE. The 1 next to the horizontal line underneath CUSTOMER and COUPLE

FIGURE 3-11

Alternatives for Representing
CUSTOMER: (a) E-R Diagram
Showing COUPLE Entity and (b)
E-R Diagram Without Couples

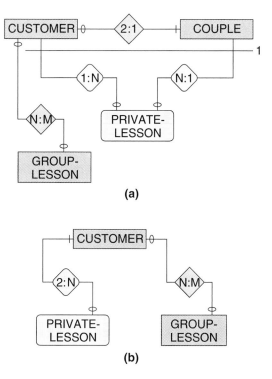

indicates that PRIVATE-LESSON must have at least one CUSTOMER or one COUPLE, which makes sense, since PRIVATE-LESSON is dependent on them.

Another alternative is not to represent couples but, instead, to model the relationship between CUSTOMER and PRIVATE-LESSON as many to many. More precisely, this relationship is one or two to many and is shown in Figure 3-11(b). Although the model is not as detailed as that in Figure 3-11(a), it may very well suffice for Jefferson's purposes.

The last relationship possibility is that between DANCE and other entities. Both customers and teachers attend dances, and the developers must decide whether it is important to store these relationships. Does Jefferson really need to know which customers attended which dances? Do Jefferson's managers really want to record attendance in a computer-based information system as customers enter the door? Do the customers want that fact recorded? Most likely, this is not a relationship that need or should be stored in the database.

The situation between DANCE and TEACHER is different. Jefferson likes some of its teachers to be present at each dance. In order to be fair about this requirement, Jefferson's management has drawn up a schedule for the teachers' attendance at dances. Developing and recording this schedule requires that the database contain the DANCE–TEACHER relationship, which is many to many.

◼ Final E-R Diagram for the Jefferson Dance Club

Figure 3-12 shows an E-R diagram for the model described in this section. We have not named the relationships in this diagram. Although doing so would make the diagrams more true to form, for our data, naming relationships would add little.

PRIVATE-LESSON's existence is dependent on CUSTOMER, but GROUP-LESSON's is not, because group lessons are scheduled long before any customer signs up, and they will be held even if no customers show up. This situation is not

FIGURE 3-12

The Final E-R Diagram
for Jefferson Dance Club

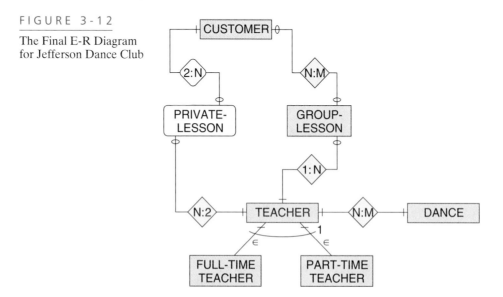

true, however, for private lessons, as they are scheduled only at the customer's request. Also notice that this model does not represent couples.

Once a model such as this is developed, its accuracy and completeness in regard to the requirements should be verified. Usually this is done with the users.

■ Evaluating the E-R Data Model

It is easier and cheaper to correct errors early in the database development process rather than later. For example, changing the maximum cardinality of a relationship from 1:N to N:M in the data modeling stage is simply a matter of recording the change in the E-R diagram. But once the database has been designed and loaded with data and application programs written to process the database, making such a change requires considerable rework, possibly even hundreds of labor hours. It is important, therefore, to evaluate the data model before designing it.

One evaluation technique is to consider the E-R data model in the context of possible queries that might be posed to a database with the structure implied by the model. For example, look at the diagram in Figure 3-12. What questions could be answered from a database that was implemented according to this design?

- Who has taught which private lessons?
- Which customers have taken a private lesson from Jack?
- Who are the full-time teachers?
- Which teachers are scheduled to attend the dance on Friday?

When evaluating an E-R data model, you can construct such questions and show them to the users, who can then be asked to draw up their own list of questions. Their questions can then be posed against the design in order to check its appropriateness. For example, suppose that the users asked which customers attended last week's Friday night dance. The designers of the data model in Figure 3-12 would conclude that their design was not correct, because it is not possible to answer this question using their E-R model. If it must be answered, a relationship between CUSTOMER and DANCE must be constructed.

Clearly, such an informal and loosely structured process cannot be used to *prove* that a design is correct. It is, however, a pragmatic technique that can be used to verify the potential correctness of a design. And it is far better than no evaluation at all!

Example 2: San Juan Sailboat Charters

San Juan Sailboat Charters is an agent that leases sailboats to customers for a fee. San Juan does not own any sailboats but instead leases them on behalf of boat owners who wish to earn income when they are not using their boats. San Juan charges a fee for its service, and it specializes in boats that can be used for multiday or weekly charters. The smallest sailboat is twenty-eight feet long, and the largest is forty-four feet long.

Each sailboat is fully equipped at the time it is leased. Most of the equipment is provided by the owners, but some is added by San Juan. The owner-provided equipment includes what is fixed on the boat, such as radios, compasses, depth indicators and other instrumentation, stoves, and refrigerators. Other owner-provided equipment is not installed as part of the boat. Such equipment includes sails, lines, anchors, dinghies, life preservers, and, in the cabin, dishes, silverware, cooking utensils, bedding, and the like. San Juan provides consumable equipment, which could also be considered supplies, such as charts, navigation books, tide and current tables, soap, dish towels, toilet paper, and similar items.

An important part of San Juan's responsibilities is keeping track of the equipment on the boat. Much of it is expensive, and some of it, particularly what is not attached to the boat, can easily be lost or stolen. Customers are responsible for all equipment during the period of their charter.

San Juan likes to keep accurate records of its customers and the charters, not only for marketing but also for recording which customers have gone on which trips. Some itineraries and weather conditions are more dangerous than others, and so San Juan also likes to know which customers have what experience.

Most of San Juan's business is bare-boat chartering, which means that no skipper or other crew is provided. In some cases, however, customers request the services of a skipper or other crew member, and so San Juan hires such personnel on a part-time basis.

Sailboats often need maintenance. San Juan is required by its contracts with the boat owners to keep accurate records of all maintenance activities and costs, including normal activities such as cleaning or engine-oil changes, and unscheduled repairs. In some cases, repairs are necessary during a charter. A boat engine, for example, might fail while the boat is far away from San Juan's facility. In this case, the customers radio the San Juan dispatcher, who determines the best facility to make the repair and sends its personnel to the disabled boat. To make these decisions, the dispatchers need information about repair facilities as well as past histories of repair quality and costs.

Before you continue reading, you might try to produce an entity-relationship diagram on your own. Examine the preceding statements and look for nouns that seem important to the design. Then check the possible relationships among the entities. Finally, if you wish, list the likely attributes for each entity or relationship.

■ Entities

The data model required for San Juan Charters is more complicated than that for the Jefferson Dance Club. Potential entities are shown in Figure 3-13(a). The equipment-related entities suggest possible subtypes, and defining subtypes is certainly a feasible alternative. So that we can illustrate another design approach, however, we will not define subtypes in this case.

Consider the equipment-related entities. Why does San Juan need to model them? The goal is not to keep track of their characteristics. We do not need to maintain data about the length chain on each anchor, for example. Instead, the requirement is just to keep track of the items and their type. This can be done without

FIGURE 3-13

Entities for San Juan
Charters

LEASE
BOAT
CUSTOMER
OWNER
EQUIPMENT
OWNER-PROVIDED-EQUIPMENT
FIXED OWNER-EQUIPMENT
REMOVABLE OWNER-EQUIPMENT
SAN-JUAN-PROVIDED-EQUIPMENT
ITINERARY/WEATHER
CHARTER
PART-TIME-CREW
SCHEDULED-MAINTENANCE
UNSCHEDULED-MAINTENANCE
REPAIRS
REPAIR-FACILITY

(a) Possible entities for San Juan Charters

LEASE or CHARTER(synonyms)
BOAT
CUSTOMER
OWNER
EQUIPMENT
ITINERARY/WEATHER
PART-TIME-CREW
SCHEDULED-MAINTENANCE
REPAIR or UNSCHEDULED-MAINTENANCE(synonyms)
REPAIR-FACILITY

(b) Entities selected for the E-R design

keeping detailed records of the particular subtypes of equipment. Thus, for this design, we place all types of equipment into the entity EQUIPMENT.

Ownership of equipment is established by defining a relationship between EQUIPMENT and OWNER. If San Juan Charters is allowed to be an instance of OWNER, all of the equipment that it owns can be carried by this relationship. Similarly, from the case description, there is no reason to define the equipment that is attached to the boat differently from that not attached. An accurate list can be produced without this division. Figure 3-13(b) shows the final list of entities. Note that LEASE and CHARTER are synonyms; they refer to the same transaction. We show both names here so that they can be related to the case description.

It is possible that SCHEDULED-MAINTENANCE should be combined with UNSCHEDULED-MAINTENANCE. One way to decide is to examine the attributes of each of these entities. If they are the same, the two entity classes should be merged into one. Also observe that REPAIR and UNSCHEDULED-MAINTE-NANCE are defined as synonyms.

FIGURE 3-14

E-R Diagram for
San Juan Charters

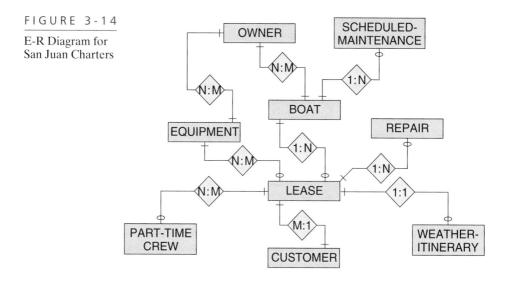

Relationships

Figure 3-14 is an entity-relationship diagram for San Juan Charters. For the most part, the relationships in this diagram are straightforward, but the relationship between EQUIPMENT and LEASE is arguable. One might say that EQUIPMENT should be related to BOAT and not to LEASE or that some EQUIPMENT should be related to BOAT (the equipment that stays with the boat) and the other equipment should be related to LEASE. These changes would be feasible alternatives to the design shown in Figure 3-14.

Notice, too, that SCHEDULED-MAINTENANCE is related to BOAT but that REPAIR (UNSCHEDULED-MAINTENANCE) is related to LEASE. This implies that no repair action is required when the boat is not being leased. Perhaps this is unrealistic.

Finally, LEASE and ITINERARY-WEATHER have a 1:1 relationship, and they also have the same identifying attributes. Therefore, it would be possible, and might even be preferable, to combine them into one entity class.

DATABASES AS MODELS OF MODELS

As you can see, there are many different ways of modeling a business situation, and the variety becomes even greater as the application grows more complex. Often, dozens of models are feasible, and it can be difficult to choose among them.

Sometimes when evaluating alternatives, project team members discuss and argue about which data model best represents the real world. These discussions are misguided. Databases do not model the real world, although it is a common misconception that they do. Rather, databases are models of the users' models of the world (or, more to the point, of their business world). The question to ask when evaluating alternative data models is not "Does this design accurately represent the real world?" but, rather, "Does this design accurately represent the users' model of his or her environment?" The goal is to develop a design that fits the users' mental conception.

In fact, Immanuel Kant and other philosophers argued that it is impossible for humans to build models of what actually exists, claiming that the essence of things is forever unknowable by humans.[6] Extending this line of argument to computer systems, Winograd and Flores stated that in societies, humans construct systems of tokens that enable them to operate successfully in the world. A series of tokens is not a model of the infinitude of reality but, rather, only a social system that enables users to coordinate their activities successfully, and nothing more can be said.[7]

Computer systems therefore need to model and represent their users' communications with one another. They do not model anything other than that system of tokens and communications. So learn to ask these questions of yourself: "Does this model accurately reflect the users' perceptions and mental models of their world? Will it help the users respond consistently and successfully with one another and with their clients?" It is pointless for one analyst to claim that his or her model is a better representation of reality. Instead, the point is to develop a model that well represents the user's model of his or her business environment.

SUMMARY

The entity-relationship model was first described by Peter Chen. With this model, entities—which are identifiable things of importance to the users—are defined. All of the entities of a given type form an entity class. A particular entity is called an instance. Entities have attributes that describe their characteristics, and one or more attributes identifies an entity.

Relationships are associations among entities. The E-R model explicitly defines relationships; each relationship has a name; and there are relationship classes as well as relationship instances.

The degree of the relationship is the number of entities participating in the relationship. Most relationships are binary. The three types of binary relationships are 1:1, 1:N, and N:M.

In entity-relationship diagrams, the entities are shown in rectangles, and the relationships are shown in diamonds. The maximum cardinality of the relationship is shown inside the diamond. The minimum cardinality is indicated by a hash mark or an oval. Relationships that connect entity instances of the same class are recursive. Attributes can be shown in an E-R diagram in ellipses or in a separate table.

A weak entity is one whose existence depends on another entity. Weak entities are shown in rectangles with rounded corners, and the relationship on which the entity depends is indicated by a diamond with rounded corners.

[6] "We cannot, indeed, beyond all possible experience, form a definitive concept of what things in themselves may be. Yet we are not at liberty to abstain entirely from inquiring into them; for experience never satisfies reason fully, but, in answering questions, refers us further and further back and leaves us dissatisfied with regard to the complete solution." Immanuel Kant, *Prolegomena to Any Future Metaphysics* (Indianapolis: Bobbs-Merrill, 1950), p. 100.

[7] Terry Winograd and F. Flores, *Understanding Computers and Cognition* (Reading, MA: Addison-Wesley, 1986).

Some entities have subtypes that define subsets of similar entities. Subtypes inherit attributes from their parent, the supertype. HAS-A relationships connect entities of different types, and the identifiers of the entities are different. IS-A relationships are subtypes, and the identifiers of the entities are the same.

Once a data model is developed, the designers should consider business rules that may restrict processing against entities. Each entity in the model should be evaluated in light of possible data additions, changes, and deletions. Deletions, in particular, often are the source of important processing restrictions. When business rules are discovered, they should be documented in the data model.

The E-R model is an important part of many CASE products. These products provide tools for constructing and storing E-R diagrams. Some CASE tools integrate the E-R constructs with data constructs in the CASE repository.

Once they are completed, E-R models should be evaluated. One technique is to list queries that could be answered using the data model. This list is then shown to the users, who are asked to think of additional questions. The design is then evaluated against these questions to ensure that the model can answer them.

Databases do not model the real world but instead model the users' model of their business world. The appropriate criterion for judging a data model is whether the model fits the users' model. Arguing about which model best fits the real world is pointless.

GROUP I QUESTIONS

3.1   Define *entity* and give an example.

3.2   Explain the difference between an entity class and an entity instance.

3.3   Define *attribute* and give examples for the entity you described in Question 1.

3.4   Explain what a composite attribute is and give an example.

3.5   Which attribute defined in your answer to Question 3 identifies the entity?

3.6   Define *relationship* and give an example.

3.7   Explain the difference between a relationship class and a relationship instance.

3.8   Define *degree of relationship*. Give an example, other than the one in this text, of a relationship greater than degree 2.

3.9   List and give an example of the three types of binary relationships. Draw an E-R diagram for each.

3.10 Define the terms *maximum cardinality* and *minimum cardinality*.

3.11 Name and sketch the symbols used in entity-relationship diagrams for (a) entity, (b) relationship, (c) weak entity and its relationship, (d) recursive relationship, and (e) subtype entity.

3.12 Give an example E-R diagram for the entities DEPARTMENT and EMPLOYEE, which have a 1:N relationship. Assume that a DEPARTMENT does not need to have any EMPLOYEE but that every EMPLOYEE does have a DEPARTMENT.

3.13 Give an example of a recursive relationship and show it in an E-R diagram.

3.14 Show example attributes for DEPARTMENT and EMPLOYEE (from Question 12). Describe the two ways that attributes can appear on or with E-R diagrams.

3.15 Define the term *weak entity* and give an example other than the one in this text.

3.16 Explain why weak entities are ambiguous. Give examples, other than those in this text, of each type of weak entity. Explain the term *ID-dependent entity*.

3.17 Describe subtype entities and give an example other than those in this text.

3.18 Explain the term *inheritance* and show how it applies to your answer to Question 17.

3.19 Explain the difference between a HAS-A relationship and an IS-A relationship, and give an example of each.

3.20 What are processing restrictions? How can an E-R diagram be used to discover such restrictions? How should such restrictions be documented?

3.21 How can CASE tools be used to construct E-R diagrams?

3.22 Describe why it is important to evaluate a data model once it has been created. Summarize one technique for evaluating a data model, and explain how that technique could be used to evaluate the data model in Figure 3.14.

GROUP II QUESTIONS

3.23 Change the E-R diagram in Figure 3-12 to include an entity LESSON. Let PRIVATE-LESSON and GROUP-LESSON be subtypes of LESSON. Modify the relationships as necessary.

3.24 Change the E-R diagram in Figure 3-12 to exclude TEACHER. Modify the relationships as necessary.

3.25 Which of the models in Figure 3-12 and in your answers to Questions 23 and 24 do you prefer? Explain the reason for your preference.

3.26 Change the E-R diagram in Figure 3-14 to include subtypes of equipment. Assume that the equipment owned by San Juan Charters pertains to LEASE and that other equipment pertains to BOAT. Model the differences between the BOAT-related equipment that is fixed on the boats and the BOAT-related equipment that is not fixed. What benefits does the added complexity of this model bring?

PROJECT

Develop an E-R diagram for the following: The Metropolitan Housing Agency (MHA) is a nonprofit organization that advocates the development and improvement of low-income housing. The MHA operates in a metropolitan area of approximately 2.2 million people in a midwestern city.

The MHA maintains data about the location, availability, and condition of low-income housing in eleven different census tracts in the metropolitan area. Within the boundaries of these tracts are approximately 250 different buildings that provide low-income housing. On average, each building contains twenty-five apartments or other units.

The MHA keeps data about each census tract, including geographic boundaries, median income of the population, elected officials, principal businesses, principal investors involved in attributes in that tract, and other demographic and economic data. It also maintains a limited amount of data about crime. For each building, the MHA stores the name, address, size, owner(s)'s name and address, mortgagor(s)'s name and address, renovations and repairs, and availability of facilities for handicapped people. In addition, the MHA keeps a list of each of the units within each building, including the type of unit, size, number of bedrooms, number of baths, kitchen and dining facilities, location in the building, and any special remarks. The MHA would like to maintain data regarding the average occupancy rates for each unit, but to date, it has been unable to collect or store such data. The MHA does, however, keep data about whether a given unit is occupied.

The MHA serves as an information clearinghouse and offers three basic services. First, it works with politicians, lobbyists, and advocacy groups to support legislation that encourages the development of low-income housing through tax incentives, developmental zoning preferences, and other legislative inducements. To accomplish this, the MHA provides information about low-income housing to state, county, and city governments. Second, through speeches, seminars, displays at conventions, and other public relations activities, the MHA strives to raise the community's consciousness about the need for low-income housing. Finally, the MHA provides information about the availability of low-income housing to other agencies that work with the low-income and homeless populations.

SEMANTIC OBJECT MODEL

This chapter discusses the semantic object model, which, like the E-R model in Chapter 3, is used to document the users' requirements and to build data models. As shown in Figure 4-1, the development team interviews users; analyzes the users' reports, forms, and queries; and from these constructs a model of the users' data. This data model is later transformed into a database design.

The particular form of the data model depends on the constructs used to build it. If an E-R model is used, the model will have entities, relationships, and the like. If a semantic model is used, the model will have semantic objects and related constructs, which are discussed in this chapter.

The E-R model and the semantic object model are like lenses through which the database developers look when studying and documenting the users' data. Both lenses work and they both ultimately result in a database design. They use different lenses to form that design, however, and because the lenses create different images, the designs they produce may not be exactly the same. When developing a database, you must decide which approach to use, just as a photographer needs to decide which lens to use. Each approach has strengths and weaknesses, which we discuss at the end of this chapter.

FIGURE 4-1

Using Different Data Models for Database Designs

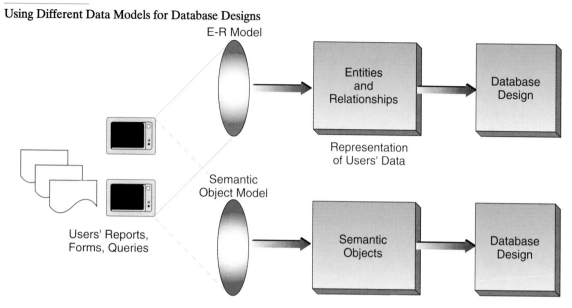

The semantic object model was first presented in the third edition of this text, in 1988. It is based on concepts that were developed and published by Codd and by Hammer and McLeod.[1]

SEMANTIC OBJECTS

The purpose of a database application is to provide forms, reports, and queries so that the users can record data and obtain the information they need about entities or objects important to their work. The main goals of the early stages of database development are to build a data model that documents the things to be represented in the database, to determine the characteristics of those things that need to be stored, and to establish the relationships among them.

In Chapter 3, we referred to these things as entities. In this chapter, we refer to them as semantic objects, or sometimes as just objects. The word *semantic* means meaning, and a semantic object is one that models, in part, the meaning of the users' data. Semantic objects model the users' perceptions more closely than does the E-R model. We use the adjective *semantic* with the word *object* to distinguish the objects discussed in this chapter from the objects defined in object-oriented programming (OOP) languages. The similarities and differences between semantic objects and OOP objects are explained at the end of this chapter.

---

[1]   E. F. Codd, "Extending the Relational Model to Capture More Meaning," *ACM Transactions on Database Systems*, December 1976, pp. 397–424; and Michael Hammer and Dennis McLeod, "Database Description with SDM: A Semantic Database Model," *ACM Transactions on Database Systems*, September 1981, pp. 351–386.

■ Defining Semantic Objects

Entities and objects are similar in some ways, and they are different in other ways. We begin with the similarities. A semantic object is a representation of some identifiable thing in the users' work environment. More formally, a semantic object is a *named collection of attributes that sufficiently describes a distinct identity.*

Like entities, semantic objects are grouped into classes. An object class has a *name* that distinguishes it from other classes and that corresponds to the names of the things it represents. Thus a database that supports users who work with records of students has an object class called STUDENT. Note that object class names, like entity class names, are spelled with capital letters. A particular semantic object is an instance of the class. Thus, 'William Jones' is an instance of the STUDENT class, and 'Accounting' is an instance of the DEPARTMENT class.

Like entities, an object has a *collection of attributes.* Each attribute represents a characteristic of the identity being represented. For instance, the STUDENT object could have attributes like Name, HomeAddress, CampusAddress, DateOfBirth, DateOfGraduation, and Major. This collection of attributes also is a *sufficient description,* which means that the attributes represent all of the characteristics that the users need in order to do their work. As we stated at the end of Chapter 3, things in the world have an infinite set of characteristics; we cannot represent all of them. Instead, we represent those necessary for the users to satisfy their information needs so that they can successfully perform their jobs. Sufficient description also means that the objects are complete in themselves. All of the data required about a CUSTOMER, for example, is located in the CUSTOMER object, and so we need not look anywhere else to find data about CUSTOMERs.

Objects represent *distinct identities;* that is, they are something that users recognize as independent and separate and that users want to track and report. These identities are the nouns about which the information is to be produced. To understand better the term *distinct identity,* recall that there is a difference between objects and object instances. CUSTOMER is the name of an object, and 'CUSTOMER 12345' is the name of an instance of an object. When we say that an object represents a distinct identity, we mean that users consider each *instance* of an object to be unique and identifiable in its own right.

Finally, note that the identities that the objects represent may or may not have a physical existence. For example, EMPLOYEEs physically exist, but ORDERs do not. Orders are, themselves, models of a contractual agreement to provide certain goods or services under certain terms and conditions. They are not physical things but, rather, representations of agreements. Thus something need not be physical in order to be considered an object; it need only be identifiable in its own right in the minds of the users.

■ Attributes

Semantic objects have attributes that define their characteristics. There are three types of attributes. *Simple attributes* have a single value. Examples are DateOfHire, InvoiceNumber, and SalesTotal. *Group attributes* are composites of other attributes. One example is Address, which contains the attributes {Street, City, State, Zip}, and another is Phone, which contains the attributes {AreaCode, LocalNumber}. *Seman-*

FIGURE 4-2

DEPARTMENT Object Diagram:
(a) **DEPARTMENT** Object and
(b) **DEPARTMENT** Object with Cardinalities

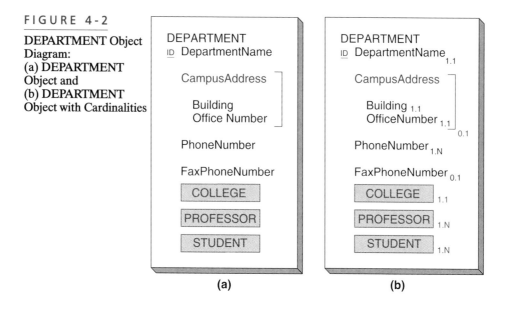

(a)   (b)

tic object attributes are attributes that establish a relationship between one semantic object and another.

To understand these statements better, look at Figure 4-2(a), which is an example of a **semantic object diagram**, or **object diagram**. Such diagrams are used by development teams to summarize the structures of objects and to present them visually. Objects are shown in portrait-oriented rectangles, in which the name of the object appears at the top. Attributes are written in order after the object name.

The DEPARTMENT object contains an example of each of the three types of attributes: DepartmentName, PhoneNumber, and FaxPhoneNumber all are simple attributes, each of which represents a single data element. CampusAddress is a group attribute containing the simple attributes OfficeNumber and Building. Finally, COLLEGE, PROFESSOR, and STUDENT each are semantic object attributes, which means that those objects are connected to and logically contained in DEPARTMENT. Stated differently, according to this model, when a user thinks about a DEPARTMENT, he or she thinks not only about DepartmentName, Address, Phone, and FaxPhone but also about the COLLEGE, PROFESSORs, and STUDENTs that are related to that department. Since COLLEGE, PROFESSOR, and STUDENT also are objects, the complete data model contains object diagrams for them, too. The COLLEGE object contains attributes of the college; the PROFESSOR object contains attributes of the faculty; and the STUDENT object contains attributes of the students

ATTRIBUTE CARDINALITY

Each attribute in a semantic object has both a minimum cardinality and a maximum cardinality. The minimum cardinality indicates the number of instances of the attribute that must exist in order for the object to be valid. Usually this number is either 0 or 1. If it is 0, the attribute is not required to have a value. If it is 1, the attribute must have a value. Although unusual, the minimum cardinality can sometimes be larger than 1. For example, the attribute PLAYER in an object called BAS-KETBALL-TEAM might have a minimum cardinality of 5, since this is the smallest number of players required to make up a basketball team.

The maximum cardinality indicates the maximum number of instances of the attribute that the object may have. It is usually either 1 or N. If it is 1, the attribute can have no more than one instance; if it is N, the attribute can have many values, and the absolute number is not specified. Sometimes the maximum cardinality is a specific number such as 5, meaning the object can contain no more than exactly five instances of the attribute. For example, the attribute PLAYER in BASKETBALL-TEAM might have a maximum cardinality of 5, since the team may have no more than five players.

Cardinalities are shown as subscripts of attributes in the format **n.m**, where n is the minimum cardinality and m is the maximum. In Figure 4-2(b), the minimum cardinality of DepartmentName is 1 and the maximum is also 1, which means that exactly one value of DepartmentName is required. The cardinality of PhoneNumber is 1.N, meaning that a DEPARTMENT is required to have at least one PhoneNumber but may have many. The cardinality of 0.1 in FaxPhoneNumber means that a DEPARTMENT may have either zero or one FaxPhoneNumber.

The cardinalities of groups and the attributes in groups can be subtle. Consider the attribute CampusAddress. Its cardinalities are 0.1, meaning a DEPARTMENT may have zero or one address (indicating the users' model is such that a DEPART-MENT's address does not have to be specified). Now examine the attributes in CampusAddress. Both OfficeNumber and Building have the cardinalities 1.1. You might be wondering how a group can be optional if the attributes in that group are required. The answer is that the cardinalities operate only between the attribute and the container of that attribute. The minimum cardinality of CampusAddress indicates that there need not be a value for address *in DEPARTMENT*. But the minimum cardinalities of OfficeNumber and Building do indicate that both OfficeNumber and Building must exist *in CampusAddress*. Thus a CampusAddress group need not appear, but if one does, it must have a value for both OfficeNumber and Building.

Showing all of the cardinalities of an object sometimes clutters the diagram. In the diagrams in this text, we assume that all simple attributes have the cardinality 0.1. As long as this is true, we do not show the cardinality of simple attributes. But if it is not true, we do show the specific cardinality. We always show the cardinalities of group and semantic object attributes.

OBJECT INSTANCES

The object diagrams for DEPARTMENT shown in Figure 4-2 is a format, or general structure, that can be used for any department. An instance of the DEPARTMENT object is shown in Figure 4-3, with each attribute's value for a particular department. The DepartmentName is Information Systems, and it is located in Room 213 of the Social Science Building. Observe that there are three values for PhoneNumber—the Information Systems Department has three phone lines in its office. Other depart-ments may have fewer or more, but every department has at least one.

Furthermore, there is one instance of COLLEGE, the College of Business, and there are multiple values for the PROFESSOR and STUDENT object attributes. Each of these object attributes is a complete object; each has all the attributes

FIGURE 4-3

An Instance of the DEPARTMENT
Object in Figure 4-2

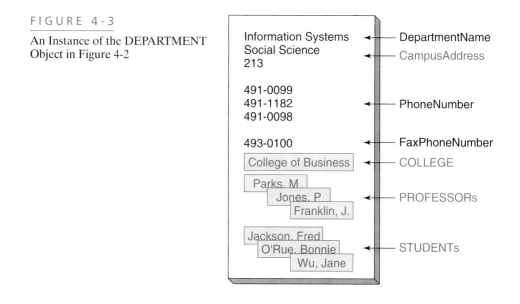

defined for an object of that type. To keep this diagram simple, only the identifying
names are shown for each of the instances of object attribute.

An object diagram is a picture of the user's perception of an object in the work
environment. Thus, in the user's mind, the DEPARTMENT object includes all of
this data. A DEPARTMENT logically contains data about the COLLEGE in which
it resides, as well as the PROFESSORs and STUDENTs who are related to that
department.

PAIRED ATTRIBUTES

The semantic object model has no one-way object relationships. If an object contains another object, the second object will contain the first. For example, if
DEPARTMENT contains the object attribute COLLEGE, then COLLEGE will
contain the matching object attribute DEPARTMENT. These object attributes are
called **paired attributes**, since they always occur as a pair.

Why must object attributes be paired? The answer lies in the way in which
human beings think about relationships. If Object A has a relationship with Object
B, then Object B will have a relationship with Object A. At the least, B is related to
A in the relationship of "things that are related to B." If this argument seems
obscure, try to envision a one-way relationship between two objects. It cannot be
done.

■ Object Identifiers

An **object identifier** is one or more object attributes that the users employ to identify
object instances. Such identifiers are potential names for a semantic object. In
CUSTOMER, for example, possible identifiers are CustomerID, CustomerName,
and CustomerPhone. Each of these are attributes that users consider to be valid
names of CUSTOMER instances. Compare these identifiers with attributes like

DateOfFirstOrder, StockPrice, and NumberOfEmployees. Such attributes are not identifiers because the users do not think of them as names of CUSTOMER instances.

A **group identifier** is an identifier that has more than one attribute. Examples are {FirstName, LastName}, {AreaCode, PhoneNumber}, and {PhoneNumber, First-Name}.

Object identifiers may or may not be unique, depending on how the users view their data. For example, InvoiceNumber is a unique identifier for ORDER, but StudentName is not a unique identifier for STUDENT. There may, for example, be two students named 'Mary Smith.' If so, the users will employ StudentName to identify a group of one or more students and then, if necessary, use values of other attributes to identify a particular member of that set.

In semantic object diagrams, object identifiers are denoted by the letters *ID* in front of the attribute. If the identifier is unique, these letters will be underlined. In Figure 4-2(b), for example, the attribute DepartmentName is a unique identifier of DEPARTMENT.

Normally, if an attribute is to be used as an identifier, its value is required. Also, generally there is no more than one value of an identifier attribute for a given object. In most cases, therefore, the cardinality of an ID attribute is 1.1, and so we use this value as a default.

There are (relatively few) cases, however, in which the cardinality of an identifier is other than 1.1. Consider, for example, the attribute Alias in the semantic object PERSON. A person need not have an alias, or he or she may have several aliases. Hence the cardinality of Alias is 0.N.

■ Attribute Domains

The **domain** of an attribute is a description of an attribute's possible values. The characteristics of a domain depend on the type of the attribute. The domain of a simple attribute consists of both a physical and a semantic description. The physical description indicates the type of data (for example, numeric versus string), the length of the data, and other restrictions or constraints (such as the first character must be alphabetic, or the value must not exceed 9999.99).

The semantic description indicates the function or purpose of the attribute—it distinguishes this attribute from other attributes that might have the same physical description. For example, the domain of DepartmentName might be defined as "the set of strings of up to seven characters that represent names of departments at Highline University." The phrase *strings of up to seven characteristics* is the physical description of the domain, and the phrase *that represent names of departments at Highline University* is the semantic description. The semantic description differentiates strings of seven characters that represent names of departments from similar strings that represent, say, names of courses or buildings or some other attribute.

In some cases, the physical description of a simple attribute domain is an **enumerated list**, the set of an attribute's specific values. The domain of the attribute PartColor, for example, might be the enumerated list 'Blue', 'Yellow', 'Red'.

The domain of a group attribute also has a physical and a semantic description. The physical description is a list of all of the attributes in the group and the order of those attributes. The semantic description is the function or purpose of the group. Thus the physical domain description of CampusAddress (in Figure 4-2) is the list OfficeNumber, Building; the semantic description is *the location of an office at Highline University.*

The domain of an object attribute is the set of object instances of that type. In Figure 4-2, for example, the domain of the PROFESSOR object attribute is the set of all PROFESSOR object instances in the database. The domain of the COLLEGE object is the set of all COLLEGEs in the database. In a sense, the domain of an object attribute is a dynamically enumerated list; the list contains all of the object instances of a particular type.

◼ Semantic Object Views

Users access the values of object attributes through database applications that provide data entry forms, reports, and queries. In most cases, such forms, reports, and queries do not require access to all of an object's attributes. For example, Figure 4-4 shows two application views of DEPARTMENT. Some attributes of DEPARTMENT (its DepartmentName, for example) are visible in both application views. Other attributes are visible in only one. For example, STUDENT is seen only in the StudentListing View, but PROFESSOR is visible in only the Staff View.

The portion of an object that is visible to a particular application is called the **semantic object view** or simply the **view**. A view consists of the name of the object plus a list of all of the attributes visible from that view.

Views are used in two ways. When developing a database they are used to develop the data model. Look at Figure 4-1 again. As shown, when developing the data model, the database and application developers work backward. That is, they

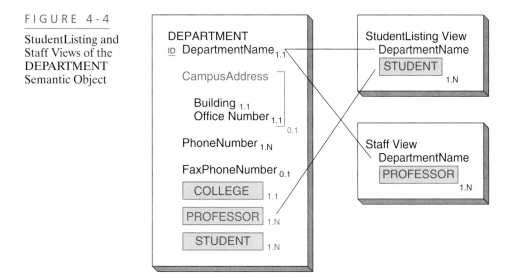

FIGURE 4-4

StudentListing and Staff Views of the DEPARTMENT Semantic Object begin with the forms, reports, and queries that the users say they need and then work backward to the database design. To do this, the team selects a required form, report, or query and determines the view that must exist in order for the form, report, or query to be created. Then the team selects the next form, report, or query and does the same. These two views are then integrated. This process is repeated until the structure of the entire database has been created.

The second way in which views are used occurs after the database structure has been created. At this point, views are constructed to support new forms, reports, and queries based on the existing database structure. Examples of this second use are shown in Part IV when we discuss database implementation.

CREATING DATA MODELS WITH SEMANTIC OBJECTS

This section illustrates a process for developing semantic objects, in which the developers examine the application interface—forms, reports, and queries—and work backward (or reverse-engineer) to derive the object structure.

For example, to model the structure of a DEPARTMENT object, we first gather all of the reports, forms, and queries based on DEPARTMENT. From them, we define a DEPARTMENT object that enables those reports, forms, and queries to be constructed. For a totally new application, however, there will be no computer-based reports, forms, or queries to examine. In this case, the developers begin by determining what objects the users need to track. Then through interviews with the users, the team finds out what object attributes are important. From this, prototypes of forms and reports can be constructed that are then used to refine the data model.

■ An Example: The Highline University Administration Database

Suppose that the administration at Highline University wants to keep track of department, faculty, and student major data. Without getting into the details of the applications, suppose that the system needs to produce four reports (Figures 4-5, 4-7, 4-9, and 4-11). Our goal is to examine these reports and, using reverse engineering, determine from them the objects and attributes that must be stored in the database.

THE COLLEGE OBJECT

Consider the first report in Figure 4-5, about a college—specifically, the College of Business. This example is only one instance of the report; Highline University has similar reports about other colleges, such as the College of Arts and Sciences and the College of Social Sciences. When creating a data model, it is important to gather enough examples to form a representative sample of all of the college reports. Here we assume that the report in Figure 4-5 is representative.

In examining the report, we find data specific to the college—such as the name, telephone number, and office of the dean—and also facts about each of the depart-

FIGURE 4-5

Example COLLEGE Report

College of Business Mary B. Jefferson, Dean			
Phone: 232-1187		Campus Address: Business Building, Room 100	
Department	Chairperson	Phone	Total Majors
Accounting	Jackson, Seymour P.	232-1841	318
Finance	HeuTeng, Susan	232-1414	211
Info Systems	Brammer, Nathaniel	236-0011	247
Management	Tuttle, Christine A.	236-9988	184
Production	Barnes, Jack T.	236-1184	212

ments within the college. This *suggests* that the database might contain COLLEGE and DEPARTMENT objects, with a relationship between the two.

These preliminary findings are documented in the object diagrams in Figure 4-6. Notice that we have omitted cardinalities from the simple attributes. The ID attributes have a cardinality of 1.1; otherwise, all the simple attributes have a cardinality of 0.1.

The cardinality of DEPARTMENT within COLLEGE is 1.N, indicating that a COLLEGE must have at least one DEPARTMENT and that it may have many. This minimum cardinality cannot be deduced from the report in Figure 4-5; rather, it was obtained by asking the users whether or not a college could exist with no departments. Their answer was no.

FIGURE 4-6

First Version of COLLEGE and DEPARTMENT Objects

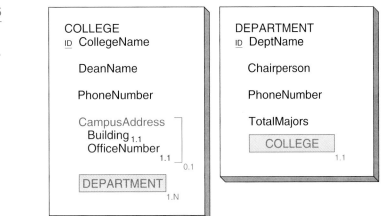

Also note that the structure of DEPARTMENT is inferred from the data shown in Figure 4-5. Since object attributes are always paired, COLLEGE is shown in DEPARTMENT, even though, strictly speaking, this fact cannot be determined from Figure 4-5. As with the DEPARTMENT attribute in COLLEGE, the users were asked to determine the cardinalities of the COLLEGE attribute. They are 1.1, meaning that a DEPARTMENT must be related to one, and only one, COLLEGE.

As an aside, we have interpreted the report in Figure 4-5 to mean that the groups of repeating data refer to DEPARTMENT as an independent object. In fact, such repeating groups are often a signal that the repeating group is data concerning another object. *This is not always the case, however.* The repeating group can also be a group attribute that happens to have several values.

You may be wondering how to tell the difference between repeating-object data and repeating-group data. To answer such questions, you must consult the users about the semantics of the data. You must ask whether this repeating-group data is only a part of the college or whether it refers to something else that stands on its own. If it is the former, it is a group attribute; if it is the latter, it is a semantic object. Also, look for other reports (or forms or queries). Do the users have one for departments? If so, then the assumption that DEPARTMENT is a semantic object would be confirmed. In fact, the personnel at Highline use two reports regarding Departments. This fact further substantiates the notion that a DEPARTMENT object must be defined.

THE DEPARTMENT OBJECT

The department report shown in Figure 4-7 contains departmental data, along with a list of the professors who are assigned to those departments. Note that this report contains data concerning the department's campus address. Since this data does not appear in the object in Figure 4-6, we need to add it to the DEPARTMENT object, as has been done in Figure 4-8. This adjustment is typical of the data modeling process. That is, the semantic objects are continually adjusted as new reports, forms, and queries are identified and analyzed.

FIGURE 4-7

Example DEPARTMENT Report

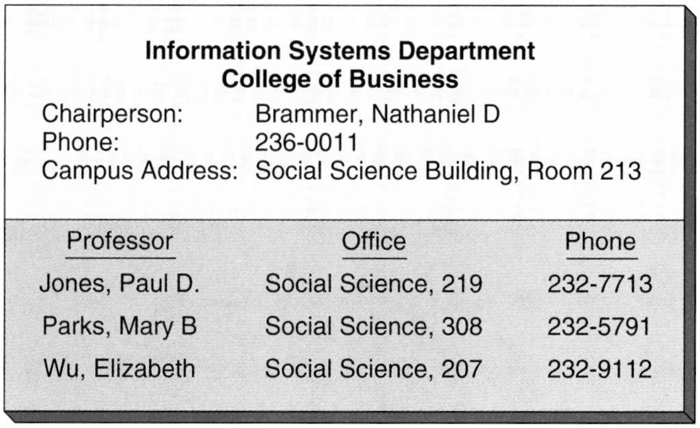

Information Systems Department
College of Business

Chairperson: Brammer, Nathaniel D
Phone: 236-0011
Campus Address: Social Science Building, Room 213

Professor	Office	Phone
Jones, Paul D.	Social Science, 219	232-7713
Parks, Mary B	Social Science, 308	232-5791
Wu, Elizabeth	Social Science, 207	232-9112

FIGURE 4-8

Adjusted
DEPARTMENT and
New PROFESSOR
Objects

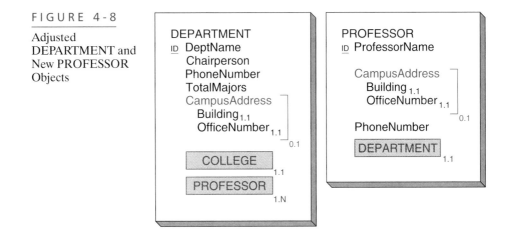

THE PROFESSOR OBJECT

The report in Figure 4-7 not only indicates that a DEPARTMENT object needs to be modeled but also, as in Figure 4-7, suggests that another object may be needed, in this case PROFESSOR. Accordingly, a PROFESSOR object was added to the model, as shown in Figure 4-8. The ID of PROFESSOR, which is ProfessorName, is not unique, which is denoted by not underlining the ID in Figure 4-8.

According to the object diagrams in Figure 4-8, a DEPARTMENT must have at least one PROFESSOR and may have several, but a PROFESSOR must have one, and only one, DEPARTMENT. Thus according to this model, joint appointments are prohibited. This restriction is part of the business rules and data semantics that must be obtained from interviews with the users.

Figure 4-9 shows a second report about a department. This one concerns a department and the students who major in that area. Having two reports about an object is typical; they are simply documenting different views of the same thing. Moreover, the existence of this second report strengthens the notion that department is an object in the minds of the users.

FIGURE 4-9

Second Example
DEPARTMENT
Report

Student Major List		
Information Systems Department		
Chairperson: Brammer, Nathaniel D Phone: 232-4146		
Major's Name	Student Number	Phone
Jackson, Robin R.	12345	237-8713
Lincoln, Fred J.	48127	237-8713
Madison, Janice A.	12345	237-8713

THE STUDENT OBJECT

The report in Figure 4-9 gives data about those students who major in that area, implying that such students are also an object. Therefore the DEPARTMENT object must contain the STUDENT object as well as the PROFESSOR object, as in Figure 4-10.

The student object in Figure 4-10 contains the attributes StudentName, StudentNumber, and PhoneNumber, the attributes listed on the report in Figure 4-9. Note that both StudentName and StudentNumber are identifiers. StudentNames are not unique, but StudentNumbers are.

Figure 4-11 is an example of another report about a student—the acceptance letter that Highline sends to its incoming students. Even though this is a letter, it is also a report; the letter was probably produced using mail merge with a word processing program.

Those data items in the letter that should be stored in the database are shown in boldface type. In addition to data regarding the student, the letter also contains data regarding the student's major DEPARTMENT and the student's adviser. Since an adviser is a PROFESSOR, this letter substantiates the need for a separate PROFESSOR object. Object diagrams from the revised PROFESSOR and STUDENT objects are shown in Figure 4-12. According to the STUDENT object, both DEPARTMENT and PROFESSOR are single valued (they have a maximum cardinality of 1). A student at this university has, at most, one major department and one adviser and is required to have both.

The STUDENT object in Figure 4-12 corresponds to the data shown in the letter in Figure 4-11. It may turn out, however, that the student actually has more than one major, in which case both PROFESSOR and STUDENT would be multivalued. This fact cannot be determined from this single form letter, and so additional letters and interviews are needed to find out whether multiple majors are permitted. Here we assume that only one major is allowed.

FIGURE 4-10

Adjusted
DEPARTMENT and
New STUDENT
Objects

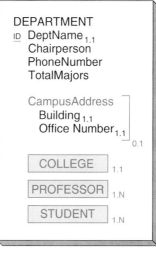

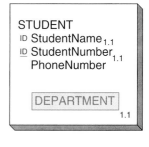

FIGURE 4-11

Acceptance Letter

> **Mr. Fred Parks**
> **123 Elm Street**
> **Los Angeles**, **CA 98002**
>
> Dear **Mr. Parks**:
>
> You have been admitted as a major in the **Accounting** Department at Highline University, starting in the **Fall Semester**, **1993**. The office of the Accounting Department is located in the **Business** Building, Room **210**.
>
> Your adviser is professor **Elizabeth Johnson**, whose telephone number is **232-8740** and whose office is located in the **Business** building, Room **227**. Please schedule an appointment with your adviser as soon as you arrive on campus.
>
> Congratulations and welcome to Highline University!
>
> Sincerely,
>
>
>
> Jan P. Smathers
> President
>
> JPS/rkp

FIGURE 4-12

Adjusted
PROFESSOR and
STUDENT Objects

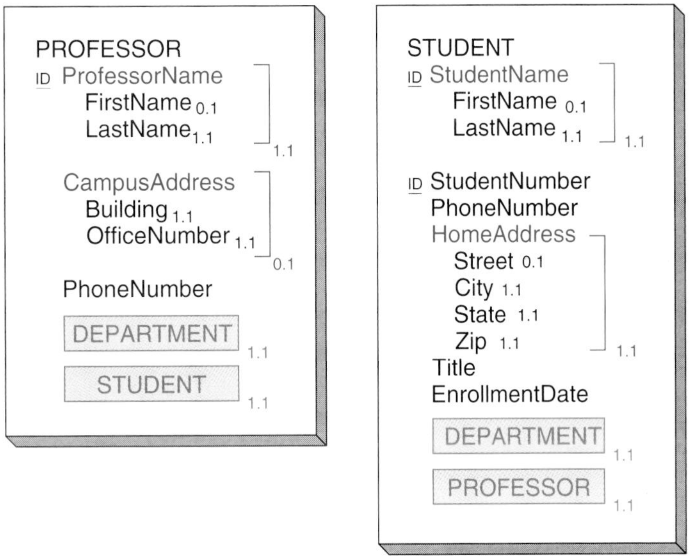

PROFESSOR
ID ProfessorName
    FirstName $_{0.1}$
    LastName $_{1.1}$ $_{1.1}$

    CampusAddress
        Building $_{1.1}$
        OfficeNumber $_{1.1}$ $_{0.1}$

    PhoneNumber

    DEPARTMENT $_{1.1}$

    STUDENT $_{1.1}$

STUDENT
ID StudentName
    FirstName $_{0.1}$
    LastName $_{1.1}$ $_{1.1}$

ID StudentNumber
    PhoneNumber
    HomeAddress
        Street $_{0.1}$
        City $_{1.1}$
        State $_{1.1}$
        Zip $_{1.1}$ $_{1.1}$
    Title
    EnrollmentDate

    DEPARTMENT $_{1.1}$

    PROFESSOR $_{1.1}$

The format of the student's name is given first in the format *first name last name* at the top of the letter and then in the format *last name* in the salutation. If presenting names in this format is a requirement, then the single attribute StudentName (in Figure 4-10) will not suffice, and instead the group FirstName, LastName must be defined. This has been done in Figure 4-12. Note also that the adviser's name is in the format *first name, last name*, which means that the name of PROFESSOR should be changed as well.

In addition, this letter indicates that names in addresses and salutations must be preceded by the title *Mr.* or *Ms.* If this is to be done, an additional attribute must be placed in STUDENT. One alternative would be to record the gender of the student and to select the title based on this attribute. Another alternative is to store the title itself. The advantage of this second alternative is that titles other than *Mr.* and *Ms.* can be stored. An example is the title *Dr.*

As currently documented, the model does not require a title other than Mr. or Ms. It seems plausible, however, that additional titles might be needed; hence the second alternative seems more robust, and therefore the attribute Title has been added to STUDENT in Figure 4-12.

Again, these changes illustrate the iterative nature of data modeling. Design decisions often need to be rethought and revised and then revised again. Such iteration does not mean that the design process is faulty; in fact, it is typical and expected.

■ Specifying Objects

Figure 4-13 shows the completed object diagrams for the Highline University database. A few changes have been made: Both DeanName and Chairperson have been modeled in the format {FirstName, LastName}, so that all names are in a similar format. And the PROFESSOR attribute in STUDENT has been renamed Adviser, to improve the precision of the model. The PROFESSOR instance that is connected to a STUDENT instance through this attribute is not just any of the STUDENT's professors; it is the particular PROFESSOR who serves as that STUDENT's adviser, and the term *Adviser* is more precise than the term *PROFESSOR*.

The domain of this attribute is unchanged. The domain of Adviser is PROFESSOR, just as the domain of the attribute PROFESSOR was PROFESSOR. This attribute still points to or connects to instances of the PROFESSOR semantic object. The name change is only that: an improvement in specifying the role that the PROFESSOR domain plays in the STUDENT semantic objects. A similar change was made in PROFESSOR. The STUDENT attribute was renamed ADVISEE, but this attribute is still connected to the STUDENT domain.

Figure 4-14 presents a tabular specification of the data model. The semantic objects and attributes are defined in the semantic object specification, and the domains are defined in the domain specification. The first table is an alternative presentation of the information in the semantic object diagrams, and its interpretation is straightforward.

The second table, the domain table, supplies information about domains that is not available from the semantic object diagrams. As we stated earlier, a domain has both a semantic and a physical description. The semantic description of each domain is shown in the Description column, and the physical description is shown in the Specification column. The Description column is self-explanatory.

The specification for domains includes a physical description and, in some cases, a set of values and a format. StudentNumber, for example, is specified as integer with values between 10000 and 99999 and with a format of five decimal digits. (In

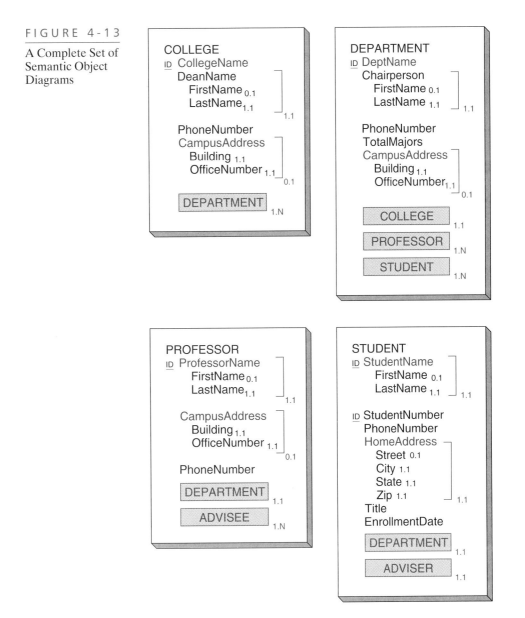

FIGURE 4-13

A Complete Set of Semantic Object Diagrams

this table, a 9 in a format specification means a decimal digit.) Other domains are documented in a similar way. Title is an example of an enumerated domain whose values for Title are Mr., Ms.. The physical description of a group domain consists of a list of the domains included in the group. The physical description of a semantic object domain is just a reference to the semantic object description.

The TotalMajors domain is an example of a fourth type of domain, the **formula domain**. Formulas represent attributes computed from other values. The Major-Count domain is the count of the STUDENT objects that are connected to a given DEPARTMENT object. We shall not try to document the means by which this computation is to be carried out in the domain definition. At this point, all that is important is documenting the need for and the specification of the formula.

FIGURE 4-14

Object Specifications for the Highline University Database:
(a) Semantic Object Specifications and (b) Domain Specifications

Object Name	Property Name	Min Card	Max Card	Key Status	Domain Name
COLLEGE	CollegeName	1	1	ID	CollegeName
	DeanName	0	1		PersonName
	PhoneNumber	0	1		Phone
	CampusAddress	1	1		CampusAddress
	Building	1	1		Building
	OfficeNumber	1	1		OfficeNumber
	DEPARTMENT	1	N		DEPARTMENT
DEPARTMENT	DeptName	1	1	ID	DeptName
	Chairperson	0	1		PersonName
	PhoneNumber	0	1		Phone
	TotalMajors	0	1		MajorFormula
	CampusAddress	1	1		CampusAddress
	COLLEGE	1	1		COLLEGE
	PROFESSOR	1	N		PROFESSOR
	STUDENT	1	N		STUDENT
PROFESSOR	ProfessorName	1	1	ID	PersonName
	CampusAddress	0	1		CampusAddress
	Building	1	1		Building
	OfficeNumber	1	1		OfficeNumber
	PhoneNumber	0	1		Phone
	DEPARTMENT	1	1		DEPARTMENT
	ADVISEE	1	N		STUDENT
STUDENT	StudentName	1	1	ID	PersonName
	StudentNumber	1	1	ID	StudentNumber
	PhoneNumber	0	1		Phone
	HomeAddress	1	1		Address
	Title	0	1		Title
	EnrollmentDate	0	1		QuarterDate
	DEPARTMENT	1	1		DEPARTMENT
	ADVISER	1	1		PROFESSOR

(a)

Name	Type[a]	Semantic Description	Physical Description
Address	G	A U.S. address	Street City State Zip
Building	S	A name of a building on campus	Text 20
CampusAddress	G	An address on campus	Building OfficeNumber
City	S	A city name	Text 25
COLLEGE	SO	One of Highline's ten colleges	See semantic object specification table
CollegeName	S	The official name of a college at Highline	Text 25
DEPARTMENT	SO	An academic department on campus	See semantic object specification table
DeptName	S	The official name of an academic department	Text 25
FirstName	S	The first-name portion of PersonName	Text 20
LastName	S	The last-name portion of PersonName	Text 30
MajorCount	F	Count of the students assigned to a given department	Integer; values {0 to 999}; format 999.
OfficeNumber	S	The number of an office on campus	Text 4
PersonName	G	First and last names of an administrator, professor, or student	FirstName LastName
Phone	S	Phone number within local area code	Text 4
PROFESSOR	SO	The name of a full-time member of Highline's faculty	See semantic object specification table
QuarterDate	S	An academic quarter and year	Text 3; values {$q99$, where q = one of {'F', 'W', 'S', 'M'} and 99 is decimal number from 00 to 99.}
State	S	A two-digit state abbreviation	Text 2
Street	S	A street address	Text 30
STUDENT	SO	A person who has been admitted for study at Highline	See semantic object specification table
StudentNumber	S	The ID assigned to a student admitted to Highline	Integer; values {10000 to 99999}; format 99999
Title	S	The title of individuals to be used in addresses	Text 3; values {Mr., Ms.}
Zip	S	A nine-digit zip code	Text 10; format 99999-9999

[a]F = formula
G = Group
S = Simple
SO = semantic object

(b)

TYPES OF OBJECTS

This section describes and illustrates seven types of objects. For each type, we examine a report or form and show how to model that report or form with an object. Later, in Chapter 6, we transform each of these types of objects into database schemas.

Three new terms are used in this section. A **single-valued attribute** is an attribute whose maximum cardinality is 1. A **multivalued attribute** is one whose maximum cardinality is greater than 1. And a **nonobject attribute** is a simple or a group attribute.

■ Simple Objects

A **simple object** is a semantic object that contains only single-valued, nonobject attributes. An example is shown in Figure 4-15. Part (a) of this figure shows two instances of a report called an *Equipment Tag*. Such tags are applied to items of office equipment in order to help keep track of inventory. These tags can be considered a report.

Figure 4-15(b) shows a simple object, EQUIPMENT, that models Equipment Tag. The attributes of the object include the items shown on the tag: EquipmentNumber, Description, AcquisitionDate, and PurchaseCost. Note that none of these attributes is multivalued and none is an object attribute. Hence, EQUIPMENT is a simple object.

■ Composite Objects

A **composite object** is a semantic object that contains one or more multivalued, nonobject attributes. The Hotel Bill shown in Figure 4-16(a) gives rise to the need for a composite object. The bill includes data that concerns the bill as a whole: InvoiceNumber, ArrivalDate, CustomerName, and TotalDue. It also contains a

FIGURE 4-15

Example of a Simple Object: (a) Reports Based on a Simple Object and (b) EQUIPMENT Simple Object

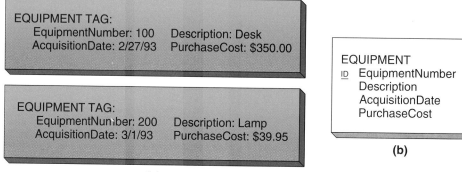

(a)

(b)

group of attributes that are repeated for services provided to the guest. Each group includes ServiceDate, ServiceDescription, and Price.

Figure 4-16(b) shows an object diagram for the HOTEL-BILL object. The attribute LineItem is a group attribute having a maximum cardinality of N, which means that the group ServiceDate, ServiceDescription, Price can occur many times in an instance of the HOTEL-BILL semantic object.

LineItem is not modeled as an independent semantic object; instead, it is considered to be an attribute within a HOTEL-BILL. This design is appropriate because the hotel does not view one line of a guest's charges as a separate thing, and so line items on the guest's bill do not have identifiers of their own. No employee attempts to enter a LineItem except in the context of a bill. The employee enters the data for bill number 1234 and then, in the context of that bill, enters the charges. Or the employee retrieves an existing bill and enters additional charges in the context of that bill.

The minimum cardinality of LineItem is 0, which means that a HOTEL-BILL object can exist without any LineItem data. This allows a bill to be started when the customer checks in and before there are any charges. If the minimum cardinality were 1, then no HOTEL-BILL could be started until there was at least one charge. This design decision must be made in light of the business rules. It may be that the hotel's policy is not to start the bill until there has been a charge. If so, then the minimum cardinality of LineItem should be 1.

A composite object can have more than one multivalued attribute. Figure 4-17(a) shows a hotel bill that has a multivalued attribute for CustomerName as well as a multivalued group for service charges. Each of these groups is independent of the

FIGURE 4-16
_____

Example of a Composite Object: (a) Report Based on a
Composite Object and (b) HOTEL-BILL Composite Object

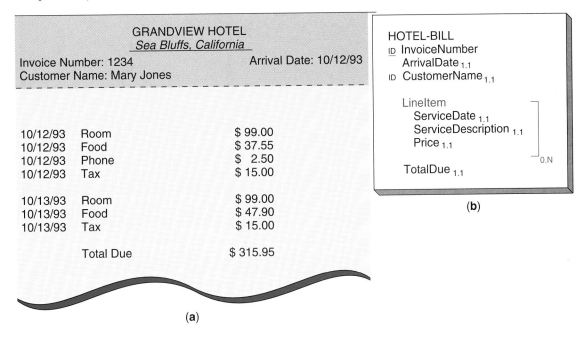

(a)

(b)

FIGURE 4-17

A Composite Object with Two Groups: (a) HOTEL-BILL with Multivalued Customer Names and (b) HOTEL-BILL with Two Multivalued Groups

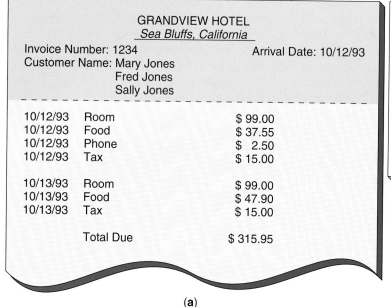

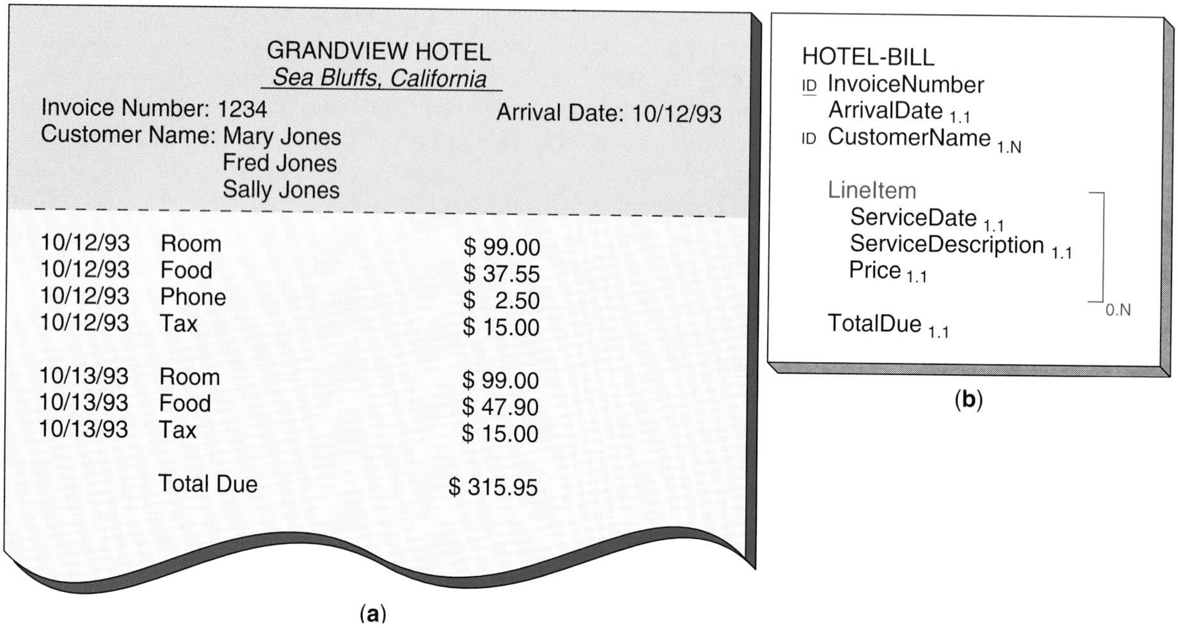

(a)

FIGURE 4-18

A Composite Object with Nested Groups: (a) HOTEL-BILL with Service Subdescriptions and (b) HOTEL-BILL with Nested Multivalued Groups

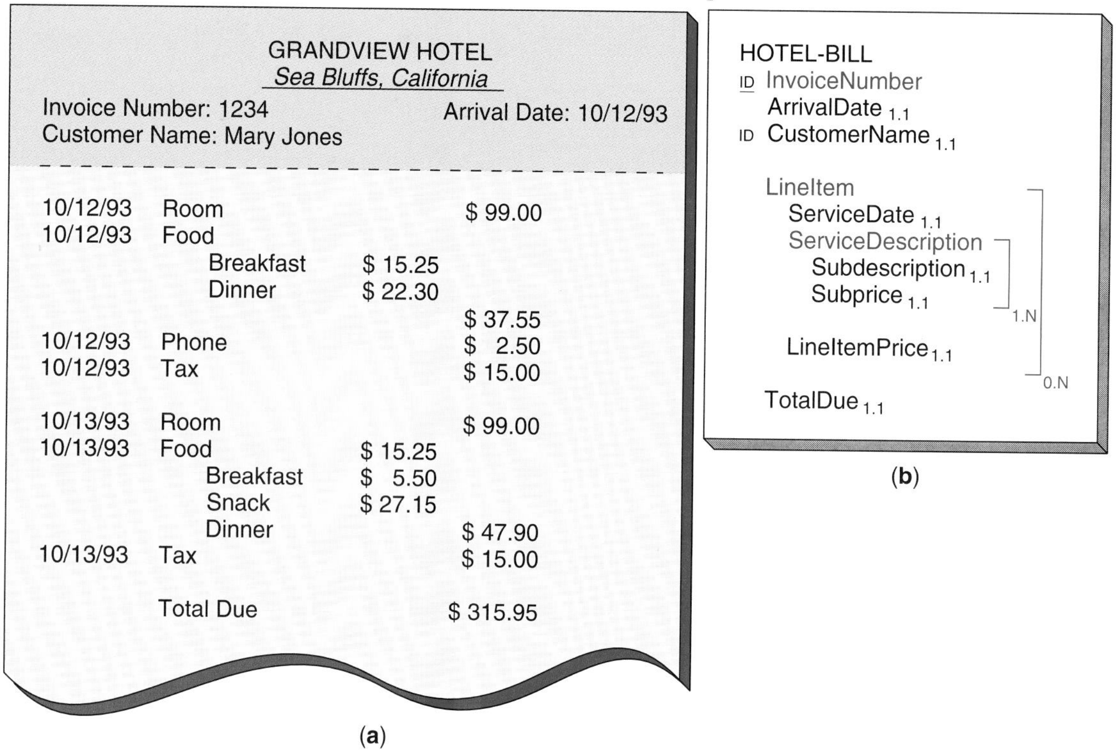

(a)

other. The second instance of customer name, for example, is not logically associated with the second LineItem.

Figure 4-17(b) is an object diagram for the hotel bill in Figure 4-17(a). CustomerName is shown as a multivalued attribute. It is not included in the bracket of service charges because the repetitions of CustomerName have nothing to do with the repetitions of services. The two are independent, as we just noted.

Both simple and group attributes can be multivalued. In Figure 4-17(a), for example, CustomerName is a multivalued, simple attribute. By itself, it is sufficient for the object to be considered a composite object.

Multivalued attributes can also be nested within one another. For example, suppose it is important to keep track of individual expenses within a LineItem. In the form in Figure 4-18(a), the charges are subdivided. Food, for example, is broken down by meal. An object diagram for such nested attributes is presented in Figure 4-18(b) and shows that any service charge can have subitems.

To repeat, a composite object is an object that contains one or more multivalued simple or group attributes. It has no object attributes.

■ Compound Objects

A **compound object** contains at least one object attribute. Figure 4-19(a) shows two different data entry forms. One form, used by the company's motor pool, is used to keep track of the vehicles. The second form is used to maintain data about the employees. According to these forms, a vehicle is assigned to at most one employee, and an employee has at most one auto assigned.

We cannot tell from these reports whether an auto must be assigned to an employee or whether every employee must have an auto. To obtain that information, we would have to ask the users in the motor pool or human resources departments. Assume that we find out that an EMPLOYEE need not have a VEHICLE but that a VEHICLE must be assigned to an employee.

Figure 4-19(b) shows object diagrams for EMPLOYEE and VEHICLE. An EMPLOYEE contains VEHICLE as one of its attributes, and VEHICLE, in turn, contains EMPLOYEE as one of its attributes. Since both EMPLOYEE and VEHICLE contain object attributes, they both are compound objects. Furthermore, since neither attribute is multivalued, the relationship from EMPLOYEE to VEHICLE is one to one, or 1:1.

In Figure 4-19(a), the Employee and Vehicle forms contain each other. That is, Vehicle Data has a field Employee assignment, and Employee Work Data has a field Auto assigned. But this is not always the case; sometimes the relationship can appear in only one direction. Consider the report and form in Figure 4-20(a), which concern two objects: DORMITORY and STUDENT. From the Dormitory Occupancy Report, we can see that users think of a dorm as having attributes regarding the dorm (Name, ResidentAssistant, Phone) and also attributes regarding the students (StudentName, StudentNumber, Class) who live in the dorm.

On the other hand, the Student Data Form shows only student data; it does not include any dormitory data. (The local address might contain a dorm address, but this, if true, is apparently not important enough to document on the form. In a database development project, this possibility should be checked out with the users in an

FIGURE 4-19

Compound Objects with 1:1 Paired Properties: (a) Example Vehicle and Employee Data Entry Forms and (b) EMPLOYEE and VEHICLE Compound Objects

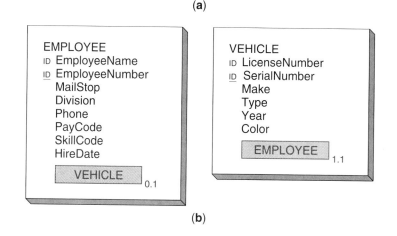

(a)

(b)

interview. Here we will assume that the Student Data Form does not include dormitory data.)

As we stated earlier, object attributes always occur in pairs. Even if the forms, reports, and queries indicate that only one side of the relationship can be seen, both sides of the relationship always exist. By analogy, a bridge that connects two islands touches both islands and can be used in both directions, even if the bridge is, by custom or law, a one-way bridge.

When no form or report can be found to document one side of a relationship, the development team must ask the users about the cardinality of that relationship. In this case, the team would need to find out how many DORMITORYs a STUDENT could have and whether a STUDENT must be related to a DORMITORY. Here let us suppose the answers to these questions are that a STUDENT is related to just one DORMITORY and may be related to no DORMITORY. Thus in Figure 4-20(b), DORMITORY contains multiple values of STUDENT, and STUDENT

FIGURE 4-20

Compound Objects with 1:N Paired Properties: (a) Example Dormitory Report and Student Data Form and (b) DORMITORY and STUDENT Compound Objects

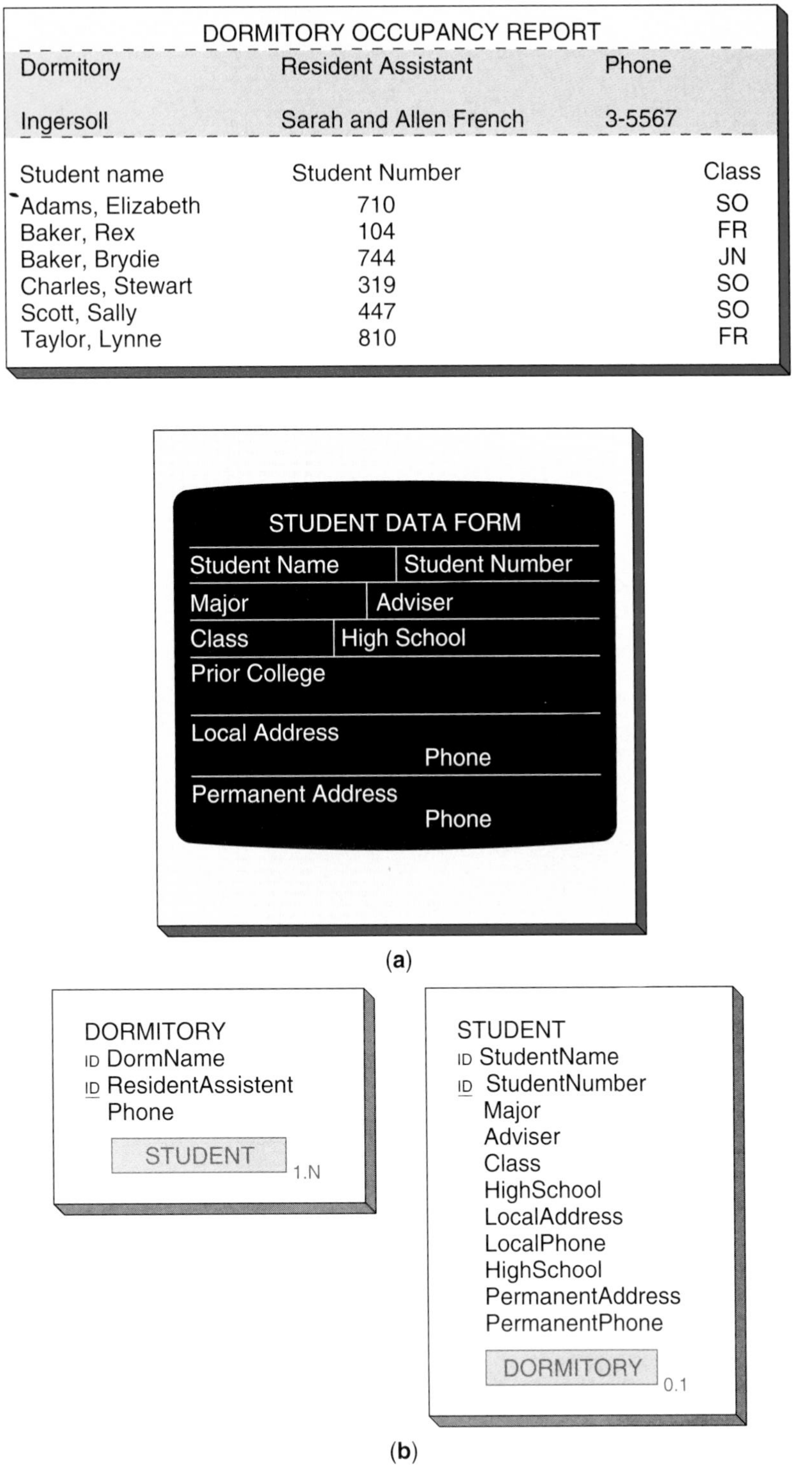

DORMITORY OCCUPANCY REPORT		
Dormitory	Resident Assistant	Phone
Ingersoll	Sarah and Allen French	3-5567

Student name	Student Number	Class
Adams, Elizabeth	710	SO
Baker, Rex	104	FR
Baker, Brydie	744	JN
Charles, Stewart	319	SO
Scott, Sally	447	SO
Taylor, Lynne	810	FR

STUDENT DATA FORM

Student Name	Student Number
Major	Adviser
Class	High School
Prior College	

Local Address
Phone

Permanent Address
Phone

(a)

DORMITORY
ID DormName
ID ResidentAssistent
Phone

STUDENT
1.N

STUDENT
ID StudentName
ID StudentNumber
Major
Adviser
Class
HighSchool
LocalAddress
LocalPhone
HighSchool
PermanentAddress
PermanentPhone

DORMITORY
0.1

(b)

contains one value of DORMITORY, and so the relationship from DORMITORY to STUDENT is one to many, or 1:N.

A third illustration of compound objects appears in Figure 4-21(a). From these two forms, we can deduce that one book can be written by many authors (from the Book Stock Data form) and that one author can write many books (from the Books in Stock, by Author form). Thus in Figure 4.21(b), the BOOK object contains many values of AUTHOR, and AUTHOR contains many values of BOOK. Hence the relationship from BOOK to AUTHOR is many to many, or N:M. Furthermore, a BOOK must have an AUTHOR, and an AUTHOR (to be an author) must have written at least one BOOK. Therefore both of these objects have a minimum cardinality of one.

Figure 4-22 summarizes the four types of compound objects. In general, OBJECT-1 can contain a maximum of one or many OBJECT-2s. Similarly, OBJECT-2 can contain one or many OBJECT-1s. We use this table when we discuss database design in Chapter 6.

FIGURE 4-21

Compound Objects with N:M Paired Properties: (a) Bookstore Data Entry Forms and (b) BOOK and AUTHOR Objects

(a)

(b)

FIGURE 4-22

Four Types of Compound Objects

Object1 Can Contain

Object2		One	Many
Can	One	1:1	1:N
Contain	Many	M:1	M:N

Hybrid Objects

As the term implies, **hybrid objects** are combinations of objects of two types. In particular, a hybrid object is a semantic object with at least one multivalued group attribute that includes a semantic object attribute.

Figure 4-23(a) is a second version of the report about dormitory occupancy shown in Figure 4-21(a). The difference is that the third column of the student data contains Rent instead of Class. This is an important difference because rent is not an attribute of STUDENT but pertains to the combination of STUDENT and DORMITORY and is an attribute of DORMITORY.

Figure 4-23(b) is an object diagram that models this form. DORMITORY contains a multivalued group with both the object attribute STUDENT and the nonobject attribute Rent. This means that Rent is paired with STUDENT in the context of DORMITORY.

Now examine the alternative DORMITORY object in Figure 4-23(c). This is an *incorrect* model of the report in Figure 4-23(a), as it shows that Rent and STUDENT are independently multivalued, which is incorrect because Rent and STUDENT are multivalued as a pair.

Figure 4-24(a) shows a form based on another hybrid object. This Sales Order form contains data about an order (Sales Order Number, Date, Subtotal, Tax, and Total), data about a CUSTOMER and a SALESPERSON, and a multivalued group that itself contains data about items on the order. Furthermore, ITEM data (item number, description, and unit price) appears within the multivalued group.

Figure 4-24(b) shows the SALES-ORDER semantic object. It contains the nonobject attributes SalesOrderNumber, Date, Subtotal, Tax, and Total. It also contains the CUSTOMER and SALESPERSON object attributes and a multivalued group that represents each line item on the sales order. The group contains nonobject attributes Quantity and ExtendedPrice and the object attribute ITEM.

The object diagrams in Figure 4-24(b) are ambiguous in one aspect that may or may not be important, depending on the application. According to the ITEM object diagram, an ITEM can be connected to more than one SALES-ORDER. But since the multivalued group LineItem is encapsulated (hidden within) SALES-ORDER, it is not clear from this diagram whether an ITEM can occur *once or many times* on the same SALES-ORDER.

In general, there are four interpretations of maximum cardinality for the paired attributes in the SALES-ORDER hybrid object:

1. An ITEM can appear on only one SALES-ORDER and in only one of the LineItems within that SALES-ORDER.

2. An ITEM can appear on only one SALES-ORDER but in many different Line-Items within that SALES-ORDER.

3. An ITEM can appear on many different SALES-ORDERs but in only one LineItem within each of those SALES-ORDERs.

4. An ITEM can appear on many different SALES-ORDERs and in many different LineItems within those SALES-ORDERs.

FIGURE 4-23

DORMITORY Hybrid Object: (a) Dormitory Report with Rent Property, (b) Correct DORMITORY and STUDENT Objects, and (c) Incorrect DORMITORY and Correct STUDENT Objects

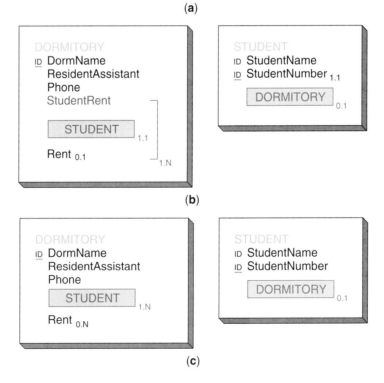

(a)

(b)

(c)

FIGURE 4-24

Hybrid SALES-ORDER and Related Objects: (a) Sales Order Form
and (b) Objects to Model Sales Order Form

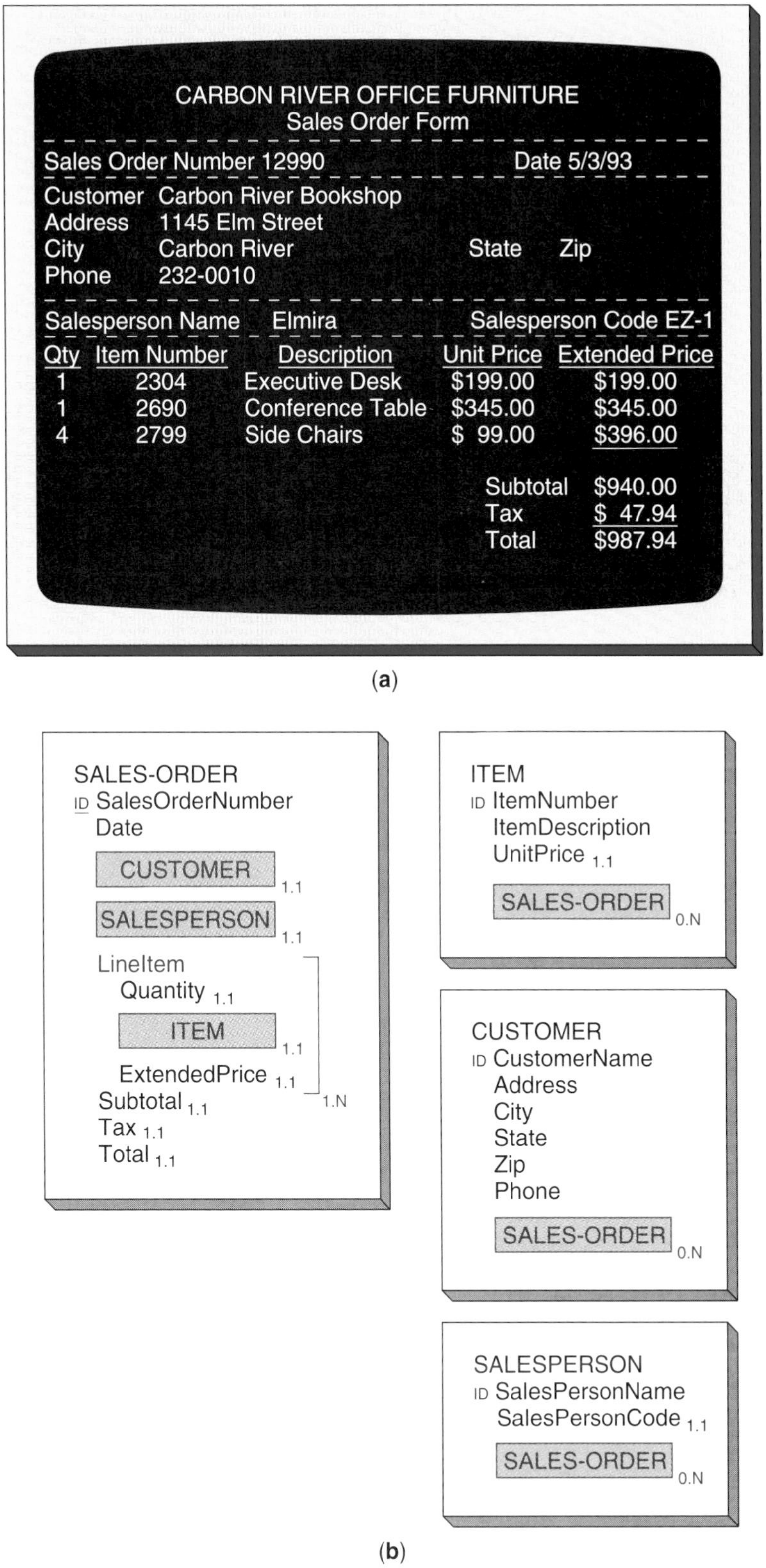

(a)

(b)

When it is important to distinguish among these cases, the following notation should be used: If either Case 1 or 2 is in force, the maximum cardinality of the hybrid object attribute should be set to 1. Thus for this example, the maximum cardinality of SALES-ORDER in ITEM is set to 1. If an ITEM is to appear in only one LineItem of the SALES-ORDER (Case 1), it should be marked as having a unique

FIGURE 4-25

Examples of the Four Cases of Maximum Cardinality in a Hybrid Object:
(a) ITEM in One LineItem of One ORDER, (b) ITEM in (Possibly)
Many LineItems of One Order, (c) ITEM in One LineItem of (Possibly)
Many Orders, and (d) ITEM in (Possibly) Many LineItems of
(Possibly) Many ORDERs

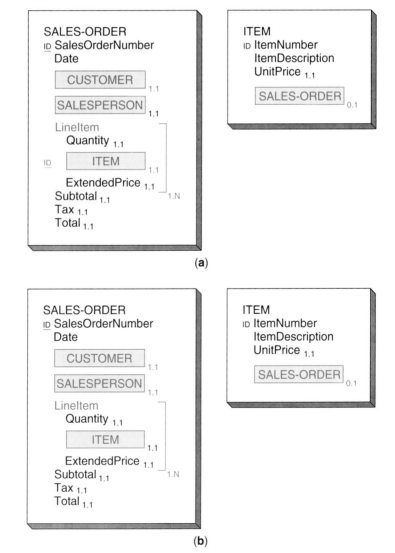

ID in that group. Otherwise (Case 2), it need not be marked. These two cases are shown in Figure 4-25 (a) and (b).

If either Case 3 or 4 is in force, the maximum cardinality of the hybrid object attribute is set to N. Thus for this example, the maximum cardinality of SALES-ORDER in ITEM is set to N. Furthermore, if an ITEM is to appear in only one LineItem of a SALES-ORDER (Case 3), it should be marked as having a unique ID in that group. Otherwise (Case 4), it need not be marked. These two cases are shown in Figure 4-25(c) and (d).

FIGURE 4-25

Continued

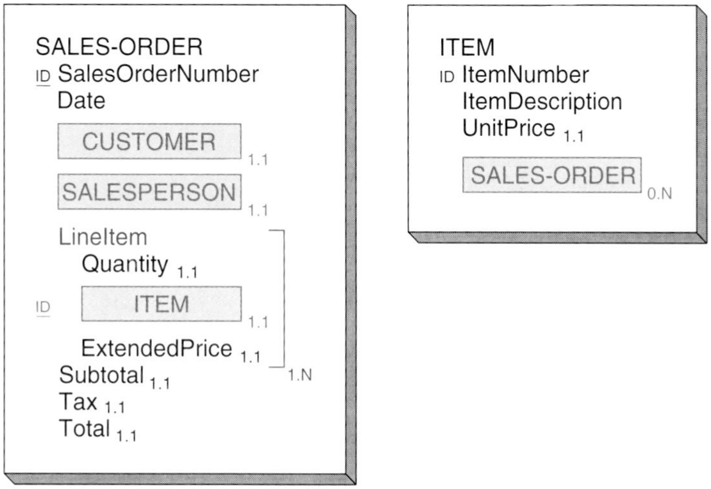

(c)

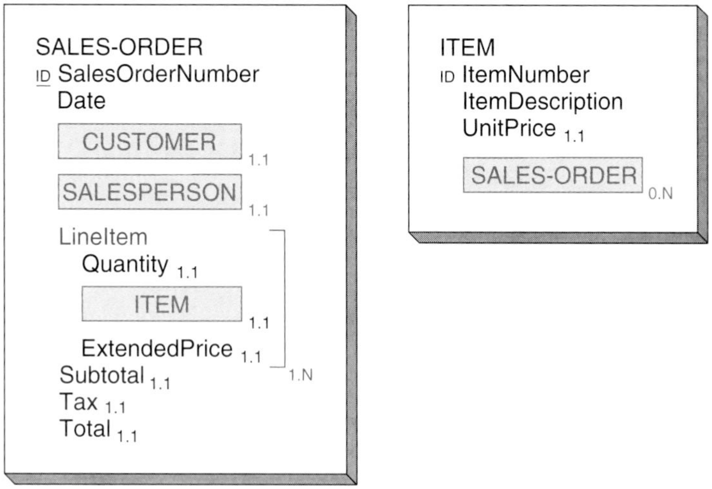

(d)

■ Association Objects

An **association object** is an object that relates two (or more) objects and stores data that is peculiar to that relationship. Figure 4-26(a) shows a report and two data entry screens that give rise to the need for an association object. The report contains data

FIGURE 4-26

Example of an Association Object: (a) Example Flight Report and Forms and (b) FLIGHT, PILOT, AIRPLANE Objects

FLY CHEAP INTERNATIONAL
Flight Planning Data Report

FLIGHT NUMBER	*FC-17*	DATE	*7/30/93*
ORIGINATING CITY	*Seattle*	DESTINATION	*Hong Kong*
FUEL ON TAKEOFF			

WEIGHT ON TAKEOFF

AIRPLANE
   Tail Number   *N1234FI*
   Type   *747-SP*
   Capacity   *148*

PILOT
   Name   *Michael Nilson*
   Base   *Los Angeles International*
   FI-ID   *33489-Z*
   Flight Hours   *18,348*

FLY CHEAP INTERNATIONAL
Pilot Summary Data Form

FCI-ID	
Name	Social Security Number
Address	
City · State Zip	
Phone	Emergency Phone
Date of Last Checkout	Hours
Date of Last Physical	

FLY CHEAP INTERNATIONAL
Airplane Data Form

Tail Number: N12324FI
Manufacturer: Boeing
Type: 747-SP
Total Airframe Hours: 112,384
Total Engine Hours: 57,998
Engine Hours Since Overhaul: 3,212
Current Capacity: 148
Range as Configured: 4,200 NM

(a)

FIGURE 4-26

Continued

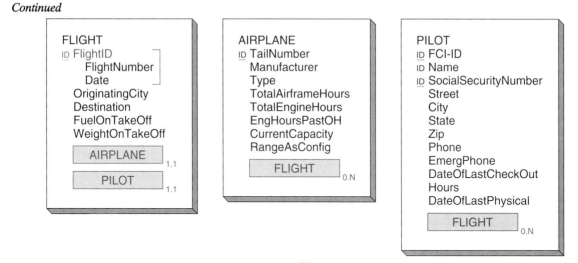

(b)

about an airline flight and data about the particular airplane and pilot assigned to that flight. The two data entry forms contain data about a pilot and an airplane.

In Figure 4-26(b), the object FLIGHT is an association object that associates the two objects AIRPLANE and PILOT and stores data about their association. FLIGHT contains one each of AIRPLANE and PILOT, but both AIRPLANE and PILOT contain multiple values of FLIGHT. This particular pattern of associating two (or more) objects with data about the association occurs frequently, especially in applications that involve the assignment of two or more things. Other examples are a JOB that assigns an ARCHITECT to a CLIENT, a TASK that assigns an EMPLOYEE to a PROJECT, and a PURCHASE-ORDER that assigns a VENDOR to a SERVICE.

For the example in Figure 4-26, the association object FLIGHT has an identifier of its own, the group {FlightNumber, Date}. Often association objects do not have identifiers of their own, in which case the identifier is the combination of the identifiers of the objects that are associated.

To understand this better, consider Figure 4-27(a), which shows a report about the assignment of architects to projects. Although the assignment has no obvious identifier, in fact, the identifier is the combination {ProjectName, Name}. These attributes, however, belong to PROJECT and ARCHITECT and not to ASSIGNMENT. The identifier of ASSIGNMENT is thus the combination of those identifiers of the things that are assigned.

Figure 4-27(b) shows the object diagrams for this situation. Both PROJECT and ARCHITECT are object attributes of ASSIGNMENT, and the group {PROJECT, ARCHITECT} is the identifier of ASSIGNMENT. This means that the combination of an instance of PROJECT and an instance of ARCHITECT identifies a particular ASSIGNMENT.

Note that the AssignmentID identifier in Figure 4-27(b) is not unique, thereby indicating that an architect may be assigned to a project more than once. If this is

FIGURE 4-27

**ASSIGNMENT Association Object: (a) Example Assignment Report
and (b) Assignment Object with Semantic Object ID**

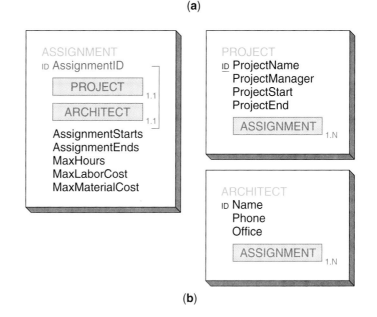

Project Assignment Report

Project Name	Abernathy House	Architect Assigned	Jackson, B.
Project Manager	Smith, J	Phone	232-8878
Project Start	11/11/93	Office Number	J-1133
Project End			

Assignment Starts	12/15/93
Assignment Ends	3/15/94
Maximum Budgeted Hours	345
Maximum Labor Cost	$27,500
Maximum Material Cost	$ 5,000

(a)

(b)

not the case, the identifier should be declared to be unique. Also, if an employee may be assigned to a project more than once and if for some reason it is important to have a unique identifier for an ASSIGNMENT, the attribute Date or some other time-indicating attribute (Week, Quarter, and so forth) should be added to the group.

■ Parent/Subtype Objects

To understand parent and subtype objects, consider the object EMPLOYEE in Figure 4-28(a). Some of the attributes in EMPLOYEE pertain to all employees, and

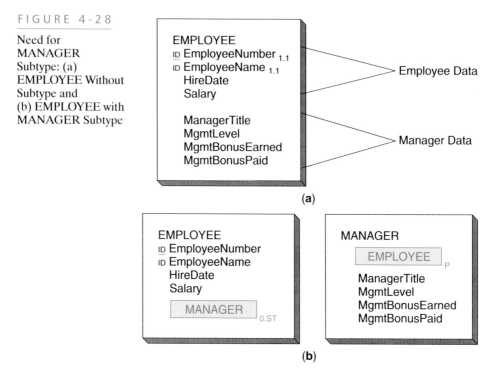

FIGURE 4-28

Need for
MANAGER
Subtype: (a)
EMPLOYEE Without
Subtype and
(b) EMPLOYEE with
MANAGER Subtype

others pertain only to employees who are managers. The object in Figure 4-28(a) is not very precise because the manager-oriented attributes are not suitable for non-manager employees.

A better model is shown in Figure 4-28(b), in which the EMPLOYEE object contains a subtype object, MANAGER. All of the manager-oriented attributes have been moved to the MANAGER object. Employees who are not managers have one EMPLOYEE object instance and no MANAGER object instances. Employees who are managers have both an EMPLOYEE instance and a MANAGER instance. In this example, the EMPLOYEE object is called a *parent object* or *supertype object*, and the MANAGER object is called a *subtype object*.

The first attribute of a subtype is the parent attribute and is denoted by the subscript P. Parent attributes are always required. The identifiers of the subtype are the same as the identifiers of the parent. In Figure 4-28, EmployeeNumber and EmployeeName are identifiers of both EMPLOYEE and MANAGER.

Subtype attributes are shown with the subscript 0.ST or 1.ST. The first digit (0 or 1) is the minimum cardinality of the subtype. If 0, the subtype is optional, and if 1, the subtype is required. (A required subtype does not make sense for this example but will for the more complicated examples to follow.) The *ST* indicates that the attribute is a subtype, or IS-A attribute.

Parent/subtype objects have an important characteristic called inheritance. A subtype acquires, or *inherits*, all of the attributes of its parent, and therefore a MANAGER inherits all of the attributes of an EMPLOYEE. In addition, the parent acquires all of the attributes of its subtypes, and an EMPLOYEE who is a MANAGER acquires all of the attributes of MANAGER.

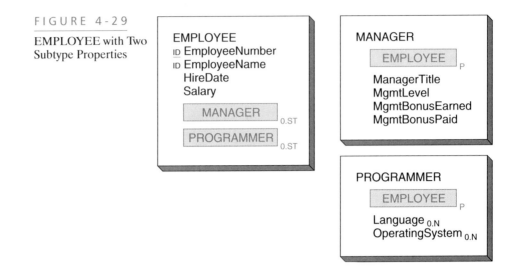

FIGURE 4-29

EMPLOYEE with Two
Subtype Properties

A semantic object may contain more than one subtype attribute. Figure 4-29 shows a second EMPLOYEE object that has two subtype attributes, MANAGER and PROGRAMMER. Since all of these attributes are optional, an EMPLOYEE can have neither, one, or both of these subtypes. This means that some employees are neither managers nor programmers, some are managers but not programmers, some are programmers but not managers, and some are both programmers and managers.

Sometimes subtypes exclude one another. That is, a VEHICLE can be an AUTO or a TRUCK, but not both. A CLIENT can be an INDIVIDUAL, a PARTNERSHIP, or a CORPORATION, but only one of these three types. When subtypes exclude one another, they are placed into a subtype group, and the group is assigned a subscript of the format $X.Y.Z$. X is the minimum cardinality and is 0 or 1, depending on whether or not the subtype group is required. Y and Z are counts of the number of attributes in the group that are allowed to have a value. Y is the minimum number required, and Z is the maximum number allowed.

Figure 4-30(a) shows three types of CLIENT as a subtype group. The subscript of the group, 0.1.1, means that the subtype is not required, but if it exists, a minimum of one and a maximum of one (or exactly one) of the subtypes in the group must exist. Note that each of the subtypes has the subscript 0.ST, meaning that they all are optional, as they must be. If they all were required, the maximum count would have to be three, not one. This notation is robust enough to allow for situations in which three out of five or seven out of ten of a list of subtypes must be required.

Even more complex restrictions can be modeled when subtypes are nested. The subtype group in Figure 4-30(b) models a situation in which the subtype CORPORATION must be either a TAXABLE-CORP or a NONTAXABLE-CORP. If it is a NONTAXABLE-CORP, it must be either GOV-AGENCY or a SCHOOL. Only a

FIGURE 4-30

Exclusive (a) and Nested (b) Subtypes

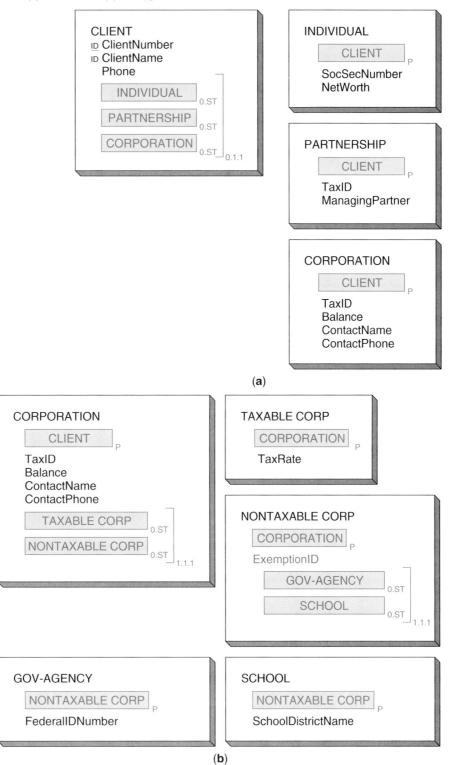

(a)

(b)

FIGURE 4-31

Example of an Archetype/Version Object

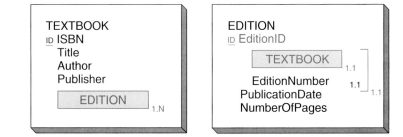

few nonobject attributes are shown in this example. In reality, if such a complex structure were required, there would likely be more attributes.

Archetype/Version Objects

The final type of object is the **archetype/version object**. An archetype object is a semantic object that produces other semantic objects that represent versions, releases, or editions of the archetype. For example, in Figure 4-31, the archetype object TEXTBOOK produces the version objects EDITIONs. According to this model, the attributes Title, Author, and Publisher belong to the object TEXT-BOOK, and the attributes EditionNumber, PublicationDate, and NumberOfPages belong to the EDITION of the TEXTBOOK.

The ID group in EDITION has two portions, TEXTBOOK and EditionNumber, a typical pattern for an ID of a version object. One part of the ID contains the archetype object, and the second part is a simple attribute that identifies the version within the archetype. Figure 4-32 shows another instance of archetype/version objects.

FIGURE 4-32

Another Example of an Archetype/Version Object

The term *object* is used in many ways today. In this chapter, we have appended the word *semantic* to *object* to distinguish the use of this term for data modeling from the use of it in object-oriented programming.

▓ A Sketch of Object-oriented Programming

Object-oriented programming (OOP) is a way of designing and coding programs. OOP is substantially different from traditional programming, as it entails an entirely new way of thinking about programming. Instead of viewing programs as sequences of instructions to be processed, OOP views programs as sets of data structures having both data elements and program behaviors.

More specifically, an OOP object is an **encapsulated structure** having both **attributes** and **methods**. The term *encapsulated* means that it is complete in itself; programs external to an object know nothing of its structure and need to know nothing of its structure. The *attributes* of OOP objects are arranged in a particular structure, and they are quite similar to the attributes of semantic objects discussed in this chapter. Finally—and this is a crucial difference—OOP objects contain *methods*, programs that OOP objects use to process themselves.

Thus an OOP object may have a method (program) to display itself, one to create itself, and one to modify itself. Consider a method that modifies a CUSTOMER object. This method, which is part of the OOP object, is a program; to modify the OOP object, this program contains instructions to obtain the current data of itself (an instance of CUSTOMER), obtain data for the modification from the user or other source, modify itself, and then store itself back in the database.

OOP objects interact by sending messages to one another. The modify method, for example, sends messages to other objects to obtain data, perform modifications, and obtain needed data. These other objects receive the messages and respond to them by executing their own methods. Since all the objects are encapsulated, none can or need know the structure of any other object. This minimizes any complexity and promotes effective cohesion.

Many objects have methods in common. To reduce the duplication in programming, objects are subclassed from more general classes. An object, say O_1, that is a subclass of another object, say O_2, inherits all the attributes and methods of O_2.

The utility of OOP methods is greatly enhanced by a characteristic called **polymorphism**. Briefly, polymorphism means that several versions of a method, say *Print*, can exist. When an object executes a call to *Print*, the compiler determines which version of the print function is appropriate and calls that version. More complex versions of *Print* can call simpler versions of *Print*. Thus functionality can be added without invalidating prior meanings and functionality.

Several terms are commonly used in OOP discussions. The structure of an object, its attributes, and it methods are called an **object class**. A group of object classes is called an **object class library**. And instances of objects are called **object instances**, or simply **objects**.

Objects are created by calling **object constructors**, programs that obtain main memory and create the structures necessary to instantiate an object. **Object destructors** are programs that unbind objects and free memory.

◾ Object-oriented DBMS (OODBMS)

Since objects are created dynamically in memory at run time, they have no existence beyond the execution of a program. Often, however, it is desirable to save an object, and so methods have been developed to provide **object persistence**. This means that the structure of the object is written out to some permanent storage such as a disk. Object persistence is difficult to provide because OOP data structures are not easily mapped to traditional file and relational database formats. A new generation of DBMS products, called object-oriented database management systems (OODBMS), are being developed that will readily provide object persistence. But the problem with these products is that they do not work with existing data structures, and few corporations are willing to reformat their data to fit the OODBMS's data store formats. It is possible that future DBMS systems will be able to provide the advantages of OOP without having to reformat all of the data.

OODBMS are not currently used to store data for typical business information systems. Although they are used in some engineering applications for computer-assisted design and computer-assisted manufacturing (CAD/CAM), these applications form a very small percentage of information systems applications. Until there is some means for commercial enterprises to painlessly translate their relational data to OODBMS, the use of such products in commercial information systems will be minimal.

◾ Similarities and Differences Between Semantic Objects and OOP

Semantic objects and OOP are both similar and different. They share a similar orientation, as both are used to model data and relationships among data; both involve constructs that encapsulate structure; and both provide for object inheritance. In these ways, they are intellectual cousins.

But they also differ. First, they operate in different domains. Semantic objects are used to model data structures that people use in business, commerce, and other administrative applications, whereas OOP is used to model data structures and methods required in computer programs. In addition, OOP provides for the definition of methods and for method inheritance and polymorphism. Semantic objects do not have methods and related structures.

It is possible that the two will merge. If ODBMS becomes popular, semantic objects could be used to model the object data that is to be stored. The concepts of methods, polymorphism, and so forth may be extended to the semantic model, and a way may be invented to model business procedures with semantic object methods: That is, the ideas of method inheritance and polymorphism may produce analogs in the domain of business rules, manual procedures, and data administration.

In summary, semantic objects and OOP have a similar intellectual orientation, but they differ with regard to methods, and they are used to address different problem domains.

COMPARING THE SEMANTIC OBJECT AND THE E-R MODEL

The E-R model and the semantic object model also have similarities and differences. They are similar in that they both are tools for understanding and documenting the structure of the users' data. They both strive to model the structure of the things in the users' world and the relationships among them.

The principal difference between the two models is one of orientation. The E-R model sees the concept of *entity* as basic. Entities and their relationships are considered the atoms, if you will, of a data model. These atoms can be combined to form what the E-R model calls *user views,* which are combinations of entities whose structure is similar to that of semantic objects.

The semantic object model views the concept of *semantic object* as basic. The set of semantic objects in a data model is a map of the essential structure of the things that the user considers important. These objects are the atoms of the users' world and are the smallest distinguishable units that the users want to process. They may be decomposed into smaller parts inside the DBMS (or application), but those smaller parts are of no interest or utility to the users.

According to the semantic object perspective, entities, as defined in the E-R model, do not exist. They are only pieces or chunks of the real entities. The only entities that have meaning to users are, in fact, semantic objects. Another way to state this is to say that semantic objects are *semantically self-contained* or *semantically complete*. Consider an example. Figure 4-33 shows four semantic objects, SALES-ORDER, CUSTOMER, SALESPERSON, and ITEM. When a user says, "Show me sales order number 2000," he or she means show all of the data modeled in Figure 4-33. That includes, among other attributes, CUSTOMER data. Because CUSTOMER is part of SALES-ORDER, the SALES-ORDER object includes CUSTOMER.

Figure 4-34 is an E-R model of this same data and contains the SALES-ORDER, CUSTOMER, SALESPERSON, LINE-ITEM, and INVENTORY entities. The SALES-ORDER entity includes the attributes OrderNumber, Date, Subtotal, Tax, and Total. Now if a user were to say, "Show me sales order number 2000" and be given only the attributes Date, Subtotal, Tax, and Total, he or she would be disappointed. Most likely the user's response would be, "Where's the rest of the data?" That is, the entity SALES-ORDER does not represent the user's meaning of the distinct identity SALES-ORDER. The entity is only a part of SALES-ORDER.

At the same time, when a user (perhaps even the same user) says, "Show me customer 12345," he or she means show all of the data modeled for CUSTOMER in Figure 4-33, including CustomerName, all of the attributes of the group Address, and all of the SALES-ORDERs for that CUSTOMER. The entity CUSTOMER in Figure 4-34 has only the attributes CustomerName, Street, City, State, Zip. If the user were to say, "Show me customer ABC" and be given only this data, he or she again would be disappointed: "No, that's only part of what I want."

According to the semantic object view, E-R entities are unnecessary. Semantic objects can be readily transformed into database designs without ever considering E-R model entities. They are halfway houses, so to speak, constructed in the process of moving away from the paradigm of the computer file to the paradigm of the user.

FIGURE 4-33

SALES-ORDER and Related Semantic Objects

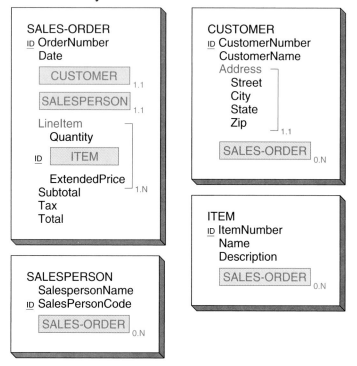

FIGURE 4-34

Entity Relationship Model of
SALES-ORDER and CUSTOMER

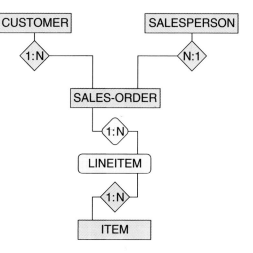

Another difference is that the semantic objects contain more metadata than do the entities. In Figure 4-33, the semantic object model records the fact that CustomerNumber is a unique identifier in the users' minds. It may or may not be used as an identifier for the underlying table, but that fact is not important to the data model. In addition, CustomerName is a nonunique identifier to the users. Furthermore, the semantic objects represent the fact that there is a semantic group of attributes called *Address*. This group contains other attributes that form the address. The fact that this group exists will become important when forms and reports are designed. Finally, the semantic objects indicate that an ITEM may relate to more than one SALES-ORDER but that it can relate to only one LineItem within that SALES-ORDER. This fact cannot be shown on the entity relationship diagram.

In the final analysis, decide which of Figures 4-33 and 4-34 gives you a better idea of what the database should contain. Most people find that the boundaries drawn around the semantic objects and the brackets around the group attributes help them get a better idea of the overall picture of the data model.

SUMMARY

Both the E-R and the semantic object models are used to interpret requirements and to build models of the users' data. These models are like lenses through which developers look when studying and documenting the users' data. Both ultimately lead to a database design.

A semantic object is a named collection of attributes that sufficiently describes a distinct identity. Semantic objects are grouped into classes, and both classes and instances of semantic objects have names. For example, the name of a class is EMPLOYEE, and the name of an instance is EMPLOYEE 2000.

Attributes represent characteristics of the identities being represented. The set of attributes is sufficient in that it represents all of the characteristics that the users need to do their work. Objects represent distinct identities, instances that the users view as independent and separate. The distinct identities represented may or may not be physical; indeed, they may themselves be representative, such as a contract.

Object attributes can be simple data items, groups, or other semantic objects. Object diagrams summarize the structure of objects. Object names are spelled in capital letters at the top of the diagram. Nonobject attributes are written with initial capitals, and attribute groups are indicated by brackets.

All attributes have a minimum cardinality that indicates how many instances of the attribute must exist in order for the object to be valid. They also have a maximum cardinality that indicates the maximum number of instances of the attribute allowed. Cardinality is written in the format m.n, where m is the minimum cardinality and n is the maximum. To reduce the clutter in an object diagram, if the cardinality of a simple value attribute is 0.1, it is not shown. But cardinality is always shown for group and object attributes.

Object attributes are always paired. If one object has a relationship with a second, the second must have a relationship with the first. Object identifiers are attributes that serve, in the users' minds, to identify objects. Identifiers can be unique or not unique. Any type of attribute can be an identifier. Identifiers are shown with the letters ID in front of the attribute. If the attribute is unique, then the letters ID are underlined. The cardinalities of an identifier are normally 1.1.

The domain of an attribute is the set of all possible values that the attribute can have. Domains have both a physical and a semantic definition. There are three types of domains: simple, group, and semantic object.

Applications process objects through users' views. A view of an object consists of the name of the object and all of the attributes visible from that view. View and object definition is often an iterative process.

The process of developing a set of object diagrams is iterative. Reports or forms are examined; an initial set of objects is documented; and the new reports and forms are then checked to reveal new objects and changes in existing objects. This process continues until all the forms and reports have been examined.

There are seven types of objects. Simple objects have no multivalued attributes and no object attributes. Composite objects have multivalued attributes but no object attributes. Compound objects have object attributes, and hybrid objects combine composite and compound objects. Association objects relate two or more other objects. Subtype objects are used to represent the specializations of objects. Finally, archetype/version objects are used to model objects that contain base data along with multiple variations, or versions.

Semantic objects and OOP share an intellectual orientation, but they differ with regard to methods and are used to address different problem domains. Both the semantic object model and the entity relationship model are tools for understanding and documenting the users' data requirements. Their primary difference is one of orientation. The E-R model considers entities as basic, whereas the semantic object model considers semantic objects as basic. The semantic object model also contains more information about the meaning of the data than does the entity relationship model.

GROUP I QUESTIONS

4.1   Explain why the E-R model and the semantic object model are like lenses.

4.2   Define *semantic object*.

4.3   Explain the difference between an object class name and an object instance name. Give an example of each.

4.4   What is required for a set of attributes to be a sufficient description?

4.5   Explain the words *distinct identity* as they pertain to the definition of a semantic object.

4.6   Explain why a line item of an order is not a semantic object.

4.7   List the three types of attributes.

4.8   Give an example of each of the following:

   a. a simple, single-valued attribute.

   b. a group, single-valued attribute.

   c. a simple, multivalued attribute.

   d. a group, multivalued attribute.

   e. a simple object attribute.

   f. a multivalued object attribute.

4.9   What is minimum cardinality? How is it used? Which types of attributes have minimum cardinality?

4.10 What is maximum cardinality? How is it used? Which types of attributes have maximum cardinality?

4.11 What are paired attributes? Why are they needed?

4.12 What is an object identifier? Give an example of a simple attribute object identifier and an example of a group attribute object identifier.

4.13 Define *attribute domain*. What are the types of attribute domain? Why is a semantic description necessary?

4.14 What is a semantic object view? Give an example of an object and two views other than those in this text.

4.15 Give an example of a simple object other than the one discussed in this chapter.

4.16 Give three examples of composite objects other than those in this chapter. One of your examples should have just one composite group; one should have two independent composite groups; and the third should have nested composite groups.

4.17 Give an example of four sets of compound objects other than those in this chapter. One set should have a 1:1 relationship; one set should have a 1:N relationship; one set should have an M:1 relationship; and one set should have an M:N relationship.

4.18 Give an example of a hybrid object other than the one in this chapter.

4.19 Give an example of one association and two compound objects other than those in this chapter.

4.20 Give an example of a supertype object with three subtype objects other than those in this chapter.

4.21 Give an example archetype/version objects other than those in this chapter.

4.22 Define the term *object* as used in object-oriented programming.

4.23 Summarize the major differences between objects in object-oriented programming and semantic objects.

4.24 Explain the similarities between the E-R model and the semantic object model.

4.25 Explain the major differences between the E-R model and the semantic object model.

4.26 Explain the reasoning that entities, as defined in the E-R model, do not truly exist.

4.27 Show how both the E-R model and the semantic object model would represent the data underlying the SALES ORDER form in Figure 4-24(a), and explain the main differences.

GROUP II QUESTIONS

4.28 Collect as many forms or reports as you can about your relationship with your college or university. Examples are acceptance letters, class schedules, transcripts, bills, class-change forms, and grades. Using the E-R model, create a data model of the entities that underlie your relationship with your school.

4.29 To answer Question 4.28, use the semantic object model instead.

4.30 Compare your answers to Questions 4.28 and 4.29. How are they similar? How are they different? Are the differences important? Do you think one model is uniformly superior to the other? Justify your answers.

Database and Database Application Design

The chapters in Part III address the design of databases and database applications. Chapter 5 presents the relational model and normalization. The relational model is important to design because it can be used to express DBMS-independent designs. Normalization is important because it is a technique for checking the quality of such a design. Given the groundwork in Chapter 5, we then consider, in Chapter 6, the process of transforming entity relationship data models into DBMS-independent, relational designs. Next, Chapter 7 describes the process for transforming semantic object data models into such designs. Finally, in Chapter 8, we address application design, and examine the relationship between database structure and application structure and processing.

CHAPTER

THE RELATIONAL MODEL AND NORMALIZATION

The relational model is important for two reasons. First, since the constructs of the relational model are broad and general, it can be used to express DBMS-independent designs. Second, the relational model is the basis for an important category of DBMS products. Being familiar with this model helps implement databases using one of these products.

This chapter presents the basics of the relational model and explains the fundamental concepts of *normalization.* We begin with the fact that not all relations are equal, that some are better than others. Normalization is a process for converting a relation that has certain problems to two or more relations that do not have these problems. Even more important, normalization can be used as a guideline for checking the desirability and correctness of relations. Much theoretical work has been done on the question of what a well-structured relation is. This work is termed *normalization* because one of the pioneers in database technology, E. F. Codd, defined various normal forms of relations. In this chapter we survey normalization, including the results of theorems that are useful and significant to database practitioners. The proofs of these theorems and a formal, more rigorous treatment of this subject can be found in the work of Date and of Ullman.[1]

---

[1] C. J. Date, *An Introduction to Database Systems* (Reading, MA: Addison-Wesley, 1992); and J. D. Ullman, *Principles of Database Systems* (New York: Computer Science Press, 1982).

THE RELATIONAL MODEL

A **relation** is a two-dimensional table. Each row in the table holds data that pertains to some thing or a portion of some thing. Each column of the table contains data regarding an attribute. Sometimes rows are called **tuples** (rhymes with "couples"), and columns are called **attributes**.

The terms *relation, tuple,* and *attribute* arose from relational mathematics, which is the theoretical source of this model. MIS professionals find more comfortable the analogous terms *file, record,* and *field,* and most users find the terms *table, row,* and *column* most sensible. Figure 5-1 summarizes this terminology.

For a table to be a relation, it must meet certain restrictions.[2] First, the cells of the table must be single valued; neither repeating groups nor arrays are allowed as values.[3] All of the entries in any column (attribute) must be of the same kind. For example, if one column contains employee numbers, it must have employee numbers for every row of the table. Each column has a unique name, and the order of the columns in the table is insignificant. Finally, no two rows (tuples) in a table may be identical, and the order of the rows is insignificant.

Figure 5-2 is a sample table. Notice that it has seven rows (tuples) made up of four columns (attributes). If we were to rearrange the order of the columns (say by placing EmployeeNumber at the far left) or to reorder the rows (perhaps in ascending sequence on Age), we would have an equivalent table.

Figure 5-2 shows one occurrence, or instance, of a table. The generalized format, EMPLOYEE (Name, Age, Sex, EmployeeNumber), is called the **relation structure**, and it is what most people mean when they use the term *relation.*

To understand the relational model and normalization, you must first understand two terms, functional dependency and key. These terms pertain to the relationships among attributes in a relation. (This is a good example of why the terminology in database technology can be confusing! A *relation* is a table. Don't confuse it with the term *relationship,* which is an association among things. Although relations can express relationships, the two terms refer to different concepts.)

FIGURE 5-1

Relational Terminology

Relational Model	Programmer	User
Relation	File	Table
Tuple (Row)	Record	Row
Attribute	Field	Column

---

[2] E. F. Codd, "A Relational Model of Data for Large Shared Databanks," *Communications of the ACM,* June 1970, pp. 377–387.

[3] This does not mean that the values must be a fixed length. A variable-length memo field, for example, is a perfectly legitimate value. Only *one* such value is allowed, however.

FIGURE 5-2

EMPLOYEE Relation

	Attribute1 Name	Attribute2 Age	Attribute3 Sex	Attribute4 EmployeeNumber
Tuple 1	Anderson	21	F	010110
Tuple 2	Decker	22	M	010100
.	Glover	22	M	101000
.	Jackson	21	F	201100
.	Moore	19	M	111100
.	Nakata	20	F	111101
Tuple 7	Smith	19	M	111111

■ Functional Dependencies

A **functional dependency** is a relationship between or among attributes. Suppose that if we are given the value of one attribute, we can obtain (or look up) the value of another attribute. For example, if we know the value of CustomerAccountNumber, we can find the value of CustomerBalance. If this is true, we can say that CustomerBalance is *functionally dependent* on CustomerAccountNumber. In more general terms, attribute Y is functionally dependent on attribute X if the value of X determines the value of Y. Or stated differently, if we know the value of X, we can obtain the value of Y.

Equations can represent functional dependencies. For example, if we know the price of an item and the quantity of items purchased, we can calculate the total price of those items, as follows:

TotalPrice = ItemPrice x Quantity

In this case, we would say that TotalPrice is functionally dependent on ItemPrice and Quantity.

The functional dependencies between attributes in a relation usually do not involve equations. For example, suppose that students have a unique identification number, SID, and that every student has one, and only one, major. Given the value of a SID, we can find out that student's major, and so Major is functionally dependent on SID. Or consider microcomputers in a computer lab. Each has one, and only one, size of main memory, and so MemorySize is functionally dependent on ComputerSerialNumber.

Unlike an equation, such functional dependencies cannot be worked out using arithmetic; instead, they are listed in the database. In fact, the expression of the functional dependencies is one of the reasons for having a database.

Functional dependencies are written using the following notation:

SID → Major
ComputerSerialNumber → MemorySize

The first expression is read as "SID functionally determines Major," "SID determines Major," or "Major is dependent on SID." The attributes on the left side of the arrow are called **determinants.**

As we pointed out, a functional dependency is a relationship among attribute values. If SID determines Major, a particular value of SID will be paired with only *one* value of Major. Conversely, a value of Major may be paired with *one or more* different values of SID.

For example, suppose the student whose SID is 123 majors in accounting. Whenever SID and Major are found together in a relation, the SID value of 123 will always be paired with the Major value of Accounting. The opposite is not true, however, as the Major Accounting may be paired with many values of SID (many students may major in accounting). Consequently, we can say that the relationship of SID with Major is many to one (N:1). In general, we can say that if A determines B, the relationship of the values of A to B is N:1.

Functional dependencies can involve groups of attributes. Consider the relation GRADES (SID, ClassName, Grade). The combination of a SID and a ClassName determines a grade, a functional dependency that is written

(SID, ClassName) → Grade

Note that both SID and ClassName are needed to determine a Grade. We cannot subdivide the functional dependency because StudentID does not determine Grade by itself.

Notice the difference in the following two patterns: If X → (Y, Z), then X → Y and X → Z. For example, if SID → (StudentName, Major), then SID → StudentName and SID → Major. But if (X, Y) → Z, then in general, it is not true that X → Y or Y → Z. So, if (SID, ClassName) → Grade, then SID by itself cannot determine Grade.

Keys

A **key** is a group of one or more attributes that uniquely identifies a row. Consider the relation ACTIVITY in Figure 5-3, whose attributes are SID, Activity, and Fee. The meaning of a row is that a student engages in the named activity for the specified fee. Assume that a student is allowed to participate in only one activity at a time. In this case, a value of SID determines a unique row, and so it is a key.

Keys can also be composed of a group of attributes taken together. For example, if students were allowed to enroll in many activities at the same time, it would be possible for one value of SID to appear in two or more rows of the table, and so SID could not uniquely identify the row. Some combination of attributes, perhaps (SID, Activity), would be required.

FIGURE 5-3

ACTIVITY Relation

ACTIVITY (SID, Activity, Fee)
Key: SID
Sample Data

SID	Activity	Fee
100	Skiing	200
150	Swimming	50
175	Squash	50
200	Swimming	50

As an aside, there is a subtle but important point in the preceding paragraph. Whether or not attributes are keys and whether or not they are functional dependencies are determined not by an abstract set of rules but, rather, by the assumptions, users' mental models, and business rules of the organization developing the database. In this example, whether SID is the key or whether (SID, Activity) is the key or whether some other combination is the key is determined entirely by the underlying semantics of the database. We must ask the users to resolve these questions. As we continue, keep in mind that all the assumptions we make about functional dependencies, keys, and the like are determined by the users' mental models.

After interviewing the users, suppose we discover that students are, in fact, allowed to participate in several activities at one time. This situation is represented by the relation ACTIVITIES, shown in Figure 5-4. As we stated, SID is *not* a key of this relation. Student 100, for example, has enrolled in both skiing and golf, and the SID value of 100 occurs in two different rows. In fact, for this relation, no single attribute is a key, so the key must be a combination of two or more attributes.

Consider the combinations of two attributes from this table. There are three possibilities: (SID, Activity), (SID, Fee), and (Activity, Fee). Is any one of these combinations a key? To be a key, it must uniquely identify a row. Again, to decide questions like this, we must ask the users. We cannot simply depend on sample data like that in Figure 5-4 or rely on our own assumptions to make the decision.

After talking with the users, suppose we find out that several activities can charge the same fee. Since this is the case, the combination (SID, Fee) cannot determine a unique row. Student 100, for example, could engage in two different activities, both of which cost $200. This would mean that the combination (100, $200) occurs twice in the table, and so this combination cannot be a key.

Can the combination (Activity, Fee) be a key? Does the combination (Skiing, $200) determine a unique row? No, it does not, because many students can participate in skiing. What about (SID, Activity)? Given what we know from the users, can a combination of values for SID and Activity determine a unique row? Yes, it can, so long as we are not required to keep records of the different occasions on which a student enrolled in a given activity. In other words, is this table to be used to record only a student's current activities, or is it supposed to keep records of past activities as well?

Again, we must consult the users to answer this question. Suppose we learn that only records of current activities are to be kept. Then the combination (SID, Activity) can determine a unique row, and consequently, (SID, Activity) is the key for this relation. If the users specified that records of current and past activities were to be

FIGURE 5-4

Relation with a Two-Attribute Key

SID	Activity	Fee
100	Skiing	200
100	Golf	65
150	Swimming	50
175	Squash	50
175	Swimming	50
200	Swimming	50
200	Golf	65

kept, the relation in Figure 5-3 would have duplicate rows. Since this is prohibited by the definition of relation, we would need to add other attributes such as Date. Every relation has at least one key. At the extreme, the key consists of all of the attributes of the relation.

Functional Dependencies, Keys, and Uniqueness

Many students confuse the concepts of functional dependencies, keys, and uniqueness. To avoid that possibility, consider the following: A determinant of a functional dependency may or may not be unique to a relation. If we know that A determines B and that A and B are in the same relation, we still do not know whether A is unique in that relation. We only know that A determines B.

For example, in the ACTIVITIES relation, Activity functionally determines Fee, and yet there can be many instances of a particular Activity in the relation. The functional dependency states only that wherever Activity occurs with Fee, it always occurs with the same value of Fee. That is, skiing always costs $200, regardless of how many times the value skiing occurs in the table.

Unlike the determinants of functional dependencies, keys are always unique. A key functionally determines the entire row. If the value of the key were duplicated, the entire tuple would be duplicated. But this is not allowed because, by definition, rows in a relation must be unique. Thus when we say that an attribute (or combination) is a key, we know that it will be unique. If (SID, Activity) is a key, then, for example, the combination (100, skiing) will occur only once in a relation.

To test your understanding of these concepts, try to explain why in the ACTIVITY relation in Figure 5-3 SID is both a determinant and a key, but Activity is a determinant and not a key. (Keep in mind that the relation in Figure 5-3 reflects the school's policy that a student may participate in, at most, one activity at a time.)

NORMALIZATION

Unfortunately, not all relations are equally desirable. A table that meets the minimum definition of a relation may not have an effective or appropriate structure. For some relations, changing the data can have undesirable consequences, called **modification anomalies.** Anomalies can be eliminated by redefining the relation into two or more relations. In most circumstances, the redefined, or **normalized,** relations are preferred.

Modification Anomalies

Again consider ACTIVITY in Figure 5-3. If we delete the tuple for Student 100, we will lose not only the fact that Student 100 is a skier but also the fact that skiing costs $200. This is called a **deletion anomaly**; that is, by deleting the facts about one entity (that Student 100 is a skier), we inadvertently delete facts about another entity (that skiing costs $200). With one deletion, we lose facts about two entities.

The same relation can be used to illustrate an **insertion anomaly.** Suppose we want to store the fact that scuba diving costs $175, but we cannot enter this data into the ACTIVITY relation until a student takes up scuba diving. This restriction seems silly. Why should we have to wait until someone takes the activity before we can record its price? This restriction is called an insertion anomaly. We cannot insert a fact about one entity until we have an additional fact about another entity.

The relation in Figure 5-3 can be used for some applications, but it obviously has problems. We can eliminate both the deletion and insertion anomalies by dividing the ACTIVITY relation into two relations, each one dealing with a different theme. For example, we can put the SID and Activity attributes into one relation (we will call the new relation STU-ACT for student activity), and we can put the Activity and Fee attributes into a relation called ACT-COST (for activity cost). Figure 5-5 shows the same sample data stored in these two new relations.

Now if we delete Student 100 from STU-ACT, we do not lose the fact that skiing costs $200. Furthermore, we can add scuba diving and its fee to the ACT-COST relation even before anyone enrolls. Thus the deletion and insertion anomalies have been eliminated.

Separating one relation into two relations has a disadvantage, however. Suppose a student tries to sign up for a nonexistent activity. For instance, Student 250 wants to enroll in racquetball. We can insert this new tuple in STU-ACT (the row would contain 250, RACQUETBALL), but should we? Should a student be allowed to enroll in an activity that is not in the relation ACT-COST? Put in another way, should the database applications somehow prevent student rows from being added if the value of the ACTIVITY is not in the ACT-COST table?

The answer to this question lies with the users' requirements. This constraint is called a **referential integrity constraint**. If the action should be prohibited, this constraint must be documented as part of the schema design. Later, in implementation, the constraint will be defined to the DBMS if the product in use provides such constraint checking. If not, the constraint must be enforced by application programs.

Suppose the user specifies that activities can exist before any student enrolls in them but that no student may enroll in an activity that does not have a fee assigned to it (that is, no activities that are not in the ACT-COST table). We can document this constraint in any of several ways in the database design: Activity in STU-ACT is a subset of Activity in ACT-COST, or STU-ACT [Activity] is a subset of ACT-COST [Activity], or STU-ACT [Activity] $\subseteq$ ACT-COST [Activity].

According to this notation, the brackets [ ] denote a column of data that is extracted from a relation. These expressions simply mean that the values in the Activity attribute of STU-ACT must exist in the Activity attribute of ACT-COST. It

normal situation

FIGURE 5-5

The Division of ACTIVITY
into Two Relations

STU-ACT (SID, Activity)
Key: SID

SID	Activity
100	Skiing
150	Swimming
175	Squash
200	Swimming

ACT-COST (Activity, Fee)
Key: Activity

Activity	Fee
Skiing	200
Swimming	50
Squash	50

also means that before we allow an Activity to be entered into STU-ACT, we must check to make sure that it is already present in ACT-COST.

■ Essence of Normalization

The anomalies in the ACTIVITY relation in Figure 5-3 can be stated in the following intuitive way: Problems occur because ACTIVITY contains facts about two different themes: which students participate in which activities and also how much each activity costs. When we add a new row, we must add data about two themes at once, and when we delete a row, we must delete data about two themes at once.

Remember your eighth-grade English teacher? He or she claimed that a paragraph should have a single theme. If a paragraph had more than one theme, we were taught to break up the paragraph in two or more paragraphs so that each paragraph would have only one theme. Similar logic applies to relations. Every normalized relation has a single theme. If it has two or more themes, it should be broken up into relations, each of which has a single theme. Every time we break up a relation, however, we may create a need for an interrelation constraint. This process is the essence of normalization. When we find a relation with modification anomalies, we eliminate them by splitting the relation into two or more separate ones, each containing a single theme.

In the remainder of this chapter, you will learn a number of rules about normalization. All of these rules are special cases of the process just described.

■ Classes of Relations

Relations can be classified by the types of modification anomalies to which they are vulnerable. In the 1970s, relational theorists chipped away at these types. Someone would find an anomaly, classify it, and think of a way to prevent it. Each time this happened, the criteria for designing relations improved. These classes of relations and the techniques for preventing anomalies are called **normal forms.** Depending on its structure, a relation may be in first normal form, second normal form, or some other normal form.

In his landmark 1970 paper, E. F. Codd defined first, second, and third normal forms (1NF, 2NF, 3NF). Later, Boyce–Codd normal form (BCNF) was specified, and then fourth and fifth normal forms were defined. As shown in Figure 5-6, these normal forms are nested. That is, a relation in second normal form is also in first

FIGURE 5-6

Relationship of
Normal Forms

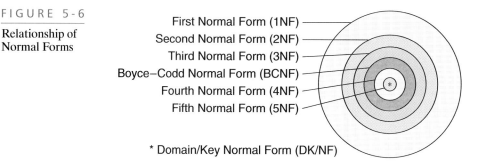

First Normal Form (1NF)
Second Normal Form (2NF)
Third Normal Form (3NF)
Boyce–Codd Normal Form (BCNF)
Fourth Normal Form (4NF)
Fifth Normal Form (5NF)

* Domain/Key Normal Form (DK/NF)

normal form, and a relation in 5NF (fifth normal form) is also in 4NF, BCNF, 3NF, 2NF, and 1NF.

These normal forms were helpful, but they had a serious limitation. No theory guaranteed that any of them would eliminate all anomalies; each form could eliminate just certain ones. This situation changed, however, in 1981 when R. Fagin defined a new normal form called **domain/key normal form (DK/NF)**. In an important paper, Fagin showed that a relation in domain/key normal form is free of all modification anomalies, regardless of their type.[4] He also showed that any relation that is free of modification anomalies is also in domain/key normal form.

Until DK/NF was defined, it was necessary for relational database designers to continue looking for more and more anomalies and more and more normal forms. Fagin's proof, however, simplified the situation. If we can put a relation in DK/NF, then we can be sure that it will have no anomalies. The trick is knowing how to put relations in DK/NF.

FIRST THROUGH FIFTH NORMAL FORMS

Any table of data that meets the definition of a relation is said to be in **first normal form**. Remember that for a table to be a relation, the following must hold: The cells of the table must be single valued, and neither repeating groups nor arrays are allowed as values. All entries in any column (attribute) must be of the same kind. Each column must have a unique name, but the order of the columns in the table is insignificant. Finally, no two rows in a table may be identical, but the order of the rows is insignificant.

The relation in Figure 5-3 is in first normal form. As we have seen, relations in first normal form can be used, but they may have modification anomalies. And as we demonstrated, we can eliminate these anomalies by changing the format of the relation, by splitting it into two or more relations. When we do this, the new relations are in some other normal form—just which one depends on the anomalies we have eliminated, as well as the ones to which the new relations are vulnerable.

■ Second Normal Form

To understand second normal form, consider the ACTIVITIES relation in Figure 5-4. This relation has modification anomalies similar to the ones we examined earlier. If we delete the tuple for Student 175, we will lose the fact that squash costs $50. Also, we cannot enter an activity until a student signs up for it. Thus the relation suffers from both deletion and insertion anomalies.

The problem with this relation is that it has a dependency involving only part of the key. The key is the combination (SID, Activity), but the relation contains a dependency, Activity → Fee. The determinant of this dependency (Activity) is only part of the key (SID, Activity). In this case, we say that Fee is *partially dependent* on

---

[4] R. Fagin, "A Normal Form for Relational Databases That Is Based on Domains and Keys," *ACM Transactions on Database Systems*, September 1981, pp. 387–415.

the key of the table. There would be no modification anomalies if Fee were dependent on all of the key. Therefore, to eliminate the anomalies, we must separate the relation into two relations.

This situation leads to the definition of second normal form: *A relation is in second normal form if all its nonkey attributes are dependent on all of the key.* According to this definition, every relation that has a single attribute as its key is automatically in second normal form. Since the key is only one attribute, by default, every nonkey attribute is dependent on *all* of the key; there can be no partial dependencies. Second normal pertains only to relations with composite keys.

ACTIVITIES can be decomposed to form two relations in second normal form. The relations are the same as those in Figure 5-5, namely, STU-ACT and ACT-COST. These relations are in second normal form because they both have single-attribute keys.

Third Normal Form

Relations in second normal form also have anomalies. Consider the HOUSING relation in Figure 5-7(a). The key is SID, and the functional dependencies are SID → Building and Building → Fee. These dependencies arise because each student

FIGURE 5-7

Elimination of Transitive
Dependency: (a) Relation
with Transitive
Dependency and (b)
Relations Eliminating the
Transitive Dependency

HOUSING (SID, Building, Fee)
Key: SID
Functional
dependencies: Building → Fee
                    SID → Building → Fee

SID	Building	Fee
100	Randolph	1200
150	Ingersoll	1100
200	Randolph	1200
250	Pitkin	1100
300	Randolph	1200

(a)

STU-HOUSING (SID, Building)
Key: SID

SID	Building
100	Randolph
150	Ingersoll
200	Randolph
250	Pitkin
300	Randolph

BLDG-FEE (Building, Fee)
Key: Building

Building	Fee
Randolph	1200
Ingersoll	1100
Pitkin	1100

(b)

lives in only one building and each building charges only one fee. Everyone living in Randolph Hall, for example, pays $1100 per quarter.

Since SID determines Building and Building determines Fee, indirectly SID → Fee. An arrangement of functional dependencies like this is called a **transitive dependency**, since SID determines Fee through the attribute Building.

Because of this transitive dependency, SID, a single attribute, is the key, and the relation is in second normal form (both Building and Fee are determined by SID). Despite this, however, HOUSING has anomalies.

What would happen if we deleted the second tuple shown in Figure 5-7(a)? We would lose not only the fact that Student 150 lives in Ingersoll Hall but also the fact that it costs $1100 to live there. This is a deletion anomaly. And how can we record the fact that the Fee for Carrigg Hall is $1500? We cannot until a student decides to move in. This is an insertion anomaly.

To eliminate the anomalies from a relation in second normal form, the transitive dependency must be removed, which leads to a definition of third normal form: *A relation is in third normal form if it is in second normal form and has no transitive dependencies.*

The HOUSING relation can be divided into two relations in third normal form. The relations STU-HOUSING (SID, Building) and BLDG-FEE (Building, Fee) in Figure 5-7(b) are examples.

The ACTIVITY relation in Figure 5-3 also has a transitive dependency. In ACTIVITY, SID determines Activity and Activity determines Fee. Therefore, ACTIVITY is not in third normal form. Decomposing ACTIVITY into the relations STU-ACT (SID, Activity) and ACT-COST (Activity, Fee) eliminates the anomalies.

■ Boyce–Codd Normal Form

Unfortunately, even relations in third normal form can have anomalies. Consider the ADVISER relation in Figure 5-8(a). Suppose the requirements underlying this relation are that a student (SID) can have one or more majors (Major), a major can have several faculty members (Fname) as advisers, and a faculty member (Fname) advises in only one major area.

Since students can have several majors, SID does not determine Major. Moreover, since students can have several advisers, SID also does not determine Fname. Thus SID, by itself, cannot be a key.

The combination (SID, Major) determines Fname, and the combination (SID, Fname) determines Major. Hence either of the combinations can be a key. Two or more attributes or attribute collections that can be a key are called **candidate keys.** Whichever of the candidates is selected to be *the* key is called the **primary key.**

In addition to the candidate keys, there is another functional dependency to consider: Fname determines Major (any faculty member advises in only one major. Therefore, given the Fname, we can determine the Major). Thus Fname is a determinant.

By definition, ADVISER is in first normal form. It is also in second normal form, since any nonkey attributes are dependent on the entire key (no matter which candidate key we select). And it also is in third normal form because it has no transitive dependencies. Despite all this, however, it has modification anomalies.

FIGURE 5-8

Boyce–Codd Normal Form:
(a) Relation in Third Normal
Form but Not in Boyce–Codd
Normal Form and (b)
Relations in Boyce–Codd
Normal Form

ADVISOR (SID, Major, Fname)

Key (primary): (SID, Major)
Key (candidate): (SID, Fname)

Functional
dependencies: Fname→Major

SID	Major	Fname
100	Math	Cauchy
150	Psychology	Jung
200	Math	Riemann
250	Math	Cauchy
300	Psychology	Perls
300	Math	Riemann

(a)

STU-ADV (SID, Fname)
Key: SID, Fname

ADV-SUBJ (Fname, Subject)
Key: Fname

SID	Fname
100	Cauchy
150	Jung
200	Riemann
250	Cauchy
300	Perls
300	Riemann

Fname	Subject
Cauchy	Math
Jung	Psychology
Riemann	Math
Perls	Psychology

(b)

Suppose Student 300 drops out of school. If we delete Student 300's tuple, we will lose the fact that Perls advises in psychology. This is a deletion anomaly. Similarly, how can we store the fact that Keynes advises in economics? We cannot until a student majors in economics. This is an insertion anomaly.

Situations like this lead to the definition of Boyce–Codd normal form (BCNF): *A relation is in BCNF if every determinant is a candidate key.* ADVISER is not in BCNF, since it has a determinant, Fname, that is not a candidate key.

As with the other examples, ADVISER can be decomposed into two relations having no anomalies. For example, the relations STU-ADV (SID, Fname) and ADV-SUBJ (Fname, Subject) have no anomalies.

Relations in BCNF have no anomalies in regard to functional dependencies, and this seemed to put the issue of modification anomalies to rest. It was soon discovered, however, that anomalies can arise from situations other than functional dependencies.

Fourth Normal Form

Consider the STUDENT relation in Figure 5-9, showing the relationship among students, majors, and activities. Suppose that students can enroll in several different majors and participate in several different activities. Since this is so, the only key is the combination of attributes (SID, Major, Activity). Student 100 majors in music and accounting, and she also participates in swimming and tennis. Student 150 majors only in math and participates in jogging.

What is the relationship between SID and Major? It is not a functional dependency because students can have several majors. A single value of SID can have many values of Major, as is also true of the relationship between SID and Activity.

This attribute dependency is called a **multivalued dependency.** Multivalued dependencies lead to modification anomalies. To begin, note the data redundancy in Figure 5-9. Student 100 has four records, each of which shows one of her majors paired with one of her activities. If the data were stored with fewer rows—say there are only two tuples, one for music and swimming and one for accounting and tennis—the implications would be misleading. It would *appear* that Student 100 swam only when she was a music major and played tennis only when she was an accounting major. But this interpretation is not logical. Her majors and her activities are completely independent of each other. So to prevent such a misleading conclusion, we store all the combinations of majors and activities.

Suppose that because Student 100 decides to sign up for skiing, we add the tuple [100, MUSIC, SKIING], as in Figure 5-10(a). The relation at this point implies that Student 100 skis as a music major but not as an accounting major. In order to keep the data consistent, we must add one row for each of her majors paired with skiing. Thus we must also add the row [100, ACCOUNTING, SKIING], as in Figure 5-10(b). This is an update anomaly—too much updating needs to be done to make a simple change in the data.

In general, a multivalued dependency exists when a relation has at least three attributes, two of them are multivalued, and their values depend on only the third attribute. In other words, in a relation R (A, B, C), a multivalued dependency exists if A determines multiple values of B, A determines multiple values of C, and B and C are independent of each other. As we saw in the previous example, SID determines multiple values of Major, and SID determines multiple values of Activity, but Major and Activity are independent of each other.

Refer again to Figure 5-9. Notice how multivalued dependencies are written: SID →→ Major, and SID →→ Activity. This is read "SID multidetermines Major, and SID multidetermines Activity." This relation is in BCNF (2NF because it is all

FIGURE 5-9

Relation with Multivalued Dependencies

STUDENT (SID, Major, Activity)
Key: (SID, Major, Activity)

Multivalued
dependencies: SID → → Major
                  SID → → Activity

SID	Major	Activity
100	Music	Swimming
100	Accounting	Swimming
100	Music	Tennis
100	Accounting	Tennis
150	Math	Jogging

FIGURE 5-10

STUDENT Relations with Insertion Anomalies: (a) Insertion of a Single Tuple and (b) Insertion of Two Tuples

STUDENT (SID, Major, Activity)
Key: (SID, Major, Activity)

SID	Major	Activity
100	Music	Skiing
100	Music	Swimming
100	Accounting	Swimming
100	Music	Tennis
100	Accounting	Tennis
150	Math	Jogging

(a)

SID	Major	Activity
100	Music	Skiing
100	Accounting	Skiing
100	Music	Swimming
100	Accounting	Swimming
100	Music	Tennis
100	Accounting	Tennis
150	Math	Jogging

(b)

key; 3NF because it has no transitive dependencies; and BCNF because it has no nonkey determinants). However, as we have seen, it has anomalies: If a student adds a major, we must enter a tuple for the new major, paired with each of the student's activities. The same holds true if a student enrolls in a new activity. If a student drops a major, we must delete each of his records containing that major. If he participates in four activities, there will be four tuples containing the major he has dropped, and each of them must be deleted.

To eliminate these anomalies, we must eliminate the multivalued dependency. We do this by building two relations, each one storing data for only one of the multivalued attributes. The resulting relations do not have anomalies. They are STU-MAJOR (SID, Major) and STU-ACT (SID, Activity), as seen in Figure 5-11.

FIGURE 5-11

Elimination of Multivalued Dependency

STU-MAJOR (SID, Major)
Key: (SID, Major)

SID	Major
100	Music
100	Accounting
150	Math

STU-ACT (SID, Activity)
Key: (SID, Activity)

SID	Activity
100	Skiing
100	Swimming
100	Tennis
150	Jogging

From these observations, we define fourth normal form in the following way: *A relation is in fourth normal form if it is in BCNF and has no multivalued dependencies.* A more intuitive understanding of multivalued dependencies will be possible after we have discussed domain/key normal form.

■ Fifth Normal Form

Fifth normal form concerns dependencies that are rather obscure. It has to do with relations that can be divided into subrelations, as we have been doing, but then cannot be reconstructed. The condition under which this situation arises has no clear, intuitive meaning. We do not know what the consequences of such dependencies are or even if they have any practical consequences. For more information about fifth normal form, refer to the work by Date that was cited earlier in this chapter.

Each of the normal forms we have discussed were identified by researchers who found anomalies with some relations that were in a lower normal form: Noticing modification anomalies with relations in second normal form led to the definition of third normal form. Although each normal form solved some of the problems that had been identified with the previous one, no one could know what problems had not yet been identified. With each step, progress was made toward a well-structured database definition, but no one could guarantee that no more anomalies would be found. In the next section we study a normal form that guarantees that there will be no anomalies of any type. When we put relations into that form, we know that even the obscure anomalies associated with fifth normal form cannot occur.

DOMAIN/KEY NORMAL FORM

In 1981, R. Fagin published an important paper in which he defined domain/key normal form (DK/NF).[5] He showed that a relation in domain/key normal form has no modification anomalies and, furthermore, that a relation having no modification anomalies must be in domain/key normal form. This finding establishes a bound on the definition of normal forms, and so no higher normal form is needed, at least in order to eliminate modification anomalies.

Equally important, DK/NF involves only the concepts of key and domain, concepts that are fundamental and close to the heart of database practitioners. They are readily supported by DBMS products (or could be, at least). In a sense, Fagin's work formalized and justified what many practitioners believed intuitively but were unable to express formally.

■ Definition

The DK/NF concept is quite simple: A relation is in DK/NF if every constraint on the relation is a logical consequence of the definition of keys and domains. Consider the important terms in this definition: constraint, key, and domain.

---

[5]   Ibid.

Constraint in this definition is intended to be very broad. Fagin defines a constraint as any rule governing static values of attributes that is precise enough to ascertain whether or not it is true. Thus, edit rules, intrarelation and interrelation constraints, functional dependencies, and multivalued dependencies are examples of constraints as Fagin has defined them. Fagin expressly excludes constraints pertaining to changes in data values, or time-dependent constraints. For example, the rule "Salesperson salary in the current period can never be less than salary in the prior period" is excluded from Fagin's definition of constraint. Except for time-dependent constraints, Fagin's definition is both broad and inclusive.

As we defined it, a *key* is the unique identifier of a tuple. The third significant term in the definition of DK/NF is *domain*. In Chapter 4, we stated that a domain is a description of an attribute's allowed values. It has two parts: a physical description and a semantic, or logical, description. The physical description is the set of values the attribute can have, and the logical description is the meaning of the attribute. Fagin's proof refers to both parts.

Informally, a relation is in domain/key normal form if enforcing key and domain restrictions causes all of the constraints to be met. Moreover, since relations in domain/key normal form cannot have modification anomalies, the DBMS can prohibit them by enforcing key and domain restrictions.

Unfortunately, there is no known algorithm for converting a relation to DK/NF, nor is it even known which relations can be converted to DK/NF. Finding, or designing, DK/NF relations is more of an art than a science. Despite this, DK/NF can be exceedingly useful for database design; indeed, DK/NF is a design objective. We wish to define our relations in a way that constraints are logical consequences of domains and keys. For many designs, this objective can be accomplished. When it cannot, the constraints must be built into the application programs that process the database. We will see more of this later in this chapter and in Chapter 8. To illustrate DK/NF we use three examples.

■ Example 1 of Domain/Key Normal Form

Consider the STUDENT relation in Figure 5-12, containing SID, GradeLevel, Building, and Fee. Building is the building in which the student lives, and Fee is the amount the student pays to live in that building.

SID functionally determines the other three attributes, so SID is a key. Assume we also know, from the requirements definition, that Building → Fee and that SIDs must not begin with 1. If we can express these constraints as logical consequences of domain and key definitions, we can be certain, according to Fagin's theorem, that there will be no modification anomalies. For this example, it will be easy.

FIGURE 5-12

Example 1 of DK/NF

STUDENT (SID, GradeLevel, Building, Fee)

Key: SID

Constraints: Building → Fee
SID must not begin with digit 1

FIGURE 5-13

Domain/Key Definition of Example 1

```
Domain Definitions

    SID          IN    CDDD, where C is decimal digit not = 1; D =
                       decimal digit
    GradeLevel   IN    {'FR', 'SO', 'JR', 'SN', 'GR'}
    Building     IN    CHAR(4)
    Fee          IN    DEC(4)


Relation and Key Definitions

    STUDENT (SID, GradeLevel, Building)
    Key: SID

    BLDG-FEE
    (Building, Fee)
    Key: Building
```

To enforce the constraint that student numbers not begin with 1, we simply define the domain for student numbers to incorporate this constraint (Figure 5-13). Enforcing the domain restriction guarantees that this constraint will be met.

Next we need to make the functional dependency Building → Fee a logical consequence of keys. If Building were a key attribute, Building → Fee would be a logical consequence of a key. Therefore the question becomes how we can make Building a key. It cannot be a key in STUDENT because more than one student lives in the same building, but it can be a key of its own relation. Thus we define the relation BLDG-FEE with Building and Fee as its attributes. Building is the key of this relation. Having defined this new relation, we can remove Fee from STUDENT. The final domain and relation definitions for this example appear in Figure 5-13.

This is the same result we obtained when converting a relation from 2NF to 3NF to remove transitive dependencies. In this case, however, the process was simpler and the result more robust. It was simpler because we did not need to know that we were eliminating a transitive dependency. We simply needed to find creative ways to make all the constraints logical consequences of domain and key definitions. The result was more robust because when converting the relation to 3NF, we knew only that it had fewer anomalies than when it was in 2NF. By converting the relation to DK/NF, we know that the relations have no modification anomalies whatsoever.

◼ Example 2 of Domain/Key Normal Form

The next example involves the relation described in Figure 5-14 and is more complicated than the previous one. The PROFESSOR relation contains data about professors, the classes they teach, and the students they advise. FID (for Faculty ID) and Fname uniquely identify a professor. SID uniquely identifies a student, but Sname does not necessarily identify a SID. Professors can teach several classes and advise several students, but a student is advised by only one professor. FIDs start with a 1, but SIDs must not start with a 1.

FIGURE 5-14

Example 2 of DK/NF

```
PROFESSOR (FID, Fname, Class, SID, Sname)
Key: (FID, Class, SID)
Constraints:      FID → Fname
                  Fname → FID
                  FID → → Class | SID
                  Fname → → Class | SID
                  SID → FID
                  SID → Fname
                  SID → Sname
                  FID must start with 1; SID must not start with 1
```

These statements can be expressed more precisely by the functional and multi-valued dependencies shown in Figure 5-14. FID and Fname functionally determine each other (in essence, they are equivalent). FID and Fname multidetermine Class and SID. SID functionally determines FID and Fname. SID determines Sname.

In more complex examples such as this one, it is helpful to consider DK/NF from a more intuitive light. Remember that the essence of normalization is that every relation should have a single theme. Considered from this perspective, there are three themes in PROFESSOR. One is the correspondence between FIDs and Fnames. Another concerns the classes that a professor teaches, and the third concerns the identification number, name, and adviser of a given student.

Figure 5-15 shows three relations that reflect these themes. The FACULTY relation represents the equivalence of FID and Fname. FID is the key and Fname is an

FIGURE 5-15

Domain/Key Definition of Example 2

```
Domain Definitions

    FID       IN   CDDD, C = 1; D = decimal digit
    Fname     IN   CHAR(30)
    Class     IN   CHAR(10)
    SID       IN   CDDD, C is decimal digit, not = 1;
                        D = decimal digit
    Sname     IN   CHAR(30)

Relation and Key Definitions

    FACULTY (FID, Fname)
    Key (primary):    FID
    Key (candidate):  Fname

    PREPARATION (Fname, Class)
    Key: Fname, Class

    STUDENT (SID Sname, Fname)
    Key: SID
```

alternative key, which means that both attributes are unique to the relation. Because both are keys, the functional dependencies FID → Fname and Fname → FID are logical consequences of keys.

The PREPARATION relation contains the correspondence of faculty and classes; it shows the classes that a professor is prepared to teach. The key is the combination (Fname, Class). Both attributes are required in the key because a professor may teach several classes. Finally, STUDENT represents the student and adviser names for a particular SID. Observe that each of these relations has a single theme. These relations express all of the constraints of Figure 5-14 as a logical consequence of domains and key definitions. These relations are, therefore, in DK/NF.

Note that separating the PREPARATION theme from the STUDENT theme has eliminated the multivalued dependencies. When we examined fourth normal form, we found that in order to eliminate multivalued dependencies, we had to separate the multivalued attributes into different relations. Our approach here is to break a relation with several themes into several relations, each with one theme. In doing that, we eliminated a multivalued dependency. In fact, we arrived at the same solution using both approaches.

■ Example 3 of Domain/Key Normal Form

The next example concerns a situation that was not addressed by any of the other normal forms but that occurs frequently in practice. This relation has a constraint among data values within a tuple that is neither a functional dependency nor a multivalued dependency.

Consider the constraints in the relation STU-ADVISER in Figure 5-16. This relation contains information about a student and his or her adviser. SID determines Sname, FID, Fname, and GradFacultyStatus and is therefore the key. FID and Fname identify a unique faculty member and are equivalent to each other, as in Example 2. Both FID and Fname determine GradFacultyStatus. Finally, the new type of constraint is that only members of the graduate faculty are allowed to advise graduate students.

FIGURE 5-16

Example 3 of DK/NF

STU-ADVISOR (SID, Sname, FID, Fname, GradFacultyStatus)

Key: SID

Constraints: FID → Fname
Fname → FID
FID and Fname → GradFacultyStatus
Only graduate faculty can advise graduate students
FID begins with 1
SID must not begin with 1
SID of graduate student begins with 9
GradFacultyStatus = $\begin{cases} 0 \text{ for undergraduate faculty} \\ 1 \text{ for graduate faculty} \end{cases}$

The domain restrictions are that SID must not begin with a 1, SID must begin with a 9 for graduate students, FID must begin with a 1, and GradFacultyStatus is 0 for undergraduate faculty and 1 for graduate faculty. With these domain definitions, the constraint that graduate students must be advised by graduate faculty can be expressed as a constraint on row values. Specifically, if the SID starts with 9, the value of GradFacultyStatus must be 1.

To put this relation in DK/NF, we proceed as in Example 2. What are the basic themes of this relation? There is one regarding faculty personnel that relates FID, Fname, and GradFacultyStatus. Since FID and Fname determine GradFacultyStatus, either of these attributes can be the key, and this relation is in DK/NF (see Figure 5-17).

Now consider the data regarding students and advisers. Although it may first appear that there is only one theme, that of advising, the constraint that only graduate faculty can advise graduate students implies otherwise. Actually, there are two themes: graduate advising and undergraduate advising. Thus Figure 5-17 contains a G-ADV relation for graduate students and a UG-ADV relation for undergraduates. Look at the domain definitions: GSID starts with a 9; Gfname is the Fname of a FACULTY tuple with GradFacultyStatus equal to 1; and UGSID must not begin with 1 or 9.

All the constraints described in Figure 5-16 are implied by the key and domain definitions in Figure 5-17. These relations are therefore in DK/NF and have no modification anomalies. To summarize, Figure 5-18 lists the normal forms and pre-

FIGURE 5-17

Domain/Key Definition of Example 3

Domain Definitions

FID	IN CDDD, where C = 1; D = decimal digit
Fname	IN CHAR (30)
Grad-faculty-status	IN [0, 1]
GSID	IN CDDD, where C = 9; D = decimal digit; graduate student
UGSID	IN CDDD, WHERE C ≠ 1 and C ≠ 9; D = decimal digit; undergraduate student
Sname	IN CHAR (30)

Additional Domain Definitions

Gfname   IN {Fname of FACULTY, where GradFacultyStatus = 1}

Relations and Key Definitions

FACULTY (FID, Fname, GradFacultyStatus)
Key: FID or Fname

G-ADV (GSID, Sname, Gfname)
Key: GSID

UG-ADV (UGSID, Sname, Fname)
Key: UGSID

FIGURE 5-18

Summary of Normal Forms

Form	Defining Characteristic
1NF	Any relation
2NF	All nonkey attributes are dependent on all of the keys.
3NF	There are no transitive dependencies.
BCNF	Every determinant is a candidate key.
4NF	There are no multivalued dependencies.
5NF	Not described in this discussion.
DK/NF	All constraints on relations are logical consequences of domains and keys.

sents the defining characteristic of each. We now turn to a different perspective on the composition of well-formed relations.

THE SYNTHESIS OF RELATIONS

In the previous section, we approached relational design from an analytical perspective. The question we asked was, Given a relation, is it in good form? Does it have modification anomalies? In this section, we look at relational design from a different perspective—a synthetic one. From this perspective, we ask, Given a set of attributes with certain functional dependencies, what relations should we form?

Observe first that two attributes, say A and B, can be related in three ways:

1. They determine each other:

   $A \rightarrow B$ and $B \rightarrow A$

Hence A and B have a one-to-one attribute relationship.

2. One determines the other.

   $A \rightarrow B$, but B not $\rightarrow A$

Hence A and B have a many-to-one relationship.

3. They are functionally unrelated.

   A not $\rightarrow B$ and B not $\rightarrow A$

Hence A and B have a many-to-many attribute relationship.

■ One-to-One Attribute Relationships

If A determines B and B determines A, the values of the attributes have a one-to-one relationship. This must be because if A determines B, the relationship between A and B is many to one. It is also true, however, that if B determines A, the relationship between B and A must be many to one. For both statements to be true at the same time, the relationship between A and B must actually be one to one (which is a special case of many to one), and the relationship between B and A is also actually one to one. Therefore the relationship is one to one.

This case is illustrated by FID and Fname in Examples 2 and 3 in the previous section on domain/key normal form. Each of these attributes uniquely identifies a faculty person. Consequently, one value of FID corresponds to exactly one value of Fname, and vice versa.

Three equivalent statements can be drawn from the example of FID and Fname:

- If two attributes functionally determine each other, the relationship of their data values is one to one.
- If two attributes uniquely identify the same thing (entity or object), the relationship of their data values is one to one.
- If two attributes have a one-to-one relationship, they functionally determine each other.

When creating a database with attributes that have a one-to-one relationship, the two attributes must occur together in at least one relation. Other attributes that are functionally determined by these (an attribute that is functionally determined by one of them is functionally determined by the other as well) may also reside in this same relation.

Consider FACULTY (FID, Fname, GradFacultyStatus) in Example 3 in the previous section. FID and Fname determine each other. GradFacultyStatus can also occur in this relation because it is determined by FID and Fname. Attributes that are not functionally determined by these attributes may not occur in a relation with them. Consider the relations FACULTY and PREPARATION in Example 2, in which both FID and Fname occur in FACULTY, but Class (from PREPARATION) may not. Class can have multiple values for a faculty member, so Class is not dependent on FID or Fname. If we added Class to the FACULTY relation, the key of FACULTY would need to be either (FID, Class) or (Fname, Class). In this case, however, FACULTY would not be in DK/NF because the dependencies between FID and Fname would not be logically implied by either of the possible keys.

These statements are summarized in the first column of Figure 5-19, and the record definition rules are listed in Figure 5-20. If A and B have a 1:1 relationship,

FIGURE 5-19

Summary of Three Types of Attribute Relationships

	Type of Attribute Relationship		
	One-to-One	Many-to-One	Many-to-Many
Relation Definition*	R(A,B)	S(C,D)	T(E,F)
Dependencies	A → B B → A	C → D D ↛ C	E ↛ F F ↛ E
Key	Either A or B	C	(E,F)
Rule for Adding Another Attribute	Either A or B → C	C → E	(E,F) → G

* The letters used in these relation definitions match those used in Figure 5-20

FIGURE 5-20

FIGURE 5-20

Summary of Rules for Constructing Relations

Concerning One-to-One Relationships

- Attributes that have a one-to-one relationship must occur together in at least one relation. Call the relation *R* and the attributes *A* and *B*.
- Either *A* or *B* must be the key of *R*.
- An attribute can be added to *R* if it is functionally determined by *A* or *B*.
- An attribute that is not functionally determined by *A* or *B* cannot be added to *R*.
- *A* and *B* must occur together in *R*, but should not occur togehter in other relations.
- Either *A* or *B* should be consistently used to represent the pair in relations other than *R*.

Concerning Many-to-One Relationships

- Attributes that have a many-to-one relationship can exist in a relation together. Assume *C* determines *D* in relation *S*.
- *C* must be the key of *S*.
- An attribute can be added to *S* if it is determined by *C*.
- An attribute that is not determined by *C* cannot be added to *S*.

Concerning Many-to-Many Relationships

- Attributes that have a many-to-many relationship can exist in a relation together. Assume two such attributes, *E* and *F*, reside together in relation *T*.
- The key of *T* must be (*E*,*F*).
- An attribute can be added to *T* if it is determined by the combination (*E*,*F*).
- An attribute may not be added to *T* if it is not determined by the combination (*E*,*F*).
- If adding a new attribute, *G*, expands the key to (*E*,*F*,*G*), then the theme of the relation has been changed. Either *G* does not belong in *T* or the name of *T* must be changed to reflect the new theme.

---

they can reside in the same relation, say R. A determines B and B determines A. The key of the relation can be either A or B. A new attribute, C, can be added to R if either A or B functionally determines C.

Attributes having a one-to-one relationship must exist together in at least one relation in order to establish their equivalence (FID of 198, for example, refers to Professor Heart). It is generally undesirable to have them occur together in more than one relation, however, because this causes needless data duplication. Often, one or both of the two attributes occur in other relations. In Example 2, Fname occurs in both PREPARATION and STUDENT in Example 2. Although it would be possible to place Fname in PREPARATION and FID in STUDENT, this generally is bad practice, because when attributes are paired in this way, one of them should be selected to represent the pair in all other relations. Fname was selected in Example 2.

Many-to-One Attribute Relationships

If attribute A determines B but B does not determine A, the relationship among their data values is many to one. In the adviser relationship in Example 2, SID determines FID. Many students (SID) are advised by a faculty member (FID), but each student is advised by only one faculty member. This, then, is a many-to-one relationship.

For a relation to be in DK/NF, all constraints must be implied by keys, and thus every determinant must be a key. If A, B, and C are in the same relation and if A determines B, then A must be the key (meaning it also determines C). If, instead, (A, B) determines C, then (A, B) must be the key. In this latter case, no other functional dependency, such as A determines B, is allowed.

You can apply these statements to database design in the following way: When constructing a relation, if A determines B, the only other attributes you can add to the relation must also be determined by A. For example, suppose you have put SID and Building together in a relation called STUDENT. You may add any other attribute determined by SID, such as Sname, to this relation. But if the attribute Fee is determined by Building, you may not add it to this relation. Fee can be added only if SID → Fee.

These statements are summarized in the center column of Figure 5-19. If C and D have an N:1 relationship, they may reside together in a relation, say S. C will determine D, but D will not determine C. The key of S will be C. Another attribute, E, can be added to S only if C determines E.

■ Many-to-Many Attribute Relationships

If A does not determine B and B does not determine A, the relationship among their data values is many to many. In Example 2, Fname and Class have a many-to-many relationship. A professor teaches many classes, and a class is taught by many professors. In a many-to-many relationship, both attributes must be a key of the relation. For instance, the key of PREPARATION in Example 2 is the combination (Fname, Class).

When constructing relations that have multiple attributes as keys, you can add new attributes that are functionally dependent on all of the keys. NumberOfTimes-Taught is functionally dependent on both (Fname, Class) and can be added to the relation. FacultyOffice, however, cannot be added because it would be dependent only on Fname, not on Class. If FacultyOffice needs to be stored in the database, it must be added to the relation regarding faculty, not to the relation regarding preparations.

These statements are summarized in the right column of Figure 5-19. If E and F have an M:N relationship, E does not determine F, and F does not determine E. Both E and F can be put into a relation T, and if this is done, the key of T will be the composite (E,F). A new attribute, G, can be added to T if it is determined by all of (E,F). It cannot be added to T if it is determined by only one of E or F.

Consider a similar, but different, example. Suppose we add ClassroomNumber to PREPARATION. Is ClassroomNumber functionally determined by the key of PREPARATION, (Fname, Class)? Most likely it is not, because a professor could teach a particular class in many different rooms.

The composite (Fname,Class) and ClassroomNumber have an M:N relationship. Since this is so, the rules in Figure 5-19 can be applied, but with E representing (Fname, Class) and F representing ClassroomNumber. Now we can compose a new relation, T, with attributes Fname, Class, and ClassroomNumber. The key becomes (Fname, Class, ClassroomNumber). In this situation, we have created a new relation with a new theme. Consider relation T, which contains faculty names, classes, and classroom numbers. The theme of this relation is therefore no longer PREPARA-TION but, rather, WHO-WHAT-WHERE-TAUGHT.

Changing the theme may or may not be appropriate. If ClassroomNumber is important, the theme does need to be changed. In that case, PREPARATION is the wrong relation, and WHO-WHERE-TAUGHT is a more suitable theme.

On the other hand, depending on user requirements, PREPARATION may be completely suitable as it is. If so, then if ClassroomNumber belongs in the database at all, it should be located in a different relation—perhaps SECTION-NUMBER, CLASS-SECTION, or some similar relation.

Multivalued Dependencies, Iteration 2

The discussion about many-to-many attribute value relationships may make the concept of multivalued dependencies easier to understand. The problem with the relation STUDENT (SID, Major, Activity) in Figure 5-9 is that it has *two* different many-to-many relationships, one between SID and Major and the other between SID and Activity. Clearly, a student's various majors have nothing to do with his or her various activities. Putting both of these many-to-many relationships in the same relation, however, makes it appear as if there is some association.

Major and Activity are independent, and there would be no problem if a student had only one of each. SID would functionally determine Major and Activity, and the relation would be in DK/NF. In this case, both the relationships between Major and SID and Activity and SID would be many to one.

Another way of perceiving the difficulty is to examine the key, (SID, Major, Activity). Since STUDENT has many-to-many relationships, all of the attributes have to be in the key. Now what theme does this key represent? We might say the combination of a student's studies and activities. But this is not one thing; it is plural. One row of this relation describes only part of the combination, and in order to get the whole picture, we need all of the rows about a particular student. In general, a row should have all of the data about one instance of the relation's theme. A row of Customer, for example, should have all the data we want about a particular customer.

Consider PREPARATION in Example 2 in the section on domain/key normal form. The key is (Fname, Class). The theme this represents is that a particular professor is prepared to teach a particular class. We need only one row of the relation to get all of the information (the relation might include NumberOfTimesTaught, AverageCourseEvaluationScore, and so on) we have about the combination of that professor and that class. Looking at more rows will not generate any more information about it.

As you know, the solution to the multivalued dependency constraint problem is to split the relation into two relations, each with a single theme. STU-MAJOR shows the combination of a student and a major. Everything we know about the combination is in a single row, and we will not gain more information about that combination by examining more rows.

DESIGN TRADE-OFFS

In this chapter we examined the concepts of normalization and demonstrated how to create tables that are in domain/key normal form. The process we used is usually suitable, but sometimes the result of normalization is not worth the cost. In this last section we look at two ways in which that can happen.

■ De-Normalization

As you know, normalized relations avoid modification anomalies, and on that ground they are preferred to unnormalized relations. Judged on other grounds, however, normalization is sometimes not worth it.

Consider this relation:

CUSTOMER (CustNumber, CustName, City, State, Zip),

where CustNumber is the key.

This relation is not in DK/NF because it contains the functional dependency Zip → (City, State), which is not implied by the key, CustNumber. Hence there is a constraint not implied by the definition of keys.

This relation can be transformed into the following two DK/NF relations:

CUSTOMER (CustNumber, CustName, Zip)

where the key is CustNumber

CODES (Zip, City, State)

where the key is Zip

These two tables are in domain/key normal form, but they most likely do not represent a better design. The unnormalized table is probably better because it will be easier to process and the disadvantages of duplicating the City and State data are not very important.

In summary, relations are sometimes purposely left unnormalized or are normalized and then de-normalized. Often this is done to improve performance. Whenever data must be combined from two separate tables, the DBMS must perform additional work. In most cases, at least two reads are required instead of one.

■ Optimization

We typically create normalized tables by splitting unnormalized tables into two or more. In some cases, there is a better way of obtaining a normalized design. For example, consider the relation

COLLEGE (CollegeName, Dean, AssistantDean)

and suppose that a college has one dean and from one to three assistant deans. In this case, the key of the table is (CollegeName, AssistantDean). This table is not in domain/key normal form because the constraint, CollegeName → Dean, is not a logical consequence of the table's key.

COLLEGE can be normalized into the relations

DEAN (CollegeName, Dean)

and

ASSISTANT-DEAN(CollegeName, AssistantDean)

But now whenever a database application needs to obtain data about the college, it must read at least two rows and possibly as many as four rows of data. An alternative to this design is to place all three AssistantDeans into the COLLEGE table, each in a separate attribute. The table would then be

COLLEGE1 (CollegeName, Dean, AssistantDean1, AssistantDean2, Assistant-Dean3)

COLLEGE1 is in domain/key normal form because all of its attributes are functionally dependent on the key CollegeName. But something has been lost. To see what, suppose that you wanted to determine the names of the COLLEGEs that had an assistant dean named 'Mary Abernathy'. To do this, you would have to look for this value in each of the three AssistantDean columns. Your query would appear something like this:

```
SELECT    CollegeName
FROM      COLLEGE1
WHERE     AssistantDean1 = 'Mary Abernathy' OR
          AssistantDean2 = 'Mary Abernathy' OR
          AssistantDean2 = 'Mary Abernathy'
```

Using the normalized design with ASSISTANT-DEAN, you would need only to state

```
SELECT    CollegeName
FROM      ASSISTANT-DEAN
WHERE     AssistantDean = 'Mary Abernathy'
```

In this example there are three possible solutions, each with advantages and disadvantages. The choice among them is an artistic one; there is no hard-and-fast rule stating how to select among them. The best choice depends on the processing characteristics of the applications that use this database.

SUMMARY

The relational model is important for two reasons: It can be used to express DBMS-independent designs, and it is the basis for an important category of DBMS-products. Normalization can be used as a guideline for checking the desirability and correctness of relations.

A relation is a two-dimensional table that has single-valued entries. All entries in a given column are of the same kind; columns have a unique name; and the order of the columns is not important. Columns are also called attributes. No two rows of a table are identical, and the order of the rows in the table is not important. Rows are also called tuples. The terms *table, file,* and *relation* are synonymous; the terms *column, field,* and *attribute* are synonymous; and the terms *row, record,* and *tuple* are synonymous.

A functional dependency is a relationship between attributes. Y is functionally dependent on X if the value of X determines the value of Y. A determinant is a group of one or more attributes on the left side of a functional dependency. For example, if X determines Y, then X is the determinant. A key is a group of one or more attributes that uniquely identifies a tuple. Every relation has at least one key; because every row is unique, in the most extreme case, the key is the collection of all of the attributes in the relation. Although a key is always unique, the determinant in a functional dependency need not be. Whether or not attributes are keys and whether or not they are attributes are determined not by an abstract set of rules but by the users' assumptions and mental models.

When updated, some relations suffer from undesirable consequences called modification anomalies. A deletion anomaly occurs when the deletion of a row loses information about two or more entities. An insertion anomaly occurs when the relational structure forces the addition of facts about two entities at the same time. Anomalies can be removed by splitting the relation into two or more relations.

There are many types of modification anomalies. Relations can be classified by the types of anomaly that they eliminate. Such classifications are called normal forms.

By definition, every relation is in first normal form. A relation is in second normal form if all nonkey attributes are dependent on all of the key. A relation is in third normal form if it is in second normal form and has no transitive dependencies. A relation is in Boyce–Codd normal form if every determinant is a candidate key. A relation is in fourth normal form if it is in Boyce–Codd normal form and has no multivalued dependencies. The definition of fifth normal form is intuitively obscure, and so we did not define it.

A relation is in domain/key normal form if every constraint on the relation is a logical consequence of the definition of domains and keys. A constraint is any constraint on the static values of attributes whose truth can be evaluated. As we defined them, domains have both a physical and a semantic part. In the context of domain/key normal form, however, domain refers only to the physical description.

An informal way of expressing domain/key normal form is to say that every relation must have only a single theme. For example, it might concern PROFESSORs or STUDENTs but not both PROFESSORs and STUDENTs at the same time.

Normalization can be considered from the standpoint of the relationship among attributes. If two attributes functionally determine each other, they have a one-to-one relationship. If one attribute functionally determines the other, but not the reverse, the attributes have a one-to-many relationship. If neither attribute determines the other, they have a many-to-many relationship. These facts can be used when constructing relations.

In some cases, normalization is not desirable. Whenever a table is split into two or more tables, interrelation constraints are created. If the cost of the extra processing of the two tables and their interrelation constraint is greater than the benefit of avoiding modification anomalies, then normalization is not recommended. In addition, in some cases, creating repeating columns is preferred to the standard normalization techniques.

GROUP I QUESTIONS

5.1   What restrictions must be placed on a table for it to be considered a relation?

5.2   Define the following terms: relation, tuple, attribute, file, record, field, table, row, column.

5.3   Define *functional dependency*. Give an example of two attributes that have a functional dependency, and give an example of two attributes that do not have a functional dependency.

5.4   If SID functionally determines Activity, does this mean that only one value of SID can exist in the relation? Why or why not?

5.5   Define *determinant.*

5.6   Give an example of a relation having a functional dependency in which the determinant has two or more attributes.

5.7   Define *key.*

5.8   If SID is a key of a relation, is it a determinant? Can a given value of SID occur more than once in the relation?

5.9   What is a deletion anomaly? Give an example.

5.10 What is an insertion anomaly? Give an example.

5.11 Explain the relationship of 1, 2, 3, BC, 4, 5, and D/K normal forms.

5.12 Define *second normal form.* Give an example of a relation in 1NF but not in 2NF. Transform the relation into relations in 2NF.

5.13 Define *third normal form.* Give an example of a relation in 2NF but not in 3NF. Transform the relation into relations in 3NF.

5.14 Define *BCNF.* Give an example of a relation in 3NF but not in BCNF. Transform the relation into relations in BCNF.

5.15 Define *multivalued dependency.* Give an example.

5.16 Why must multivalued dependencies exist in pairs?

5.17 Define *fourth normal form.* Give an example of a relation in BCNF but not in 4NF. Transform the relation into relations in 4NF.

5.18 Define *domain/key normal form.* Why is it important?

5.19 Transform the following relation into DK/NF. Make and state the appropriate assumptions about functional dependencies and domains.

EQUIPMENT (Manufacturer, Model, AcquisitionDate, BuyerName, BuyerPhone, PlantLocation, City, State, ZIP)

5.20 Transform the following relation into DK/NF. Make and state the appropriate assumptions about functional dependencies and domains.

INVOICE (Number, CustomerName, CustomerNumber, CustomerAddress, ItemNumber, ItemPrice, ItemQuantity, SalespersonNumber, SalespersonName, Subtotal, Tax, TotalDue)

5.21 Answer Question 5.20 again, but this time add attribute CustomerTaxStatus (0 if nonexempt, 1 if exempt). Also add the constraint that there will be no tax if CustomerTaxStatus = 1.

GROUP II QUESTIONS

5.22 Consider the following relation definition and sample data:

PROJECT (ProjectId, EmployeeName, EmployeeSalary)
Where ProjectId is the name of a work project
EmployeeName is the name of an employee who works on that project
EmployeeSalary is the salary of the employee whose name is Employee-Name

PROJECT Relation

ProjectID	EmployeeName	EmployeeSalary
100A	Jones	64K
100A	Smith	51K
100B	Smith	51K
200A	Jones	64K
200B	Jones	64K
200C	Parks	28K
200C	Smith	51K
200D	Parks	28K

Assuming that all of the functional dependencies and constraints are apparent in this data, which of the following statements is true?

a. ProjectID → EmployeeName
b. ProjectID → EmployeeSalary
c. (ProjectID, EmployeeName) → EmployeeSalary
d. EmployeeName → EmployeeSalary
e. EmployeeSalary → ProjectID
f. EmployeeSalary → (ProjectID, EmployeeName)

Answer these questions:

g. What is the key of PROJECT?
h. Are all nonkey attributes (if any) dependent on all of the key?
i. In what normal form is PROJECT?
j. Describe two modification anomalies from which PROJECT suffers.
k. Is ProjectID a determinant?
l. Is EmployeeName a determinant?
m. Is (ProjectID, EmployeeName) a determinant?
n. Is EmployeeSalary a determinant?
o. Does this relation contain a transitive dependency? If so, what is it?
p. Redesign this relation to eliminate the modification anomalies.

5.23 Consider the following relation definition and sample data:

PROJECT-HOURS (EmployeeName, ProjectID, TaskID, Phone, TotalHours)
Where EmployeeName is the name of an employee
ProjectID is the name of a project
TaskID is the name standard work task
Phone is the employee's telephone number
TotalHours is the hours worked by the employee on this project

PROJECT-HOURS Relation

EmployeeName	ProjectID	TaskID	Phone	TotalHours
Don	100A	B-1	12345	12
Don	100A	P-1	12345	12
Don	200B	B-1	12345	12
Don	200B	P-1	12345	12
Pam	100A	C-1	67890	26
Pam	200A	C-1	67890	26
Pam	200D	C-1	67890	26

Assuming that all of the functional dependencies and constraints are apparent in this data, which of the following statements is true?

a. EmployeeName → ProjectID

b. EmployeeName →→ ProjectID

c. EmployeeName → TaskID

d. EmployeeName →→ TaskID

e. EmployeeName → Phone

f. EmployeeName → TotalHours

g. (EmployeeName, ProjectID) → TotalHours

h. (EmployeeName, Phone) → TaskID

i. ProjectID → TaskID

j. TaskID → ProjectID

Answer these questions:

k. List all of the determinants.

l. Does this relation contain a transitive dependency? If so, what is it?

m. Does this relation contain a multivalued dependency? If so, what are the unrelated attributes?

n. Describe the deletion anomaly that this relation contains.

o. How many themes does this relation have?

p. Redesign this relation to eliminate the modification anomalies. How many relations did you use? How many themes does each of your new relations contain?

5.24 Consider the following domain, relation, and key definitions:

DOMAIN DEFINITIONS

EmployeeName	IN	CHAR(20)
PhoneNumber	IN	DEC(5)
EquipName	IN	CHAR(10)

Location	IN	CHAR(7)
Cost	IN	CURRENCY
Date	IN	YYMMDD
Time	IN	HHMM where HH between 00 and 23 and MM between 00 and 59

Definitions of Relation, Key, and Constraint

EMPLOYEE (EmployeeName, PhoneNumber)

    Key: EmployeeName

    Constraints: EmployeeName $\rightarrow$ PhoneNumber

EQUIPMENT (EquipmentName, Location, Cost)

    Key: EquipmentName

    Constraints: EquipmentName $\rightarrow$ Location

                EquipmentName $\rightarrow$ Cost

APPOINTMENT (Date, Time, EquipmentName, EmployeeName)

    Key: (Date, Time, EquipmentName)

    Constraints: (Date, Time, EquipmentName) $\rightarrow$ EmployeeName

Modify the definitions to add this constraint: An employee may not sign up for more than one equipment appointment.

CHAPTER

DATABASE DESIGN USING ENTITY-RELATIONSHIP MODELS

In Chapter 3 we discussed the specification of data models using the entity-relationship model, and in Chapter 5 we studied the relational model and normalization. In this chapter, we bring these subjects together to illustrate the transformation of users' requirements expressed in entity-relationship models into relational database designs. These designs are independent of any particular DBMS. In the next chapter we show how to transform semantic object data models into relational designs.

This chapter has two main sections. In the first, we show how to transform entity-relationship data models into relational designs. Normalization is important to this process because entities can contain more than one semantic theme. After demonstrating how to represent entities, we examine the representation of relationships using the relational model.

The second section applies the concepts described in the first section, illustrating the transformation of entity-relationship models into the representation of four common data structures. These structures are special cases of E-R constructs, and the techniques shown in the first section are applied to represent them with relations. We give these structures special attention only because they occur so frequently as common patterns of entities and relationships.

TRANSFORMATION OF ENTITY-RELATIONSHIP MODELS INTO RELATIONAL DATABASE DESIGNS

Chapter 3 demonstrated how to express user data requirements in an entity-relationship model. With this model, those things that users want to track are represented by **entities**, and the relationships among those entities are represented by explicitly defined **relationships.** As defined in the E-R model, relationships can be of any degree, but as we pointed out, most of the relationships encountered in practical database management are of degree 2, or **binary relationships.** This section describes how to transform entities and binary relationships into the terms of the relational model.

■ Representing Entities with the Relational Model

In general, the representation of entities by means of a relational model is straightforward. We begin by defining a relation for each entity. The name of the relation is the name of the entity, and the attributes of the relation are the attributes of the entity. Then we examine each relation according to the normalization criteria discussed in Chapter 5. It may or may not be necessary to change this initial design.

The example in Figure 6-1 is the entity shown in Figure 3-1. The CUSTOMER entity contains the following attributes: CustNumber, CustName, Address, City, State, Zip, ContactName, and PhoneNumber. To represent this entity with a relation, we define a relation for the entity and place the attributes in it as columns. If we know from the data model which attribute identifies this entity, that attribute will become the key of the relation. Otherwise, we must ask the users or otherwise investigate the requirements to determine what attribute or attributes can identify an entity. In this case, we assume that CustNumber is the key. In this figure, as in others to follow, the keys of the relations are underlined.

FIGURE 6-1

Representation of an Entity with a
Relation: (a) CUSTOMER Entity
and (b) Relation Representing
CUSTOMER Entity

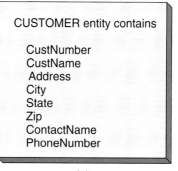

CUSTOMER entity contains

CustNumber
CustName
Address
City
State
Zip
ContactName
PhoneNumber

(a)

CUSTOMER (<u>CustNumber</u>, CustName, Address, City,
State, Zip, ContactName, PhoneNumber)

(b)

THE ROLE OF NORMALIZATION

During the requirements phase, the only stipulation placed on an entity is that it be important to the user. No attempt is made to determine whether the entity fits any of the criteria for normalization discussed in Chapter 5. Therefore once a relation has been defined for an entity, it should be examined according to the normalization criteria.

Consider, for example, the CUSTOMER relation in Figure 6-1(b). Is it in DK/NF? To find out, we need to know the constraints on this relation. Without a full description of the underlying requirements, we do not know all of the constraints, such as all of the domain constraints. But we can discover some of requirements just from the names of the attributes and knowledge about the nature of the business.

First, CustNumber determines all of the other attributes, because the unique values of CustName, Address, City, State, Zip, ContactName, and PhoneNumber can be determined from a given value of CustNumber. There are other constraints, however, that arise from other functional dependencies. Zip determines City and State, and ContactName determines PhoneNumber. As we stated in Chapter 5, to create a set of relations in DK/NF, we need to make these additional functional dependencies a logical consequence of domains and keys, and we can do that by defining the three relations shown in Figure 6-2. Observe that the key of CUSTOMER is CustNumber, the key of ZIP-TABLE is Zip, and the key of CONTACT is ContactName.

The design in Figure 6-2 is in DK/NF, and so there are no modification anomalies. That is, we can add new zip codes and new contacts without having to add a customer with the new zip code or contact. Furthermore, when we delete the last customer in a given zip code, we do not lose the city and state for that zip code. But as we pointed out at the end of Chapter 5, this design is too pure; it is so broken up that it will be difficult to use.

In this case the original CUSTOMER relation may be preferable. Even though it contains modification anomalies, they may not be too important. For example, without a CUSTOMER, it is probably not necessary to maintain the phone number of the contacts in another company. That is, we do not need to know that Jones's phone number is 555–1234 if the company for whom Jones works is not a customer.

FIGURE 6-2

Representing the Customer Entity with Relations in Domain/Key Normal Form

CUSTOMER (<u>CustomerNumber</u>, Address, Zip, ContactName)

ZIP-TABLE (<u>Zip</u>, City, State)

CONTACT (<u>ContactName</u>, PhoneNumber)

Interrelation constraints:

>   Zip in CUSTOMER must exist in Zip in ZIP-TABLE
>   ContactName in CUSTOMER must = a ContactName in CONTACT

FIGURE 6-3

Entity with Appropriate Normalization: (a) SALES-COMMISSION Entity, (b) Representing SALES-COMMISSION with a Single Relation, and (c) Representing SALES-COMMISSION with Domain/Key Normal Form Relations

SALES-COMMISSION entity contains

SalespersonNumber
SalespersonName
Phone
CheckNumber
CheckDate
CommissionPeriod
TotalCommissionSales
CommissionAmount
BudgetCategory

(a)

SALES-COMMISSION (SalespersonNumber, SalespersonName, Phone, CheckNumber, CheckDate, CommissionPeriod, TotalCommissionSales, CommissionAmount, BudgetCategory)

Functional dependencies:
    CheckNumber is key
    SalespersonNumber determines SalespersonName, Phone,
        BudgetCategory
    (SalespersonNumber, CommissionPeriod) determines
        TotalCommissionSales, CommissionAmount

(b)

SALESPERSON(SalespersonNumber, SalespersonName, Phone,
    BudgetCategory)
SALES (SalespersonNumber, CommissionPeriod,
    TotalCommissionSales, CommissionAmount)
COMMISSION-CHECK (CheckNumber, CheckDate, SalespersonNumber,
    CommissionPeriod)

(c)

In other examples it is clearer that the DK/NF design is preferable. Consider the SALES-COMMISSION entity in Figure 6-3. If we attempt to represent this entity with one relation, as shown in Figure 6-3(b), the result is a confused mess of attributes with many potential modification anomalies.

This relation obviously contains more than one theme. On examination, it contains a theme about salespeople, a theme about sales during some period, and a theme about sales commission checks. The relations in DK/NF that represent this entity are shown in Figure 6-3(c). Intuitively, this design seems superior to that in Figure 6-3(b); it is more straightforward and better fitting.

To summarize the discussion so far, when representing an entity with the relational model, the first step is to construct a relation that has all of the entity's attributes as columns. Then the relation is examined against the normalization criteria. In many cases the design can be improved by developing sets of relations in DK/NF.

DK/NF relations are not always preferred, however. If the relations are contrived and difficult to work with, a non-DK/NF design may be better. Performance can also be a factor. Having to access two or three relations to obtain the data needed about a customer may be prohibitively time-consuming.

Regardless of our decision about whether to normalize, we should examine every entity's relation(s) against the normalization criteria. That is, if we are going to sin, we should make an informed and conscious decision to do so. In the process, we also learn the types of modification anomalies to which the relations are vulnerable.

REPRESENTATION OF WEAK ENTITIES

Before turning to the representation of E-R model relationships, consider the relational representation of weak entities. Recall that a weak entity depends for its existence on another entity. If the weak entity is not ID dependent, it can be represented using the techniques described in the last section. But this existence dependency needs to be recorded in the relational design so that no application will create a weak entity without its proper parent (the entity on which the weak entity depends). Moreover, a processing constraint needs to be implemented so that when the parent is deleted, the weak entity is also deleted. These rules should be described in the relational design.

This situation is slightly different if the weak entity also is ID dependent. In Figure 6-4(a), LINE-ITEM is an ID-dependent weak entity. It is weak because its existence depends on INVOICE, and it is ID dependent because it has no name separate from INVOICE.

Consider what would happen if we merely established a relation for LINE-ITEM and set the attributes of the relation to be the same as the attributes of the entity. Such a relation is shown in Figure 6-4(b). What is the key of this relation? Because the weak entity depends on another entity, it does not have a complete key, and in fact, this relation could very well have duplicate rows. (This would happen if two invoices had the same quantity of the same item on the same line of the invoice.) The problem is that the relation in Figure 6-4(b) has no unique identifier.

FIGURE 6-4

Relational Representation of a Weak Entity: (a) Example Weak Entity, (b) Relation Representing LINE-ITEM with No Key, and (c) LINE-ITEM Relation with Proper Key (Partly from INVOICE)

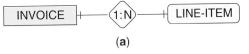

(a)

LINE-ITEM (LineNumber, Qty, ItemNumber, Description, Price, ExtPrice)

(b)

LINE-ITEM (InvoiceNumber, LineNumber, Qty, ItemNumber, Description, Price, ExtPrice)

(c)

For an ID-dependent weak entity, it is necessary to add the key of the parent entity to the weak entity's relation, and this added attribute becomes part of the weak entity's key. Thus in Figure 6-4(c), we have added InvoiceNumber, the key of INVOICE, to the attributes in LINE-ITEM. The key of LINE-ITEM is the composite (InvoiceNumber, LineNumber). With relations that represent ID-dependent weak entities, the key always is composite. Now consider the representation of E-R model relationships.

Representing Binary HAS-A Relationships

There are two types of relationships in the E-R model: HAS-A relationships among entities of different logical types and IS-A relationships among entities that are subtypes of a common logical type. In this section we consider HAS-A relationships; later we discuss IS-A relationships.

REPRESENTING ONE-TO-ONE RELATIONSHIPS

The simplest form of binary relationship is a one-to-one (1:1) relationship, in which an entity of one type is related to no more than one entity of another type. In the example of EMPLOYEE and AUTO, suppose that an employee is assigned exactly one automobile and an auto is assigned to exactly one employee. An E-R diagram for this relationship is shown in Figure 6-5.

Representing a 1:1 relationship with the relational model is straightforward. First each entity is represented with a relation, and then the key of one of the relations is placed in the other. In Figure 6-6(a), the key of EMPLOYEE is stored in AUTO, and in Figure 6-6(b), the key of AUTO is stored in EMPLOYEE.

When the key of one relation is stored in a second relation, it is called a **foreign key.** In Figure 6-6(a), EmployeeNumber is a foreign key in AUTO, and in Figure 6-6(b), LicenseNumber is a foreign key in EMPLOYEE. In this figure, foreign keys are shown in italics, but sometimes you may see foreign keys depicted by a dashed underline. In still other cases, foreign keys are not denoted in any special way. In this text, when there is a danger of confusion, we show foreign keys in italics, but most of the time, they do not receive any special notation.

For a 1:1 relationship, the key of either table can be placed as a foreign key in the other table. In Figure 6-6(a) the foreign key *EmployeeNumber* is placed in AUTO. With this design, we can navigate from EMPLOYEE to AUTO or from AUTO to EMPLOYEE. In the first case, we have an employee and want the auto assigned to that employee. To get the employee data, we use EmployeeNumber to obtain the employee's row in EMPLOYEE. From this row, we obtain the LicenseNumber of the auto assigned to that employee. We then use this number to look up the auto data in AUTO.

Now consider the other direction. Assume that we have an auto and want the employee assigned to that auto. Using the design in Figure 6-6(a), we access the

FIGURE 6-5

Example of a 1:1 Relationship

**Alternatives for Representing 1:1 Relationships: (a) Placing the Key of
EMPLOYEE in AUTO and (b) Placing the Key of AUTO in EMPLOYEE**

EMPLOYEE (<u>EmployeeNumber</u>, EmployeeName, Phone, . . .)

AUTO (<u>LicenseNumber</u>, SerialNumber, Color, Make, Model, . . .*EmployeeNumber*)

(a)

EMPLOYEE (<u>EmployeeNumber</u>, EmployeeName, Phone, . . .*LicenseNumber*)

AUTO (<u>LicenseNumber</u>, SerialNumber, Color, Make, Model, . . .)

(b)

EMPLOYEE table and look up the row that has the given license number. The data about the employee who has been assigned that auto appears in that row.

We take similar actions to travel in either direction for the alternative design, in which the foreign key of *LicenseNumber* is placed in EMPLOYEE. Using this design, to go from EMPLOYEE to AUTO, we go directly to the AUTO relation and look up the row in AUTO that has the given employee's number as its value of EmployeeNumber. To travel from AUTO to EMPLOYEE, we look up the row in AUTO having a given LicenseNumber. From this row, we extract the EmployeeNumber and use it to access the employee data in EMPLOYEE. Here we are using the term *look up* to mean "find a row given a value of one of its columns." Later, when we discuss particular DBMS models, we demonstrate how this is done.

Although the two designs in Figure 6-6 are equivalent in concept, they may be different in performance. For instance, if a query in one direction is more common than a query in the other, we may prefer one design to the other. Also, if the DBMS product is much faster in lookups on primary keys versus lookups on foreign keys, we might also prefer one design to another.

Figure 6-7 shows another 1:1 relationship, in which each EMPLOYEE has a JOB-EVALUATION and each JOB-EVALUATION corresponds to a particular employee. Observe from the hash marks that the relationship is mandatory in both directions. When the relationship is 1:1 and is mandatory in both directions, it is likely that the records are describing different aspects of the same entity, especially if, as is the case in Figure 6-7, both entities have the same key. When this occurs, the records should generally be combined into one relation. Learn to regard such 1:1 mandatory relationships with suspicion.

The separation of an entity into two relations can sometimes be justified. One justification concerns performance. For example, suppose that the JOB-EVALUATION data is lengthy and is used far less frequently than is the other employee data. In these circumstances it may be appropriate to store JOB-EVALUATIONs in a separate table so that the more common requests for nonevaluation employee data can be processed faster.

Suspicious 1:1 Relationship

Better security is the second reason for separating the two records. If the DBMS does not support security at the data item level, the JOB-EVALUATION data may need to be separated in order to prevent unauthorized users from accessing it. Or it may be desirable to place JOB-EVALUATION in a separate table so that the table can be placed on disk media that are kept in special locked facilities.

Do not conclude from this discussion that all 1:1 relationships are inappropriate; only those that appear to describe different aspects of the same entity are questionable. For example, the 1:1 mandatory relationship between EMPLOYEE and AUTO is quite suitable because each relation describes a different entity.

REPRESENTING ONE-TO-MANY RELATIONSHIPS

The second type of binary relationship is one to many (1:N), in which an entity of one type can be related to many entities of another type. Figure 6-8 is an E-R diagram of a one-to-many relationship between professors and students. In this relationship, PROFESSOR is related to the many STUDENTs that he or she advises. The oval means that the relationship between PROFESSOR and STUDENT is optional; that is, a professor need not have any advisees. The bar across the line at the other end means that a STUDENT row must correspond to a PROFESSOR row.

The terms **parent** and **child** are sometimes applied to relations in 1:N relationships. The parent relation is on the *one* side of the relationship, and the child relation is on the *many* side. In Figure 6-8(a), PROFESSOR is the parent entity, and STUDENT is the child entity.

Figure 6-8 shows two other one-to-many relationships. In Figure 6-8(b), a DORMITORY entity corresponds to many STUDENT entities, but a STUDENT entity corresponds to one DORMITORY. Furthermore, a dormitory does not have to have any students assigned to it, nor is a student required to live in a dormitory.

In Figure 6-8(c), a CUSTOMER is related to many APPOINTMENT entities, and a particular APPOINTMENT corresponds to only one CUSTOMER. Moreover, a CUSTOMER may or may not have an APPOINTMENT, but every APPOINTMENT must correspond to a CUSTOMER.

Representing 1:N relationships is simple and straightforward. First each entity is represented by a relation, and then the key of the relation representing the parent entity is placed in the relation representing the child entity. Thus to represent the

FIGURE 6-8

Examples of One-to-Many Relationships: (a) Optional-to-Mandatory 1:N Relationship, (b) Optional-to-Optional 1:N Relationship, and (c) 1:N Relationship with Weak Entity

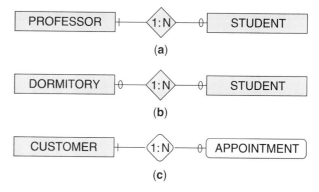

FIGURE 6-9

Relational Representation of PROFESSOR and STUDENT Entities in
Figure 6-8(a)

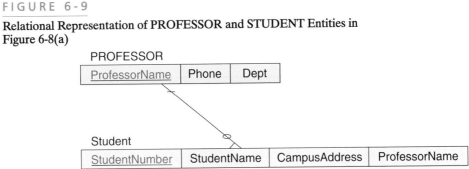

ADVISES relationship of Figure 6-8(a), we place the key of PROFESSOR, ProfessorName, in the STUDENT relation, as shown in Figure 6-9.

Figure 6-9 is an example of what is sometimes called a **data structure diagram**, in which relations are shown in rectangles with lines representing relationships and the key attributes are underlined. A fork, or crow's foot, on a relationship line indicates a many relationship.

In Figure 6-9, the fork at the STUDENT end of the relationship line means that there can be many STUDENT rows for each PROFESSOR. No fork at the other end means that each STUDENT can be advised by, at most, one PROFESSOR. As with E-R diagrams, hash lines are used to denote mandatory relationships, and ovals denote optional ones.

Notice that with ProfessorName stored as a foreign key in STUDENT, we can process the relationship in both directions. Given a StudentNumber, we can look up the appropriate row in STUDENT and get the name of his or her adviser from the row data. To obtain the rest of the PROFESSOR data, we use the professor name obtained from STUDENT to look up the appropriate row in PROFESSOR. To determine all of the students advised by a particular faculty member, we look up all rows in STUDENT having the professor's name as a value for ProfessorName. Student data is then taken from those rows.

Contrast this situation with one representing 1:1 relationships. In both cases, we store the key of one relation as a foreign key in the second relation. In a 1:1 relationship it does not matter which key is moved to the second relation. But in a 1:N relationship, it does matter. *The key of the parent relation must be placed in the child relation.*

To understand this better, notice what would happen if we tried to put the key of the child into the parent relation. Since attributes in a relation can have only a single value, there is room in any professor's record for only one student. Consequently, such a structure cannot be used to represent the "many" side of the 1:N relationship. Again, to represent a 1:N relationship, we place the key of the parent relation in the child relation.

Figure 6-10 shows the representation of the CUSTOMER and APPOINTMENT entities. Here we represent each entity with a relation. As we stated, APPOINTMENT is an ID-dependent weak entity, and so it has a composite key consisting of the key of the entity on which its key depends plus an attribute from itself. In this case, the key is

FIGURE 6-10

Relational Representation of the Weak Entity in Figure 6-8(c)

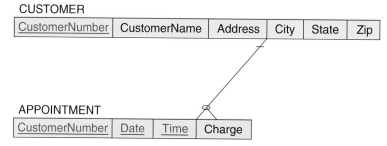

Interrelation constraint:
CustomerName in APPOINTMENT must exist in CustomerNumber in CUSTOMER

(CustomerNumber, Date, Time). Now to represent the 1:N relationship, we would normally add the key of the parent to the child. In this case, however, the key of the parent (CustomerNumber) is already part of the child, and so we do not need to add it; the relationship is already represented. (Verify this for yourself by determining how you would look up data to process the relationship in both directions.)

REPRESENTING MANY-TO-MANY RELATIONSHIPS

The third and final type of binary relationship is many to many (M:N), in which an entity of one type corresponds to many entities of the second type, and an entity of the second type corresponds to many entities of the first type.

Figure 6-11(a) presents an E-R diagram of the many-to-many relationship between students and classes. A STUDENT entity can correspond to many CLASS entities, and a CLASS entity can correspond to many STUDENT entities. Notice that both participants in the relationship are optional: A student does not need to be enrolled in a class, and a class does not need to have any students. Figure 6-11(b) gives sample data.

Many-to-many relationships cannot be directly represented by relations in the same way that one-to-one and one-to-many relationships are. To understand why

FIGURE 6-11

Example of an M:N Relationship: (a) E-R Diagram of STUDENT to CLASS Relationship and (b) Sample Data for STUDENT to CLASS Relationship

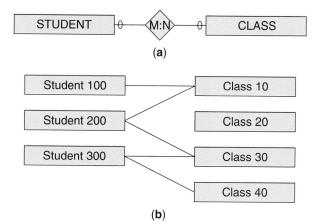

FIGURE 6-12

Incorrect Representation of an M:N Relationship

SID	Other STUDENT Data
100	. . .
200	. . .
300	. . .

STUDENT

ClassNumber	ClassTime	Other CLASS Data	SID
10	10:00 MWF	. . .	100
10	10:00 MWF	. . .	200
30	3:00 TH	. . .	200
30	3:00 TH	. . .	300
40	8:00 MWF	. . .	300

CLASS

this is so, try using the same strategy we did for 1:1 and 1:N relationships—placing the key of one relation as a foreign key in the other relation. First define a relation for each of the entities; call them STUDENT and CLASS. Now try to put the key of STUDENT (say StudentNumber) in CLASS. Because multiple values are not allowed in the cells of a relation, we have room for only one StudentNumber, so what do we do with the second student enrolled in that class?

The same problem will occur if we try to put the key of CLASS (say ClassNumber) in STUDENT. We can readily store the identifier of the first class in which a student is enrolled, but we have no place to store the identifier of the second and subsequent classes.

Figure 6-12 shows another (*but incorrect*) strategy. In this case, we have stored a row in the CLASS relation for each STUDENT enrolled in one class, and so there

FIGURE 6-13

Representing an M:N Relationship: (a) Relations Needed to Represent STUDENT to CLASS Relationship and (b) Example Data for STUDENT to CLASS Relationship

STUDENT (<u>StudentNumber</u>, StudentName)

CLASS (<u>ClassNumber</u>, ClassName)

STU-CLASS (*<u>ClassNumber</u>*, *<u>StudentNumber</u>*)

(a)

100	Jones, Mary
200	Parker, Fred
300	Wu, Jason

100	10
200	10
200	30
300	30
300	40

10	Accounting
20	Finance
30	Marketing
40	Database

(b)

FIGURE 6-14

Data Structure Diagram for STUDENT to CLASS Relationship

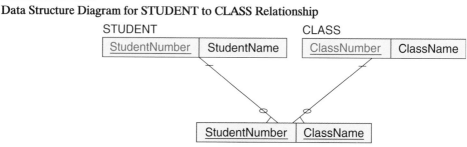

are two records for Class 10 and two for Class 30. The problem with this scheme is that we duplicate the class data and thus create modification anomalies.

Many rows will need to be changed if, say, Class 10's schedule is modified. Also consider the insertion and deletion anomalies: How can we schedule a new class until a student has enrolled? And what will happen if Student 300 drops out of Class 40? Obviously, this strategy is unworkable.

The solution to this dilemma is to create a third relation that represents the relationship itself. An instance of such a relation is shown in Figure 6-13, the correspondence of students to classes. Such relations are called **intersection relations** because each row of such a relation documents the intersection of a particular student with a particular class. Notice in Figure 6-13(b) that there is one row in the intersection relation for each line between STUDENT and CLASS in Figure 6-11(b).

The data structure diagrams for the STUDENT-CLASS relationship appear in Figure 6-14. The relationship from CLASS to STU-CLASS is 1:N, and the relationship from STUDENT to STU-CLASS is also 1:N. In essence, we have decomposed the M:N relationship into two 1:N relationships. The key of STU-CLASS is the combination of the keys of both of its parents, (SID, ClassNumber). The key for an intersection relation is always the combination of parent keys.

■ Representing Recursive Relationships

A recursive relationship is a relationship among entities of the same class. Recursive relationships are not fundamentally different from other HAS-A relationships and can be represented using the same techniques. The only complication is that entities in recursive relationships have relationships with entities of their own class. As with nonrecursive HAS-A relationships, there are three types of recursive relationships: 1:1, 1:N, and N:M; Figure 6-15 shows an example of each.

Consider first the SPONSOR relationship in Figure 6-15(a). As with a 1:1 relationship, one person can sponsor another person, and each person is sponsored by no more than one person. Figure 6-16(a) shows sample data for this relationship.

To represent 1:1 recursive relationships, we take an approach nearly identical to that for regular 1:1 relationships: We can place the key of the person being sponsored in the row of the sponsor, or we can place the key of the sponsor in the row of the person being sponsored. Figure 6-16(b) shows the first alternative, and Figure

FIGURE 6-15

Examples of Recursive Relationships: (a)
1:1 Recursive Relationship, (b) 1:N
Recursive Relationship, and (c) N:M
Recursive Relationship

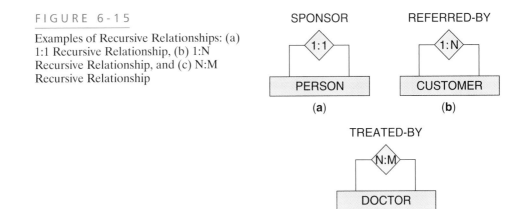

FIGURE 6-15

Examples of Recursive Relationships: (a)
1:1 Recursive Relationship, (b) 1:N
Recursive Relationship, and (c) N:M
Recursive Relationship

6-16(c) shows the second. Both work, and so the choice depends on issues like performance.

This technique is identical to that for nonrecursive 1:1 relationships, except that both the child and parent rows reside in the same relation. You can think of the process as follows: Pretend that the relationship is between two different relations. Determine where the key goes, and then combine the two relations into a single one.

FIGURE 6-16

Example of a 1:1 Recursive Relationship:
(a) Sample Data for 1:1 Recursive
Relationship, (b) First Alternative for
Representing a 1:1 Recursive Relationship,
and (c) Second Alternative for Representing
a 1:1 Recursive Relationship

Person

Jones
Smith
Parks

Myrtle
Pines

(a)

Person	PersonSponsored
Jones	Smith
Smith	Parks
Parks	null
Myrtle	Pines
Pines	null

(b)

Person	PersonSponsoredBy
Jones	null
Smith	Jones
Parks	Smith
Myrtle	null
Pines	Myrtle

(c)

FIGURE 6-17

Example of a 1:N Recursive
Relationship: (a) Sample Data for
the REFERRED-BY Relationship
and (b) Representing a 1:N Recursive
Relationship by Means of a Relation

Customer Number	Referred These Customers
100	200, 400
300	500
400	600, 700

(a)

CUSTOMER Relation

CustomerNumber	CustomerData	ReferredBy
100	. . .	null
200	. . .	100
300	. . .	null
400	. . .	100
500	. . .	300
600	. . .	400
700	. . .	400

(b)

FIGURE 6-18

Example of an M:N Recursive Relationship:
(a) Sample Data for the TREATED-BY
Relationship and (b) Representing an M:N
Recursive Relationship by Means of Relations

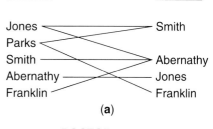

Provider	Receiver
Jones	Smith
Parks	
Smith	Abernathy
Abernathy	Jones
Franklin	Franklin

(a)

DOCTOR relation

Name	OtherAttributes
Jones	. . .
Parks	. . .
Smith	. . .
Abernathy	. . .
O'Leary	. . .
Franklin	. . .

TREATMENT-INTERSECTION relation

Physician	Patient
Jones	Smith
Parks	Smith
Smith	Abernathy
Abernathy	Jones
Parks	Franklin
Franklin	Abernathy
Jones	Abernathy

(b)

To illustrate, consider the REFERRED-BY relationship in Figure 6-15(b). This is a 1:N relationship, as shown in the sample data in Figure 6-17(a). When this data is placed in a relation, one row represents the referrer, and the other rows represent those who have been referred. The referrer row takes the role of the parent, and the referred rows take the role of the child. As with all 1:N relationships, we place the key of the parent in the child. In Figure 6-17(b), we place the name of the referrer in all the rows that have been referred.

Now consider M:N recursive relationships. Examine the TREATED-BY relationship in Figure 6-15(c) with the sample data shown in Figure 6-18(a). As with other M:N relationships, we must create an intersection table that shows all pairs of doctors. The name of the doctor in the first column is the one who provided the treatment, and the name of the doctor in the second column is the one who received the treatment. This structure is shown in Figure 6-18(b).

Recursive relationships are thus represented in the same way as are other relationships. The rows of the tables can take two different roles, however. Some are parent rows, and others are child rows. If a key is supposed to be a parent key and if the row has no parent, its value will be null. If a key is supposed to be a child key and the row has no child, its value will be null.

Representing IS-A Relationships (Subtypes)

The strategy for representing subtypes, or IS-A relationships, is somewhat different from the strategy used for HAS-A relationships. Consider the example of CLIENT with attributes ClientNumber, ClientName, and AmountDue. Suppose that there are three subtypes of CLIENT, namely, INDIVIDUAL-CLIENT, PARTNERSHIP-CLIENT, and CORPORATE-CLIENT, with the following attributes:

INDIVIDUAL-CLIENT: Address, SocialSecurityNumber

PARTNERSHIP-CLIENT: ManagingPartnerName, Address, TaxIdentificationNumber

CORPORATE-CLIENT: ContactPerson, Phone, TaxIdentificationNumber

To represent this structure by means of relations, we define one relation for the supertype (CLIENT) and one relation for each subtype. Then we place each of the attributes of the supertype into the relation that represents it and each of the attributes of the subtypes into the relations that represent them. At this point, the subtype relations do not have a key. To create a key, we add the key of the supertype, or ClientNumber, to each of the subtypes. The final list of relations is

CLIENT (ClientNumber, ClientName, AmountDue)

INDIVIDUAL-CLIENT (ClientNumber, Address, SocialSecurityNumber)

PARTNERSHIP-CLIENT (ClientNumber, ManagingPartnerName, Address, Tax IdentificationNumber)

CORPORATE-CLIENT (ClientNumber, ContactPerson, Phone, TaxIdentification Number)

Note that with this structure, the relationship between a row in CLIENT and a row in one of the subtypes is 1:1. No client has more than one row in a subtype relation, and each subtype corresponds uniquely to one row of the supertype. Depending on the restrictions of the application, it might be possible for a row in CLIENT to correspond to multiple rows, each in a different subtype. But no row of CLIENT can correspond to more than one row in the *same* subtype relation.

It is possible for one or more of the subtypes to have a key of its own. For example, the application may call for a CorporateClientNumber that is distinct from ClientNumber. In that case, the key of CORPORATE-CLIENT is CorporateClient-Number. Since the relationship between CLIENT and CORPORATE-CLIENT is 1:1, it can be established by placing the key of one in the other. Most often, it is considered better aesthetically to place the key of the supertype relation in the key of the subtype relation. For this case, the structure of CORPORATE-CLIENT is

CORPORATE-CLIENT (CorporateClientNumber, ClientNumber, ContactPerson, Phone, TaxIdentificationNumber)

EXAMPLE

Figure 6-19(a) is a copy of the E-R diagram introduced in Chapter 3 as Figure 3-9. It contains all of the basic elements used in E-R diagrams. To represent this diagram by means of relations, we begin by establishing one relation for each entity. We assume the keys as follows:

RELATION	KEY
EMPLOYEE	EmployeeNumber
ENGINEER	EmployeeNumber
TRUCK	LicenseNumber
SERVICE	InvoiceNumber
CLIENT	ClientNumber
ENGINEER-CERTIFICATION	(Employee , CertificationName)
CERTIFICATION	CertificationName

The next step is to examine each of these relations against the normalization criteria. The example does not tell us what attributes must be represented, and so we cannot determine the constraints. We will assume that these relations are in DK/NF, although in practice, we would need to check out that assumption against the attribute lists and constraints. For now, we will focus on the representation of relationships. The relations and their key attributes (including foreign keys) are listed in Figure 6-19(b).

The relationship between EMPLOYEE and ENGINEER is already represented, since the relations have the same key, EmployeeNumber. ENGINEER and TRUCK have a 1:1 relationship and so can be related by placing the key of one in the other. Since a truck must be assigned to an employee, there will be no null values if we place EmployeeNumber in TRUCK, and so we will do so.

For the 1:N relationship between ENGINEER and SERVICE, we place the key of ENGINEER (the parent) in SERVICE (the child). The relationship between SERVICE and CLIENT is M:N, and so we must create an intersection relation. Since this relationship has an attribute, Fee, we add that attribute to the intersection relation. For the 1:N recursive relationship, REFERRED-BY, we add the attribute

FIGURE 6-19

**Relational Representation of an Example E-R Diagram: (a) E-R Diagram
from Chapter 3 and (b) Relations Needed to Represent This E-R Diagram**

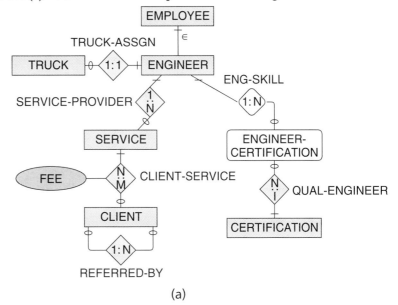

(a)

EMPLOYEE (<u>EmployeeNumber</u>, other nonkey EMPLOYEE attributes . . .)

ENGINEER (<u>EmployeeNumber</u>, other nonkey ENGINEER attributes . . .)

TRUCK (<u>LicenseNumber</u>, other nonkey TRUCK attributes, *EmployeeNumber*)

SERVICE (<u>InvoiceNumber</u>, other nonkey SERVICE attributes, *EmployeeNumber*)

CLIENT (<u>ClientNumber</u>, other nonkey CLIENT attributes, *ReferredBy*)

SERVICE-CLIENT (<u>InvoiceNumber</u>, <u>ClientNumber</u>, Fee)

ENGINEER-CERTIFICATION (<u>EmployeeNumber</u>, <u>CertificationName</u>, other nonkey
ENGINEER-CERTIFICATION attributes)

CERTIFICATION (<u>CertificationName</u>, other nonkey CERTIFICATION attributes)

(**b**)

ReferredBy to CLIENT. The name *ReferredBy* implies, correctly, that the key of the
parent—the one client doing the referring—is being placed in the relation.

Since ENGINEER-CERTIFICATION is ID-dependent on ENGINEER, we
know that EmployeeNumber must be part of its key; thus the key is a composite
(EmployeeNumber, CertificationName). The dependency relationship is 1:N and so
will be carried by EmployeeNumber. Finally, the relationship between CERTIFICA-
TION and ENGINEER-CERTIFICATION is 1:N, and so we would normally add
the key of CERTIFICATION (the parent) to ENGINEER-CERTIFICATION. But
that key is already part of the relation, so we need not do this.

Study this example to make sure that you understand the various types of relationships and how they are expressed in terms of the relations. All of the elements of the E-R model are present in this diagram.

TREES, NETWORKS, AND BILLS OF MATERIALS

Although neither the E-R model nor the semantic object model makes any assumptions about patterns of relationships among entities, some occur often enough that they have been given special names. These patterns are trees, simple networks, complex networks, and bills of materials. We introduce the concept of these patterns here, in the context of the E-R model, so that you can see in Chapters 10, 11, and 12 how they apply to particular DBMS products.

■ Trees

A **tree**, or **hierarchy**, as it is sometimes called, is a data structure in which the elements of the structure have only one-to-many relationships with one another. Each element has at most one parent. Figure 6-20 is an example of a tree. According to standard terminology, each element is called a **node,** and the relationships among the elements are called **branches.** The node at the top of the tree is called the **root** (what a metaphor—the roots of real trees are normally at the bottom!). In Figure 6-20, Node 1 is the root of the tree.

Every node of a tree, except the root, has a **parent**, which is the node immediately above it. Thus Node 2 is the parent of Node 5; Node 4 is the parent of Node 8; and so on. As we stated earlier, trees are distinguished from other data structures in that every node has at most one parent. We say *at most one parent* because the root node has no parent.

The descendants of a node are called **children.** In general, there is no limitation on the number of children that a node may have. Node 2 has two children, Nodes 5 and 6; Node 3 has no children; and Node 4 has three children, Nodes 7, 8, and 9. Nodes having the same parent are called **twins,** or **siblings.** For example, Nodes 5 and 6 are twins or siblings.

Figure 6-21(a) illustrates a tree of entities in which you can see several one-to-many relationships among entities in a university system. Colleges consist of many departments, which in turn have many professors and many administrative employ-

FIGURE 6-20

Example of a Tree

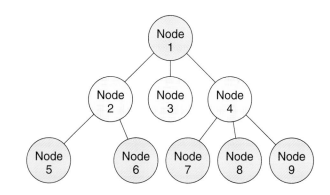

ees. Finally, professors advise many students who have received many grades. There are six different entity types in this structure, but all of the relationships are 1:N.

To represent a tree of entities using the relational model, we simply apply the concepts described in earlier sections of this chapter. First we transform each entity into a relation. Then we examine the relations generated against the normalization criteria and subdivide the relations if necessary. We represent the 1:N relationships by storing the key of the parent in the child. Figure 6-21(b) is a data structure diagram corresponding to the tree in Figure 6-21(a).

In summary, a hierarchy, or tree, is a collection of records organized in such a way that all relationships are 1:N. All records have exactly one parent, except the root, which has no parent. A hierarchy can be represented by a set of relations using the methods defined earlier. Hierarchies are common in businesses, especially in manufacturing applications.

FIGURE 6-21

Representation of a Tree by Means of Relations: (a) Tree Composed of Entities and (b) Representation of This Tree by Means of Relations

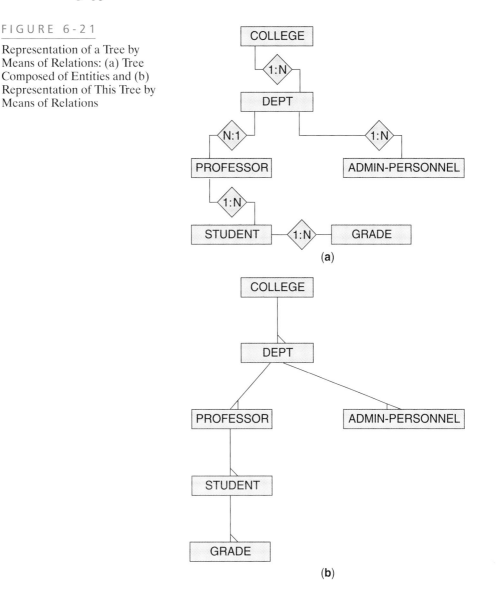

FIGURE 6-22

Example of a Simple
Network

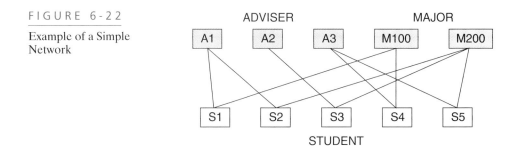

Simple Networks

A **simple network** is also a data structure of elements having only one-to-many relationships. In a simple network, however, the elements may have more than one parent as long as the parents are different types. For example, in the simple network shown in Figure 6-22, each STUDENT entity has two parents, an ADVISER entity and a MAJOR entity. The data structure in Figure 6-22 is not a tree because STUDENT entities have more than one parent.

Figure 6-23(a) shows the general structure of this simple network. Notice that all relationships are one to many but that STUDENT has two parents. In this figure, the parent records are on top, and the children records are beneath them. This arrangement is convenient but not essential. You may see simple networks depicted with parents beside or below the children. You can identify simple networks in such arrangements by the fact that a single record type participates as a child in two (or more) one-to-many relationships.

To represent a simple network of entities with the relational model, we follow the procedures described earlier. First we transform each entity into a relation and normalize the relations if necessary. Then we represent each 1:N relationship by storing the key of the parent relation in the child relation. The result of this process for the network in Figure 6-23(a) is shown in Figure 6-23(b).

FIGURE 6-23

Representation of a Simple Network
by Means of Relations: (a) Simple
Network Composed of Entities and
(b) Its Representation by Means of
Relations

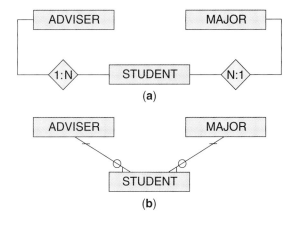

FIGURE 6-24

Representation of a Complex Network by Means of Relations: (a) Complex Network Composed of Entities and (b) Its Representation by Means of Relations

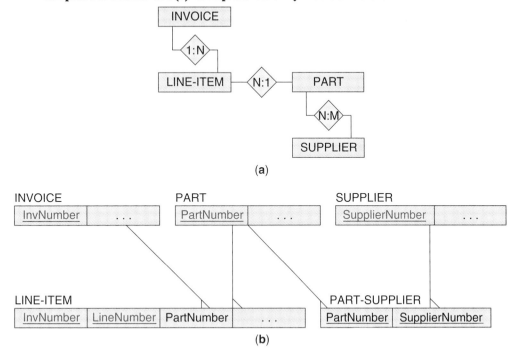

(a)

(b)

Complex Networks

A **complex network** is a data structure of elements in which at least one of the relationships is many-to-many. The complex network in Figure 6-24(a) illustrates the relationships among invoices, line items, parts, and suppliers. Two of the three relationships are 1:N, and the third is M:N. Since there is at least one many-to-many relationship, this structure is called a complex network.

As we just pointed out, M:N relationships have no direct representation in the relational model. Consequently, before this structure can be stored in relational form, we must define an intersection relation. In Figure 6-24(b), the intersection relation is PART-SUPPLIER.

Bills of Materials

A **bill of materials** is a special data structure that occurs frequently in manufacturing applications. In fact, such structures provided a major impetus for the development of database technology in the 1960s.

Figure 6-25 is an example of a bill of materials, which shows the parts that constitute products. When viewed from the standpoint of a given product, say Product A, this data structure is a hierarchy. But because a part can be used in more than one product, this structure is actually a network. For example, the part ABC100 has two parents, Product A and Product B.

FIGURE 6-25

FIGURE 6-25

Example of a Bill
of Materials

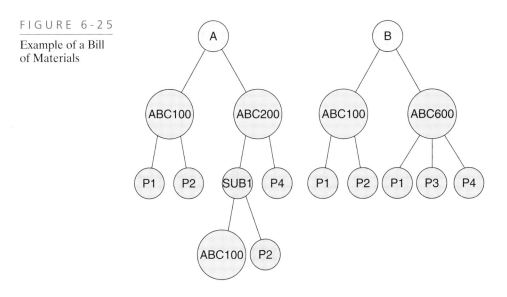

A bill of materials can be represented by means of relations in several ways. The most common is to consider it as an M:N recursive relationship. A part (or product or assembly or subassembly or whatever) contains many elements. At the same time, there may be many elements that contain it. Figure 6-26(a) shows the general data structure of the M:N recursive relationship, and Figure 6-26(b) shows an instance of the intersection relation created to represent this bill of materials.

FIGURE 6-26

Representation of a
Bill of Materials with
Relations: (a)
Relations Representing
a Bill of Materials and
(b) Data for the
ELEMENT
RELATIONSHIP
Intersection Relation

ELEMENT

ElementNumber	Other element data . . .

ContainedBy   Contains

ELEMENT RELATIONSHIP

Contained By	Contains

(a)

Contained By	Contains
A	ABC100
A	ABC200
B	ABC100
B	ABC600
ABC100	P1
ABC100	P2
ABC200	SUB1
ABC200	P4
ABC600	P1
ABC600	P3
ABC600	P4
SUB1	ABC100
SUB1	P2

Observe element A
contains an ABC100
and element ABC100
is contained by an A

(b)

SUMMARY

To transform entity-relationship data models, each entity is represented by a relation. The attributes of the entity become the attributes of the relation. Once the relation has been created, it must be examined against normalization criteria, and divided into two or more relations if necessary.

There are three types of HAS-A relationships in the E-R model: 1:1, 1:N, and N:M. To represent a 1:1 relationship, we place the key of one relation into the other relation. One-to-one relationships sometimes indicate that two relations have been defined on the same entity and so should be combined into one relation.

To represent a 1:N relationship, we place the key of the parent in the child. Finally, to represent an M:N relationship, we create an intersection relation that contains the keys of the other two relations.

Recursive relationships are relationships in which the participants in the relationship arise from the same entity class. There are three types: 1:1, 1:N, and N:M. The types are represented in the same way as are nonrecursive relationships. For 1:1 and 1:N relationships, we add a foreign key to the relation that represents the entity. For an N:M recursion, we create an intersection table that represents the M:N relationship.

Supertype and subtype entities (IS-A relationships) are also represented by relations. One relation is defined for the supertype entity, and other relations are defined for each subtype. Usually the keys of the relations are the same, and the relationship among the rows is defined through those keys. If they are not the same, the key of the subtype relation can be placed in the supertype relation or the key of the supertype relation can be placed in the subtype. Most often, the key of the supertype relation is placed in the subtype relation.

Binary relationships can be combined to form three types of more complicated structures. A tree is a collection of record types in which each record has exactly one parent, except the root, which has no parent. In a simple network, records may have multiple parents, but the parents must be of different types. In a complex network, records have multiple parents of the same type. Another way of saying this is that in a complex network, at least one of the binary relationships is M:N.

A bill of materials is a data structure frequently seen in manufacturing applications. Such structures can be represented by M:N recursive relationships.

GROUP I QUESTIONS

6.1   Explain how E-R entities are transformed into relations.

6.2   Why is it necessary to examine relations transformed from entities against normalization criteria? Under what conditions should the relations be altered if they are not in DK/NF? Under what conditions should they not be altered?

6.3   Explain how the representation of weak entities differs from the representation of strong entities.

6.4   List the three types of binary relationships and give an example of each. Do not use the examples in this text.

6.5   Define *foreign key* and give an example.

6.6   Show two different ways to represent the 1:1 relationship in your answer to Question 6.4. Use data structure diagrams.

6.7   For your answers to Question 6.6, describe a method for obtaining data about one of the entities, given the key of the other. Describe a method for obtaining data about the second entity, given the key of the first. Describe answers for both of your alternatives in Question 6.6.

6.8   Why are some 1:1 relationships considered suspicious? Under what conditions should relations in a 1:1 relationship be combined into one relation?

6.9   Define the terms *parent* and *child* and give an example of each.

6.10 Show how to represent the 1:N relationship in your answer to Question 6.4. Use a data structure diagram.

6.11 For your answer to Question 6.10, describe a method for obtaining data for all of the children, given the key of the parent. Describe a method for obtaining data for the parent, given a key of the child.

6.12 For a 1:N relationship, explain why you must place the key of the parent in the child, rather than placing the key of the child in the parent.

6.13 Give examples of binary 1:N relationships, other than those in this text, for

   a. An optional-to-optional relationship.

   b. An optional-to-mandatory relationship.

   c. A mandatory-to-optional relationship.

   d. A mandatory-to-mandatory relationship.

   Illustrate your answer using data structure diagrams.

6.14 Show how to represent the N:M relationship in your answer to Question 6.4. Use a data structure diagram.

6.15 For your answer to Question 6.14, describe a method for obtaining the children for one entity, given the key of the other. Also describe a method for obtaining the children for the second entity, given the key of the first.

6.16 Why is it not possible to represent N:M relationships with the same strategy used to represent 1:N relationships?

6.17 Explain the meaning of the term *intersection relation.*

6.18 Define three types of recursive binary relationships and give an example of each.

6.19 Show how to represent the 1:1 recursive relationship in your answer to Question 6.18. How does this differ from the representation of 1:1 nonrecursive relationships?

6.20 Show how to represent the 1:N recursive relationship in your answer to Question 6.18. How does this differ from the representation of 1:N nonrecursive relationships?

6.21 Show how to represent the M:N recursive relationship in your answer to Question 6.18. How does this differ from the representation of M:N nonrecursive relationships?

6.22 Give an example of a supertype and subtypes, and show how to represent it using relations.

6.23 Define tree, simple network, and complex network.

6.24 Give an example of a tree structure other than one in this text, and show how to represent it by means of relations.

6.25 Give an example of a simple network other than one in this text, and show how to represent it by means of relations.

6.26 Give an example of a complex network other than one in this text, and show how to represent it by means of relations.

6.27 What is a bill of materials? Give an example other than the one in this text, and show how to represent your example by means of relations.

GROUP II QUESTIONS

6.28 Transform the entity-relationship diagram for the Jefferson Dance Club (Figure 3-12) into relations. Express your answer with a data structure diagram, and show the interrelation constraints.

6.29 Transform the entity-relationship diagram for San Juan Charters (Figure 3-14) into relations. Express your answer with a data structure diagram, and show the interrelation constraints.

DATABASE DESIGN WITH SEMANTIC OBJECT MODELS

This chapter discusses the transformation of semantic object models into relational database designs. First we describe the transformation of each of seven common types of semantic objects. Then we illustrate these concepts by showing the semantic object modeling and relational representation of various real-world objects.

TRANSFORMATION OF SEMANTIC OBJECTS INTO RELATIONAL DATABASE DESIGNS

Chapter 4 introduced the semantic object data model and defined seven types of semantic objects. In this section, we present methods for transforming each of those seven types into relations. When working with semantic objects, normalization problems are less likely than they are when working with the entity-relationship models because the definition of semantic objects usually separates semantic themes into group attributes or objects. Thus when transforming an object into relations, the relations are generally either already in domain/key normal form or are in very close to domain/key normal form.

FIGURE 7-1

Relational Representation of Example Simple Object: (a) EQUIPMENT Object Diagram and (b) Relation Representing EQUIPMENT

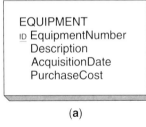

EQUIPMENT
ID EquipmentNumber
Description
AcquisitionDate
PurchaseCost

(a)

EQUIPMENT (EquipmentNumber, Description, AcquisitionDate, PurchaseCost)

(b)

■ Representing Simple Objects

Figure 7-1 illustrates the transformation of a simple object into a relation. Recall that a simple object has no multivalued attributes and no object attributes. Consequently, simple objects can be represented by a single relation in the database.

Figure 7-1(a) is an example of a simple object, EQUIPMENT, which can be represented by a single relation, as shown in Figure 7-1(b). Each attribute of the object is defined as an attribute of the relation, and the identifying attribute, EquipNumber, becomes the key attribute of the relation, denoted by underlining Equipment-Number in Figure 7-1(b).

The general transformation of simple objects is illustrated in Figure 7-2. Object OBJECT1 is transformed into relation R1. The attribute that identifies OBJECT1 instances is O1; it becomes the key of relation R1. Nonkey data is represented in this and subsequent figures with ellipses (. . .).

Since a key is an attribute that uniquely identifies a row of a table, only unique identifiers—those with the ID underlined—can be transformed into keys. If there is no unique identifier in the object, then one must be created, by either creating a new attribute that is a unique identifier or combining the existing attributes to form a unique identifier.[1]

FIGURE 7-2

General Transformation of Simple Object
into a Relation

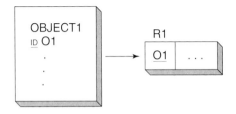

---

[1] In some situations, database developers create a unique key, called a *surrogate key*, that identifies each row of a relation. Since it has no semantic meaning, this key is hidden from the users by the application. When a user creates a new row in a form, the application creates, behind the scenes, a new value for the surrogate key, but the user never sees the keys or is even aware of its existence. Such keys are used to give a unique identity to objects that do not have a unique identifier useful to the user.

▦ Transformation of Composite Objects

A composite object is an object that has one or more multivalued simple or group attributes but no object attributes. Figure 7-3(a) shows an example composite object, HOTEL-BILL. To represent this object, one relation is created for the base object, HOTEL-BILL, and an additional relation is created for the repeating group attribute, DailyCharge. This relational design is shown in Figure 7-3(b).

In the key of DAILY-CHARGE, InvoiceNumber is underlined because it is part of the key of DAILY-CHARGE, and it is italicized because it is also a foreign key. (It is a key of HOTEL-BILL.) ChargeDate is underlined because it is part of the key of DAILY-CHARGE, but it is not italicized because it is not a foreign key.

In general, composite objects are transformed by defining one relation for the object itself and another relation for each multivalued attribute. In Figure 7-4(a), object OBJECT1 contains two groups of multivalued attributes, each of which is represented by a relation in the database design. The key of each of these tables is the composite of the identifier of the object plus the identifier of the group. Thus the representation of OBJECT1 is a relation R1 with key O1, a relation R2 with key (O1, G1), and a relation R3 with key (O1, G2).

The minimum cardinality from the object to the group is specified by the minimum cardinality of group attribute. In Figure 7-4(a), the minimum cardinality of Group1 is 1 and that of Group2 is 0. These cardinalities are shown as a hash mark (on R2) and an oval (on R3) in the data structure diagram. The minimum cardinality from the group to the object is, by default, always 1, because a group cannot exist if the object that contains that group does not exist. These minimum cardinalities are shown by hash marks on the relationship lines into R1.

FIGURE 7-3

Relational Representation of Example Composite Object: (a) HOTEL-BILL Object Diagram and (b) Relations Representing HOTEL-BILL

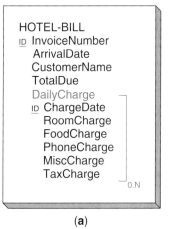

(a)

HOTEL-BILL (<u>InvoiceNumber</u>, ArrivalDate, CustomerName, TotalDue)

DAILY-CHARGE (<u>*InvoiceNumber*</u>, <u>ChargeDate</u>, RoomCharge, FoodCharge, PhoneCharge, MiscCharge, TaxCharge)

(b)

FIGURE 7-4

General Transformation of Composite Objects: (a) Composite Object with Separate Groups and (b) Composite Object with Nested Groups

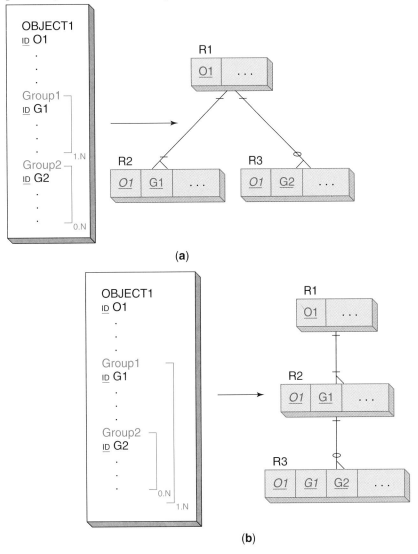

(a)

(b)

As we noted in Chapter 4, groups can be nested. Figure 7-4(b) shows an object in which Group2 is nested within Group1. When this occurs, the relation representing the nested group is made subordinate to the relation that represents its containing group. In Figure 7-4(b), relation R3 is subordinate to relation R2. The key of R3 is the key of R2, which is (O1, G1) plus the identifier of Group2, which is G2; thus the key of R3 is (O1, G1, G2).

Make sure that you understand why the keys in Figure 7-4(b) are constructed as they are. Also note that some attributes are underlined and italicized and some are simply underlined, because some attributes are both local and foreign keys and some are just local keys.

FIGURE 7-5

Four Types of Compound Objects

Object1 Can Contain

		One	Many
Object2 Can Contain	One	1:1	1:N
	Many	M:1	M:N

Transformation of Compound Objects

The relational representation of compound objects is similar to the representation of entities. In fact, compound objects and entities are in many ways quite similar.

As we stated in Chapter 4, an object, OBJECT1, can contain one or many instances of a second object, OBJECT2, and OBJECT2 can contain one or many instances of the first object, OBJECT1. This leads to the object types shown in Figure 7-5.

All of these relationships involve some variation of one-to-one, one-to-many, or many-to-many relationships. Specifically, the relationship from OBJECT1 to OBJECT2 can be 1:1, 1:N, or N:M, whereas the relationship from OBJECT2 to OBJECT1 can be 1:1, 1:M, or M:N. To represent any of these, we need only address these three types of relationships.

REPRESENTING ONE-TO-ONE COMPOUND OBJECTS

Consider the assignment of a LOCKER to a health club MEMBER. A LOCKER is assigned to one MEMBER, and each MEMBER has one, and only one, LOCKER. Figure 7-6(a) shows the object diagrams. To represent these objects with relations, we define a relation for each object, and as with 1:1 entity relationships, we place the key of either relation in the other relation. That is, we can place the key of MEMBER in LOCKER or the key of LOCKER in MEMBER. Figure 7-6(b) shows the

FIGURE 7-6

Example Relational Representation of 1:1 Compound Objects: (a) Example 1:1 Compound Objects and (b) Their Representation

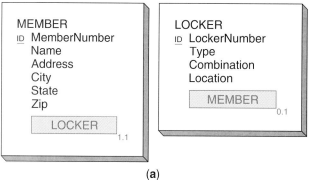

(a)

MEMBER (<u>MemberNumber</u>, Name, Address, City, State, Zip, *LockerNumber*)

LOCKER (<u>LockerNumber</u>, Type, Combination, Location)

(b)

FIGURE 7-7

FIGURE 7-7

General Transformation of 1:1
Compound Objects

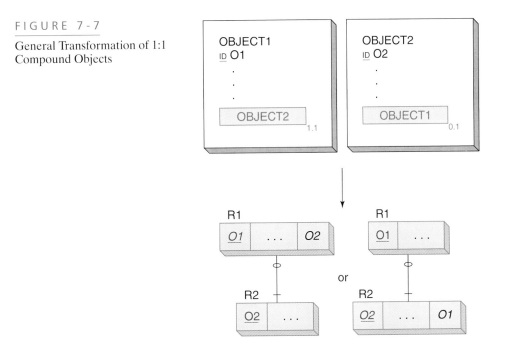

placement of the key of LOCKER in MEMBER. Note that LockerNumber is underlined in LOCKER because it is the key of LOCKER and is italicized in MEMBER because it is a foreign key in MEMBER.

In general, for a 1:1 relationship between OBJECT1 and OBJECT2, we define one relation for each object, R1 and R2. Then we place the key of either relation (O1 or O2) as a foreign key in the other relation, as in Figure 7-7.

FIGURE 7-8

Example Relational Representation of 1:N Compound Objects: (a) Example 1:N Compound Objects and (b) Their Representation

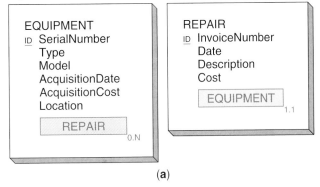

(a)

EQUIPMENT (<u>SerialNumber</u>, Type, Model, AcquisitionDate, AcquisitionCost, Location)

REPAIR (<u>InvoiceNumber</u>, Date, Description, Cost, *SerialNumber*)

(b)

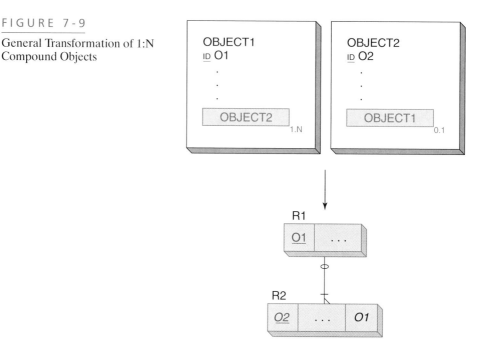

FIGURE 7-9

General Transformation of 1:N
Compound Objects

REPRESENTING ONE-TO-MANY AND MANY-TO-ONE RELATIONSHIPS

Now consider 1:N relationships and N:1 relationships. Figure 7-8(a) shows an example of a 1:N object relationship between EQUIPMENT and REPAIR. An item of EQUIPMENT can have many REPAIRs, but a REPAIR can be related to only one item of EQUIPMENT.

The objects in Figure 7-8(a) are represented by the relations in Figure 7-8(b). Observe that the key of the parent (the object on the one side of the relationship) is placed in the child (the object on the many side of the relationship).

Figure 7-9 shows the general transformation of 1:N compound objects. Object OBJECT1 contains many objects OBJECT2, and object OBJECT2 contains just one OBJECT1. To represent this structure by means of relations, we represent each object by means of a relation and place the key of the parent in the child. Thus in Figure 7-9 the attribute O1 is placed in R2.

If OBJECT2 were to contain many OBJECT1s and OBJECT1 were to contain just one OBJECT2, we would use the same strategy but reverse the role of R1 and R2. That is, we would place O2 in R1.

The minimum cardinalities in either case are determined by the minimum cardinalities of the object attributes. In Figure 7-9, OBJECT1 requires at least one OBJECT2, but OBJECT2 does not necessarily require an OBJECT1. These cardinalities are shown in the data structure diagram as an oval on the R1 side of the relationship and as a hash mark on the R2 side of the relationship. These values are simply examples; either or both objects could have a cardinality of 0, 1, or some other number.

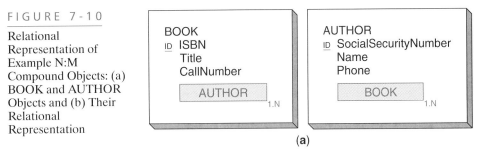

FIGURE 7-10

Relational
Representation of
Example N:M
Compound Objects: (a)
BOOK and AUTHOR
Objects and (b) Their
Relational
Representation

BOOK (ISBN, Title, CallNumber)

AUTHOR (SocialSecurityNumber, Name, Phone)

BOOK-AUTHOR-INT (*ISBN*, *SocialSecurityNumber*)
(b)

REPRESENTING MANY-TO-MANY RELATIONSHIPS

Finally, consider M:N relationships. As with M:N entity relationships, we define three relations, one for each of the objects and a third intersection relation. The intersection relation represents the relationship of the two objects and consists of the keys of both of its parents. Figure 7-10(a) shows the M:N relationship between BOOK and AUTHOR. Figure 7-10(b) depicts the three relations that represent these objects: BOOK, AUTHOR, and BOOK-AUTHOR-INT, the intersection relation. Notice that BOOK-AUTHOR-INT has no nonkey data. Both the attributes

FIGURE 7-11

General Transformation of M:N
Compound Objects into
Relations

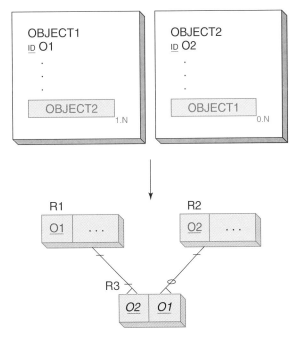

ISBN and SocialSecurityNumber are underlined and in italics because they each are local and foreign keys.

In general, for two objects that have an M:N relationship, we define a relation R1 for object OBJECT1, a relation R2 for object OBJECT2, and a relation R3 for the intersection relation. The general scheme is shown in Figure 7-11. Note that the attributes of R3 are always O1 and O2. For M:N compound objects, R3 never contains nonkey data. The importance of this statement will become clear when we contrast M:N compound relationships with association relationships.

FIGURE 7-12

Relational Representation of Example Hybrid Object: (a) Example Hybrid Object and (b) Relational Representation of SALES-ORDER and Related Objects

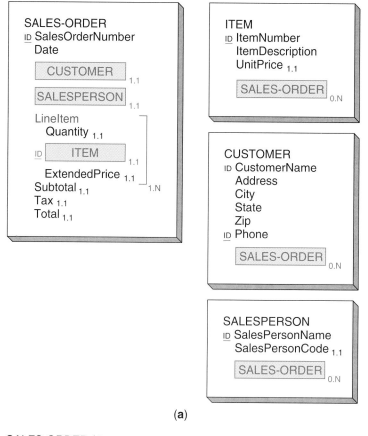

(a)

SALES-ORDER (SalesOrderNumber, Date, Subtotal, Tax, Total, *Phone, SalespersonName*)

CUSTOMER (CustomerName, Address, City, State, Zip, Phone)

SALESPERSON (SalesPersonName, SalesPersonCode)

LINE-ITEM (*SalesOrderNumber, ItemNumber*, Quantity, ExtendedPrice)

ITEM (ItemNumber, ItemDescription, UnitPrice)

(b)

FIGURE 7-13

Four Cases of Hybrid Object Cardinality

Case	Description	Example
1	OBJECT2 relates to one instance of OBJECT1 and appears in only one group instance within that object.	ITEM relates to one ORDER and can appear on only one LineItem of that ORDER.
2	OBJECT2 relates to one instance of OBJECT1 and appears in possibly many group instances within that object.	ITEM relates to one ORDER and can appear on many LineItems of that ORDER.
3	OBJECT2 relates to possibly many instances of OBJECT1 and appears in only one group instance within each object.	ITEM relates to many ORDERs and can appear on only one LineItem of that ORDER.
4	OBJECT2 relates to possibly many instances of OBJECT1 and appears in possibly many group instances within those objects.	ITEM relates to many ORDERs and can appear on many LineItems of that ORDER.

■ Hybrid Objects

Hybrid objects can be transformed into relational designs using a combination of the techniques for composite and compound objects. Figure 7-12(a) shows SALES-ORDER, a hybrid object, and related objects. To represent this object by means of relations, we establish one relation for the object itself and another relation for each of the contained objects CUSTOMER and SALESPERSON. Then, as with a composite object, we establish a relation for the multivalued group, which is LineItem. Since this group contains another object, ITEM, we also establish a relation for ITEM. All of the one-to-many relationships are represented by placing the key of the parent relation in the child relation, as shown in Figure 7-12(b).

The example in Figure 7-12 is deceptively simple. As we mentioned in Chapter 4, there are actually four cases of hybrid objects, which are summarized in Figure 7-13.

Cases 3 and 4 are more common than Cases 1 and 2, so we consider them first. OBJECT1 in Figure 7-14 shows two groups; Group1 illustrates Case 3 and Group2 illustrates Case 4.

Group1 has a maximum cardinality of N, which means that there can be many instances of Group1 within an OBJECT1. Furthermore, since OBJECT2 is marked as *ID*, this means that a particular OBJECT2 can appear in only one of the Group1 instances within an OBJECT1. Thus OBJECT2 acts as an identifier for Group1 within OBJECT1.

(The SALES-ORDER in Figure 7-12 illustrates this case. ITEM is an identifier of LineItem, so a given ITEM can appear on only one LineItem in a particular ORDER. But an ITEM can appear on many ORDERs.)

Now consider the relational representation of Group1 in Figure 7-14. A relation, R1, is created for OBJECT1, and a relation, R2, is created for OBJECT2. In addition, a third relation, R-G1, is created for Group1. The relationship between R1 and

FIGURE 7-14

General Transformation of Hybrid Object into Relations

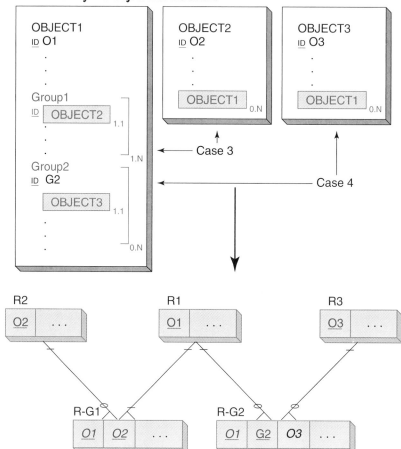

R-G1 is 1:N, so we place the key of R1 (which is O1) into R-G1; the relationship between R2 and R-G1 is also 1:N, so we place the key of R2 (which is O2) in R-G1. Since an OBJECT2 can appear with a particular value of OBJECT1 only once, the composite (O1, O2) is unique to R-G1 and can be made the key of that relation.

Now consider Group2. OBJECT3 does not identify Group2, and so OBJECT3 can appear in many Group2 instances in the same OBJECT1. (The SALES-ORDER in Figure 7-12 would be like this if ITEM were not *ID* in LineItem. This means that an ITEM could appear many times on the same ORDER.) Since OBJECT3 is not the identifier of Group2, we assume that some other attribute, G2, is the identifier.

In Figure 7-13, we create a relation R3 for OBJECT3 and another relation R-G2 for Group2. The relationship between R1 and R-G2 is 1:N, so place the key of R1 (which is O1) into R-G2. The relationship between R3 and R-G2 is also 1:N, so place the key of R3 (which is O3) into R-G2.

Now, however, unlike Group1, (O1, O3) cannot be the key of R-G2 because an O3 can be paired with a given O1 many times. That is, the composite (O1,O3) is not unique to R-G2, and so the key of R-G2 must be (O1, G2).

Case 1 is similar to Case 3 except for the restriction that an OBJECT2 can be related to only one OBJECT1. The relations in Figure 7-14 will still work, but we must add the key of R1 (which is O1) to R2 and establish the restriction that (O1, O2) of R-G1 must equal (O1,O2) of R2.

Case 2 is similar to Case 4 except for the restriction that an OBJECT3 can be related to only one OBJECT1. Again, the relations in Figure 7-14 will work, but we must add the key of R1 (which is O1) to R3 and establish the restriction that (O1,O3) of R-G2 is a subset of (O1,O3) in R3 (see Questions 7.7 and 7.8).

■ Association Objects

An association object is an object that associates two other objects. It is a special case of compound objects that most often occurs in assignment situations. Figure 7-15(a) shows a FLIGHT object that associates an AIRPLANE with a PILOT.

To represent association objects, we define a relationship for each of the three objects, and then we represent the relationships among the objects using one of the strategies used with compound objects. In Figure 7-15(b), for example, one relation is defined for AIRPLANE, one for PILOT, and one for FLIGHT. The relationships between FLIGHT and AIRPLANE and between FLIGHT and PILOT are 1:N, and

FIGURE 7-15

Relational Representation of Example Association Object: (a) FLIGHT Association Object and Related Objects and (b) Relational Representation of AIRPLANE, PILOT, and FLIGHT Objects

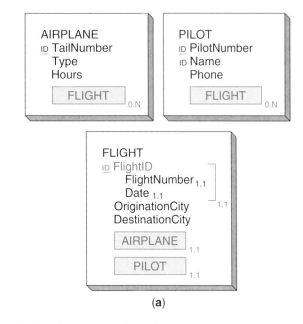

(a)

AIRPLANE (TailNumber, TypeHours)

PILOT (PilotNumber, Name, Phone)

FLIGHT (FlightNumber, Date, OriginationCity, DestinationCity, TailNumber, PilotNumber)

(b)

FIGURE 7-16

General Transformation of Association Objects into Relations

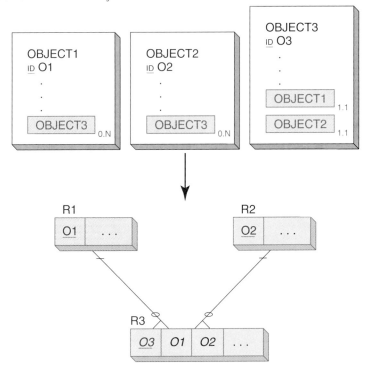

so we place the keys of the parent in the children. In this case, we place the key of AIRPLANE and the key of PILOT in FLIGHT.

FLIGHT contains a key of its own. Although it contains foreign keys, these keys are only attributes and are not part of FLIGHT's key. But this is not always the case. If FLIGHT had no key of its own, its key would be the combination of the foreign keys of the objects that it associates. Here that combination would be {AirplaneNumber, PilotNumber, Date}.

In general, when transforming association object structures into relations, we define one relation for each of the objects participating in the relationship. In Figure 7-16, OBJECT3 associates OBJECT1 and OBJECT2. In this case, we define R1, R2, and R3, as shown. The key of each of the parent relations, O1 and O2, appears as foreign key attributes in R3, the relation representing the association object. If the association object has no unique identifying attribute, the combination of the attributes of R1 and R2 will be used to create a unique identifier.

Note the difference between the association relation in Figure 7-16 and the intersection relation in Figure 7-11. The principal distinction is that the association table carries data that represents some aspect of the combination of the objects. The intersection relation carries no data; its only reason for existence is to specify which objects have a relationship with one another.

▨ Parent/Subtype Objects

Parent (also called *supertype*) and subtype objects are represented in a way similar to that for 1:1 compound objects. We define a relation for the parent object and one for each of the subtype objects. The key of each of these relations is the key of the parent.

Figure 7-17(a) shows a parent object, PERSON, that includes two mutually exclusive subtypes, STUDENT and PROFESSOR. Figure 7-17(b) shows a relational representation of these three objects. Each object is represented by a table, and the key of all of the tables is the same.

The relations in Figure 7-17(b) pose a problem, however. The application program still needs to look in both the STUDENT and PROFESSOR tables to determine the type of PERSON. If an entry is found in STUDENT, the person is a student; if an entry is found in PROFESSOR, the person is a professor. This is an indirect and possibly slow way to determine the type of a person, and if, as may happen, the PERSON is of neither type, both tables will have been searched for no reason. Because of this problem, a type indicator attribute is sometimes placed in the parent table.

FIGURE 7-17

Representation of Example Parent and Subtypes: (a) PERSON Parent and STUDENT and PROFESSOR Subtypes, (b) Relational Representation of Parent and Subtypes, and (c) Alternative Representations of the Parent Relation

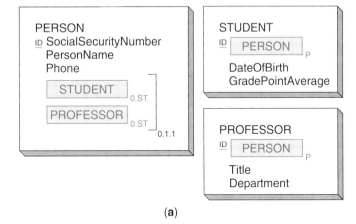

(a)

PERSON (<u>SocialSecurityNumber</u>, PersonName, Phone)

STUDENT (<u>SocialSecurityNumber</u>, DateOfBirth, GradePointAverage)

PROFESSOR (<u>SocialSecurityNumber</u>, Title, Department)

(b)

PERSON1 (<u>SocialSecurityNumber</u>, PersonName, Phone, PersonType)

PERSON2 (<u>SocialSecurityNumber</u>, PersonName, Phone, StudentType, ProfessorType)

(c)

Figure 7-17(c) shows two variations of a type indicator. In the first variation, relation PERSON1, the type of object is stored in the attribute PersonType. Possible values of this attribute are 'Neither', 'STUDENT', or 'PROFESSOR'. The application would obtain the value of this attribute and thereby determine whether a subtype exists and, if so, which type it is.

A second possibility is shown in the relation PERSON2, to which two attributes have been added, one for StudentType and another for ProfessorType. Each of the attributes is a Boolean variable; the allowed values are true or false. Note that if, as is the case here, a person can only be of one type, then if one of these values is true, the other one must be false.

In general, designs of type PERSON1 are better when the subtypes are mutually exclusive. Designs of type PERSON2 are better when the subtypes are not exclusive.

A general scheme for representing subtypes is shown in Figure 7-18. One relation is created for the parent and one each for the subtypes. The key of all of the relations is the identifier of the parent. All relationships between the parent and the subtype are 1:1. Note the bar across the relationship lines and the presence of the subtype group's cardinality. The value shown, 0.1.1, means that no subtype is required but, if present, at most one of the subtypes is allowed.

FIGURE 7-18

General Transformation of Parent/
Subtype Objects into Relations

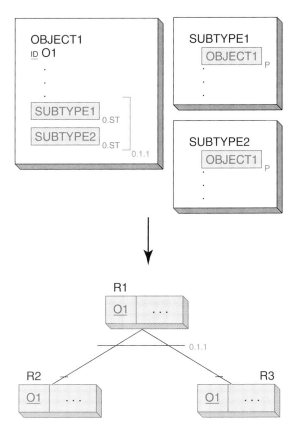

(Recall that in general, the format of group cardinality is **r.m.n.**, where *r* is a Boolean true or false depending on whether or not the subtype group is required, *m* is the minimum number of subtypes that must have a value within the group, and *n* is the maximum number of subtypes that may have a value within the group. In a group of five subtypes, therefore, the cardinality of 1.2.4 indicates that the subtype group is required, that at least two subtypes must have a value, and that a maximum of four subtypes may have a value.)

Archetype/Version Objects

Archetype/version objects are compound objects that model various iterations, releases, or instances of a basic object. The objects in Figure 7-19(a) model software products for which there are various releases. Examples of such products are Excel, WordPerfect, and Paradox for Windows, and examples of releases are Release 2.0, Release 3.0, and Release 4.0 of Excel.

The relational representation of PRODUCT and RELEASE is shown in Figure 7-19(b). One relation is created for PRODUCT, and another is created for RELEASE. The key of RELEASE is the combination of the key of PRODUCT and the local key (ReleaseNumber) of RELEASE.

Figure 7-20 shows the general transformation of archetype/version objects. Attribute O1 of R2 is both a local and a foreign key, but O2 is only a local key.

FIGURE 7-19

Relational Representation of Example Archetype/Version Objects: (a) PRODUCT Archetype and RELEASE Version Objects and (b) Relational Representation of PRODUCT and RELEASE

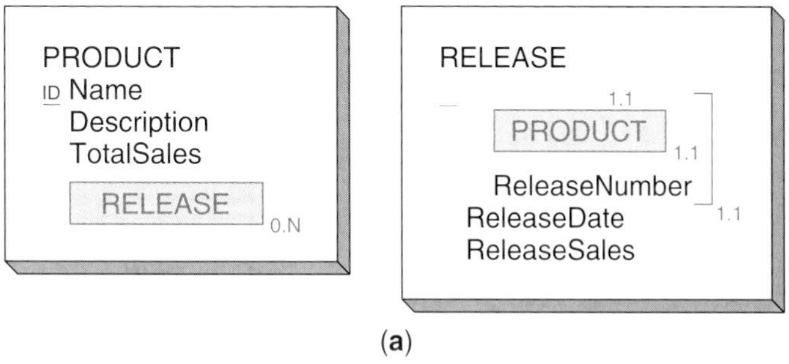

(a)

PRODUCT (<u>Name</u>, Description, TotalSales)

RELEASE (*<u>Name</u>*, <u>ReleaseNumber</u>, ReleaseDate, ReleaseSales)

(b)

FIGURE 7-20

General Transformation of
Archetype/Version Objects

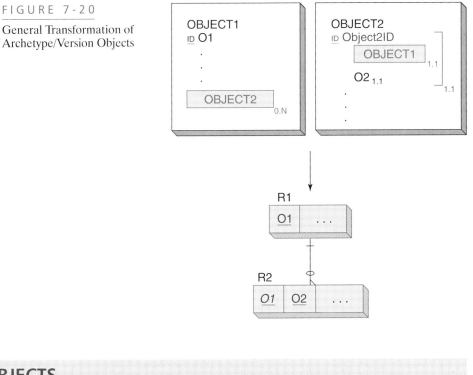

SAMPLE OBJECTS

To reinforce the concepts presented in this chapter, we now consider several example objects taken from actual businesses, presented in increasing order of complexity. We model the underlying object and represent it in relations using the methods described in this chapter.

■ Subscription Form

Figure 7-21(a) shows a magazine subscription form. At least two object structures could represent this form. If the publishers of *Fine Woodworking* consider a subscriber to be an attribute of a subscription, a subscription could be a simple object represented as a single relation, as in Figure 7-21(b).

If this company has only a single publication and no plans to produce additional publications, the design in Figure 7-21(b) will work. If, however, this company has several publications and if a customer may subscribe to more than one of them, this design will duplicate the customer data for each publication. This will not only waste file space for the publisher but will also exasperate the customer because, for example, he or she will be required to submit address changes for each publication of the same publisher.

If the publisher has several publications or plans to have several publications, a better design would be to model subscriber as a separate object, as shown in Figure 7-21(c). CUSTOMER is a 1:N compound object and is represented by the relations in this figure.

FIGURE 7-21

Alternative Representations of Subscription: (a) Subscription Order Form, (b) Subscription Modeled as One Object, and (c) Subscription Modeled as Two Objects

Fine Wood ▲▲▲▲▲Working

To subscribe

☐ 1 year (6 issues) for just $18 — 20% off the newsstand price.
(Outside the U.S. $21/year.—U.S. funds, please)

☐ 2 years (12 issues) for just $34 — save 24%
(Outside the U.S. $40/2 years—U.S. funds, please)

Name _____

Address _____

City _____ State _____ Zip _____

☐ My payment is enclosed.   ☐ Please bill me.

Please start my subscription with ☐ *current issue* ☐ *next issue*.

(a)

SUBSCRIPTION
ID SubNumber
StartDate
EndDate
AmtDue
Name
Address
City
State
Zip
PayCode

SUBSCRIPTION

SubNumber	StartDate	EndDate	AmtDue	Name	Address

City	State	Zip	PayCode

(b)

FIGURE 7-21

(Continued)

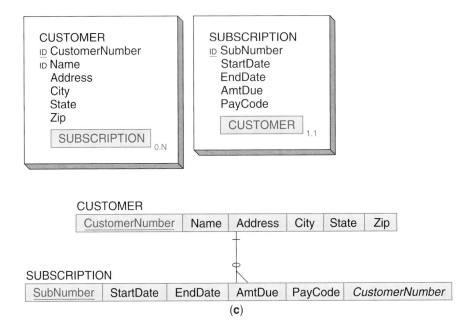

(c)

Product Description

Figure 7-22(a) shows the description of a popular packaged-goods product. Whereas Figure 7-21(a) shows a generic form, Figure 7-22(a) shows an instance of a specific report about a cereal product. The reports for all of Kellogg's cereal products use this format.

Figure 7-22(b) shows a composite object that could underlie this report. We say *could* because there are many different ways that this object could be represented. Also, further investigation may reveal other objects that are not apparent in this one report. For example, USDA Recommendation may be a semantic object in its own right.

For illustration purposes, we make different assumptions about the Nutrient and USDARecDailyAllow groups. The CEREAL-PRODUCT object assumes that every element of the Nutrient group—namely, calories, protein, carbohydrate, fat, cholesterol, sodium, and potassium—is required in every instance of this object. We do not assume this for the USDARecDailyAllow group, because only at least one instance of this group must exist.

The report in Figure 7-22(a) has many interpretations and could be modeled in several different ways. In an actual development project, it would be important to obtain as many other reports about other cereal products and about the ingredients and nutritional information in this report. These other documents would most likely give additional structure to this semantic object.

Figure 7-22(c) shows the relational representation for the CEREAL-PRODUCT object. The minimum cardinality of 7 is shown by placing the numeral 7 next to

FIGURE 7-22

Cereal Product Representation: (a)
Cereal Product Report, (b) CEREAL-
PRODUCT Object Diagram, and (c)
Relational Representation of CEREAL-
PRODUCT

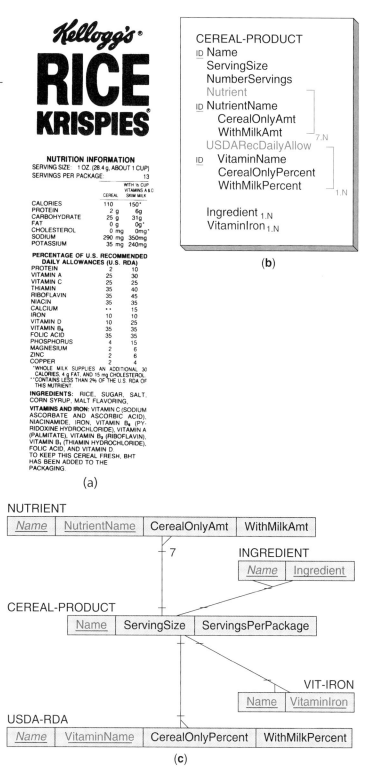

(a)

(b)

(c)

the required hash mark on the relationship line. Foreign keys have been placed as described previously for composite objects.

Traffic-warning Citation

Figure 7-23(a) shows an instance of the traffic-warning citation form used in the state of Washington. The designer of this form has given us important clues to the underlying objects of this form. Notice that portions of the form are distinguished by rounded corners, indicating that different sections pertain to different objects. Also, some groups of attributes have names, indicating the need for group attributes.

Figure 7-23(b) is one way to illustrate the underlying objects of the traffic-warning citation. Although we cannot be certain from just this one form, there are certain clues that lead us to believe that the driver, vehicle, and officer are independent objects. First, the data concerning each of these subjects is in a separate section on the form. But more important, each section has its fields that are undoubtedly iden-

FIGURE 7-23

Representation of a Correction Notice: (a) Example Form, (b) CORRECTION-NOTICE Object Diagram, and (c) Relational Representation of CORRECTION-NOTICE

WASHINGTON STATE PATROL CORRECTION NOTICE

NAME Kroenke, David M
LAST FIRST
ADDRESS 5053 88 Ave SE
CITY Mecer Island STATE Wa ZIP CODE 98040
DRIVERS LICENSE 00000 STATE Wa M F BIRTH DATE 2127 46 HGT 6 WGT 165 EYES Bl
VEHICLES LICENSE AAA000 STATE Wa COLOR YEAR 90 MAKE Saab TYPE 900
VIN
REGISTERED OWNER
ADDRESS
VIOLATION DATE MO 11 DAY 7 YEAR 91 TIME HOUR: 935 DIST 2 DETACH 17
LOCATION 17 MILES E OF Enumckum ON SR410
VIOLATIONS Writing text while driving
OFFICERS SIGNATURE S Scott PERSONNEL NUMBER 850
[X] This is a warning, no further action is required.
[ ] You are released to take this vehicle to a place of repair. Continued operation on the roadway is not authorized.
[ ] CORRECT VIOLATION(S) IMMEDIATELY. Return this signed card for proof of compliance within 15/30 days. (if this box checked)
X DRIVERS SIGNATURE

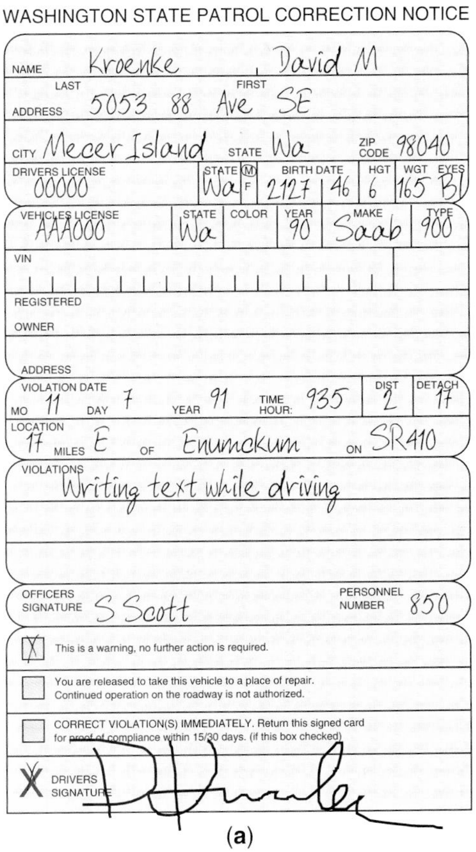

(a)

FIGURE 7-23

(Continued)

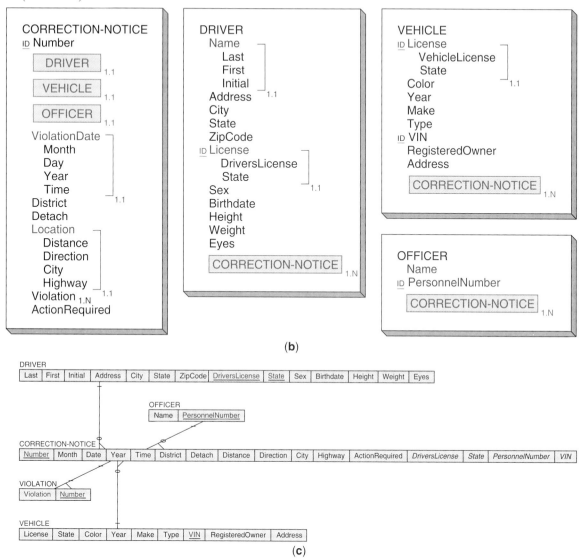

(b)

(c)

tifying attributes of something apart from CORRECTION-NOTICE. For example, {DriversLicense, State} uniquely identifies a driver; VehicleLicense, State and VIN (Vehicle Identification Number) identify registered vehicles; and PersonnelNumber identifies an officer. These key fields obviously are determinants, and so objects were defined for each. The relation representation of these diagrams appears in Figure 7-23(c).

SUMMARY

The transformation of semantic objects into relations depends on the type of object. Simple objects are represented by a single relation. The nonobject attributes are carried as attributes of the relation.

Composite objects require two or more relations for their representation. One relation contains the single-valued attributes of the object. Another relation is constructed for each multivalued simple or group attribute. The key of the relations representing the multivalued attributes is always a composite key that contains the key of the object plus an identifier of the composite group within that object.

At least two relations are required to represent a compound object. Each relation has its own distinct key. There are four different types of compound objects—one to one, one to many, many to one, and many to many—which are represented by inserting foreign keys. For one-to-one relationships, the key of either table is placed in the other table, and for one-to-many and many-to-one relationships, the key of the parent is placed in the child relation. Finally, for many-to-many relationships, an intersection table is created that carries the keys of both relations.

Hybrid objects are represented by creating a table for the multivalued group attribute of the composite object and placing the key of the relation representing the noncomposite object into that table. The four cases of hybrid are listed in Figure 7-14.

Association objects require at least three relations for their representation, one for each of the objects involved. Each relation has its own key, and the relation representing the association object contains, as foreign keys, the keys of the other two objects.

Parent and subtype objects are represented by creating a relation for the parent and one for each subtype. The key of all relations is normally the same. An identifier attribute is sometimes placed in the parent to indicate the object's type.

For archetype/version objects, one relation is created for the archetype object and a second is created for the version. The key of the version's relation always contains the key of the archetype.

GROUP I QUESTIONS

7.1   Give an example of a simple object other than one in this text. Show how to represent this object by means of a relation.

7.2   Give an example of a composite object other than one in this text. Show how to represent this object by means of relations.

7.3   Give an example of a 1:1 compound object other than one in this text. Show two ways to represent it by means of relations.

7.4   Give an example of a 1:N compound object other than one in this text. Show how to represent it by means of relations.

7.5   Give an example of an M:1 compound object other than one in this text. Show how to represent it by means of relations.

7.6   Give an example of a M:N compound object other than one in this text. Show how to represent it by means of relations.

7.7   Give an example of a Case 1 (see Figure 7-13) hybrid object. Show how to represent it by means of relations.

7.8   Give an example of a Case 2 (see Figure 7-13) hybrid object. Show how to represent it by means of relations.

7.9   Give an example of an association and related objects other than one in this text. Show how to represent these objects by means of relations. Assume that the association object has an identifier of its own.

7.10   Do the same as for Question 9, but assume that the association object does not have an identifier of its own.

7.11   Give an example of a parent object with at least two exclusive subtypes. Show how to represent these objects by means of relations. Use a type indicator attribute.

7.12   Give an example of a parent object with at least two nonexclusive subtypes. Show how to represent these objects by means of relations. Use a type indicator attribute.

7.13   Find an example of a form on your campus that would be appropriately modeled with a simple object. Show how to represent this object by means of a relation.

7.14   Find an example of a form on your campus that would be appropriately modeled with a composite object. Show how to represent this object by means of relations.

7.15   Find an example of a form on your campus that would be appropriately modeled with one of the types of a compound object. Show how to represent these objects by means of relations.

7.16   Find an example of a form on your campus that would be appropriately modeled with a hybrid object. Classify the object according to Figure 7-14, and show how to represent these objects by means of relations.

7.17   Find an example of a form on your campus that would be appropriately modeled with an association and related objects. Show how to represent these objects by means of relations.

7.18   Find an example of a form on your campus that would be appropriately modeled with parent/subtypes objects. Show how to represent these objects by means of relations.

7.19   Find an example of a form on your campus that would be appropriately modeled with archetype/version objects. Show how to represent these objects by means of relations.

PROJECTS

7.20 In Figure 7-13, give a different example for each of the four cases in the right column. Show how each of your examples would be represented with relations.

7.21 Suppose you are working on a project to develop a database to support a student microcomputer lab at a university. Consider the following statements describing various objects and relationships:

   a. Students must be enrolled in certain courses in order to use the microcomputer lab.

   b. Students can make appointments to use the lab by reserving a certain computer for use at a certain time.

   c. Each computer has a certain amount of memory and might also have special peripherals attached (such as a mouse, a speech synthesizer, or a special keyboard).

   Perform the following tasks:

   a. Draw the object diagrams for STUDENT, COURSE, COMPUTER, PERIPHERAL, and APPOINTMENT.

   b. What type (simple, composite, compound, hybrid, association, parent/subtype, archetype/version) is each of the objects?

   c. Transform the object diagrams into relation diagrams, and underline the key of each relation.

   d. Identify the foreign keys in each relation.

7.22 Modify Figures 7-22(b) and (c) to add the reports shown in Figure 7-24.

FIGURE 7-24

Reports for Question 22

FDA REPORT #6272
Date: 06/30/93
Issuer: Kellogg's Corporation
Report Title: Product Summary by Ingredient

Corn	Corn Flakes
	Krispix
	Nutrigrain (Corn)
Corn syrup	Rice Krispies
	Frosted Flakes
	Sugar Pops
Malt	Rice Krispies
	Sugar Smacks
Wheat	Sugar Smacks
	Nutrigrain (Wheat)

(a)

SUPPLIERS LIST
Date: 06/30/93

Ingredient	Supplier	Price
Corn	Wilson	2.80
	J. Perkins	2.72
	Pollack	2.83
	McKay	2.80
Wheat	Adams	1.19
	Kroner	1.19
	Schmidt	1.22
Barley	Wilson	0.85
	Pollack	0.84

(b)

FIGURE 7-25

Reports for Question 7.23

West Side Story

Based on a conception of Jerome Robbins

Book by ARTHUR LAURENTS
Music by LEONARD BERNSTIEN
Lyrics by STEPHEN SONDHEIM

Entire Original Production Directed
and Choreographed by JEROME ROBBINS

Originally produced on Broadway by Robert E. Griffith and Harold S. Prince
by arrangment with Roger L. Stevens
Orchestration by Leonard Bernstein with Sid Ramin and Irwin Kostal

HIGHLIGHTS FROM THE COMPLETE RECORDING

Maria . . . . KIRI TE KANAWA
Tony . . . . JOSE CARRERAS
Anita . . . . TATIANA TROYANOS
Riff . . . . KURT OLLMAN
and MARILYN HORNE singing "Somewhere"

Rosalia . . . . Louise Edeiken	Diesel . . . . Marty Nelson
Consuela . . . . Stella Zambalis	Baby John . . . . . . Stephen Bogardus
Fancisca . . . . Angelina Reaux	A-rab . . . . Peter Thom
Action. . . . . David Livingston	Snowboy. . . . . Todd Lester
	Bernardo. . . . Richard Harrell

1	**Jet Song** (Riff, Action, Baby John, A-rab, Chorus)	[3'13]
2	**Something's Coming** (Tony)	[2'33]
3	**Maria** (Tony)	[2'56]
4	**Tonight** (Maria, Tony)	[5'27]
5	**America** (Anita, Rosalia, Chorus)	[4'47]
6	**Cool** (Riff, Chorus)	[4'37]
7	**One Hand, One Heart** (Tony, Maria)	[5'38]
8	**Tonight (Ensemble)** (Entire Cast)	[3'40]
9	**I Feel Pretty** (Maria, Chorus)	[3'22]
10	**Somewhere** (A Girl)	[2'34]
11	**Gee OFicer Krupke** (Action, Snowboy, Diesel, A-rab, Baby John, Chorus)	[4'18]
12	**A Boy Like That** (Anita, Maria)	[2'05]
13	**I Have a Love** (Maria, Anita)	[3'30]
14	**Taunting Scene** (Orchestra)	[1'21]
15	**Finale** (Maria, Tony)	[2'40]

7.23 Using the album cover shown in Figure 7-25 as a guide, perform the following
      tasks:

      a. Draw the object diagrams for the underlying objects ARTIST, ROLE, and
         SONG.

      b. Identify the relationships among those objects. What types of objects are
         they (simple, composite, and so on)?

      c. Indicate for each participant in a relationship whether it is optional or
         mandatory.

      d. Transform the object diagrams into relation diagrams.

      What is the key of each relation? What foreign keys appear in each relation?

DATABASE
APPLICATION DESIGN

Chapter 8 discusses the design of database applications. Since this is not a text on systems development, we address only those aspects of application design that pertain directly to database processing and technology.

This chapter assumes that the users' data model has been expressed in terms of semantic objects, in order to show more clearly how the users' data model drives application design. Even though this fact is true whether the data model is expressed in entity relationship terms or in semantic object terms, it is more obvious when semantic objects are used.

We begin with a case to illustrate design concepts. This case will also be used in Chapter 11 where it is the basis for a discussion of database implementation. Next we describe the nature of database applications, object views, materializations, and the design of application forms and reports. Finally, the chapter concludes with a summary of application program design.

CASE APPLICATION: VIEW RIDGE GALLERY

View Ridge Gallery is a small art gallery that sells contemporary fine art, including lithographs, original paintings, and photographs. All of the lithographs and photos are signed and numbered, and most of the art is priced between $1000 and $25,000. View Ridge has been in business for twenty-seven years, has one full-time owner, three salespeople, and two workers who make frames, hang art in the gallery, and prepare art works for shipment.

View Ridge holds openings and other gallery events to attract customers to the gallery. Art is also placed on display in local companies, restaurants, and in other public places. View Ridge owns all of the art that it sells; it holds no items on a consignment basis.

Application Requirements

View Ridge wants to build database applications to satisfy the requirements shown in Figure 8-1. First, both the owner and the salespeople want to keep track of their customers and their art-purchasing interests. The salespeople need to know whom to contact when new art arrives, and they also need this information so that they can create personal written and verbal communications with their customers.

In addition, the database should record the customers' art purchases so that the salespeople can devote more time to the most active buyers. They also sometimes use the purchase records to identify the location of the art, because the gallery occasionally repurchases hard-to-find art for resale. The database application also should have a form for adding new works that the gallery purchases.

View Ridge wants its database application to provide a list of artists and works that have appeared in the gallery. The owner would also like to be able to determine how fast an artist's work sells and at what sales margins, and the database application should produce a list of current inventory for periodic physical inventory counts. Finally, View Ridge would like the database to produce reports that would reduce the work of the gallery's part-time bookkeeper/accountant.

Database Design

Figure 8-2(a) shows the structure of the objects required to support the gallery's database. CUSTOMER and ARTIST are compound objects, and WORK is a hybrid object whose unique identifier is the group {ARTIST, Title, and Copy}. The multi-valued group Transaction represents the gallery's purchase and sale of the work.

FIGURE 8-1

Summary of Requirements for the View Ridge Gallery Database Applications

Track customers and their purchasing interests.

Record customers' art purchases.

Record gallery's purchases.

List the artists and works that have appeared in the gallery.

Report how fast an artist's works have sold and at what margin.

List current inventory.

List product reports to be used by the gallery's bookkeeper/accountant.

FIGURE 8-2

Database Design for View Ridge Gallery: (a) Objects Required for the View Ridge Gallery Database, (b) Relational Representation of View Ridge Gallery's Objects, and (c) Relational Representation Using Surrogate Keys

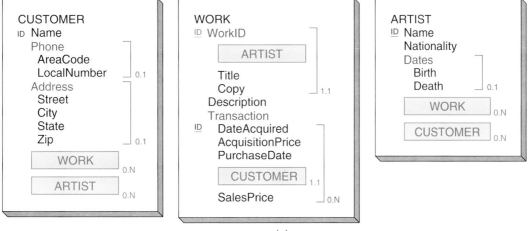

(a)

CUSTOMER (<u>CustNumber</u>, Name, AreaCode, LocalNumber, Street, City, State, Zip)

WORK (<u>ArtistName</u>, <u>Title</u>, <u>Copy</u>, Description)

TRANSACTION (<u>*ArtistName*</u>, <u>*Title*</u>, <u>*Copy*</u>, <u>DateAcquired</u>, AcquisitionPrice, PurchaseDate, *CustNumber*, SalesPrice)

ARTIST (<u>ArtistName</u>, Nationality, Birthdate, DeceasedDate)

CUSTOMER-ARTIST-INT (<u>CustNumber</u>, <u>ArtistName</u>)

(b)

CUSTOMER (<u>CustomerID</u>, Name, AreaCode, LocalNumber, Street, City, State, Zip)

WORK (<u>WorkID</u>, ArtistName, Title, Copy, Description)

TRANSACTION (<u>TransactionID</u>, *WorkID*, DateAcquired, AcquisitionPrice, PurchaseDate, *CustomerID*, SalesPrice)

ARTIST (<u>ArtistID</u>, ArtistName, Nationality, Birthdate, DeceasedDate)

CUSTOMER-ARTIST-INT (<u>*CustomerID*</u>, <u>*ArtistID*</u>)

(c)

Since a given work can pass through the gallery several times (because of repurchases and trade-ins), Transaction is multivalued. WORK is a hybrid object because it contains the object attribute CUSTOMER.

View Ridge wants to be able to track its customers' interests: in which artists is a particular customer interested, and which customers have an interest in a particular artist? These requirements are supported by placing the multivalued attribute ARTIST in CUSTOMER and the multivalued attribute CUSTOMER in ARTIST.

The relational representation of the View Ridge objects is shown in Figure 8-2(b). Since the CUSTOMER object does not have a unique identifier, one must be created to use as a key. Here we have added an identifying number, CustNumber. The maximum cardinality of the Phone and Address groups is 1, so the attributes in those groups can be folded into the CUSTOMER table. These groups, in fact, do not appear in the table as groups; instead, the group information is used later to construct forms.

The key of WORK consists of the key of ARTIST plus Title and Copy. The only nonkey attribute of WORK is Description. Since the Transaction attribute is multi-valued, a table must be created for it. Its key is the key of the object in which it is contained plus the key of the group, which is DateAcquired. Note that CustNumber is carried as a foreign key in TRANSACTION.

The ARTIST object is represented by a single table, and ArtistName can be used as the table key, since artist's names are modeled as being unique. The intersection table CUSTOMER-ARTIST-INT must be created to carry the M:N relationship between CUSTOMER and ARTIST.

The design in Figure 8-2(b) could be improved by replacing the data keys with surrogate keys. Remember that such keys are supplied by the application system, as hidden identifiers that are maintained, behind the scenes, for the user. Such a design is shown in Figure 8-2(c), in which the names of the surrogate keys are constructed by appending the letters ID to the name of the table.

The design in Figure 8-2(c) is better because less data is duplicated. The columns (ArtistName, Title, Copy) need not be copied into the Transaction table. Since there may be many transactions for a given work, this savings may be appreciable. The cost is that application programs must be developed to create and maintain the surrogate key values.

CHARACTERISTICS OF DATABASE APPLICATIONS

The purpose of a database application is to create, update, delete, and display objects at the direction of the users while at all times protecting the security and integrity of the database. Ideally, an application provides an easy-to-use interface for authorized users who are making authorized requests with valid and accurate data. Also ideally, it presents the equivalent of a closed door to unauthorized users, and it provides informative and helpful error messages to authorized users who are making unauthorized requests or mistakes or who are attempting to process invalid data. Often, however, these ideals cannot be fully achieved because of limitations in the DBMS products, time and budget restrictions, limits in the developers' knowledge or abilities, or other constraints.

◼ Create, Update, Delete, and Display Objects

The database application's first task is to create, update, delete, and display objects. As you know from earlier chapters, objects are not stored in the database. Rather, they are transformed and stored as sets of relations. Before objects can be processed, therefore, the application must construct them from the underlying relations or, as we sometimes say, the application must **materialize objects.**

Objects are created by obtaining data from users or other sources and storing it in the database. To update the data, the object data is read from the relations, and the appropriate changes are made. To delete the data, all object data is removed from the underlying relations. The data can be displayed by reporting it (on paper or other external media) or by showing object structures on video display devices.

Creating, updating, and deleting objects are the bulk of the application's and the application developers' work. When objects are modified in this way, the data must be correctly changed while the constraints are enforced. Although DBMS products should enforce many constraints automatically, in practice few do. It thus often falls on the application program to enforce domain, intrarelation, and interrelation constraints.

In addition, if the database is concurrently processed, updating must be controlled so that the actions of one user do not interfere with those of another. Finally, update processing must be structured so that in the event of a failure, the database can be recovered.

Objects are seldom queried. Most DBMS products currently support the querying of *relations*, but not *objects*. Chapter 10 discusses SQL, the ANSI standard query language. This language is relation oriented, and so the users themselves must construct objects from underlying relations. Since few users have the knowledge or patience to construct objects from relations, such languages are most often used only for querying simple objects. If the objects are more complex, users turn to an application program that constructs the object from the underlying relations.

■ Provide Facilities for Controlling Processing

The next phrase in a database's application is *at the direction of the users.* That is, an application must provide a means for the user to direct and control its activity. Three means are used. First, the user learns a set of **commands** to issue, like the following:

UPDATE CUSTOMER WHERE CustNum = 12345
SET CustBalance TO 1350

The advantage of command-driven applications is that they are direct and to the point; the user need not fuss with menus or other structures. The disadvantage is that the end user must learn and remember the commands and their syntax. Command-driven applications are used for those few commands that are used frequently. Teller processing at a bank or airline reservation processing probably use command-driven applications.

The second means are application **menus**. Here the user is given one or more menus from which to make choices. Menus that the View Ridge Gallery could use are shown in Figure 8-3. Their advantage is that the end user need not remember command syntax or even which commands are suitable in a particular situation, because the system leads the user through the appropriate choices. The disadvantage of menu-driven applications is that they seem cumbersome to experienced users.

A new style of control interface has begun to emerge, made popular by Apple Macintosh microcomputers and products like Microsoft's Windows. This interface is

FIGURE 8-3

Example Menus for Use by the
View Ridge Gallery

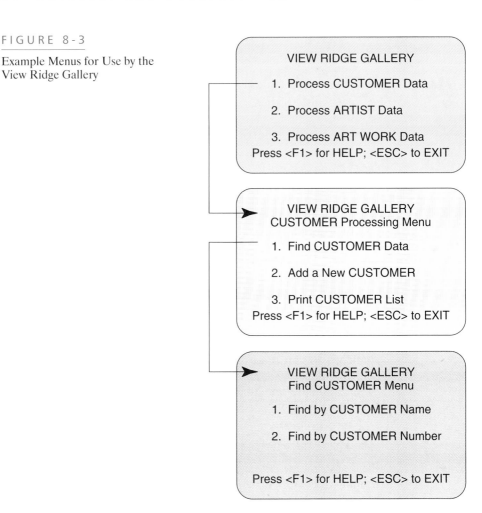

an outgrowth of menu-oriented control and is called a **graphical user interface,** or
GUI. Such interfaces include pull-down menus, icons, dialogue boxes, mice, and
other facilities that greatly enhance the application's ease of use. Because of their
intuitive nature and the standardized mode of processing, such interfaces will
become common for database applications in the near future. Figure 8-4 shows an
example of GUI menus that View Ridge might use.

FIGURE 8-4

Example Graphical User Interface (GUI) Menu

■ Protect Security and Integrity

The phrase *while at all times protecting the security and integrity of the database* means that the application should be designed so that only authorized users can perform authorized activities with valid data. Again, this is far easier to state as a goal than it is to accomplish in practice. Application designers, however, must keep in mind this goal at all times.

End users inevitably make keystroke mistakes, and so the data that they receive (on source documents, for example) often is incorrect. Or end users try to perform operations out of sequence or to perform invalid operations. And they try to perform operations that they are not trained, qualified, or authorized to perform. Applications should therefore be designed to prevent as many such activities as possible.

There are several ways in which the application developer can protect security and integrity. First, passwords and other controls can be established, as described in Chapter 15. Second, the developer can encode constraint enforcement into update programs. In addition, forms can be designed to eliminate errors. A twenty-five-character text field can be displayed in a window of only twenty-five spaces, for example. Menus can be designed so that only those commands suitable for a particular context can be executed in it.

Security and integrity protection must be incorporated into the applications from the start. All too often this is done only after problems have been detected, and at this point, it is usually far more difficult to implement such protection.

■ A Continuum of Applications

A database application is the interface between the user and the database. Although all applications have the functions described in the previous section, not all are equivalent. In fact, there is a continuum of applications. On the high end, some provide extensive services on behalf of the user. They obtain data from several relations, combine it in accordance with an object structure, and display and manage updates of the data in a sophisticated GUI. While doing this, the application is constantly monitoring database integrity, ensuring that the user is not violating any constraints, and performing only authorized activities. All of these activities are organized and structured so as to maximize the application's performance.

At the other end of the spectrum are applications that do little more than list tables. In Chapter 10, in our discussion of SQL, we point out that the sophisticated end user could use this language as a bare-bones application. But such an application would only process data in tables; there would be little formatting, no object structuring, and little data integrity checking.

■ Overview of Application Development

There are many ways to design database applications. Indeed, this subject has been discussed extensively in the literature. In this section, we present only an overview of an object-oriented method of designing an application.

Figure 8-5 summarizes the general process of developing database applications. It has three steps: requirements, design, and implementation.

FIGURE 8-5

Principal Steps in Developing
Database Applications

Requirements Phase
  Interview users
  Build data flow diagrams
  Determine data flows
  Determine processes that operate on data flows
  Specify application groups

Design Phase
  Design application control facilities
  Design forms
  Design reports
  Specify program logic

Implementation Phase
  Build applications
    with DBMS application facilities
    with code generation systems
    with programming

During requirements, the functions of applications are determined. As shown in Figure 8-5, data flow diagrams are constructed out of business activities and show the necessary data flows and processes. Often, especially for organizational and large work-group databases, requirements are divided into groups, each of which is then referred to as a particular application. For example, a personnel and payroll system might be divided into *administration, compensation,* and *benefits* applications.

Once the application functions are known, the applications are designed. The term **application design** covers more than the design of application programs' structure and logic. It also applies to the design of the user interfaces: control facilities such as commands and menus, the structure and behavior of forms, and the definition of reports.

Once the application(s) has been designed, it is implemented in a variety of ways. On one end of the continuum, programs may be written entirely from scratch using a third-generation language like COBOL; at the other end, the default application facilities of the DBMS may be used. In between these extremes are applications that combine application-specific programming with DBMS-provided forms and reports. In this chapter we are concerned with only the design phase of application development, in particular, the design of the database and of the applications that process it.

OBJECT AND VIEW MATERIALIZATION

One of the functions of a database application is to materialize objects. To understand this, consider the objects in Figure 8-2(a). Suppose that the gallery has just received a shipment of Mark Tobey lithographs and that the salespeople in the gallery want to know which customers have expressed an interest in Tobey's works. In this case, the salespeople do not want a list of all of the attributes in ARTIST; they just want the names and phone numbers of those customers who are interested in Mark Tobey. An example is shown in Figure 8-6.

To produce the list in Figure 8-6, the database application must construct the object from the underlying relations. It must find the row in ARTIST for Mark Tobey, find all of the rows in the CUSTOMER-ARTIST-INT table that pertain to Mark Tobey, and, from each row, extract the value of CustNumber (according to the design in Figure 8-2[b]). This value of CustNumber is then used to look up the customers' names and phone numbers in the CUSTOMER table.

The process just described is what is meant by materializing an object. In general, such materialization is one of the most important functions of an application, as it saves the user from having to understand all of the tables and from learning how to bring the data in those tables together.

FIGURE 8-6

List of Customers Interested in a Given Artist

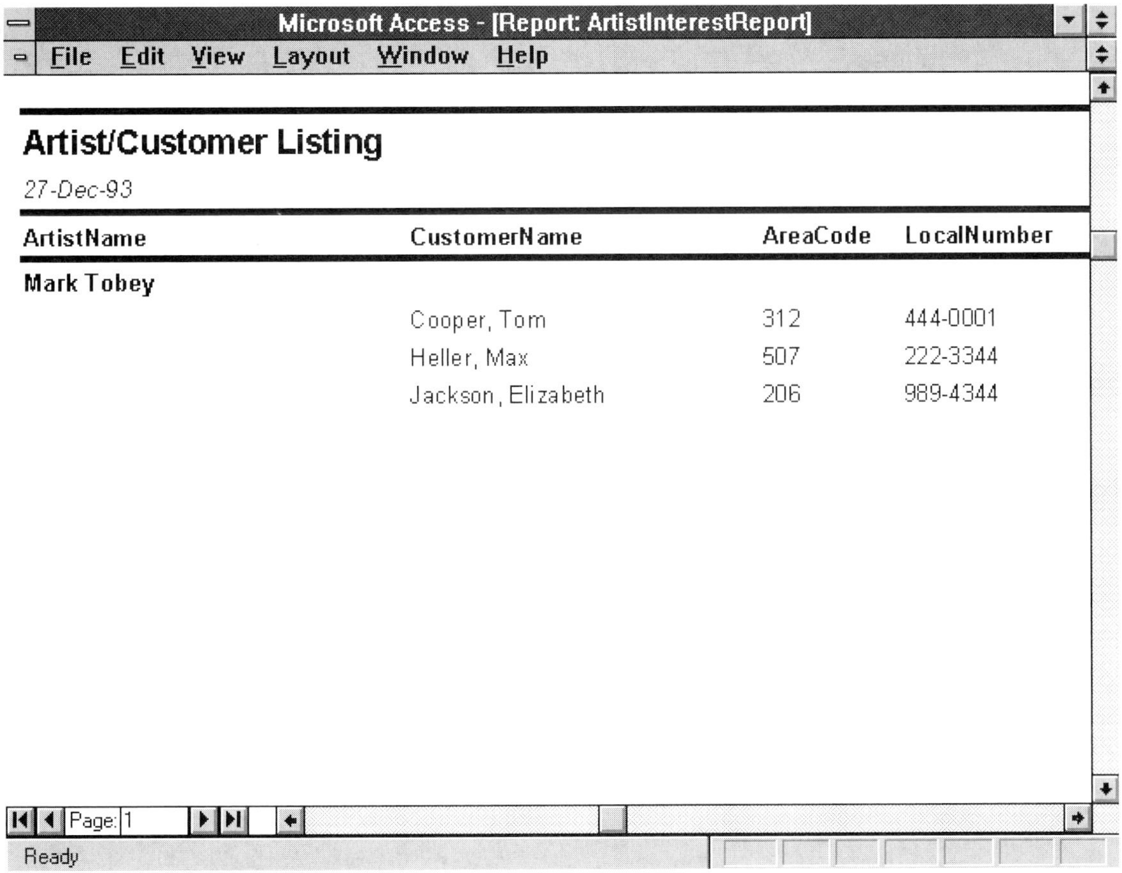

ArtistName	CustomerName	AreaCode	LocalNumber
Mark Tobey			
	Cooper, Tom	312	444-0001
	Heller, Max	507	222-3344
	Jackson, Elizabeth	206	989-4344

FIGURE 8-7

Hierarchical Relationships of Object, View, and Materialization

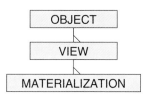

Object Views

As it turns out, in most applications, the users seldom want to see all of the data in an object at any one time; they usually want to process a subset of the object's data. In Figure 8-6, for example, the salespeople did not want to see all of Mark Tobey's works, nor did they want to see all of the data about customers interested in Mark Tobey. They wanted only a subset of the ARTIST data.

The need to process subsets of objects occurs because although the users process the same object, they often do not see this object from the same perspective. For instance, the needs of salespeople who want to know who might buy a Tobey lithograph are different from those of the gallery's owner, who wants to know how profitable Tobey's work has been for the gallery.

An **object view,** or **user view** or **view,** is a named subset of an object that a particular user or group of users uses. A view is described by naming the object on which it is based and listing the attributes of the object that are visible from that view.

The definition of views is especially important to security and control. With views, sensitive data can be hidden from all but authorized users. For example, a personnel administration system contains an object called EMPLOYEE, which includes Salary. Because not all users may need to work with Salary data, one view can be defined for the EMPLOYEE object to enable those who need Salary to see it, and another view can be defined without Salary for those who do not need its data.

A view is a list of an object's visible attributes. In most cases, users want more than just a list of attribute values; they also want the view data to be formatted. That is, they want labels, lines, boxes, indentations, control breaks, and the like. A view plus this formatting data is called a **materialization.** Normally, object views are processed by application programs that add the formatting data to produce the materialization, and so we can restate one of the purposes of an application program to be to produce materializations of views of objects.

To summarize, a view is a list of attributes of an object. A materialization of a view is a view plus formatting data that exhibits that view in a particular format. Objects, views, and materializations have a hierarchical relationship, as shown in Figure 8-7. An object can have many views, and each view can have many materializations. In most cases, the application program receives the view data and constructs the materialization.

FORM DESIGN

A **form** is a screen display that is most often used for data entry and edit. Forms can also be used to report data, but in most cases, when developers speak of forms, they mean those used for data entry and edit.

Some forms are easy to use and result in few data entry errors. Others seem awkward and contrived and are difficult to use without creating errors. In this section, we discuss and illustrate several principles of good form design.

■ The Form Structure Should Reflect the Object Structure

First, to seem natural and be easy to use, *the structure of a form must reflect the structure of the object that it materializes.* Look at the form in Figure 8-8, which is a materialization of a view of the CUSTOMER object in the View Ridge database (Figure 8-2[a]).

The structure of this form reflects the structure of the CUSTOMER object. One section of the form has the basic customer data such as Name, Phone, and Address. The second section shows the customer's ARTIST interests. Finally, the third section lists the customer's purchases (of WORKs). Users find this form easy to use because the attributes are grouped in a way that reflects their understanding of the structure of the customer data.

In general, when designing a form, all of the data from a single relation should be placed in one contiguous section of the form. Assuming that the database is in

FIGURE 8-8

Materialization of View of CUSTOMER Object

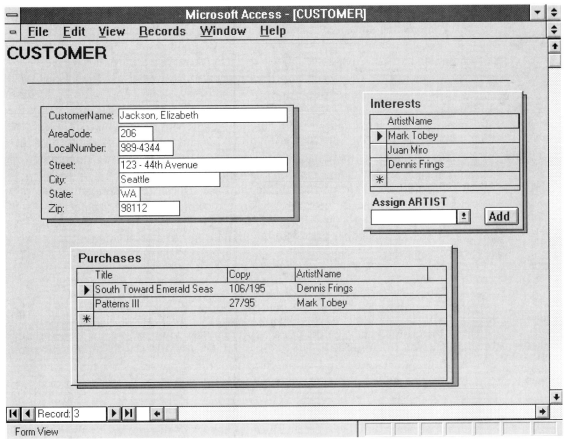

domain/key normal form (which it should be), each relation should pertain to a specific theme, and the user should expect to have in one location all of the data for that theme. Thus CUSTOMER, ARTIST (labeled Interests), and WORK (labeled Purchases) are contiguous on the form in Figure 8-8.

There is one exception to this rule: Attributes in the base relation of the object (here, the relation CUSTOMER) are sometimes not placed contiguously. Suppose, for example, that CUSTOMER had a simple attribute named TotalPurchases. If we followed this rule, we would place TotalPurchases in the first section of the form. But it would be more sensible to the users to place that attribute at the end of the form, after all of the purchases have been listed.

The form in Figure 8-8 is not the only acceptable form of this view. Purchases could be placed before Interests, for example. The base CUSTOMER data could be rearranged to be more horizontal in appearance. CustomerName, AreaCode, and LocalNumber could be placed in one column, and Street, City, State, and Zip could be placed in another. All of these alternatives enable the structure of the form to reflect the structure of the underlying objects.

The Semantics of the Data Should Be Graphically Clear

Another characteristic of a well-designed form is that the semantics of the data are graphically clear. Consider the base customer data section of the CUSTOMER form in Figure 8-8. Observe that there is a small space between the data entry box for CustomerName and AreaCode but that there is no such space between AreaCode and LocalNumber. In fact, AreaCode and LocalNumber are placed adjacent to each other, and Street, City, State, and Zip are also placed adjacent to one another.

To understand why this is done, refer again to Figure 8-2(a). The CUSTOMER semantic object has a group attribute named Phone and another group attribute named Address. Since both of these attributes have a maximum cardinality of 1, they are—from the standpoint of the relational design—not really required. In fact, they do not appear in the relations in Figure 8-2(b) or (c). The only purpose of these group attributes is to semantically associate AreaCode with LocalNumber and Street and City, State, and Zip with one another.

The purpose of the vertical spacing in the CUSTOMER form is to make these associations graphically clear. Most users are comforted by the arrangement of the attributes in the CUSTOMER form. Knowing that phone number consists of AreaCode and LocalNumber, they find the graphically close association of those two to be very sensible.

The Form Structure Should Encourage Appropriate Action

The structure of forms should make it easy to perform appropriate actions and difficult to perform inappropriate or erroneous actions. For example, the field for entering State in the form in Figure 8-8 is small. Clearly, the user is supposed to enter only a two-digit state abbreviation. But a better design would allow only two digits to be entered, and the best design would present the states in a drop-down list and allow the user to choose from only that list.

In Figure 8-8, some fields in the form are white, and others are gray. The forms in this application have been designed so that the user can enter data only in the white spaces; the gray data items cannot be changed. Thus the user cannot type into the

Interests grid and instead must select from the combo box at the bottom of the grid. When the user clicks on the arrow, a drop-down list of available artists is displayed, as shown in Figure 8-9. If the user wants to add a new artist, he or she presses the button labeled Add, and the application brings the artist form to the screen.

Now suppose that the user wants to change some artist data—say the spelling of Mark Tobey's name. The designer of the form in Figure 8-8 made it impossible to change that data in this form. Instead, the user places the mouse pointer on the name Mark Tobey and double-clicks the left button on the mouse. When this is done, the application displays the ARTIST form shown in Figure 8-10. The user can then change the spelling of Mark Tobey in this form.

The form in Figure 8-8 cannot be used to change artist data, but the one in Figure 8-10 can. Why? The relationship between ARTIST and CUSTOMER is many to many. If the user could change artist data from the CUSTOMER form, the user would be changing data not only for this particular customer's linkage to that artist but also for all customers' linkages to that artist. This action, however, is not apparent in the form in Figure 8-8. According to that form, the user is aware only that Elizabeth Jackson is somehow connected to Mark Tobey.

FIGURE 8-9

Form with Drop-down List Box

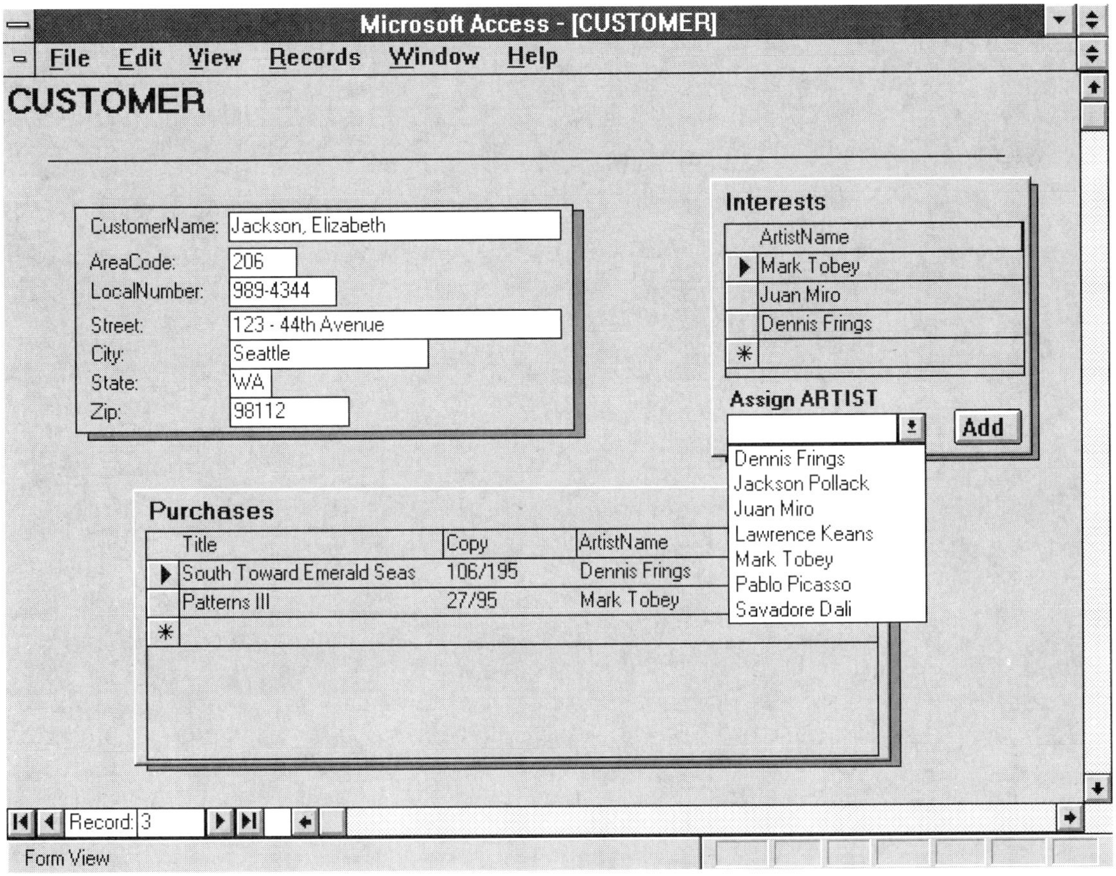

FIGURE 8-10

Materialization of View of ARTIST Object

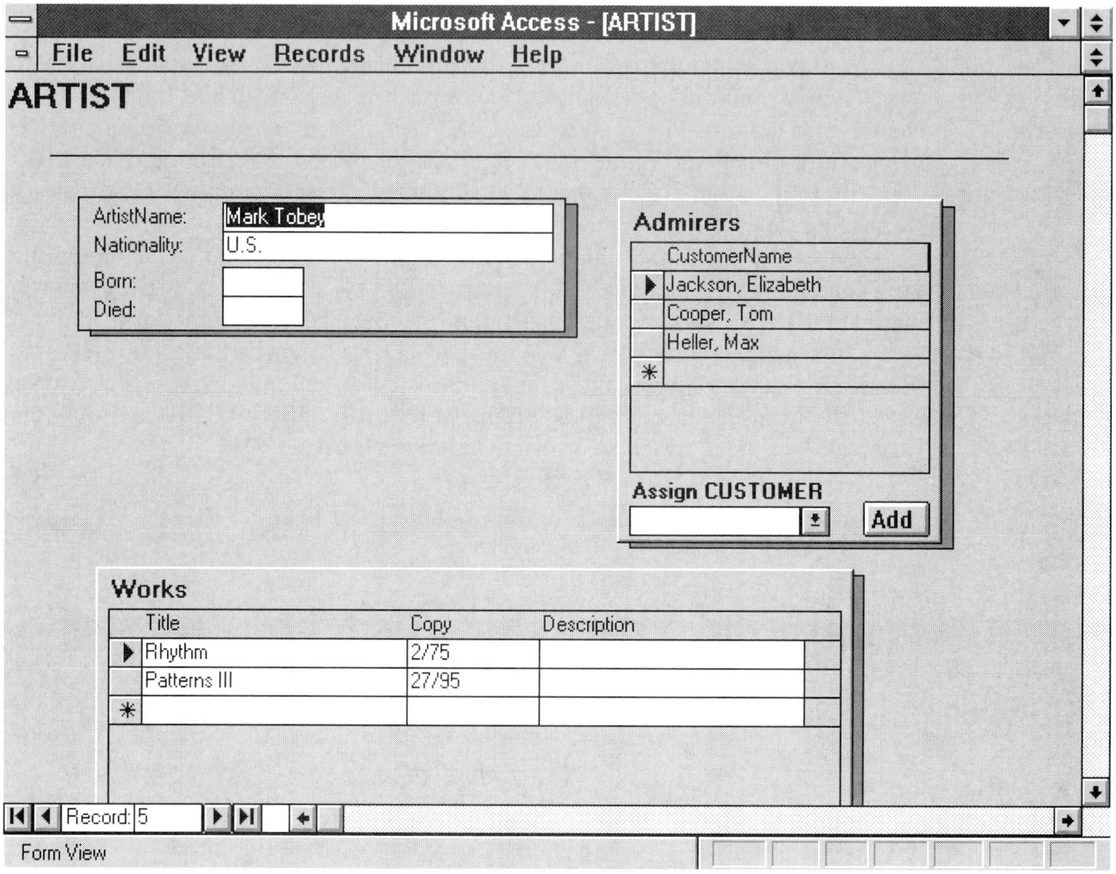

When making changes in the artist data using the form in Figure 8-10, however, the user is aware that this change is affecting not only Elizabeth Jackson but also Tom Cooper and Max Heller. The structure of the forms thus makes it difficult for the user to make mistakes that he or she may or may not know are mistakes.

■ Forms in a GUI Environment

A number of form features peculiar to GUI systems can dramatically facilitate the use of database applications.

DROP-DOWN LIST BOXES

A drop-down list box is a GUI control that presents a list of items from which the user can choose. There are two types of list boxes. With one type, the list is fixed; users cannot add to it. With the other, users can both add to and select from the list. The choice between the two types depends on the requirements of the application. The list box shown in Figure 8-9 has a fixed list; the users cannot add to the list.

List boxes have a number of advantages over data entry text boxes. First, human beings find it easier to *recognize* than to *recollect*. For example, in the form in Figure 8-9, it is easier to choose an artist's name from the list than it is to remember all of the artists' names. It is also easier to recognize a name than it is to spell it correctly. Finally, list boxes can be set up to display only those values present in the database, which means that the user cannot enter an invalid item.

OPTION BUTTONS AND GROUPS

An **option button,** or **radio button,** is a display device that enables users to select one alternative condition or state from a list of possibilities. For example, suppose the gallery decides that it needs to track the tax status of its customers. Assume that tax status has two possibilities, Taxable and Nontaxable, and that these possibilities are mutually exclusive. An option group like the one shown in Figure 8-11 could be used to gather this data. Because of the way that the option group works, if the user selects Taxable, then Nontaxable is automatically removed from the list. If the user selects Nontaxable, then Taxable is automatically removed.

FIGURE 8-11

CUSTOMER Form with Option Button Group

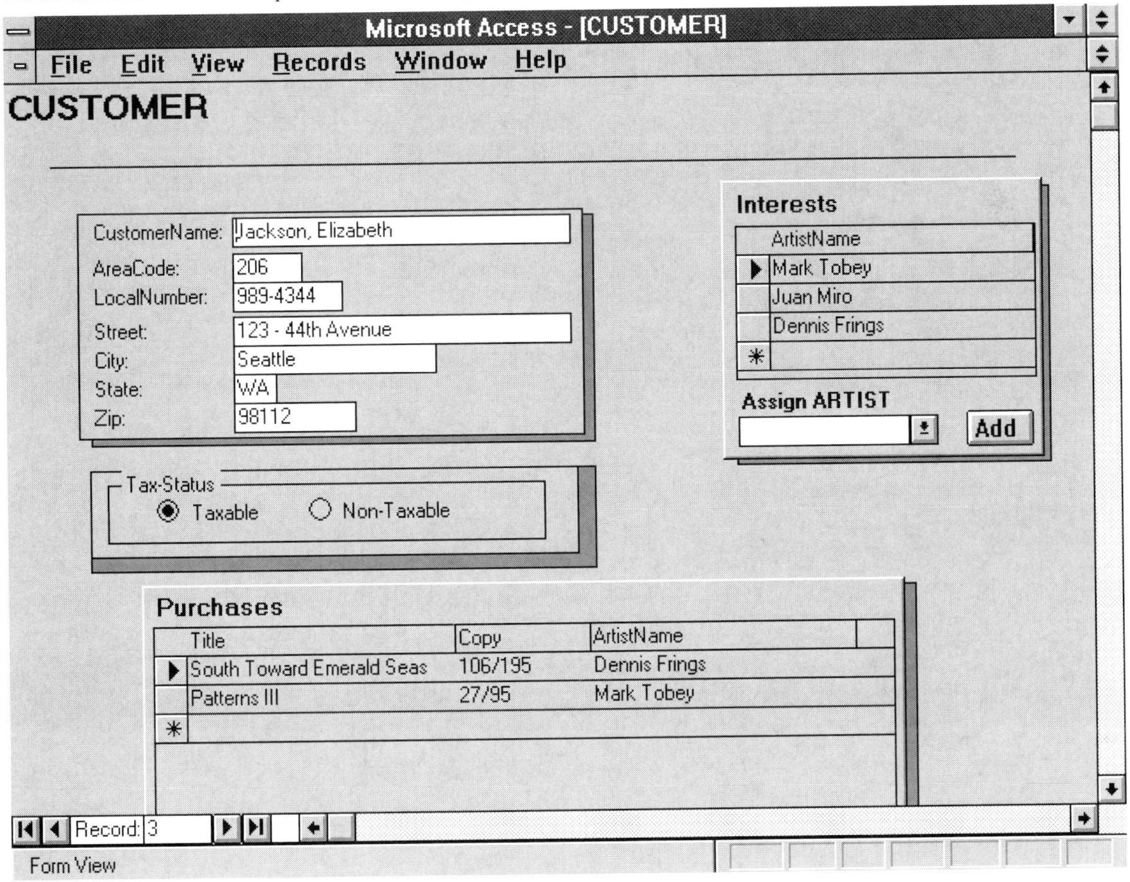

Behind the form, the application program must store data in a table column that represents the radio button selected. For this example, the column is named TaxStatus. One of two possible ways for storing the option button data is used. One is to store an integer number from 1 to the number of buttons. In this example, one of the values 1 or 2 would be stored. The second option is to store a text value that describes the option chosen. The possibilities are Yes or No.

CHECK BOXES

Check boxes are similar to option buttons except that the alternatives in a group of check boxes are not mutually exclusive—more than one alternative may be chosen. Suppose, for example, that the gallery wants to record the type or types of art in which its customers are interested. The possible types are Lithographs, Oils, Pastels, and Photographs, shown in a series of check boxes in the version of the CUSTOMER form in Figure 8-12. The user selects or *checks* the appropriate boxes.

There are a number of ways of representing check boxes in relations. One common and simple way is to define a Boolean-valued column for each item in the

FIGURE 8-12

CUSTOMER Form with Check Boxes

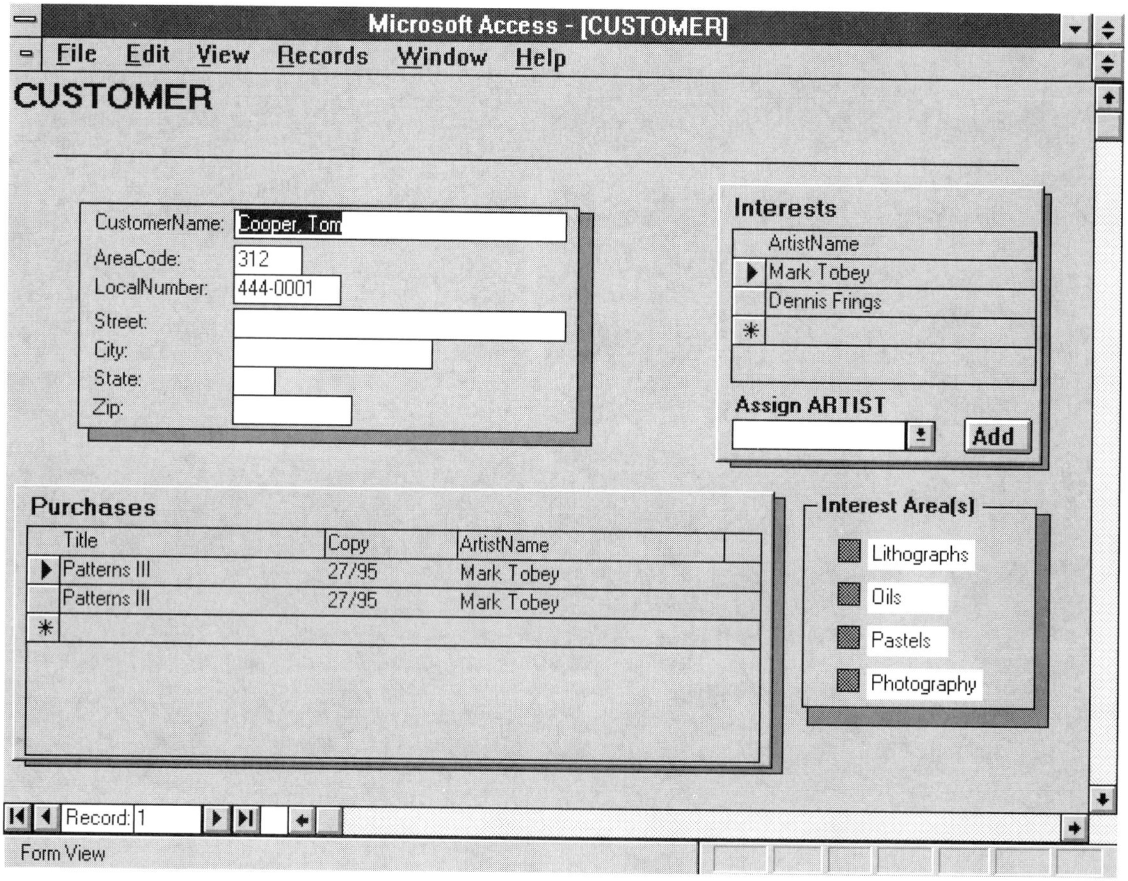

check box group. The value of each of such columns is binary; that is, it can be 1 or 0, representing yes or no. There are other possibilities, such as encoding bits in a byte, although they are not important to our discussion.

■ Cursor Movement and Pervasive Keys

Another consideration in forms design is the action of the cursor. The cursor should move through the form easily and naturally. This usually means that the cursor follows the end user's processing pattern as he or she reads the source data entry documents. If forms are used to enter data over the telephone, the cursor should control the flow of the conversation. In this case, its movement should progress in a manner that the customer finds natural and appropriate.

Now let us turn to the action of the cursor during and after an exception condition. Suppose that in using the form in Figure 8-10, an error is made—perhaps an invalid state code is entered. The form should be processed so that the cursor moves to a logical location. For example, the application might display a list box of available state values and place the cursor on a logical position in the list—perhaps on the first state that starts with the first letter the user entered. When the state is selected, the cursor should move back to Zip, the next appropriate space on the form.

The actions of special-purpose keys such as ESC and function keys should be *consistent* and *pervasive*. If ESC is used to exit forms, use it consistently for this purpose and none other (except for actions that are logically equivalent to exiting from forms). The actions of the keys should be consistent throughout the application. That is, if ESC is used to exit from one form, it should be used to exit from all forms. If F1 is used to delete data in one form, it should be used to delete data in all forms. Otherwise, habits formed in one portion of the application must be disregarded or relearned in other portions of the application. This is wasteful, frustrating, and aggravating, and it causes errors. Although these comments may seem obvious, attention to such details is what makes a form easy and convenient to use.

REPORT DESIGN

The subject of report design, even more so than form design, has been discussed extensively in texts on application development. We will not duplicate or even attempt to summarize those discussions here but, rather, look at several concepts directly related to the notion of a report as a materialization of a semantic object.

■ Report Structure

The principles of effective report design are similar to those for form design. In fact, it is possible to consider a report as a display-only form. Just as forms should, *the structure of a report should reflect the structure of the underlying object.* This means that data from one table should generally be located in one contiguous group on the report. As with forms, one exception to this rule is that the base relation of the object (for example, the CUSTOMER relation for the CUSTOMER object), may be separated on the report. Attribute groups, like Phone, should also be located together and distinguished in some way.

Figure 8-13 shows a sample report for the View Ridge Gallery—the data for each work of art and the transaction for each work of art—and computes the gross margin by work and artist, as well a grand total.

The structure of the report in Figure 8-13 reflects the structure of the WORK object. The section for each work begins with the name of the work, which includes artist, title, and copy. Next is a section of repeating lines that shows the transactions for the work. Within each section, the name of the customer has been found from the CUSTOMER table.

We describe in Chapter 11 how this report is produced. For now, just note that its structure does, in fact, reflect the fundamental structure of the object. Because of this characteristic, the report seems useful and familiar to its users.

FIGURE 8-13

Sales Listing Report

Sales Listing
15-Nov-93

ArtistName	Title		Copy		
Dennis Frings	**South Toward Emerald Sea**		**106/195**		
DateAcquired	AcquisitionPrice	DateSold	Sold To	SalesPrice	GrossMargin
4/17/86	$750.00	5/3/86	Heller, Max	$1,000.00	$250.00
3/15/93	$1,200.00	5/11/93	Jackson, Elizabeth	$1,800.00	$600.00
	Total margin for South Toward Emerald Seas, Copy 106/195				$850.00
	Total margin for Dennis Frings				$850.00
Mark Tobey	**Patterns III**		**27/95**		
DateAcquired	AcquisitionPrice	DateSold	Sold To	SalesPrice	GrossMargin
7/3/71	$7,500.00	9/11/71	Cooper, Tom	$10,000.00	$2,500.00
1/4/86	$11,500.00	3/18/86	Jackson, Elizabeth	$15,000.00	$3,500.00
9/11/91	$17,000.00	10/17/91	Cooper, Tom	$21,000.00	$4,000.00
	Total margin for Patterns III, Copy 27/95				$10,000.00
Mark Tobey	**Rhythm**		**2/75**		
DateAcquired	AcquisitionPrice	DateSold	Sold To	SalesPrice	GrossMargin
4/8/90	$17,000.00	7/14/90	Heller, Max	$27,000.00	$10,000.00
	Total margin for Rhythm, Copy 2/75				$10,000.00
	Total margin for Mark Tobey				$20,000.00
	Grand Total:				$20,850.00

■ Implied Objects

Consider the request "Print all WORKs Sorted by Total Margin." At first glance, this appears to be a request to print a report about the object WORK. The words *sorted by*, however, indicate that more than one WORK is to be considered. In fact, this request is not based on the object WORK but, rather, is based on the object SET OF ALL WORKs. The report in Figure 8-13 shows data for multiple WORKs and is, in fact, based on the object SET OF ALL WORKs, not on the object WORK.

The human mind is so quick to shift from the object *OBJECT-A* to the object *SET OF ALL OBJECTS-A* that we normally do not even know there has been a change. When developing database applications, however, it is important to notice this shift. It is also important to classify the shift. Consider three ways in which sorting can change the nature of the base object: (1) sorting by object identifier; (2) sorting by nonidentifier, nonobject columns; and (3) sorting by attributes contained in object attributes.

SORTED BY OBJECT IDENTIFIER

If the report is to be sorted by an attribute that is an identifier of object, the true object is a simple collection of those objects. Thus an ARTIST report sorted by ArtistName is a report about the object SET OF ALL ARTISTS. For most DBMS report-writing products, a report about the object SET OF ALL X is no more difficult to produce than a report about object X. It is important to know, however, that there has been a shift in object type.

SORTED BY NONIDENTIFIER, NONOBJECT COLUMNS

When a user needs a report sorted by an attribute that is a nonidentifier of the object, the true object in the user's mind is most likely a totally different type of object. For example, the user wants to produce a report about ARTIST sorted by Nationality. Such a report is actually a materialization of a NATIONALITY object, not a materialization of the ARTIST object. Similarly, if the user asks for a report about CUSTOMER sorted by AreaCode, the report is actually based on an object called PHONE-REGION, or some similar object. Figure 8-14 shows an example PHONE-REGION implied object.

Some objects such as NATIONALITY or PHONE-REGION are **implied objects**; that is, their existence can be inferred by the fact that the user asked for such a report. If it makes sense to the user to ask for something as a sort value, then that something must be an object in the user's mind, regardless of whether it is modeled in the database or not.

FIGURE 8-14

PHONE-REGION Implied Object

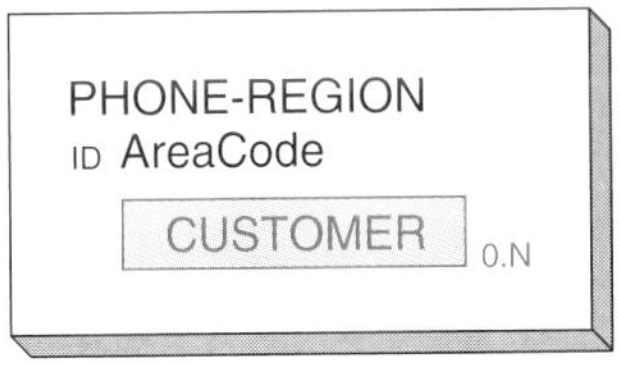

SORTED BY ATTRIBUTES CONTAINED IN OBJECT ATTRIBUTES

The third way in which reports can be sorted is by attributes contained in object attributes. For example, the user might ask for a report about WORKs sorted by Birthdate of ARTIST. ARTIST is an object attribute of WORK, and Birthdate is an attribute contained in ARTIST. In this case, the user is actually asking for a report about an implied object (say TIME or ARTISTIC PERIOD) that contains many ARTISTs, each of which includes many WORKs in the gallery.

Understanding this switch in objects may ease the task of developing the report. Proceeding as if WORK were the base object of the report will make the report logic contrived. If WORK is considered the base, the materializations of WORK objects that include ARTIST and Birthdate must be created for all WORK objects, stored on disk, and then sorted by Birthdate. On the other hand, if this report is about an implied object that contains ARTIST, which in turn contains WORK, then ARTIST objects can be created and sorted by Birthdate and WORK objects treated as multivalued rows in each ARTIST object.

APPLICATION PROGRAM DESIGN

Literally hundreds of books have been written about application program design, and so it is not necessary here to summarize even the basic schools of thought concerning this subject. Instead, we focus only on those aspects of program design that pertain directly to database processing.

■ The Structure of Application Program Logic

Some experts, notably Michael Jackson and those who follow his line of reasoning, state that the structure of a program should mirror the structure of the data that it processes.[1] If one adheres to that design philosophy, the data model and database design will offer rich and valuable guidelines for designing the structure of application logic.

Consider, for example, an application program that displays a CUSTOMER object. Pseudocode for the logic of such a program is shown in Figure 8-15. Observe the similarity in the structure of the object and that of the pseudocode. In the first section, the program obtains a value for the key of CUSTOMER. Then the customer data is displayed, and a grid is set up to show the multivalued attribute WORK.

Next the program loops through all of the WORK rows that have CustNumber equal to the given number. For each such row, the identifying data is displayed, and ARTIST Nationality is obtained and displayed. Then another grid and loop are set up to process each of the TRANSACTION rows that pertain to this particular WORK.

In general, any program that processes a multivalued attribute must contain an iteration logic structure for that attribute. If there are nested multivalued attributes, there will be nested iterations, and if there are serial multivalued attributes, there will be serial iterations in the program.

---

[1] Michael Jackson, *Principles of Program Design* (New York: Academic Press, 1975).

FIGURE 8-15

Pseudocode for Program to Display CUSTOMER and Related WORK Objects

Get CustNumber from User.

Display form headings for CUSTOMER.

Read CUSTOMER table using CustNumber as key.

Display Name, AreaCode, LocalNumber, Street, City State, Zip on form.

Read First WORK row using CustNumber as foreign key.

Display column headings for WORK display grid.

Do Until WORK.EndOfFile.

  Display ArtistName, Title, Copy, Description on form.

  Read ARTIST row using ArtistName as key.

  Display ArtistName, Nationality on form.

  Read First TRANSACTION row using (ArtistName, Title, Copy) as p
  key.

  Display column headings for TRANSACTION display grid.

  Do Until TRANSACTION.EndOfFile.

    Display DateAcquired, AcquisitionPrice, PurchaseDate, SalesPric
    on form.

    Read Next TRANSACTION row using (ArtistName, Title, Copy) a:
    partial key.

  End Do.

  Display Column footings for TRANSACTION display grid.

  Read Next WORK row using CustNumber as foreign key.

End Do.

Display column footings for WORK display grid.

[Logic to process the ARTIST property of CUSTOMER could go here.}

Display column footings for CUSTOMER form.

Relationship Constraint Checking

The processing of updates for database applications differs in one important regard from the processing of updates in nondatabase applications: When processing updates, the application must be certain to preserve the constraints defined in the

Example of a Mandatory-to-Mandatory Constraint: (a) Sample Mandatory-to-Mandatory Relationship and (b) Sample Data for It

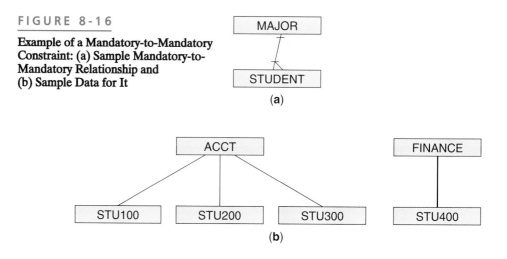

database data. In this section we consider constraints that arise from relationships, and in the next, we look at other types of constraints.

Figure 8-16 depicts the relationship between MAJOR and STUDENT relations. As shown, a MAJOR must have at least one STUDENT, and a STUDENT must have exactly one MAJOR. When users update either of these relations, the application program must make sure that these constraints are not violated (we assume in this section that such checking is not done by the DBMS). In Figure 8-16(b), for example, if a user attempted to delete the row for Student 400, the application program should deny this request. If the request were allowed, the row for FINANCE would not have a child row, and the mandatory constraint would be violated. Similarly, a new MAJOR, say BIOLOGY, cannot be added until there is a student who is majoring in that subject.

A row that exists inappropriately without a required parent or child is sometimes called a **fragment**, and child rows that exist without a mandatory parent are sometimes called **orphans.** One of the functions of an application program is to prevent the creation of fragments and orphans.

TYPES OF RELATIONSHIP CONSTRAINT

The means of preventing fragments depends on the type of constraint. Figure 8-17 shows examples of the four possible kinds of constraints: mandatory to mandatory (M–M), mandatory to optional (M–O), optional to mandatory (O–M), and optional to optional (O–O). These constraints are shown on one-to-many relationships, but the same four types also apply to one-to-one relationships. We need not be concerned with many-to-many relationships constraints, as they will have been converted to one-to-many relationships by defining the intersection tables.

Constraints can be violated whenever there are changes in the key attributes (whether local or foreign), because changes in key values have the effect of changing the parent–child relationship. For example, in Figure 8-15(b), changing the major of Student 300 from ACCT to FINANCE reassigns that student to the finance department. Although this results in a change of parent, it does not cause a constraint violation.

FIGURE 8-17

Examples of the Four Types of Relationship Constraints: (a) Mandatory-to-Mandatory (M–M) Constraint, (b) Mandatory-to-Optional (M–O) Constraint, (c) Optional-to-Mandatory (O–M) Constraint, and (d) Optional-to-Optional (O–O) Constraint

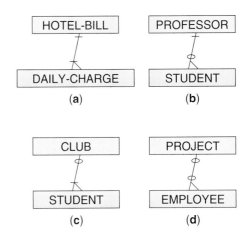

Such a violation will be committed, however, if the major of Student 400 is changed to ACCT. When this is done, FINANCE no longer has any majors, and so the M–M constraint between MAJOR and STUDENT is violated. As another example, in Figure 8-17(a), a change in the HOTEL-BILL InvoiceNumber invalidates the relationship carried by the foreign key, InvoiceNumber, in DAILY-CHARGE. All of the DAILY-CHARGE rows for the changed invoice become orphans.

Figure 8-18 presents rules for preventing fragments for each of these types of constraints. Figure 8-18(a) concerns actions on the parent row, and Figure 8-18(b) concerns actions on the child rows. As these figures indicate, we want to insert new rows, modify key data, and delete rows. Figure 8-18 lists the rules for one-to-many relationships; the rules for one-to-one relationships are similar.

RESTRICTIONS ON UPDATES TO PARENT ROWS

The first row of Figure 8-18(a) concerns M–M constraints. A new parent row can be inserted only if at least one child row is being created at the same time, which can be done by inserting a new child row or by reassigning a child from a different parent (however, this latter action may itself cause a constraint violation).

A change in the key of a parent is permitted in an M–M relationship only if the values in the corresponding foreign key in the child rows also are changed in the new value. (It is possible to reassign all of the children to another parent and then create at least one new child for the parent, but this seldom is done.) Thus, changing the Invoice in HOTEL-BILL is allowed as long as the Invoice is changed in all the appropriate DAY-CHARGE rows as well.

Finally, a parent of an M–M relationship can be deleted as long as all of the children also are deleted or are reassigned.

In regard to M–O constraints, a new parent can be added without restriction, since parents need not have children. For the relationship in Figure 8-17(b), a new PROFESSOR row can be added without restriction. A change in the parent's key value, however, is permitted only if the corresponding values in the child rows are changed as well. If a PROFESSOR in the relationship in Figure 8-17(b) changes his or her key, the value of Adviser in all of that professor's advisees' rows also must be changed.

FIGURE 8-18

Rules for Preventing Fragments: (a) Conditions for Allowing Changes in Parent Records and (b) Conditions for Allowing Changes in Child Records

Proposed Action on Parent

		Insert	Modify (key)	Delete
	M-M	Create at least one child	Change matching keys of all children	Delete all children OR Reassign all children
Type of Rela-tionship	M-O	OK	Change matching keys of all children	Delete all children OR Reassign all children
	O-M	Insert new child OR Appropriate child exists	Change key of at least one child OR Appropriate child exists	OK
	O-O	OK	OK	OK

(a)

Proposed Action on Child

		Insert	Modify (key)	Delete
	M-M	Parent exists OR Create parent	Parent with new value exists (or create one) AND Sibling exists	Sibling exists
Type of Rela-tionship	M-O	Parent exists OR Create parent	Parent with new value exists OR Create parent	OK
	O-M	OK	Sibling exists	Sibling exists
	O-O	OK	OK	OK

(b)

Finally, in a relationship with an M–O constraint, the parent row can be deleted only if all the children are deleted or reassigned. For the PROFESSOR–STUDENT relationship, all of the student rows would probably be reassigned.

For O–M constraints, a parent can be inserted only if at least one child is added at the same time or if an appropriate child already exists. For the O–M relationship between CLUB and STUDENT in Figure 8-17(c), for example, a new club can be added only if an appropriate STUDENT row can be created (by either adding a new student or changing the value of Club in an existing STUDENT). Alternatively, an appropriate student row may already exist.

Similarly, the key of the parent of an O–M relationship may be changed only if a child is created or if a suitable child row already exists. That is, the Ski Club can change its name to Scuba only if at least one skier is willing to join Scuba or if a student has already enrolled in Scuba. There are no restrictions on the deletion of a parent row in an O–M relationship.

The last type of relationship constraint, O–O, is shown in Figure 8-17(d). There are no restrictions on any type of update on rows in an O–O relationship. Both PROJECT and EMPLOYEE rows can be updated as necessary.

RESTRICTIONS ON UPDATING CHILD ROWS

The rules for preventing fragments when updating child rows are shown in Figure 8-18(b) and are similar to those in Figure 8-18(a). The one notable difference is that in several cases, child rows can be modified or deleted as long as sibling rows exist. For example, in an M–M constraint, a child row can be deleted as long as there are siblings in existence. (The last child never leaves home!) For the M–M constraint in Figure 8-17(a), a particular DAY-CHARGE row can be deleted as long as at least one remains.

With the exception of the considerations regarding siblings, the rules for avoiding fragments when processing child rows are similar to those for parents. Make certain you understand each statement in Figure 8-18(b).

Many of the rules in Figure 8-18 offer several alternatives, and so the application program developer must select one of them. The choice depends on the requirements of the application. The point to remember is that you must consider such constraints when designing and developing application programs.

■ Other Types of Constraint Checking

There are types of constraints besides those that arise from relationships. One common constraint is uniqueness. In some cases, the values of attributes or of composites of attributes must be unique. Many DBMS products are capable of enforcing this type of constraint, and if so, the application program is freed of the burden.

With regard to uniqueness, observe that requiring the composite (AreaCode, LocalNumber) to be unique is different from requiring the attributes (AreaCode) and (LocalNumber) to be independently unique. The second case is far more restrictive than the first. For example, in the first case, there can be only one (206, 325–1876). In the second case, there can be only one 206 and only one 325–1876. Some DBMS products do not support composite uniqueness, and as you can see, this can be a problem.

Another common type of constraint is null values, or unknown values. For example, if the value of ShippingMode is null, this means that the shipping mode is unknown. Null is not the same as zero (for numeric attributes) or a blank (for text attributes).

Nulls can arise in one of two ways. Either no value has ever been entered into the database, or no value is appropriate. These two are not logically the same. If ShippingMode has the value null, it might mean that the mode of shipment is unknown or that a value is inappropriate. A SALES-ORDER used for consulting services does not have a meaningful ShippingMode.

We discuss nulls further in later chapters. For now, it is enough to know that some DBMS products can enforce the constraint that *nulls are not allowed*. Others cannot, however, and in that case, the enforcement is up to the application program.

Finally, some constraints do not fall into any of these types. There might be the constraint that if the SALESPERSON resides in a region east of the Mississippi, the value of ShippingMode cannot equal 1-Day. Few DBMS products provide robust means of defining and enforcing such constraints. Today, almost all products require that such constraints be written into the application program.

■ The Use of Application Programs in Backup and Recovery

We address strategies for providing backup and recovery in Chapter 15. For now, however, you should know that the backup and recovery of concurrently processed databases requires application programs to define transaction boundaries to the DBMS. These boundaries, called **logical transactions** or **logical units of work,** define a set of atomic actions. By atomic, we mean that either all of the actions are performed or none of them is.

To understand the need for atomicity, suppose that a user is entering data for a new WORK, and after several TRANSACTIONS have been created, the computer system fails. In this case, only a portion of the WORK data has been entered into the database. When the system recovers and the user reenters the WORK, it is possible that some TRANSACTIONs will be duplicated.

To prevent this from happening, the application program can define boundaries of atomicity for the DBMS. The means by which this is done varies from DBMS product to DBMS product, but in general, before processing any transactions, the application issues a command like START TRANSACTION (other terms are used synonymously). Then the application program processes the users' requests to a logically consistent end point (the end of a WORK object, for example).

If all processing has been done correctly, the application program will issue a command like END TRANSACTION, COMMIT, or some other equivalent command. At this point, the DBMS makes permanent all the changes in the database. If there has been a problem during processing, the application program will issue a command like ROLL BACK, thus telling the DBMS to remove all the changes made since the START TRANSACTION command. If the application program is abnormally terminated because of a system failure or an unexpected program termination, no END TRANSACTION command will be received, and the DBMS will remove the provisional changes.

The reason for introducing this topic here is that the definition of an object also defines the boundaries of the logical transaction. The start transaction is issued when the application program begins work on the object, and the end transaction is issued when all the object attributes have been processed.

SUMMARY

The purpose of a database application is to create, update, delete, and display objects (or views of entities) at the users' direction while at all times protecting the security and integrity of the database. Before objects can be processed, they must be constructed, or materialized, from the underlying relations. When objects are updated, the data must be correctly modified while the constraints are enforced. Furthermore, if the database is concurrently processed, the updates must be controlled so that the actions of one user do not interfere with those of another.

The application must provide a means for the user to direct and control activities. Three strategies are used. With command-driven applications, the users are given a set of commands to do their work. The commands are direct and to the point, but users must memorize them and their syntax. Menu-driven applications provide a list of items from which users choose. Recently, a new style of control interface, the graphical user interface, has been devised and includes pull-down menus, icons, dialogue boxes, mice, and other facilities.

Database applications must protect the security and integrity of the database. They should be designed to enable authorized users to perform authorized activities, to provide accurate and helpful error messages when mistakes are made, and to prohibit unauthorized users and unauthorized activities.

Database applications differ in character along a continuum. At the high end, some applications offer extensive services on behalf of the user; they materialize complicated objects and present them in a sophisticated GUI. At the other end of the continuum, some applications do little more than list tables.

There are three steps in developing database applications: requirements, design, and implementation. During the requirements, the application functions are determined. During the design, both the user interface and the application program structure and logic are designed, and during the implementation, the application development facilities of the DBMS are used in conjunction with programming languages to build the applications.

Applications materialize objects by combining data from one or more relations in accordance with the defined object structure. An object view is a subset of an object utilized by a particular user or group of users. Views can be described by naming the object on which they are based and listing the visible attributes. A materialization of a view is a view plus display data such as labels, lines, boxes, and other window dressing. An object can have many views, and a view of an object can have many materializations.

A form is a screen display that is most often used for data entry and edit, although forms are sometimes used for display. Not all forms are equal. For a form to be easy to use, its structure must reflect the structure of the object that it materializes. Forms should also make the semantics of the data graphically evident, and they should be structured so as to encourage the appropriate action.

Several form features are peculiar to GUI systems, including drop-down list boxes, option buttons, and check boxes. Such facilities are effective ways of materializing objects. Forms should be designed so that the movement of the cursor is natural to the user—for both normal use and exceptions. Moreover, the meaning and use of keys should be consistent throughout the application.

Reports also should be designed so that their structure reflects the structure of the object they materialize. Report sorting often implies the existence of other objects. If the sorting is done by the object identifier, the report concerns a collection of objects of this type. If the sorting is done by a nonidentifier attribute, the report concerns an object of a different type, called an implied object. If the sorting is done by an attribute contained in an object attribute, the report is about an implied object of that other object. The report will be easier to produce if the entry point of the object is considered to be the relation from which the sort field arises.

When designing application programs, the structure of the application program logic should also reflect the structure of the object that it processes. Multivalued attributes or groups require iteration structures.

Application programs have an important role in enforcing data constraints. There are four types of relationship constraints: M–M, M–O, O–M, and O–O. Changes in key values can alter relationships and possibly violate these constraints. Such changes should be disallowed when necessary.

Other types of constraints include attribute value uniqueness constraints and null values constraints. In some cases, composites of attributes are constrained to be unique. Null values indicate either that a value is unknown or that it is inappropriate. Sometimes the constraint is that null values are not allowed for attributes.

For backup and recovery in concurrent systems, application programs must define transaction boundaries with START TRANSACTION, END TRANSACTION, and ROLL BACK commands (or their equivalent). Object definitions can be used to establish these boundaries.

GROUP I QUESTIONS

8.1   State the purpose of a database application.

8.2   Explain the special tasks that the application must perform when adding, updating, or deleting objects.

8.3   Explain why relations are more frequently queried than objects.

8.4   What are the three principal means by which users control applications? Summarize the advantages and disadvantages of each.

8.5   What does GUI stand for, and how does it relate to database applications?

8.6   Summarize the role of database applications with regard to security and integrity.

8.7   Describe the continuum of applications discussed in this chapter.

8.8   Name the three steps in application development discussed in this chapter, and summarize the basic tasks for each.

8.9   Explain the term *materialize objects*.

8.10 Define *view*. What constitutes a view?

8.11 Explain the difference between the terms *materialize an object* and *materialize a view of an object*.

8.12 Diagram the relationship of objects, views, and materializations.

8.13 Define *form*.

8.14 Explain the meaning of the phrase *a form should reflect object structure*. Why is a form with this characteristic easy to use?

8.15 Give a general rule for locating data on a form. What data should be physically contiguous?

8.16 Describe a circumstance in which it would make sense to place data from the base relation of an object at both the top and the bottom of a form that materializes a view of that object.

8.17 Explain the meaning of the phrase *data semantics should be graphically evident*. Why is this important?

8.18 Explain the meaning of the phrase *form structure should encourage appropriate action.*

8.19 What is a drop-down list box? Describe three advantages of such controls.

8.20 What is an option button? An option button group? Under what conditions would these controls be useful on a form? How would the underlying data be stored?

8.21 What are check boxes? Under what conditions would they be useful on a form? How would the underlying data be stored?

8.22 Describe the general design considerations regarding the cursor's movement on a form.

8.23 What is a pervasive key? Why are such keys desirable?

8.24 What should the relationship be between reports and object structures?

8.25 Explain why sorting implies a change in the object being processed.

8.26 Consider the object STUDENT with identifier StudentNumber and nonidentifier, nonobject attribute DateEnrolled. Suppose that STUDENT contains a single-valued object attribute DORMITORY, which contains an attribute DormName. Describe the object implied when producing reports about STUDENT that are sorted in the following way:

a. by Student.

b. by DateEnrolled.

c. by StudentLastName (a nonobject attribute of STUDENT).

d. by DormName.

8.27 What general rule pertains to the relationship of the structure of a program and the structure of an object that it processes?

8.28 What is a fragment? An orphan?

8.29 Describe four types of relationship constraint. Give an example of each type, other than those in this book.

8.30 Explain the use of the rules in Figure 8-18 for each type of relationship constraint in your answer to Question 8.29.

8.31 What is a null value? What meaning does a null value have?

8.32 What roles does an application have in enforcing rules concerning null values?

8.33 What role does an application have in enforcing rules concerning uniqueness constraints?

8.34 How does the statement that FirstName must be unique and LastName must be unique differ from the statement that (FirstName, LastName) must be unique? Which of these two statements is more restrictive?

8.35 What is a logical unit of work? What is a set of atomic actions? Why are these important?

8.36 What role does an application have in defining logical units of work?

GROUP II QUESTIONS

8.37 Consider a database application that is used to manage the access of students to a microcomputer lab at a university. Assume that the application is used to schedule student appointments for equipment at the lab and also to check out optional hardware or software. Assume too that only authorized students may use the lab and that therefore students must be preenrolled in the database before they can schedule an appointment. Finally, assume that when a student schedules an appointment, he or she must indicate the class for which the appointment was made. This means class data must also be stored. Finally, assume that the objects in Figure 8-19 are to be stored.

a. Transform the objects in Figure 8-19 into normalized relations, and indicate the key of each relation.

b. Design a data entry form for the STUDENT and the APPOINTMENT objects. Be certain your forms follow the design guidelines in this chapter.

FIGURE 8-19

Objects for Question 37

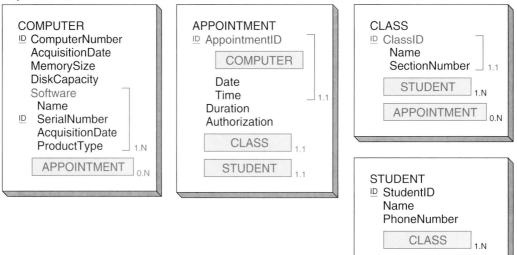

c. Design a report to display the COMPUTER object. Be certain your report follows the design guidelines in this chapter. Explain how the underlying object changes when this report is sorted by ComputerNumber, by AcquisitionDate, and by StudentName.

d. Show the basic logic of an application program that creates a new APPOINTMENT. Assume that all required CLASS, STUDENT, and COMPUTER objects already exist.

e. Do you think there should be a separate object for SOFTWARE? Justify your answer. How would the application change if there were a separate SOFTWARE object?

8.38 Modify Figure 8-18 to describe the update rules for one-to-one relationships. Explain each entry.

Database Implementation with the Relational Model

Part IV considers database implementation using the relational model. It begins, in Chapter 9, with a discussion of relational data manipulation. First we look at the types of relational data manipulation languages, and then we explain the basic operators of relational algebra and illustrate its use.

Chapter 10 describes Structured Query Language, or SQL. This language has been endorsed by the American National Standards Institute as the language of choice for manipulating databases, and it also is the primary data manipulation language for commercial relational DBMS products.

The concepts presented in these two chapters are illustrated in Chapters 11 and 12. In Chapter 11 we describe the implementation of a database for the View Ridge Gallery case introduced in Chapter 8. The implementation uses Microsoft Access, a relational DBMS for personal computers. Chapter 12 shows the implementation of a different case using IBM's DB2, a DBMS product for large mainframe computers.

FOUNDATIONS OF RELATIONAL IMPLEMENTATION

This and the next three chapters discuss the implementation of databases using DBMS products based on the relational model. We begin by defining relational data definition, reviewing relational terminology, and explaining how a design is defined to the DBMS. Next we turn to space allocation and database data creation. The remainder of the chapter addresses relational data manipulation: first, a survey of four types of relational data manipulation language (DML), then the three common modes of DML interfaces to the DBMS, and finally, the basic operators of relational algebra and example queries expressed in terms of relational algebra.

DEFINING RELATIONAL DATA

Several tasks must be performed when implementing a relational database. First, the structure of the database must be defined to the DBMS. To do this, the developer uses a data definition language (DDL) or some equivalent means (such as a graphical display) to describe the structure. Then the database is allocated to physical storage media and filled with data. In this section we will discuss each of these tasks, but first we will review the relational terminology.

■ Review of Terminology

As stated in Chapter 5, a **relation** is a table that has several properties:

1. The entries in the relation are single valued; multiple values are not allowed. Hence the intersection of a row and a column contains only one value.

2. All the entries in any column are of the same kind. For example, one column may contain customer names, and another, birthdates. Each column has a unique name, and the order of the columns is not important to the relation. The columns of a relation are called **attributes.** Each attribute has a **domain,** which is a physical and logical description of allowed values.

3. No two rows in the relation are identical, and the order of the rows is not important (see Figure 9-1). Each row of the relation is known as a tuple.

Figure 9-1 is an **example**, or **occurrence**. The generalized format, PATIENT (Name, Age, Gender, AccountNumber, Physician), is the **relation structure** and is what most people mean when they use the term *relation.* (Recall from Chapter 5 that an underlined attribute is a key.) If we add constraints on allowable data values to the relation structure, we then have a **relational schema.**

Although relations are defined in the formal terms *relation*, *attribute*, and *tuple*, the informal terms *table, column,* and *row* are often used synonymously. Sometimes, too, the terms *file, field,* and *record* are used as synonyms. These terms are summarized in Figure 9-2.

CONFUSION REGARDING THE TERM *KEY*

The term **key** is a common source of confusion when implementing relational databases, because it has different meanings between the design and the implementation stages. During the design, the term *key* refers to one or more columns that uniquely identify a row in a relation. As we explained in Chapter 5, we know every

FIGURE 9-1

Occurrence of PATIENT Relation Structure

	Col 1 (or Attribute 1)	Col 2	Col 3	Col 4	Col 5
	Name	Age	Gender	Account Number	Physician
Row 1 (or Tuple 1)	Riley	56	F	147	Lee
Row 2	Murphy	17	M	289	Singh
Row 3	Krajewski	25	F	533	Levy
Row 4	Ting	67	F	681	Spock
Row 5	Dixon	17	M	704	Levy
Row 6	Abel	41	M	193	Singh

FIGURE 9-2

Summary of Relational Terminology

Term	Meaning
Relation (or Table) (or File)	Two-dimensional table
Attribute (or Column) (or Field) (or Data Item)	Column of a relation
Tuple (or Row) (or Record)	Row in a relation
Domain	Physical and logical description of allowed values
Relation structure	Format of relation
Occurrence	Relation structure with data
Relational schema	Relation structure plus constraints
Key	Group of one or more attributes that uniquely identifies a tuple in a relation
Logical key	Same as key
Physical key (or Index)	A group of one or more attributes that is supported by a data structure that facilitates fast retrieval or rapid sequential access

relation has a key because every row is unique; at the limit, the composite of every column in the relation is the key. Usually the key is composed of one or two columns, however.

During implementation, the term *key* is used differently. For most relational products, a key is a column on which the DBMS builds an index or other data structure. This is done to access rows quickly by means of that column's value. Such keys need not be unique, and often, in fact, they are not. They are constructed only to improve performance. (See the Appendix for information about such data structures.)

For example, consider the relation ORDER (<u>OrderNumber</u>, OrderDate, Cust-Number, Amount). From the standpoint of relational *design*, the key of this relation is OrderNumber, since the underline means OrderNumber uniquely identifies rows of the relation. From the standpoint of relational *implementation,* however, any of the four columns could be a key. OrderDate, for example, could be defined as a key. If it is, the DBMS will create a data structure so that ORDER rows can be quickly accessed by the value of OrderDate. Most likely there will be many rows for a given value of OrderDate. Defining it as this type of key says nothing about its uniqueness.

Sometimes the terms **logical key** and **physical key** are used to distinguish between these two meanings of key. A logical key is a unique identifier, whereas a physical key is a column that has a special data structure defined for it in order to improve access performance. A logical key need not be a physical key, and a physical key need not be a logical key.

INDEXES

Since a physical key is usually an index, some people reserve the term *key* for a logical key and use the term *index* for a physical key. In this text, we use the term *key* to mean a logical key, and we use the term *index* to mean a physical key.

There are three reasons for defining indexes. One is to allow rows to be quickly accessed by means of the indexed attribute's value. The second is to facilitate sorting rows by that attribute. For instance, in ORDER, OrderDate might be defined as a key so that a report showing orders by dates can be more quickly generated.

A third reason for building an index concerns uniqueness. Although indexes do not have to be unique, when the developer wants a column to be unique, an index is created by the DBMS. This index is used to ensure no duplicated values are accepted by the DBMS. With most relational DBMS products, a column or group of columns can be forced to be unique by using the keyword UNIQUE when defining the appearance of a column in a table.

■ Implementing a Relational Database

In this text, we use the relational model to express database designs. Since we have done so, we can proceed directly from designing the database to implementing it. There is no need to transform the design during the implementation stage; we simply define the existing relational design to the DBMS.

The situation is different when we implement databases using DBMS products based on data models other than the relational model. For example, when implementing a database for a CODASYL DBTG DBMS, we must convert the relational design to a CODASYL DBTG design and then define the converted design to the DBMS product. You will see examples of such design transformations in Chapters 13 and 14.

DEFINING THE DATABASE STRUCTURE TO THE DBMS

There are a number of different means by which the structure of the database is described to the DBMS, depending on the DBMS product being used. With some products, a text file is constructed that describes the database structure. The language used to describe such a structure is sometimes called the **data definition language,** or DDL. The DDL text file names the tables in the database, names and describes the columns of those tables, defines indexes, and describes other structures such as constraints and security restrictions. Figure 9-3 shows the typical data definition language used for defining a simple relational database for a hypothetical DBMS. A more realistic example of such a language for the DBMS product DB2 is shown in Chapter 12.

Some DBMS products do not require that the database be defined by DDL in text file format. One common alternative is to provide a graphical means for defining the structure of the database. With Paradox, for example, the developer is shown a graphical list structure and asked to fill in the table and column names in the appropriate places (see Figure 9-4).

In general, graphical definition facilities are easier to use than textual DDL is. In Figure 9-4, the developer does not have to remember that field names are restricted to a certain number of characters because the form provides space only for the maximum number of characters allowed. For the text file, there is no such graphical constraint, and the developer does not find out that a mistake has been made until the DBMS definition utility reports an error message. A systems flowchart for defining the database structure is shown in Figure 9-5.

Regardless of the means by which the database structure is defined, the developer must name each table, define the columns in that table, and describe the physical format (for example, TEXT 10) of each column. Also, depending on the facilities of the DBMS, the developer may specify constraints that the DBMS is to enforce. Column values can be defined to be NOT NULL or UNIQUE, for example. Some products also allow the definition of range and value constraints (Part less than 10000 or Color equal to one of ['Red', 'Green', 'Blue'], for example). Finally, inter-

FIGURE 9-3

Example DDL Text File for Database Definition

```
CREATE SCHEMA PHYSICIAN

CREATE TABLE PATIENT

        ( Name                 CHARACTER VARYING (35) NOT NULL,
          Age                  SMALLINT,
          Gender               CHARACTER VARYING (10),
          AccountNumber        INTEGER NOT NULL,
          PhysicianName_FK1    CHARACTER VARYING (35) NOT NULL,

          PRIMARY KEY ( AccountNumber ),
          FOREIGN KEY ( PhysicianName_FK1 )
              REFERENCES PHYSICIAN
        )

CREATE TABLE PHYSICIAN

        ( PhysicianName        CHARACTER VARYING (35) NOT NULL,
          AreaCode             CHARACTER VARYING (3),
          LocalNumber          CHARACTER VARYING (8) NOT NULL,

          PRIMARY KEY (PhysicianName)
        )
```

FIGURE 9-4

Example of Graphical Relation Definition

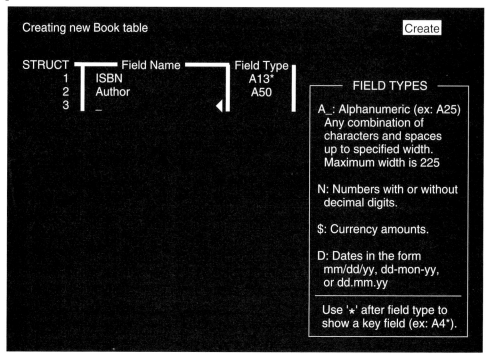

FIGURE 9-5

Defining a Database

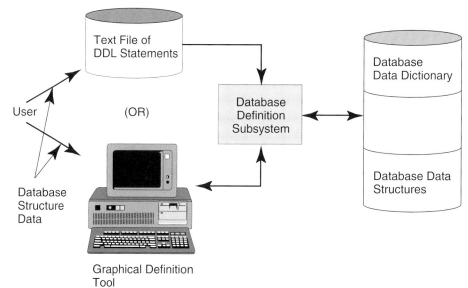

relation constraints can be defined. An example is that DeptNumber in EMPLOYEE must match a value of DeptNumber in DEPARTMENT.

With many products, the developer can also define passwords and other control and security facilities. As shown in Chapter 15, a number of different strategies can be used. Some strategies place controls on data constructs (passwords on tables, for example), and others place controls on people (the user of password X can read and update tables T1 and T2).

ALLOCATING MEDIA SPACE

In addition to defining the structure of the database, the developer must allocate database structures to physical media. Again, the specific tasks depend on the particular DBMS product used. For a personal database, all that needs to be done is to assign the database to a directory and give the database a name. The DBMS then allocates storage space automatically.

Other DBMS products, especially those used for work-group and enterprisewide applications, require more work. To improve performance and control, the distribution of the database data across disks and channels must be carefully planned. For example, depending on the nature of application processing, it may be advantageous to locate certain tables on the same disk, or it may be important to ensure that certain tables are not located on the same disk.

Consider, for example, an order object that is composed of data from ORDER, LINE-ITEM, and ITEM tables. Suppose that when processing an order, the application retrieves one row from ORDER, several rows from LINE-ITEM, and one row from ITEM for each LINE-ITEM row. Furthermore, the LINE-ITEM rows for a given order tend to be clustered together, but the ITEM rows are not at all clustered. Figure 9-6 illustrates this situation.

Now suppose that an organization concurrently processes many orders and has one large, fast disk and one smaller, slower disk. The developer must determine the

FIGURE 9-6

Example Data for Three Tables Representing an Order

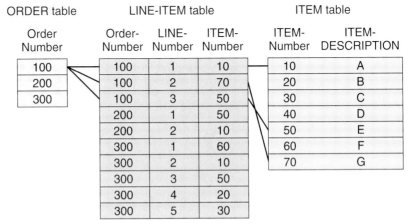

Note: For a given order, LINE-ITEM rows are clustered, but ITEM rows are not.

best place to locate the data. One possibility is that the performance will be better if the ITEM table is stored on the larger, faster disk and the ORDER and LINE-ITEM data on the smaller, slower disk. Or perhaps the performance will be better if the ORDER and LINE-ITEM data for prior months' orders is placed on the slower disk and all the data for this month's orders is placed on the faster disk.

We cannot answer this question here, as the answer depends on the amount of data, the processing characteristics of the DBMS and the operating system, the size and speed of the disks and channels, and the application-processing requirements of all applications that use the database. The point is that factors such as these must be considered when allocating media space to the database.

CREATING THE DATABASE DATA

Once the database has been defined and allocated to physical storage, it can be filled with data. The means by which this is done depends on the application requirements and the features of the DBMS product. In the best case, all of the data is already in a computer-sensible format, and the DBMS has features and tools to facilitate importing the data from magnetic media. In the worst case, all of the data must be entered via manual keyboarding using application programs created from scratch by the developers. Most data conversions lie between these two extremes.

Once the data is input, it must be verified for accuracy. Verification is a labor-intensive and tedious but important task. Often, especially for large databases, it is well worth the time and expense for the development team to write verification programs. Such programs count the number of records of various categories, compute control totals, perform reasonableness checks on data item values, and provide other kinds of verification.

RELATIONAL DATA MANIPULATION

So far in this text, we have discussed the design of relational databases and the means by which such designs are defined to the DBMS. Whenever we have referred to processing relations, we have done so in a general and intuitive manner. Although this is fine for discussing designs, to implement applications, we need clear, unambiguous languages for expressing processing logic.

◼ Categories of Relational Data Manipulation Language

To date, four different strategies for relational data manipulation have been proposed. **Relational algebra,** the first of the strategies, defines operators that work on relations (akin to the operators +, −, and so forth, of high school algebra). Relations can be manipulated using these operators to achieve a desired result. But relational algebra is hard to use, partly because it is procedural. That is, when using relational algebra we must know not only *what* we want but also *how* to get it.

Relational algebra is infrequently used in commercial database processing. Although a few commercially successful DBMS products do provide relational algebra facilities, these facilities are seldom used because of their complexity. Even so, we will discuss relational algebra here, as it helps clarify relational manipulation and establishes a foundation on which to learn SQL.

Relational calculus is a second type of relational data manipulation. Relational calculus is nonprocedural; it is a language for expressing what we want without expressing how to get it. Recall the variable of integration in calculus, which ranges over an interval to be integrated. Relational calculus has a similar variable. For **tuple relational calculus**, the variable ranges over the tuples of a relation, and for **domain relational calculus**, the variable ranges over the values of a domain. Relational calculus is derived from a branch of mathematics called **predicate calculus**.

Unless you are going to become a theoretician of relational technology, you will probably not need to learn relational calculus. It is seldom used in commercial database processing, and the little use it once had is declining in importance. Therefore, we will not discuss relational calculus in this text.

Although relational calculus is hard to understand and use, its nonprocedural property is highly desirable. Therefore, DBMS designers looked for other nonprocedural techniques, which led to the third and fourth categories of relational DML.

Transform-oriented languages are a class of nonprocedural languages that transform input data expressed as relations into results expressed as a single relation. These languages provide easy-to-use structures for expressing what is desired regarding the data supplied. SQUARE, SEQUEL, and SEQUEL's offspring, SQL, all are transform-oriented languages. We study SQL in depth in the next chapter.

The fourth category of relational DML is **query-by-example** (QBE). Systems based on this technology, such as Borland's Paradox and Microsoft Access, offer the user a picture of a relation's structure. The user fills in an example of what he or she wants, and the system responds with actual data in that format (see Figure 9-7).

FIGURE 9-7

Example of Graphical Query

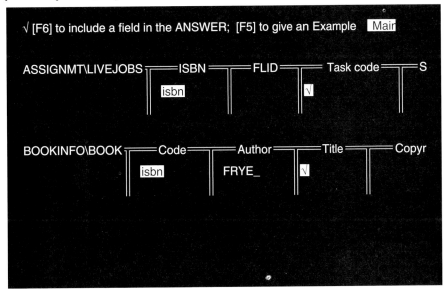

- Relational algebra
- Relational calculus
- Transform-oriented languages (such as SQL)
- Query-by-example

If you are able to understand relational algebra and SQL, you will find it easy to use a graphical-oriented DBMS product, and so we will not discuss this category further here. The four categories of relational DML are summarized in Figure 9-8.

DML Interfaces to the DBMS

As we pointed out in Chapter 2, there are several different ways that users can interface to a database: They can use the form and report capabilities supplied by the DBMS. They can access the database via a query/update language, and they can process the database through application programs that access the database by means of DBMS commands.

DATA MANIPULATION BY MEANS OF FORMS

Most relational DBMS products include tools for building forms. Some of these are created automatically when a table is defined, but others must be created by the developer, perhaps with intelligent assistance like that provided by Access's Wizards. A form may be tabular, like a spreadsheet, in which case it shows multiple rows at a time, or the form may show each row as an independent entity. Figures 9-9 and 9-10 show an example of each for the PATIENT table in Figure 9-1.

Name	Age	Gender	AccountNumber	Physician
Riley	56	F	147	Lee
Abel	41	M	193	Singh
Murphy	17	M	289	Singh
Krajewski	25	F	533	Levy
Ting	67	F	681	Spock
Dixon	17	M	704	Levy

FIGURE 9-10

Example of a Single-Row
Default Screen Form

PATIENT DATA UPDATE FORM

Name	Krajewski
Age	25
Gender	F
Account-number	533
Physician	Levy

With most products, some flexibility is provided in the processing of the forms and reports. For example, rows can be selected for processing based on column values, and they can also be sorted. The table in Figure 9-9 is sorted by Account-Number.

Many of the default forms present data from only a single relation at a time. If data is required from two or more relations, then customized forms must be created using DBMS tools. It is possible for both multitable and multirow forms to be created using such tools. The use of such tools is very specific to the product, however, and so we will not discuss them further here. Some of the tools for Microsoft Access are described in Chapter 11.

QUERY/UPDATE LANGUAGE INTERFACE

The second type of interface to a database is via a **query/update language,** or simply a **query language.** (Although most such languages perform both query and update, they are generally referred to as query languages.) With this type, the user enters query commands that specify actions on the database. The DBMS decodes the commands and carries out the appropriate actions. Figure 9-11 shows the programs involved in query processing.

FIGURE 9-11

Programs Involved in Query Processing

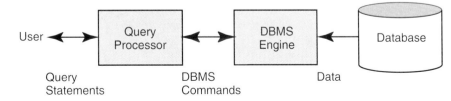

The single most important query language is SQL. To give you an idea of query languages, consider the following SQL statement that processes the relation PATIENT (Name, Age, Gender, <u>AccountNumber</u>, Physician) shown in Figure 9-1:

```
SELECT      Name, Age
FROM        PATIENT
WHERE       Age > 50
```

This SQL query statement extracts all the rows from the relation PATIENT in which the patient's age is greater than 50. It then displays the Name and Age for the qualifying rows in a second table. The results of such an operation on the data in Figure 9-1 are shown in Figure 9-12.

Query languages were developed to provide a robust interface to the database that does not require writing traditional computer programs in a procedural language. This was especially important before the advent of the microcomputer. At that time, when most databases resided on mainframes, there was not enough processing power at the users' terminals to create and process the sophisticated forms and reports that are so common today. Query languages were thus a way of giving the nonprogramming user access to a database.

Although query languages are simpler than computer-programming languages, they have generally proved to be too complicated for the average end user. Consequently, many end users have specialists write the query procedures, which are stored as files. Such procedures can be written to be parameter driven, thereby enabling the users to execute them when they change the data. As an example, the following command invokes a query procedure called BILLING and gives it a date value:

```
DO BILLING FOR BDATE = '9/15/93'
```

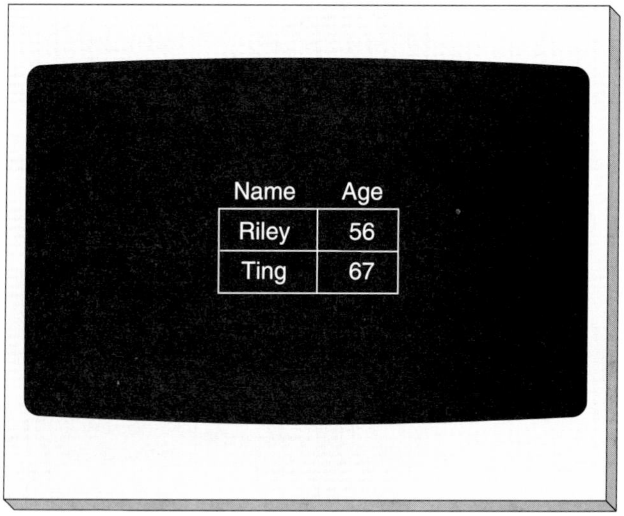

FIGURE 9-12

Result of Example Query

Stored queries are similar in character to the BATCH files on DOS systems, although the commands are processed by the DBMS and not by the operating system (COMMAND.COM in DOS).

When query procedures are stored and processed in this way, there is, in fact, little difference in concept between them and the stored programs that are written in a traditional programming language. The primary justification for their use is productivity, as stored query procedures are often quicker for the specialist to write.

There is one group of end users who are an exception and who have found it feasible and desirable to learn a query language and write their own queries: business professionals working in decision-support environments. An example is a group of financial planners who process corporate databases to develop a series of what–if financial analyses. Such end users are generally well-educated professionals who have been given specialized training in the query language, the DBMS, and the structure of the databases they access.

APPLICATION PROGRAM INTERFACE

The third type of data access interface is through application programs written in programming languages such as COBOL, BASIC, REXX, Pascal, and C. In addition, some application programs are written in languages provided by the DBMS vendors, of which the dBASE programming language is the best known.

There are two styles of application program interface to the DBMS. In one, the application program makes subroutine calls to routines in a subroutine library provided with the DBMS. For example, to read a particular row of a table, the application program calls the DBMS read routine and passes parameters that indicate the table to be accessed, the data to be retrieved, the criteria for row selection, and the like.

Accessing the DBMS via a subroutine call can be complicated. The parameters to be passed may be complex, and often complicated shared data areas must be set up and maintained. Such programming is time-consuming and often error prone. To overcome these disadvantages, many DBMS products offer a second style of program interface in which they define a set of high-level data access commands. These commands—which are peculiar to database processing and not part of any standard language—are embedded in the application program code.

The application program, with embedded commands, is then submitted to a precompiler provided by the DBMS vendor. This precompiler translates the data access statements into valid subroutine calls and data structure definitions. In this process, the precompiler sets up parameter sequences for the calls and defines data areas that will be shared between the application program and the DBMS. The precompiler also inserts program logic to maintain the data areas. Then the precompiled routine is submitted to the language compiler. Figure 9-13 shows the relationships of the programs involved in this process.

In addition to its role in query processing, SQL is also used as a data access language in application programs. In this mode, SQL statements are embedded in the programs and translated into subroutine calls by a precompiler. Training costs and learning time are reduced, since the same language can be used for access to both query and application programs.

FIGURE 9-13

Processing Program with Embedded DML Statements

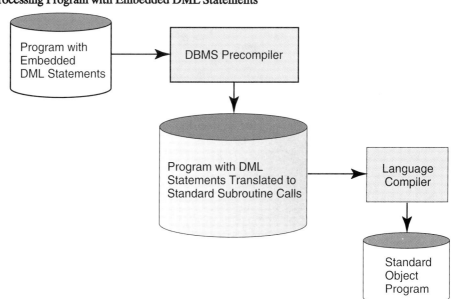

There is one problem to be overcome, however. SQL is a transform-oriented language that accepts relations, manipulates them, and outputs a result relation. Thus it deals with relations one at a time. Almost all application programs are row (record) oriented; that is, they read one row, process it, read the next row, and so forth. Such programs deal with a row at a time.

Thus there is a mismatch in the basic orientation of SQL and application program languages. To correct for this mismatch, the results of SQL statements are assumed, in the application program, to be files. To illustrate, assume that the following SQL statements (the same as those earlier) are embedded in an application program:

```
SELECT      Name, Age
FROM        PATIENT
WHERE       Age > 50
```

The result of these statements is a table with two columns and N rows. In order to accept the results of this query, the application program is written to assume that these statements have produced a file with N records. The application opens the query, processes the first row, processes the next row, and so forth, until the last row has been processed. This logic is the same as that for processing a sequential file. You will see examples of such application programs in Chapter 12. For now, just be aware that there is a mismatch in the basic orientation of SQL (relation oriented) and programming languages (row, or record, oriented) and that this mismatch must be corrected when programs access a relational database via SQL.

RELATIONAL ALGEBRA

Relational algebra is similar to the algebra you learned in high school, but with an important difference. In high school algebra, variables represented numbers, and operators like $+$, $-$, $\times$, and $/$ operated on numeric quantities. In relational algebra, however, the variables are relations, and the operators manipulate relations to form new relations. For example, the union operation combines the tuples of one relation with the tuples of another relation, thereby producing a third relation. In fact, relational algebra is *closed*, which means that the results of one or more relational operations are *always* a relation.

Relations are sets. The tuples of a relation can be considered elements of a set, and so operations that can be performed on sets can also be performed on relations. We first show four such set operators and then discuss other operators that are peculiar to relational algebra. Before proceeding, however, consider the following sample relations that we will use in this and the next chapter.

■ Relational Operators

Figure 9-14 shows six relations and their attribute and domain definitions. Note that the attribute Name is used in several relations. When we refer to a specific attribute, we qualify it with its relation name. Accordingly, Name in CLASS is sometimes denoted as CLASS.Name.

Also, observe that the physical description of the Ages and the ClassSizes domains is the same, yet the domains are different. This is because their logical description is different; they are not the same semantically, since they do not represent the same attributes. The integer 21 in Ages represents 21 years, but the same integer 21 in ClassSizes refers to the number of people in a class. Thus the value 21 represents two entirely different characteristics.

In the following discussion, character values are shown in single quotes, and those characters not in quotes represent names. Thus 'ROOM' differs from Room because 'ROOM' is a value, whereas Room is, say, a domain name. In regard to numeric data, those numbers not in quotes refer to numeric quantities, and those numbers in quotes refer to character strings. Thus, 123 is a number, and '123' is a string of the characters '1', '2', and '3'.

UNION

The **union** of two relations is formed by adding the tuples from one relation to those of a second relation to produce a third relation. The order in which the tuples appear in the third relation is not important, but duplicate tuples must be eliminated. The union of relations A and B is denoted A + B.

For this operation to make sense, the relations must be **union compatible**; that is, each relation must have the same number of attributes, and the attributes in corresponding columns must come from the same domain. If, for example, the third attribute of one relation comes from the Ages domain, the third attribute of the second relation must also come from the Ages domain.

FIGURE 9-14

Examples of Relations and Domains: (a) Relation Definitions, (b) Attribute Domains, and (c) Domain Definitions

1. JUNIOR (<u>Snum</u>, Name, Major)
2. HONOR-STUDENT (<u>Number</u>, Name, Interest)
3. STUDENT (<u>SID</u>, Name, Major, GradeLevel, Age)
4. CLASS (<u>Name</u>, Time, Room)
5. ENROLLMENT (<u>StudentNumber</u>, ClassName, PositionNumber)
6. FACULTY (<u>FID</u>, Name, Department)

(a)

	Attribute	Domain
1.	Snum	PeopleIdentifiers
	JUNIOR.Name	PeopleNames
	Major	SubjectNames
2.	Number	PeopleIdentifiers
	HONOR-STUDENT.Name	PeopleNames
	Interest	SubjectNames
3.	SID	PeopleIdentifiers
	STUDENT.Name	PeopleNames
	Major	SubjectNames
	GradeLevel	Classes
	Age	Ages
4.	CLASS.Name	ClassNames
	Time	ClassTimes
	Room	Rooms
5.	StudentNumber	PeopleIdentifiers
	ClassName	ClassNames
	PositionNumber	ClassSizes
6.	FID	PeopleIdentifiers
	FACULTY.Name	PeopleNames
	Department	SubjectNames

(b)

In Figure 9-14, the JUNIOR and the HONOR-STUDENT relations are union compatible because they both have three attributes, and the corresponding attributes come from the same domain. JUNIOR.Snum and HONOR-STUDENT.Number come from the domain PeopleIdentifiers; JUNIOR.Name and HONOR-STUDENT.Name have the domain PeopleNames; and JUNIOR.Major and HONOR-STUDENT.Interest have the domain SubjectNames. The relations JUNIOR and CLASS both have three attributes, but they are **union incompatible** because the three attributes do not have the same domain.

FIGURE 9-14

Continued

Domain Name	Format
PeopleIdentifiers	Decimal (3)
PeopleNames	Char (8) (unrealistic, but handy for these examples)
SubjectNames	Char (10)
Classes	One of [FR, SO, JR, SN, GR]
Ages	Decimal from 0 to 100
ClassNames	Char (5)
ClassTimes	Char (5) format: DDDHH, where D is one of [M, T, W, R, F, or blank], and HH is decimal between 1 and 12
Rooms	Char (5) format: BBRRR, where BB is a building code, and RRR, is a room number
ClassSizes	Decimal from 0 to 100

(c)

Figure 9-15 shows the union of two instances of the JUNIOR and HONOR-STUDENT relations. Note that the tuple, [123, JONES, HISTORY], which occurs in both relations, is not duplicated in the union.

DIFFERENCE

The **difference** of two relations is a third relation containing tuples that occur in the first relation but not in the second. The relations must be union compatible. The difference of JUNIOR and HONOR-STUDENT is shown in Figure 9-16. As in arithmetic, the order of the subtraction matters, and so A – B is not the same as B – A.

INTERSECTION

The **intersection** of two relations is a third relation containing the tuples that appear in both the first and second relations. Again, the relations must be union compatible. In Figure 9-17 the intersection of JUNIOR and HONOR-STUDENT is the single tuple, [123, JONES, HISTORY], which is the only tuple that occurs in both JUNIOR and HONOR-STUDENT.

PRODUCT

The **product** of two relations (sometimes called the **Cartesian product**) is the concatenation of every tuple of one relation with every tuple of a second relation. The

FIGURE 9-15

JUNIOR and HONOR-STUDENT Relations and Their Union: (a) Example JUNIOR Relation, (b) Example HONOR-STUDENT Relation, and (c) Union of JUNIOR and HONOR-STUDENT Relations

Snum	Name	Major
123	JONES	HISTORY
158	PARKS	MATH
271	SMITH	HISTORY

(a)

Number	Name	Interest
105	ANDERSON	MANAGEMENT
123	JONES	HISTORY

(b)

Snum or Number	Name	Major or Interest
123	JONES	HISTORY
158	PARKS	MATH
271	SMITH	HISTORY
105	ANDERSON	MANAGEMENT

(c)

product of relation A (having m tuples) and relation B (having n tuples) has m times n tuples. The product is denoted A $\times$ B or A TIMES B. In Figure 9-18, the relation STUDENT has four tuples, and the relation ENROLLMENT has three. STUDENT TIMES ENROLLMENT therefore has twelve tuples, which are shown in Figure 9-19. (Incidentally, the resulting relation in Figure 9-19 contains some meaningless tuples. Other operations, shown later, would need to be performed in order to extract any meaningful information from this relation. This is simply an illustration of the product operator.)

PROJECTION

Projection is an operation that selects specified attributes from a relation. The result of the projection is a new relation with the selected attributes; in other words, a projection chooses columns from a relation. For example, consider the STUDENT relation data in Figure 9-18, from which the projection of STUDENT on Name and Major attributes, denoted with brackets as STUDENT [Name, Major], is shown in Figure 9-20(a). The projection of STUDENT on Major and GradeLevel, denoted as STUDENT [Major, GradeLevel], appears in Figure 9-20(b).

Note that although STUDENT has four tuples to begin with, the projection STUDENT [Major, GradeLevel] has only three. A tuple was eliminated because

FIGURE 9-16

JUNIOR Minus HONOR-STUDENT Relation

Snum	Name	Major
158	PARKS	MATH
271	SMITH	HISTORY

FIGURE 9-17

Intersection of JUNIOR and HONOR-STUDENT Relations

Snum or Number	Name	Major or Interest
123	JONES	HISTORY

FIGURE 9-18

Examples of (a) STUDENT and (b) ENROLLMENT Relations

SID	Name	Major	GradeLevel	Age
123	JONES	HISTORY	JR	21
158	PARKS	MATH	GR	26
105	ANDERSON	MANAGEMENT	SN	27
271	SMITH	HISTORY	JR	19

(a)

StudentNumber	ClassName	PositionNumber
123	H350	1
105	BA490	3
123	BA490	7

(b)

FIGURE 9-19

Product of the STUDENT and ENROLLMENT Relations in Figure 9-18

SID	Name	Major	GradeLevel	Age	Student-Number	Class-Number	Position-Number
123	JONES	HISTORY	JR	21	123	H350	1
123	JONES	HISTORY	JR	21	105	BA490	3
123	JONES	HISTORY	JR	21	123	BA490	7
158	PARKS	MATH	GR	26	123	H350	1
158	PARKS	MATH	GR	26	105	BA490	3
158	PARKS	MATH	GR	26	123	BA490	7
105	ANDERSON	MANAGEMENT	SN	27	123	H350	1
105	ANDERSON	MANAGEMENT	SN	27	105	BA490	3
105	ANDERSON	MANAGEMENT	SN	27	123	BA490	7
271	SMITH	HISTORY	JR	19	123	H350	1
271	SMITH	HISTORY	JR	19	105	BA490	3
271	SMITH	HISTORY	JR	19	123	BA490	7

FIGURE 9-20

Projections of STUDENT Relation: (a) STUDENT [Name, Major] and (b) STUDENT [Major, GradeLevel]

Name	Major
JONES	HISTORY
PARKS	MATH
ANDERSON	MANAGEMENT
SMITH	HISTORY

(a)

Major	GradeLevel
HISTORY	JR
MATH	GR
MANAGEMENT	SN

(b)

after the projection was completed, the tuple [HISTORY, JR] occurred twice. Because the result of projection is a relation and because relations cannot contain duplicate tuples, the redundant tuple is eliminated.

Projection can also be used to change the order of attributes in a relation. For example, the projection STUDENT [Age, GradeLevel, Major, SID] reverses the order of STUDENT attributes (see Figure 9-14 for the original order). This feature can sometimes be used to make two relations union compatible.

SELECTION

Whereas the projection operator takes a vertical subset (columns) of a relation, the **selection** operator takes a horizontal subset (rows). Projection identifies those *attributes* to be included in the new relation, and selection identifies those *tuples* to be included in the new relation. Selection is denoted by specifying the relation name, followed by the keyword WHERE, followed by a condition involving attributes. Figure 9-21(a) shows the selection of the relation STUDENT WHERE Major = 'MATH', and Figure 9-22(b) shows the selection of STUDENT WHERE Age < 25.

JOIN

The **join** operation is a combination of the product, selection, and (possibly) projection operations. The join of two relations, say A and B, operates as follows: First, form the product of A times B. Then do a selection to eliminate some tuples (the

FIGURE 9-21

Examples of Relational Selection: (a) STUDENT WHERE Major = 'Math' and (b) STUDENT WHERE Age < 25

SID	Name	Major	GradeLevel	Age
158	PARKS	MATH	GR	26

(a)

SID	Name	Major	GradeLevel	Age
123	JONES	HISTORY	JR	21
271	SMITH	HISTORY	JR	19

(b)

FIGURE 9-22

Examples of Joining STUDENT and ENROLLMENT Relations: (a) Equijoin and (b) Natural Join

SID	Name	Major	Grade-Level	Age	Student-Number	Class-Name	Position-Number
123	JONES	HISTORY	JR	21	123	H350	1
123	JONES	HISTORY	JR	21	123	BA490	7
105	ANDERSON	MANAGEMENT	SN	27	105	BA490	3

(a)

SID	Name	Major	GradeLevel	Age	ClassName	PositionNumber
123	JONES	HISTORY	JR	21	H350	1
123	JONES	HISTORY	JR	21	BA490	7
105	ANDERSON	MANAGEMENT	SN	27	BA490	3

(b)

criteria for the selection are specified as part of the join). Then (optionally) remove some attributes by means of projection.

Consider the STUDENT and ENROLLMENT relations shown in Figure 9-18. Suppose we want to know the sizes of the classes for each student. To find this out, we need to join STUDENT tuples by matching ENROLLMENT tuples based on the SID. We denote such a join as STUDENT JOIN (SID = StudentNumber) ENROLLMENT. The meaning of this expression is "Join a STUDENT tuple to an ENROLLMENT tuple if SID of STUDENT equals StudentNumber of ENROLLMENT."

To form this join, we first find the product of STUDENT and ENROLLMENT, an operation shown in Figure 9-19. Next we SELECT those tuples from the product where SID of STUDENT equals StudentNumber of ENROLLMENT (there are only three). This operation leads to the relation in Figure 9-22(a). Note that two attributes are identical: SID and StudentNumber (Snum). One of these is redundant, so we eliminate it (in this case, we choose StudentNumber) with projection. The result is the join in Figure 9-22(b). The join in Figure 9-22(a) is called the **equijoin,** and the one in Figure 9-22(b) is called the **natural join.** Unless otherwise specified, when people say join, they mean the natural join.

Because forming the product of two large relations is time-consuming, the algorithm used by a DBMS to join two relations will be different from that described here. The result will be identical, however.

Joining on conditions other than equality also is possible. For example, STUDENT JOIN (SID not = StudentNumber) ENROLLMENT, or STUDENT JOIN (SID < FID) FACULTY. The latter join would result in tuples in which the student numbers are lower than the faculty numbers. Such a join may have meaning if, say, PeopleIdentifiers were assigned in chronological order. Such a join would portray pairs of students and teachers in such a way that the student would appear to have been at the institution longer than the teacher had.

There is one important limit on the conditions of a join: The attributes in the condition must arise from a common domain, and so STUDENT JOIN (Age =

FIGURE 9-23

Summary of Relational Algebra Operations

Type	Format	Example
Set operations	+, –, intersection, product	STUDENT [Name] – JUNIOR [Name]
Selection	SELECT relation WHERE condition	SELECT CLASS WHERE Name = 'A'
Projection	relation [list of attributes]	STUDENT [Name, Major, Age]
Join	relation 1 JOIN (condition) relation 2	STUDENT JOIN (SID = StudentNumber) ENROLLMENT

ClassSize) ENROLLMENT is *illogical*. Even though the values of Age and Class-Size are compatible, they do not arise from the same domain. Semantically, this type of a join makes no sense. (Unfortunately, many relational DBMS products permit such a join.)

■ Expressing Queries in Relational Algebra

Figure 9-23 summarizes the basic relational operations just discussed. Standard set operations include +, –, intersection, and product. Selection chooses specific tuples (rows) from a relation in accordance with the conditions for attribute values. Projection chooses specific attributes (columns) from a relation by means of the attribute name. Finally, join concatenates the tuples of two relations in accordance with a condition on the values of attributes.

We now turn to how relational operators can be used to express queries, using the relations STUDENT, CLASS, and ENROLLMENT from Figure 9-14; sample data is shown in Figure 9-24. Our purpose is to demonstrate the manipulation of relations. Although you will probably never use relational algebra in a commercial environment, these examples will help you understand how relations can be manipulated.

1. What are the names of all students?

STUDENT [Name]

This is simply the projection of the Name attribute of the STUDENT relation, and the result is

JONES
PARKS
BAKER
GLASS
RUSSELL
RYE

FIGURE 9-24

Example Data for Relations Defined in Figure 9-14: (a) STUDENT Relation, (b) ENROLLMENT Relation, and (c) CLASS Relation

SID	Name	Major	GradeLevel	Age
100	JONES	HISTORY	GR	21
150	PARKS	ACCOUNTING	SO	19
200	BAKER	MATH	GR	50
250	GLASS	HISTORY	SN	50
300	BAKER	ACCOUNTING	SN	41
350	RUSSELL	MATH	JR	20
400	RYE	ACCOUNTING	FR	18
450	JONES	HISTORY	SN	24

(a)

StudentNumber	ClassName	PositionNumber
100	BD445	1
150	BA200	1
200	BD445	2
200	CS250	1
300	CS150	1
400	BA200	2
400	BF410	1
400	CS250	2
450	BA200	3

(b)

Name	Time	Room
BA200	M-F9	SC110
BD445	MWF3	SC213
BF410	MWF8	SC213
CS150	MWF3	EA304
CS250	MWF12	EB210

(c)

Duplicate names have been omitted. Although the names JONES and BAKER actually occur twice in the relation STUDENT, repetitions have been omitted because the result of a projection is a relation, and relations may not have duplicate tuples.

2. What are the student numbers of all students enrolled in a class?

ENROLLMENT [StudentNumber]

This is similar to the first query, but the projection occurs on the relation ENROLL-MENT. The result is

100
150
200
300
400

Again, duplicate tuples have been omitted.

3. What are the student numbers of all students not enrolled in a class?

STUDENT [SID] − ENROLLMENT [StudentNumber]

This expression finds the difference of the projection of two relations: STUDENT [SID] has the student numbers of all students, and ENROLLMENT [StudentNumber] has the student numbers of all students enrolled in a class. The difference is the number of students not enrolled in a class. The result is

450

4. What are the numbers of students enrolled in the class 'BD445'?

ENROLLMENT WHERE ClassName = 'BD445' [StudentNumber]

This expression selects the appropriate tuples and then projects them onto the attribute StudentNumber. The result is

100
200

5. What are the names of the students enrolled in class 'BD445'?

STUDENT JOIN (SID = StudentNumber) ENROLLMENT WHERE ClassName = 'BD445' [STUDENT.Name]

To answer this query, data from both STUDENT and ENROLLMENT is needed. Specifically, student names must come from STUDENT, whereas the condition "enrolled in BD445" must be checked in ENROLLMENT. Since both relations are needed, they must be joined. After STUDENT and ENROLLMENT have been joined, the selection is applied, followed by a projection on student names. The result is

JONES
BAKER

As we stated earlier, when two or more relations are considered, attribute names can be duplicated. Therefore, for clarity, the relation name may be prefixed to the attribute name. Thus, in our example, the projection is on [STUDENT.Name]. In this example, this prefix was added only for clarity, since the attribute names are different. But when attribute names are identical (a join involving STUDENT and CLASS yields two attributes, both called Name), the prefix is required. Consider the following query:

6.   What are the names and meeting times of 'PARKS' classes?

To answer this, we must bring together data in all three relations. We need STUDENT data to find PARKS's student number; we need ENROLLMENT data to learn which classes PARKS is in; and we need CLASS data to determine the class meeting times.

STUDENT WHERE Name = 'PARKS' JOIN (SID = StudentNumber)
ENROLLMENT JOIN (ClassName = Name) CLASS [CLASS.Name, Time]

This expression first selects PARKS's tuple and joins it to matching ENROLLMENT tuples. Then the result is joined to matching CLASS tuples. Finally, the projection is taken to print classes and times. The result is

| BA200 | M-F9 |

We must specify CLASS.Name; simply specifying Name is ambiguous because both STUDENT and CLASS have an attribute called Name.

There are other, equivalent ways of responding to this query. One is

STUDENT JOIN (SID = StudentNumber) ENROLLMENT JOIN (ClassName = Name) CLASS WHERE STUDENT.Name = 'PARKS' [CLASS.Name, Time]

This expression differs from the first one because the selection on PARKS is not done until after all of the joins have been performed. Assuming that the computer performs the operations as stated, this latter expression will be slower than the former one because many more tuples will be joined.

Such differences are a major disadvantage of relational algebra. To the user, two equivalent queries should take the same amount of time (and hence cost the same). Imagine the frustration if one form of a query costs $1.17 and another costs $4,356. To the unwary and unsophisticated user, the cost difference appears capricious. To eliminate this problem, the DBMS must optimize relational algebra expressions before processing them.

SUMMARY

Several tasks must be carried out when implementing a relational database. First the structure of the database must be defined to the DBMS. Then file space needs to be allocated, and finally the database is filled with data.

The relational model represents and processes data in the form of tables called relations. The columns of the tables are called attributes, and the rows are called tuples. The values of the attributes arise from domains. The terms *table, column,* and *row* and *file, field,* and *record* are used synonymously with the terms *relation, attribute,* and *tuple,* respectively.

The use of the term *key* can be confusing because it is used differently in the design and implementation stages. During design, the term means a logical key, which is one or more attributes that uniquely define a row. During implementation, the term means a physical key, which is a data structure used to improve performance. A logical key may or may not be a physical key, and a physical key may or may not be a logical key. In this text we use key to mean logical key and index to mean physical key.

Since we are using the relational model to express database designs, there is no need to transform the design during the implementation stage. We simply define the relational design to the DBMS. Two ways of defining the design are to express it in a DDL text file or to use a graphical data definition tool. In either case, the tables, columns, indexes, constraints, passwords, and other controls are defined to the DBMS.

In addition to defining the database structure, the developers must allocate media space for the database. With multiuser systems, such allocation can be important to the DBMS's effective performance. Finally, the database is filled with data using tools provided by the DBMS vendor, programs developed by the vendor, or both.

The four categories of relational data manipulation language are relational algebra, relational calculus, transform-oriented languages, and query-by-example. Relational algebra consists of a group of relational operators that can be used to manipulate relations to obtain a desired result. Relational algebra is procedural. The transform-oriented languages offer a nonprocedural means to transform a set of relations into a desired result. SQL is the most common example.

There are three means of accessing a relational database. One is to use the form and report facilities provided by the DBMS. A second is to use a query/update language, of which SQL is the most common. A third is through application programs.

Application program interfaces can be either by subroutine call or special-purpose database commands that are translated by a precompiler. The processing orientation of the relational model is relation at a time, but the orientation of most programming languages is row at a time. Some means must be devised to correct for this mismatch.

Relational algebra is used to manipulate relations to obtain a desired result. The operators are union, difference, intersection, product, projection, selection, and join.

GROUP I QUESTIONS

9.1 Name and describe the three tasks necessary to implement a relational database.

9.2 Define *relation, attribute, tuple,* and *domain.*

9.3 Explain the use of the terms *table, column, row, file, field,* and *record.*

9.4 Explain the difference between a relational schema and a relation.

9.5 Define *key, index, logical key,* and *physical key.*

9.6 Describe three reasons for using indexes.

9.7   Under what conditions is it necessary to transform the database design during the implementation stage?

9.8   Explain the term *data definition language.* What purpose does it serve?

9.9   How can a database structure be defined other than through a text file?

9.10 What aspects of a database design need to be defined to the DBMS?

9.11 Give an example, other than the one in this text, in which the allocation of the database to physical media is important.

9.12 Describe the best and worst extremes for loading the database with data.

9.13 Name and briefly explain four categories of relational DML.

9.14 Describe how relational data can be manipulated by means of forms.

9.15 Explain the role of query languages in relational data manipulation. How do stored queries differ from application programs? Why are they used?

9.16 Describe the two styles of application program interface to the database. In your answer, explain the role of a precompiler.

9.17 Describe the mismatch between the orientation of the SQL and the orientation of most programming languages. How is this mismatch corrected?

9.18 How does relational algebra differ from high school algebra?

9.19 Why is relational algebra *closed*?

9.20 Define *union compatible.* Give an example of two relations that are union compatible and two that are union incompatible.

Questions 9.21 through 9.23 refer to the following two relations:

COMPANY (Name, NumberEmployees, Sales)
MANUFACTURERS (Name, PeopleCount, Revenue)

9.21 Give an example of a union of these two relations.

9.22 Give an example of a difference of these two relations.

9.23 Give an example of an intersection of these two relations.

Questions 9.24 through 9.28 refer to the following three relations:

SALESPERSON (Name, Age, Salary)
ORDER (Number, CustName, SalespersonName, Amount)
CUSTOMER (Name, City, IndustryType)

An instance of these relations is shown in Figure 9-25. Use the data in those tables for the following problems:

9.24 Give an example of the product of SALESPERSON and ORDER.

9.25 Show an example of

SALESPERSON[Name, Salary]
SALESPERSON[Age, Salary]

Under what conditions will SALESPERSON [Age, Salary] have fewer rows than SALESPERSON does?

9.26 Show an example of a select on SALESPERSON Name, on SALESPERSON Age, and on both SALESPERSON Name and Age.

FIGURE 9-25

Sample Data for Questions 9-24 Through 9-28

Name	Age	Salary
Abel	63	120,000
Baker	38	42,000
Jones	26	36,000
Murphy	42	50,000
Zenith	59	118,000
Kobad	27	34,000

SALESPERSON

Number	CustName	SalespersonName	Amount
100	Abernathy Construction	Zenith	560
200	Abernathy Construction	Jones	1800
300	Manchester Lumber	Abel	480
400	Amalgamated Housing	Abel	2500
500	Abernathy Construction	Murphy	6000
600	Tri-City Builders	Abel	700
700	Manchester Lumber	Jones	150

ORDER

Name	City	IndustryType
Abernathy Construction	Willow	B
Manchester Lumber	Manchester	F
Tri-City Builders	Memphis	B
Amalgamated Housing	Memphis	B

CUSTOMER

9.27 Show an example of an equijoin and a natural join of SALESPERSON and ORDER in which the Name of SALESPERSON equals the SalespersonName of ORDER.

9.28 Show relational algebra expressions for

a. The names of all salespeople.

b. The names of all salespeople having an ORDER row.

c. The names of salespeople not having an ORDER row.

d. The names of salespeople having an order with ABERNATHY CONSTRUCTION.

e. The ages of salespeople having an order with ABERNATHY CONSTRUCTION.

f. The city of all CUSTOMERS having an order with salesperson JONES.

STRUCTURED QUERY LANGUAGE

Structured Query Language, or SQL, is the most important relational data manipulation language in use today. It has been endorsed by the American National Standards Institute (ANSI) as the language of choice for manipulating databases, and it is the data access language used by many commercial DBMS products, including DB2, SQL/DS, ORACLE, INGRES, SYBASE, SQL Server, dBASE IV, Paradox, and Microsoft Access. Because of its popularity, SQL has become the standard language for information interchange among computers. Since there is a version of SQL that can run on almost any computer and operating system, computer systems may exchange data by passing SQL requests and responses to one another, a capability that is likely to expand in the future.

The development of SQL began at IBM's San Jose research facilities in the mid-1970s under the name SEQUEL. Several versions of SEQUEL were released, and in 1980 the product was renamed SQL. Since then, IBM has been joined by many other vendors in developing products for SQL. The American National Standards Institute has taken over the role of maintaining SQL and periodically publishes updated versions of the SQL standard.

This chapter discusses the core of SQL as described in the 1991 ANSI standard.[1] The constructs and allowed expressions in a particular implementation of

---

[1] American National Standards Institute, *American National Standard for Information System–Database Language–SQL*, ANSI Publication X3.135-1991.

SQL (for example, in INGRES or SQL Server) may differ in minor ways from the ANSI standard, in part because many of the DBMS products were developed before there was agreement on the standard and also because vendors added capabilities to their products to gain a competitive advantage. From a marketing perspective, simply supporting the ANSI standard may be judged as not enough sizzle.

SQL commands can be used interactively as a query language, or they can be embedded in application programs. In the latter case, they are processed by a precompiler, as described in Chapter 9. Thus SQL is *not* a programming language (like COBOL); rather, it is a *data sublanguage,* or a *data access language,* that is embedded in other languages.

In this chapter, we present interactive SQL statements, which need to be adjusted and modified when they are embedded in programs, as we describe in Chapter 12. Here we are concerned only with data manipulation statements, although there also are SQL commands for data definition and control, examples of which are given in Chapter 12 in regard to the DBMS product DB2.

SQL is a transform-oriented language that accepts one or more relations as input and produces a single relation as output. The result of every SQL query is a relation; even if the result is a single number, that number is considered to be a relation with a single row and a single column. Thus SQL, like relational algebra, is *closed.*

QUERYING A SINGLE TABLE

In this section, we consider SQL facilities for querying a single table. We will discuss multitable and update statements later in this chapter. By custom, SQL reserved words such as SELECT and FROM are written in capital letters. Also, SQL statements are normally written in multiple lines as illustrated in this chapter. SQL language compilers do not require either capitals or multiple lines, however. These conventions are used only to provide better clarity to humans who read the SQL statements.

We use the same set of six relations with which we illustrated relational algebra in Chapter 9. The structure of those relations is shown in Figure 10-1, and sample data for three of them appears in Figure 10-2.

▨ Projections Using SQL

To form a projection with SQL, we name the relation to be projected and list the columns to be shown. Using standard SQL syntax, the projection STUDENT [SID, Name, Major] is specified as:

```
SELECT      SID, Name, Major
FROM        STUDENT
```

FIGURE 10-1

Relations Used for SQL Examples

1. JUNIOR (Snum, Name, Major)
2. HONOR-STUDENT (Number, Name, Interest)
3. STUDENT (SID, Name, Major, GradeLevel, Age)
4. CLASS (Name, Time, Room)
5. ENROLLMENT (StudentNumber, ClassName, PositionNumber)
6. FACULTY (FID, Name, Department)

	Attribute	Domain
1.	Snum	PeopleIdentifiers
	JUNIOR.Name	PeopleNames
	Major	SubjectNames
2.	Number	PeopleIdentifiers
	HONOR-STUDENT.Name	PeopleNames
	Interest	SubjectNames
3.	SID	PeopleIdentifiers
	STUDENT.Name	PeopleNames
	Major	SubjectNames
	Grade-level	Classes
	Age	Ages
4.	CLASS.Name	ClassNames
	Time	ClassTimes
	Room	Rooms
5.	Student-number	PeopleIdentifiers
	Classname	ClassNames
	Position-number	ClassSizes
6.	FID	PeopleIdentifiers
	FACULTY.Name	PeopleNames
	Department	SubjectNames

The keywords SELECT and FROM are always required; the columns to be obtained are listed after the keyword SELECT; and the table to be used is listed after the keyword FROM. The result of this projection for the data in Figure 10-2 is

HISTORY
ACCOUNTING
MATH
HISTORY
ACCOUNTING
MATH
ACCOUNTING
HISTORY

FIGURE 10-2

Sample Data Used for SQL Examples: (a) STUDENT Relation, (b) ENROLLMENT Relation, and (c) CLASS Relation

SID	Name	Major	Grade-level	Age
100	JONES	HISTORY	GR	21
150	PARKS	ACCOUNTING	SO	19
200	BAKER	MATH	GR	50
250	GLASS	HISTORY	SN	50
300	BAKER	ACCOUNTING	SN	41
350	RUSSELL	MATH	JR	20
400	RYE	ACCOUNTING	FR	18
450	JONES	HISTORY	SN	24

(a)

StudentNumber	ClassName	PositionNumber
100	BD445	1
150	BA200	1
200	BD445	2
200	CS250	1
300	CS150	1
400	BA200	2
400	BF410	1
400	CS250	2
450	BA200	3

(b)

Name	Time	Room
BA200	M-F9	SC110
BD445	MWF3	SC213
BF410	MWF8	SC213
CS150	MWF3	EA304
CS250	MWF12	EB210

(c)

Do not confuse the keyword SELECT with the relational algebra operator selection. SELECT is an SQL verb that can be used to perform a relational algebra projection, selection, and to specify other actions. Selection, on the other hand, differs from SELECT because it is the relational algebra operation of obtaining a subset of rows from a table.

Consider another example:

```
SELECT      Major
FROM        STUDENT
```

The result of this operation is the following table:

HISTORY
ACCOUNTING
MATH
HISTORY
ACCOUNTING
MATH
ACCOUNTING
HISTORY

As you can see, this table contains duplicate rows, and consequently, in a strict sense, this table is not a relation. In fact, SQL does not automatically eliminate duplicates because such removal can be very time-consuming and, in many cases, is not desirable or necessary.

If duplicate rows must be removed, the qualifier DISTINCT must be specified, as follows:

SELECT   DISTINCT Major
FROM   STUDENT

The result of this operation is the relation

HISTORY
ACCOUNTING
MATH

■ Selections Using SQL

The relational algebra selection operator is also performed with the SQL SELECT command. An example is the following:

SELECT   SID, Name, Major, GradeLevel, Age
FROM   STUDENT
WHERE   Major = 'MATH'

This SELECT expression specifies the names of all the table's columns. FROM specifies the table to be used, and the new phrase, WHERE, provides the condition(s) for the selection. The format SELECT–FROM–WHERE is the fundamental structure of SQL statements. The following is an equivalent form of the preceding query:

SELECT   *
FROM   STUDENT
WHERE   Major = 'MATH'

The asterisk (*) means that all columns of the table are to be obtained. The result of both of these queries is

200	BAKER	MATH	GR	50
350	RUSSELL	MATH	JR	20

We can combine the selection and projection as follows:

SELECT   Name, Age
FROM   STUDENT
WHERE   Major = 'MATH'

The result is

BAKER	50
RUSSELL	20

Several conditions can be expressed in the WHERE clause. For example, the expression

SELECT   Name, Age
FROM   STUDENT
WHERE   Major = 'MATH' AND Age > 21

obtains the following:

The conditions in WHERE clauses can refer to a set of values. To do this, the keyword IN or NOT IN may be used. Consider

SELECT   Name
FROM   STUDENT
WHERE   Major IN ['MATH', 'ACCOUNTING']

Notice that multiple values can be placed inside the brackets. This expression means "Display the names of students who have either a math or an accounting major." The result is

PARKS
BAKER
BAKER
RUSSELL
RYE

The expression

SELECT   Name
FROM   STUDENT
WHERE   Major NOT IN ['MATH', 'ACCOUNTING']

causes the names of students other than math or accounting majors to be presented. The result is

JONES
GLASS
JONES

The expression MAJOR IN means the value of the Major column can equal *any* of the listed majors. This is equivalent to the logical OR operator. The expression MAJOR NOT IN means the value must be different from *all* the listed majors.

Sorting

The rows of the result relation can be sorted by the values in one or more columns. Consider the following example:

SELECT   Name, Major, Age
FROM   STUDENT
WHERE   Major = 'ACCOUNTING'
ORDER BY   Name

This query will list the accounting majors in ascending sequence by value of name. The result is

BAKER	ACCOUNTING	41
PARKS	ACCOUNTING	19
RYE	ACCOUNTING	18

More than one column can be chosen for sorting. If so, the first column listed will be the major sort field, the next column the next major sort field, and so on. Columns can also be declared to be ascending (ASC) or descending (DESC), as shown in the next statement:

SELECT   Name, Major, Age
FROM   STUDENT
WHERE   GradeLevel IN ['FR', 'SO', 'SN']
ORDER BY   Major ASC, Age DESC

The result is

BAKER	ACCOUNTING	41
PARKS	ACCOUNTING	19
RYE	ACCOUNTING	18
GLASS	HISTORY	50
JONES	HISTORY	24

ORDER BY can be combined with any of the SELECT statements.

SQL Built-in Functions

SQL provides five built-in functions: COUNT, SUM, AVG, MAX, and MIN.[2] Although COUNT and SUM sound similar, they actually are different. COUNT computes the number of rows in a table, whereas SUM totals numeric columns. AVG, MAX, and MIN also operate on numeric columns: AVG computes the average value, and MAX and MIN obtain the maximum and minimum values of a column in a table.

The query expression

```
SELECT      COUNT(*)
FROM        STUDENT
```

counts the number of STUDENT rows and displays this total in a table with a single row and single column:

With the exception of GROUP BY (considered later), built-in functions cannot be mixed with column names in the SELECT statement. Thus

```
SELECT      Name, COUNT (*)
```

is not allowed.

Consider the expressions

```
SELECT      COUNT (Major)
FROM        STUDENT
```

and

```
SELECT      COUNT (DISTINCT Major)
FROM        STUDENT
```

---

[2] Sometimes built-in functions are referred to as *aggregate functions* to distinguish them from program languages' built-in functions such as SUBSTRING.

The first expression counts all majors, including duplicates, and the second counts only unique majors. The results are

and

8

3

respectively.

The special functions can be used to request a result, as in the preceding examples. In most implementations of SQL, and in the ANSI standard SQL, the built-in functions *cannot* be used as part of a WHERE clause.

■ Built-in Functions and Grouping

To increase their utility, built-in functions can be applied to groups of rows within a table. Such groups are formed by collecting those rows (logically, not physically) that have the same value of a specified column. For example, students can be grouped by major, which means that one group will be formed for each value of MAJOR. For the data in Figure 10-2, there is a group of HISTORY majors, a group of ACCOUNTING majors, and a group of MATH majors.

The SQL keyword GROUP BY instructs the DBMS to group together those rows that have the same value of a column. Consider

```
SELECT      Major, COUNT (*)
FROM        STUDENT
GROUP BY    Major
```

The result of this expression is

HISTORY	3
ACCOUNTING	3
MATH	2

The rows of the STUDENT table have been logically grouped by the value of MAJOR, and the COUNT function sums the number of rows in each group. The result is a table with two columns, the major name and the sum. For subgroups, both columns and built-in functions can be specified in the SELECT statement.

In some cases, we do not want to consider all of the groups. For example, we might form groups of students having the same major and then wish to consider only those groups that have more than two students. In this case, we use the SQL HAVING clause to identify the subset of groups we want to consider.

The following SQL statements can list the majors that have more than two students and also the count of students in each of those majors.

```
SELECT      Major, COUNT (*)
FROM        STUDENT
GROUP BY    Major
HAVING      COUNT (*) > 2
```

Here, groups of students having the same major are formed, and then groups having more than two students are selected. (Other groups are ignored.) The major and the count of students in these selected groups are produced. The result is

| HISTORY | 3 |
| ACCOUNTING | 3 |

For even greater generality, WHERE clauses can be added as well. Doing so, however, can create ambiguity. For example,

```
SELECT      Major, AVG (Age)
FROM        STUDENT
WHERE       GradeLevel = 'SN'
GROUP BY    Major
HAVING      COUNT (*) >
```

The result of this expression will differ depending on whether the WHERE condition is applied before or after the HAVING condition. To eliminate this uncertainty, the SQL standard specifies that WHERE clauses are to be applied first. Accordingly, in the preceding statement, the operations are: select the senior students; form the groups; select the groups that meet the HAVING condition; display the results. In this case, the result is

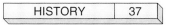

| HISTORY | 37 |

(Incidently, this query is not valid for all implementations of SQL. For some implementations, the only attributes that can appear in the SELECT phrase of a query with GROUP BY are attributes that appear in the GROUP BY phrase and built-in functions of those attributes. Thus in this query, only MAJOR and built-in functions of MAJOR would be allowed.)

QUERYING MULTIPLE TABLES

In this section we extend our discussion of SQL to include operations on two or more tables. The STUDENT, CLASS, and ENROLLMENT data in Figure 10-2 are used to illustrate these SQL commands.

■ Retrieval Using Subquery

Suppose we need to know the names of those students enrolled in the class BD445. If we know that students with SIDs of 100 and 200 are enrolled in this class, the following will produce the correct names:

```
SELECT     Name
FROM       STUDENT
WHERE      SID IN [100, 200]
```

Usually we do not know the SIDs of students in a class, but we do have a facility for finding those out. Look at the expression

```
SELECT     StudentNumber
FROM       ENROLLMENT
WHERE      ClassName = 'BD445'
```

The result of this operation is

These are the student numbers we need. Now when combining the last two queries, we obtain the following:

```
SELECT     Name
FROM       STUDENT
WHERE      SID IN
           (SELECT   StudentNumber
           FROM      ENROLLMENT
           WHERE     ClassName = 'BD445' )
```

Observe that the second SELECT, called the subquery, is enclosed in parentheses.

It may be easier to understand these statements if you work from the bottom and read up. The last three statements obtain the student numbers for people enrolled in BD445, and the first three statements produce the names for the two students selected. The result of this query is

JONES
BAKER

This strategy can be very useful, although for this operation to be semantically correct, SID and StudentNumber must come from the same domain.

Subqueries can consist of three or even more tables. For example, suppose we want to know the names of the students enrolled in classes on Monday, Wednesday, and Friday at 3 o'clock (denoted as MWF3 in our data). First, we need the names of those classes that meet at that time:

```
SELECT      CLASS.Name
FROM        CLASS
WHERE       Time = 'MWF3'
```

(Since we are dealing with three different tables, we qualify the column names with table names to avoid confusion and ambiguity. Thus CLASS.Name refers to the column Name in the relation CLASS.)

Now we get the identifying numbers of students in these classes with the following expression:

```
SELECT      ENROLLMENT.StudentNumber
FROM        ENROLLMENT
WHERE       ENROLLMENT.ClassName IN
            (SELECT   CLASS.Name
             FROM     CLASS
             WHERE    Time = 'MWF3')
```

This yields

100
200
300

which are the numbers of the students in the class MWF3. To get the names of those students, we specify

```
SELECT      STUDENT.Name
FROM        STUDENT
WHERE       STUDENT.SID IN
            (SELECT   ENROLLMENT.StudentNumber
             FROM     ENROLLMENT
             WHERE    ENROLLMENT.ClassName IN
                      (SELECT CLASS.Name
                       FROM   CLASS
                       WHERE  CLASS.Time = 'MWF3'))
```

The result is

JONES
BAKER
BAKER

This strategy works well as long as the attributes in the answer come from a single table. If, however, the result comes from two or more tables, we have a problem. For example, suppose we want to know the names of students and the names of their classes. Say we need SID, StudentName, and ClassName. In this case, the results come from two different tables (STUDENT and ENROLLMENT), and so the subquery strategy will not work.

◼ Joining with SQL

To produce the SID, StudentName, and ClassName for every student, we must join the STUDENT table with the ENROLLMENT table. The following statements will do this:

```
SELECT      STUDENT.SID, STUDENT.Name, ENROLLMENT.ClassName
FROM        STUDENT, ENROLLMENT
WHERE       STUDENT.SID = ENROLLMENT.StudentNumber
```

Recall that a join is the combination of a product operation, followed by a selection, followed (usually) by a projection. In this expression, the FROM statement expresses the product of STUDENT and ENROLLMENT, and then the WHERE statement expresses the selection. The meaning is "Select from the product of STUDENT and ENROLLMENT those rows in which SID of STUDENT equals StudentNumber of ENROLLMENT." Finally, after the selection, the projection of the student number, name, and class name is taken. The result is

100	JONES	BD445
150	PARKS	BA200
200	BAKER	BD445
200	BAKER	CS250
300	BAKER	CS125
400	RYE	BA200
400	RYE	BF410
400	RYE	CS250
450	JONES	BA200

The WHERE clause can contain qualifiers in addition to those needed for the join. For example,

```
SELECT      STUDENT.SID, ENROLLMENT.ClassName
FROM        STUDENT, ENROLLMENT
WHERE       STUDENT.SID = ENROLLMENT.StudentNumber
   AND      STUDENT.Name = 'RYE'
   AND      ENROLLMENT.PositionNumber = 1
```

The additional qualifiers here are STUDENT.Name = 'RYE' and ENROLLMENT.PositionNumber = 1. This operation will list the student number and class name of all students named RYE who were first to enroll in a class. The result is

400	BF410

When data is needed from more than two tables, we can use a similar strategy. In the next example, three tables are joined:

SELECT   STUDENT.SID, CLASS.Name, CLASS.Time, ENROLLMENT.Position-Number
FROM   STUDENT, ENROLLMENT, CLASS
WHERE   STUDENT.SID = ENROLLMENT.StudentNumber
   AND   ENROLLMENT.ClassName = CLASS.Name
   AND   STUDENT.Name = 'BAKER'

The result of this operation is

200	BD445	MWF3	2
200	CS250	MWF12	1
300	CS150	MWF3	1

Comparison of SQL Subquery and Join

A join can be used as an alternative way of expressing many subqueries. For example, we used a subquery to find the students enrolled in the class BD445. We can also use a join to express this query:

SELECT   STUDENT.Name
FROM   STUDENT, ENROLLMENT
WHERE   STUDENT.SID = ENROLLMENT.StudentNumber
   AND   ENROLLMENT.ClassName = 'BD445'

Similarly, the query "What are the names of the students in class MWF at 3?" can be expressed as

SELECT   STUDENT.NAME
FROM   STUDENT, ENROLLMENT, CLASS
WHERE   STUDENT.SID = ENROLLMENT.StudentNumber
   AND   ENROLLMENT.ClassName = CLASS.Name
   AND   CLASS.Time = 'MWF3'

Although join expressions can substitute for many subquery expressions, they cannot substitute for all of them. For instance, subqueries that involve EXISTS and NOT EXISTS (discussed in the next section) cannot be represented by joins.

Similarly, subqueries cannot be substituted for all joins. When using a join, the displayed columns may come from any of the joined tables, but when using a subquery, the displayed columns may come from only the table named in the FROM expression in the first SELECT. For example, suppose we want to know the names of classes taken by undergraduates. We can express this as a subquery:

SELECT   DISTINCT ClassName
FROM   ENROLLMENT

WHERE   StudentNumber IN
           (SELECT   SID
           FROM   STUDENT
           WHERE   GradeLevel NOT = 'GR')

or as a join:

SELECT   DISTINCT ENROLLMENT.ClassName
FROM   ENROLLMENT, STUDENT
WHERE   ENROLLMENT.StudentNumber = STUDENT.SID
   AND   STUDENT.GradeLevel NOT = 'GR'

But if we want to know both the names of the classes and the grade levels of the undergraduate students, we must use a join. A subquery will not suffice because the desired results come from two different tables. That is, the names of the classes are stored in ENROLLMENT, and the names of the students are stored in STUDENT. The following obtains the correct answer:

SELECT   DISTINCT ENROLLMENT.ClassName, STUDENT.GradeLevel
FROM   ENROLLMENT, STUDENT
WHERE   ENROLLMENT.StudentNumber = STUDENT.SID
   AND   STUDENT.GradeLevel NOT = 'GR'

The result is

BA200	SO
CS150	SN
BA200	FR
BF410	FR
CS250	FR
BA200	SN

■ EXISTS and NOT EXISTS

EXISTS and NOT EXISTS are logical operators whose value is either true or false depending on the presence or absence of rows that fit the qualifying conditions. For example, suppose we want to know the student numbers of students enrolled in more than one class.

SELECT   DISTINCT StudentNumber
FROM   ENROLLMENT A
WHERE   EXISTS
   (SELECT   *
   FROM   ENROLLMENT B
   WHERE   A.StudentNumber = B.StudentNumber
     AND   A.ClassName NOT = B.ClassName)

In this example, both the query and the subquery refer to the ENROLLMENT table. To prevent ambiguity, these two uses of ENROLLMENT have been assigned a different name. In the first FROM statement, ENROLLMENT is assigned the temporary and arbitrary name A, and in the second FROM statement, it is assigned another temporary and arbitrary name, B.

The meaning of the subquery expression is this: Find two rows in ENROLLMENT having the same student number but different class names. (This means that the student is taking more than one class.) If two such rows exist, then the logical value of EXISTS is true. In this case, we present the student number in the answer. Otherwise, the logical value of the EXISTS is false, and so we do not present that SID in the answer.

Another way of viewing this query is to imagine two separate and identical copies of the ENROLLMENT table. Call one copy Table A and the other copy Table B. We compare each row in A with each row in B. First we look at the first row in A and the first row in B. In this case, since the two rows are identical, both the StudentNumbers and the ClassNames are the same, and so we do not display the SID.

Now look at the first row in A and the second row in B. If the StudentNumbers are the same and the ClassNames are different, we display the StudentNumber. Essentially, we are comparing the first row of ENROLLMENT with the second row of ENROLLMENT. For the data in Figure 10-2, neither the StudentNumbers nor the ClassNames are the same.

We continue comparing the first row of A with each row of B. If the conditions are ever met, we print the StudentNumber. When all of the rows in B have been examined, we move to the second row of A and compare it with all the rows in B (actually, if we are considering the nth rows in A, only those rows greater than n need to be considered in B).

The result of this query is

| 200 |
| 400 |

To illustrate the application of NOT EXISTS, suppose we want to know the names of students taking all classes. Another way of stating this is that we want the names of students such that there are no classes that the student did not take. The following expresses this:

```
SELECT      STUDENT.Name
FROM        STUDENT
WHERE       NOT EXISTS
     (SELECT      *
      FROM        ENROLLMENT
      WHERE       NOT EXISTS
           (SELECT      *
            FROM        CLASS
```

```
WHERE        CLASS.Name = ENROLLMENT.ClassName
AND          ENROLLMENT.StudentNumber= STUDENT.SID))
```

This query has three parts. In the bottom part, it finds classes the student did take. The middle part determines whether any classes were found that the student did not take. If not, then the student is taking all classes, and his or her name is displayed.

This query may be difficult to understand. If you have trouble with it, use the data in Figure 10-2 and follow the instructions. For that data, the answer is that no student is taking all classes. You might try to change the data so that a student does take all classes. Another way to look at this query is to try to solve it in a way other than with NOT EXISTS. The problems you encounter will help you understand why NOT EXISTS is necessary.

A final example combines many SQL concepts and illustrates the power of this data sublanguage. Suppose we want to know the names of graduate students taking classes only with other graduate students.

```
SELECT      A.Name
FROM        STUDENT A
WHERE       STUDENT.GradeLevel = 'GR'
     AND  NOT EXISTS
     (SELECT        *
     FROM           ENROLLMENT B
     WHERE          STUDENT.SID = B.StudentNumber
          AND   B.ClassName IN
          (SELECT     C.ClassName
          FROM        ENROLLMENT C
          WHERE       B.ClassName = C.ClassName
               AND        C.StudentNumber IN
               (SELECT    D.SID
               FROM       STUDENT D
               WHERE      C.StudentNumber =D.SID
               AND D.GradeLevel NOT = 'GR')))
```

The meaning of this query is "Present the names of students where there is no row in ENROLLMENT that matches the student with a class that is one of the classes that are matched with students who have a grade level other than graduate." The result of this query is

JONES

The last three queries are complicated, but you should not presume from this that SQL need always be this way. Actually, compared with the alternatives, SQL is simple. These last three queries are difficult only because we are solving queries that are logically quite complex. For most day-to-day problems, however, SQL queries are far simpler and straightforward.

CHANGING DATA

SQL has provisions for changing data in tables by inserting new rows, deleting rows, and modifying values in existing rows. SQL also can change the data structure, although we will not explore this until we study DB2 in Chapter 12.

■ Inserting Data

Rows can be inserted into a table one at a time or in groups. To insert a single row, we state

```
INSERT    INTO  ENROLLMENT
          VALUES (400, 'BD445', 44)
```

If we do not know all of this data—for instance, if we do not know PositionNumber—we could say

```
INSERT    INTO ENROLLMENT
          (StudentNumber, ClassName)
          VALUES (400, 'BD445')
```

PositionNumber could then be added later. Note that this causes the value of PositionNumber to have a null value in the new row.

We can also copy rows in mass from one table to another. For example, suppose we want to fill the JUNIOR table defined in Figure 10.1.

```
INSERT    INTO JUNIOR
      VALUES
      (SELECT   SID, Name, Major
      FROM      STUDENT
      WHERE     GradeLevel = 'JR')
```

The contained SELECT, and all of the SQL SELECT expressions developed in the previous two sections, can be used to identify the rows to be copied. This feature offers quite powerful capabilities.

■ Deleting Data

As with insertion, rows can be deleted one at a time or in groups. The following example deletes the row for Student 100:

```
DELETE    STUDENT
WHERE     STUDENT.SID = 100
```

Note that if Student 100 is enrolled in classes, this delete will cause an integrity problem, as the ENROLLMENT rows having StudentNumber = 100 will have no corresponding STUDENT row.

Groups of rows can be deleted as shown in the next two examples, which delete all enrollments for accounting majors as well as all accounting majors.

```
DELETE      ENROLLMENT
WHERE       ENROLLMENT.StudentNumber IN
    (SELECT      STUDENT.SID
     FROM        STUDENT
     WHERE       STUDENT.Major = 'ACCOUNTING')
DELETE      STUDENT
WHERE       STUDENT.Major = 'ACCOUNTING'
```

The order of these two operations is important, for if it were reversed, none of the ENROLLMENT rows would be deleted because the matching STUDENT rows would already have been deleted.

■ Modifying Data

Rows can also be modified one at a time or in groups. The keyword SET is used to change a column value. After SET, the name of the column to be changed and then the new value or way of computing the new value is specified. Consider two examples:

```
UPDATE      STUDENT
SET         PositionNumber = 44
WHERE       SID = 400
```

and

```
UPDATE      STUDENT
SET         PositionNumber = MAX(PositionNumber) + 1
WHERE       SID = 400
```

In the second UPDATE statement, the value of the column is calculated using the MAX built-in function. Some implementations of SQL, however, may not allow the built-in function to be used as an argument in the SET command.

To illustrate mass updates, suppose the name of a course has been changed from BD445 to BD564. In this case, to prevent integrity problems, both the ENROLLMENT and the CLASS tables must be changed.

```
UPDATE      ENROLLMENT
SET         ClassName = 'BD564'
WHERE       ClassName = 'BD445'

UPDATE      CLASS
SET         ClassName = 'BD564'
WHERE       ClassName = 'BD445'
```

Remember that mass updates can be quite dangerous. The user is given great power—power that when used correctly can rapidly perform the task at hand but when used incorrectly can cause serious problems.

SUMMARY

SQL is today's most important relational data manipulation language. It has become the standard for information exchange among computers, and its popularity continues to grow. SQL statements that operate on a single table include SELECT, SELECT with WHERE, SELECT with GROUP BY, and SELECT with GROUP BY and HAVING. SQL also contains the built-in functions of COUNT, SUM, AVG, MAX, and MIN.

Operations on two or more tables can be done using subquery, joins, EXISTS, and NOT EXISTS. Subqueries and joins perform many of the same operations, but they do not completely substitute for one another. Subqueries require that the attributes retrieved arise from a single relation, but joins do not. On the other hand, some queries are possible with subqueries and EXISTS and NOT EXISTS that are impossible with joins.

The SQL statements for data modification include INSERT, DELETE, and UPDATE commands, which are used to add, remove, and change data values.

In this chapter we presented the basic SQL commands in generic form, and in the next two chapters we use these commands to process a database using commercial DBMS products.

GROUP I QUESTIONS

The questions in this group refer to the following three relations:

SALESPERSON (<u>Name</u>, Age, Salary)
ORDER (<u>Number</u>, CustName, SalespersonName, Amount)
CUSTOMER (<u>Name</u>, City, IndustryType)

An instance of these relations is shown in Figure 10-3. Use the data in those tables and show the SQL statements to display or modify data as indicated in the following questions:

10.1 Show the ages and salaries of all salespeople.

10.2 Show the ages and salaries of all salespeople but omit duplicates.

10.3 Show the names of all salespeople under thirty years old.

10.4 Show the names of all salespeople who have an order with ABERNATHY CONSTRUCTION.

10.5 Show the names and salary of all salespeople who do not have an order with ABERNATHY CONSTRUCTION, in ascending order of salary.

10.6 Compute the number of orders.

FIGURE 10-3

Sample data for Group I questions

Name	Age	Salary
Abel	63	120,000
Baker	38	42,000
Jones	26	36,000
Murphy	42	50,000
Zenith	59	118,000
Kobad	27	34,000

SALESPERSON

Number	CustName	SalespersonName	Amount
100	Abernathy Construction	Zenith	560
200	Abernathy Construction	Jones	1800
300	Manchester Lumber	Abel	480
400	Amalgamated Housing	Abel	2500
500	Abernathy Construction	Murphy	6000
600	Tri-City Builders	Abel	700
700	Manchester Lumber	Jones	150

ORDER

Name	City	IndustryType
Abernathy Construction	Willow	B
Manchester Lumber	Manchester	F
Tri-City Builders	Memphis	B
Amalgamated Housing	Memphis	B

CUSTOMER

10.7 Compute the number of different customers who have an order.

10.8 Compute the average age of a salesperson.

10.9 Show the name of the oldest salesperson.

10.10 Compute the number of orders for each salesperson.

10.11 Compute the number of orders for each salesperson, considering only orders for an amount exceeding 500.

10.12 Show the names and ages of salespeople who have an order with ABERNATHY CONSTRUCTION in descending order of age (use a subquery).

10.13 Show the names and ages of salespeople who have an order with ABERNATHY CONSTRUCTION, in descending order of age (use a join).

10.14 Show the age of salespeople who have an order with a customer in MEMPHIS (use a subquery).

10.15 Show the age of salespeople who have an order with a customer in MEMPHIS (use a join).

10.16 Show the industry type and ages of the salespeople of all orders for companies in MEMPHIS.

10.17 Show the names of salespeople who have two or more orders.

10.18 Show the names and ages of salespeople who have two or more orders.

10.19 Show the names and ages of salespeople who have an order with all customers.

10.20 Show an SQL statement to insert a new row into CUSTOMER.

10.21 Show an SQL statement to insert a new name and age into SALESPERSON; assume that salary is not determined.

10.22 Show an SQL statement to insert rows into a new table, HIGH-ACHIEVER (Name, Age), in which to be included, a salesperson must have a salary of at least 100,000.

10.23 Show an SQL statement to delete customer ABERNATHY CONSTRUCTION.

10.24 Show an SQL statement to delete all orders for ABERNATHY CONSTRUCTION.

10.25 Show an SQL statement to change the salary of salesperson JONES to 45,000.

10.26 Show an SQL statement to give all salespeople a 10 percent pay increase.

10.27 Assume that salesperson JONES changes his name to PARKS. Show the SQL statements that make the appropriate changes.

GROUP II QUESTIONS

10.28 Find out about a relational DBMS product such as Paradox for Windows, Microsoft Access, or Informix. For the product you select, explain how its SQL syntax differs from that used in this chapter. Answer the following questions in your response:

a. How are single-table queries expressed?

b. What built-in functions does it have? What limits are set on their use?

c. How are subqueries expressed?

d. How are joins expressed?

e. Are EXISTS and NOT EXISTS supported? If so, how do they differ from the syntax shown in this chapter?

RELATIONAL IMPLEMENTATION ON A PERSONAL COMPUTER

The goal of this chapter is to bring together the chapters on database and application design with the chapters on relational implementation and show how all these topics are used in the development of a database application. To do this, we will build a database and application that meets several important application requirements for the View Ridge Gallery, a case introduced in Chapter 8.

The concepts of this chapter are illustrated using Microsoft Access, a Windows-based DBMS product. We use Access because it is modern and popular and has many features, and you are likely to encounter it sometime in your career. But this choice is not meant to be an endorsement of Access over other similar products such as Borland's Paradox for Windows and other GUI-based DBMS products.

IMPLEMENTING A RELATIONAL APPLICATION

A database is a model of the users' model of their business activities, and so to implement it, we must first have such a model. Here we assume that the model has already been developed and that it has been expressed in terms of semantic objects.

We use the semantic objects shown in Figure 11-1 as the basis of our discussion. They are a subset of the objects described for the View Ridge Gallery in Chapter 8; that is, the model has been simplified by omitting the Transaction group property

FIGURE 11-1

Modified View Ridge Gallery Objects

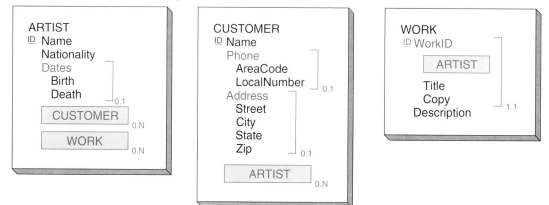

from the WORK semantic object. This has been done to avoid complexities that are not important to the purposes of this chapter.

CREATING THE DATABASE SCHEMA

Figure 11-2 shows the relations that represent the objects in Figure 11-1. These relations use data columns as keys; surrogate keys are not used. The N:M relationship between ARTIST and CUSTOMER is carried in the intersection relation ARTIST_CUSTOMER_INT. Note that the columns of this table are both local and foreign keys, and so they are both underlined and italicized. The 1:N relationship from ARTIST to WORK is carried by the column ArtistName. Note that it, too, is both underlined and italicized in the WORK table.

To define these tables to Access, we must create a new database. This has been done in Figure 11-3. The box in the upper left-hand portion of the screen is called the database container, and it has six buttons: Table, Query, Form, Report, Macro,

FIGURE 11-2

Relations Representing the Objects in Figure 11-1

ARTIST (<u>ArtistName</u>, Nationality, Birthdate, DeceasedDate)

CUSTOMER (<u>CustomerNumber</u>, Name, AreaCode, LocalNumber, Street, City, State, Zip)

ARTIST_CUSTOMER_INT (<u>*ArtistName*</u>, <u>*CustomerNumber*</u>)

WORK (<u>*ArtistName*</u>, <u>Title</u>, <u>Copy</u>, Description)

FIGURE 11-3

An Empty Microsoft Access Database

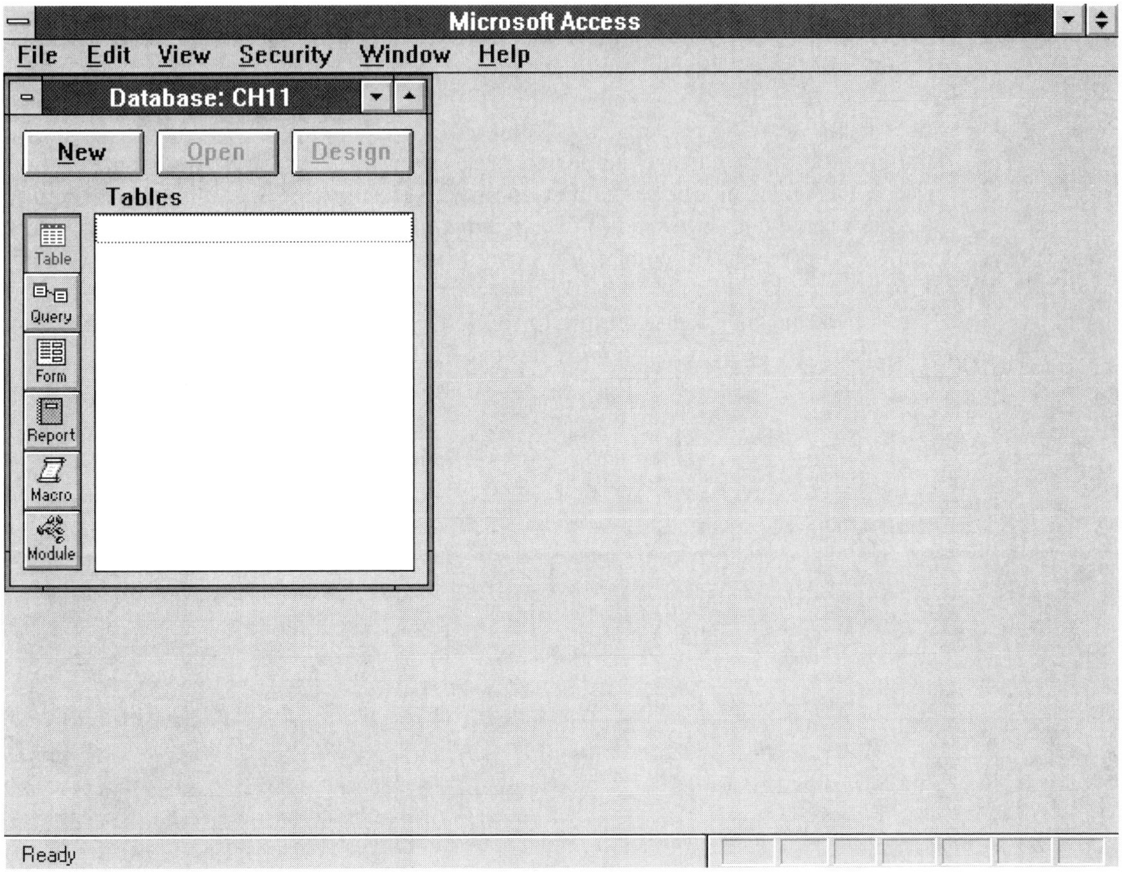

and Module. When the developer presses one of those buttons, a list of items of that category appears in the list box to the right of the column of buttons. Hence, pressing the Tables button causes a list of tables to be displayed. But since this database is empty, nothing appears in this list in Figure 11-3.

In this text, we will be concerned with only the first four buttons. The last two, Macros and Modules, pertain to the development of application program logic. Macros are groups of high-level actions, akin to what we earlier referred to as stored procedures. Modules are groups of Microsoft Access Basic programs; this language is a GUI-oriented version of BASIC that is similar to Microsoft's Visual Basic. Any further discussion of the functions of these buttons will take us too far afield from database processing, however, so consult the Access documentation for more information.[1]

---

[1] *Microsoft Access User's Guide*, Microsoft Corporation, Doc. DB26141-1092, 1992.

■ Creating Tables

To create a table in Access, the developer presses the Table button and then the NEW button: This brings up a screen like that shown in Figure 11-4. To define the columns of the table (referred to as fields in Access), the developer types the names of the fields in the Field Name column of the form and enters the data type of each field in the second column. Only Number and Text fields are needed in this table. Other data types that are supported are Date/Time, Currency, Boolean, Counter (Access assigns a unique sequential number to each row of the table), and Memo (a large, variable-length text field). The third column of this form, labeled Description, can contain optional documentation about the column, but it is left blank in Figure 11-4.

Notice the small key icon just to the left of the CustomerNumber Field Name. This means that CustomerNumber has been set to be the key of the table.

FIGURE 11-4

Microsoft Access Table Definition Form

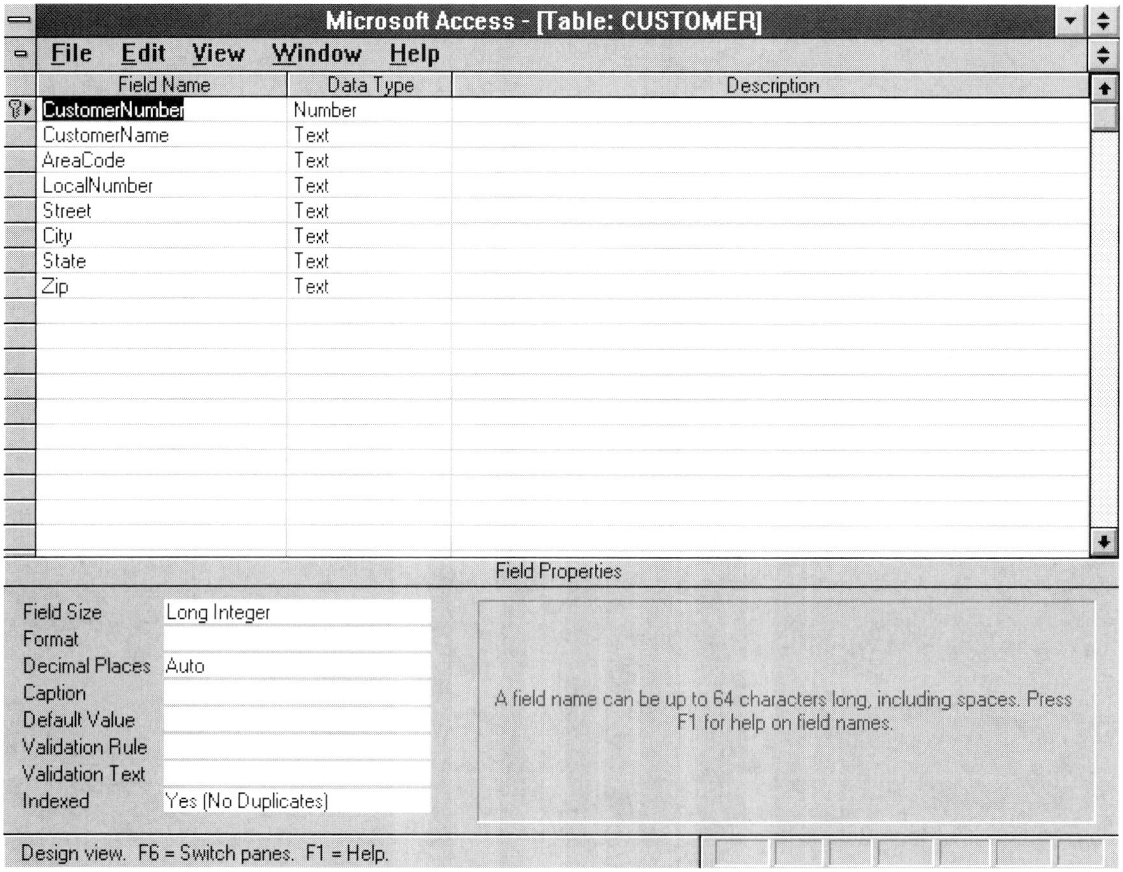

The bottom of the table definition form contains additional data about each property. In Figure 11-4, the focus is on the CustomerNumber field, and so the additional properties of that field are shown in the bottom of this form. The Field Size is shown as Long Integer (this means a 32-bit integer); Decimal Places are set to automatic; and the Indexed property has been set to Yes (No Duplicates). This means that Access is to create and maintain a unique index for the CustomerNumber property. The Indexed Property was automatically set by Access for this column when it was defined as a key column. If the developer knows that other columns are to be used to access directly a row or for sorting, those columns, too, can be defined as Indexed. CustomerName is a likely candidate for a nonunique index because users are likely to access rows by means of CustomerName.

When the table definition has been completed, the developer closes the window, and Access prompts for a table name. The developer then enters the name CUSTOMER to save this table under that name.

The other tables in Figure 11-2 would be defined in a similar manner. The column names are entered, the properties are set, keys are defined, and the table is saved under the appropriate name.

■ Defining Relationships

Once the tables have been created, the relationships among them can be defined. Access recognizes both one-to-one and one-to-many relationships. The advantage of defining relationships to Access is that when rows of two tables need to be connected (in a JOIN, a multitable form, or a report), Access uses the defined relationship as the default way of combining the two tables. This can spare the developer both time and confusion.

Figure 11-5 shows a form that is used to do this with Access. To open this form, the developer clicks Edit, Relationships. Then the table on the one side of the relationship (or, in the case of one to one, one of the two tables) is entered into the Primary Table combo box. The type of relationship is indicated by clicking the appropriate option button, and the name of the second table in entered in the Related Table combo box.

The key fields of the primary table are listed in the middle part of the form. The developer matches each such field (there is only one in Figure 11-5), with a field of the related table. In this case, both fields are named ArtistName (see Figure 11-2). Then the developer clicks the Add button.

Access allows the developer to select a type of interrelation constraint checking. If she checks Enforce Referential Integrity, Access will not allow her to enter a value of ArtistName in WORK that does not already exist in ARTIST. In addition, if a row of ARTIST is deleted that has one or more dependent rows of WORK, either the deletion of ARTIST will be disallowed, or all of the dependent WORK rows will be deleted when the ARTIST row is deleted. If desired, the referential integrity check should be made before pressing the Add button.

Access also provides some capabilities for defining data value restriction constraints, which are defined in the Table definition form, in the Field Properties section. We will not consider them here.

FIGURE 11-5

Defining a Relationship Between ARTIST and WORK

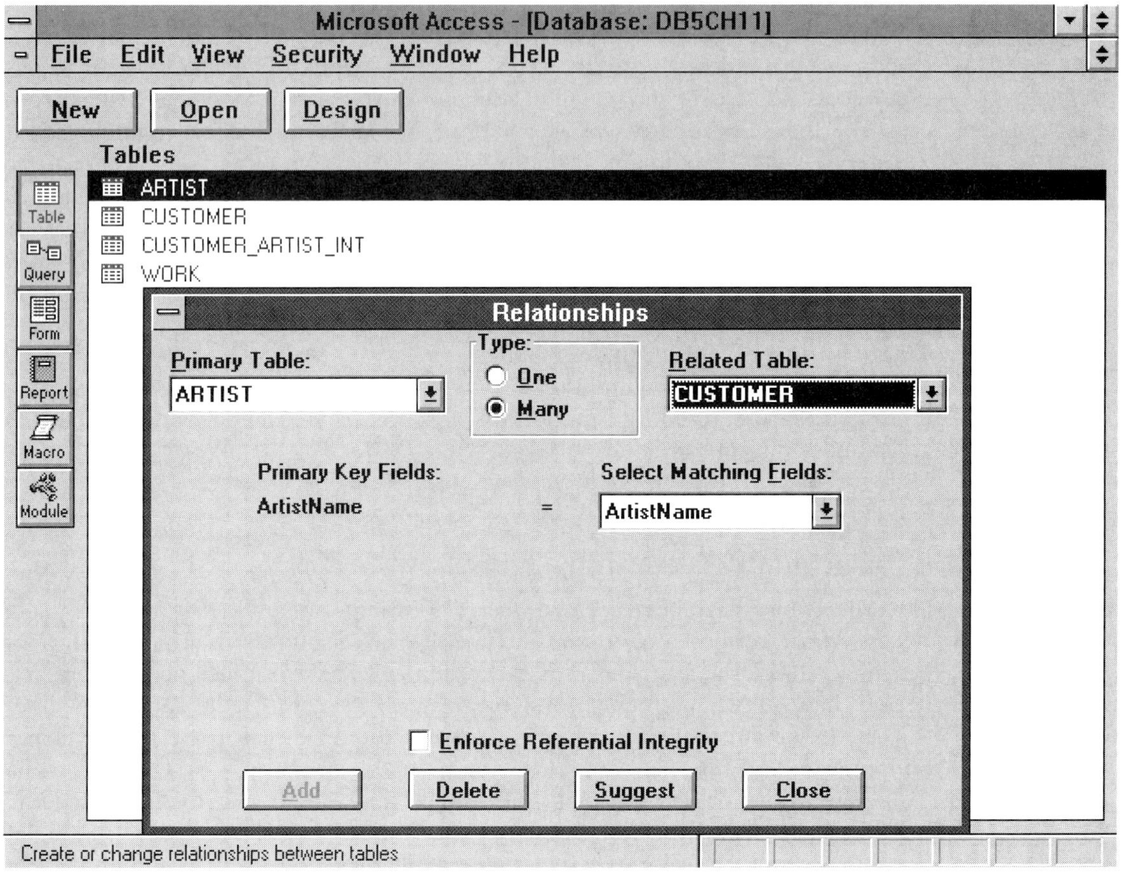

Creating Queries

Queries are used for three purposes in Access: as a means for the user to pose ad hoc questions on the data, as the basis of forms and reports, and as the basis of multivalued controls such as combo boxes. In this section, we consider the development of queries that can be used for any or all of these purposes. Later we demonstrate how to bind a query to a form, report, or other control.

Single-Table Queries

Queries can be defined either by using a variation of query by example, called graphical QBE, or by entering SQL statements directly. Figure 11-6 shows an example of defining a single-table query using QBE. The top part of this form is the table on which the query is based, with the key of the table in boldface type.

FIGURE 11-6

Using Access QBE to Define a Single-Table Query

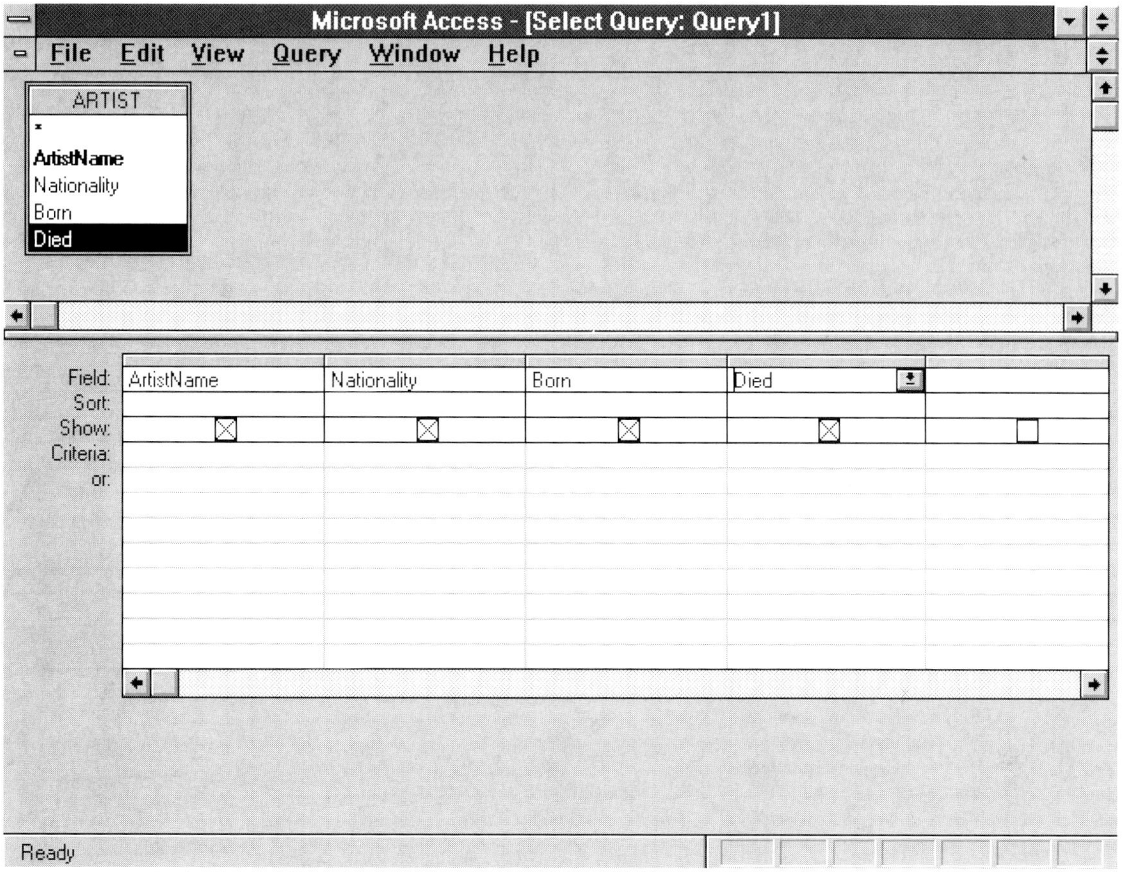

To include a field in the query, the field name is dragged from the table box and dropped on a column of the query grid in the bottom part of the form. If the column is to be used for sorting, the sort criteria are entered on the second row of the grid. If the box is checked, the column will appear in the result of the query. Search criteria can be added to the additional rows of the grid. For example, if the expression < #1/1/50# were added to the Criteria row of the Born column in the grid in Figure 11-6, only those ARTISTs that were born before 1950 would be part of the query result.[2]

Figure 11-7 shows an Access SQL expression equivalent to the query in Figure 11-6. Access SQL is quite similar to the standard SQL discussed in Chapter 10, except that the keyword *DISTINCT* has been changed to *DISTINCTROW* in Access,

---

[2] Dates are enclosed in pound signs in Access so that the expression parser in Access can distinguish dates from division operations.

FIGURE 11-7

Access Version of SQL Statement for the Query in Figure 11-6

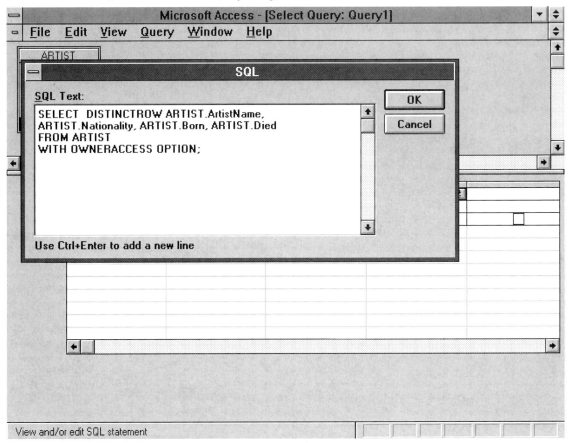

and the phrase OWNERACCESS has been appended to the query. This phrase concerns Access's security implementation and is beyond the scope of our discussion. Finally, all Access SQL statements must be terminated with a semicolon.

Multitable Queries

Figure 11-8 is a query of three tables. The developer has instructed Access to include these three tables in the query (by selecting the Add Table dialogue [not shown], which can be activated by the Query menu choice at the top of the form in Figure 11-8). The lines between the tables represent table relationships, which Access automatically draws. This first line shows that ARTIST is related to

FIGURE 11-8

Using Access QBE to Define a Three-Table Query

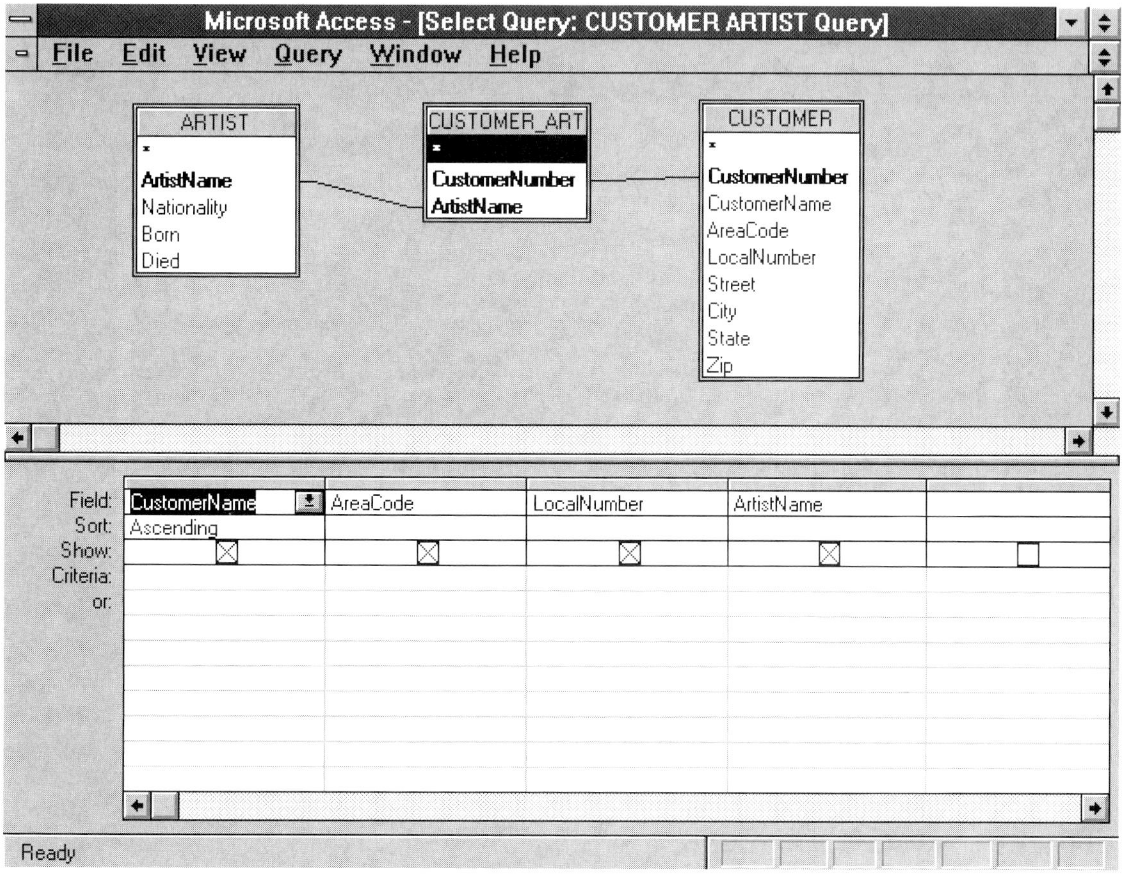

ARTIST_CUSTOMER_INT (the table name is cut off in Figure 11-8), by the field ArtistName in both tables.

Those fields that are to appear in the query can also be dragged and dropped, as with a single-table query. For the query in Figure 11-8, CustomerName, AreaCode, LocalNumber, and ArtistName are to appear.

The SQL statement for the query in Figure 11-8 is shown in Figure 11-9. The join expression in this statement is similar to the syntax shown in Chapter 9 for the relational algebra JOIN. The term INNER JOIN is used to indicate that null values in join fields are to be ignored when forming the join.

The sample data for the query in Figure 11-9 is shown in Figure 11-10. Observe that the rows of this table are sorted by CustomerName, as indicated in the query definition.

FIGURE 11-9

Access SQL Statement for the Query in Figure 11-8

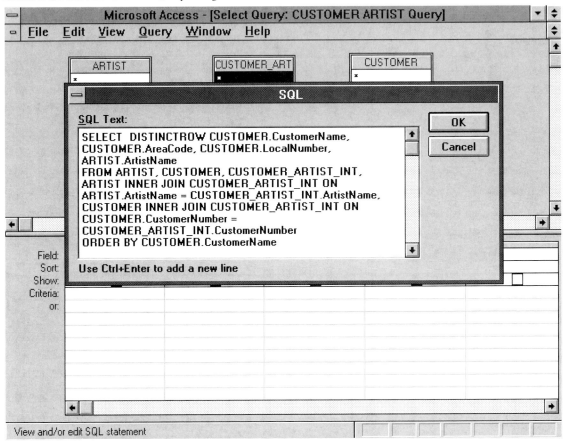

CREATING FORMS

An Access form is used to display rows from a table or query. Since queries can combine several tables, an Access form may be based on data from several tables. When creating a form, the designer must first create the table or query and then bind that table or query to the form. The term **bind** means to associate logically the table or query with the form.

Access forms consist of an arrangement of GUI controls. Examples of the types of controls available are labels, text boxes, combo boxes, and subform regions. Each control has a set of properties that can be changed. These properties govern characteristics such as caption, color, font type, font size, position on the form, width, and length. Some controls are bound to tables or columns of tables, and the particular entity to which a control is bound is a property that can be set or changed by the developer.

FIGURE 11-10

Sample Result of the Query in Figure 11-9

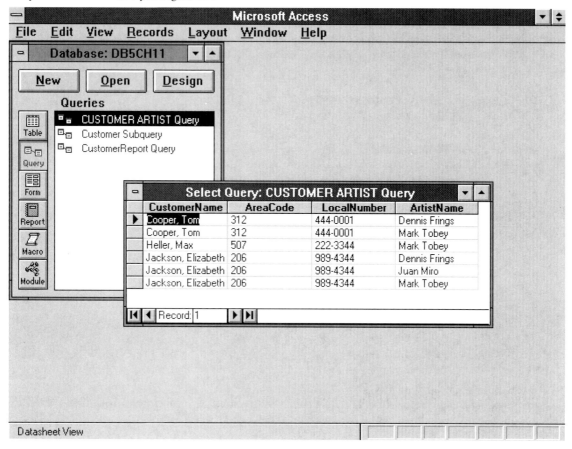

To create a new form, the developer presses the Form button in the database container and then presses the New button, thereby bringing up a blank form. He then places controls on the form. Figure 11-11 shows a form that is in the process of being created. The long vertical window is the Access Toolbox, which contains tools that can be used to create controls of various types. In Figure 11-11, the user has clicked the arrow tool, which is used to select controls on the form.

Figure 11-11 shows two controls. The first is the label "View Ridge Gallery," and the second is the label "Artist Data." The second control is in the process of being created in Figure 11-11; that is, the user is typing the phrase "Artist Data" into the text label.

The properties of the form and the controls on the form can be viewed by opening a property window (a selection under the View menu choice). Figure 11-12 shows the property window with the properties of the text label being created. Note

FIGURE 11-11

Access Form Definition and Toolbox

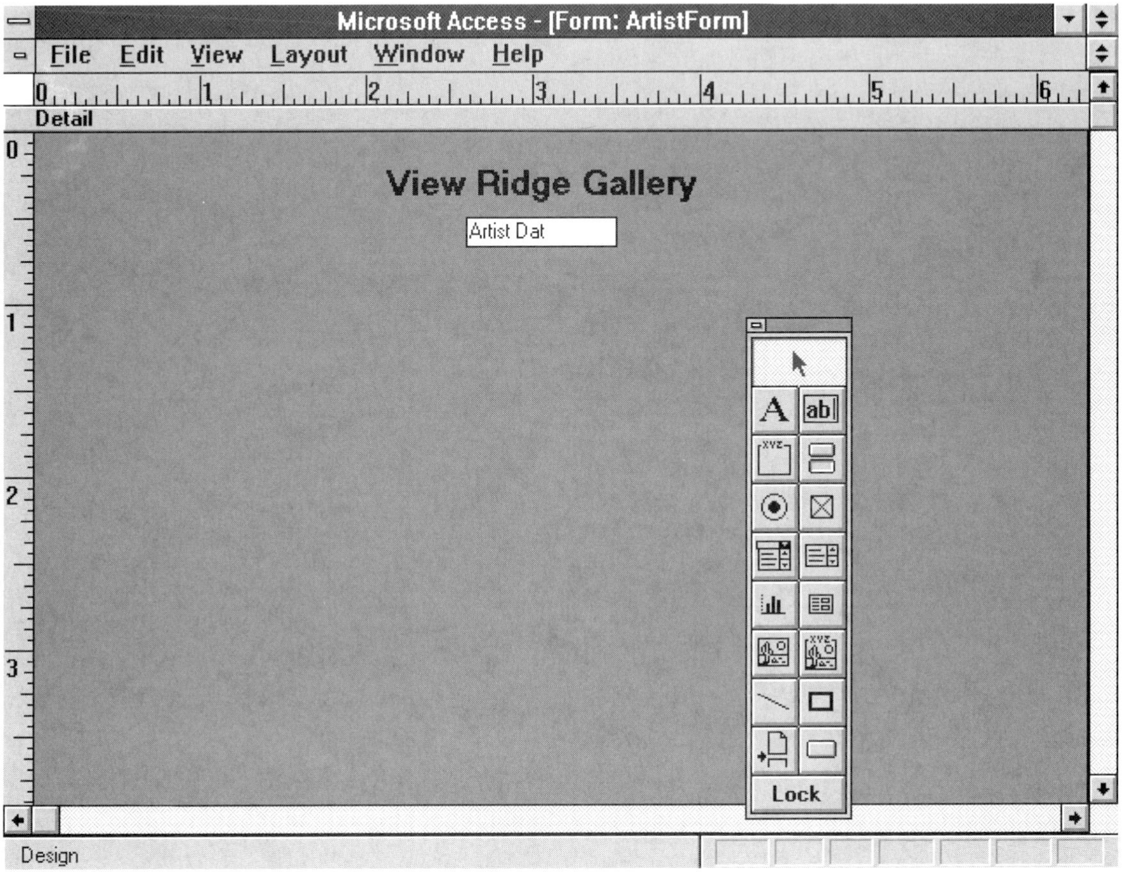

that the Caption property is set to Artist Data (the caption of the label). The other properties shown are not important to this discussion.

■ Binding a Relation to a Form

As stated, forms can be used to show the data from the row of a table or query. To do this, the relation must be bound to the form, and Figure 11-13 demonstrates how this is done. The properties of the form are made visible by clicking on a region of the form. Then the property Record Source is clicked. When this is done, a list box containing the names of tables and queries is displayed, and the developer chooses a name from this list to bind that name to the current form. In Figure 11-13 the table ARTIST has been bound to the form, and so at this point, any of the columns of ARTIST are available to be bound to the form.

FIGURE 11-12

Properties for a Text Label

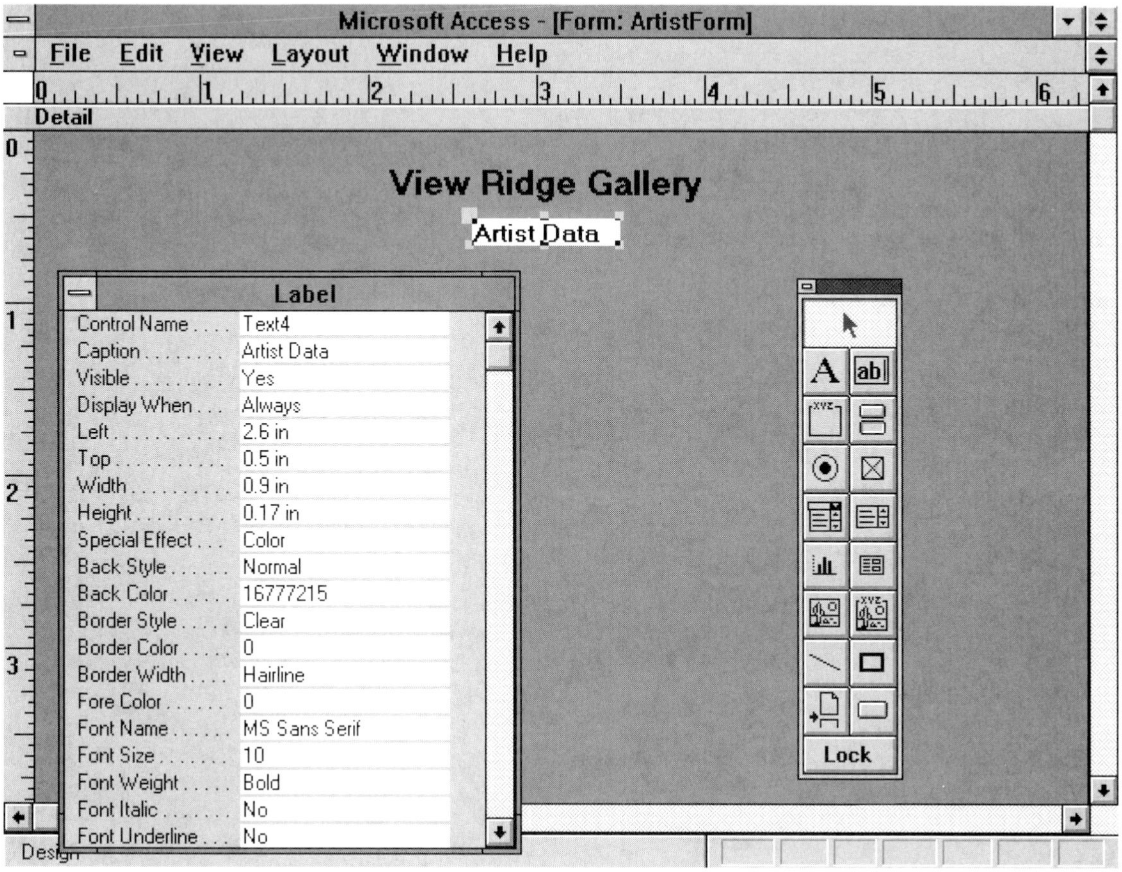

◼ Binding a Column to a Text Box Control

Figure 11-14 shows the form after several text boxes have been created. Each text box has a label and a box that will contain column data. The first text box has the label "Artist Name" and has been bound to the column ArtistName. Nationality has also been created.

In Figure 11-14, the developer is in the process of binding the Born column of the ARTIST table to a text box, by setting the Control Source property to Born. To make this association, the developer clicks on the Control Source entry field, and a list box appears with the names of all the columns in the table or query. Figure 11-14 shows the expanded list box.

Every control has a name. The control being bound in Figure 11-14 is named Field15, and this value is shown in the property list under Control Name. The names

FIGURE 11-13

Binding a Relation to a Form

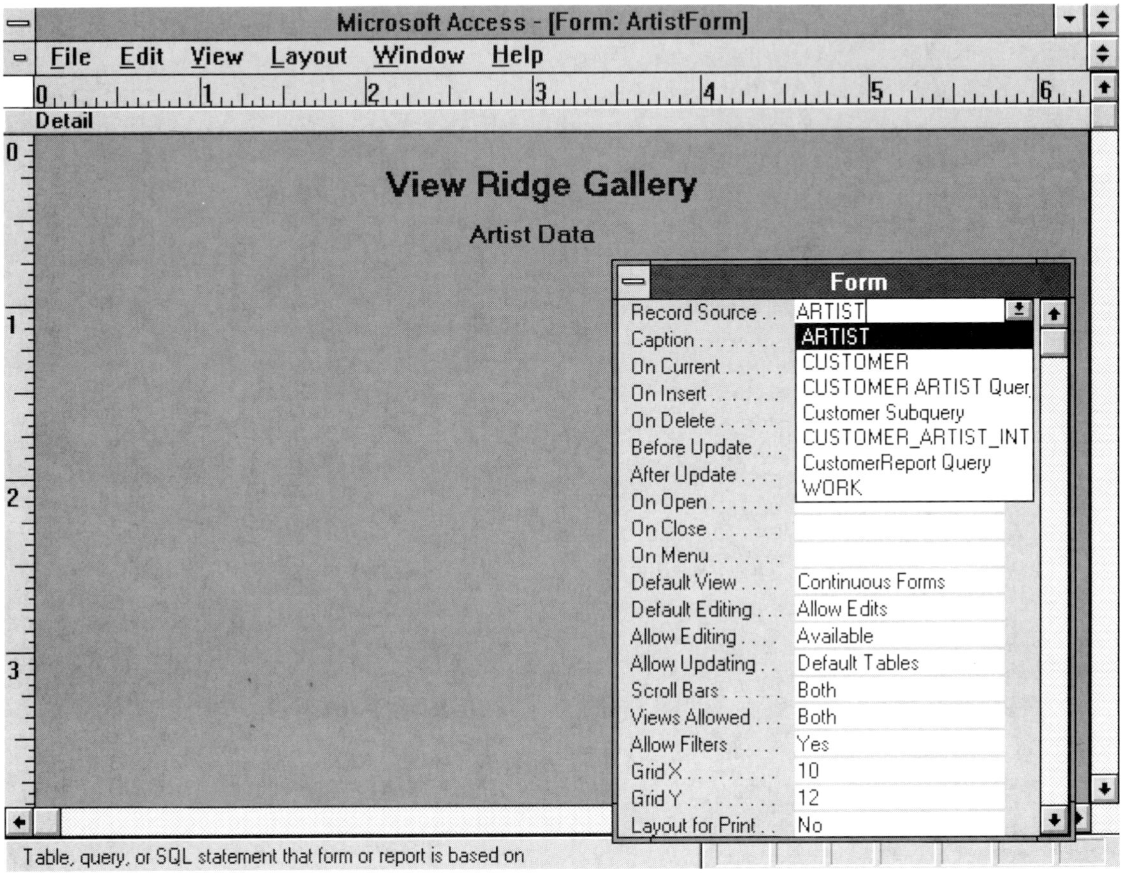

of the controls are not important to this application, as they are used primarily by macros and Access Basic programs that need to refer programatically to values in the controls on the form. Other properties of the text box pertain to its format, the number of decimal places to be shown, validation rules, and so forth.

The properties Before Update, After Update, On Enter, and so forth down to On Dbl Click represent events that can apply to the text box. For example, after the user changes the value in the text box and moves to another control on the form, Access generates the event After Update. By placing the name of the macro or BASIC function into the After Update property, the developer can specify that a particular macro or BASIC function be called at that point.[3] Other properties in the form are not important now to our discussion.

---

[3]   Actually, so that Access can tell the difference between a macro and a function, function names must be preceded by an equals sign. Thus to call the function CHECKVALUE, the developer would enter =CHECKVALUE() into the property.

FIGURE 11-14

Binding a Column to a Text Box

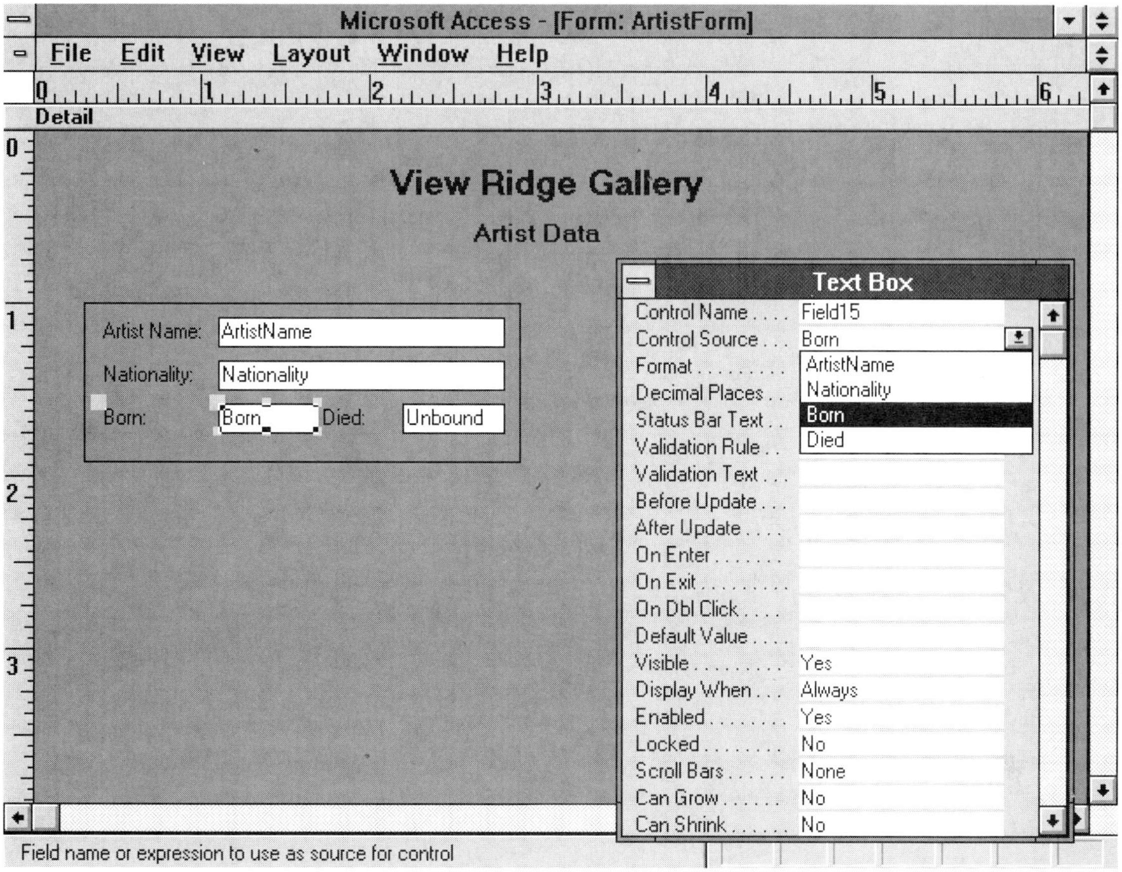

Subform Control

The Artist Data form must contain a grid that has one row for each of the artist's works that the gallery has carried. (Look ahead to the finished form in Figure 11-19. The grid just referred to is at the bottom of the form and contains the columns Title, Copy, and Description.)

To create such a grid, the developer must first create a subform that has the required columns. Figure 11-15 shows the creation of such a form called WORK Subform. The Record Source of the form is the table WORK, and it contains headings labeled "Title," "Copy," and "Description." In addition, the subform contains three text boxes that have been bound to the Title, Copy, and Description columns of the WORK table, respectively.

Figure 11-16 shows how the subform is bound to the Artist Data form. A subform control has been drawn on the form and appears as a white rectangle in Figure 11-16, partially covered by the property list. The Source Object property of this sub-

FIGURE 11-15

Creating a WORK Subform

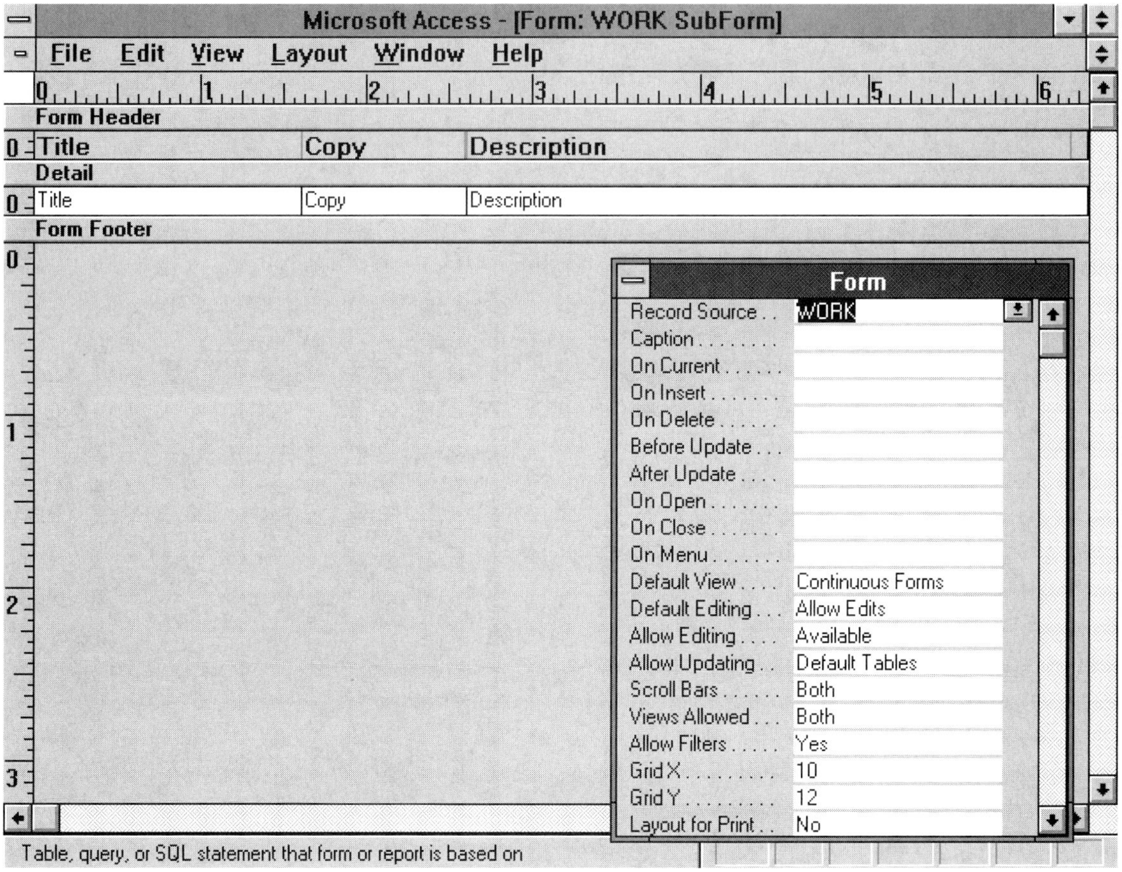

form control has been set to WORK Subform, the name of the subform created in Figure 11-15.

To match a row of ARTIST with the proper rows of WORK, the Link Child Fields and Link Master Fields properties must be set. Here they both are set to ArtistName, which means that the value of ArtistName in the master form (Artist Data) is to be matched with values of ArtistName in the subform. Since the subform is bound to the WORK table, all rows in WORK that have a value of ArtistName that matches the value of ArtistName in the Artist Data form are to be displayed.

■ Binding a Table or Query to a Combo Box Control

A combo box or a list box contains a list of values. Access allows combo or list boxes to contain multicolumn lists. Thus, several columns from a table or query can be bound to and appear in a combo or list box. In Figure 11-17, the CUSTOMER table

FIGURE 11-16

Binding the WORK Subform to the ARTIST Form

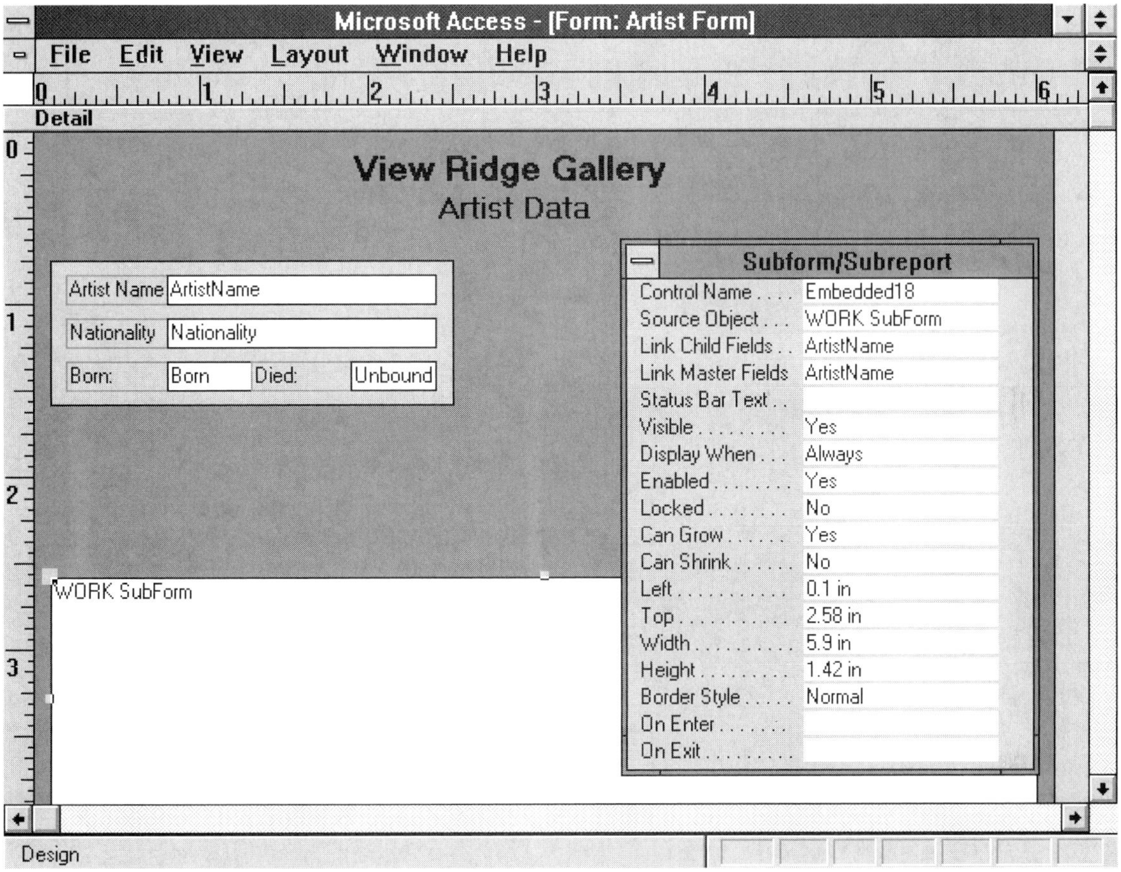

is being bound to a combo box on the Artist Data form, so that the user can click on the combo box to select a customer that has an interest in the artist being displayed.

The combo box is bound to the table by entering CUSTOMER into the Row Source property. The Column Count has been set to 2 to indicate that the combo box is to contain the first two columns of the CUSTOMER table, CustomerNumber and CustomerName. The property Bound Column has been set to 1 to indicate that the value of the first column of the entry selected is to be bound to the form. Finally, the Column Widths property has been set to "0 in; 1.2 in," specifying the width of the first column in the text box as 0 and the width of the second as 1.2 inches.

These property settings state that the combo box will contain the first two columns of all the rows of CUSTOMER and that the first column will not be shown but the second one will, in a column 1.2 inches wide. Furthermore, when the user chooses a row from this list box, the value of the first column of that row (which will be CustomerNumber), will be bound to the form.

FIGURE 11-17

Binding a Relation to a Combo Box

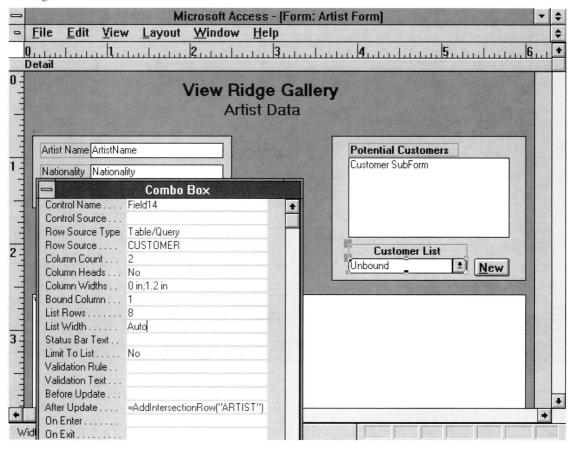

Observe that the After Update property has been set to call a function named AddIntersectionRow and is passing a parameter to that function, whose value is "ARTIST." This function, which was written by the developer, takes the values of ArtistName and CustomerNumber that have been bound to the form and adds a new row to the ARTIST–CUSTOMER–INT table with those two values.

The subform region labeled Customer Subform in Figure 11-17 has been bound to a subform, as was done for the WORK subform. The Customer Subform, however, is not bound to a table but instead to a query named CUSTOMER Subquery, shown in Figure 11-18. This query contains ArtistName from the intersection table and CustomerNumber and CustomerName from the CUSTOMER table. The result of this query is to create a table with the artists' names bound to data concerning the customers interested in those artists.

The Link Child Fields and Link Master Fields of the Customer Subform are set to ArtistName so that the master form (Artist Data) will be bound to the CUS-

FIGURE 11-18

Customer Subquery

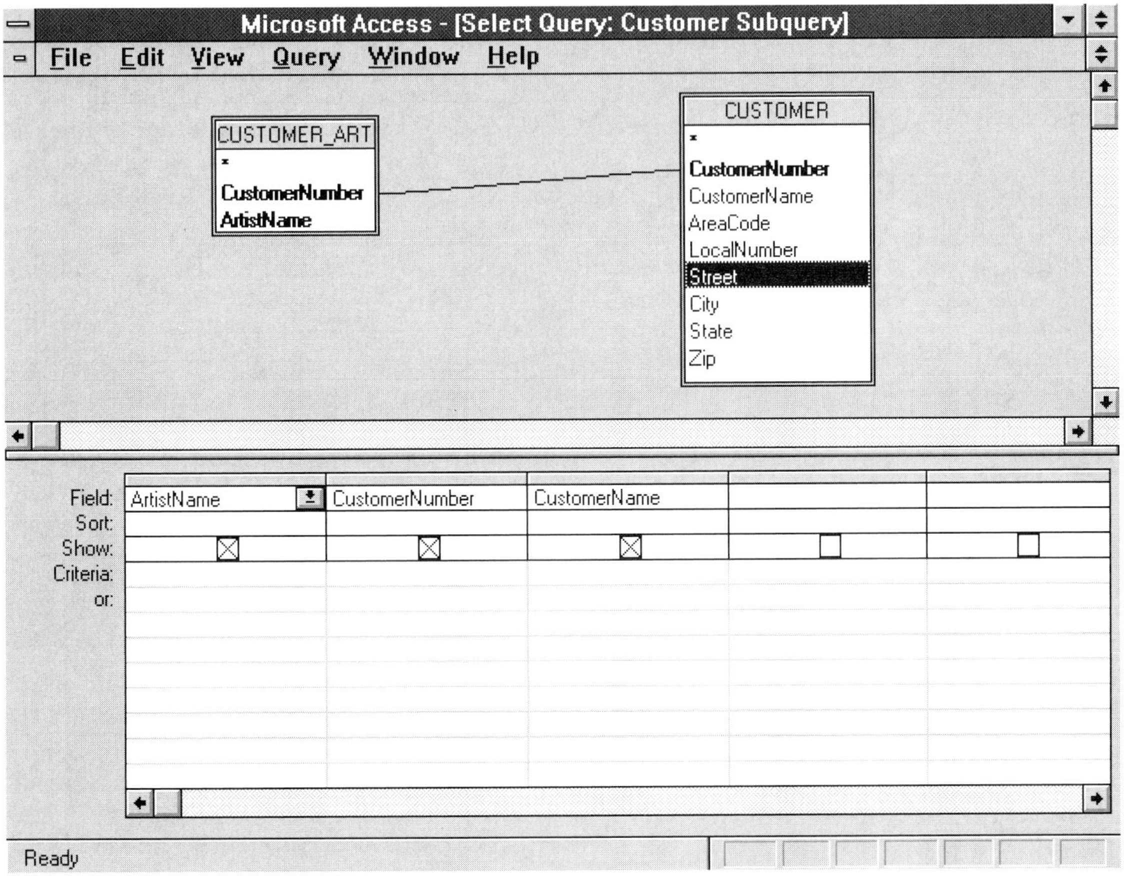

TOMER Subform by Artist name. The result of all of these bindings is that when the user clicks on a customer name in the combo box, the function AddIntersection-Row is called. This function adds a row to the ARTIST–CUSTOMER–INT table and causes the CUSTOMER Subquery to be requeried, which adds the new name to the query for the current ARTIST. The change in the subquery causes the Artist form to be repainted, and when it is, the new value of CUSTOMER is added to the CUSTOMER subform. The final form is shown in Figure 11-19, the way the form will appear when the user clicks the Customer List combo box.

◼ Creating Reports

The process of creating reports with Microsoft Access is similar to that of creating forms. In many ways, the creation of reports is easier, since reports are display-only documents.

FIGURE 11-19

The Finished Artist Data Form

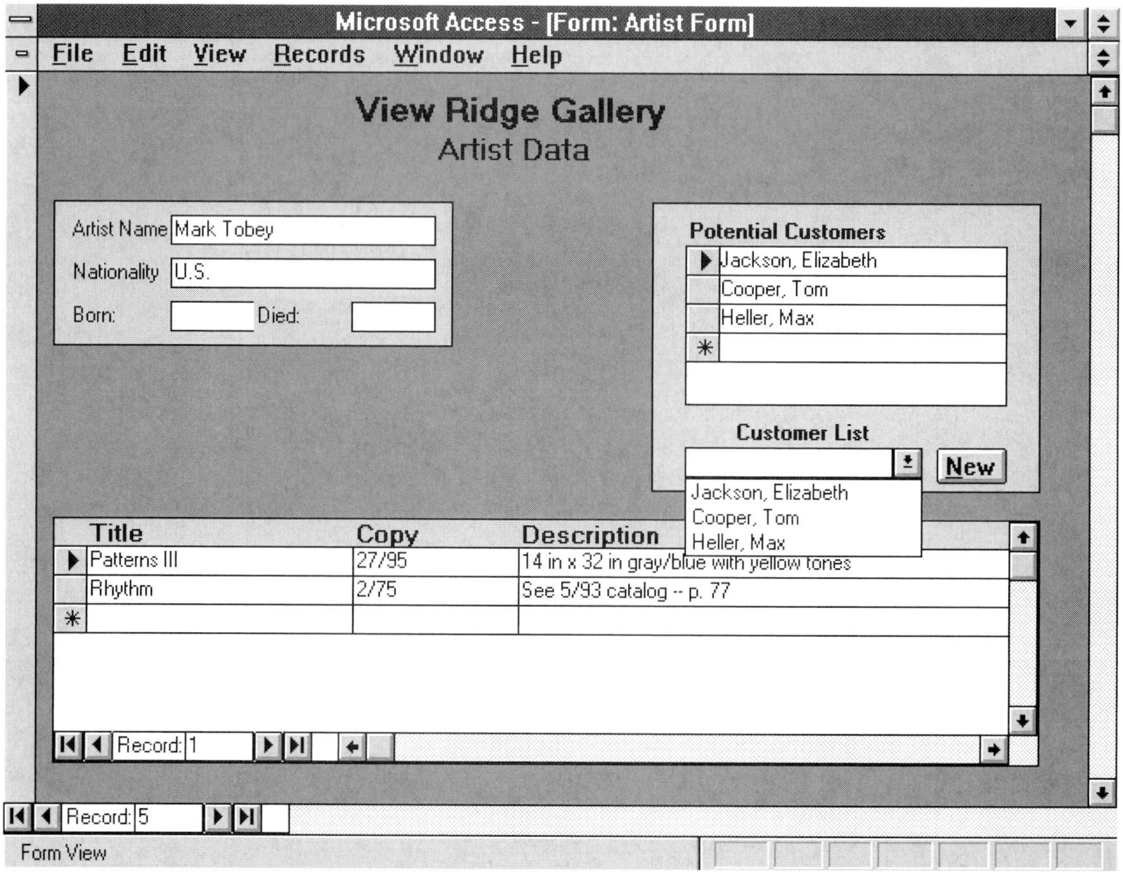

Each report is based on a query. To create the query, the developer first must decide which columns of which tables will be required and then construct a query with those columns. For example, suppose that the salespeople at the View Ridge Gallery want a report, sorted by CustomerName, that includes the names of those artists in which their customers have expressed an interest. Suppose also that the salepeople want a list of all the works of those artists that the gallery has ever carried.

Note the wording in the last paragraph. The works to be listed are not the works that the customers have purchased but all of the works that the gallery has ever carried for the artists in which the customers have expressed an interest.

Figure 11-20 shows the query that would be required for the report just described. It uses all four tables, although it does not show any columns from the ARTIST–CUSTOMER–INT table, which is used simply to link a CUSTOMER and an ARTIST. Sample results of this query are shown in Figure 11-21.

FIGURE 11-20

Query to Be Used to Generate Customer Report

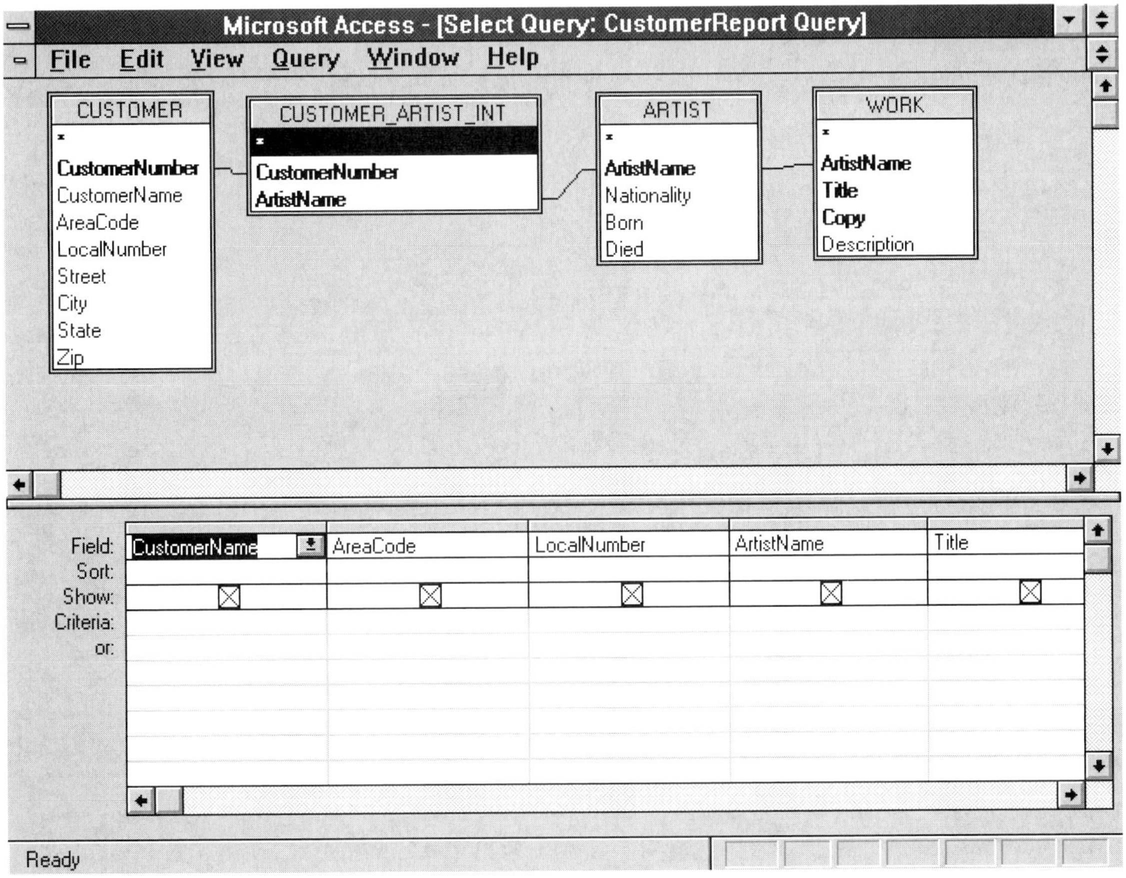

◼ Grouping

Report grouping offers a function similar to that of the SQL GROUP BY command. When a column is used for grouping, the underlying query or table is sorted by that column, and a group is defined for each set of rows with the same value of the column.

The report requirements indicate that the report data is to be grouped by customer and, within customer, grouped by artist. Then all of the works for a given artist are to be listed. Figure 11-22 shows an example of the report for the sample data in Figure 11-21.

Examine the data for the third customer, Elizabeth Jackson. Because she has expressed an interest in two artists, their works are listed after their names. The report is consistent, as the same works are listed for Mark Tobey under Elizabeth

FIGURE 11-21

Sample Data for the Customer Report Query

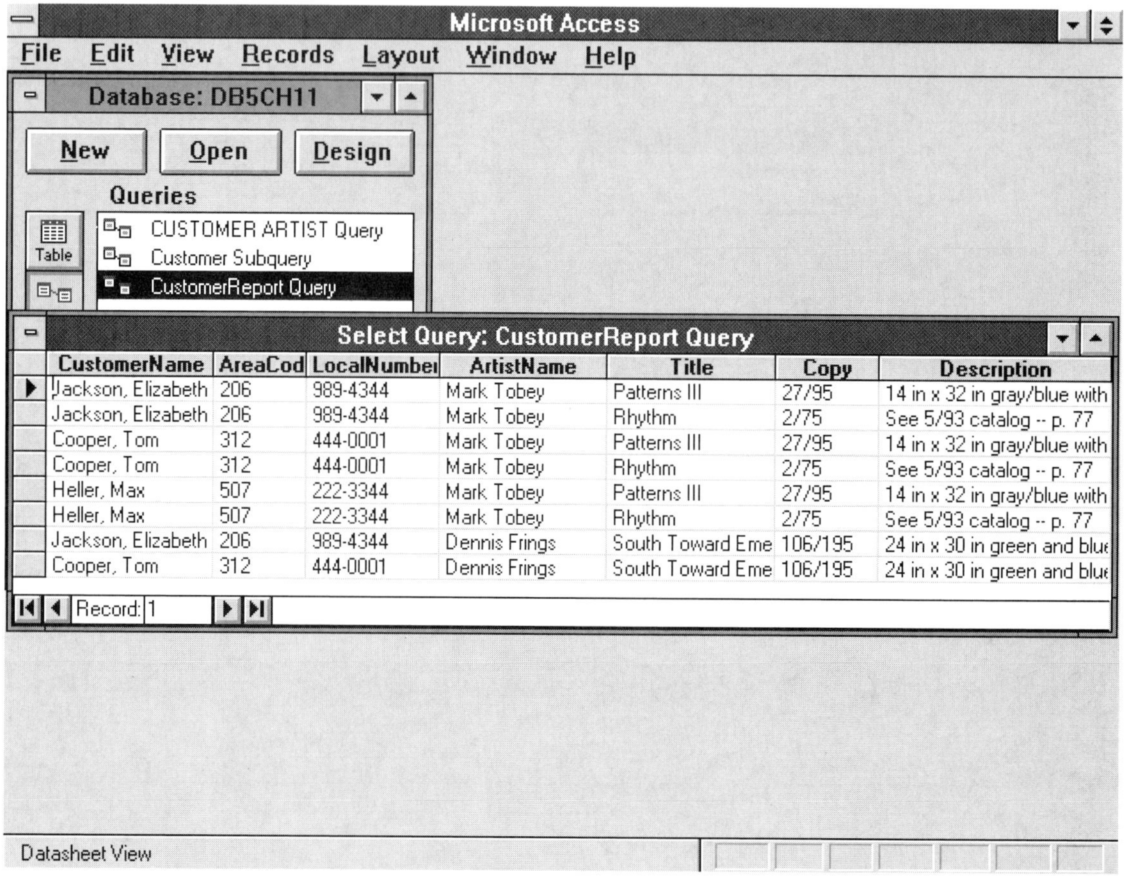

Jackson as are listed for Mark Tobey under Max Heller. Again, the works shown are those that the gallery has carried, not the works purchased by a particular customer.

■ Defining the Report

To create a report with Access, the developer presses the Report button in the database container window and then the New button. Next he enters the table or query on which the report is to be based. The result of these actions is the form in Figure 11-23. Notice that the Record Source property of the report will need to be set to CustomerReport Query, the name of the query in Figure 11-20.

To define the needed groups, the developer selects Sorting and Grouping from the View menu, and a subwindow like the one in Figure 11-24 appears. The names

FIGURE 11-22

Example of the Customer Interests Report

Customer Interests Report
27-Dec-93

Customer: **Cooper, Tom**   Phone: **312** - **444-0001**

Artist Dennis Frings

Title	Copy	Description
South Toward Emerald Seas	106/195	24 in x 30 in green and blue abstra

Artist Mark Tobey

Title	Copy	Description
Patterns III	27/95	14 in x 32 in gray/blue with yello
Rhythm	2/75	See 5/93 catalog – p. 77

Customer: **Heller, Max**   Phone: **507** - **222-3344**

Artist Mark Tobey

Title	Copy	Description
Patterns III	27/95	14 in x 32 in gray/blue with yello
Rhythm	2/75	See 5/93 catalog – p. 77

Customer: **Jackson, Elizabeth**   Phone: **206** - **989-4344**

Artist Dennis Frings

Title	Copy	Description
South Toward Emerald Seas	106/195	24 in x 30 in green and blue abstra

Artist Mark Tobey

Title	Copy	Description
Patterns III	27/95	14 in x 32 in gray/blue with yello
Rhythm	2/75	See 5/93 catalog – p. 77

of columns to be used for the grouping are entered in the first column of this window. In Figure 11-24, the developer has typed CustomerName in the first row and ArtistName in the second. The Group Header and Group Footer properties of both these groups were set to yes, which causes Access to create a set of heading and footing areas for Customer and another set for ArtistName. Sometimes such headings and footings are called **report bands**, and a report writer that can support such bands is called a **banded report writer**.

FIGURE 11-23

Building an Access Report

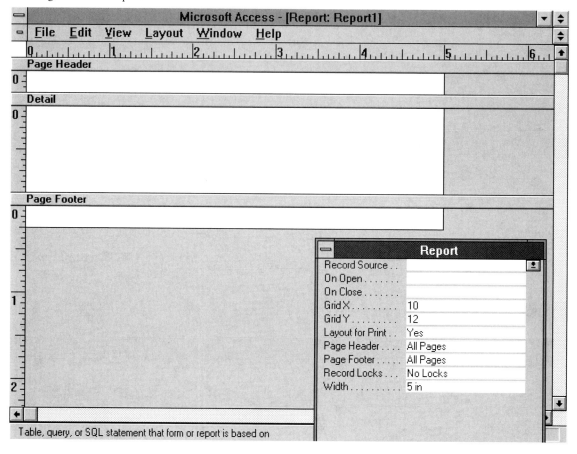

Once this structure has been created, the labels and text boxes are created and moved into the correct bands and positions within the bands. Additional formatting can be done by placing horizontal or vertical lines on the report. In this report a thick line has been drawn to be displayed before each new Customer group, as can be seen in Figure 11-25.

To improve the readability of this report, the developer has enlarged the font used to display the customer name and also has used boldface type for the customer and artist data and the headings of the work data.

In addition to the bands shown here, it also is possible to create page headers and footers that are placed at the top and bottom of each page when the page is printed. The location of such headers and footers varies depending on the data and the characteristics of the printer used to print the report.

FIGURE 11-24

Defining the Group Structures

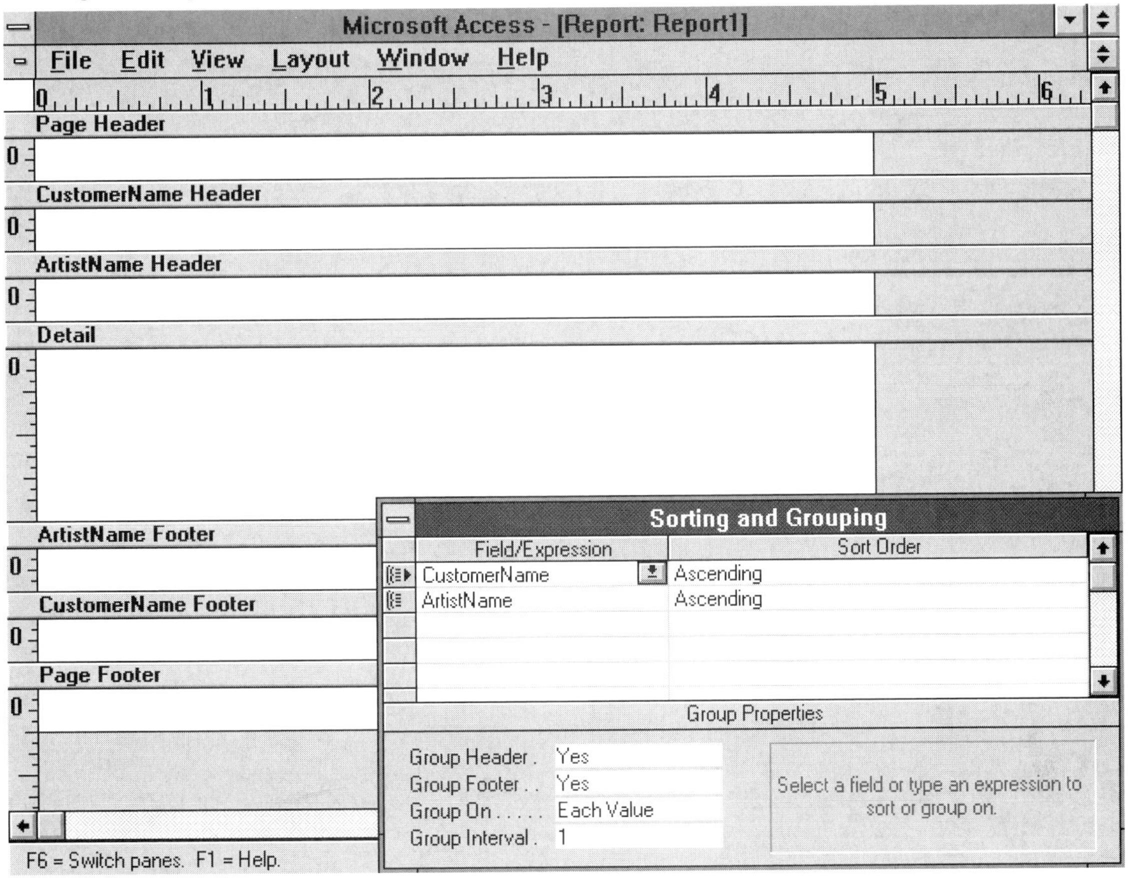

SUMMARY

A database is a model of the users' model, and so a data model representation of the users' model must be created before implementation can start. The four main components of a database application are tables, queries, forms, and reports.

To create tables in Access, the developer initiates the table definition form and then enters the name and data type of each column (called *field* in Access) of that form. Other properties of the column are entered as well.

Relationships are defined in a separate form. Access recognizes both one-to-one and one-to-many relationships. Relationships are defined by identifying the column of the child table that matches the column on the parent table. Once the relationships have been defined, they are used as a default for joins and multitable forms and reports. A form of referential integrity can also be specified.

FIGURE 11-25

Access Report Definition

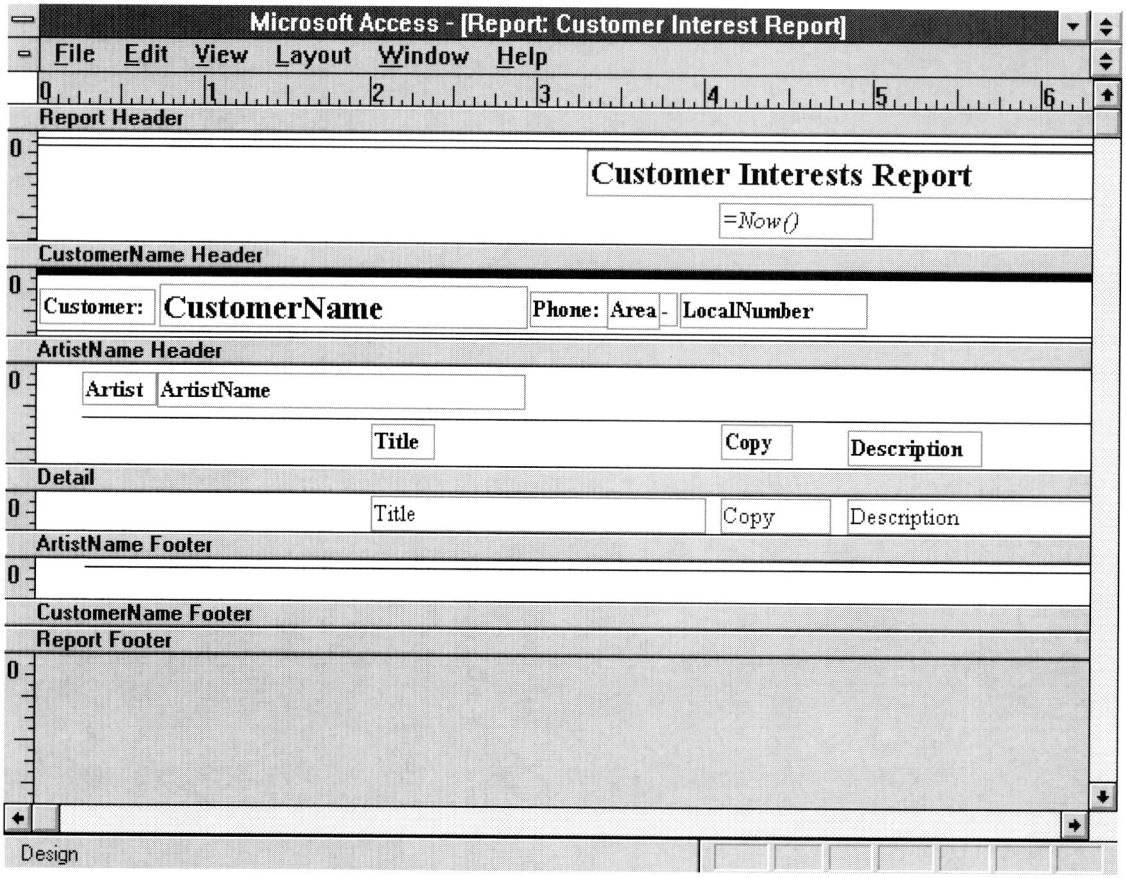

Queries are used for three purposes in Access: as a means of asking ad hoc questions about the data, as the basis of forms and reports, and as the basis of multivalued controls such as combo boxes. Queries can be defined using Access's version of QBE, or the SQL for the query can be entered directly.

Forms are created by binding various elements of the database to the form and its controls. A table or query is bound to the form itself. Columns of the table are bound to text boxes; subforms are bound to subform controls; and tables or queries are bound to combo boxes. The form itself and every control on the form has properties including the binding of the control, its physical characteristics, and possibly the names of the macros of the Access Basic functions to be called when particular events take place.

Reports, like forms, are based on queries or tables. Grouping and sorting are supported. Headers and footers (also called **bands**) can be defined for each group that is defined. Once the structure of the report has been created, text labels, text boxes, and other graphical symbols are added to the appropriate positions of the form.

GROUP I QUESTIONS

11.1   What must exist before the database and database application can be implemented? Why?

11.2   Name a modern, GUI-based DBMS product other than Microsoft Access.

11.3   Redefine the relations in Figure 11-2 to use surrogate keys.

11.4   What is the Access database container? What does it contain?

11.5   What are the six components of an Access database?

11.6   What is an Access field? How does it differ from a table column?

11.7   List the field data types that are supported by Access.

11.8   What is a table key in Access? What is the difference between a key and an index in Access?

11.9   Briefly describe how relationships are defined in Access.

11.10 How is referential integrity supported by Access?

11.11 What are the three uses of queries in Access?

11.12 What are the two ways that queries can be created in Access? Which do you think is better? Why?

11.13 Explain the use of the term *bind* in regard to database application development in Access.

11.14 Explain how table or query data is made available to a form.

11.15 What is the purpose of a text box? What is bound to text boxes?

11.16 What is the purpose of control properties?

11.17 What is an event? What kinds of events can happen to text boxes?

11.18 How is an Access macro or BASIC function bound to an event?

11.19 What is a subform control? What is it used for?

11.20 How are the rows of the main form connected to the rows of the subform?

11.21 What is the purpose of a combo box?

11.22 Describe the function of the following combo box properties: Row Source, Column Count, and Bound Column.

11.23 In the example in the text, the After Update property of the combo box was set to AddIntersectionRow. Describe the purpose of this function.

11.24 What is the essential difference between the functions of a form and those of a report?

11.25 What happens when a column is used for grouping?

11.26 What is a report band? What is its function?

GROUP II QUESTIONS

11.27 Get a copy of Microsoft Access. Implement the View Ridge Gallery example, but use the semantic objects shown in Figure 8-2(a). Use data keys rather than surrogate keys, and create a form for CUSTOMER that includes WORK data but not ARTIST data. CUSTOMER relates directly to the Transaction group property, but that property is encapsulated in WORK and hence is hidden from CUSTOMER. Thus the apparent relationship is between CUSTOMER and WORK. Using these statements and the gallery's information needs, design the form for CUSTOMER and implement it using Access.

11.28 Obtain a copy of a GUI-based DBMS product other than Access, such as Paradox for Windows. Using that product, implement the database and application described in this chapter.

RELATIONAL IMPLEMENTATION WITH DB2

In Chapter 9 we discussed the processes of implementing relational databases and developed a foundation of relational processing using relational algebra. Chapter 10 presented SQL, the most important relational data manipulation language, and Chapter 11 illustrated the implementation of a small database using Microsoft Access, a DBMS frequently used on personal computers.

Chapter 12 continues this discussion by presenting the implementation of an example database using DB2, a DBMS product for large IBM mainframes. We begin by considering a case that concerns information problems faced by the marketing department of a manufacturing company and then outline the features and functions of an information system that can solve those problems. This information system has a relational database, and we define both the objects and the relations that should be stored in it. Next we look at Database2 or, as it is more frequently called, DB2. We examine not only its data definition and data manipulation features but also those features that support concurrent processing, backup and recovery, and database security. Finally, we explore those portions of the relational application developed for the manufacturing company, including interactive DB2 queries and a COBOL program that contains embedded DB2 commands.

This chapter is long, as it includes a case, a description of the features and functions of DB2, and an application of DB2 to the case. Although we could have chosen a shorter case or a simpler product, this would not demonstrate the complexities in developing large-enterprise databases and applications.

DB2 is typical of mainframe DBMS products designed to provide fast, highly reliable performance while processing hundreds of concurrent transactions per minute. Such products are complicated and thus require considerable expertise and knowledge on the part of systems and database administrators. Unlike microcomputer DBMS products, mainframe DBMS products are not designed to be easy to use and install but instead are intended to offer high performance and reliability. This chapter provides the only exposure in this text that you will have to such products. Therefore, read this chapter in part to appreciate the difference between a DBMS for personal applications and one for large organizational applications. Finally, we have omitted from our discussion many of the important and useful features and functions of DB2, but you can learn about them in the publications *DB2 System and Database Administration Guide* and *DB2 Application Programming Guide,* both published by IBM.

CASE STUDY: KDK APPLIANCES

KDK Appliances manufactures major kitchen appliances, such as refrigerators, ranges, microwave ovens, and dishwashers. The company markets its products to independent dealers that then sell them to the public. Currently, its market is mainly the northeastern United States, but KDK plans to open soon new sales regions in the Midwest and Canada. Each sales region is serviced by several salespeople who call on dealers and explain KDK's product line, dealer-training program, incentives, and local advertising programs. It is possible for one dealer to work with more than one KDK salesperson.

KDK has a large mainframe computer that handles all order processing, inventory control, personnel, and accounting functions. Stored in this mainframe are files and databases that track sales and other data to meet various reporting requirements. In addition to the large mainframe computer, KDK has a smaller mainframe computer in its Information Center that processes extracts of operational data that are periodically downloaded (copied) from the large mainframe. No updating of data takes place in the Information Center; instead this is done by the carefully controlled programs running on the large mainframe (see Figure 12-1).

The purpose of the Information Center is to support the planning and analysis functions. It is staffed by operations personnel, systems administrators, database administrators, and systems analysts, in addition to the functional business personnel who perform business studies. The Information Center uses the IBM relational product DB2. It has installed additional programs to provide on-line concurrent access, but those programs are not within the scope of our discussion.

■ Problems

The marketing department plays a key role in the success of the company's plans to expand. It now employs eight product managers (PMs), each responsible for a particular line of products (one for refrigerators, one for ranges, and so forth). As part of their duties, the PMs develop an annual product plan for each major product (for example, a major product is a particular refrigerator model or a specific type of microwave oven). The product plan establishes, among other things, the sales goals

FIGURE 12-1

Relationship Among KDK's Computers

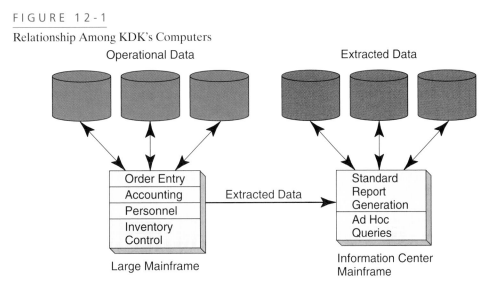

for the product and the budget for its marketing. These marketing expenses include advertising, dealer training, salesperson training, and dealer promotions.

In order to spend the marketing dollars wisely, the PMs want to access data stored in the computer. They need to know, for example, product sales by region and by salesperson and the effect of some aspect of marketing (say, advertising) on product sales. All the PMs know that the information they want can be produced from data stored in the Information Center's computer.

Instant response time is not vital, because the PMs usually need quarterly, monthly, or weekly summaries of data. For example, instant access to a particular order is not important. (In contrast, consider how important response time is when performing the order entry function on KDK's large operational mainframe.)

All of the PMs are either familiar with SQL or willing to learn it. None is a programmer, though, and none has the time or interest to learn COBOL. Nonetheless, the PMs want the following questions answered: Which dealers participated in our shared advertising program this month? What was the total sales figure for product 45678 in March? How does that compare with its sales in April?

KDK Appliances sponsors a co-op advertising program and employs several agencies to create advertising campaigns for various media, including newspapers (daily and weekly), periodicals (weekly and monthly), television, and radio. Much of KDK's advertising is shared with its dealers, which means that in addition to the advertising copy promoting a specific KDK product, a dealer's name, address, and logo appear in the ad (see Figure 12-2). Thus although KDK products are the central focus of the ad, a local dealer can share in the benefits by sharing the cost of the ad.

Some, though not all, dealers take advantage of this arrangement. The shared costs (percentages of the cost borne by KDK and the dealer) vary from one ad to another and from one dealer to another, so the sales and marketing personnel must establish the shared costs of each ad.

FIGURE 12-2

Advertisement for a KDK Product

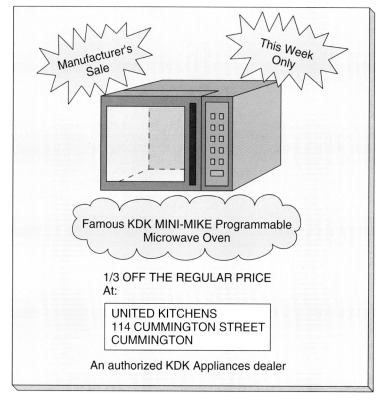

An Overview of the Solution

After studying these problems and talking them over with several of the product managers, one of the systems analysts proposed that KDK develop a database system on the Information Center's computer, which could be used to store and process the data needed to answer the product managers' questions. This data would be periodically extracted from KDK's operational mainframe computer. (The frequency depends on how up-to-date the data needs to be. The analyst suggested that they begin downloading data once a week. If that proves unsatisfactory, it can be downloaded more or less frequently.)

Some of the information that the PMs need is highly predictable. For example, each wants a monthly report summarizing his or her product's sales by region, dealer, and salesperson. The analyst decided to write application programs in COBOL to produce those reports, and the programs will be run on a regular schedule. In addition to the regular anticipated reports, the analyst suggested that each PM learn how to use SQL to make simple ad hoc queries. More complex queries will be handled by Information Center personnel.

■ Security Precautions for a Database

Because the Information Center handles extracts of data for all divisions of the company, certain security precautions must be taken to protect the data and to ensure the privacy of proprietary information. First, the Information Center systems analysts must be authorized by the company's database administrator to extract sales and other data from the operational database on the large mainframe. Second, because the operational database on the large mainframe contains vast amounts of private data (such as the employees' salaries), only that data necessary to assess product sales will be extracted.

Third, because many employees use the Information Center terminals to perform queries, this database will be made available to PMs only. All other employees (except for Information Center personnel) will be prevented from using it. Fourth, the PMs will be authorized to use only this database; they will not have access to databases established for other user departments. The Information Center will assign each PM an identification number that will serve as a password for access to the database.

Finally, data will be downloaded only from the mainframe computer. None of the extracted data will be updated, and no data will be sent back to the large mainframe. The extracted data will be merely a snapshot of the data in the operational database, a work copy that can be destroyed when the PMs are finished with it.

■ Defining Objects

To develop the proposed system, the analyst first had to identify the semantic objects in which the PMs were interested. To start, the analyst and the PMs examined reports, transactions, and other entities. Let us first consider the reports and identify the underlying objects needed to construct them.

PRODUCT SALES SUMMARY REPORTS

Figure 12-3 shows three examples of the product sales summaries that the PMs need each month. Figure 12-3(a) is a sample PRODUCT SALES SUMMARY BY SALESPERSON report that contains data about products (product number, name, description, price), salespeople (name), and sales (total units sold by each salesperson). This suggests the existence of PRODUCT, SALESPERSON, and SALE objects, but we will not be sure until all reports, transactions, and so forth have been examined.

The PRODUCT SALES SUMMARY BY DEALER report (Figure 12-3[b]) contains data about products (product number, name, description, price), dealers (name), and sales (total units sold to each dealer). Thus, in addition to the objects mentioned, it is likely that a DEALER object will exist as well.

The third summary report, PRODUCT SALES SUMMARY BY REGION (Figure 12-3[c]), contains data about products (product number, name, description, price), regions (region number), and sales (total units sold in each region). In addition to the potential objects already identified—PRODUCT, SALESPERSON, SALE, and DEALER—another possible object is found: REGION.

FIGURE 12-3

PRODUCT SALES SUMMARY Reports: (a) SALES SUMMARY BY SALESPERSON Report, (b) SALES SUMMARY BY DEALER Report, and (c) SALES SUMMARY BY REGION Report

```
          PRODUCT SALES SUMMARY BY SALESPERSON
- - - - - - - - - - - - - - - - - - - - - - - - - - - - - -
Product Number:  87224

Name/Description: Mini-Mike Programmable compact microwave
                  oven

Price:              $194.99


          SALESPERSON              UNITS SOLD
          John Eberle                 280
          Margaret Gosselin           200
          Hans Jensen                  50
                          TOTAL      530
```

(a)

```
          PRODUCT SALES SUMMARY BY DEALER
- - - - - - - - - - - - - - - - - - - - - - - - - - - - - -
Product Number:  87224

Name/Description: Mini-Mike Programmable compact microwave
                  oven

Price:              $194.99


          DEALER                             UNITS SOLD
          Lisbon Furniture and Appliances        30
          Parks Department Store                200
          United Kitchens                        50
          Gem Appliances                        100
          Rich Appliance Co.                    100
          Sounds Terrific                        50
                                  TOTAL        530
```

(b)

```
          PRODUCT SALES SUMMARY BY REGION
- - - - - - - - - - - - - - - - - - - - - - - - - - - - - -
Product Number:  87224

Name/Description: Mini-Mike Programmable compact microwave
                  oven

Price:              $194.99


          REGION              UNITS SOLD
            2                    200
            5                    330
                    TOTAL      530
```

(c)

■ DEALER ACTIVITY SUMMARY Report

Figure 12-4 shows an example of the DEALER ACTIVITY SUMMARY report, which contains data about dealers (number, name, address, telephone number), sales (invoice number, data, invoice total), and advertisements (advertisement name, date, cost, and dealer's share). We have already identified DEALER and SALE (an invoice is the record of sale) as potential objects, and the DEALER ACTIVITY SUMMARY report suggests a few more attributes of these objects, such as the dealers' addresses, telephone numbers, and invoice numbers. This report also indicates that advertisements are possible objects.

Figure 12-5 illustrates our findings so far. The potential objects are PRODUCT, SALESPERSON, SALE (or INVOICE), REGION, DEALER, and ADVERTISE-MENT. But this is by no means a complete and final list, as these objects show only the beginning of our investigation. Study the object diagrams in Figure 12-5, making sure you understand them before continuing.

SALES INVOICE DOCUMENT

Product managers derive much information about product sales from one important document: the sales invoice. An invoice for each sale is completed by a salesperson. An *actual* invoice captures many details about the dealer, the product(s) sold, and the dollar amounts of the transaction, discounts, credits, balance due, and shipping charges. All invoice details are entered into KDK's large operational mainframe computer. Keep in mind that the PMs need only a subset of the data on an actual

FIGURE 12-4

DEALER ACTIVITY SUMMARY Report

DEALER ACTIVITY SUMMARY

#6644   (617) 479-5555
J&S Department Store
75 Rock Road
Plymouth, MA 02787

Purchases to Date

Invoice #	Date	Total
1013	01/02/92	15349.81
1071	02/01/92	22467.00
1296	03/02/92	18949.37
1380	04/01/92	36755.29
	TOTAL	93620.47

Advertising to Date

Ad Name	Date	Ad Cost	Dealer's Share (%)
Ultra	03/10/92	250.00	67
Free Time	02/15/92	400.00	67
St. Paddy's Sale	03/14/92	600.00	67
Ultra	03/15/92	250.00	60

FIGURE 12-5

Preliminary Objects for KDK Appliances

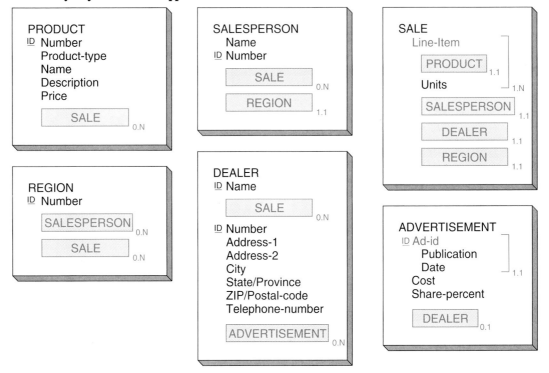

invoice. An invoice as viewed by a product manager is illustrated in Figure 12-6. It contains data about the invoice (number, sale date, total), salesperson (number, name), dealer (name, address), and items sold (line item number, product number, name, price, quantity sold, extended price).

It is easy to see that what we have just described as an *invoice* is really an embellishment of what we have been calling a *sale.* Because the PMs are more likely to use the term *invoice* than *sale* (this was discovered by talking to the PMs), we modify the object diagrams from Figure 12-5, replacing the SALE object with the updated INVOICE object. The results are shown in Figure 12-7.

ADVERTISING

We noted earlier that KDK advertises its products to consumers in various media, such as print and television. An ad that can be run in, say, a newspaper is referred to as an *ad-copy.* Each ad-copy is given a title by the advertising agency that developed it. When a particular ad-copy is actually run in a newspaper on a certain date at a certain cost, it is referred to as an *advertisement.* Thus, an ad-copy called "Free Time" emphasizing the time-saving features of various KDK appliances might be

FIGURE 12-6

Product Manager's View of an Invoice

	INVOICE 1001			02/01/93
	SOLD TO:		SALES REP:	#5762
	Lisbon Furniture and Appliances			Paula Jasinski
	692 S. Ellington Rd.			
	South Windsor, CT 06114			

	Number	Name	Price	Qty	Extended-price
1	80911	Kitchen Valet	$1,699.99	2	$ 3,399.98
2	87755	Mini-Mike	344.99	20	6,899.80
3	93861	E. Range-white	679.99	15	10,199.85
4					
5					
6					
				TOTAL	$20,499.63

FIGURE 12-7

Modified Objects for KDK Appliances

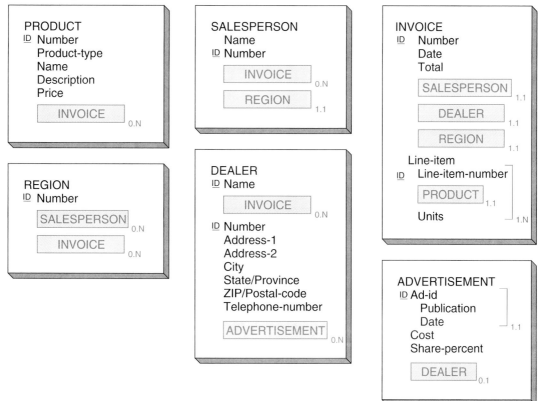

FIGURE 12-8

KDK Objects After Modification for AD-COPY Object

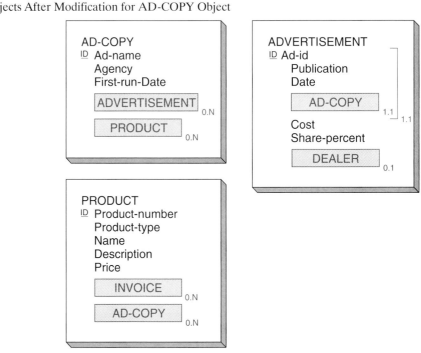

run in several newspapers over a period of three or four months. Each time it is run it is termed an advertisement.

As we already noted, each advertisement may be shared with a local appliance dealer, as long as the dealer agrees to share the cost of the ad. Because each ad-copy can target several products and because each advertisement can be shared with a dealer, the product managers need to track various aspects of advertising. After all, a large portion of each PM's budget is spent on advertising.

The underlying objects in the system's advertising are AD-COPY and ADVERTISEMENT, and object diagrams for them are shown in Figure 12-8. This more complete definition of the ADVERTISEMENT object replaces the one in Figure 12-7.

FINAL VERSION

Using object diagrams like the ones in Figures 12-7 and 12-8, the analyst reviewed with the PMs his understanding of the problems, thereby giving each of them an opportunity to correct or confirm what the analyst had done. One point that the analyst raised during this review concerned the REGION object. He wanted to be sure that the PMs did not need any data about a region. When the product managers agreed that they did not need any more data, the analyst decided to drop the REGION object. Thus modified, the object diagrams seemed acceptable, and the analyst went to the next step, translating the object definitions into relation definitions.

FIGURE 12-9

Relationship Between INVOICE and
LINE-ITEM

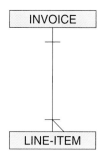

■ Defining Relations

The Information Center analyst at KDK Appliances followed the guidelines described in Chapter 7 for transforming objects into relations. Let us consider the INVOICE object first.

INVOICE

INVOICE is a hybrid object because the line-item composite group contains an object attribute. Thus the INVOICE object is represented by several relations. One contains general information about an invoice, and another contains the line items associated with the invoice. The relations have a one-to-many relationship, and both relations are mandatory (see Figure 12-9). The formats of the two relations are

INVOICE (<u>Number</u>, Date, Total, *Salesperson.Number*, *Dealer.Number*)

LINE-ITEM (<u>*Invoice.Number*</u>, <u>Line-item-number</u>, *Product.Number*, Quantity, Extended-price)

Observe that the keys are underlined and the foreign keys are shown in italics. Those columns that are both local and foreign keys are shown in underlined italics. An example of the INVOICE and LINE-ITEM relations is given in Figure 12-10. Notice that the key for INVOICE (Invoice.Number) is part of the key for LINE-ITEM.

Three foreign keys appear in the INVOICE and LINE-ITEM relations, namely, Salesperson.Number, Dealer.Number, and Product.Number. These keys are needed to establish the one-to-many relationships between DEALER and INVOICE, between SALESPERSON and INVOICE, and between PRODUCT and INVOICE.

DEALER AND SALESPERSON

The DEALER object in Figure 12-7 is a compound object because it contains multi-valued object attributes, INVOICE and ADVERTISEMENT. There is a 1:N relationship in both cases.

Similarly, the SALESPERSON object in Figure 12-7 is a compound object, and it has a 1:N relationship with INVOICE. In Figure 12-11 we have added the DEALER and SALESPERSON relations to the diagram from Figure 12-9. The relationships between SALESPERSON and INVOICE and between DEALER and

FIGURE 12-10

Sample Data in INVOICE and LINE-ITEM Relations

Number	Date	Salesperson.Number	Dealer.Number	Total
10982	03/12/93	8555	2425	38549.05
75214	03/12/93	1755	4528	60472.95
63911	03/15/93	5762	6178	12249.92
41200	03/18/93	5762	6644	147997.70

INVOICE relation

Invoice. Number	Line-item-number	Product. Number	Quantity	Extended-price
10982	001	14365	50	14999.50
10982	002	74961	30	17999.70
10982	003	87033	15	5549.85
75214	001	87214	25	4874.75
75214	002	87224	100	25999.00
75214	003	87033	80	29599.20
63911	001	56271	3	3749.97
63911	002	80911	5	8499.95
41200	001	15965	200	129998.00
41200	002	74961	30	17999.70

LINE-ITEM relation

INVOICE are mandatory to optional, which means that an invoice must be associated with a salesperson and a dealer but that a salesperson or a dealer does not have to have any invoices. The relation formats are

DEALER (<u>Number</u>, Name, Address-1, Address-2, City, State/Province, ZIP/Postal-code, Telephone)

SALESPERSON (<u>Number</u>, Name, Region)

FIGURE 12-11

Result of Adding DEALER and SALESPERSON Relations to Figure 12-9

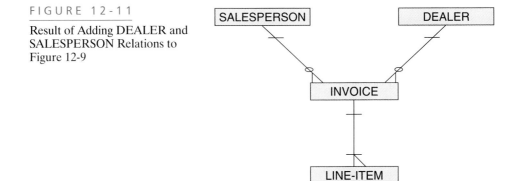

Sample data for the SALESPERSON and DEALER relations is shown in Figure 12-12. Following the guidelines established in Chapter 7, the 1:N relationship between DEALER and INVOICE has been represented by placing the key field of DEALER (Dealer.Number) in the INVOICE relation. Similar comments hold for the relationship between SALESPERSON and INVOICE.

PRODUCT

Another object in Figure 12-7 is PRODUCT. According to the object diagram, there is an N:1 relationship between a product and an invoice. More specifically, there is an N:1 relationship between a line item and a product. A certain product—say, a dishwasher—can be found on line items from the various invoices issued to many different dealers, and this can be represented in relations as shown in Figure 12-13.

The relational format for the PRODUCT relation is

PRODUCT (<u>Number</u>, Name, Description, Price)

The 1:N relationship between PRODUCT and LINE-ITEM has been established by placing Product.Number in the LINE-ITEM relation. Sample data for the PRODUCT relation can be found in Figure 12-14.

ADVERTISEMENT AND AD-COPY

Two more objects, ADVERTISEMENT and AD-COPY (see Figure 12-8), need to be transformed into relations. A dealer can share the cost of several advertisements, but any advertisement features at most one dealer. Thus there is a 1:N relationship between a dealer and an advertisement.

Similarly, one ad-copy can be run several times in many newspapers, and so there is a 1:N relationship between an ad-copy and an advertisement. Adding these relations to the ones in Figure 12-13, we arrive at the result in Figure 12-15.

The next relationship to be incorporated is that between PRODUCT and AD-COPY. Each product can be featured in several ads, and each ad can specify several products. Thus we have an N:M relationship between PRODUCT and AD-COPY.

Recall from Chapter 7 that many-to-many relationships are represented by creating an intersection relation containing only those keys from the two other relations. In this case, an intersection relation called PRODUCT-AD is defined, in which each row contains a product number and an ad-name. Here the PRODUCT-AD relation is added to the ones from Figure 12-15, and the result is Figure 12-16.

The formats for these three new relations are

AD-COPY (<u>Ad-name</u>, Agency, First-run-date)

ADVERTISEMENT (<u>Publication</u>, <u>Date</u>, *Ad-name*, Cost, Share-percent, *Dealer.Number*)

PRODUCT-AD (*<u>Ad-name</u>*, *<u>Product.Number</u>*)

Sample data for the AD-COPY and ADVERTISEMENT relations appears in Figure 12-17 and for PRODUCT-AD in Figure 12-18.

FIGURE 12-12

Sample Data for SALESPERSON and DEALER Relations

Number	Name	Region
1043	Ronald Hunt	1
2711	John Eberle	5
8555	Margaret Gosselin	2
5762	Paula Jasinski	4
1755	Hans Jensen	5
6042	Lawrence Smithers	1
2814	Maxine Whittier	3

SALESPERSON relation

Number	Name	Address-1	Address-2	City	State	Zip	Phone
6178	Gem Appliances	1005 Farmington Ave.	-0-	W. Hartford	CT	06754	(203) 555-4312
2425	S. K. Lafferty	Prestige Park	Building 43	E. Hartford	CT	06832	(203) 555-6789
6624	Rich Appliance Co.	17 Whiting Street	Suite 4143	New Britain	CT	06588	(203) 555-6609
0212	Lisbon Furniture & Appliances	692 Ellington Road	-0-	South Windsor	CT	06551	(203) 677-4582
9356	Gallo's Appliance Outlet	P.O. Box 344	264 Park Road	W. Hartford	CT	06431	(203) 549-6772
4516	United Kitchens	114 Cummington Street	-0-	Cummington	MA	07231	(617) 438-0065
9101	Parks Department Store	21 Main Street	-0-	Worcester	MA	07488	(617) 756-2295
6644	J&S Department Store	75 Rock Road	-0-	Plymouth	MA	02787	(617) 555-9734
4528	Sounds Terrific	1433 W. Northeast Highway	Suite 5678	Boston	MA	07665	(617) 885-4000

DEALER relation

FIGURE 12-13

PRODUCT Relation Added to Diagram in
Figure 12-11

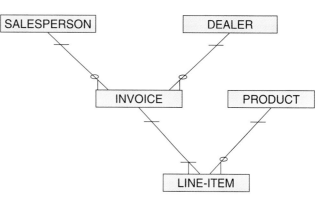

FIGURE 12-14

Sample Data for PRODUCT Relation

Number	Name	Description	Price
392761	Electric range–white	Electric range	$299.99
393861	Electric range–white	Electric range; self-clean; window	$679.99
393863	Electric range–toast	Electric range; self-clean; window	$689.99
393867	Electric range–avocado	Electric range; self-clean; window	$689.99
370351	Gas range–white	Gas range; 21-inch	$279.99
370353	Gas range–toast	Gas range; 21-inch	$289.99
374961	Gas range–white	Gas range; 36-inch; continuous clean	$599.99
374963	Gas range–toast	Gas range; 36-inch; continuous clean	$599.99
374976	Gas range–avocado	Gas range; 36-inch; continuous clean	$599.99
380551	Fifth-burner kit	Gas range 5th burner to replace griddle	$19.99
787214	Mini-mike	Compact microwave oven	$194.99
787224	Mini-mike	Programmable compact microwave oven	$259.99
787755	Mity-mike	Programmable solid-state full-size microwave oven	$344.99
787033	Mity-mike	#87755 with carousel	$369.99
415965	Ultra wash	Electronic dishwasher	$649.99
414365	Dishwasher	18-inch; 2-level dishwasher	$299.99
417375	Dishwasher–P	Dishwasher-portable	$409.99
416037	Dishwasher–sp	Space saver dishwasher	$249.99
556681	Porcelain-plus	Refrigerator; porcelain-on-steel; 25.8 cu ft	$1,599.99
556271	Quiet Cold	Frost-free refrigerator; ice maker	$1,249.99
580911	Kitchen Valet	Refrigerator; all-electronic; customized panels	$1,699.99
580922	KDK Limited Edition	Refrigerator; frost-free; special use compartments	$2,549.99
593252	Mini-fridge	Compact refrigerator	$99.00
593286	Mini-fridge	Compact refrigerator/freezer	$174.99
594605	Compact-fridge	3.6 cu ft compact refrigerator	$219.99
594911	Compact-fridge	#94605 with push-button defrost	$299.99

FIGURE 12-15

Addition of AD-COPY and ADVERTISEMENT Relations to Those in Figure 12-13

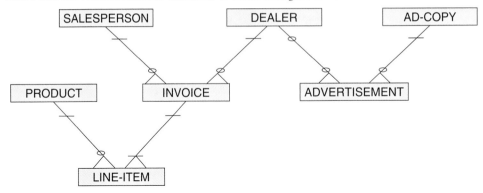

FIGURE 12-16

Addition of PRODUCT-AD Relation to Those in Figure 12-15

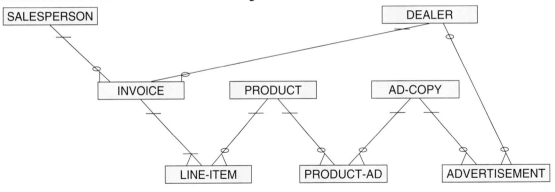

■ KDK Case Summary

All the objects identified earlier can be constructed from data stored in the relations we defined. Reports summarizing product sales based on various criteria (such as salesperson, region, and dealer), reports that analyze advertising, and much more can be readily extracted from the database.

The next step is to implement the database structure, that is, to define tables, fields, and constraints; to assign passwords; to establish security procedures; and to allocate file space. After doing that, the analyst tests the database structure by downloading some sample data from the mainframe and making various queries. Finally, when no errors can be found in the testing, KDK can download the sales data from the mainframe computer and begin to use the newly established database in the Information Center.

Once the database exists, queries can be processed using a version of SQL that is provided with DB2. More complicated reports will need to be produced by applica-

FIGURE 12-17

Sample Data for AD-COPY and ADVERTISEMENT Relations

Ad-name	Agency	First-run-date
Dishwashers	On-Target Ads	03/10/93
Free Time	Haskins	02/15/93
Microwaves	On-Target Ads	03/12/93
Presidents	Haskins	02/03/93
Ranges	On-Target Ads	02/01/93
St. Paddy's Sale	J&J Marketing	03/12/93
The Bachelor	J&J Marketing	01/04/93
The Fridge	Haskins	02/01/93
Ultra	J&J Marketing	03/10/93
Working Woman	Haskins	03/01/93

AD-COPY relation

Publication	Date	Ad-name	Cost	Share%	Dealer.Num
Herald	02/01/93	Ranges	300.00	25.	6644
Free Press	02/01/93	Ranges	320.00	33.	6178
Free Press	02/03/93	Presidents	450.00	50.	4528
Sentinel	02/15/93	Free Time	400.00	33.	6178
Herald	02/17/93	Free Time	350.00	50.	6178
Herald	02/19/93	Ranges	300.00	40.	4516
Sentinel	03/10/93	Dishwashers	400.00	50.	9101
Times	03/10/93	Ultra	250.00	33.	6644
Courier	03/11/93	Ultra	280.00	40.	0212
Sentinel	03/12/93	Working Woman	500.00	40.	9356
Times	03/14/93	St. Paddy's Sale	600.00	33.	6644
Times	03/14/93	The Bachelor	550.00	25.	4516
Herald	03/15/93	Ultra	250.00	40.	6644

ADVERTISEMENT relation

tion programs. These programs will be written in COBOL and tested before they can be used to produce the product managers' reports.

DB2: THE PRODUCT

Database2 (DB2) is IBM's relational database management system for large main-frame computers that run IBM's MVS operating system. Another popular IBM DBMS, called IMS, is based on the hierarchical (DL/I), rather than the relational, model. IMS is an older, and therefore more established, database product that was already installed in many companies before the relational model was developed. To allow its customers flexibility in their choice of DBMS products, IBM designed DB2

FIGURE 12-18

Sample Data for PRODUCT-AD Relation

Ad-name	Product.Number	Ad-name	Product.Number
Dishwashers	17375	Ranges	93861
Dishwashers	16037	Ranges	93863
Dishwashers	14365	Ranges	93867
Free Time	70351	Ranges	74967
Free Time	16037	Ranges	74963
Free Time	92761	Ranges	80551
Microwaves	87033	St. Paddy's Sale	15965
Microwaves	87224	St. Paddy's Sale	93867
Microwaves	87755	St. Paddy's Sale	94605
Microwaves	87214	St. Paddy's Sale	74967
Presidents	93286	The Bachelor	15965
Presidents	80551	The Bachelor	87755
Presidents	93861	The Bachelor	93867
Presidents	74961	The Fridge	56681
Presidents	80922	The Fridge	80922
Presidents	14365	Ultra	15965
Presidents	93252	Working Woman	93867
Ranges	92761	Working Woman	87033
Ranges	74961	Working Woman	87755

to coexist with IMS, and so DB2 allows the same application program to access both IMS and DB2 database data. User organizations can take advantage of the newer relational product without having to abandon or convert all of their hierarchical applications. We consider IMS in the next chapter.

■ Key Features

DB2 uses SQL to perform all database operations: data definition, data access, data manipulation, and authorization functions. The user enters the SQL statements at a computer terminal. This mode employs an interactive terminal interface program called DB2I, but SQL statements can also be embedded in application programs written in assembler language, COBOL, PL/I, FORTRAN, or C. Later in this chapter we present examples of both interactive commands and COBOL programs containing SQL instructions.

DB2 is well suited to a multiuser environment, as it allows users to create and modify tables, views, and other database structures; to define and modify database security parameters; and to execute various database utilities on-line. Most functions can be performed—within certain limits—even while others are using the database.

DB2's mechanisms for recovery in the event of a system failure are especially important in a multiuser environment. DB2 includes features for activity logging and transaction reprocessing, thus increasing system reliability. Because DB2 is just one of several subsystems that may be operating at the time of a system failure, its recovery processing is coordinated with that of other subsystems that may be present, such as CICS or other communications control programs.

DB2 enables a person—database designer, database administrator, or end user—to define and manipulate various constructs.[1] Constructs include databases, tables, views, and indexes, to name a few. In the next section, we examine DB2 constructs and some SQL data definition (DDL) statements.

■ DB2 Data Definition Language

This section briefly describes each DB2 construct, including the resources that application programmers (and sometimes end users) need to understand, such as tables and views, as well as the resources that database designers and database administrators (DBAs)[2] need to understand, such as storage groups and table spaces. We also present SQL statements to define several objects for KDK Appliances' Information Center database. The DB2 constructs we study are tables, views, table spaces, indexes, index spaces, databases, and storage groups. Although a few other DB2 constructs exist, they are not important to our discussion.

TABLES

Like all products based on the relational model, DB2 stores data as **tables** with rows and columns. DB2 can retrieve and change data in a table, insert and delete rows, and add new columns to an existing table.

VIEWS

A DB2 **view** is a virtual table derived from one or several base tables and not physically stored in the database (although the table data is). Views can be accessed and manipulated much as tables are, using many of the same SQL data manipulation statements used for tables. Indeed, a user often cannot tell whether he or she is processing a table or a view. Examples of a base table and a view of it are illustrated in Figure 12-19.

Database users, including application programmers and end users, need to know only about tables and views. But database designers and DBAs need to understand not only tables and views but also physical database storage, including table spaces, indexes, index spaces, data bases, and storage groups.

TABLE SPACES

A **table space** is a collection of one or more VSAM data sets (this is the name of standard nondatabase IBM mainframe files) used to store database data on mag-

---

[1] IBM uses the term *object* instead of construct, and we substitute this term here to avoid confusion between semantic objects and DB2 objects.

[2] DB2 allows separate passwords for *system administrators* and *database administrators*. A system administrator can access and change constructs for all databases on the DB2 system, whereas a database administrator is restricted to a particular database.

FIGURE 12-19

Example of (a)
EMPLOYEES (base table)
and (b) EMPLOYEE-
DIRECTORY (view of
EMPLOYEES)

Name	Salary	Hire-date	Office	Extension
Walker	21800	12/88	321	246
Berg	36500	10/85	411	647
Dean	42900	02/91	308	795
Hsiu	36500	09/88	307	581
Cameratta	40000	03/83	419	669

(a)

Name	Office	Extension
Walker	321	246
Berg	411	647
Dean	308	795
Hsiu	307	581
Cameratta	419	669

(b)

netic disk. Both user and system tables are stored in table spaces (see Figure 12-20).
A table space can hold approximately 64 billion bytes of data, although that size is
not practical.

Table spaces are DB2's recoverable units. If the database system crashes, the
table spaces will be recovered, not the databases or individual tables. Perhaps you
can see why huge table spaces (such as 64 billion bytes of data), though theoretically

FIGURE 12-20

Table Spaces and Tables

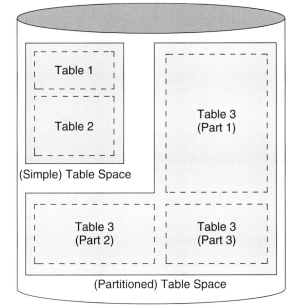

DASD (Disk) Volume

possible, are in reality seldom defined, as recovering a table space that large would be very difficult and time-consuming.

A table space can be either a **simple table space** or a **partitioned table space.** A simple table space can hold one or more tables, whereas a partitioned table space holds exactly one table. The DBA would probably define a partitioned table space for a very large table. Each partition would contain a part of the table based on the range of values in one or more columns. For example, each partition might contain taxpayer data based on Social Security Number. Partitions are independent of one another and can be reorganized and recovered individually.

Simple table spaces might contain several small, related tables. For example, the DBA might establish one table space for each user department and use each table space to store all the tables pertinent to a particular department. If an application requires exclusive use of a table, it issues a LOCK TABLE statement. This statement locks an entire table space and prevents other tables in it from being accessed. If separate table spaces "belong" to individual user departments, it is less likely that users from different departments will interface with one another.

INDEXES

A DB2 **index** is an index as defined in earlier chapters. Indexes are used to reduce table access time and to place the table data in a logical sequence, regardless of its physical sequence. Multiple indexes can be defined for a single table. Consider the table in Figure 12-21(a). (In this example, the rows are numbered to represent relative locations within the table, but in practice, record addressing is far more com-

FIGURE 12-21

Indexes on CUSTOMER Table: (a) CUSTOMER Table, (b) INDEX for Name, and (c) Index for CustomerNumber

RowNumber	CustNumber	Name	CreditLimit	ZIPcode
1	10	Smith	3000	06413
2	20	Jones	3000	95060
3	30	Whittaker	2000	07814
4	40	Murphy	3000	62200
5	50	Wang	3000	08142
6	60	Youngblood	2000	62200
7	70	Jones	2000	95060

(a)

Name	RowNumber
Jones	2
Jones	7
Murphy	4
Smith	1
Wang	5
Whittaker	3
Youngblood	6

(b)

CustNumber	RowNumber
10	1
20	2
30	3
40	4
50	5
60	6
70	7

(c)

plex, as discussed in the Appendix.) The rows might be stored in the sequence in which they appear in the figure. Now suppose that a user frequently needs to access the data by means of customer name. The index illustrated in Figure 12-21(b) can be used to find a specific name and the location of a row in the CUSTOMER table that has that name. Using the index will be much faster than sequentially searching the table.

Similarly, suppose another user often accesses the table by means of customer number. The index in Figure 12-21(c) would be useful in that case. Of course, the table in Figure 12-21 is very small, as it is only an example. KDK's real CUS-TOMER table has thousands of rows. In fact, using indexes on such a small table would probably downgrade performance. Not only does index searching require time, but every addition or deletion to the CUSTOMER table also requires updating the indexes.

Subject to concurrent processing restrictions, indexes can be defined at any time. An index is a physical construct, completely separate from the table to which it is related. As we mentioned, DB2 automatically maintains an index once it is created. In fact, after an index is defined for a table, DB2 decides without any direction from a user or a programmer when, if ever, to use it. In other words, once an index has been defined, neither a user nor an application programmer actually references it.

INDEX SPACES

An **index space** is an area of disk storage in which DB2 stores an index (see Figure 12-22). When an index is created, DB2 automatically allocates an index space for it.

FIGURE 12-22

DB2 Indexes Stored in
Index Spaces

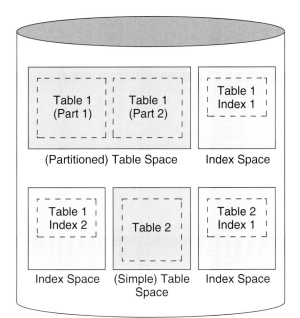

(Partitioned) Table Space

Index Space

Index Space

(Simple) Table
Space

Index Space

DASD (Disk) Volume

FIGURE 12-23

DB2 Storage Groups

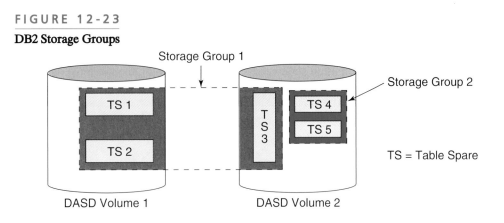

DATA BASES

IBM uses the term **data base** (two words) to define a collection of DB2 tables and indexes and the storage areas that hold them. Several DB2 data bases can exist on the same computer system. DB2 is designed to use a data base as an operational unit, meaning that it can *start* a data base (make it available), *stop* a data base (make it unavailable), and assign *authorization* to use a data base (allow users to access the data).

Users and application programmers do not deal directly with data bases any more than they deal with table spaces or indexes. Rather, they refer only to tables and views and are shielded from needing to know anything about the underlying database structures.

STORAGE GROUPS

A **storage group** is a group of disk volumes on which DB2 allocates space for user databases (see Figure 12-23). DB2 manages its own data set[3] allocation unless the system administrator overrides this feature, thereby enabling DB2 to keep track of available disk space and locates tables, indexes, and other database constructs in that space. It also releases disk space for use when it becomes available, such as when an index or a table is dropped. The system administrator can also define, locate, and delete data sets. Sometimes this is done when tuning, or optimizing, the database system.

■ **Using DB2 to Create Tables, Views, and Indexes**

DB2 uses its version of the SQL data definition language (DDL) to define the DB2 constructs. In this section and in the sections that follow, we will illustrate SQL DDL by defining several constructs—tables, views, and indexes—for the Information Center database at KDK Appliances.

---

[3] Data set is an IBM term for a file. A data set is a named collection of data used to hold table and index data.

DEFINING A TABLE

DB2 uses the SQL CREATE statement to define its constructs. In Chapter 10 we examined only the data manipulation functions of SQL, and in this chapter we add data definition statements. Before defining a table, we must decide on the names of all the columns and their data types and lengths and whether we wish to allow null values.

The allowable DB2 data types for field values are summarized in Figure 12-24. As we stated earlier, a **null value** is a field value that is unknown or not applicable. A null value is different from a zero or a blank value. For example, a customer balance of zero is different from an unknown customer balance. You can prohibit null values from specific columns when you create a table by coding the phrase NOT NULL. If the column does not have this phrase, the nulls will be allowed.

Consider the SALESPERSON relation for which sample data appears in Figure 12-12. The following CREATE statement defines it:

```
CREATE TABLE SALESPERSON
    (NUMBER      CHAR (4)        NOT NULL,
     NAME        CHAR (20)       NOT NULL,
     REGION      DECIMAL (1))
```

The next SQL statement creates the PRODUCT relation for the sample data shown in Figure 12-14:

```
CREATE TABLE PRODUCT
    (TYPE          CHAR (1)        NOT NULL,
     NUMBER        CHAR (5)        NOT NULL,
     NAME          CHAR (25)       NOT NULL,
     DESCRIPTION   CHAR (50),
     PRICE         DECIMAL (7,2)   NOT NULL)
```

DEFINING A VIEW

The CREATE statement can also be used to define a view. To do this, you include a SELECT statement that describes the view. The following CREATE statement defines a view of PRODUCT that includes only product numbers and prices:

FIGURE 12-24

Some Allowable DB2 Data Types

INTEGER	31-bit signed binary values
SMALLINT	15-bit signed binary values
FLOAT	Floating-point values
DECIMAL(p,q)	Packed decimal values of p (1 to 15) digits; a number of decimal places (q) to the right of the decimal point may be specified
CHAR(n)	Fixed-length text data n (1 to 254) characters long
VARCHAR(n)	Variable-length text data up to n (1 to 32674) characters

```
CREATE VIEW PRICELIST
    AS      SELECT      NUMBER, PRICE
            FROM        PRODUCT
```

The view PRICELIST can be manipulated in exactly the same way as a table is. Data is retrieved from a view using the same SQL statements used for a table. If the view is a subset of rows or columns of a single table, it can be used to update base table data. But views that are the result of a join operation cannot be used to update table data.

The next statement creates a view that contains only those rows in the PRODUCT relation for refrigerators (the Type field contains a 5):

```
CREATE VIEW REFRIGERATORS
    AS      SELECT      *
            FROM        PRODUCT
            WHERE       TYPE = '5'
```

By specifying SELECT * we include all of the columns, and by specifying WHERE TYPE = '5' we include only those rows for refrigerators. This view can be used to update base table data.

Consider a third view. Assume that KDK wants a particular user to have only restricted access to the DEALER and ADVERTISEMENT relations, that is, only those dealers who have participated in the advertising (see Figures 12-12 and 12-17). We might define an appropriate joined view in this way:

```
CREATE VIEW ACTIVEDEALER
        AS      SELECT      DEALER.NUMBER, DEALER.NAME,
                            TELEPHONE, ADVERTISEMENT.DATE,
                            COST, SHARE-PERCENT
                FROM        DEALER, ADVERTISEMENT
                WHERE       DEALER.NUMBER =
                            ADVERTISEMENT.DEALER-NUMBER
```

Since this view is based on a join, it cannot be used to update base table data.

DEFINING AN INDEX

Indexes are usually defined and dropped by the DBA or system administrator. As we mentioned earlier, neither users nor application programmers ever reference an index; rather, DB2 decides when to use it and which one to use.

One reason to use an index, as described in the previous section, is to speed up the processing. Several indexes can be defined for one table, thereby allowing rapid access on many different fields. Another reason for defining an index on a table is that an index can force the uniqueness of the values of a column (or multiple columns). For example, the dealer number in KDK's DEALER relation must be unique (although the dealer's name, address, ZIP, and so forth do not need to be unique). The way to establish the uniqueness of the dealer number field is to issue this CREATE statement:

```
CREATE      UNIQUE INDEX XDEALER
            ON DEALER (NUMBER)
```

In the next example, since UNIQUE is not specified, the resulting index might include duplicate telephone numbers. Incidentally, the index value is assumed to be ascending (ASC) unless otherwise specified (DESC):

```
CREATE      INDEX XDLRPHONE
            ON DEALER (PHONE DESC)
```

USING DB2 TO CHANGE A TABLE

Often when we design a database, we are unable to anticipate all of the user's needs. And even if we could, the needs change over time, and consequently we sometimes need to modify our database design. Notice that we are not talking about changing the data stored in the tables (that happens all the time, of course) but, rather, the structure of tables themselves.

DB2 offers two ways to modify table specifications: by dropping and then recreating the table and by using the ALTER statement. The ALTER statement can be used only for adding a column to an existing table.

To remove a column or to change a column's data type or length or to change whether null values are allowed, we must drop the table and recreate it. We illustrate how to drop a table in the next section. For now, just be aware that when you drop a table, you lose the table data as well as all the views and indexes based on that table.

To make structure changes other than adding a new column, follow these steps:

1. Define a new table with all the changes and a different name.
2. Copy the table data from the old table to the new one.
3. Define all indexes on the new table.
4. Drop the old table (this loses all the views of it, too).
5. Restore the original table name as a view of the new table. This allows applications that once referenced the old table to remain unchanged, because the new view is processed in exactly the same way as the old table.
6. Define views like the ones defined for the old table. These can be exact duplicates of the old views because you can base a view on another view, just as you can base a view on a table. (Of course, if a view contains a column that has just been dropped, that view is no longer valid.)
7. Authorize users to use the new table and views.

Clearly, this type of database modification is done only by a DBA or someone who is authorized by the DBA.

The second option for changing a table design uses the ALTER statement, with which we can add a column to an existing table. For instance, to add a salary column to the SALESPERSON relation, we would use the following statement:

```
ALTER      TABLE SALESPERSON
           (ADD SALARY DECIMAL (7,2))
```

■ Using DB2 to Delete Tables and Views

The DBA periodically needs to eliminate tables from the database. Users are rarely authorized to do this, because they could inadvertently delete data they do not realize that another user needs. In the previous section, we saw how the DBA might need to delete a table in order to change its structure.

Deleting a table erases not only the table but also all its dependent views and indexes. Thus a table should not be dropped without careful thought. To delete the ADVERTISEMENT table from its database, KDK's DBA would issue the following DROP statement:

```
DROP        TABLE ADVERTISEMENT
```

The table and all its data would be deleted from the table space, as well as all the indexes and views associated with it.

The DROP statement can also be used to delete views. For instance, the DBA might authorize a user to create views and then to delete them when they are no longer useful. It is unlikely, however, that a user would be authorized to drop views that might be used by anyone else. That responsibility (and control) should remain with the DBA. This notwithstanding, however, we could delete the ACTIVEDEALER view by issuing the following statement:

```
DROP        VIEW ACTIVEDEALER
```

Any applications that used that view (or views based on that view) would no longer work.

SUMMARY OF DB2 CREATION FACILITIES

DB2 allows the DBA or user to define, modify, and delete various database constructs—tables, views, table spaces, indexes, index spaces, data bases, and storage groups. Users and application programmers are concerned only with tables and views. In addition to tables and views, the DBA and database designers need to understand the underlying physical structures and database storage.

■ Using DB2 SQL to Manipulate Data

There are some differences between the DB2 statements used by interactive users and those used by application programmers that occur because of differences in the users' and the programmers' environments. Interactive users want results to be displayed immediately on a screen, whereas application programmers want the DBMS to place the values of columns and rows into program variables.

INTERACTIVE DATA MANIPULATION

Interactive DB2, or DB2I, supports all of the SQL statements described in Chapter 10. Because the format is the same as shown in that chapter, we will not go over it again. The user simply types the commands, as shown in Chapter 10, at the DB2I prompt.

ACCESSING DB2 FROM COBOL

DB2 application programs can be written in COBOL, PL/I, FORTRAN, C, and assembler language, and SQL statements can be embedded in programs written in any of these languages. The examples used in this text are embedded in COBOL programs.

As shown in Figure 12-25, all application programs that access DB2 must first be processed by the DB2 **precompiler.** The precompiler analyzes program source statements and processes those that are flagged SQL statements (you will see how later). The precompiler inserts into the program the required **table formats**, which are already written in the host language and stored on disk. It also builds for each SQL statement a **data base request module,** or DBRM, which it stores for later use. And

FIGURE 12-25

Steps in Developing an Application Program with DB2

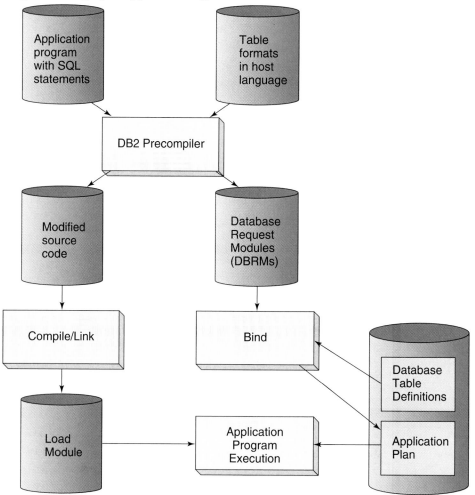

the precompiler replaces the SQL statements with host-language call statements to access the DBRMs. As illustrated in Figure 12-25, the modified source code is then input to a standard language compiler for normal compilation.

The Bind process uses the DBRMs, database table definitions, available indexes, and other database data to determine the access paths for each SQL request. It stores these in the database data as an **application plan,** which is loaded when the first SQL call is executed.

To enable the DB2 precompiler to recognize the statements intended for it, all SQL statements are embedded in keywords. Specifically, every SQL statement is preceded by the keyword EXEC SQL and followed by the keyword END-EXEC. In COBOL, the keyword END-EXEC is followed by a period unless the SQL statement is located in an IF statement. The general format of a DB2 SQL statement in a COBOL program is

EXEC SQL statement END-EXEC.

Only one statement can be included between the keywords. Multiple SQL statements require multiple EXEC SQL. . .END-EXEC statements. DB2 SQL statements are embedded in the DATA DIVISION and the PROCEDURE DIVISION.

SQL STATEMENTS IN THE DATA DIVISION

Two types of statements are embedded in the DATA DIVISION. The first describes data items that are used to pass **database data** between the application program and DB2. The second type describes the **system data** shared by the application program and DB2.

Figure 12-26 shows part of a COBOL program that processes the SALESPERSON table defined earlier. The DATA DIVISION includes data item definitions for

FIGURE 12-26

SQL Statements Embedded in COBOL Program

```
DATA DIVISION.
WORKING-STORAGE SECTION.
EXEC  SQL   BEGIN DECLARE SECTION          END-EXEC.
01      SALESPERSON.
        05      SALESPERSON-NUM            PICTURE X(4).
        05      SALESPERSON-NAME           PICTURE X(20).
        05      SALES-REGION               PICTURE 9  COMP-3.
EXEC  SQL   END DECLARE SECTION            END-EXEC.
EXEC  SQL   INCLUDE SQLCA   END-EXEC.
PROCEDURE DIVISION.
        MOVE '5762' TO SALESPERSON-NUM.
        EXEC SQL
                SELECT NAME, REGION
                INTO :SALESPERSON-NAME, :SALES-REGION
                FROM SALESPERSON
                WHERE NUMBER = :SALESPERSON-NUM
        END-EXEC.
```

all three columns of SALESPERSON. These columns have been renamed: NUM-BER is SALESPERSON-NUM, NAME is SALESPERSON-NAME, and REGION is SALES-REGION. The correct correspondence of names is established in the PROCEDURE DIVISION.

The data types and lengths of data items do match, although COBOL uses a different vocabulary than SQL does. For example, when we created the table using SQL, we defined SPNUM as CHAR(4), whereas the equivalent COBOL definition for SALESPERSON-NUM is PICTURE X(4).

All the data items that DB2 and the application program share are grouped together, thereby enabling the precompiler to identify them. (We show these statements in the WORKING-STORAGE SECTION, but they could be located elsewhere in the DATA DIVISION.) The DECLARE SECTION is used to define those data items that will be used to transfer database data between the application program and DB2. That group of data item definitions is preceded by the DB2 keywords BEGIN DECLARE SECTION and is terminated with the message END DECLARE SECTION. In Figure 12-26, the definition of SALESPERSON is found in the DECLARE SECTION.

In addition to database data, the application program and the DBMS also need to share system data. For example, after each SQL statement is executed, DB2 sets a return code that indicates whether an error occurred. Both DB2 and the application program need access to this return code.

System data is defined in the program with the DB2 SQL message INCLUDE SQLCA (which stands for SQL Communications Area). When the precompiler processes this INCLUDE message, it inserts the data definitions in Figure 12-27(a) into the application program.

For brevity, Figure 12-27(b) describes only a few of the data items in SQLCA. Knowing all of them would contribute little to your understanding of DB2, but the one data item you must know is SQLCODE. SQLCODE is set by DB2 after each SQL command is executed. If the command is executed normally, SQLCODE is set to zero. If an unusual but normal condition occurs, SQLCODE is set to a positive value. For example, end-of-data is indicated by the value 100. If an abnormal, unexpected condition occurs, SQLCODE is set to a negative value. Insufficient VSAM file space is an example of an abnormal unexpected event.

SQL STATEMENTS IN THE PROCEDURE DIVISION

SQL statements in the PROCEDURE DIVISION instruct DB2 to perform some action. For example, the SELECT statement in Figure 12-26 causes DB2 to extract from the database the name and region of Salesperson 5762 and to place those values in the data items called SALESPERSON-NAME and SALES-REGION. This SQL statement is almost identical to the format followed when writing interactive SQL commands. The exception is the INTO clause that tells DB2 the name of the **host variable** (or variables) into which DB2 will place the value(s) it obtains from the database.

One problem for the DB2 precompiler is distinguishing between the data names defined in the database and those defined locally within the application program. If all names are unique, it can process the statements correctly. But it is impossible to guarantee that the application programmer will always choose data names not

FIGURE 12-27

DB2 Communications Area: (a) COBOL Description of SQLCA and (b) Content of Selected SQLCA Data Items

```
01    SQLCA.
      05    SQLCAID         PICTURE X(8).
      05    SQLCABC         PICTURE S9(9) COMPUTATIONAL.
      05    SQLCODE         PICTURE S9(9) COMPUTATIONAL.
      05    SQLERRM
            49   SQLERRML   PICTURE S9(4) COMPUTATIONAL.
            49   SQLERRMC   PICTURE X(70).
      05    SQLERRP         PICTURE X(8).
      05    SQLERRD         OCCURS 6 TIMES
                            PICTURE S9(9) COMPUTATIONAL.

      05    SQLWARN.
            10   SQLWARN0   PICTURE X(1).
            10   SQLWARN1   PICTURE X(1).
            10   SQLWARN2   PICTURE X(1).
            10   SQLWARN3   PICTURE X(1).
            10   SQLWARN4   PICTURE X(1).
            10   SQLWARN5   PICTURE X(1).
            10   SQLWARN6   PICTURE X(1).
            10   SQLWARN7   PICTURE X(1).
      05    SQLEXT          PICTURE X(8).
```

(a)

Data-item	Content
SQLCODE	Return code. Set by DB2 after each command. Zero indicates successful operation. Positive value indicates normal condition (such as end of data). Negative value indicates abnormal error.
SQLERRM	Error message. Set when SQLCODE is less than 0.
SQLERRP	Name of DB2 routine detecting error. Set when SQLCODE is less than 0.
SQLERRD	DB2 system status.
SQLWARN	Warning flags. Set for conditions such as data-item truncation (receiving data-item too small); null values encountered when processing SUM, AVG, MIN, or MAX; recovery from deadlock; and so forth.

(b)

already used in the database. Consequently, a colon (:) precedes the names of program variables used within any embedded SQL statement.

As we stated in Chapter 9, COBOL (as well as many other programming languages) is designed to process data one record at a time. That is, a typical COBOL program retrieves one record, processes it, retrieves the next one, processes it, and so forth, until all the records have been handled. DB2, however, processes tables. That is, a DB2 SELECT statement always returns a table of data. (The example in Figure 12-26 is unusual in that it only returns one row; most SELECT statements return many rows.) This distinction between COBOL file processing and DB2 relation processing is important to the application programmer who might be tempted to think that SQL statements correspond to simple READ and WRITE statements. They do not.

The application programmer would be better served by thinking of DB2 as a vehicle for retrieving an entire input data set, or pseudofile, from the database. Then the data is processed one row at a time. To do this, we define a cursor within the application program.

A **cursor** is a pointer that operates on a SELECT statement, indicating the row to be processed within the pseudofile generated by the SELECT statement. In Figure 12-28, for example, the cursor CURRENT is defined to operate on the SELECT statement that will retrieve the names of all the salespeople in Region 5. In subsequent statements the program uses CURRENT to process sequentially the retrieved rows. As you can see in Figure 12-28, the logic is similar to that of sequential file processing. The cursor is opened (similar to opening a file); the first row is fetched (similar to a read); and a loop is executed to process the rest of the data (similar to processing an entire file). The processing stops when SQLCODE is returned with a value of 100, indicating the end-of-data. For now we will ignore other types of error processing.

The format of the FETCH statement is

FETCH cursor-name INTO dataname(s)

FIGURE 12-28

Using the Cursor to Process Sequentially a Set of Database Records

```
PROCEDURE DIVISION.
        .
        .
        .
        .
        MOVE 5 TO SALES-REGION.
        EXEC SQL DECLARE CURRENT CURSOR FOR
            SELECT NAME FROM SALESPERSON
            WHERE REGION = :SALES-REGION
        END EXEC.
        .
        .
        .
        EXEC SQL OPEN CURRENT END-EXEC.
        EXEC SQL FETCH CURRENT INTO :SALESPERSON-NAME END-EXEC.
        PERFORM PROCESS-FETCH UNTIL SQLCODE NOT = 0.
        EXEC SQL CLOSE CURRENT END-EXEC.
        .
        .
        .
PROCESS-FETCH.
        (Instructions to process SALESPERSON-NAME go here.)
        EXEC SQL FETCH CURRENT INTO :SALESPERSON-NAME END-EXEC.
```

The datanames in the FETCH statement must match the column names identified in the SELECT statement in which the cursor is defined. More details about the programming techniques used with DB2 appear in the example at the end of this chapter.

■ DB2 Concurrent Processing

Because DB2 allows concurrent processing, it must provide facilities to control and limit users' interference. This is done by means of locks. Two types of locks employed by DB2 are shared locks and exclusive locks. When an application reads database data, DB2 acquires a **shared lock** on the data, which allows other applications to read the same data. Applications that wish to modify that data must wait, however, until the lock has been released, to ensure that everyone has access to the most current data.

When an application needs to modify data (DB2 knows this by analyzing the SQL statements in the application), DB2 acquires an **exclusive lock** on the data, which prevents all other applications from accessing the data. When the application is finished with the data, the lock is released, thereby giving other applications access to the updated data. If DB2 did not acquire exclusive locks, a second application could possibly use the old version of the data while it was being updated by the first application, and this would compromise the integrity of the stored data.

In addition to choices regarding the type of lock, DB2 offers options regarding the **level,** or **locksize.** The two locking units in DB2 are table spaces and pages. (Recall that a table space is an area of disk storage in which one or several base tables are stored. Table spaces are made up of **pages,** 4k-byte blocks of disk space. Pages generally contain parts of tables.) Although you might expect DB2 to apply locks to tables or even to rows within tables, this is not the case. When an exclusive lock is acquired for a table space, no application can access the data in *any* table stored in that table space.

When establishing a new database, the DBA can specify the lock level within a table space, through the LOCKSIZE option of the CREATE TABLESPACE command. The format is

LOCKSIZE = ANY | PAGE | TABLESPACE

If the DBA specifies TABLESPACE, then locks (either shared or exclusive) will be applied to the entire table space in which a referenced table resides. This option improves the performance of the application, but in doing so, it can seriously delay other applications needing access to something in that table space.

If the DBA selects PAGE, the locks initially are applied at the page level (DB2 may escalate the lock to the table level if it detects poor performance). Although locking at the page level results in fewer conflicts than does locking at the table space level, more resources are required to administer it.

Finally, if the DBA specifies ANY, then DB2 selects the appropriate level, depending on the number of pages that may be required to fulfill an application's needs. If only a few pages are referenced, page-level locks will be applied. On the other hand, if many pages are required, table space–level locks will be applied. ANY is the default value for the LOCKSIZE option, and so the DBA does not need to specify the LOCKSIZE option when creating a table space. By default, DB2 can be allowed to select the proper level of locking based on the type of SQL request and the number of pages involved.

As we mentioned, locks are completely transparent to end users and application programmers. DB2 automatically does all the necessary locking and unlocking.

COMMIT AND ROLLBACK

All DB2 table data modifications must be either committed or discarded. When a change is committed, it is final and becomes part of the actual database data. When a commitment is made, all the page locks placed on that data are released, and the updated data is made available to other applications. A commitment is automatically executed when an application terminates normally, but it can also be explicitly invoked with the SQL COMMIT statement.

Sometimes DB2 table modifications need to be discarded, for example, when an end user wants to terminate a transaction while it is being carried out. To discard the changes, the application program issues an SQL ROLLBACK statement, which returns the tables to their original state (the state after the most recent COMMIT), thus eliminating any pending updates to the table. At that point, all page locks are released, and other applications have access to the unchanged data.

DB2 AND DEADLOCK

When two or more applications are deadlocked, DB2 resolves the problem by examining the number of records that each application has written and terminates the application(s) with the fewest changes since the last commitment. The more active application is selected to continue processing. (See Chapter 15 for a more comprehensive discussion of deadlock.)

■ DB2 Backup and Recovery

DB2 stores the before images and after images of all database changes on a transaction log. Changes are written to the log before they are written to the database, and DB2 periodically checks itself. At the checkpoints, all changes residing in system buffers are written to the database, and a checkpoint record is written to the log. At the time of a checkpoint, therefore, the log and DB2 databases are synchronized.

DB2 can recover from a system failure by first applying all the before images created since the most recent checkpoint and then applying all the after images of committed transactions. As a result, all committed changes can endure the crash, although those transactions in progress at the time of the crash must be restarted.

Databases are stored on disks and are therefore vulnerable to physical damage. Should the disk be damaged, the database must be recreated from backup copies, which means that the users' organization must periodically save the database. In DB2, this is done by means of utility programs that copy table spaces (that is, the physical storage areas that contain table data). DB2 includes an option that allows the users' organization to make backup copies of only those pages in a table space that have been modified since the latest backup. This option can save much time because unchanged pages are not copied unnecessarily.

■ DB2 Security

DB2 provides two types of security mechanisms to protect the database: restricting access via views, and limiting processing capabilities to particular users.

VIEWS

Views provide data security at the field level. Remember that a view is a subset of columns, rows, or both derived from one or more base tables. To prevent a user from accessing any data in a base table except the fields that he or she needs to access, the DBA simply defines a view of the table and authorizes the user to access it but not the base table. We explained how to use SQL to create a view earlier in this chapter, so the following two examples are presented without further explanation.

The following SQL creates a view of KDK's DEALER table that allows access only to the dealers' names and telephone numbers:

```
CREATE VIEW DLRPHONES
      AS SELECT NAME, TELEPHONE
      FROM DEALER
```

The user of the next view is given access to only those dealers' records in the state of Massachusetts:

```
CREATE VIEW MASSDLRS
      AS SELECT *
      FROM DEALER
      WHERE STATE/PROVINCE = 'MA'
```

LIMITING ACCESS TO DB2 RESOURCES

DB2 is able to control access to various database resources, including tables, views, databases, utility programs, the DB2 catalog, and table spaces. Because DB2 users (both end users and application programmers) access only tables and views, we will only discuss them. Though not shown here, system administrators and database administrators have access to all other database resources as well.

DB2 can control access to data in tables and views, so that users can be authorized to issue SELECT, INSERT, DELETE, and UPDATE statements against a table or view. The columns that may be updated can be specified, and the use of the ALTER command to change a table definition can be restricted.

IDENTIFYING USERS

Because DB2 is used in the MVS environment, many users can access it concurrently from a variety of other subsystems, such as IMS and CICS transaction managers, TSO, and batch jobs. Although you need not understand all these subsystems, it is important to know that each has a means of identifying authorized users. For instance, TSO terminal users have a log-on ID that identifies them; a batch job has a special parameter on the job card; and IMS users have a sign-on ID or a logical terminal name (thus the equipment, not the person, is authorized to access the system). Other systems have similar authorization IDs.

DB2 uses the connecting subsystem's ID to identify the DB2 user and assigns capabilities to access resources according to permissions granted to those IDs. Permissions are given via the SQL GRANT statement:

GRANT capability resource-list

    TO authorization-ID-list

    (WITH GRANT OPTION)

The capabilities that can be granted to users are the following:

- ALTER   The definition of the specified tables may be altered.
- DELETE   Rows may be deleted from the specified tables or views.
- INSERT   Rows may be inserted into the specified tables or views.
- SELECT   Rows may be selected from the specified tables or views.
- UPDATE The values for the specified list of columns in the specified tables or views may be updated.

The resource list for most users is simply the names of tables or views for which they will have the specified capabilities. The authorization-ID list is the list of user IDs to whom the specified authorization is being granted. The authorization-ID list can also be the keyword PUBLIC, which grants authority to all users. Here are some examples that illustrate the GRANT command:

- All users are allowed to look at the DEALER table:

  GRANT SELECT ON TABLE DEALER TO PUBLIC

- An application program can insert new records into the ADVERTISEMENT table:

  GRANT INSERT ON TABLE ADVERTISEMENT TO PROG87

- A user known by the ID TERM 14 is allowed to access the view DLRPHONES:

  GRANT SELECT ON VIEW DLRPHONES TO TERM 14

- Two users are allowed to change table definitions for the DEALER and SALESPERSON tables:

  GRANT ALTER ON TABLE DEALER, SALESPERSON TO USER5, USER7

- An application program is allowed to delete SALESPERSON records:

  GRANT DELETE ON TABLE SALESPERSON TO PERS000

When the DB2 database is installed, the system administrator is given total control over all resources. He or she may grant authority to or revoke authority from any other individual, including DBAs, by means of the GRANT statement. Of course, the resources and capabilities available to the system administrator include many options besides those just described.

The GRANT statement contains an optional clause: WITH GRANT OPTION. When used, this clause enables the grantee to give others the same capabilities over the same resources. Thus one can pass along authorization to others. Consider this example:

GRANT SELECT ON AD-COPY TO MURPHY WITH GRANT OPTION

This gives Murphy permission to read the AD-COPY table and allows her to authorize other users to do the same.

In addition to the explicit authorization conveyed by the GRANT command, the creator of a construct is automatically given full authority WITH GRANT OPTION over that construct, and this cannot be revoked unless the construct itself is deleted from the database.

If authority is revoked (by means of the REVOKE command), it has a cascading effect; that is, the specified privilege is revoked not only from the named authorized ID but also from anyone else to whom that authorized ID granted this privilege. Suppose that User A were granted the authority to read a table with the GRANT option and subsequently granted that privilege to User B. When User A is transferred to another department and his authority to read the table is revoked, User B's authority stemming from the GRANT is also automatically revoked. The following illustrates this sequence of events:

1. DBA:

GRANT SELECT ON TABLE PRODUCT TO USERA WITH GRANT OPTION
(User A can now read the PRODUCT table.)

2. User A:

GRANT SELECT ON TABLE PRODUCT TO USERB
(Users A and B can now read the PRODUCT table.)

3. DBA:

REVOKE SELECT ON TABLE PRODUCT FROM USERA
(Neither User A nor User B can read the PRODUCT table.)

RELATIONAL IMPLEMENTATION USING DB2

This section discusses the implementation of KDK's Information Center database using DB2. A summary of KDK's database design appears in Figures 12-29 and 12-30.

First we create the database using interactive DB2 commands, and then we illustrate several on-line queries that product managers (or Information Center personnel) might execute. Finally, we present an application program that produces one of the standard reports that the PMs need.

FIGURE 12-29

Summary of Relations for KDK Appliances' Information Center Database

INVOICE	(Number, Date, Total, Salesperson.Number, Dealer.Number)
LINE-ITEM	(Invoice.Number, Line-item-number, Product.Number, Quantity, Extended-price)
DEALER	(Number, Name, Address-1, Address-2, City, State/Province, ZIP/Postal-code, Telephone)
SALESPERSON	(Number, Name, Region)
PRODUCT	(Number, Name, Description, Price)
AD-COPY	(Ad-name, Agency, First-run-date)
ADVERTISEMENT	(Publication, Date, Ad-name, Cost, Share-percent, Dealer.Number)
PRODUCT-AD	(Ad-name, Product.Number)

Creating the Database Structure

The interactive DB2 statements to create the database structure (KDKICB) presented in Figures 12-29 and 12-30 are shown in Figure 12-31. As you can see, the statements are straightforward. Having completed the design earlier, we need only specify the format of each table and column using DB2.

Keep in mind that this database will be used for queries only—it will be neither updated nor altered. It is a snapshot of corporate operational data downloaded from the mainframe database to be analyzed by the product managers. All updates are made to the operational data in a carefully controlled environment. Therefore, other than authorizing each PM to access (SELECT) the tables, no other authority is granted. No one needs to alter, delete, or update any of the data. And because all the PMs are given access to all the columns in all the tables, no views are necessary.

Examples of Interactive Queries

Figure 12-32 shows four sample queries of KDK's Information Center database. The first lists the names of dealers who shared advertising with KDK during the month of March. The DB2 word DISTINCT eliminates duplicate names from the list. Although the name of a dealer who shared more than one ad with KDK should appear several times in the list, we will print it only once.

This example uses the subquery technique. Recall from Chapter 10 that subqueries allow us to narrow the scope of our search through the database by qualifying one level of query with another. Reading from the bottom up, the first example in Figure 12-32 begins by building a list of numbers for those dealers who shared with KDK the cost of advertising during March. Then, moving up to the next SELECT statement, it extracts the dealers' names from the DEALER table for all whose numbers appeared in the first list. Finally, the DISTINCT option causes the DBMS to eliminate duplicate names.

FIGURE 12-30

Table Descriptions for
KDK's Information Center
Database

INVOICE	
Number	Char (4)
Date	Numeric YYMMDD
Total	Numeric 9999.99
Salesperson.Number	*
Dealer.Number	*
LINE-ITEM	
Invoice.Number	*
Line-item-number	Numeric 999 positive integer
Product.Number	*
Quantity	Numeric 999 positive integer
Extended-price	Computed numeric 9(6).99
DEALER	
Number	Char(4)
Name	Char(45)
Address-1	Char(25)
Address-2	Char(25)
City	Char(15)
State/Province	Char(2)
ZIP/Postal-code	Char(10)
Telephone	Char(10)
SALESPERSON	
Number	Char(4)
Name	Char(20)
Region	Numeric 9
PRODUCT	
Type	Numeric 9
Number	Char(5)
Name	Char(25)
Description	Char(50)
Price	Numeric 99999.99
AD-COPY	
Ad-name	Char(15)
Agency	Char(30)
First-run-date	Numeric YYMMDD
ADVERTISEMENT	
Publication	Char(10)
Date	Numeric YYMMDD
Ad-name	*
Cost	Numeric 9999.99
Share-percent	Numeric 999.99
	E.g., 30% is 30.00
Dealer.Number	*
PRODUCT-AD	
Ad-name	*
Product.Number	*

*Definitions for foreign keys are shown in the foreign relations.

The second example in Figure 12-32 also uses the subquery technique, only this time it is more complex. Once again we interpret the statement by reading it from the bottom up. We begin by building a list of product numbers for refrigerators (Type = '5'). Then we build a list of invoice numbers that contain line items for any of those products. Next we extract the dealers' numbers for all of those invoices occurring in March, and finally we build a list of dealers' names, eliminating duplicates. This is the list of dealers who purchased refrigerators during March.

FIGURE 12-31

Interactive DB2 Statements to Create Tables for KDK's Information Center Database

```
CREATE  TABLE        INVOICE
        (NUMBER                    CHAR(4)         NOT NULL,
        DATE                       DECIMAL(6)      NOT NULL,
        TOTAL                      DECIMAL(7,2)    NOT NULL,
        SALESPERSON-NUMBER         CHAR(4)         NOT NULL,
        DEALER-NUMBER              CHAR(4)         NOT NULL)
CREATE  TABLE        LINE-ITEM
        (INVOICE-NUMBER            CHAR(4)         NOT NULL,
        LINE-ITEM-NUMBER           DECIMAL(3)      NOT NULL,
        PRODUCT-NUMBER             CHAR(5)         NOT NULL,
        QUANTITY                   DECIMAL(3)      NOT NULL,
        EXTENDED-PRICE             DECIMAL(8,2)    NOT NULL)
CREATE  TABLE        DEALER
        (NUMBER                    CHAR(4)         NOT NULL,
        NAME                       CHAR(45)        NOT NULL,
        ADDRESS-1                  CHAR(25),
        ADDRESS-2                  CHAR(25),
        CITY                       CHAR(15)
        STATE/PROVINCE             CHAR(10),
        ZIP/POSTAL-CODE            CHAR(10),
        TELEPHONE                  CHAR(10))
CREATE  TABLE        SALESPERSON
        NUMBER                     CHAR(4)         NOT NULL,
        NAME                       CHAR(20)        NOT NULL,
        REGION                     DECIMAL(1)).
CREATE  TABLE        PRODUCT
        (TYPE                      CHAR(1)         NOT NULL,
        NUMBER                     CHAR(5)         NOT NULL,
        NAME                       CHAR(25)        NOT NULL,
        DESCRIPTION                CHAR(50),
        PRICE                      DECIMAL(7,2)    NOT NULL)
CREATE  TABLE        AD-COPY
        (AD-NAME                   CHAR(15)        NOT NULL,
        AGENCY                     CHAR(30),
        FIRST-RUN-DATE             DECIMAL(6))
CREATE  TABLE        ADVERTISEMENT
        (PUBLICATION               CHAR(10)        NOT NULL,
        DATE                       DECIMAL(6)      NOT NULL,
        AD-NAME                    CHAR(15)        NOT NULL,
        COST                       DECIMAL(6,2)    NOT NULL,
        SHARE-PERCENT              DECIMAL(5,2),
        DEALER-NUMBER              CHAR(4))
CREATE  TABLE        PRODUCT-AD
        (AD-NAME                   CHAR(15)        NOT NULL,
        PRODUCT-NUMBER             CHAR(5)         NOT NULL)
```

The third illustration in Figure 12-32 extracts data from several tables in order to give the user the desired results. Product names and descriptions come from the PRODUCT table. Advertisements, which are dated, are stored in the ADVERTISE-MENT table. But advertisements are not directly associated with any product—they are associated with advertising copy by means of the Ad-name column. Similarly,

FIGURE 12-32

Sample Interactive DB2 Queries Against KDK's Database

```
1.    List the dealers who participated in shared advertising during the month of March:
      SELECT DISTINCT NAME FROM DEALER
      WHERE DEALER. NUMBER IN
            SELECT DEALER-NUMBER
            FROM ADVERTISEMENT
            WHERE ADVERTISEMENT. DATE BETWEEN 880301 AND 880331
2.    List the dealers who purchased refrigerators (product type = 5) in March:
      SELECT DISTINCT NAME FROM DEALER
      WHERE DEALER. NUMBER IN
            SELECT DEALER-NUMBER FROM INVOICE
            WHERE   DATE BETWEEN 880301 AND 880331
            AND     INVOICE. NUMBER IN
                  SELECT INVOICE-NUMBER FROM LINE-ITEM
                  WHERE LINE-ITEM. PRODUCT-NUMBER IN
                        SELECT NUMBER FROM PRODUCT
                        WHERE TYPE = '5'
3.    List the products that were advertised in March:
      SELECT NUMBER, NAME, DESCRIPTION FROM PRODUCT
      WHERE PRODUCT. NUMBER IN
            SELECT DISTINCT PRODUCT-NUMBER FROM PRODUCT-AD
            WHERE   PRODUCT-AD. AD-NAME = ADVERTISEMENT. AD-NAME
            AND     ADVERTISEMENT. DATE BETWEEN 880301 AND 880331
4.    Print the total sales for product #94605 for the month of March. Then print it for the
      month of April:
      CREATE VIEW PRODUCTSALES
            (DATE, PRODUCT, EXTENDED-PRICE)
            AS SELECT DATE, PRODUCT-NUMBER, EXTENDED-PRICE
                  FROM INVOICE, LINE-ITEM
                  WHERE LINE-ITEM. INVOICE-NUMBER = INVOICE. NUMBER
                  AND   LINE-ITEM. PRODUCT-NUMBER = '94605'
      SELECT SUM (EXTENDED-PRICE)
      FROM PRODUCTSALES
      WHERE DATE BETWEEN 880301 AND 880331
      SELECT SUM (EXTENDED-PRICE)
      FROM PRODUCTSALES
      WHERE DATE BETWEEN 880401 AND 880430
```

products are not associated directly with an advertisement, but with advertising copy by means of the Ad-name column in the PRODUCT-AD table.

We begin by joining the PRODUCT-AD table and the ADVERTISEMENT table, matching on Ad-name. Then we extract unique (distinct) product numbers, but only for advertisements that ran in March. Finally, we extract from the PRODUCT table the name and description for each product number we have identified.

The fourth example of a query in Figure 12-32 begins by building a view (the join of two tables) and then selecting total sales figures from the view. The view is made up of sales data for Product 94605, taken from the INVOICE table (date) and the LINE-ITEM table (product number, extended price). Having established this subset of the larger base tables, we can ask DB2 to calculate the two sales totals by invoking the SUM built-in function in the SELECT statement. Two SELECT statements are needed, of course, one for each month.

■ Application Program Example

Figure 12-33 presents a COBOL program that prints the report shown in Figure 12-3(c), entitled PRODUCT SALES SUMMARY BY REGION. In this section we examine the COBOL program, noting the placement of DB2 commands. Although this example is written in COBOL, SQL can also be embedded in PL/I, FOR-TRAN, C, and assembler language programs.

Looking at the WORKING-STORAGE SECTION of the DATA DIVISION, we find the definition of those variables that will hold data values as they are retrieved by DB2 from the database. These variables are defined following the SQL message BEGIN DECLARE SECTION. Notice that each SQL statement is surrounded by the precompiler keywords EXEC SQL and END-EXEC.

Within the DECLARE SECTION we have defined a sale record, made up of six fields. Later, in the PROCEDURE DIVISION, the data for this sale record can be found in four different database tables. The words END DECLARE SECTION signal the end of the DECLARE SECTION.

The next instruction in the WORKING-STORAGE SECTION directs the precompiler to copy SQLCA into the COBOL program. Again, this is a list of parameters shared by the DBMS and the application program. The most important field in SQLCA is SQLCODE, as described earlier.

The remainder of the WORKING-STORAGE SECTION defines the work areas and report formats to be used by the program. These are normal COBOL entries that are not affected by the need to use DB2.

In the PROCEDURE DIVISION we find a mixture of SQL statements and ordinary COBOL instructions. The first sequence of instructions in the PROCEDURE DIVISION defines a cursor (C-1) that will be used to retrieve data from the database. The SELECT statement on which the cursor operates is lengthy, but it is easily understood. To print the report seen in Figure 12-3, we need a set of sales records containing product numbers, names and descriptions, prices, quantities sold, and regions, which are found in several different database tables.

The SELECT specifies a join of four tables. The join conditions are specified in the where clause that starts

WHERE LINE-ITEM.INVOICE.NUMBER = INVOICE.NUMBER, etc.

Finally, the ORDER BY clause specifies that the rows (records) should be made available to the program sorted by region number within product number.

Having established the cursor, we now have a conceptual pseudofile that contains all the newly constructed sales records in the desired sequence. The rest of the program follows ordinary sequential file-processing logic, testing for two control-level breaks (one on region number and the other on product number).

First we open the output report file, and then we issue SQL statements to prepare the database data to be processed:

OPEN C-1

We use the cursor to retrieve the first database row in the sale pseudofile,

FETCH C-1 INTO :SALE-RECORD

FIGURE 12-33

COBOL Program to Produce PRODUCT SALES SUMMARY BY REGION Report

```
IDENTIFICATION DIVISION.
PROGRAM-ID.   DB2-EXAMPLE.
ENVIRONMENT DIVISION.
CONFIGURATION SECTION.
SPECIAL-NAMES.
     (special names go here)
INPUT-OUTPUT SECTION.
FILE-CONTROL.
     SELECT    (SELECT statements for non-database files go here)
DATA DIVISION.
FILE SECTION.
     FD          (FDs for non-database files go here)
WORKING-STORAGE SECTION.
*
*      DECLARE VARIABLES FOR USE WITH DB2
*
       EXEC SQL   BEGIN DECLARE SECTION   END EXEC.
  01   SALE-RECORD.
       05  PRODUCT-NUMBER            PICTURE X(05).
       05  PRODUCT-NAME              PICTURE X(25).
       05  PRODUCT-DESC              PICTURE X(50).
       05  QUANTITY-SOLD             PICTURE S999         COMP-3.
       05  UNIT-PRICE                PICTURE S9 (5) V99   COMP-3.
       05  SALE-REGION               PICTURE S9           COMP-3.
       EXEC SQL   END DECLARE SECTION      END EXEC.
*      REQUEST DB2 TO COPY INTO COBOL PROGRAM
*      DEFINITIONS FOR DB2 COMMUNICATIONS AREA.
*
       EXEC SQL   INCLUDE SQLCA            END-EXEC.
*
*      DEFINE NON-DATABASE VARIABLES
*
  77   PRODUCT-NUMBER HOLD          PICTURE X(5).
  77   REGION-HOLD                  PICTURE X.
  77   SUM-UNITS-THIS-REGION        PICTURE 999          COMP-3 VALUE 0.
  77   SUM-UNITS-THIS-PRODUCT       PICTURE 99999        COMP-3 VALUE 0.
  01   PAGE-HEADER-1.
       05  FILLER                   PICTURE X(24)    VALUE SPACES.
       05  FILLER                   PICTURE X(31)
           VALUE 'PRODUCT SALES SUMMARY BY REGION'.
       05  FILLER                   PICTURE X(25)    VALUE SPACES.
  01   GROUP-1.
       05  FILLER                   PICTURE X(16)
           VALUE 'PRODUCT NUMBER:'.
```

placing the data values into the fields we defined in the DECLARE SECTION. The word SALE-RECORD is preceded by a colon (:) to help the precompiler determine that SALE-RECORD is a program variable and not a database term. This FETCH SQL statement effectively reads the first sale record from the pseudofile.

The next instruction sequence saves the product number and region values in work areas and writes the first set of report headers. Now the program is ready to process the first record. The program starts the loop called PROCESS–AND–FETCH and remains in this program loop until no more "sale records" are left in the database

FIGURE 12-33

Continued

```
        05  PRODUCT-NUMBER-OUT        PICTURE X(05).
        05  FILLER                    PICTURE X(59)    VALUE SPACES.
    01  GROUP-2.
        05  FILLER                    PICTURE X(16)
            VALUE 'DESCRIPTION:'
        05  NAME-OUT                  PICTURE X(25).
        05  FILLER                    PICTURE X(39)    VALUE SPACES.
    01  GROUP-3.
        05  FILLER                    PICTURE X(16)    VALUE SPACES.
        05  DESCRIPTION-OUT           PICTURE X(50).
        05  FILLER                    PICTURE X(14)    VALUE SPACES.
    01  GROUP-4.
        05  FILLER                    PICTURE X(16)
            VALUE 'PRICE:'
        05  PRICE-OUT                 PICTURE $(6).99.
        05  FILLER                    PICTURE X(55)    VALUE SPACES.
    01  COLUMN-HEADERS.
        05  FILLER                    PICTURE X(30)    VALUE SPACES.
        05  FILLER                    PICTURE X(24)
            VALUE 'REGION                UNITS SOLD'.
        05  FILLER                    PICTURE X(26)    VALUE SPACES.
    01  REGION-TOTAL-LINE.
        05  FILLER                    PICTURE X(32)    VALUE SPACES.
        05  REGION-OUT                PICTURE X.
        05  FILLER                    PICTURE X(13)    VALUE SPACES.
        05  UNITS-SOLD-OUT            PICTURE ZZ9.
        05  FILLER                    PICTURE X(31)    VALUE SPACES.
    01  PRODUCT-TOTAL-LINE.
        05  FILLER                    PICTURE X(36)    VALUE SPACES.
        05  FILLER                    PICTURE X(08).
            VALUE 'TOTAL'
        05  TOTAL-OUT                 PICTURE ZZZZ9.
        05  FILLER                    PICTURE X(31)    VALUE SPACES.
PROCEDURE DIVISION.
    EXEC SQL
        DECLARE C-1 CURSOR FOR
        SELECT PRODUCT. NUMBER, PRODUCT. NAME,
              PRODUCT. DESCRIPTION, LINE-ITEM. QUANTITY,
              PRODUCT. PRICE, SALESPERSON. REGION
        FROM PRODUCT, SALESPERSON, LINE-ITEM, INVOICE
        WHERE LINE-ITEM. INVOICE. NUMBER = INVOICE. NUMBER
            AND INVOICE. SALESPERSON. NUMBER = SALESPERSON. NUMBER
            AND LINE-ITEM. PRODUCT. NUMBER = PRODUCT. NUMBER
        ORDER BY PRODUCT. NUMBER, SALESPERSON. REGION
    END-EXEC.
    OPEN OUTPUT REPORT-FILE.
    EXEC SQL   OPEN C-1            END-EXEC.
```

(UNTIL SQLCODE = 100). When that eventually happens, the program closes the cursor, releasing those resources to other users of this database, and terminates the program normally.

Within the main program loop, PROCESS–AND–FETCH, we find only one SQL statement. The last command in the loop is

FIGURE 12-33

Continued

```
        EXEC SQL   FETCH C-1 INTO :SALE-RECORD     END-EXEC.
        MOVE PRODUCT-NUMBER TO PRODUCT-NUMBER-HOLD.
        MOVE SALE-REGION TO REGION-HOLD.
        PERFORM ISSUE-HEADERS.
        PERFORM PROCESS-AND-FETCH UNTIL SQLCODE = 100.
        EXEC SQL   CLOSE C-1 END EXEC.
        PERFORM ISSUE-REGION-TOTAL.
        PERFORM ISSUE-PRODUCT-TOTAL.
        CLOSE REPORT-FILE.
        EXIT PROGRAM.
  *
    PROCESS-AND-FETCH.
        IF PRODUCT-NUMBER NOT EQUAL PRODUCT-NUMBER-HOLD
        THEN PERFORM ISSUE-REGION-TOTAL
            PERFORM ISSUE-PRODUCT-TOTAL
        ELSE
            IF REGION-NUMBER NOT EQUAL REGION-HOLD
            THEN PERFORM ISSUE-REGION-TOTAL
            ELSE NEXT SENTENCE.
        ADD QUANTITY-SOLD TO SUM-UNITS-THIS REGION.
        ADD QUANTITY-SOLD TO SUM-UNITS-THIS-PRODUCT.
        EXEC SQL   FETCH C-1 INTO :SALE-RECORD   END-EXEC.
    ISSUE-REGION-TOTAL.
        MOVE SUM-UNITS-THIS-REGION TO UNITS-SOLD-OUT.
        MOVE REGION-HOLD TO REGION-OUT.
        MOVE REGION-TOTAL-LINE TO (printer record goes here).
        PERFORM WRITE-LINE.
        MOVE 0 TO SUM-UNITS-THIS-REGION.
        MOVE SALE-REGION TO REGION-HOLD.
    ISSUE-PRODUCT-TOTAL.
        MOVE SUM-UNITS-THIS-PRODUCT TO TOTAL-OUT.
        MOVE PRODUCT-TOTAL-LINE TO (printer record goes here).
        PERFORM WRITE-LINE.
        MOVE 0 TO SUM-UNITS-THIS-PRODUCT.
        MOVE PRODUCT-NUMBER TO PRODUCT-NUMBER-HOLD.
        PERFORM ISSUE-HEADERS.
    ISSUE-HEADERS.
        MOVE PAGE-HEADER-1 TO (printer record goes here).
        PERFORM WRITE-NEW-PAGE.
        MOVE PRODUCT-NUMBER TO PRODUCT-NUMBER-OUT.
        MOVE GROUP-1 TO (printer record goes here).
        PERFORM WRITE-LINE.
        MOVE PRODUCT-NAME TO NAME-OUT.
        MOVE GROUP-2 TO (printer record goes here).
        PERFORM WRITE-LINE.
        MOVE PRODUCT-DESC TO DESCRIPTION-OUT.
```

FETCH C-1 INTO :SALE-RECORD

This instruction, like an ordinary COBOL READ, reads the next sequential row
from the pseudofile, replacing the one just processed. As we mentioned, the loop is
executed until all appropriate data has been retrieved from the database. The
remaining COBOL paragraphs contain no SQL statements. They are used simply to

FIGURE 12-33

Continued

```
            MOVE GROUP-3 TO (printer record goes here).
            PERFORM WRITE-LINE.
            MOVE UNIT-PRICE TO PRICE-OUT.
            MOVE GROUP-4 TO (printer record goes here).
            PERFORM WRITE-LINE.
            MOVE COLUMN-HEADERS TO (printer record goes here).
            PERFORM WRITE-LINE.
        WRITE-NEW-PAGE.
            (instructions for printing line at top of page go here)
        WRITE-LINE.
            (instructions for writing a line go here).
```

format and produce the SALES SUMMARY report and would be no different if a sequential input file had been used.

Note that because KDK Appliances' Information Center database is being used exclusively for analyzing data, no database changes are illustrated. If changes in the table data were made in an application program, either the COMMIT SQL statement would be invoked whenever a change were to be made permanent (perhaps after each valid record update), or the ROLLBACK SQL command would be invoked if the program discovered an error partway through an update. Also, a COMMIT would automatically be invoked when the program terminated. However, COMMITS are unnecessary in this sample program because it does not update the database.

SUMMARY

KDK Appliances, a manufacturing company, needed to analyze sales data from its operational database. The most effective and least disruptive way to do this was to download sales data from the operational database onto a smaller mainframe computer located in the company's Information Center. Then the snapshot of the operational data could be studied by product managers so that they would have the data they needed to make timely decisions and to plan marketing strategies. KDK Appliances chose Database2 (DB2) as its relational database management system.

After identifying the various objects that the product managers needed, we developed a relational database design. First we drew a set of object diagrams and then converted them to relation diagrams. With the design completed, we turned to the database management system DB2 for implementation.

DB2 is an IBM product used to process relational databases on large computers operating under MVS. DB2 uses the language SQL to define, access, and manipulate data and to grant authorizations. SQL statements can be issued interactively or be embedded into application programs written in COBOL, PL/I, FORTRAN, C, or assembler language.

DB2 allows users to define various database constructs such as tables, views, table spaces, indexes, index spaces, data bases, and storage groups. Users—both on-line end users and application programmers—refer only to tables and views. The database administrator, or someone performing other system functions, is concerned with physical database storage and organization and thus deals with other DB2 constructs as well.

Database constructs can be defined, modified, and deleted, and DB2 includes SQL statements to perform all those functions.

SQL data manipulation language as implemented in DB2 contains all the relational functions studied in Chapter 10. In addition to reading a database, we can insert records, update stored data, and delete rows from a table. The SQL statements for these four functions are SELECT, INSERT, UPDATE, and DELETE.

When SQL statements are embedded in an application program, the entire program must first be processed by the DB2 precompiler. The precompiler finds all SQL statements (indicated in COBOL by the keywords EXEC SQL. . .END-EXEC) and translates them into equivalent host-language instructions. It builds database request modules, stores them on disk, and inserts call statements into the program to access them. Thus the application programmer needs to know little about the inner workings of the database management system, as the precompiler effectively shields the programmer from it.

In order to process a multiple-row query, the application programmer needs to define a cursor, a pointer that acts on a SELECT statement. Although the SELECT statement does not actually generate a file, you can imagine that a cursor defines a pseudofile in which DB2 will store the rows it retrieves. Then the set of retrieved rows can be processed one at a time, as if in a sequential file.

DB2 handles any problems of concurrent processing by using locks on portions of a database. Shared locks allow multiple concurrent access to the same data. But if any application needs to modify data, DB2 acquires an exclusive lock. No other application can access data that has an exclusive lock on it. When the lock is released, all applications have access to the updated data. The exclusive lock ensures the integrity of the data.

DB2 can lock either table spaces (which might include several tables) or pages (which contain tables or parts of tables). Locking pages causes less interference with other concurrent users but costs more to administer. Trade-offs like these are common in information processing.

DB2 logs all database changes before they are committed, or written, to the database. Database modifications that are not yet committed can be eliminated by issuing the ROLLBACK command. This might be necessary if a processing error is detected or a system failure occurs. The system log enables DB2 to recover data in the event of a system crash, by applying all before images of the database since the latest checkpoint and then all after images of the committed transactions (that had been logged). Any transactions in progress at the time of the crash must be restarted.

GROUP I QUESTIONS

12.1. Why did KDK Appliances decide to download only its sales data from its operational mainframe computer? What effect will that decision have on the processing privileges that the product managers will eventually be granted regarding the Information Center database?

12.2 Why does the INVOICE, as defined for the Information Center database, contain fewer fields than does the actual invoice used for operational processing?

12.3 What is the purpose of the PRODUCT-AD relation?

12.4 Describe two modes of DB2 access.

12.5 Define *table*, *view*, and *base table*, and describe their relationships with one another.

12.6 How can a view be used to make the database more secure?

12.7 Which database constructs are referenced by users and application programmers?

12.8 Describe the relationship among data base, storage group, table space, page, index space, table, and index.

12.9 Write the DB2 SQL statement that creates a table, an index, and a view. Assume that the table contains CustomerName, Address, and AccountNumber. Build an index on AccountNumber, assuming that the view presents unique customer names.

12.10 Show the DB2 statement to add a CustomerAge column to your answer to Question 12.9.

12.11 Write the DB2 statement(s) that would add these records to the customer table in your answer to Question 10:

Mike Thompson, Madison, 456, 45

Paula Hand, New Haven, 722, 20

Karen Munroe, Gales Ferry, 076, 27

12.12 Show the DB2 statement that drops the table, index, and view defined in Question 12.9.

12.13 Explain the role of the DB2 precompiler.

12.14 How does the precompiler know which instructions are SQL instructions and which belong to the host language?

12.15 Explain the role of the cursor in DB2 processing.

12.16 Explain the difference between a shared lock and an exclusive lock.

12.17 Why is an exclusive lock required when the data is going to be modified?

12.18 What two lock sizes are supported by DB2? What is the advantage of each over the other?

12.19 What is the purpose of the COMMIT statement? Of the ROLLBACK statement?

12.20 How does DB2 handle deadlock?

12.21 Explain how DB2 can recover from a system crash and from damage to the database.

12.22 Explain the role of the GRANT statement. How can GRANT authority be given to another user?

12.23 Explain the role of the REVOKE statement. What is the cascade effect of REVOKE?

GROUP II QUESTIONS

12.24 Locate a company that is using DB2. Determine how long it has had the system, why it chose DB2, and how well DB2 has worked out. Does the company use DB2 interactively, is it used in application programs, or both? Do users develop any on-line inquiries using DB2? If possible, obtain a copy of an application program, and explain the meaning of each embedded SQL statement. How does DB2 identify the application program as an authorized user? How often does the company back up its database? Does it copy the entire database, or does it back up only those pages changed since the previous backup? Has this company ever had to recover the database? What problems, if any, did it experience? Has performance ever been a problem? If so, what did the company do to improve it? Explain whether you believe that DB2 has been an effective DBMS for that company.

12.25 Locate a company that uses a mainframe relational DBMS other than DB2, and answer Question 12.24 for this DBMS.

Database Implementation with Hierarchical and Network Data Models

Part V considers the implementation of databases using DBMS products based on the hierarchical and network data models. Unlike the relational model, which can be used for both transaction and ad hoc processing, these models are used exclusively for transaction processing applications.

Chapter 13 summarizes the characteristics of transaction processing and then introduces Data Language/I, a data model developed by IBM and the sole surviving hierarchical data model. Chapter 14 presents the CODASYL DBTG data model, the most important network model. The CODASYL DBTG model was used for the design of the interface of a dozen or so DBMS products in the early to mid-1970s.

Today, databases structured according to the hierarchical and network models are far less common than those structured according to the relational model. There still are thousands of such databases, however, and most of them are used for large, organizational database processing. Because these models continue to be important and because you may be called upon at some time to convert a hierarchical or network database to a relational database, knowing something about these models will be helpful.

TRANSACTION PROCESSING AND DATA LANGUAGE/I

The previous four chapters were concerned with database implementation using the relational model. As described, the relational model can support all types of databases processing, including operational transaction processing systems, decision support and other ad hoc processing systems, and personal database systems. In fact, the relational model is the basis of most databases today. There are, however, two important classes of DBMS products besides the relational model. Such DBMS products are used exclusively for transaction processing systems that support organizational operations. They are seldom used for decision support or other ad hoc processing and never used for personal database applications.

One of these classes, the hierarchical data model, represents data in the form of hierarchies or trees. Data Language/I is the sole surviving member of this class and the subject of this chapter. The second class is the network model, which represents data in terms of one-to-many relationships. The most important version of the network model is the CODASYL DBTG model, and it is the subject of Chapter 14.

The hierarchical and network models were created during the very earliest period of database processing, before the commercial viability of the relational model. Their chief importance lies in the multitudes of existing information systems based on them, for few new information systems are developed now using these models.[1] Thus these models are important primarily because you may be called upon to maintain existing information systems based on them or because you may participate in the conversion to the relational model of a database using one of these models.

We begin with the characteristics of transaction processing, its history, and the databases that support transaction processing. Then we consider the hierarchical data model as implemented in IBM's Data Language I (or *DL/I*), the components of DL/I, and how they are used to represent various types of objects. Finally, we look at the DL/I data manipulation language commands and their use. We discuss transaction processing here because it is the chief application of both the DL/I and the CODASYL DBTG data models. This does not mean, however, that products based on the relational model cannot support transaction processing; they can, as you saw for DB2 in Chapter 12.

TRANSACTION PROCESSING

To understand transaction processing systems, consider the needs of a flourishing business. Goods are purchased and sold. Clients come and go. Money is earned and spent. Time passes. At some point, somebody (perhaps an owner, a tax agent, an employee, or an auditor) asks, "What is the state of the business?" or "How much money did we make last month?" or "What were your travel expenses in 1993?" or "How much have I contributed to the stock option plan?" We could answer these questions by taking the person on a tour of the company and saying, "Here's the business, see for yourself!" Such a response would be unhelpful if not downright rude, because this person wants a report of the measurement of some *aspect* of the business's operation, not a tour of the entire enterprise.

To provide more realistic answers to questions like these, businesses maintain accounting and operational records. They gather names, inventory goods, count money, and so forth and then store these measurements. In some businesses, records of these measurements (or a portion of them) are stored in an **operational database.** Such a database is a **model** of a user's model of the business's operational aspects, representing conditions in the organization. Business, however, is dynamic, and conditions change, and as they do, the model must be changed as well. Otherwise, over time, the model will come to bear little resemblance to the business.

A **transaction** is the representation of an event in the business. Examples are orders, receipts, transfers, and the like. A transaction processing application accepts the transaction data and processes it in accordance with rules embedded in its logic. During this processing, the program modifies the operational database accordingly and produces records of the transaction, which are sometimes called **real outputs.** The term *real output* is used to differentiate between program outputs that are changes in the database data and program outputs that are communicated in some

---

[1]   But this does not mean that no new information systems are developed using these models. Some organizations, particularly those that have made a substantial investment in systems based on one of these models, continue to produce new, nonrelational systems, although this is a very small percentage of the new databases being created today.

FIGURE 13-1

Role of Transaction Processing Program

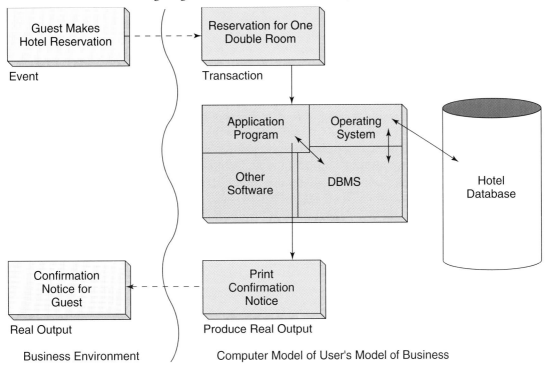

Event   Transaction

Real Output   Produce Real Output

Business Environment   Computer Model of User's Model of Business

way to the business environment. An example of a real output is the confirmation of a hotel reservation.

This distinction is important because outputs to a database can be readily changed if they are incorrect, whereas once real outputs have been communicated, they are difficult to change. Normally, compensating transactions must be processed in order to change real outputs. In the case of a hotel reservation confirmation, if an error is made, the reservation must be changed or canceled, and this action must be communicated to the customer. The environment of a transaction processing application is illustrated in Figure 13-1.

■ Characteristics of Transaction Processing

Transaction processing applications differ in character from other applications studied in this text. First, transaction processing applications support basic business operations, by servicing teller lines at banks, authorizing credit card transactions, making hotel reservations, and the like. Fast performance with a quick response time is critical. Businesses cannot afford to have customers waiting long for the transaction processing system to respond, and so the turnaround time from the input of the transaction to the production of real outputs must be a few seconds or less.

Transaction processing systems must also be reliable. Perhaps nothing is more frustrating to business employees and customers than being unable to complete a sale or other business transaction because "the computer is down." To be effective, the failure rate of a transaction processing application must be very low. Furthermore, when the system does fail, quick and accurate recovery is essential. Comprehensive backup and recovery, including transaction logging, rollback, and rollforward (see Chapter 15) are mandatory for most transaction processing applications.

Unlike other types of database applications, flexibility is less important to transaction processing applications. In fact, flexibility is sometimes undesirable. Transaction processing is standardized processing; businesses want every transaction to be processed in the same way, regardless of the clerk, the customer, or the time of day. If transaction processing applications were flexible, there would be too many opportunities for nonstandard operations. In addition, business operations change slowly. For example, commercial airlines cannot frequently change the way they accept airline reservations. The social system of travel agents, customers, and employees is too large and therefore cannot adapt readily to change.

Since transaction processing supports business operations, control is important. For example, in order to prevent an employee from defrauding the company by creating bogus purchase orders and then authorizing their payment (and stealing the cash), a company might distribute duties and responsibilities among employees. In this case, some employees may be authorized to issue purchase orders, and other employees may authorize the payments. For the sake of control, these two activities must be performed by different employees. In such an environment, a transaction processing application that supports purchasing should enforce this separation of duties and authorities by allowing purchasing agents access to only purchasing data and payment clerks access to only payment data.

Transaction processing applications usually have a restricted view of the database. There is no need, for example, for an order entry program to have access to accounts payable data. If both order data and payables data are stored in the database, they can be controlled better if the view of the order entry program is restricted to order data. Thus transaction processing subsets of the database are often defined, and the scope of the database available to a transaction program is restricted to a particular subset. This subset is called an **application view,** or **subschema.**

As we stated, an operational database is a model of the business or organization, and as such, it is a valuable asset and needs to be protected. Only authorized users should have access to the database, and they should be able to perform only authorized actions. Most transaction processing–oriented DBMS products provide security facilities. The DBA must therefore ensure that applications take advantage of them and must supplement them with programs and manual procedures when necessary.

Finally, the environment of typical transaction processing applications differs substantially from that of personal and ad hoc or decision support database applications. Because of the importance of reliability and control, the computers that support transaction processing usually reside in a closed and controlled environment. Access to such environments is monitored, and only authorized personnel are allowed for authorized purposes. The characteristics of transaction processing systems are summarized in Figure 13-2.

FIGURE 13-2

Characteristics of Trans-
action Processing Systems

- Fast performance with quick response time
- Reliable processing
- Quick and accurate recovery
- Controlled processing
- Restricted views of database for application programs
- Data protected via DBMS security mechanisms
- Equipment usually located in closed environment

◼ Databases for Transaction Processing

Database processing began with transaction processing applications. In the early and mid-1960s, many efforts at data integration failed, although systems designers knew that their file processing was inadequate and that some type of data modeling that facilitated the definition and processing of record relationships was needed. Many approaches and techniques were attempted, which, over time, were divided into three categories.

THREE DATA MODELS

By the early 1970s, three different methods of modeling data were generally recognized: the hierarchical data model, the network data model, and the relational data model. According to the **hierarchical data model**, all data relationships must be transformed into hierarchies, or trees, before they can be defined in the database. Although it is possible to transform any object structure into hierarchies, the transformation is sometimes contrived. The most important and popular database product based on the hierarchical data model is **Data Language I,** or DL/I, which was developed and is marketed by IBM.

The **network data model** readily represents one-to-many relationships, and therefore it can be used to represent directly all the object types discussed in Chapter 7, except many-to-many compound objects. Such objects must be transformed into one-to-many relationships, just as we did for the relational model in previous chapters. The most important network data model is the CODASYL DBTG (Conference on Data Systems Languages, Data Base Task Group) model.

The **relational data model** is the third data model. It was defined in 1970 but had little practical significance until relational DBMS products became available in the early 1980s. However, the development of the relational model during the 1970s and 1980s has contributed much to the understanding and theory of data modeling. Furthermore, as seen in previous chapters, the relational model is a useful tool for designing databases and implementing databases that are directly processed by end users.

PREDEFINED RELATIONSHIPS

Both the hierarchical and the network data models require that relationships be predefined. That is, all relationships must be anticipated and defined before implementing the database. Adding new relationships to an existing database is more difficult with these two models than it is using the relational model, because of the method used for representing relationships.

Unlike the relational model, in which relationships are established by data values, the hierarchical and network models represent relationships by means of separate **data structures,** such as indexes and linked lists (see the Appendix). These data structures must be established by the DBMS before the relationships can be represented. Consider the ramifications of this approach.

For transaction processing applications, the representation of relationships in data structures has two advantages over storing relationships within the data. First, performance is likely to be better (at least with the currently available technologies). When relationships are predefined, data structures can be selected for and tuned to the workload. Most relational DBMS products cannot begin to match the performance of well-tuned hierarchical and network DBMS products.

The second advantage is control. For transaction processing applications, the restriction that relationships must be predefined can be very desirable. Transaction processing needs to be standardized, because most organizations do not want the users of transaction processing applications to be able to perform ad hoc processing of data. Furthermore, the requirements for most transaction processing applications evolve slowly. In most cases, there is ample time to adjust the database structure as new requirements emerge. Consequently, what is generally viewed as an advantage of relational database processing is often regarded as unnecessary or undesirable for transaction processing. (Even still, more and more transaction processing is being done on relational databases.)

■ Implementing Databases for Transaction Processing

The process of implementing a database structured according to the hierarchical and network models must be extended from that described in previous chapters. As shown in Figure 13-3, we begin by defining reports, forms, and form-processing logic. From these we define objects, and then we transform object definitions into a relational database design. If we were using a relational database, we would then develop applications and implement them as discussed in Chapters 8 through 12. But if the database is to be organized using either the hierarchical or the network data models, we must perform an additional step: We must first convert the relational design to a hierarchical or network database design. This process will be demonstrated later in this chapter for hierarchical models and in the next chapter for network models.

Keep in mind that although we will describe the use of the hierarchical and network data models for transaction processing, relational DBMS products can be used for transaction processing as well. In some microcomputer database applications, particularly those involving multiuser processing on LANs, relational DBMS products are used for transaction processing. Here, however, the workload is considerably smaller than it is for most minicomputer or mainframe transaction processing applications. In any case, Figure 13-3 shows that relational database designs can be used for databases implemented with any of the three models.

The last step in Figure 13-3 is identifying the application views. As we pointed out, control and security are essential to transaction processing applications, and an application's view of data is often restricted to a portion of the database. When

FIGURE 13-3

Steps in Designing Databases

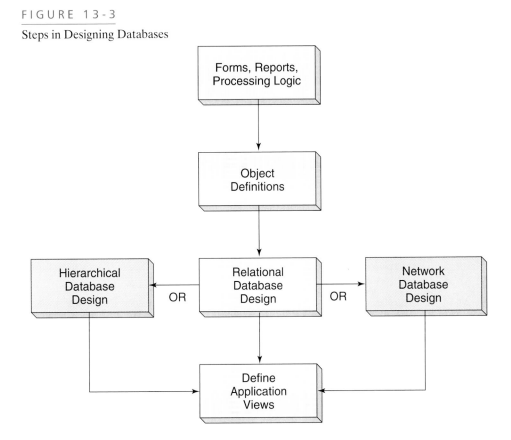

designing this view, the designer must determine the objects that an application needs to access and the views of those objects. Once the views have been defined, the database can be designed, and the database and views can be created. We explore this topic further when we describe the hierarchical and network data models.

DATA LANGUAGE/I

IBM and North American Aviation jointly developed DL/I in the 1960s as an outgrowth of data processing needs in the aerospace industry. DL/I is a language for processing a database, and its most popular implementation is IMS, or Information Management System, which for years was IBM's primary transaction processing–oriented DBMS (DB2 has now taken over this role). Actually, IMS is both a communications processor and a database management system, so it would be more correct to say that DL/I is implemented in IMS/DB, which is the database portion of IMS. DL/I uses hierarchies (trees) to represent relationships, which means that the users' objects must be transformed into tree representations before they can be processed using DL/I.

FIGURE 13-4

STUDENT Data Base Record

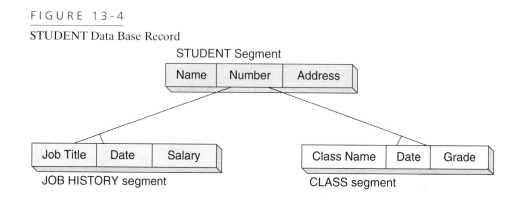

In DL/I terms, fields are grouped into **segments,** or the nodes of tree structures. Remember from Chapter 6 that a **tree** is a collection of records and relationships in which each record has at most one parent and all relationships are one to many between parent and child. (Throughout this discussion, we use the DL/I term *segment* rather than record or row.) DL/I refers to a particular tree structure (a collection of related segments) as a **data base record.** (*Data base* is two words in DL/I.)

A sample STUDENT data base record is sketched in Figure 13-4. The forked line notation used throughout this text is not part of DL/I notation but is used here for consistency. Each STUDENT segment has Name, Number, and Address fields. Also, under each STUDENT segment are a variable number of JOB HISTORY and CLASS segments. An occurrence of the STUDENT data base record is shown in Figure 13-5.

FIGURE 13-5

STUDENT Data Base Record Occurrence

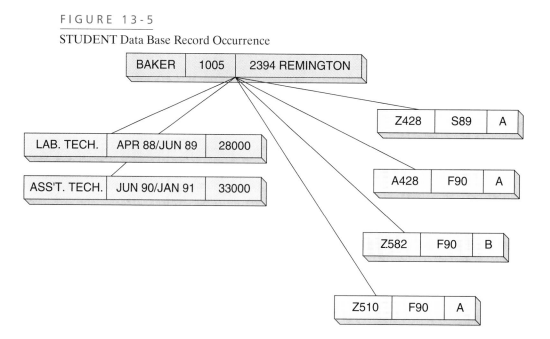

FIGURE 13-6

FACULTY Data Base Record

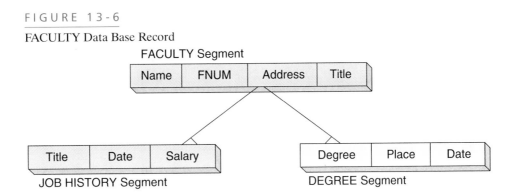

In DL/I, a **data base** is composed of data base records, which can be occurrences of the same record type or of several different record types. For example, a DL/I data base could consist of occurrences of the STUDENT data base record in Figure 13-4 and the FACULTY data base record in Figure 13-6. The data base would comprise all occurrences of each data base record type. Figure 13-7 summarizes the DL/I data structures.

Data base records are defined by means of a **data base description.** In the DBMS product IMS, a set of assembly-language macro instructions indicates the structure of each data base record. (Note that this is different from the relational language SQL we examined earlier. SQL includes both data definition and data manipulation statements, whereas DL/I is for data manipulation only. This reflects DL/I's age, as it was developed before having a convenient means of defining data was judged important.) Figure 13-8 depicts a portion of the data base description for the STUDENT data base record in Figure 13-4. The format of this description is unique to IMS.

Each segment description is headed by a SEGM macro that names the segment, shows its total length, and gives the name of the parent if there is one. The first segment, or **root,** has no parent. Each field within a segment is represented by a FIELD

FIGURE 13-7

Summary of DL/I Data Structures

Data Structure	Description
Field	Smallest unit of data
Segment	Group of fields; segments must be related by hierarchical structure; each segment has a sequence field used for logical ordering
Data base record	Hierarchically structured group of segments
Data base	Collection of data base record occurrences of one or more data base record types

FIGURE 13-8

Description of Data Base for STUDENT Data Base Record in Figure 13-4

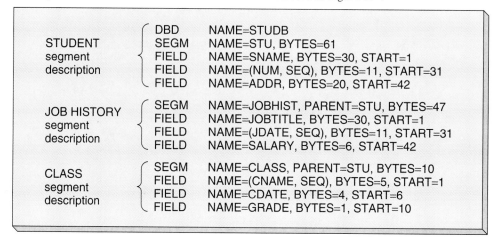

macro that indicates the field's name, length, and starting position in the segment. One field in each segment is designated as the **sequence field** and is used to order the occurrences of a given segment type. The order is a logical one; although it may appear to the application program that the segments are in order of sequence field, the physical ordering of the segments may be different.

In Figure 13-8, the STUDENT segment is named STU and is 61 bytes long. The STU record is composed of an SNAME field in bytes 1 through 30, a NUM field in bytes 31 through 41, and an ADDR field in bytes 42 through 61. (Because DL/I uses uppercase letters, all names are spelled in capitals.) The sequence field for STU segments is NUM.

JOB HISTORY segments are called JOBHIST and are composed of JOBTITLE, JDATE, and SALARY fields. CLASS segments are called CLASS and have CNAME, CDATE, and GRADE fields.

The data base description is assembled and can be stored in object form in a library to be called into main memory when needed. Consequently, each application programmer need not perform the time-consuming process of writing the data base description for his or her program.

■ Representation of Objects in DL/I

This section explains the representation of objects using DL/I, beginning with one method by which trees are represented in physical storage.

PHYSICAL REPRESENTATION OF TREES

In order to appreciate the way in which DL/I eliminates data duplication, you must first understand how trees are represented in physical storage. We describe one technique in this section, but see the Appendix for more information.

FIGURE 13-9

Three Objects Used by a University Library

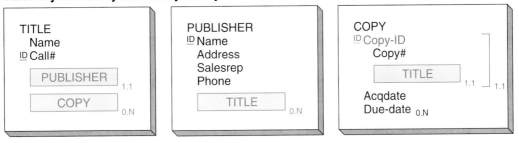

Figure 13-9 presents object diagrams of three objects used in a university library. TITLE contains data about a particular book title as well as two object attributes, PUBLISHER and COPY. PUBLISHER contains data about a publisher and its salesperson as well as the object attribute TITLE. COPY contains data about a copy of a TITLE as well as a multivalued attribute, Due-date. This repeating attribute contains all of the dates on which that book copy has been due.

These three objects can be represented by the hierarchical data structure shown in Figure 13-10(a), in which each rectangle is defined as a DL/I segment. The sample data for this hierarchy is shown in Figure 13-10(b). Since this is a hierarchy, it can be represented by DL/I in a straightforward fashion.

There are many ways in which a tree like the one in Figure 13-10 can be represented in physical storage. In fact, IMS supports several different methods. One technique, shown in Figure 13-11, is called the **child and twin pointer** method.

Figure 13-11 assumes that each segment is stored in a separate physical record. Although this is unrealistic, it is convenient for our purposes. In practice, many segments would be blocked into a single physical record. But because dealing with

FIGURE 13-10

Hierarchical Data Structure: (a) Hierarchy of Objects and (b) Sample Data

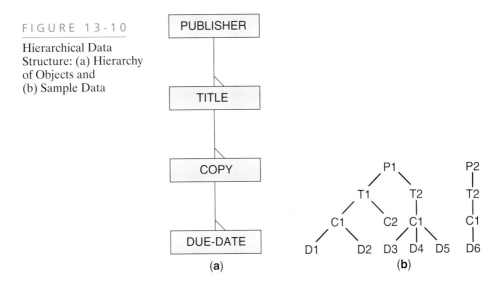

FIGURE 13-11

Child and Twin Pointer Representation
of the Hierarchy in Figure 13-10

Record Number	Key Data	Nonkey Data	Pointers Child	Pointers Twin
1	P1	· · ·	2	12
2	T1	· · ·	4	3
3	T2	· · ·	6	0
4	T1 C1	· · ·	7	5
5	T1 C2	· · ·	0	0
6	T2 C1	· · ·	9	0
7	T1 C1 D1	· · ·	0	8
8	T1 C1 D2	· · ·	0	0
9	T2 C1 D3	· · ·	0	10
10	T2 C1 D4	· · ·	0	11
11	T2 C1 D5	· · ·	0	0
12	P2	· · ·	13	0
13	T3	· · ·	14	0
14	T3 C1	· · ·	15	0
15	T3 C1 D6	· · ·	0	0

blocking and unblocking would not contribute to an understanding of the topic at hand, we have chosen to omit it and thus to simplify the illustration. Each record is addressed by its relative position in the file. For example, the record containing the segment for PUBLISHER P2 is located at address 12.

Each record in Figure 13-11 has three sections. One contains the key of the segment; one contains nonkey data; and one contains two pointers, or the addresses of other related segments. The first pointer is a **child pointer.** If a segment has any children, this pointer will contain the address of the record holding the first child segment. If the segment has no children, this pointer will be zero.

The second pointer is a **twin pointer.** If a segment has any siblings (segments of the same type having the same parent segment), this pointer will contain the address of the record holding the next sibling segment. If there are none (or no more), this pointer will be zero. Examine Figure 13-11 and make sure that you understand how the pointers represent the tree in Figure 13-10. For practice, follow the pointers from P1 through T2 to the due date D5.

This data structure allows records to be inserted and deleted without reorganizing the file. The pointers are simply changed (see the Appendix for more information about this process). We will come back to this example to demonstrate how duplicated data can be eliminated. Next let us consider the transformation of simple networks into trees.

TRANSFORMING SIMPLE NETWORKS INTO TREES

Figure 13-12(a) shows an expansion of the library objects in Figure 13-9. The PUBLISHER and TITLE objects are the same, and the COPY object is the same except that a STUDENT object attribute has been added to it. The fourth object is STUDENT, which represents those students who check out copies of titles.

FIGURE 13-12

Representation of Objects with Simple Network: (a) Four Objects Used by a University Library and (b) Simple Network for These Objects

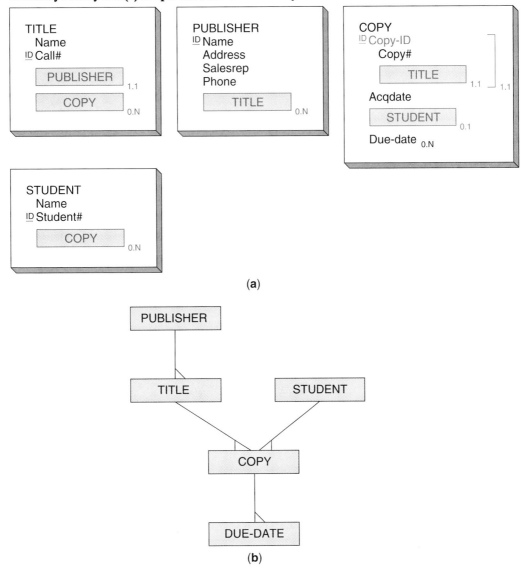

(a)

(b)

The design of a data base that represents these four objects is shown in Figure 13-12(b). Observe that this data structure is *not* a hierarchy because COPY has two parents of different types, TITLE and STUDENT. In fact, this structure is a **simple network.**

Since this structure is not a hierarchy, it cannot be directly represented in DL/I but must first be transformed into a hierarchy. Figure 13-13(a) shows such a transformation. Two trees have been generated, one for each parent of COPY. Notice

FIGURE 13-13

Representing a Simple Network with Trees: (a) Two Trees with Duplication and (b) Sample Data

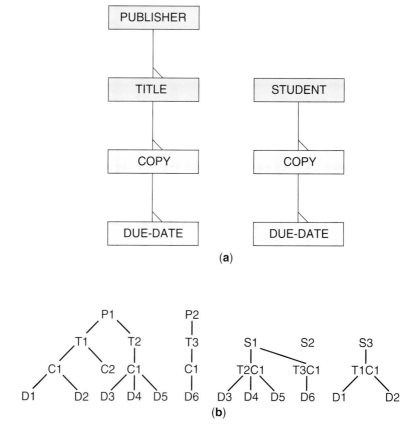

that in doing this, the data of COPY and of all of its children has been duplicated, as shown in Figure 13-13(b).

In general, it always is possible to transform a simple network into trees, although there will be some data duplication. For every node that has two parents, we create two trees.

A NOTE ON COMPLEX NETWORKS

In Chapter 6, three types of data structures were based on binary record relationships: trees, simple networks, and complex networks. A relational design, however, includes only two of these, trees and simple networks. Complex networks are eliminated from relational designs because the only objects that generate them, M:N compound objects, are represented in a relational design as simple networks containing an intersection relation (see Chapter 7 for a review of this representation).

According to the process illustrated in Figure 13-3, we first produce a relational design before transforming it into DL/I. Hence, complex networks already have been transformed into simple networks, and so, for DL/I, you need to know only how to transform simple networks into trees.

ELIMINATING DATA DUPLICATION

We eliminate data duplication by storing the data once and representing all subsequent references to that data by means of pointers. In Figure 13-14(a), the PUBLISHER/TITLE/COPY/DUE-DATE tree is stored intact, as shown in Figure 13-11. In contrast, the STUDENT/COPY/DUE-DATE tree is not stored in that form. Rather, the children segments of STUDENT contain **pointers** to data rather than data, as in Figure 13-14(b).

Figure 13-14(c) shows how these structures can be stored using the child and twin pointer scheme. The first fifteen records of this file are the same as those in Figure 13-11. These records represent the PUBLISHER/TITLE/COPY/DUE-DATE tree. Records 16 through 21 represent the STUDENT/COPY/DUE-DATE

FIGURE 13-14

Child and Twin Pointer Representation of a Simple Network: (a) Eliminating Data Duplication with Pointers, (b) Pointers for Data in Figure 13–13(b), and (c) Child and Twin Pointer Representation of a Simple Network

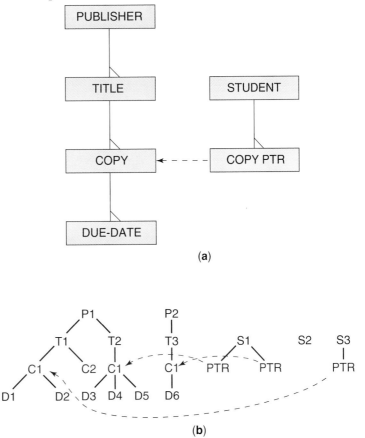

FIGURE 13-14

(Continued)

Record Number	Key Data	Nonkey Data	Pointers Child	Twin
1	P1	· · ·	2	12
2	T1	· · ·	4	3
3	T2	· · ·	6	0
4	T1 C1	· · ·	7	5
5	T1 C2	· · ·	0	0
6	T2 C1	· · ·	9	0
7	T1 C1 D1	· · ·	0	8
8	T1 C1 D2	· · ·	0	0
9	T2 C1 D3	· · ·	0	10
10	T2 C1 D4	· · ·	0	11
11	T2 C1 D5	· · ·	0	0
12	P2	· · ·	13	0
13	T3	· · ·	14	0
14	T3 C1	· · ·	15	0
15	T3 C1 D6	· · ·	0	0
16	S1	· · ·	19	17
17	S2	· · ·	0	18
18	S3	· · ·	21	0
19	T2 C1	PTR = 6	0	20
20	T3 C1	PTR = 14	0	0
21	T1 C1	PTR = 4	0	0

(c)

tree. Observe that the nonkey data fields of COPY children (such as T2, C1) have been replaced by pointers to segments containing actual COPY data.

Using this strategy, both trees can be represented without duplicating the COPY or DUE-DATE data. The strategy is not without risk, however, because **fragments,** or children segments that become logically detached from a parent, may be created. For instance, suppose a STUDENT segment is linked to a COPY of a TITLE and that the TITLE segment and its children segments (COPY and DUE-DATE) are deleted from the data base. The COPY pointer under the STUDENT segment now points to an invalid location and is therefore a fragment. Similarly, a student may not check out a book until the copy has been stored in the PUBLISHER, TITLE, COPY, DUE-DATE hierarchy.

Such dynamic constraints are unlike the constraints we have encountered before. Although the relationship between STUDENT and COPY is optional to optional, once a student is related to a COPY segment, that segment cannot be deleted. Neither can a STUDENT segment be related to a COPY segment that has not already been entered. Because such constraints are not enforced by IMS, this task falls to the application programmer.

This situation is unfortunate because if application programs are incorrectly written so that the constraints are not enforced or are enforced incorrectly, then fragments will exist in the database and will be difficult to detect until the user makes errors. Furthermore, the presence of one fragment creates the suspicion that more may exist, a suspicion that is exceedingly difficult to investigate.

REPRESENTATION OF THE LIBRARY EXAMPLE

To demonstrate the transformation of a relational design to DL/I, consider the expanded set library objects shown in Figure 13-15. This group contains one example of most of the object types described in Chapter 7, namely, composite objects; 1:1, 1:N, and M:N compound objects; and association objects. COPY is a composite object because it contains Due-date as a multivalued nonobject attribute. The 1:1 compound objects are STUDENT and VIDEO (students are allowed to check out only one videocassette at a time). The 1:N compound objects are PUBLISHER and TITLE. The M:N compound objects are AUTHOR and TITLE because an author can write many books and a book can be written by many authors. The association object is COPY, which documents the relationship between a TITLE and the STUDENT who checks it out.

A relational design for these objects is shown in Figure 13-16. Note that there is one relation for each object. The names of the relations are slightly different from the object names, in order to differentiate the two. In addition to these six relations, the relation DUE-DATE represents the repeating group in the COPY object, and the intersection relation TA-INT represents the M:N relationship between TITLE and AUTHOR. To be certain you understand this design, identify which relations make up each object.

FIGURE 13-15

Six Objects Used by a University Library

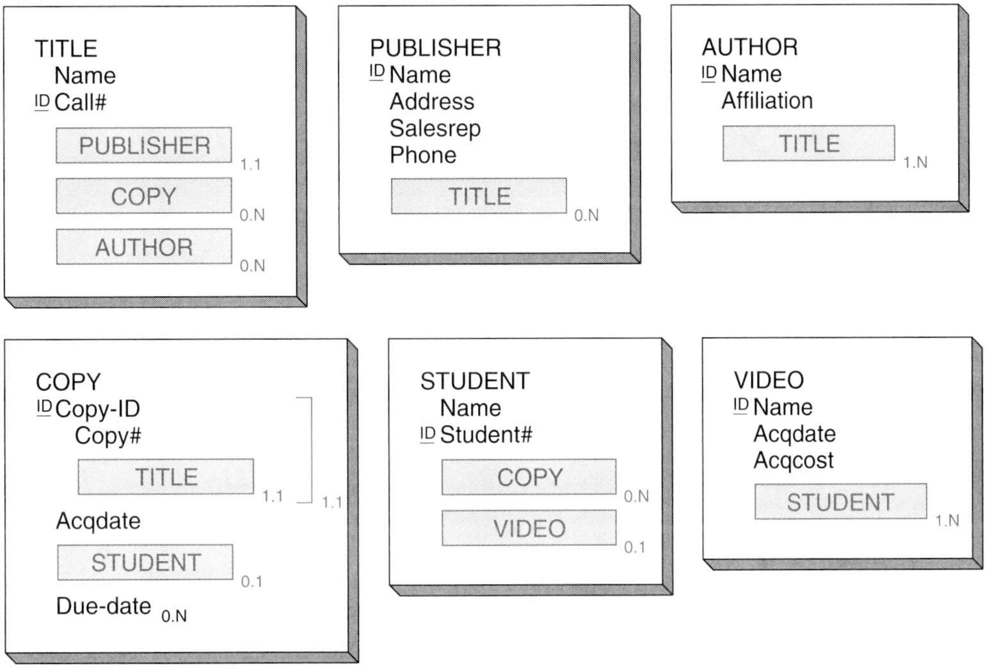

FIGURE 13-16

Relational Design for
the Objects in Figure
13-15

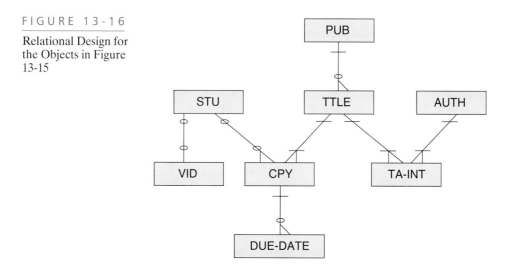

The relational design in Figure 13-16 is not a hierarchy because two relations, CPY and TA-INT, have more than one parent. Therefore, we must create two trees for each of these relations, a total of four trees. This has been done in Figure 13-17(a) (only three trees appear because the middle tree in this figure holds two of them). Consider CPY first. Since both TTLE and STU are parents of CPY, we need to construct one tree for each of them. Thus you see in Figure 13-17(a) the STU/CPY/DUE-DATE tree (part of the leftmost tree in that figure) and the PUB/TTLE/CPY/DUE-DATE tree (part of the middle tree). STU also has a child, VID, which we can add under STU without causing a problem, thereby completing that tree.

Now consider the TA-INT relation in Figure 13-16. The purpose of TA-INT is to represent many titles for a given author and many authors for a given title. Thus we want a tree with AUTH as parent and TTLE as child, and a tree with TTLE as parent and AUTH as child. This representation is also shown in Figure 13-17(a). AUTH/TTLE/CPY/DUE-DATE is shown as a separate tree. The TTLE/AUTH relationship has been represented within the PUB/TTLE/CPY/DUE-DATE tree by adding the AUTH relation under TTLE. Figure 13-17(a) therefore shows four trees (two for each of the relations that have two parents), but two of them have been combined under the common parent TTLE.

The trees in Figure 13-17(a) have considerable data duplication, which we can eliminate with pointers, as shown in Figure 13-17(b). Concerning CPY, we must choose either to put the data under TTLE and the pointers under STU or to put the pointers under TTLE and the data under STU. The choice between the two depends on the workload and the type of physical data structure used to store the trees. As a general rule, the data should be stored as part of the tree that is used most frequently. However, the particulars of this depend on specific features of IMS and are not relevant to our discussion here.

FIGURE 13-17

Representing Hierarchies for DL/I Processing: (a) Logical Data Base Records for the Data Base in Figure 13-16 and (b) Physical Data Base Records for the Data Base in Figure 13-16

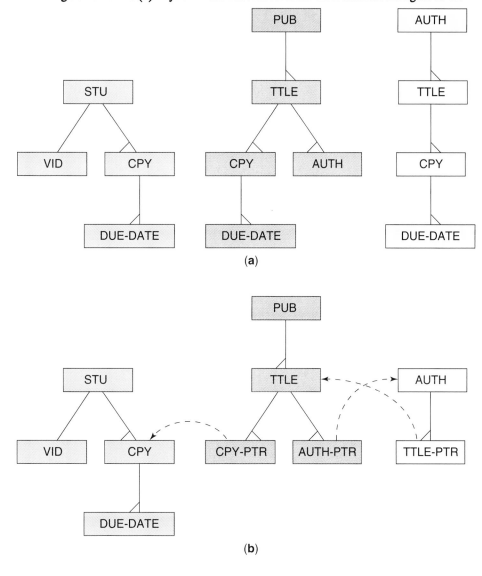

Logical and Physical Records

DL/I divides a data base into physical and logical constructs. The terms **physical data base** (PDB) and **physical data base record** (PDBR) are used to describe the data as it exists in data storage. The terms **logical data base** (LDB) and **logical data base record** (LDBR) are used to describe the data as it appears to the application programs that process it. LDBRs differ from PDBRs in either of two ways. An

LDBR may be a subset of a PDBR, or an LDBR may contain portions of two or more PDBRs and represent tree structures that are not present in the PDBRs. The trees sketched in Figure 13-17(a) are LDBRs, as they represent data as it appears to an application program. Conversely, the trees sketched in Figure 13-17(b) are PDBRs.

To understand LDBRs that are subsets of PDBRs, consider the PDBR STU/CPY/VID/DUE-DATE tree in Figure 13-17(b). Personnel at the video check-out desk need not have access to CPY and DUE-DATE data, as the application that checks out videocassettes requires only STU and VID data. To meet this need, the data base developers define an LDBR containing only STU/VID; this LDBR is a subset of the STU/CPY/VID/DUE-DATE PDBR. All three of the LDBRs in Figure 13-17(a) are examples of LDBRs that contain relationships not present in the PDBRs. Consider the LDBR AUTH/TTLE/CPY/DUE-DATE. The PDBR that represents this tree is AUTH/TTLE-PTR. Clearly, the LDBR is constructed from data in two PDBRs. The data base developer defines PDBRs and LDBRs using macro instructions similar to those shown in Figure 13-8. The specific instructions are beyond the scope of this text.

■ Application Views

For reasons of control, application programs are generally not allowed to access the entire data base. Instead, they are given access to **views** of objects. With DL/I, a view of an object is represented by an LDBR, and so an application view in DL/I consists of the definition of one or more LDBRs.

Consider the university library applications. The video checkout desk needs access to STUDENT and VIDEO data, and so an LDBR consisting of STU/VID would be defined for the application programs that support the video checkout station. The book checkout desk needs access to STUDENT and COPY data, and so an LDBR consisting of STU/CPY would be defined for the applications that support this function. The acquisitions desk needs access to PUBLISHER, TITLE, COPY, and DUE-DATE (to be able to determine how frequently the copies are used) data, and so an LDBR with only this data would be defined for the programs serving that department. Similarly, LDBRs would be defined for the reference desk, the overdue fines collection clerk, and so forth.

The prevention of fragments needs to be carefully considered when defining these LDBRs and their processing. Because of the way that networks are represented, dynamic constraints can exist in addition to normal relationship constraints (M–M, M–O, and so forth). As discussed in the section on eliminating data duplication, data that is pointed to from one PDBR must be deleted with great care. Otherwise, pointers to the addresses vacated by the deleted data will become invalid. Because IMS does not provide facilities for defining and enforcing such dynamic constraints, they must be enforced by application programs. But unfortunately, the constraints may not be apparent to the programmers, who see only a particular LDBR's view of the data base.

In addition, an application program can actually delete data that is not visible in its LDBR. Since this is the case, the application programmer must be told which operations can be performed on the data in each view. With IMS, processing rights and authorities that limit allowable actions can be defined for each LDBR. As discussed in Chapter 15, these authorities need to be carefully thought out during the data base design stage.

DL/I DATA MANIPULATION LANGUAGE

DL/I processes data in segments; DL/I statements can retrieve, update, insert, and delete segments. Unlike SQL, which can be used interactively or be embedded in application programs, DL/I statements must be embedded in application programs. DL/I is not an interactive query language. (Keep in mind that DL/I was one of the earliest database languages, used exclusively for transaction processing by information systems professionals and not by end users.)

Using DL/I, the application programmer defines an input/output (I/O) work area that is shared by the application program and the DBMS product. To insert or update a segment, the application program places new data in the work area; the DBMS takes the data from there to modify the data base. When the DBMS retrieves data from the data base, it places it in the work area for the program to access. System status data, such as completion flags and error flags, is also placed in the work area by the DBMS so the application program can examine it.

The DL/I syntax that is presented in this section is very general; it is possible that it could apply to almost any programming language. Unlike DB2, IMS does not have a precompiler. Instead, DL/I commands are executed by calling a DBMS subroutine from the host program. The parameters of a data base subroutine call specify the command type, search criteria, and other data. The format of data base subroutine calls depends on the host language. We will present only the DL/I commands; we will not be concerned with the particulars of the programming language. To illustrate the DL/I data manipulation commands, consider the LDBR in Figure 13-18, which is based on the PUB/TTLE/AUTH-PTR/CPY-PTR PDBR in Figure 13-17(b).

FIGURE 13-18

Sample LDBR for Data Base
in Figure 13-17(b)

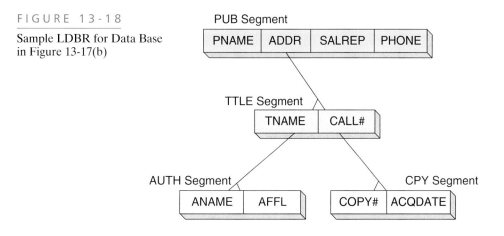

■ GET UNIQUE (GU)

GET UNIQUE (GU) is a command used to read a particular segment into the I/O work area. For example, the statement

GU   PUB   (SALREP = 'JONES')

causes the first PUB segment with the SALREP value of JONES to be placed into the I/O work area. Thus, if the occurrences in Figure 13-19 are the first ones in the data base, the segment P2,NYC,JONES,(212)555–1776 will be placed in the work area. The following statements cause the first AUTH with name A3 of TTLE T2 to be placed in the work area:

GU   PUB
        TTLE (TNAME = 'T2')
        AUTH (ANAME = 'A3')

If no such segment exists, the DBMS will set an appropriate return code in the work area.

The DBMS searches for the desired segment by starting at the first occurrence of the LDBR, at the first T2 occurrence of the TTLE segment (assuming that there could be more than one), and at the first A3 occurrence of the AUTH segment (again assuming that there could be more than one). The order of the segments is

FIGURE 13-19

Two Occurrences of the LDBR in Figure 13-18

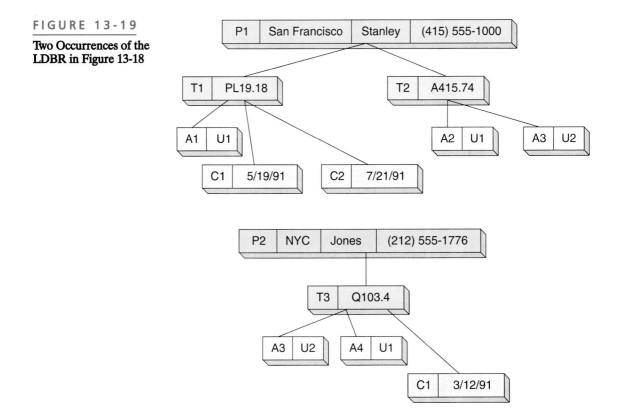

determined by the sequence fields in each segment (see Figure 13-8). For this LDBR, assume the following sequence fields:

SEGMENT	SEQUENCE FIELD
PUB	PNAME
TTLE	TNAME
AUTH	ANAME
CPY	COPY

To find the first occurrence of AUTH A3 in TTLE T2, we examine the segments in the following order: P1 (PUB) segment, T1, T2 (TTLE segments) and, finally, A2, A3 (AUTH segments). The segment read into the work area is A3.

The qualifying data after the GU command is called a **segment search argument** (SSA). In general, an SSA is the name of a segment, which may be followed by a condition. As shown, there can be one SSA for each segment in the hierarchical path for the segment to be retrieved.

◼ GET NEXT (GN)

GET NEXT (GN) is a command used to read the next segment. Next implies that there be a current segment to start from, so it is necessary to indicate a current segment before issuing a GN command. For example, the statements

```
GU      PUB
        TTLE (TNAME = 'T1')
GN      TTLE
```

cause the first TTLE segment in the data base with TNAME field equal to T1 to be placed in the I/O work area. This establishes a current position. (There most likely would be some program instructions to process that segment following the GU command, but we have omitted them.) The GN statement reads the next TTLE segment. For the occurrence in Figure 13-19, the T1 segment is read first, followed by the T2 segment. If a subsequent GN TTLE command is executed, the DBMS will attempt to find another TTLE segment under the current PUB segment. There is none for this occurrence, so it searches under the next PUB segment (P2) and reads the T3 occurrence of TTLE.

A third execution of GN TTLE causes the DBMS to look for the next TTLE segment. Since there are no more in the P2 occurrence of PUB, the DBMS searches the next LDBR occurrence for a TTLE segment and, if it finds one, places it in the work area. The search will continue to the end of the data base if necessary. If no TTLE segment remains in the data base, appropriate status data will be set.

When the GN statements are executed, the DBMS selects the next occurrence of the segment named. If there is no such occurrence under the current parent, the DBMS will switch to the next parent. The application program may need to know, however, when the DBMS selects a segment from a new parent. For example, if the second GN TTLE statement is executed as discussed in the preceding paragraph, the program may need to know that a new PUB segment has been retrieved.

To provide this information, when a segment is read, data regarding the path leading to the segment is placed in the work area. IMS places the *fully concatenated key* of the retrieved segment in the work area. This key is the concatenation of all sequence fields of segments leading to the segment, along with the sequence field of the segment. For example, the fully concatenated key for the A4 AUTH segment is P2 T3 A4. After the second GN TTLE command is executed as described, the DBMS returns the key P2 T3, and the application program can detect the new PUB segment by means of the change in PUB sequence field in the key. Now consider another example. The commands

```
GU       PUB
         TTLE       (TNAME = 'T1')
GN       TTLE       (CALL# > 'P')
```

cause the T1 TTLE segment to be read, followed by the next TTLE segment with a call number starting with a letter beyond P in the collating sequence. Consequently T3 is read next. The important point here is that sequential retrieval can be either *qualified* (with a condition after the segment name) or *unqualified* (with no condition).

Another type of sequential retrieval command requests the next segment regardless of its type. For example, the commands

```
GU       PUB
         TTLE       (TNAME = 'T1')
GN
```

cause the T1 segment of TTLE to be read, followed by the A1 AUTH segment. A subsequent GN command reads the C1 CPY segment.

As an aside, this LDBR does not include DUE-DATE segments (or, as sometimes expressed in DL/I, this LDBR *is not sensitive to* DUE-DATE segments). When the GN commands are executed, no DUE-DATE data is presented to the application program; the DBMS automatically skips it. IMS never presents to an application any data to which the application is not sensitive.

■ GET NEXT WITHIN PARENT (GNP)

GET NEXT WITHIN PARENT (GNP) is a command that sequentially retrieves segments under one parent. When all segments under that parent have been read, end-of-data status is returned to the program. For example, when the commands

```
GU       PUB
         TTLE       (TNAME = 'T1')
GNP      TTLE
GNP      TTLE
```

are executed, the T1 and T2 segments of P1 are read. The second GNP command does not return data; rather, it causes the end-of-data status flag to be set. Contrast this with the statements

```
GU       PUB
         TTLE (TNAME = 'T1')
GN       TTLE
GN       TTLE
```

Here, the second GN command retrieves the T3 TTLE segment.

■ Get Hold Commands

GET HOLD UNIQUE (GHU), GET HOLD NEXT (GHN), and GET HOLD NEXT WITHIN PARENT (GHNP) operate like their Get counterparts except they inform the DBMS to prepare for a change in or deletion of the retrieved segment. They are used with Replace and Delete commands. When the program replaces or deletes a segment, it first issues a Get Hold command for the segment. DBMS retrieves the segment and "holds" it; then Replace or Delete can be issued.

■ REPLACE (REPL)

Replace is used to modify data within a segment. For example, the commands

```
GHU     PUB
        TTLE (TNAME = 'T2')
```

(here the application program changes TTLE data)

```
REPL
```

causes the DBMS to retrieve the T2 TTLE segment and replace it with the changed data. (In this and several following examples, the program processing is in lowercase letters. Syntax is dependent on the language used and is omitted.)

The following instruction sequence sets the acquisition date of titles to 1/1/93.

```
GHU   PUB
        TTLE
        CPY
DOWHILE data remains
        Set ACQDATE = '1/1/93'
        REPL
        GHN   CPY
END-DO
```

The GHU command obtains the first CPY segment; GHN obtains subsequent ones.

Another example changes the acquisition date for titles published in New York City. The logic appears in Figure 13-20 and requires the GHN and GHNP commands:

```
GU    PUB (ADDR = 'NYC')
        (set status-1 = 1 if data exists; 0 otherwise)
DOWHILE status-1 = 1
        GHNP TTLE
            CPY
        (set status-2 = 1 if data exists; 0 otherwise)
        DOWHILE status-2 = 1
            (set ACQDATE = '1/1/91')
            REPL
            GHNP TTLE
                CPY
            (set status-2 = 1 if data exists; 0 otherwise)
        END-DO
        GN    PUB (ADDR = 'NYC')
        (set status-1 = 1 if data exists; 0 otherwise)
END-DO
```

FIGURE 13-20

Logic Required to Change Acquisition Dates for New York City Publishers

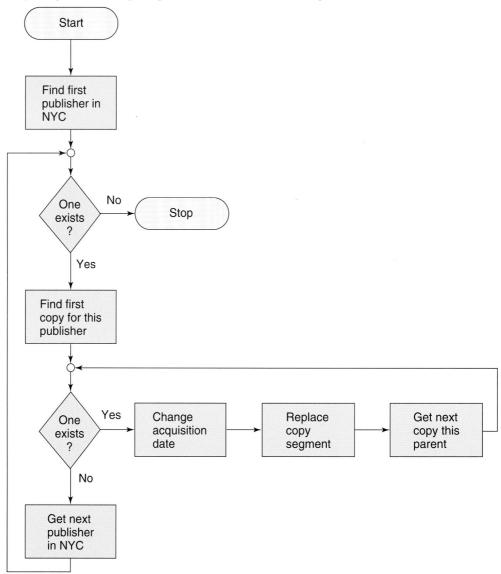

The GU command attempts to find the first publisher located in New York City. If one exists, the loop is executed for that publisher. The program attempts to obtain the first CPY in that publisher. If one exists, its ACQDATE is changed and replaced. The program attempts to read the next CPY in the current publisher parent. If one exists, it, too, is changed and replaced, and so forth. When there is no CPY in the current publisher parent, the program tries to find the next publisher in NYC. If one exists, the outer loop is repeated again.

■ DELETE (DLET)

Delete operates in conjunction with the Get Hold commands in a manner similar to Replace. The commands

```
GHU        PUB (PNAME = 'P1')
           TTLE (TNAME = 'T1')
           AUTH (ANAME = 'A1')

DLET
```

delete the A1 segment under T1 and P1 from the data base. When a segment is deleted, any subordinate segments are also deleted (including ones invisible to the application). Thus the commands

```
GHU        PUB (PNAME = 'P1')
           TTLE (TNAME = 'T1')
           CPY (COPY# = 1)

DLET
```

delete not only the C1 copy segment under T1 and P1 but also all of the DUE-DATE segments under that copy. Therefore any subordinate segments to which the application is not sensitive are deleted.

Deleting invisible data is dangerous and not recommended. In order to prevent it from happening, the database administrator, database designers, and application programmers must communicate clearly with one another and establish and enforce standards. They also should review the designs. Otherwise, application programmers may write application code that appears to them to be correct but that in fact is causing errors—errors that the programmers could not know might exist.

■ INSERT (INSRT)

Insert is used to create a new segment. For example, the statements (instructions to place new AUTH data in I/O work area)

```
INSERT     PUB (PNAME d= 'P1')
           TTLE (TNAME = 'T2')
           AUTH
```

insert a new AUTH segment into the data base. Since the AUTH sequence field is ANAME, the new segment is logically inserted in order of that field. For example, if the new value of ANAME is A4, the new AUTH segment will be inserted logically as the last AUTH segment under the T2 parent.

■ Summary of DL/I Data Manipulation Commands

Figure 13-21 summarizes the DL/I data manipulation commands, all of which operate on the logical structure of the data as seen by an application program. Since the physical structure of the data may be quite different from the logical structure, the DBMS must translate the logical activity into actions on the physical data structures. The application is independent of the physical structures and is freed from maintaining them.

FIGURE 13-21

Summary of DL/I Data Manipulation Commands

Name	Function
Get Unique (GU)	Retrieve a particular segment.
Get Next (GN)	Retrieve the next segment.
Get Next within Parent (GNP)	Retrieve the next segment under a particular parent.
Get Hold Unique (GHU) Get Hold Next (GHN) Get Hold Next within Parent (GHNP)	Similar to preceding commands but used to obtain a segment to be modified or deleted.
Replace (REPL) Delete (DLET)	Used in conjunction with Get Hold commands to modify or delete a segment.
Insert (INSRT)	Insert a new segment.

SUMMARY

DBMS products based on the hierarchical and network data models are used to support transaction processing systems. These products were created during the earliest years of database processing, and their importance lies in the many existing databases whose structure is based on them. Few new databases use these models. Their chief importance to you is in maintaining existing applications or converting databases to the relational model.

An operational database is a model of the important aspects of a business. Transaction processing applications update such databases to keep them current. Such transactions, which are representations of business events, are processed both to change the data and to generate real outputs. Real outputs cannot be undone in the case of error. Rather, compensating transactions must be generated.

Transaction processing applications differ in character from decision support or personal applications. Transaction processing systems must have a fast response time. They should not fail often, and when they do, they must be able to be recovered quickly and accurately. Unlike decision support applications, transaction processing applications do not need to be flexible—in fact, because business processing is standardized processing, flexibility may be undesirable. Control, however, is very important. One means of control is using views that restrict a database system user's view of the data. Another form of control is placing the computer equipment in a restricted environment.

Three data models evolved to support transaction processing: the hierarchical data model, the network data model, and the relational data model. The sole surviving hierarchical data model is the IBM language DL/I. The most important network model is the CODASYL DBTG data model, which is discussed in the next chapter.

Both the hierarchical and the network data models require that relationships be predefined, because relationships are carried in data structures such as linked lists, not in the data, as is done with the relational model. Although predefinition reduces flexibility, it does have two advantages: better performance and greater control.

When developing databases based on the hierarchical or network data models, we must add another step to the development process. During implementation, the DBMS-independent relational design must be converted to the hierarchical or network design.

DL/I uses terminology substantially different from that of the relational model. In DL/I, a row or record is called a segment. A segment is a group of fields. One field in the segment is designated as the sequence field; it is used to logically order the segments. A tree is made up of several related segments. An instance of a tree is a data base record (DL/I spells data base as two words). Data base records are defined by means of a data base description. A data base is composed of data base records of one or more types.

DL/I is hierarchical. Because the segments in a data base record can have at most one parent, in order to represent networks (relationships in which a child has more than one parent), the network must be decomposed into trees with data duplication. This duplication is then eliminated through the use of pointers or other data structures. The child and twin pointer scheme illustrated in this chapter is one example.

DL/I uses the term *physical data base record* (or PDBR) to refer to physically stored data and the term *logical data base record* (or LDBR) to refer to application views of data. An LDBR differs from a PDBR in one of two ways: It may be a subset of a PDBR, or it may contain portions of two or more PDBRs. An application view is a set of one more LDBRs.

DL/I statements to retrieve, modify, insert, and delete segments must be embedded in application programs; thus, DL/I cannot be used interactively. DL/I data base requests are carried out by issuing subroutine calls from the application program. IMS, the product in which DL/I is implemented, does not include a pre-compiler.

Basic DL/I commands are GET UNIQUE, GET NEXT, GET NEXT within PARENT, GET HOLD UNIQUE, GET HOLD NEXT, GET HOLD NEXT within PARENT, REPLACE, DELETE, and INSERT. Each of these commands operates on an LDBR.

GROUP I QUESTIONS

13.1 Explain the difference in the range of application of DBMS products based on the hierarchical, network, and relational models.

13.2 Explain how a database is a model of the users' model of an organization.

13.3 What is a transaction?

13.4 What is a real output? Why is the distinction between real outputs and other outputs important?

13.5 Summarize the basic characteristics of a transaction processing application.

13.6 Why is flexibility not desirable in a transaction processing system?

13.7 Summarize the nature of the three data models that support transaction processing systems.

13.8 Describe the advantages of the fact that relationships in a hierarchical or network data model must be predefined.

13.9 How must the implementation process be extended when developing databases based on the hierarchical and network models?

13.10 Define the DL/I terms *field, segment, data base record,* and *data base.*

13.11 What DL/I structure corresponds to a node on a tree?

13.12 How are DL/I data base records defined? Does DL/I include data definition language as well as data manipulation language?

13.13 Describe the child and twin pointer scheme, and illustrate it with an example other than the one in this text.

13.14 Why must simple networks be transformed into trees before they can be stored for processing by DL/I?

13.15 Why, if you follow the data base design process described in this text, do you not need to transform complex networks into trees before storing them for DL/I processing?

13.16 How does DL/I eliminate data duplication, even though logically more than one tree can contain the same (duplicate) data?

13.17 What is the danger in deleting a segment that is being pointed to by another segment in the data base?

13.18 How can an application program delete data to which it is not sensitive?

13.19 What is the difference between a physical data base record and a logical data base record? In what two ways does an LDBR differ from a PDBR?

13.20 What is an application view? What is its role?

GROUP II QUESTIONS

13.21 Consider the following organizational chart:

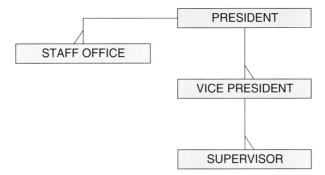

a. Sketch an occurrence of this structure.

b. What in this example constitutes a DL/I segment? A data base record? The total data base?

13.22 Assume that each segment in Question 13.21 has Name, Address, Employee-number, and Salary fields. Write a data base description similar to the one in Figure 13-8 for this data base.

13.23 Sketch the hierarchical structure and logical pointers necessary to model the following data base records in DL/I:

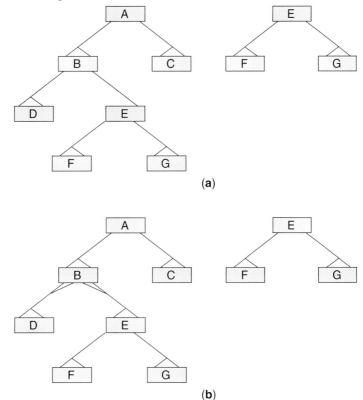

13.24 Assume that a data base consists of three separate PDBs, as follows:

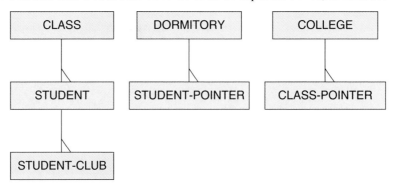

Describe the LDBR required to respond to the following requests:

   a. Get the names of all students in a class taught by the College of Business.

   b. Find the name of every student club that has at least one member living in Green Dormitory.

The data following Question 13.29 pertains to Questions 13.25 through 13.29. The sequence fields are underlined.

13.25 Describe the results of the following retrievals:

   a. GU   FACTORY
             PRODUCT (COST = 40)
             PART

   b. GU   FACTORY
             WREHOUSE (NAME = 'W2')
             DISTRBTR

   c. GU   FACTORY
             PRODUCT (COST = 40)
             PART (NUM-REQ = 24)
      GN   PART
      GN   PART
      GN   PART
      GN   PART

   d. GU   FACTORY
             PRODUCT (COST = 40)
      GNP   PART
      GNP   PART

13.26 What will happen when the last GN PART statement is executed in Question 13.25(c)? How will the user be able to detect this?

13.27 What will happen if another GNP PART statement is executed immediately after those in Question 13.25(d)?

13.28 Show the DL/I statements needed to specify the following actions:

a. Delete the | PRT6 | 24 | segment under PRD2.

b. Delete all data concerning warehouse W3.

c. Delete all data concerning factory F1.

d. Delete all products costing more than $45.

13.29 Show the DL/I statements needed to perform the following modifications and additions. In doing so, also describe the actions that must be performed by language-unique commands:

a. Modify PRD2 to show a cost of $85.

b. Modify the cost of all products to be 10 percent greater.

c. Add distributor D11 to warehouse W2 and distribute D14 to warehouse W3.

d. Add to factory F1: PRD4, COST $105, with parts PRT2, 26 required, and PRT4, 31 required.

e. Change the cost of PRD1 to $45 and add PRT6, 21 required to it.

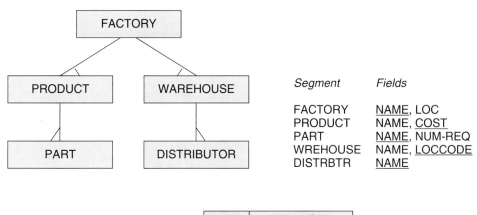

Segment	Fields
FACTORY	NAME, LOC
PRODUCT	NAME, COST
PART	NAME, NUM-REQ
WREHOUSE	NAME, LOCCODE
DISTRBTR	NAME

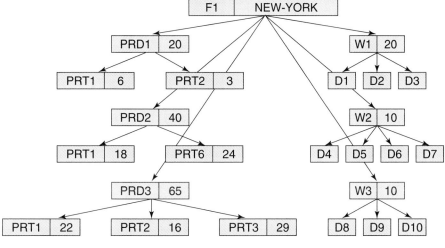

First Factory PDBR

THE CODASYL
DBTG MODEL

This chapter introduces a third data model that is frequently used to build databases to support transaction processing. The network data model derives its name from the fact that it enables simple networks to be represented directly, without the transformations required for the hierarchical data model. Although at one time there were several varieties of network models, the only one of consequence today is the CODASYL DBTG data model.

We begin with a brief history of this model and its features and functions, starting with the data definition components. Next we illustrate how these components are used to represent each of the object types discussed in this text. After that, we examine application views, or subschemas as they are called in the DBTG model, and finally we look at the DBTG data manipulation language in the context of the library database introduced in Chapter 13.

THE HISTORY OF THE CODASYL DBTG DATA MODEL

The CODAYSL DBTG data model was developed by a group known as the CODASYL (Conference on Data Systems Languages) Data Base Task Group (hence the name CODASYL DBTG). The CODASYL committee is best known as the group that developed the standards for COBOL. The CODASYL data model evolved over several years, and several transaction-oriented DBMS products are based on it. Today, however, those DBMS products are on the wane. Several reasons account for the decline of the DBTG model. First, it is complex and incohesive. For example, a statement in a schema definition can combine with a seemingly unrelated operation in an application program to produce strange and unexpected results. Consequently, designers and programmers must be very careful when building DBTG databases and applications. Second, the model has a decidedly COBOL flavor to it (for an example, examine Figure 14-18), and this similarity has been an issue in organizations in which COBOL is not the language of choice. Furthermore, the development of the CODASYL database model was heavily politicized, and so the committee had to contend with the tendency to include everyone's favorite idea. Finally, in fairness to this model, it originated very early in the history of database technology. Although it incorporated many important concepts, mistakes were also made. Indeed, some people believe that the model was developed too soon— before the essential concepts of database technology were known and had been explored.

The history of the CODASYL model is complex. Three different versions were developed, and although the data model was twice submitted to the American National Standards Institute (ANSI) for consideration as a national standard, it was never accepted. Instead, in August 1986, the relational model and SQL were recognized as the national database standard.

The basic functions and features of the three versions of the CODASYL model are the same. Most of the commercial DBMS products based on this model are based on the earliest one, developed in 1971. The later 1978 and 1981 models changed some of the language and syntax (the 1971 model had inappropriately used COBOL reserved words), added features to support the definition of constraints, and made other changes. The discussion in this chapter centers on the 1981 model, but when it is important to know how earlier models differ from this version, we also describe concepts from them.

Strictly speaking, only the 1971 version was called the CODASYL *DBTG* model. In subsequent versions, the DBTG was dropped. Common industry practice, however, refers to all versions of this model as the DBTG model, and we follow that practice.

As you read this chapter, keep in mind that you are learning about a *model* that was used as the basis for the design of many transaction-oriented DBMS products such as IDMS/R, IDS, and DMS-170. The developers of these products conformed to the model to greater and lesser degrees. Although you will not find a product that exactly fits the CODASYL DBTG model (of any version), their core features and functions do conform to its basic philosophy and orientation.

The DBTG model (1971) introduced the terms **data definition language** (DDL) and **data manipulation language** (DML). As you know from earlier discussions in this text, the DDL is the language used to describe the structure of the database, and the DML is the language used to describe the processing of the database. Recall that DL/I, discussed in Chapter 13, does not include a DDL, and so the CODASYL model was an improvement over it and the earlier database products that included only data manipulation facilities.

CODASYL DBTG DATA DEFINITION LANGUAGE

The 1981 version of the CODASYL model provides three different types of database view. The **schema** is the complete logical view of the database, the entire database as viewed by the database administrator or other humans. A **subschema** is a view of the database as it appears to an application program. A subschema is a subset of the database and, in the 1978 and 1981 models, is allowed to have records that are constructed by joining records in the schema. This is similar to a view composed of relation joins, as discussed in Chapter 12. The **data structure description** is the third type of view, and it maps schema records, fields, and relationships to physical storage. It is the view of the database as it appears in physical storage. Because data structure descriptions were introduced in the second (1978) version of the model, they are not widely used, and as it is unlikely that you will ever encounter them, we omit them from our discussion.

As shown in Figure 14-1, users interact with the database by means of an application program (no interactive query language exists). One or more users can execute a single program. Each user has a **user working area** (UWA) that contains database and control data for a particular user (it is similar to the DL/I input–output work area described in Chapter 13). The execution of a program by one of the users

FIGURE 14-1

CODASYL DBTG Program/Data View Relationships

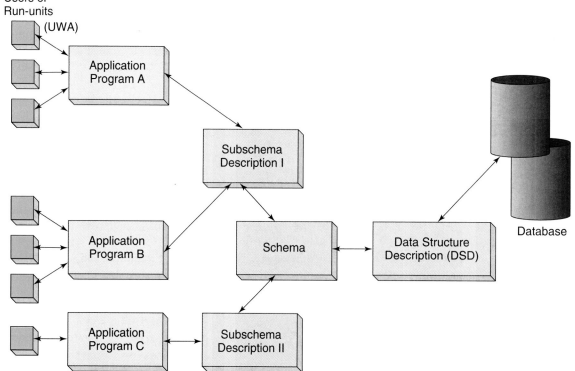

is called a **run-unit.** Figure 14-1 shows three run-units for Application Program A, and the application programs view the database through a subschema. The programs may share subschemas, or each may have its own.

■ Data Definition Constructs

Database designers use the basic data definition constructs in CODASYL DBTG to define schemas and subschemas. The three fundamental building blocks are data-items, records, and sets. A fourth construct, area, was present in early editions of the model but has since been dropped.

DATA-ITEMS

A **data-item** is a field that corresponds to an attribute or column in the relational model. Data-items have names and formats, and examples are Name, Character 25; Address, Character 40; Amount, Fixed 6.2. Although data-items come from domains, the domain concept is not recognized by the DBTG model.

RECORDS

A **record** is a collection of data-items, and Figure 14-2 shows several examples of DBTG records. Unlike the relational model, this model allows **vectors,** which are repetitions of a data-item (like GPA in Figure 14-2[b]), and it allows repeating groups, such as the data-items Course Name and Grade in Figure 14-2(c). Although such repeating groups are allowed, they are unnecessary and generally not recommended. Repeating groups were developed to represent composite objects, but a better way of representing them is with two record types and a set.

SETS

A **set** is a one-to-many relationship between records. Sets have *owners* and *members.* The owner of a set is the parent, and in Figure 14-3, ACCOUNTING is the owner of one set, and MARKETING is the owner of another set. Members of a set are the children in the one-to-many relationship. In Figure 14-3, Jones, Parks, and Williams are the members of the set owned by ACCOUNTING.

Figure 14-3 shows two occurrences of a general structure representing instances of a one-to-many relationship between the DEPARTMENT and FACULTY records, and Figure 14-4 is a generalized representation of this relationship. The general structure, such as the one in Figure 14-4, is called the *set,* and examples of the structure, such as those in Figure 14-3, are called *instances,* or *occurrences,* of the set.

To define a set, we specify a set name and identify the type of record that will be the owner and the type (or types) of the records that will be the members. For example, in Figure 14-5, the set STU-MAJOR has MAJOR owner records and STUDENT member records; the set ORDER-ITEM has ORDER owner records and ITEM member records; and the set STU-HISTORY has STUDENT owner records and CLASS-GRADE member records.

The DBTG model has specific rules regarding set definition. First, a set can have only one type of record as owner, although one or more record types can be members. Figure 14-6(a) shows the set ACTIVITY: The owner record is CLUB, and the member records are PROFESSOR and STUDENT. Figure 14-6(b) shows two

FIGURE 14-2

CODASYL DBTG Record Types: (a) Record Composed of Data-Items, (b) Record Composed of Data-Items and a Vector Data-Aggregate, (c) Record with Repeating Group, and (d) Record with Nested Repeating Group

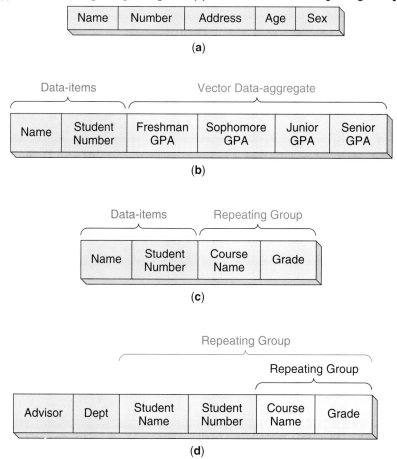

FIGURE 14-3

Two Occurrences of DEPT-FAC Set

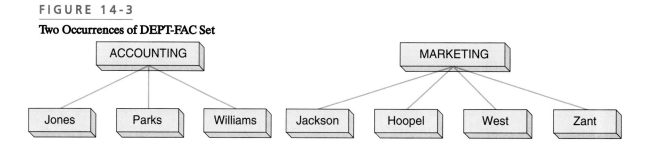

FIGURE 14-4

General Form of CODASYL DBTG Set

FIGURE 14-5

Example of CODASYL DBTG Sets

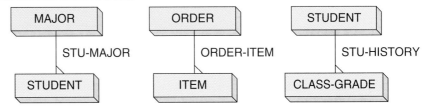

FIGURE 14-6

Set with (a) Two Member Record Types and (b) Example Occurrences of Them

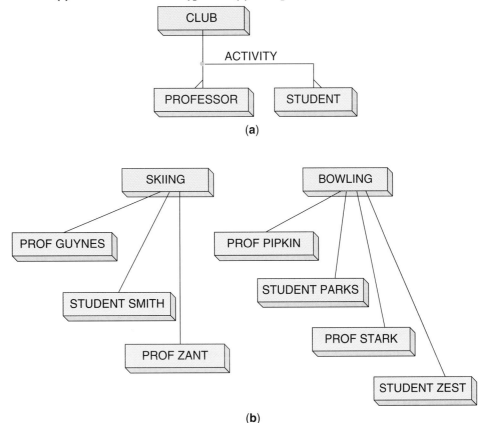

instances of this set, in which both PROFESSOR and STUDENT records are members of the SKIING and BOWLING clubs.

According to the DBTG model, a member record can belong to only one instance of a particular set; that is, a record may not have two parents in the same set. This means, in Figure 14-6, that Professor Guynes can have only the SKIING parent record; he may not have BOWLING as well. Furthermore, Professor Pipkin can have only the BOWLING record as a parent and not SKIING as well. If faculty members are allowed to belong to more than one club, a DBTG set cannot be used to represent this relationship. In fact, if faculty members were allowed to belong to two clubs, this would be an instance of an M:N relationship.

Although a record cannot have two owners in the *same* set, a record may have two owners if they are in *different* sets. For example, a professor may have one ACTIVITY owner and one JOB-TITLE owner. Figure 14-7 extends Figure 14-6 to allow this possibility. Professor Guynes, for example, has both SKIING and FULL PROFESSOR records as parents.

These restrictions on set membership mean that a set can readily be used to represent 1:1 and 1:N relationships and can directly represent composite objects, 1:1 and 1:N compound objects, association objects, and any hybrid objects that do not

FIGURE 14-7

Example of Two-Owner Record in Different Sets: (a) Record Belonging to Two Different Sets and (b) Instance of This Set Structure

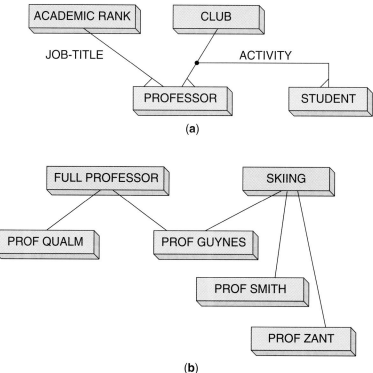

Summary of Set Characteristics

- A set is a collection of records.
- There are an arbitrary number of sets in the database.
- Each set has one owner record type and one or more member record types.
- Each owner record occurrence defines a set occurrence.
- There are an arbitrary number of member record occurrences in one set occurrence.
- A record may be a member of more than one set.
- A record may not be a member of two occurrences of the same set.

include an M:N compound object. M:N compound objects cannot be represented because M:N relationships cannot be represented directly with DBTG sets. The characteristics of sets are summarized in Figure 14-8.

AREAS

Until 1981 the CODASYL DBTG model included a fourth data definition construct called an *area* (1971), or *realm* (1978). This fourth construct referred to a collection of records and sets that could be allocated to a physical entity such as a file, disk, or similar physical storage unit. But all versions of the DBTG model were indefinite about how records or sets were to be placed into areas (or realms). The decision regarding the use of this construct was therefore left to the DBMS product designers.

In 1981 the area (realm) construct was deleted from the CODASYL model because it was considered to be a physical construct and therefore inappropriate to a schema or subschema description, and so we will not consider this construct further in this chapter.

■ CODASYL DBTG Representation of Objects

The process for developing a database according to the CODASYL DBTG model is similar to that used for developing DL/I databases. It differs only in the last step. We collect forms, reports, and other evidence of users' views; develop a data model; convert the data model to a DBMS-independent relational design; and, finally, convert the relational design to a CODASYL DBTG design. To illustrate this conversion we use the six objects defined for the library in Chapter 13. The relations underlying these objects are summarized in Figure 14-9.

SIMPLE OBJECTS

The DBTG representation of a simple object is straightforward. A record is defined for the object, and its attributes are represented by data-items.

FIGURE 14-9

Sample Objects and Relations: (a) Objects in the Library Database and (b) a Relational Representation of an Object in the Library Database

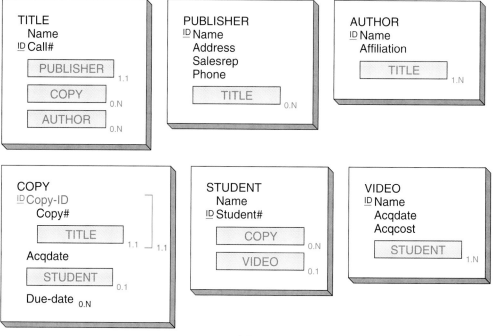

(a)

TTLE (Name, <u>Call#</u>, *Pname*)
PUB (<u>Pname</u>, Address, Salesrep, Pphone)
AUTH (<u>Aname</u>, Affiliation)
TA-INT (*<u>Call#</u>*, *<u>Aname</u>*)
CPY (<u>Call#</u>, <u>Copy#</u>, Acqdate, *Student#*)
STU (<u>Student#</u>, Sname, Sphone)
DUE-DATE (<u>Call#</u>, <u>Copy#</u>, <u>Date-due</u>)
VID (<u>Vname</u>, Acqdate, Acqcost, *Student#*)

(b)

COMPOSITE OBJECTS

To represent a composite object in the DBTG model, we define two record types and a set. One record type represents the object, and the second represents the composite group of attributes in the object. The set represents the relationship.

Consider the composite group DUE-DATE in the COPY object in Figure 14-9, consisting of the multivalued attribute DUE-DATE. The relational representation of CPY and DUE-DATE is shown in Figure 14-10(a), and the DBTG representation is shown in Figure 14-10(b). Observe that the one-to-many relationship is represented by a CODASYL DBTG set. As in earlier discussions, the oval indicates an

FIGURE 14-10

Representation of Composite Object: (a) Relational Design and (b) CODASYL DBTG Design (Information-bearing Set)

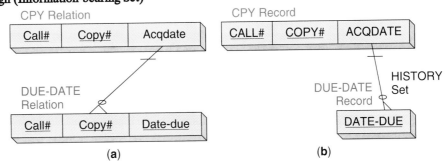

optional relationship, and a hash mark indicates a mandatory relationship. Thus, a CPY need not have a DUE-DATE, but a DUE-DATE must have a CPY.

One important difference between the relational representation and the DBTG representation is that in the relational representation, the relationship between DUE-DATE and CPY is carried in the foreign key (Call#, Copy#), but in the CODASYL representation, the relationship is not carried in the data. The foreign key (Call#, Copy#) does *not* appear in the DUE-DATE record. When a DUE-DATE record is created, the record itself is inserted into a particular instance of the HISTORY set. From that point on, the DBMS is responsible for maintaining this association by means of physical location, pointers, or some other method. Unlike the relational model, the relationship is carried in **overhead data** maintained by the DBMS and not in the data itself.

The set in Figure 14-10(b) is sometimes called an **information bearing set,** since it carries the information about which DUE-DATE records belong to which CPY records. Database practitioners disagree about the desirability of information bearing sets. On one hand, information bearing sets reduce the amount of data duplication (Title and Copy in this case). But on the other hand, the use of information bearing sets can be risky. If, for some reason, the overhead structure is lost or becomes suspect, there is no way of determining which DUE-DATE records belong to which CPY records. Also, some people believe that burying data in overhead structures is philosophically wrong. Instead, some believe, it should be visible to the user and not hidden from everyone but the DBMS.

Examples can be constructed to support both positions. If the composite key is large, so that there is considerable duplication of data, a strong case can be made for information-bearing sets. Otherwise there is little harm in carrying along the duplicate key data, and this redundancy does improve the reliability of the database. We talk about both types in this and the next chapter.

1:1 COMPOUND OBJECTS

To represent a 1:1 compound object, we define a record for each object and a set for the relationship. Since the relationship is 1:1, it does not matter which record is the parent and which is the child. In general, performance usually is better if the record

FIGURE 14-11

Representation of 1:1
Compound Object: (a)
Relational Design and (b)
CODASYL DBTG Design
(Non-information-bearing Set)

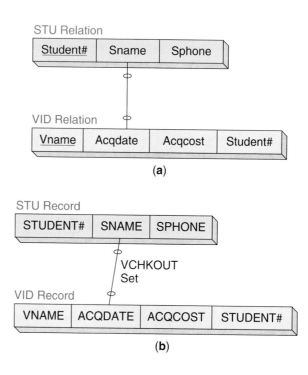

(a)

(b)

more frequently used as the entry point is the parent (the actual answer depends on the workload, the DBMS, and the supporting data structures). Thus, if student data is more commonly accessed followed by video, STU should be the parent. But if video data is more frequently accessed, followed by student data, then VID should be the parent. These comments pertain to the frequency with which the *relationship* is used, although VID may be accessed by itself, without accessing STU, or the reverse. What matters is identifying the record most frequently accessed first whenever the relationship is processed.

Figure 14-11 shows both the relational representation of the STUDENT and VIDEO objects and a DBTG representation. Notice that VCHKOUT is a non-information bearing set, since STUDENT is carried as a data-item of VID.

The DBTG model provides no direct means of limiting the number of child records that can belong to a set (in this case, a student is allowed only one videocassette at a time). However, we can require the STUDENT data-item in VID to be unique, thereby limiting the number of videos for a student to one.

1:N COMPOUND OBJECTS

A 1:N compound object is represented by defining two record types and a set. Each object is stored in a record, and the set represents the relationship. The record on the 1 side of the relationship is the parent, and the record on the N side is the child. That is, the record having the foreign key in the relational design is the child record of the set in the DBTG design. Figure 14-12 shows the DBTG representation of the PUBLISHER and TITLE objects from Figure 14-9. PUB is the parent of the PUBLISHING set, and TTLE is the child.

FIGURE 14-12

Representation of 1:N Compound Object: (a) Relational Design and (b) CODASYL DBTG Design (Non-information-bearing Set)

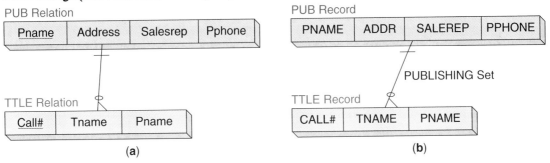

(a)   (b)

Since PNAME is included in the TTLE record, PUBLISHING is a non-information-bearing set. One advantage of this arrangement is that if a report or form requires TTLE data plus the name of the publisher, then including PNAME in TTLE saves DBMS processing. The appropriate PUB record need not be accessed to obtain the name. But if the report or form requires data besides Pname—say, Phone—the lookup will be necessary.

M:N COMPOUND OBJECTS

M:N compound objects cannot be represented directly in the DBTG model. They must be converted to simple networks with intersection data, as is done with the relational model. Figure 14-13(a) shows the relational representation of the TITLE and AUTHOR objects from Figure 14-9. TA-INT has been created to represent the M:N relationship.

The DBTG representation of the simple network consists of three records and two sets, as shown in Figure 14-14. One record is defined for each object and a third for the intersection data. The sets represent the M:N relationship.

To find all the authors of a given book, the program would access all the TA-INT children in the T-A set and, for each child record, obtain the A-T parent. To find all the titles written by a particular author, the program would access all the TA-INT children of the A-T set and, for each one, obtain the T-A parent.

The intersection record of an M:N object *never* contains data beyond the identities of the related records. If it did, we would call it an association object, not an M:N compound object.

The sets shown in Figure 14-13 are non-information bearing sets. If information bearing sets were to be used here, the records would have no data whatsoever, only pointers or other overhead. There is nothing wrong with that fact; it simply indicates that the function of an intersection record is to represent the relationship. If the relationship is carried in information bearing sets, there is no need for data.

ASSOCIATION OBJECTS

Figure 14-14 shows the DBTG representation of the association object COPY, with its associate objects STUDENT and TITLE. To define the association object COPY,

FIGURE 14-13

Representation of M:N Compound Object: (a) Relational Design and (b) CODASYL DBTG
Design (Two Non-information-bearing Sets)

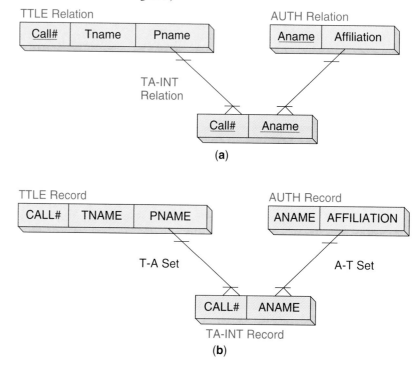

we define one record for each object and two sets, one for the 1:N relationship
between COPY and TITLE, and one for the 1:N relationship between COPY and
STUDENT.

This structure is similar to the one in Figure 14-13 except that the record that is
the child of the two sets is itself an object seen by the user as an entity establishing
the relationship between two other objects. We would have discovered this during the
design phase, when we might have found a form or report about copies. This fact
would have told us that eventually a program would need to access the CPY record as
an entry point.

Conversely, the TA-INT record in Figure 14-13 is not an independent object. No
program will ever access TA-INT as an entry point. Rather, TA-INT is used as a
bridge between related TITLE and AUTHOR records. Stated in another way, CPY
will contain data of its own, but TA-INT will not.

In this example, CHECKOUT is an information bearing set, but COLLECTION
is not information bearing. The decision to structure these sets in this manner is
arbitrary. Since Call# is part of the key of CPY, it is already carried in the data and
not by the set. But since Student is not part of the key, that relationship can be carried by the set. On the other hand, Student# could have been placed in the CPY
record, making COLLECTION a non-information bearing set. There is no com-
pelling reason to choose one way or the other–they both work. (Contrast this with

FIGURE 14-14

Representation of Association Object: (a) Relational Design and (b) CODASYL DBTG Design

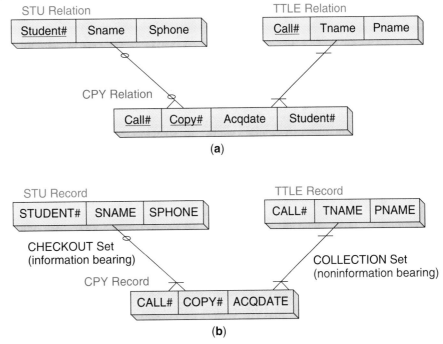

(a)

(b)

the relational model in which relationships *must* be carried in the data because information bearing sets do not exist.)

■ DBTG Set Ordering

According to the DBTG model, member records of a set can be ordered in a variety of ways. Figure 14-15 lists the possibilities. If the set order is FIRST, when new records are placed in a set occurrence, they will be placed in the first position. Subsequently, when the set members are accessed, the new record will be the first one retrieved. This placement is logical, supported by the underlying data structures. The physical placement is unknown and unimportant except to the DBMS itself. If

FIGURE 14-15

CODASYL DBTG Set Member Ordering Options

FIRST
LAST
NEXT
PRIOR
SYSTEM DEFAULT
SORTED

the set order is LAST, new records will be placed in the last position. In this case, set members will be ordered chronologically in the database.

If the order is NEXT, new members will be placed in the next position after the most recently accessed member record of the set. To use this option, at least one set record must already have been accessed in order to establish a position. The new record is placed immediately after the most recently accessed record. If the most recently accessed record of the set were the owner, the new record would be placed at the start of the set members. If the order is PRIOR, the new record will be inserted just before the most recently accessed set record. If that record is the owner, the new record will be placed at the end of the set.

If the set is ordered by SYSTEM DEFAULT, the database designer is stating that the order is immaterial to the applications, that the DBMS can determine the order. Finally, set members can be SORTED on the value of a data-item they contain. If they are, the name of the data-item will be identified in a separate KEY clause. Figure 14-16 shows the set ordering we will use for sets in the library database.

As long as records belong to sets, they can be ordered within the set. For some applications, however, the entire file of records must be sorted, regardless of the sets to which the file's records might belong. In order to do this, the DBTG provides system sets.

A **system set** is a special set with only one occurrence for each type of record, an occurrence owned by the DBMS. To provide sequential processing, the set is defined as an ordered set based on one or more data-items in the record. Thus, if TTLE records are to be sorted by Call, a system set having TTLE records as members and ORDER of Call would be created. We have labeled this system set TITLE-SEQ in Figure 14-16. The TTLE records can then be processed in Call order.

■ Set Membership

The DBTG model provides a group of commands to put records into set occurrences, to take records from set occurrences, and to move records around within set occurrences. We discuss these commands in the section on the DML. The allowable commands depend on the definition of **set membership**, which involves two concepts: getting members into set occurrences and, once in, getting them out.

FIGURE 14-16

Set Ordering for the Library Database

Set Name	Order
PUBLISH	Sorted by TNAME
T-A	System default
A-T	System default
COLLECTION	Sorted by COPY#
CHECKOUT	Last
VCHKOUT	Last (but immaterial)
HISTORY	Last
TITLE-SEQ	Sorted by TNAME

FIGURE 14-17

Set Insertion and Set Retention Status

Retention status

	FIXED	MANDATORY	OPTIONAL
AUTO-MATIC	DBMS puts record in set at time of creation. Once in, it cannot be taken out.	DBMS puts record in set at time of creation. It can be moved to another occurrence with RECONNECT.	DBMS puts record in set at time of creation. It can be disconnected, reconnected, or connected.
MANUAL	Application program puts record into set. Once in, it cannot be taken out.	Application program puts record into set. It can be moved to another occurrence with RECONNECT.	Application program puts record into set. It can be disconnected, reconnected, or connected.

Insertion status

SET INSERTION STATUS

When we define a set in the schema, we must give it an **insertion status,** either AUTOMATIC or MANUAL. If the insertion status is AUTOMATIC, whenever a member record is created, the DBMS will automatically insert the record into the set. If the insertion status is MANUAL, a member record will not be put into a set occurrence until the application program executes a special command, CONNECT.

SET RETENTION STATUS

When a set is defined in the schema, it must be given a **retention status**, FIXED, MANDATORY, or OPTIONAL. If FIXED, then once a record is placed in a set occurrence, it must remain in *that* occurrence of the set. To change its set membership, the record must be deleted from the database and recreated. If the retention status is MANDATORY, then once a record is placed in a set occurrence, it must always belong to a set occurrence; however, the occurrence need not be the initial one. Thus MANDATORY sets require that once a record is put into a set occurrence, it must stay in *some* occurrence of the set. A special command, RECONNECT, is used to move a member record from one occurrence to another. Finally, if the retention status is OPTIONAL, member records can be removed, inserted, and moved from set occurrence to set occurrence without restriction. Figure 14-17 summarizes the interaction of set insertion and retention status.

◼ Constraints

The DBTG model provides partial support for domain, intrarelation, and interrelation (record) constraint enforcement. The DBTG support for constraint enforcement has evolved over time in different versions of the model. We describe the capabilities of the 1981 model here. Because the DBTG model was evolving at the same time that the need for constraint enforcement was only beginning to be apparent, constraint enforcement was not thoroughly developed.

DOMAIN CONSTRAINTS

The DBTG model does not recognize the concept of domain, and so data-items are independently defined to have a particular physical appearance and particular constraints. If two or more data-items are based on the same domain, it is up to the database developer to know this and to ensure that the physical descriptions and constraints are defined in the same way.

The manner in which data-item formats are defined is rather open-ended. Various versions of the model offer a variety of data-items and formats for data-item specification. Basically, the model includes common data formats such as CHARACTER, FIXED, CURRENCY, DATE, and TIME. In addition, the length of the data-items and the number of places to the right of the decimal point (where appropriate) can also be specified.

Besides format descriptions, the 1981 DBTG provides a means of limiting the allowed data-item values, through the CHECK statement in the schema definition. The following are some examples of CHECK statements:

CHECK IS NOT EQUAL 0

CHECK IS LESS THAN 500

CHECK IS NOT NULL

The first two CHECK statements enforce range restrictions on allowable values. The last one ensures the existence of a value in a mandatory field, such as a key field. CHECK statements are located in the schema definition next to the data-item that they limit. Examples are shown in the next section (see Figure 14-18).

INTRARECORD CONSTRAINTS

The DBTG model supports one type of intrarelation constraint: **uniqueness**. Record instances can be defined to be unique based on one or more data-items, considered singly or as composites. For example, suppose the record type TTLE contains the data-item TNAME. (As with DL/I, the DBTG model does not support lowercase letters, and so data-items are spelled in capital letters for this model.) The following statement can be inserted in the schema to ensure that duplicate titles are prohibited:

DUPLICATES NOT ALLOWED FOR TNAME

Such statements are located in the schema in the section defining the record having the constraint. Consider another example involving the record CPY, which contains the data-items CALL# and COPY#. The statement

DUPLICATES NOT ALLOWED FOR CALL#, COPY#

states that the composite (CALL#, COPY#) must be unique. There may be records having duplicate CALL# values (for different copies of the same book) and records having duplicate COPY# values (for copy numbers of different titles), but the combination of a particular call number with a particular copy number must be unique.

FIGURE 14-18

Definition of Library Schema

```
SCHEMA NAME IS LIBRARY
        RECORD NAME IS PUB
                DUPLICATES ARE NOT ALLOWED FOR PNAME
                PNAME                   TYPE IS    CHARACTER    10
                                        CHECK IS   NOT NULL
                ADDRESS                 TYPE IS    CHARACTER    25
                SALPSN                  TYPE IS    CHARACTER    20
                PPHONE                  TYPE IS    FIXED        10

        RECORD NAME IS TTLE
                DUPLICATES ARE NOT ALLOWED FOR CALL#
                DUPLICATES ARE NOT ALLOWED FOR TNAME
                CALL#                   TYPE IS    CHARACTER    8
                                        CHECK IS   NOT NULL
                TNAME                   TYPE IS    CHARACTER    50
                                        CHECK IS   NOT NULL
                PNAME                   TYPE IS    CHARACTER    10
                                        CHECK IS   NOT NULL
        RECORD NAME IS CPY
                DUPLICATES ARE NOT ALLOWED FOR CALL#, COPY#
                CALL#                   TYPE IS    CHARACTER    8
                                        CHECK IS   NOT NULL
                COPY#                   TYPE IS    FIXED        2
                                        CHECK IS   NOT NULL
                ACQDATE                 TYPE IS    DATE

        RECORD NAME IS AUTH
                DUPLICATES ARE NOT ALLOWED FOR ANAME
                ANAME                   TYPE IS    CHARACTER    30
                                        CHECK IS   NOT NULL
                AFFILIATION             TYPE IS    CHARACTER    30

        RECORD NAME IS TA-INT
                DUPLICATES ARE NOT ALLOWED FOR CALL#, ANAME
                CALL#                   TYPE IS    CHARACTER    8
                                        CHECK IS   NOT NULL
                ANAME                   TYPE IS    CHARACTER    30
                                        CHECK IS   NOT NULL     7

        RECORD NAME IS STU
                DUPLICATES ARE NOT ALLOWED FOR STUDENT#
                STUDENT#                TYPE IS    FIXED        10
                                        CHECK IS   NOT NULL
                SNAME                   TYPE IS    CHARACTER    30
                SPHONE                  TYPE IS    FIXED
```

(Continued)

```
RECORD NAME IS VID
        DUPLICATES ARE NOT ALLOWED FOR VID#, VCOPY#
        DUPLICATES ARE NOT ALLOWED FOR STUDENT#
        VID#                        TYPE IS      FIXED          5
                                    CHECK IS     NOT NULL
        VCOPY#                      TYPE IS      FIXED          2
                                    CHECK IS     NOT NULL
        VNAME                       TYPE IS      CHARACTER      40
        STUDENT#                    TYPE IS      FIXED          10

RECORD NAME IS DUE-DATE
        DATE-DUE                    TYPE IS      DATE
                                    CHECK IS     NOT NULL

SET NAME IS PUBLISH
        OWNER IS PUB
        ORDER IS SORTED BY DEFINED KEYS
        MEMBER IS TTLE
        INSERTION IS AUTOMATIC, RETENTION IS FIXED
        KEY IS ASCENDING TNAME
        SET SELECTION IS BY VALUE OF PNAME

SET NAME IS T-A
        OWNER IS TTLE
        ORDER IS SYSTEM DEFAULT
        MEMBER IS TA-INT
        INSERTION IS AUTOMATIC, RETENTION IS FIXED
        CHECK IS CALL# IN TTLE = CALL# IN TA-INT
        SET SELECTION IS BY VALUE OF CALL#

SET NAME IS A-T
        OWNER IS AUTH
        ORDER IS SYSTEM DEFAULT
        MEMBER IS TA-INT
        INSERTION IS AUTOMATIC, RETENTION IS FIXED
        CHECK IS ANAME IN AUTH = ANAME IN TA-INT
        SET SELECTION IS BY VALUE OF ANAME

SET NAME IS COLLECTION
        OWNER IS TTLE
        ORDER IS BY DEFINED KEYS
        MEMBER IS CPY
        INSERTION IS AUTOMATIC, RETENTION IS FIXED
        KEY IS ASCENDING COPY#
        SET SELECTION IS STRUCTURAL CALL# = CALL#
```

FIGURE 14-18

(Continued)

```
        SET NAME IS CHECKOUT
                OWNER IS STU
                ORDER IS LAST
                MEMBER IS CPY
                INSERTION IS MANUAL, RETENTION IS OPTIONAL
                SET SELECTION IS BY VALUE OF STUDENT#

        SET NAME IS VCHKOUT
                OWNER IS STU
                ORDER IS LAST
                MEMBER IS VID
                INSERTION IS MANUAL, RETENTION IS OPTIONAL
                SET SELECTION IS BY VALUE OF STUDENT#

        SET NAME IS HISTORY
                OWNER IS CPY
                MEMBER IS DUE-DATE
                ORDER IS LAST
                INSERTION IS AUTOMATIC, RETENTION IS FIXED
                SET SELECTION IS BY VALUE OF CALL#, COPY#

        SET NAME IS TITLE-SEQ
                OWNER IS SYSTEM
                ORDER IS BY DEFINED KEYS
                MEMBER IS TTLE
                INSERTION IS AUTOMATIC, RETENTION IS FIXED
                KEY IS ASCENDING TNAME
```

Consider the difference in the DUPLICATE statement for CPY (immediately preceding) and the following two statements for TTLE:

DUPLICATES NOT ALLOWED FOR TNAME

DUPLICATES NOT ALLOWED FOR Call#

The two statements for TTLE define uniqueness for data-items independently, and the single statement for CPY defines uniqueness for the composite (CALL#, COPY#).

INTERRECORD CONSTRAINTS

The DBTG model provides partial support for the definition of interrecord constraints, or referential integrity, through two facilities. One is the definition of set retention status, and the second is a version of the CHECK command.

Consider Figure 14-17 in light of the four types of binary record relationships (M–M, M–O, O–M, and O–O). If the retention status of a set member is either FIXED or MANDATORY, that record will always be in a set, and hence it will always have a parent. Thus either of these two values of retention status can be used to enforce the parent side of M–M or M–O constraints. Moreover, defining a set as

OPTIONAL means that a parent may or may not exist and thus can be used to define the parent side of O–M or O–O constraints.

Set insertion status does not facilitate the definition of interrecord constraints. In fact, some database practitioners find it to be more confusing than helpful. AUTO-MATIC/FIXED and AUTOMATIC/MANDATORY definitions provide for a consistent enforcement of M–x (meaning either M–M or M–O) constraints. MANUAL/FIXED and MANUAL/MANDATORY provide such enforcement once the record is placed in a set. However, MANUAL insertion status allows a child record to be stored in the database before the parent is stored.

Set insertion and retention status concern a child record's requirement for a parent; they do not consider a parent record's requirement for a child. Insertion and retention status therefore do not concern the enforcement of x–M constraints. Unfortunately, such constraints must be enforced by application programs.

The 1981 model provided a version of the CHECK statement that enforces values in foreign keys. As such, it can be used only for non-information bearing sets (sets in which the key of the parent is stored as a foreign key in the child record). For example, consider the TTLE and CPY records just discussed, in which CALL in CPY is a foreign key from TTLE. The following CHECK statement, placed in the set definition portion of the schema, enforces a match between the key and the foreign key:

CHECK IS CALL# IN TTLE = CALL# IN CPY

This statement, which is associated with a set—say, COLLECTION—makes sense only if CALL is located in both records. With this statement, whenever a record is placed into a set occurrence, the values of CALL must match. This is another way of enforcing an M–x constraint.

Perhaps you are beginning to get a feel for the inconsistent and eclectic nature of this model. Such a CHECK statement leans in the direction of interrelation constraints in the relational model. Yet its presence is somewhat confusing laid on top of the rest of the DBTG model. Such is the nature of emerging technology.

A SCHEMA DEFINITION FOR THE LIBRARY DATABASE

Figure 14-18 presents a schema definition for the library database design shown in Figure 14-9. There are many ways that the DBTG model can be used to represent this database, and Figure 14-18 is one of them, showing options that another database designer might not have chosen. With this model, there can be several feasible definitions for the database because it is so open-ended.

The schema definition has two main parts. The first concerns the definition of record structures, and the second, the definition of sets.

■ Defining Records

Examine the definition of the PUB record in Figure 14-18. The first statement declares that values of PNAME must be unique. Following that, the data-items are described. Notice the CHECK statement that enforces the domain constraint that PNAME may not be null.

The definition of TTLE is next. Here, two different statements declare that both TNAME and CALL# are to be unique. Since these statements are separate, they imply that the value of TNAME and the values of CALL# each must be unique. As we stated earlier, this is different from declaring that a composite group is unique. An example of composite data-item uniqueness can be found in the definition of the next record, CPY, in which the DUPLICATES statement declares that the composite (CALL#, COPY#) must be unique.

The remaining record definitions are similar, although one unusual statement appears in the definition of VID. In this record, STUDENT is required to be unique. Since a set is defined with STU as the parent and VID as the child, this relationship would normally be one to many, as the same value of STUDENT could appear in many different instances of VID. With the declaration that STUDENT must be unique, however, the same STUDENT can appear in only one VID record. This declaration therefore turns what would normally be a one-to-many relationship into the one-to-one relationship required in the design.

Defining Sets

In Figure 14-18, one set is defined for each one-to-many relationship shown in Figure 14-9. The first set, PUBLISH, represents the relationship between PUB and TTLE. The owner record of this set is PUBLISH, and the member record is TTLE. The records in the set are to be maintained in sorted order of TNAME, defined by two statements in the set definition. The first, ORDER IS SORTED BY DEFINED KEYS, indicates that the order is to be kept by a value of one or more data-items in the member record. The particular data-item is then identified by the statement KEY IS ASCENDING TNAME. The fourth statement in the set definition specifies the set insertion and the retention status. AUTOMATIC, FIXED was chosen here because every book must have a publisher, and the publisher of a book cannot change.

The last statement in the set definition specifies how the DBMS is to identify a particular set occurrence when it needs one. There are several situations in which this is necessary, as we will see when discussing the DML. One instance: Since the insertion status of TTLE is AUTOMATIC, when a new TTLE record is created, the DBMS must insert it into an instance of the PUBLISH set. The question is, Which instance of that set? The SET SELECTION statement specifies how the DBMS is to identify such a set instance. This particular statement decides that the DBMS should use the value of PNAME to identify a PUB record. The new TTLE record is to be inserted into the set occurrence owned by that PUB record.

The remaining sets also are defined in Figure 14-18. The sets T-A and A-T represent the M:N relationship between titles and authors. Both of these sets are non–information bearing, since they contain the keys of their parents. The order is SYSTEM DEFAULT, which means that the application developers are not concerned about the order of the member records in the set. Other statements are similar to those for PUBLISH, except that these sets include a CHECK clause.

Consider the set T-A. The CHECK clause in this set definition tells the DBMS to enforce the constraint that the values of CALL in TTLE and TA-INT must match. Since the insertion status is AUTOMATIC, the retention status is FIXED, and the set selection is by value of CALL#, this CHECK clause is redundant. Unless the DBMS code is wrong, it should be impossible for nonmatching values of CALL# to occur in the same set.

Observe that the set insertion and retention status, the SET SELECTION, and the CHECK statements all interact. To determine the impact of any one of these three statements, look at the other two. This interaction, which is used to enforce interrecord constraints, is, unfortunately, complicated and sometimes a bit mysterious. It requires that both the database designer and the application programmer know and remember the action of these statements. If the programmer does not understand this interaction, the results may be surprising.

The COLLECTION set represents the one-to-many relationship between TTLE and CPY. It is similar to the other set definitions except for the SET SELECTION statement, which is a combination of SET SELECTION and a CHECK statement. It indicates that the DBMS should preserve the interrecord constraint that the owner and member records in this set always have the same CALL# value. When the DBMS needs a set occurrence for some reason, it should select the one that will enable this constraint to be maintained. In addition, no data-item changes that would violate this constraint are to be allowed. This statement is equivalent to the combination of CHECK and SET SELECTION statements shown in the definitions for the sets T-A and A-T. Such a statement can be used only for non-information bearing sets.

The CHECKOUT set is similar to the other sets except that its INSERTION STATUS is MANUAL and RETENTION is OPTIONAL. Records are placed into this set by means of application programs, and they can be removed without restriction. This is appropriate, since copies of books can be checked out and returned dynamically. The order of this set is LAST, meaning that the member records will occur in the set in chronological order and that the book checked out first will be the first record in the set.

CHECKOUT and the next set, VCHKOUT, are the only sets in this database that have MANUAL and OPTIONAL status. The other records and sets represent more permanent conditions. For example, authors of book titles do not change. In this database, only the allocations of students to books or videos change. The last set is a system set containing all of the TTLE records in the database. Its purpose is to provide a logical ordering of TTLE records by CALL#.

The schema definition we just reviewed includes the major facilities of the 1981 DBTG DDL. It differs from earlier versions primarily in that it includes CHECK clauses and that keys and SET SELECTION statements are handled slightly differently. If you understand these statements in this schema, you should have little trouble understanding the statements in the schema definitions of DBMS products based on other versions of the DBTG model.

■ Defining Subschemas

Application programs do not access the database schema directly; instead, they view the database by way of subschemas. These subschemas are basically subsets of the schema. (The 1981 model does allow the definition of virtual records through joins of actual records. One implementation of this model, the product IDMS/R, uses this feature extensively.)

Unfortunately, there currently is no accepted DBTG standard for subschema descriptions. The 1981 schema language is incompatible with the 1978 subschema language (the last date for which a subschema standard was published). Work was never finished to reconcile these two because industry interest in this model waned as the relational model gained popularity. We show here a subschema as typically implemented in a commercial DBTG product.

■ Subschemas for the Library Database

To illustrate the definition and use of CODASYL DBTG subschemas, we consider two subschemas for the library database. Figure 14-19(a) shows the structure of the PURCHASE subschema, used by application programs in the purchasing depart-

FIGURE 14-19

Sample of Subschema Structures: (a) PURCHASE Subschema and (b) BORROW Subschema

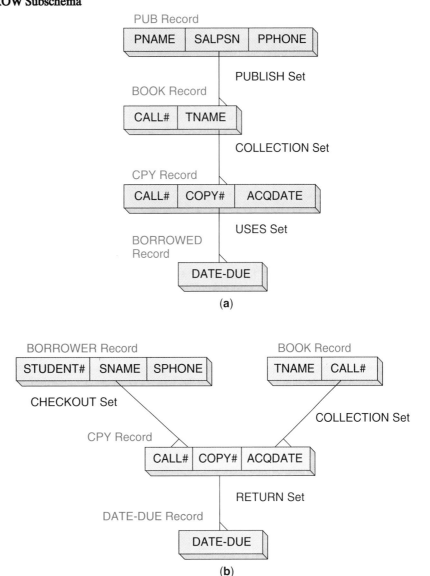

FIGURE 14-20

Format of Subschema Description, 1978 Specification

```
TITLE DIVISION.
 (subschema name)
MAPPING DIVISION.
ALIAS SECTION.
 (alternate names for records, sets, or data-items)
STRUCTURE DIVISION.
RECORD SECTION.
 (records and data-items that are to appear in the subschema)
SET SECTION.
 (sets to appear in the subschema)
```

ment. The second subschema, BORROW, is shown in Figure 14-19(b). BORROW is used by the checkout desk when books are lent.

PURCHASE SUBSCHEMA

The general format of a subschema description is shown in Figure 14-20. Each sub-schema description has three divisions. The TITLE DIVISION contains the name of the subschema; the MAPPING DIVISION contains alias descriptions; and the STRUCTURE DIVISION indicates the records, data-items, and sets in the schema that are present in the subschema.

Figure 14-21(a) has a subschema description for PURCHASE. In the MAP-PING DIVISION, the record TTLE is renamed BOOK, and the record DUE-DATE is renamed BORROWED. In addition, the set HISTORY is renamed USES, and the data-item DATE-DUE is named USE-DATE. The application program that accesses this subschema must use these aliases rather than the names in the schema description. AD is a keyword that stands for *alias definition.*

The RECORD SECTION of this subschema redefines the PUB record to omit the ADDRESS data-item. All the data-items in BOOK, CPY, and BORROWED should be part of the PURCHASE subschema. Finally, in the SET SECTION, the sets PUBLISH, COLLECTION, and USES are declared to be included in PUR-CHASE. SD is a keyword that stands for *set definition.*

BORROW SUBSCHEMA

The subschema BORROW is defined in Figure 14-21(b). The structure of the description is the same as that for PURCHASE. BORROW includes the BOOK (alias for TTLE), BORROWER (alias for STU), CPY, and DUE-DATE records. The sets included are COLLECTION, CHECKOUT, and RETURN (alias for HIS-TORY).

These figures are the essence of the CODASYL DBTG model's facility for sub-schema description. In the next chapter we demonstrate how these concepts were implemented in an actual DBMS product. For now, we use both the schema and subschema descriptions to illustrate the DML commands.

FIGURE 14-21

Example Subschema Definitions for Library Database: (a) PURCHASE Subschema Definition and (b) BORROW Subschema Description

```
TITLE DIVISION.
SS PURCHASE WITHIN LIBRARY.
MAPPING DIVISION.
ALIAS SECTION.
AD      RECORD TTLE IS BOOK.
AD      RECORD DUE-DATE IS BORROWED.
AD      SET HISTORY IS USES.
AD      DATE-DUE IS USE-DATE.
STRUCTURE DIVISION.
RECORD SECTION.
01      PUB.
        05                  PNAME      PIC X(10).
        05                  SALPSN     PIC X(20).
        05                  PHONE      PIC 9(10).
01      BOOK ALL.
01      CPY ALL.
01      BORROWED ALL.
SET SECTION.
SD      PUBLISH.
SD      COLLECTION.
SD      USES.
```

(a)

```
TITLE DIVISION.
SS BORROW WITHIN LIBRARY.
MAPPING DIVISION.
ALIAS SECTION.
AD      RECORD TTLE IS BOOK.
AD      RECORD STU IS BORROWER.
AD      SET HISTORY IS RETURN.
STRUCTURE DIVISION.
RECORD SECTION.
01      BOOK.
        05                  TNAME      PIC X(50).
        05                  CALL#      PIC X(8).
01      BORROWER ALL.
01      CPY ALL.
01      DUE-DATE ALL.
SET SECTION.
SD      COLLECTION.
SD      CHECKOUT.
SD      RETURN.
```

(b)

CODASYL DBTG DATA MANIPULATION LANGUAGE

This section presents the essence of the DBTG DML, its general concepts and single-record processing. Finally, we discuss DML processing of several records using sets.

■ General DML Concepts

Most CODASYL DBTG data manipulation commands have two steps. First, a FIND command is issued to identify the record to be acted on. The FIND command does not read or otherwise process the indicated record; it simply identifies a record for the DBMS to locate. After a record has been identified, a second DML command can be issued to perform an operation on it. Typical patterns are FIND, GET; or FIND, MODIFY; or FIND, ERASE.[1]

The only DML command that does not follow this pattern is STORE. Since this command inserts a new record into the database, there is nothing to be found before it is executed.

As we stated, every DBTG run-unit (a particular user connected to a particular program) has a user working area (UWA). The records in the subschema are stored in the UWA. For the PURCHASE subschema, there are four records in the UWA: PUB, BOOK, CPY, and BORROWED. For the BORROW subschema, they are BOOK, BORROWER, CPY, and DUE-DATE. The UWA contains other data as well, in particular, currency indicators and special registers.

CURRENCY INDICATORS

Currency indicators are place markers. When the program issues a FIND command, a record is found and its identity is stored in a special variable called a **currency indicator.** Subsequently, when a GET, MODIFY, ERASE, or other command is issued, the DBMS references the currency indicator to determine which record to act on. Currency indicators also are used as reference points for sequential-processing commands such as FIND NEXT or FIND PRIOR.

There are several currency indicators, one for every record type and set type in the subschema. These indicators identify the most recently processed record of a type or in a set. The run-unit itself has a currency indicator that identifies the most recently processed record of any type. The PURCHASE subschema has currency indicators for the PUB, BOOK, CPY, and BORROWED records; for the PUBLISH, COLLECTION, and USES sets; and for the run-unit that is processing the subschema. For the BORROW subschema there are indicators for the BOOK, BORROWER, CPY, and DUE-DATE records; for the COLLECTION, CHECKOUT, and RETURN sets; and for the run-unit that is processing this subschema. Initially, all of these currency indicators are null, indicating that no record has been accessed. As the records are processed, the DBMS updates the currency indicator values.

The currency indicators can be envisioned as variables in a table. Figure 14-22 lists those for the BORROW subschema as it is processed. The top row shows the

---

[1] Because the combination FIND, GET is so common, some products have defined a special command for the combination. IDMS/R, for example, defines the OBTAIN command as the combination FIND, GET. The options and syntax of OBTAIN are the same as for FIND.

FIGURE 14-22

Currency Indicators for the BORROW Subschema

Currency Indicator For

Statement	RUN-UNIT	BOOK	BORROWER	CPY	DUE-DATE	COLLECTION	CHECKOUT	RETURN
Initial	NULL	NULL	NULL	NULL	NULL	NULL	NULL	NULL
FIND BORROWER with STUDENT# = 150	BORROWER 150	NULL	BORROWER 150	NULL	NULL	NULL	BORROWER 150	NULL
FIND CPY R726.8.L, COPY 3	CPY R726.8.L COPY 3	NULL	BORROWER 150	CPY R726.8.L COPY 3	NULL	CPY R726.8.L COPY 3	CPY R726.8.L COPY 3	CPY R726.8.L COPY 3

initial status of all the currency indicators. The indicator in the first column is the current of run-unit (the most recently processed record of any type), and the indicators in other columns refer to the record and set types as listed.

The FIND command sets the currency indicator values. For example, when a FIND command is executed to FIND the BORROWER record with STUDENT equal to 150, the currents of run-unit, BORROWER, and CHECKOUT all are set to point to the record for BORROWER 150 (see the second row in Figure 14-22). If a FIND command were then issued to locate the CPY record with CALL equal to "R726.8.L" and COPY equal to "3," the currents of run-unit, CPY, CHECKOUT, COLLECTION, and RETURN would be set to point to the CPY record having "R726.8.L", COPY "3." The modified currency indicators are shown in the third row. Notice that the current of BORROWER is not affected by the second FIND command.

SPECIAL REGISTERS

Special registers are also kept in the UWA. Unlike machine registers (you might remember them from a systems architecture or assembly-language course), these "registers" are simply data fields in which the DBMS places system information for the application program to access, such as return codes and error messages. For example, after a DML command is executed, the DBMS places a return code in a register called DB-STATUS. If the command is executed without problems, it sets DB-STATUS to zero. Other values of DB-STATUS indicate an error or an unusual situation. One common use of DB-STATUS is to signal end-of-data. Other special registers are DB-SET-NAME, DB-DATA-NAME, and DB-RECORD NAME. The first two are set only when an error is made. The DBMS places in these registers the names of the record and the data-item it was processing at the time of the error. DB-RECORD-NAME is set when an error occurs and also whenever a FIND or STORE command has been executed. This data is useful when the application program is processing records in a set that has more than one record type as members.

■ DBTG DML for Single-Record Processing

The following examples show how FIND is used in conjunction with other commands to process the database. The commands are shown in pseudocode form, and the particular syntax of each depends on the language in which they are embedded and on the particular implementation of the DBTG model.

Suppose we want to read the BORROWER record for STUDENT 150. The following commands will do this:

```
MOVE "150" TO STUDENT# IN BORROWER
FIND ANY BORROWER USING STUDENT#
GET BORROWER
```

The FIND command sets the currents of run-unit, BORROWER, and CHECKOUT to point to the record for Student 150. Then the GET command places the record into the BORROWER record area in the UWA. GET always operates on the current of the run-unit record.

Suppose we want to read all the CPY records for a book with the call number R726.8.L:

```
MOVE "R726.8.L" TO Call# IN CPY
FIND ANY CPY USING Call#
DOWHILE DB-STATUS = 0
            GET CPY
            (process CPY data)
            FIND DUPLICATE CPY USING Call#
END-DO
```

DB-STATUS is used here to control the loop processing. This code assumes that DB-STATUS will be set to a value other than zero only at the end-of-data. A more sophisticated (and appropriate) algorithm would examine the value of DB-STATUS to ensure that no other condition or error had occurred. The first FIND specifies that ANY record can qualify, and the next FIND specifies DUPLICATE. This keyword means that the desired record must have the same value of CALL that the current of CPY contains.

To illustrate the elimination of records, suppose we want to delete all CPY records of the book having the call number R726.8.L60:

```
MOVE "R726.8.L" TO Call# IN CPY
FIND FOR UPDATE ANY CPY USING Call#
DOWHILE DB-STATUS = 0
            ERASE CPY
            FIND FOR UPDATE DUPLICATE CPY USING Call#
END-DO
```

The logic is similar to that for the GET, except that the ERASE command is used in this example. Also, the words FOR UPDATE are added to the FIND command. These keywords inform the DBMS that an update is to occur, and accordingly, the DBMS locks the record for the run-unit. This is similar to the DL/I GET HOLD commands described in the previous chapter.

To illustrate the modification of records, suppose that the BORROWER with STUDENT of 150 changes her name to WILLIS:

```
MOVE "150" TO STUDENT# IN BORROWER
FIND FOR UPDATE ANY BORROWER USING STUDENT#
GET BORROWER
IF DB-STATUS = 0
    THEN MOVE "WILLIS" TO SNAME IN BORROWER
        MODIFY SNAME
    ELSE do error processing
END-IF
```

In this case, the MODIFY statement indicates that only the SNAME data-item has been changed. If no data-item is listed, the DBMS is to assume that the entire record (or this subschema's view of it) has been changed.

To create a new record, we first build it in the UWA and then issue a STORE command. The following statements insert a BORROWER record into the database:

```
MOVE "2000" TO STUDENT# IN BORROWER
MOVE "CALBOM" TO SNAME IN BORROWER
MOVE "5258869" TO PHONE IN BORROWER
STORE BORROWER
```

After the STORE command, the new record is the currents of run-unit, BORROWER, and CHECKOUT.

Although not shown, the program should examine DB-STATUS to determine whether the command executed successfully. In fact, DB-STATUS should be examined after every DBMS command. In these and the following examples, we sometimes omit this examination and subsequent error processing, in order to simplify the discussion. Remember, however, that actual application programs should examine DB-STATUS after every command and do the appropriate error processing.

■ Processing Multiple Records with Sets

Sets are used to process records by relationship. Three commands are used to insert and remove records from sets, and then several different formats of the FIND command are used to process the records in sets.

INSERTING INTO AND REMOVING RECORDS FROM SETS

The DBTG model provides three commands for processing set members: CONNECT, DISCONNECT, and RECONNECT. The first command places a record into a set; the second removes a record from a set; and the third changes the set membership.

The allowed use of these commands depends on the set insertion and retention status. The insertion status governs the use of CONNECT, and the retention status governs the use of DISCONNECT and RECONNECT. If the insertion status is AUTOMATIC, then CONNECT is unnecessary, at least when the record is created. (If the set retention status is OPTIONAL, the record may be removed from its initial set assignment and later placed in a new set using CONNECT.) If the insertion status is MANUAL, then CONNECT must be used to place the record into a set. If the retention status is FIXED, then DISCONNECT and RECONNECT are invalid. If the retention status is MANDATORY, then RECONNECT is valid, but DISCONNECT is not. If the retention status is OPTIONAL, both of these commands are valid.

The COLLECTION and CHECKOUT sets in the BORROW subschema represent the two extremes. COLLECTION is AUTOMATIC/FIXED, and CHECKOUT is MANUAL/OPTIONAL. None of these commands is valid for COLLECTION. Since the insertion status is AUTOMATIC, CONNECT is unnecessary. Since the retention status is FIXED, neither DISCONNECT nor RECONNECT is valid.

On the other hand, all of these commands are necessary and valid for CHECKOUT. CONNECT must be used to place a record into CHECKOUT, and both RECONNECT and DISCONNECT may then be used.

CONNECT places the current of the member record type into the current of the set. To illustrate its operation, suppose that Student 150 wishes to check out copy 2 of the book with the call number R726.8.L. The following statements can do this:

MOVE "R726.8.L" to Call#

MOVE "2" TO COPY#

FIND ANY CPY USING CALL#, COPY#

MOVE "150" TO STUDENT#

FIND ANY BORROWER USING STUDENT#

CONNECT CPY TO CHECKOUT

The first FIND command establishes copy 2 of R726.8.L as the current of CPY. The second FIND then establishes Student 150 as the current of the CHECKOUT set. The copy is then placed in the set with CONNECT. Since the SET SELECTION clause is BY VALUE OF STUDENT, the second FIND command is not necessary. If it were not there, the DBMS would use the value of STUDENT to determine the set occurrence for the CONNECT command.

DISCONNECT operates in a similar fashion. The current of member record type is removed from the current of set. The following commands take copy 2 of R726.8.L from the set owned by Student 150:

MOVE "R726.8.L" to CALL#

MOVE "2" TO COPY#

FIND ANY CPY USING CALL#, COPY#

MOVE "150" TO STUDENT#

FIND ANY BORROWER USING STUDENT#

DISCONNECT CPY FROM CHECKOUT

As with CONNECT, the second FIND statement is unnecessary, since the SET SELECTION is BY VALUE OF STUDENT.

RECONNECT operates by disconnecting the current of a record type from its occurrence in a set and connecting it to the current occurrence of that same set. For example, the following commands reassign copy 2 of book R726.8.L from Student 150 to Student 400:

MOVE "R726.8.L" to CALL#

MOVE "2" TO COPY

FIND ANY CPY USING CALL#, COPY#

MOVE "400" TO STUDENT#

FIND ANY BORROWER USING STUDENT#

RECONNECT CPY TO CHECKOUT

The first FIND command establishes the current of CPY, and the next one establishes Student 400 as the current of CHECKOUT. The record is then moved from Student 150's set occurrence to Student 400's set occurrence.

As we stated, when the set insertion status is AUTOMATIC, the DBMS connects records to sets when they are created. An appropriate record must be available to serve as the parent at the time the new record is created. For example, when a new CPY record is created, it is automatically inserted into a COLLECTION set. The appropriate BOOK record must exist in the database:

MOVE "PS477.5C" TO CALL# IN CPY
MOVE "3" TO COPY# IN CPY
MOVE "11/14/87" TO ACQDATE IN CPY
STORE CPY

When the STORE command is executed, CPY is automatically inserted into the COLLECTION set occurrence of which PS477.5C is the parent. If this BOOK does not exist, an error will result.

The new CPY record is connected to the appropriate set because of the STRUCTURAL SET SELECTION statement in the definition of COLLECTION. This statement means, when necessary, find a parent record of COLLECTION that will make the CALL in the child record equal to the CALL in the parent record. Since the insertion status of COLLECTION is AUTOMATIC, the DBMS must find such a parent when the STORE is executed.

Processing a MANDATORY set is similar except that once a record is placed in a set (either MANUAL or AUTOMATIC, depending on its insertion status), only the RECONNECT command may be used. DISCONNECT is not allowed.

SET MEMBERSHIP AND ERASE COMMANDS

If a record owns a set occurrence, special considerations will apply when the record is deleted. The application program can request that all children (and children of children, and so forth) be erased when the record is erased, or it can be more selective.

Suppose we want to delete a BOOK record and all of the CPY and DUE-DATE records that pertain to this book. The following statements can do this for the book whose call number is Q360.C33:

MOVE "Q360.C33" TO CALL#
FIND FOR UPDATE ANY BOOK USING CALL#
ERASE ALL BOOK

The keyword ALL in this ERASE command directs the DBMS to erase all CPY records (and all DUE-DATE records belonging to the set owned by CPY).

If ALL is not specified in the ERASE command, the result will depend on the retention status of the owned sets. If the retention status is FIXED, the ERASE will be successful, and all the owned children records will be erased as well. If the retention status is MANDATORY, the ERASE will be disallowed. If it were allowed, the remaining child records would be fragments. Their retention status is MANDATORY, and they must reside in a set. If the DBMS were to erase their parent, it would not know what to do with the fragments.

If the retention status is OPTIONAL, the ERASE will be allowed, and any child records will be disconnected from the set, but they will remain in the database.

USING SETS FOR RECORD RETRIEVAL

Once records have been placed in sets, set membership can be used to retrieve records by relationships. Or in the terminology of this text, sets and set membership can be used to construct objects from records.

Suppose we want to process a view of the STUDENT object that contains both BORROWER and CPY records. Say we want to retrieve the call numbers of all the books on loan to Student 400. The following statements do this:

```
MOVE "400" TO STUDENT#
FIND ANY BORROWER USING STUDENT#
FIND FIRST CPY WITHIN CHECKOUT
DOWHILE DB-STATUS & 0
        GET CPY
        (process CPY record to display CALL#)
        FIND NEXT CPY WITHIN CHECKOUT
END-DO
```

The first FIND command establishes the currents of both BORROWER and CHECKOUT. The next FIND command sets the current of CPY to the first record in the set owned by the BORROWER with STUDENT of 400. The first record is then processed, and the next one is identified with the FIND NEXT command. In addition to FIND FIRST and FIND NEXT, this model also provides FIND LAST and FIND nth, where n is the ordinal position of the record in the set. This last option is useful only if the set members are ordered in some manner.

Suppose we want not only the call numbers of all books on loan to Student 400 but also the titles. Titles are stored in TTLE records, and therefore we must retrieve the owner of each CPY record. Thus we start with student, find a CPY record owned by that student, find the parent of that record, and then repeat this for the next CPY record owned by that student. This can be done as follows:

```
MOVE "400" TO STUDENT#
FIND ANY BORROWER USING STUDENT#
FIND FIRST CPY WITHIN CHECKOUT
DOWHILE DB-STATUS & 0
        GET CPY
        FIND OWNER WITHIN COLLECTION
        GET TTLE
        (process CPY and TTLE records to display CALL#
and
           title)
        FIND NEXT CPY WITHIN CHECKOUT
END-DO
```

The FIND OWNER statement establishes the owner of the CPY record as the current of run-unit.

THE CODASYL DBTG MODEL AS A MODEL

The CODASYL DBTG model is a rich, comprehensive, and complicated model. Because of its long history and the many different versions, committees, companies, and people involved, it is inconsistent and difficult to comprehend. As a model, however, it is rich enough to encompass the expression of database designs and application program logic for transaction processing databases and applications.

You may think of this situation as analogous to using pseudocode for specifying program logic. Pseudocode is vague in some ways, but it is entirely adequate for expressing program logic. Of course, when the logic is expressed in a programming language, the vagueness is replaced with statements that have one, and only one, interpretation to the language compiler. So it is with this model. The DBTG model can be used to express designs and logic, and within the parameters of the model, the statements can mean what you want them to mean. Once the database is implemented, however, and a particular DBMS product is used, then the statements available and their function and meaning become precise.

SUMMARY

Like the hierarchical data model, the network data model is the basis for many DBMS products that perform transaction processing. The most significant network data model is known as the CODASYL DBTG data model, named after the committee that developed it. The most significant difference between the network data model and the hierarchical data model is that simple networks can be represented directly in the network model. Thus it was an improvement over the earlier hierarchical model.

The history of the CODASYL DBTG data model is a long one. Essentially, many people helped develop it, and its many options and formats reflect the views of these many participants. It is a rich but not very cohesive model.

The DBTG model introduced the concepts of both a data definition and a data manipulation language for DBMS products. Unlike DL/I, which has no database definition facilities, products based on the DBTG model provide both languages.

A schema is a logical view of the entire database as seen by the database administration. A subschema is a subset of the database, like a view in the relational model. A subschema is the application program's view of the database.

All user interactions with the database are carried out by means of application programs (there is no interactive query language in the model). An application program can be run by one or more users. Each user has his or her own user work area for passing data to and from the DBMS.

The building blocks used for DBTG data definition are data-items (or fields), records (collections of data-items), and sets (a set is a one-to-many relationship between records). These building blocks can be used to represent all the object types we have discussed in this text: composite, compound, and association. When defining the database, it is easy to transform the relational database definition into the DBTG database definition.

When defining DBTG sets, we specify various options such as how the members will be ordered, how they will be placed in a set occurrence (insertion status), and how, if at all, a member can be removed from a set occurrence (retention status). These options allow us to enforce some database constraints. However, the DBTG model does not provide complete and comprehensive facilities for enforcing all constraints.

Among the constraints the DBTG model does enforce are domain constraints (allowable values and mandatory existence), intrarecord constraints (uniqueness, of both individual data-item values and composite data-item values), and interrecord constraints (referential integrity, by means of set retention status and the CHECK command).

The DBTG model also offers a data manipulation language. Generally, the database is accessed in two steps: The first is used to identify the record to be acted on, and the second performs some operation. The DBTG FIND statement is used to identify a record. When executed, the FIND statement sets the value of one or more currency indicators.

A currency indicator is a place marker that points to the most recently identified record in a record type, set, or run-unit. Each execution of a FIND may modify one or several of these place markers. After a currency indicator is set, a subsequent instruction can access the record to which it is pointing.

Special registers are data-items in the user work area whose values are set by the DBMS to report on the status of the system. They can be accessed by the application program. Special registers are used to indicate error conditions, end-of-data, the name of the most recently processed record, and so forth.

DBTG commands are available to read, insert, modify, and delete database records. DBTG DML can be used to access and process individual database records and to process sets. The syntax shown in this chapter is generic; the exact syntax varies with the DBMS product.

GROUP I QUESTIONS

14.1   Explain the relationship among user, run-unit, application program, subschema, schema, database, and DBMS.

14.2   Define *data-item*. How are data-items related to domains? How are domains defined using the DBTG model?

14.3   Define *record* as used in the DBTG model.

14.4   Define the following terms and explain their purpose: set, owner, member, set occurrence.

14.5   Give an example of a set structure, and sketch two occurrences of this set.

14.6   Consider the following tree: School districts have schools, and schools have pupils (one record type) and teachers (another record type). Teachers have past assignments. Show a DBTG representation of this tree, and describe two occurrences.

14.7   Consider the following simple network: Fathers have children, and teachers teach children. Show a DBTG representation of this simple network, and describe two occurrences.

14.8   Consider the following complex network: Children have many hobbies, and a hobby is enjoyed by many children. Show a DBTG representation of this complex network, and describe two occurrences.

14.9   List the DBTG currency indicators, and describe situations in which each would be used.

14.10 Explain how most DBTG DML operations are executed in two steps.

For Questions 14.11 through 14.16, provide pseudocode similar to that used in this chapter, based on the following model:

SALESPERSON with data-items NAME, AGE, SALARY
ORDER with data-items NUMBER, CUST-NAME, SALESPERSONNAME, AMOUNT
CUSTOMER with data-items NAME, CITY, INDUSTRY-TYPE
SET SALE with owner SALESPERSON and member ORDER
SET PURCHASE with owner CUSTOMER and member ORDER

14.11 Retrieve

    a. Customer with name ABC CONSTRUCTION.

    b. Order with number 12345.

    c. All orders for customer ABC CONSTRUCTION.

14.12 Delete all orders for salesperson PARKS.

14.13 Change the industry type of ABC Construction to type J (assume that INDUSTRY-TYPE is a character data-item).

14.14 Store a new SALESPERSON record: The name is CURTIS, the age is 39, and the salary is 65,000.

14.15 Change the name of customer ABC Construction to SoftSystems, and change the ORDER records as well, assuming that the retention status of PURCHASE is

    a. OPTIONAL

    b. MANDATORY

    c. FIXED

14.16 Assume that both SALE and PURCHASE are MANUAL, OPTIONAL sets.

    a. Create an ORDER record and place it in the correct set occurrences of PURCHASE and SALE.

    b. Change the name of a customer in an ORDER record, and RECONNECT it to the correct occurrence (assume that the record is already in an occurrence).

    c. Remove all ORDERs for customer JONES from the sets to which they belong.

GROUP II QUESTIONS

14.17 Modify Figure 14-10(b) to make it a non-information bearing set. Modify Figures 14-11(b), 14-12(b), and 14-13(b) to make all sets information bearing ones. Modify Figure 14-14(b) to make CHECKOUT a non-information bearing set, and COLLECTION an information bearing set. Are any of these reversals impossible to carry out? Why?

14.18 Compare and contrast the DBTG model with the relational model. Which model is easier to understand? Which do you think would be easier to use? For what applications would the DBTG model be preferable to the relational model? For what applications would the relational model be preferable to the DBTG model?

14.19 Locate a company in your community that uses a CODASYL DBTG DBMS. Talk to some of the people who work there, and find out how the schemas and subschemas are designed. If possible, get a copy of a schema, subschema, and application program, and compare them with the concepts described in this chapter.

Administration

Part VI turns to the subjects of data administration and database administration. As you will learn, the difference between these two topics concerns scope. The scope of data administration is wide, encompassing data throughout the entire organization, whereas the scope of database administration is narrow, pertaining to a particular database rather than to the organization as a whole. Chapter 15, the sole chapter in this part, also discusses reliability and security, two important concerns of database administration.

DATA ADMINISTRATION AND DATABASE ADMINISTRATION

Data is an important organizational asset, and so organizations must establish policies, procedures, standards, and similar management structures to ensure that the data is both protected and well utilized. Data administration and database administration are two organizational functions that have these responsibilities. This chapter begins by describing the need for data administration, its challenges, and its basic functions. The next section addresses database administration, reliability, and security, looking at some of the problems that can occur and solutions to them. Solutions can be either *pro*active (preventing the problems) or *re*active (responding to failure). The chapter concludes with a model of security and describes several types of database security schemes.

The first half of this chapter concerns broad management issues, and the second half describes specific techniques and technology. This combination may seem odd, but it does reflect the nature of these functions. Data administration and database administration require both management and diplomacy skills and technical competency. Accordingly, it is often difficult to know the nature of the work of someone who has the title of data administrator or database administrator. Such a person could be management oriented and concerned with the large issues of effective data usage in the organization, or he or she could be technically oriented and narrowly focused on the details of database design and implementation, DBMS tuning, and the like. As you read this chapter, keep these differences in mind.

DATA AS AN ORGANIZATIONAL ASSET

An organization's data is as much of a resource as are its plant, equipment, and financial assets. Data is time-consuming and expensive to acquire, and it is important not only to an organization's operations and management but also to its product's quality and delivery. Data often serves to establish and maintain the organization's competitive advantage. For example, consider the value of a customer list to a mail-order company or the value of price and volume histories to a stock broker. Because of its value, organizational data should be managed as other organizational assets are. In recognition of this need, many organizations have established offices of data administration and database administration, to guard and protect the data and also to ensure that it is used effectively.

In some ways, data administration is to data what the controller is to money. The responsibility of a controller is to ensure not only that financial assets are protected and accounted for but also that they are effectively used. Storing an organization's money in a vault can protect it, but it will not be effectively used. Instead, it must be invested in ways that advance the organization's goals and objectives. Similarly, with data administration, simply protecting the data is not enough. Data administration and database administration must also try to increase the utility of the organization's data.

DATA ADMINISTRATION

The terms **data administration** and **database administration** both are used in industry. In some cases the terms are considered synonymous; in other cases they have different meanings. In this text, we use the term *data administration* to refer to a function that applies to all of the organization. Sometimes the term *global database administration* is used instead of *data administration*. The term *database administration* refers to a function that is specific to a particular database, including the systems that process that database.

■ Need for Data Administration

To understand the need for data administration, consider the analogy of a university library. The typical university library contains hundreds of thousands of books, journals, magazines, government reports, and so forth, but they offer no utility while they are on the bookshelves. To be useful, they must be made available to people who have an interest in and need for them.

Clearly, the library must have some means of describing its collection so that potential users can determine what is available. At first glance, this might seem like a trivial problem. You might say, "Well, build a card catalog." But much work must be done to be able to do that. How should the library's works be identified? How should they be described? Even more basic, what constitutes a work? How can we accommodate different ways of identifying works (ISBN, Dewey decimal system, government report number, or whatever)? How do we help people find things that they may not know exist?

Other complications arise. Suppose the university is so large that it has several libraries. In this case, how are the collections to be managed as one resource? Furthermore, some departments may maintain their own libraries. Are these to be made part of the university system? Many professors have extensive personal libraries. Should these be part of the system?

■ Challenges of Data Administration

The library analogy does not go far enough, however, as organizational data administration is considerably more difficult than library administration. First, it is not at all clear what constitutes a work in an organization. Libraries contain books, periodicals, and so forth, but organizational data comes in myriads of formats. Organizations have traditional data records, but they also have documents, spreadsheets, graphics and illustrations, technical drawings, audio and video files, and so forth. How should all of these be described? What are the basic categories of organizational data? These questions are important because their answers determine how the data will be organized, managed, protected, and accessed.

Most organizations have many names for the same thing. For instance, a telephone number can be described as a PhoneNumber, Phone, TelephoneNumber, EmployeePhone, DeptPhone, and so forth. Which of these names is preferable? When a graphic designer places a telephone number on a new form, what label should he or she use? When a programmer writes a new program, what name should he or she use for the program variable that holds the telephone number? Clearly, there are economies in using the same name, at least for many applications.

There also are many ways of representing the data element. A phone number can be represented as a ten-digit integer, a ten-digit text field, a thirteen-digit text field in the form *(nnn)nnn-nnnn,* a twelve-digit text field in the form *nnn-nnn-nnnn,* or in still other formats. Which of these should be allowed? Which, if any, should be the standard?

Such differences between organizational data and library materials are miniscule, however, when compared with the next difference: People must be able to change organizational data.

In contrast, consider what would happen at the library if people checked out books, wrote in them, tore out pages, added pages, and then put the books back on the shelves. Or, even worse, suppose someone checked out three books, made changes in all three, checked them back in, and told the librarian: "Either change all of these or none of them."

When people change data, however, they do not immediately change the data in the database. Instead, they read a copy of the data into the application program, change it there, and then attempt to replace the official copy of the data with their changed copy. In multiuser systems, because several people may be doing this at the same time, it clearly is possible for users' activities to interfere with one another.

In addition to all of these operationally oriented challenges, there are organizational issues. For example, data can mean organizational power; hence changes in data control can mean changes in power. Thus, behind the tasks of data administra-

FIGURE 15-1

Challenges of Data
Administration

- Many types of data exist.
- Basic categories of data are not obvious.
- The same data can have many names.
- The same data can have many descriptions and formats.
- Data is changed — often concurrently.
- Political - organizational issues complicate operational issues.

tion lie all sorts of political issues. A discussion of these is beyond the scope of this text, but they are important nonetheless. The challenges for data administration are summarized in Figure 15-1.

Functions of Data Administration

Because of the challenges just described, data administration is complex. To protect the data while at the same time increasing its utility to the organization, a number of different functions or tasks must be performed. As shown in Figure 15-2, these activities can be grouped into several different categories.

MARKETING

First and foremost, data administration is responsible for declaring its existence and selling its services to the rest of the organization. Employees need to know that data administration exists, that there are policies, standards, and guidelines that pertain to organizational data and the reasons for them, and they need to be given reasons for respecting and following data administration rules, guidelines, and restrictions.

As Vinden points out, data administration must be, in the final analysis, a service function, and the users must perceive it in that way.[1] Thus, data administration activities must be communicated to the organization in a positive, service-providing light. Employees must believe that they have something to gain from data administration. Otherwise, the function becomes all cost and no benefit to the users, and it will be ignored.

DATA STANDARDS

For organizational data to be managed effectively, it must be organized coherently. If each department, function, or employee were to choose a different definition for a data item or for the means by which data items are to be named or described, the result would be chaos. It would be impossible even to compile an inventory of data, let alone manage it. Consequently, many organizations decide that important data

---

[1] Robin J. Vinden, *Data Dictionaires for Database Administration* (Blue Ridge Summit, PA: TAB Books, 1990), p. 18.

FIGURE 15-2

Functions of Data
Administration

Marketing
- Communicate existence of data administration to organization.
- Explain reason for existence of standards and policies.
- Describe in a positive light the services provided.

Data Standards
- Establish standard means for describing data items. Standards include name, definition, description, processing restrictions, and so forth.
- Establish data proponents.

Data Policies
- Establish organizationwide data policy. Examples are security, data proponency, and distribution.

Forum for Data Conflict Resolution
- Establish procedures for reporting conflicts.
- Provide means for hearing all perspectives and views.
- Have authority to make decision to resolve conflict.

Return on Organization's Data Investment
- Focus attention on value of data investment.
- Investigate new methodologies and technologies.
- Take proactive attitude toward information management.

items will be described in a standard way. For example, data administration may decide that every data item of importance to the organization will be described by a standard name, definition, description, set of processing restrictions, and the like. Once this structure is determined, the next question is who will set the values of these standard descriptions. For example, who will decide the standard name or standard-processing restrictions?

In most organizations, the data administration group does not determine the standard descriptions. Instead, each item is assigned a **data proponent,** a department or other organizational unit in charge of managing that data item. The proponent is given the responsibility for establishing and maintaining the official organizational definitions for the data items assigned to it. Even though the data administration group may be the proponent of some data items, most proponents come from other departments.

You may encounter the term *data owner*, which is generally used in the same way that the term *data proponent* is used in this text. We avoid the term here because it implies a degree of propriety that does not exist. Both legally and practically, the organization is the one and only owner of the data. Although some group or groups have a legitimate claim to a greater degree of authority over particular data than others do, these groups do not own that data. Hence we use the term *data proponent* instead.

To summarize, the foundation of data administration is a system of data standards. The data administration group is responsible for working with users and management to develop a workable system of standards, which must be documented and communicated to the organization by some effective means. Procedures for assessing the employees' compliance with the standards also must be established.

DATA POLICIES

Another group of data administration functions concerns data policies. To illustrate the need for such policies, first consider data security. Every organization has data that is proprietary or sensitive, and data administration is responsible for developing a security system to protect it. Questions like the following need to be addressed: What security schemes should be put in place? Does the organization need a multilevel security system similar to that of the military? Or would a simpler system suffice? The security policy must also decide what is required for someone to have access to sensitive data, what agreements they must sign to do so. What about employees of other organizations? Should sensitive data be copied? How should employees be trained with regard to security? What should be done when security procedures are violated?

A second type of data policy concerns data proponents and processing rights. What does being a data proponent mean? What rights does the proponent have that other groups do not? Who decides who will become a data proponent, and how can this be changed?

A third example of the need for data policy concerns the distribution of data, such as whether official data should be distributed on more than one computer and, if so, which, if any, should be the official copy. What processing should allowed on distributed data? Should data that has been distributed be returned to the official data store? If so, what checks must there be to validate it before accepting it?

FORUM FOR DATA CONFLICT RESOLUTION

To be effective, organizational data must be shared, but humans have difficulty sharing. Consequently, the organization must be prepared to address disputes regarding data proponents, processing restrictions, and other matters.

The first responsibility of data administration in this regard is to establish procedures for reporting conflicts. When one user's or group's needs conflict with another's, the groups need a way to make their conflict known in an orderly manner. Once the conflict has been acknowledged, established procedures should allow all involved parties to present their case. Data administration staff, perhaps in conjunction with the data proponents involved, then must resolve the conflict. This scenario assumes that the organization has granted to data administration the authority to make and enforce the resulting decision.

Data administration provides a forum for resolving conflicts that apply to the entire organization. Database administration also provides a forum for resolving conflicts, but those that pertain to a particular database.

INCREASING THE RETURN ON THE ORGANIZATION'S DATA INVESTMENT

A final function for data administration is the need to increase the organization's return on its data investment. Data administration is the department that asks such questions as, Are we getting what we should be getting from our data resource? If so, can we get more? If not, why not? Is it all worthwhile? This function involves all of the others: It includes marketing, the establishment of standards or policies, conflict resolution, and so forth. Sometimes this function also means investigating new techniques for storing, processing, or presenting data; new methodologies and technology; and the like.

The successful fulfillment of this role requires a *proactive* attitude toward information management. Relevant questions are whether we can use information to increase our market position, our economic competitiveness, and our overall net worth. Data administration must work closely with the organization's planning and development departments to anticipate rather than just react to the need for new information requirements.

DATABASE ADMINISTRATION

Whereas the scope of activity for data administration is the entire organization, the scope of activity for database administration is restricted to a particular database and the systems that process it. Database administration operates within the framework provided by data administration to facilitate the development and use of a particular database and its applications. The acronym **DBA** is used to refer to both the function *database administration* and the job title *database administrator.*

Chapter 1 described the various levels of databases and database applications, and the database administration function exists at all of them, although it varies in complexity. Database administration is considerably simpler for personal than for work-group applications, and database administration for work-group applications is, in turn, considerably simpler than for organizational applications.

Often personal database administration is informal. For example, individuals follow simple procedures for backing up their database, and they keep minimal records for documentation. In this case, the person who uses the database performs the DBA functions. More administration is required for work-group applications, and typically one or two persons fulfill this function on a part-time basis.

At the organizational level, database administration responsibilities are often too time-consuming and too varied to be handled even by a single full-time person. Supporting a database with dozens or hundreds of users requires considerable time as well as both technical knowledge and diplomatic skills and usually is handled by an office of database administration. The manager of the office is often known as the *database administrator*, and in this case, the acronym *DBA* refers to either the office or the manager.

The overall responsibility of the DBA is to facilitate the development and use of the database within the context of guidelines set out by data administration. Usually this means balancing the conflicting goals of protecting the database and maximizing its availability and benefit to users.

The DBA also is responsible for the development, operation, and maintenance of the database and its applications, specifically

- Managing the database structure.
- Managing data activity.
- Managing the DBMS.
- Establishing the database data dictionary.
- Providing for database reliability.
- Providing for database security.

■ Managing the Database Structure

Managing the database structure includes participating in the initial database design and implementation as well as controlling and managing changes in it. Ideally, the DBA is involved early in the development of the database and its applications, participates in the requirements study, helps evaluate alternatives, including the DBMS to be used, and helps design the database structure. For large, organizational applications, the DBA usually is a manager who supervises the work of technically oriented database design personnel.

Once the database has been designed, it is implemented using the DBMS product, and the database data is created. The DBA participates in the development of procedures and controls to ensure high integrity and quality of the database data.

Users' requirements change; users find better ways to accomplish their goals; database technology changes; and DBMS vendors upgrade their products. All changes in the database structure or procedures need to be carefully managed. Change in the database structure is usually an evolutionary—not a revolutionary—process.

CONFIGURATION CONTROL

After a database and its applications have been implemented, requests for changes are inevitable. For example, requests can arise from new requirements or can result from an inadequate understanding of the requirements. In any case, the changes must be made with regard to the entire database community, because the impact of the changes is seldom felt by only one application. In some cases, the DBA may decide that even though a particular change has a negative effect on one or a few users, it is in the best interests of the company to make it. Accordingly, she should carefully explain her decision to the affected user group.

Effective database administration should include procedures and policies by which users can register their need for change, the entire community can discuss the impacts of the change, and a decision can be made to implement or not the proposed change.

Because of the size and complexity of a database and its applications, changes sometimes have unexpected results. The DBA thus must be prepared to repair the database and to gather sufficient information to diagnose and correct the problem that caused the damage. The database is most vulnerable to failure after a change.

DOCUMENTATION

The DBA's final responsibility in managing the database structure is documentation. It is extremely important to know what changes have been made, how they were made, and when they were made. A change in the database structure may cause an error that is not revealed for six months, and without proper documentation of the change, diagnosing the problem is next to impossible. Dozens of job reruns may be required to identify the point at which certain symptoms first appeared, and for this reason, it also is important to maintain a record of the test procedures and test runs made to verify a change. If standardized test procedures, test forms, and record-keeping methods are used, recording the test results does not have to be time-consuming.

Although maintaining documentation is tedious and unfulfilling, the effort pays off when disaster strikes and the documentation is the difference between solving and not solving a major (and costly) problem. Today, a number of products are emerging that ease the burden of documentation. Many CASE tools, for example, can be used to document logical database designs. Data dictionaries also provide documentation assistance, and other products that read and interpret the database data structures maintained by popular DBMS products are available.

Another reason for carefully documenting changes in the database structure is to use historical data properly. If, for example, marketing wants to analyze three-year-old sales data that has been in the archives for two years, it will be necessary to know what structure was current at the time the data was last active. Records that show the changes in the structure can be used to answer that question. A similar situation arises when a six-month-old backup copy of data must be used to repair a damaged database (although this should not happen, sometimes it does). The backup copy can be used to reconstruct the database to the state it was in at the time of the backup. Then transactions and structural changes can be made in chronological

FIGURE 15-3

Summary of the DBA's Responsibilities for Managing the Database Structure

Participate in Database and Application Development
- Assist in requirements stage and evaluation of alternatives.
- Play an active role in database design and creation.
- Develop procedures for integrity and quality of database data.

Facilitate Changes to Database Structure
- Seek community-wide solutions.
- Assess impact on all users.
- Provide configuration control forum.
- Be prepared for problems after changes are made.
- Maintain documentation.

order to restore the database to its current state. Figure 15-3 summarizes the DBA's responsibilities for managing the database structure.

Management of Data Activity

Although the DBA protects the data, she does not process it. The DBA is not a user of the system, and consequently, she does not manage *data values.* Rather, the DBA manages *data activity.* The database is a shared resource, and the DBA provides standards, guidelines, control procedures, and documentation to ensure that the users work in a cooperative and complementary fashion when processing database data.

Because of the abundance of interrelated activity, database processing must be standardized. Providing database standards is one aspect of managing data activity: Every database field must have a standard name and format; every database record must have a standard name, format, and access strategies; and every database file must have a standard name and relationships with other files. The DBA establishes these standards in a manner that satisfies most of the needs of all the database users. Those organizations with an effective data administration will already have many of these standards, in which case the DBA may broaden them and ensure that they are enforced. Once established, the details of standardization are recorded in the DBMS **data dictionary**, which both the systems developers and the users can query to determine exactly what data is being maintained, the names and formats of the data items, and their relationships.

Another aspect of managing data activity is establishing data proponents, access, and modification rights. Since the data is a shared resource, there may be problems regarding processing rights. The DBA and the relevant data proponents should consider each shared data item and determine the access and modification rights of particular applications and users. This should be done with regard for the greater community's benefit rather than that of one particular application, group, or user. Once processing rights have been determined, they can be implemented by the DBMS, by applications that process the database via the DBMS, or by both.

Problems may appear when two or more user groups are authorized to modify the same data. One such problem, the **lost update problem,** occurs when the work of one user is overwritten by the work of a second user. The DBA is responsible for identifying the possibilities of such problems and for creating procedures and standards for avoiding them. This means ensuring that the DBMS's facilities are used properly by both programmers and users and also establishing processing schedules and other manual procedures. For example, in some cases the DBA may restrict certain activities by user groups to certain periods of the day to avoid concurrency problems that can hurt the system's overall performance.

Another important concern for the DBA in managing data activity is devising recovery techniques and procedures. Although the DBMS performs one part of the recovery process, the users are critical. The DBA must anticipate failures and develop standardized procedures for handling them, and the users must know what to do while the system is down and what to do first when the system is back up again. The operations staff must know how to initiate a database recovery process, which backup copies of the database to use, how to schedule the rerunning of lost work

FIGURE 15-4

Summary of the DBA's
Responsibilities for Managing
Data Activity

- Establish database standards consistent with data administration standards.
- Establish and maintain data dictionary.
- Establish data proponencies.
- Work with data proponents to develop data access and modification rights.
- Develop, document, and train staff on backup and recovery procedures.
- Publish and maintain data activity standards documentation.

(because other systems are using the computer resources, too, priorities need to be established and enforced), and so on. If a communications control program is in use (a likely situation in an on-line multiuser database environment), the recovery of its processing must be coordinated with the database recovery. All of these problems are the DBMS's responsibility.

Finally, the DBA is responsible for publishing and maintaining documentation regarding the data activity, including database standards, data retrieval and access rights, recovery procedures, and policy enforcement. Good documentation is especially important because it is needed by users throughout the organization. As with all documentation, keeping it current is a major and unpopular task.

Many DBMS products provide utility services to assist in managing data activity. Some systems record the names of users and application programs that access (or are authorized to access) objects in the database. In this case, the DBMS data dictionary can be queried to determine which programs can access a particular record and what actions each can take. Figure 15-4 summarizes the DBA's responsibilities for managing data activity.

Management of the DBMS

In addition to managing data activity and the database structure, the DBA must manage the DBMS itself. She should compile and analyze statistics concerning the system's performance and identify potential problem areas. Keep in mind that the database is serving many user groups. The DBA needs to investigate all complaints about the system's response time, accuracy of data, ease of use, and so forth. If changes are needed, the DBA must plan and implement them.

The DBA must periodically (and continually) monitor the users' activity on the database. DBMS products include features that collect and report statistics. Some of these reports may indicate, for example, which users have been active, which files and perhaps which data items have been used, and which access methods have been employed. Error rates and types can also be captured and reported. The DBA ana-

FIGURE 15-5

Summary of the DBA's
Responsibilities for Managing
the DBMS Product

- Generate database application performance reports.
- Investigate user performance complaints.
- Assess need for changes in database structure or application design.
- Modify database structure.
- Evaluate and implement new DBMS features.
- Tune the DBMS.

lyzes this data to determine whether a change to the database design is needed to improve performance or ease the users' tasks. If so, the DBA will make it.

The DBA should analyze run-time statistics on database activity and performance. When a performance problem is identified (by either a report or a user's complaint), the DBA must determine whether a modification of the database structure or system is appropriate. Examples of possible structure modifications are establishing new keys, purging data, deleting keys, and establishing new relationships among objects.

When the vendor of the DBMS being used announces new product features, the DBA must consider them in light of the overall needs of the user community. If she decides to incorporate the new DBMS features, the users must be notified and trained in their use. Accordingly, the DBA must manage and control changes in the DBMS as well as in the database structure.

Other changes in the system for which the DBA is responsible vary widely, depending on the DBMS product as well as other software and hardware in use. For example, changes in other software (such as the operating system or a communications control program) may mean that some DBMS parameters must be modified. The DBA must therefore also tune the DBMS product to other software in use.

The DBMS options are initially chosen when little is known about how the system will perform in the particular user environment. Consequently, operational experience and performance analysis over a period of time may reveal that a change is necessary. Even if the performance seems acceptable, the DBA may want to alter the options and observe the effect on performance. This process is referred to as *tuning*, or *optimizing*, the system. Figure 15-5 summarizes the DBA's responsibilities for managing the DBMS product.

Establishing the Database Data Dictionary

A DBMS data dictionary is an important tool for the database administrator. It is actually a user-accessible catalog of data concerning the database, and its importance can be demonstrated by the following problem: A development team creates a database consisting of 20 tables and 300 columns. Seventy-five application programs regularly process this database. Suppose that adhering to a new tax law requires changes in the way that employees' taxes are calculated and in the formats of the data fields that are used. Before modifying either the data or the programs, the manager of data processing should assess the impact of these changes (in order to allocate people and testing facilities, to develop user training, and so forth). He also needs to know which programs reference which data items.

If a data dictionary is in place, then a simple query (just like a query against data) can answer the manager's question. But if there is no cross-referencing mechanism in place, then each application program must be studied (usually by application programmers) to determine whether it references the data items in question. Obviously, the first of the approaches is much faster and probably much more accurate.

Data dictionaries are not new. In fact, many data processing managers developed their own cross-referencing systems long before databases became popular. Now, however, many DBMS products include an integrated data dictionary option. As we pointed out in Chapter 12, IBM incorporates a user-accessible catalog in its DB2 relational database product. Other manufacturers offer similar options.

Some data dictionaries are active, and some are passive. An active data dictionary is one whose entries are automatically modified by the software whenever changes are made in the database structure. In contrast, passive data dictionaries need to be updated separately when changes are made in the database; otherwise, they will not accurately reflect the state of the database. Active data dictionaries usually cost more, but they ensure currency; however, they are not available with every DBMS product. Although passive data dictionaries are less expensive than active ones, more effort is required to keep them up-to-date. But either one greatly aids the DBA in recording and tracking data names, formats, relationships, and cross-references.

DATABASE RELIABILITY

An important responsibility of the DBA is the reliability of the database, ensuring that the programs and procedures provide for the data's reliability in light of machine malfunctions, program bugs, and human errors. For single-user, personal databases, little is required. Procedures should be developed to save copies of the database data periodically and to keep records of processing since the save so that any lost work can be duplicated.

In a multiuser environment, the situation is more complicated. First, users process the database concurrently, and so there is always the possibility that one user's work may interfere with another's. In addition, recovery after failure is more complicated. Simply reprocessing the transactions is undesirable, not only because of the duplication of manual work involved, but also because in a multiuser environment the results of the reprocessing may differ from the original. If so, the documents (confirmation of orders, for example), generated during the first processing and those during the second processing may not match.

Next we turn to controlling concurrent processing and then look at backup and recovery.

■ Characteristics of Multiuser Processing

In a multiuser environment, users submit work in units called **transactions**, also known as **atomic transactions** and **logical units of work** (LUWs). A transaction is a series of actions to be taken on the database such that either all of them are per-

FIGURE 15-6

Comparison of the Results of Applying Serial Actions Versus a Multiple-Step Transaction: (a) Two out of Three Activities Successfully Completed, Resulting in Database Anomalies, and (b) No Change Made Because Entire Transaction Not Successful

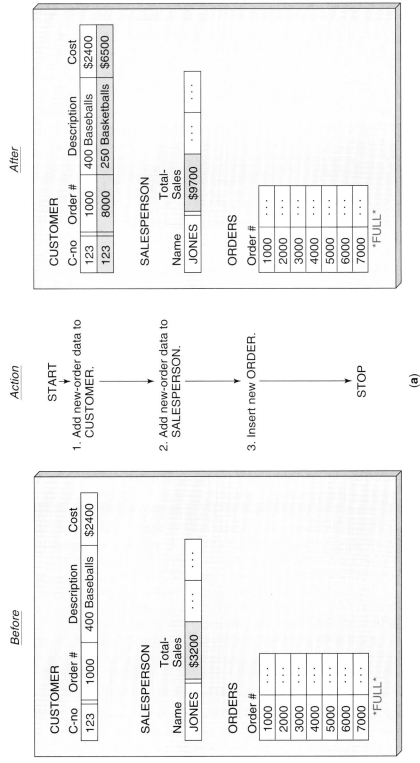

FIGURE 15-6
(Continued)

Before

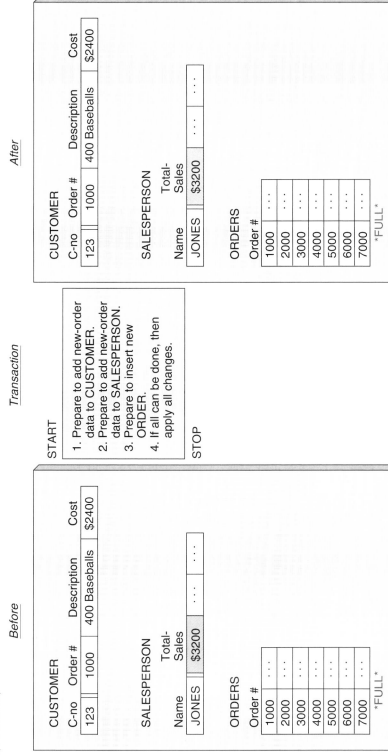

Transaction

START

1. Prepare to add new-order data to CUSTOMER.
2. Prepare to add new-order data to SALESPERSON.
3. Prepare to insert new ORDER.
4. If all can be done, then apply all changes.

STOP

After

CUSTOMER

C-no	Order #	Description	Cost
123	1000	400 Baseballs	$2400

SALESPERSON

Name	Total-Sales	
JONES	$3200	...

ORDERS

Order #
1000
2000
3000
4000
5000
6000
7000

FULL

(b)

461

formed successfully or none of them is performed at all, in which case the database remains unchanged. For example, suppose that a transaction to enter a customer order includes the following actions:

1. Change the customer record with the new order data.
2. Change the salesperson record with the new order data.
3. Insert a new order record into the database.

Suppose the last step failed, perhaps because of insufficient file space. Imagine the confusion that would ensue if the first two changes were made, but not the third one. The customer might receive an invoice for an item never received, and a salesperson might receive a commission on an item never sent to the customer.

Figure 15-6 compares the results of performing these activities as a series of independent steps (Figure 15-6[a]) and as an atomic transaction (Figure 15-6[b]). Notice that when the steps are carried out atomically and one fails, no changes are made in the database. Thus, defining and processing logical units of work is a requirement for multiuser systems.

When two transactions are interleaved, which is common in the multiuser environment, it is termed *concurrent processing*. In almost all cases (the exception concerns certain, special-purpose hardware), the CPU of the machine processing the database executes only one instruction at a time. Rather than devoting all the CPU's time to a single transaction until it is completed and then starting on the next one, and so forth, the operating system instead switches CPU services among the waiting tasks so that some portion of each of them is carried out in a given period of time.

This switching among tasks is done so quickly that two people seated at terminals side by side, processing the same database, may believe that their two transactions are completed simultaneously, but in reality, the two transactions are interleaved. The CPU performs instructions for one task, then switches to the second,

FIGURE 15-7

Example of Concurrent Processing of Two Users' Tasks

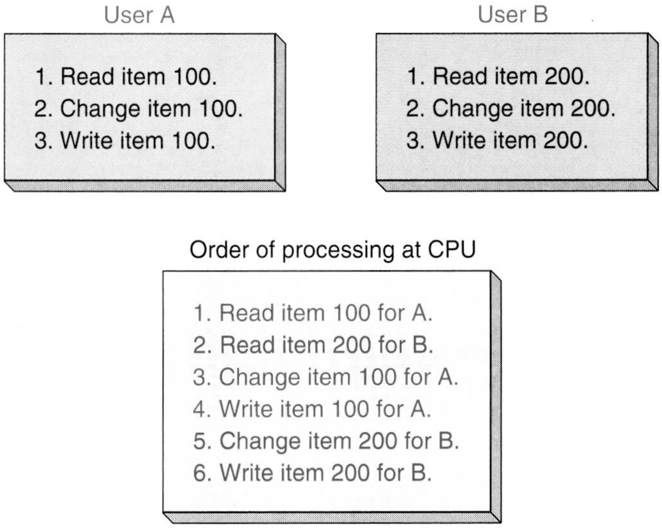

User A

1. Read item 100.
2. Change item 100.
3. Write item 100.

User B

1. Read item 200.
2. Change item 200.
3. Write item 200.

Order of processing at CPU

1. Read item 100 for A.
2. Read item 200 for B.
3. Change item 100 for A.
4. Write item 100 for A.
5. Change item 200 for B.
6. Write item 200 for B.

then back to the first, and so forth. Although humans cannot perceive that the interleaving has taken place, it has.

Figure 15-7 shows two concurrent transactions. User A's transaction reads Item 100, changes it, and rewrites it in the database. User B's transaction takes the same actions, but on Item 200. The CPU processes User A until it encounters an I/O interrupt or some other delay for User A. The operating system shifts control to User B. The CPU now processes User B until an interrupt, at which point the operating system passes control back to User A. To the users, the processing appears to be simultaneous, but actually it is interleaved, or concurrent.

LOST UPDATE PROBLEM

The concurrent processing illustrated in Figure 15-7 poses no problems because the users are processing different data. But suppose that both users want to process Item 100. For example, User A wants to order 5 units of Item 100, and User B wants to order 3 units of the same item.

Figure 15-8 illustrates the problem. User A reads Item 100's record into a user work area. According to the record, there are 10 items in inventory. Then User B reads Item 100's record into another user work area. Again, according to the record there are 10 in inventory. Now User A takes 5, decrements the count of items in its user work area to 5, and rewrites the record for Item 100. Then User B takes 3, decrements the count in its user work area to 7, and rewrites the record for Item 100. The database now shows, incorrectly, that there are 7 Item 100s in inventory. To review: We started with 10 in inventory, User A took 5, User B took 3, and the database shows that 7 are in inventory. Clearly we have a problem.

FIGURE 15-8

Lost Update Problem

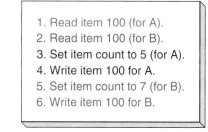

Note: The change and write in Steps 3 and 4 are lost.

Both users obtained current data from the database. But when User B read the record, User A already had a copy that it was about to update. This situation is called the **lost update problem** or the **concurrent update problem.** There is another, similar problem called the **inconsistent read problem** that we discuss in Chapter 17.

One remedy for the inconsistencies caused by concurrent processing is to prevent multiple applications from obtaining copies of the same record when the record is about to be changed. This approach is called **resource locking.**

■ Resource Locking

To prevent concurrent processing problems, data retrieved for update must not be shared among users. (In this sense, the term *user* refers to the user of the DBMS, not necessarily the end user. Thus, a user can be either a person seated at a terminal using the DBMS query/update facility or an application program that calls the DBMS for service.)

To prevent such sharing, the DBMS can place **locks** on data that is retrieved for update. Figure 15-9 shows the order of processing using a lock command. User B's transaction must wait until User A is finished with Item 100's record. Using this strategy, User B can read Item 100's record only after User A has completed the modification. In this case, the final item count stored in the database is 2, as it should be. (We started with 10, A took 5, and B took 3, leaving 2.)

FIGURE 15-9

Concurrent Processing with Explicit Locks

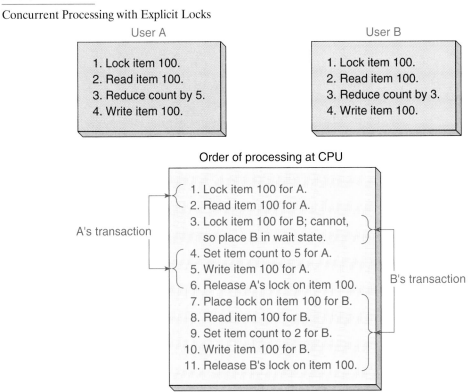

LOCK TERMINOLOGY

Locks can be placed either automatically by the DBMS or by a command issued to the DBMS from the application program or query user. Locks placed by the DBMS are called **implicit locks**; those placed by command are called **explicit locks.**

In the preceding example, the locks were applied to rows of data. Not all locks are applied at this level, however. Some DBMS products lock at the page level, some at the table level, and some at the database level. The size of a lock is referred to as the **lock granularity.** Locks with large granularity are easy for the DBMS to administer but frequently cause conflicts. Locks with small granularity are difficult to administer (there are many more details for the DBMS to keep track of and check), but conflicts are less common.

Locks also vary by type. An **exclusive lock** locks the item from access of any type. No other transaction can read or change the data. A **shared lock** locks the item from change but not from read. That is, other transactions can read the item as long as they do not attempt to alter it.

SERIALIZABLE TRANSACTIONS

However the DBMS and application program accomplish the locking, they must make sure that the database suffers from no anomalies due to concurrent processing. That is, when two or more transactions are processed concurrently, the results in the database should be logically consistent with the results that would have been achieved had the transactions been processed in an arbitrary serial fashion. A scheme for processing concurrent transactions in this way is said to be **serializable.**

Serializability can be achieved by a number of different means. One way is to process the transaction using **two-phased locking.** With this strategy, transactions are allowed to obtain locks as necessary, but once the first lock is released, no other lock can be obtained. Transactions thus have a **growing phase,** in which the locks are obtained, and a **shrinking phase,** in which the locks are released. The rationale for two-phased locking is discussed in Chapter 17.

A special case of two-phased locking is used with a number of DBMS products, including DB2. With it, locks are obtained throughout the transaction, but no lock is released until the COMMIT or ROLLBACK command is issued. This strategy is more restrictive than two-phase locking requires, but it is easier to implement.

In general, the boundaries of a transaction should correspond to the definition of the object it is processing. Following the two-phase strategy, the rows of each relation in the object are locked as needed. Changes are made, but the data is not committed to the database until all of the object has been processed. At this point, changes are made in the actual database, and all locks are released.

Consider an order entry transaction that involves an object CUSTOMER-ORDER that is constructed from data in the CUSTOMER table, the SALESPERSON table, and the ORDER table. To make sure that the database will suffer no anomalies due to concurrency, the order entry transaction begins by issuing all of its locks (on CUSTOMER, SALESPERSON, and ORDER) and concludes by making all the database changes and then releasing all its locks.

Many DBMS products use the two-phase locking strategy. One example is IBM's DB2 relational database product. The DB2 COMMIT command makes all the database changes and then releases all the locks. Thus, by definition, COMMIT ends a transaction. Refer to Chapter 17 for more information on this subject.

FIGURE 15-10

Deadlock

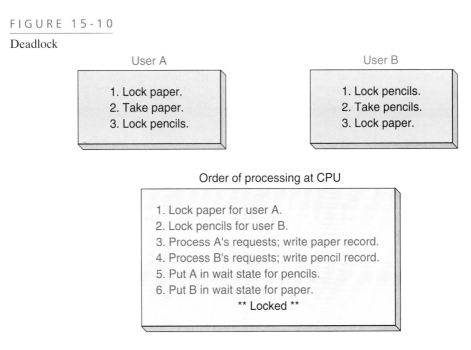

DEADLOCK

Although locking solves one problem, it introduces another. Consider what might happen if two users want to order two items from inventory. Suppose A wants to order some paper, and if she can get the paper, she wants to order some pencils. Then suppose User B wants to order some pencils, and if he can get the pencils, he wants to order some paper. The order of processing could be that shown in Figure 15-10.

What has happened? Users A and B are locked in a condition known as **deadlock**, or sometimes the **deadly embrace**. Each is waiting for a resource that the other person has locked. There are two common ways of solving this problem: preventing the deadlock from occurring or allowing the deadlock to occur and then breaking it.

Deadlock can be prevented in several ways. One is to allow users to have only one lock at a time. In essence, users must lock all the resources they want at once. If User A in the illustration had locked both the paper and the pencil records at the beginning, the embrace would never have taken place.

The other strategy is to allow the deadlock to occur, detect it, and then break it. Unfortunately, there is only one way to break deadlock: kill one of the transactions. In the situation in Figure 15-10, one of the two transactions must be aborted. When that happens, the lock is released, and the other transaction can process the database unhindered. Obviously any changes the killed transaction has made in the database must be undone, and we discuss the techniques for this in the next section.

■ Database Recovery

Computer systems, database oriented or not, can fail. Hardware fails. Programs have bugs. Human procedures contain errors, and people make mistakes. All of these can and do occur in database-processing applications.

When a database becomes inoperable, especially an on-line system, several problems must be addressed. First, from a business standpoint, business functions must continue. For example, customer orders, financial transactions, and packing lists must be completed manually. Later, when the computer is running again, the data can be entered. Second, computer operations personnel must as quickly as possible to restore the system to a usable state, as close as possible to what it was when the system crashed. Third, users must know what to do when the system becomes available again. Some work may need to be reentered, and users must know how far back they need to go.

Performing a recovery may be exceedingly difficult. It is impossible simply to fix the problem and resume processing where it was interrupted. Even if no data is lost during a failure (which assumes that all types of memory are nonvolatile—an unrealistic assumption), the timing and scheduling of computer processing are too complex to be accurately recreated. Enormous amounts of overhead data and processing would be required for the operating system to be able to restart processing precisely where it was interrupted. It is simply not possible to roll back the clock and put all the electrons in the same configuration they were in at the time of the failure. Thus, two approaches are possible: recovery via reprocessing, and recovery via rollback/rollforward.

RECOVERY VIA REPROCESSING

Since processing cannot be resumed at a precise point, the next best alternative is to go back to a known point and reprocess the workload from there. The simplest form of this type of recovery is to make a copy periodically of the database (called a **database save**) and to keep a record of all transactions that have been processed since the save. Then when there is a failure, the operations staff can restore the database from the save and reprocess all the transactions.

Unfortunately, this simple strategy is normally infeasible. First, reprocessing transactions takes the same amount of time as does processing them in the first place. If the computer is heavily scheduled, the system may never catch up.

Second, when transactions are processed concurrently, events are asynchronous. Slight variations in human activity, such as a user inserting a floppy disk more slowly or a user reading an electronic mail message before responding to an application prompt, may change the order of the execution of concurrent transactions. Therefore, whereas Customer A got the last seat on a flight during the original processing, Customer B may get the last seat during reprocessing. For these reasons, reprocessing is seldom a viable form of recovery for concurrent processing systems.

RECOVERY VIA ROLLBACK/ROLLFORWARD

A second approach is to make a copy periodically of the database (the database save) and to keep a log of the changes made by transactions against the database since the save. Then when there is a failure, one of two methods can be used. By using **rollforward,** the database can be restored to the save, and all valid transactions since the save are reapplied. (We are not reprocessing the transactions, as the application programs are not involved in the rollforward. Instead, the processed changes, as recorded in the log, are reapplied.)

The other method is **rollback**, in which we undo changes made by erroneous or partially processed transactions, by undoing the changes they have made in the database. Then the valid transactions that were in process at the time of the failure are restarted.

Both of these methods require that a **log** be kept of the transaction results, which contains a record of the data changes in chronological order. Transactions are written to the log before they are applied to the database. If the system crashes between the time a transaction is logged and the time it is applied, then at worst there is a record of an unapplied transaction. If the transactions were applied before they were logged, it would be possible (as well as undesirable) to change the database but have no record of the change. If this happened, an unwary user might reenter an already completed transaction.

In the event of a failure, the log is used both to undo and redo transactions, as shown in Figure 15-11. To undo a transaction, the log must contain a copy of every database record (or page) before it was changed. Such records are called **before-images.** A transaction is undone by applying before-images of all its changes to the database.

FIGURE 15-11

Undo and Redo Transactions: (a) Removing Changes in the Database (Rollback) and (b) Reapplying Changes in the Database (Rollforward)

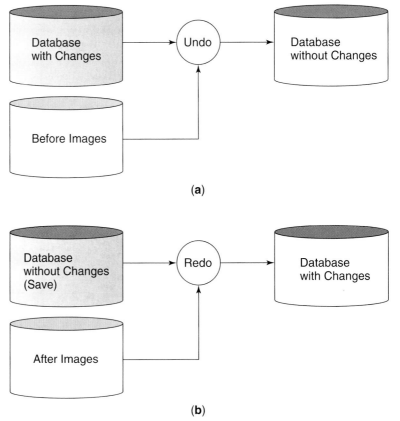

(a)

(b)

To redo a transaction, the log must contain a copy of every database record (or page) after it was changed. These records are called **after-images.** A transaction is redone by applying after-images of all its changes to the database. Possible data items of a transaction log are shown in Figure 15-12(a).

For this example log, each transaction has a unique name for identification purposes. Furthermore, all images for a given transaction are linked together with pointers. One pointer points to the previous change made by this transaction (the reverse pointer), and the other points to the next change made by this transaction (the forward pointer). A zero in the pointer field means that this is the end of the list. The DBMS recovery subsystem uses these pointers to locate all records for a particular transaction. Figure 15-12(b) shows an example of the linking of log records.

Other data items in the log are the time of the action; the type of operation (START marks the beginning of a transaction, and COMMIT terminates a transaction, thereby releasing all locks that were in place); the object acted on, such as record type and identifier; and finally, the beforeimages and afterimages.

Given a log with both before-images and after-images, the undo and redo actions are straightforward (to describe, anyway). To undo the transaction in Figure 15-13,

FIGURE 15-12

Transaction Log: (a) Possible Data Items in a Log Record and (b) Log Instance for Three Transactions

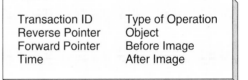

Transaction ID	Type of Operation
Reverse Pointer	Object
Forward Pointer	Before Image
Time	After Image

(a)

Relative
Record
Number

1	OT1	0	2	11:42	START		
2	OT1	1	4	11:43	MODIFY	CUST 100	(old value)	(new value)
3	OT2	0	8	11:46	START		
4	OT1	2	5	11:47	MODIFY	SP AA	(old value)	(new value)
5	OT1	4	7	11:47	INSERT	ORDER 11		(value)
6	CT1	0	9	11:48	START		
7	OT1	5	0	11:49	COMMIT		
8	OT2	3	0	11:50	COMMIT		
9	CT1	6	10	11:51	MODIFY	SP BB	(old value)	(new value)
10	CT1	9	0	11:51	COMMIT		

(b)

FIGURE 15-13

Example of a Recovery Strategy: (a) ORDER Transaction and (b) Recovery Processing to Undo an ORDER Record

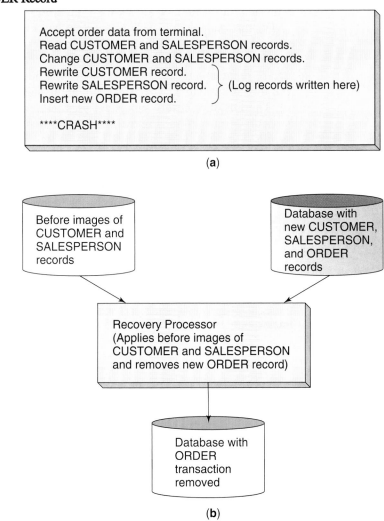

Accept order data from terminal.
Read CUSTOMER and SALESPERSON records.
Change CUSTOMER and SALESPERSON records.
Rewrite CUSTOMER record.
Rewrite SALESPERSON record.   } (Log records written here)
Insert new ORDER record.

****CRASH****

(a)

Before images of CUSTOMER and SALESPERSON records

Database with new CUSTOMER, SALESPERSON, and ORDER records

Recovery Processor
(Applies before images of CUSTOMER and SALESPERSON and removes new ORDER record)

Database with ORDER transaction removed

(b)

the recovery processor simply replaces each changed record with its before-image. When all before-images have been restored, the transaction is undone.

To redo a transaction, the recovery processor starts with the version of the database at the time the transaction started and applies all after-images. This action assumes that an earlier version of the database is available from a database save. If it is necessary to restore a database to its most recent save and then to reapply all transactions, much processing time may be required. To minimize this problem, DBMS products provide a facility called **checkpoint.**

A checkpoint command provides a point of synchronization between the database and the transaction log. To perform a checkpoint, the DBMS refuses to accept any new requests; it finishes processing any outstanding requests; and it empties its buffers. The DBMS then waits until the operating system notifies it that all outstanding write requests to the database and to the log have been completed. At this point, the log and the database are synchronized. A checkpoint record is then written to the log. When the database needs to be recovered, only those after-images for transactions that started after the checkpoint need to be applied.

Checkpoints may be inexpensive operations, and often it is feasible to take three or four checkpoints per hour (or more). In this way, no more than fifteen or twenty minutes of processing need to be recovered. Some DBMS products automatically checkpoint themselves, making human intervention unnecessary.

As you can imagine, the ability to restore the database system to a usable state is critical in most situations. (It might not be so critical in a single-user environment. First, only one individual is inconvenienced, and second, the system is probably not so heavily scheduled that reprocessing work is infeasible.) Although DBMS products include some of the recovery features we have discussed, remember that people play a vital role in backup and recovery. The DBA should establish procedures that computer center personnel and users should follow in the event of a system crash, and people must be trained in those procedures.

DATABASE SECURITY

Database processing can provide far greater productivity than other types of processing can, but unfortunately, such processing also increases the company's vulnerability. With a database, the company's data—a valuable resource—is centralized and made readily accessible. In fact, DBMS products are designed to maximize this accessibility.

This situation is great for the authorized user. But unfortunately, DBMS products are also easy for unauthorized users—and criminals—to use. Recognizing the problem of unauthorized use, most DBMS vendors have incorporated security features into their products. To the greatest extent possible, these features allow only identifiably authorized users (people or programs) to access the data, and they can restrict the types of processing on the data.

Not all users (and programmers) who are authorized to access a database system have complete access to all of the data. Some users have access to more data than other users do, and some have more extensive processing rights as well. For example, some users can modify or delete records, but other users cannot. In the database environment, not all users enjoy the same privileges.

In *Database Security and Integrity,* Fernandez, Summers, and Wood developed a model of database security.[2] Their model is essentially a table of processing permissions, or **authorization rules.** As shown in Figure 15-14, the table has four columns representing subjects, objects[3], actions, and authorization constraints. A row in this

---

[2] E. B. Fernandez, R. C. Summers, and C. Wood, *Database Security and Integrity* (Reading, MA: Addison-Wesley, 1981).

[3] This use of the term *object* is more general than *semantic object*, as it refers to some element or entity of the database or database application.

FIGURE 15-14

Sample of Authorization Rules

Subject	Object	Action	Authorization Constraint
PGM OE104I	ORDER Record	Insert	Amount less than $500,000
Sally Smith	ORDER Record	Read	None
Payroll Dept	EMPLOYEE Record	Read	Hourly workers
Payroll Dept	EMPLOYEE Record	Modify	Hourly workers
Payroll Dept	EMPLOYEE Record	Insert	Hourly workers
Payroll Supv	EMPLOYEE Record	Delete	Hourly workers
Payroll Supv	Read Permission of EMPLOYEE Records	Grant	To payroll personnel

table indicates that the named subject has permission to take the indicated action on the listed object, subject to the stated authorization constraints. Thus, row 1 indicates that the program OE104J is authorized to insert ORDER records as long as the amount of the order is less than $500,000.

Although no DBMS product provides security in the form of this model, the model is an effective framework for understanding security capabilities and can help the DBA when determining users' processing rights and responsibilities. Next we examine the four columns in the model.

Subjects

A **subject** is any identifiable user or user group that can process the database. Examples of subjects are particular people (Sally Smith), groups of people (everyone in the payroll department), people operating in particular roles (a teller making deposit transactions), application programs, and remote computers.

Determining whether someone who claims to be a subject really is that subject is difficult. People can be identified by fingerprints, voice prints, and passwords, to name a few. Passwords are by far the most commonly used identifiers in a computer environment. Computer equipment is identified by hardware configuration (say, the line connected to port 4) and by the presence or absence of specialized signals. Programs are usually identified by name or specialized protocol.

In the database environment, the subject desiring access to an object provides his, her, or its identifier (name or password, for example). For verification, the DBMS looks up the name of the object and other data in a table and, if it is found, allows the subject access to the object.

Objects

The second column of the security table in Figure 15-14 contains objects, the database units to be protected by security. Examples of objects (using relational terminology) are databases, relations, rows, columns, views, the DBMS, programs, transactions, and knowledge of status (for example, the existence or nonexistence of an attribute).

The term *granularity,* which was used earlier to refer to the size of locks, is also sometimes used to refer to the size of security objects. A security system that allows access to (or prevents access from) only the entire database as a unit has large granularity. Conversely, a security system that allows access to or prevents access from a particular attribute has small granularity.

Small-granularity security systems allow close control over data. The users' access can be limited to the data needed to perform a function. On the other hand, security systems with small granularity require more overhead processing to administer. If a DBMS must check the authorization every time a user accesses any attribute of any row, processing will be slow and expensive.

Choosing the granularity of a security system involves a trade-off between closely tailored security and processing efficiency. As security increases, efficiency decreases. Although the DBMS enforces the security that is put in place, the DBA is responsible for determining what security is needed.

Actions

The action column in Figure 15-14 identifies what the subject can do to the object. Possibilities include reading, inserting, deleting, modifying, creating, destroying, and granting. Inserting and creating sound similar, but they differ as follows: Inserting means adding data to an existing structure, and creating means building the structure. Thus a subject can insert a row (record) or create the structure of a table. Similarly, deleting means removing data, and destroying means eliminating data and structure.

The grant action refers to giving a permission (such as permission to modify data) to another subject. In Figure 15-14 the last row of the table specifies that the payroll supervisor has the authority to grant permission to payroll personnel to read employee records.

Usually the DBA is given sweeping grant authority by the DBMS. That is, when the DBMS is installed, someone must be identified to the system to grant authority to all other individuals. This is usually the DBA. Furthermore, some DBMS products automatically assign grant authority to anyone who creates a new table. That person, in turn, can then grant permission to perform actions on that table to whomever he or she chooses, which thereby constitutes ownership of that data.

Authorization Constraints

Authorization constraints specify limitations on permissions concerning subject, object, and action. Several examples of authorization constraints are shown in Figure 15-14. For example, the payroll department can process EMPLOYEE records for hourly workers. If this table contains all the authorization constraints on the database then the payroll department could process records *only* for hourly workers and not for supervisory or executive employees. Supervisory and executive payroll would be processed outside of the database system.

■ Security in DBMS Products

No commercial DBMS provides as general a security capability as that shown in Figure 15-14. Rather, DBMS products usually offer a subset of capabilities. The DBA therefore should determine security requirements and augment the capabilities of the DBMS product in areas where it is lacking.

SUBJECT-ORIENTED SECURITY

With subject-oriented security, the subject is defined to the DBMS, and each is allocated permissions. Before allowing him (or her or it) to perform a database action, the DBMS confirms that he has such authority. If the subject does not have permission, the DBMS will not permit the user's request. The table in Figure 15-15 illustrates permissions that have been assigned to one subject. In this case the subject is a program. The table tells us that all ORDER transactions are authorized to read CUSTOMER, SALESPERSON, and ORDER records. ORDER transactions may insert only ORDER records, but they may modify all three types of records. ORDER transactions are not authorized to delete any data, nor can they grant any rights to other subjects.

OBJECT-ORIENTED SECURITY

Another approach to security defines authorizations from the standpoint of objects. In this case, each object has an authorization matrix that shows what actions can be taken by various subjects on that object. Most often the subjects are defined by passwords. For example, in Figure 15-16 those subjects who can provide the password SESAME can read, insert, modify, and delete SALESPERSON records. People who supply the password ABALONE can read SALESPERSON records but take no other action.

COMBINATION OF SUBJECT- AND OBJECT-ORIENTED SECURITY

Some DBMS products provide both subject- and object-oriented security. In this case, both subjects and objects have authorization matrices.

CONSTRAINTS VIA PROGRAMMABLE EXITS

Constraints on authorization rules are not generally supported by DBMS products, although some DBMS products have an indirect way of enforcing authorization con-

FIGURE 15-15

Subject-oriented Security Example: Permissions Granted to the Program Processing ORDER Transactions

		Objects		
		CUSTOMER Records	SALESPERSON Records	ORDER Records
Actions	Read	Y	Y	Y
	Insert	N	N	Y
	Modify	Y	Y	Y
	Delete	N	N	N
	Grant	N	N	N

FIGURE 15-16

Entity-oriented Security Example: Permissions Granted for SALESPERSON Records

Object: SALESPERSON Record

		Subjects Who Know Password SESAME	Subjects Who Know Password ABALONE
	Read	Y	Y
	Insert	Y	N
Actions	Modify	Y	N
	Delete	Y	N
	Grant	N	N

straints. They exit to (call) user-written programs whenever a specified action is performed on a specified object. (The event properties described for Microsoft Access in Chapter 11 are examples of such exits.) The program can then provide the logic to enforce the constraint. Note that end users do not generally write such programs; rather, they are usually developed by professional programmers. Consider an example.

Suppose that no order in excess of $50,000 is to be accepted after 3:00 P.M. on a Friday or the day before a holiday. Instead, such orders are to be referred to a supervisor. In this case, the database designer specifies that whenever an ORDER record is created, a special program is to be called. This program will determine whether these conditions are true. If so, the program will not allow the insert and will instead send a message to a supervisor.

User exits provide a great deal of flexibility, as they can supplement the DBMS's capabilities or compensate for deficiencies in a particular DBMS product. Their advantage is flexibility and greater control and security. But exits to user-written routines have disadvantages as well. For instance, the user organization must develop and test these routines, and such routines add overhead to the system. They may need to be dynamically loaded (copied into computer memory from disk storage each time they are needed) and therefore degrade the system's performance.

In terms of security, then, a DBMS includes facilities for identifying subjects and allowing them to access the database, for restricting the actions that subjects can perform, for limiting objects that subjects can access, and for allowing user-developed routines to be incorporated into normal processing. Thus the *operation* of a security system is one function of the DBMS, but as we described earlier, establishing the *policies and administration* of a security system is a function of data administration or database administration.

SUMMARY

Data is an important organizational asset and must be administered so as to protect it while at the same time maximizing its usefulness to the organization. The functions of data administration and database administration serve this need.

The scope of data administration is the entire organization. Data administration is responsible for determining what data is to be protected and for establishing data standards, policies, proponents, and other managerial guidelines and constraints to ensure the data's quality and usefulness. The functions of data administration include marketing its services, setting data standards and policies, providing a forum for resolving conflicts, and taking other measures to increase the organization's return from its data investment.

The scope of database administration is a particular database and the applications that process that database. Functions include managing the database structure, establishing frameworks to manage data activity, and managing the DBMS software. In addition, the database administration is responsible for establishing and managing the database data dictionary.

The database management system contains features essential to a multiuser environment. The primary functions of a DBMS are storing, retrieving, and modifying data. Other features include controlling concurrent processing, providing backup and recovery services, and providing facilities to establish an appropriate level of database security.

Concurrent updates can be a problem if two users attempt to modify the same record at once. When this happens, anomalies can occur in the database. DBMS products solve this problem by locking the resources whenever the data might be changed. Locks prevent other users from accessing a record until the transaction is completed and the lock is released.

Concurrent processing can also be a problem if two users each lock resources that the other one needs. This situation, called deadlock, can be resolved by the DBMS by terminating one of the transactions and undoing any changes it made in the database.

In the event of a system failure, the database must be restored to a usable state as quickly as possible. Any transactions in progress at the time of the crash must be reapplied, and any processing that was done manually while the system was down must be entered. Recovery can be by means of straightforward reprocessing or rollback/rollforward. The latter strategy is almost always preferred.

Transaction logs must be maintained to ensure that all lost work is reapplied. Checkpoints can be taken more frequently than database saves. Although they require some overhead, checkpoints minimize the amount of reprocessing that needs to be done in the event of a failure.

Database security means allowing only authorized subjects to perform authorized actions on specified objects, subject to any managerial constraints. Once established by the DBA, many of these access and processing rights are enforced by the DBMS. Constraints that are not enforced by the DBMS can be enforced by user-written subroutines.

GROUP I QUESTIONS

15.1   Describe the two purposes of data administration and database administration.

15.2   Explain the difference between data administration and database administration.

15.3   How is the data administrator analogous to the company controller?

15.4   Explain the necessity of data administration. What would be likely to happen if there were no data administration?

15.5   Summarize the marketing function of data administration.

15.6   Summarize the data standards function of data administration.

15.7   What is a data proponent? What functions does it serve? What is the difference between a data proponent and a data owner?

15.8   Summarize the data policy function of data administration.

15.9   Explain the need for a forum to resolve data conflicts.

15.10 What can data administration do to help increase an organization's return on its data investment?

15.11 Describe the need for database administration. What would be likely to happen if there were no database administration?

15.12 Explain how database administration is likely to vary among personal, workgroup, and organizational databases.

15.13 Summarize the DBA's responsibilities for managing the database structure.

15.14 What is configuration control? Why is it necessary for databases?

15.15 Describe two situations to which database system documentation is important.

15.16 Summarize the DBA's responsibilities for managing database activity. What are data access and modification rights? Why are they important?

15.17 Summarize the DBA's responsibilities for managing DBMS software.

15.18 What is the function of a data dictionary? Explain the difference between a passive and an active data dictionary.

15.19 Define *transaction, atomic transaction,* and *logical unit of work.*

15.20 What is concurrent processing? Under what conditions is concurrent processing a problem?

15.21 Describe the lost update problem.

15.22 Explain the difference between explicit and implicit locks.

15.23 Define *lock granularity.* What are the general differences between large and small lock granularity?

15.24 Explain the difference between an exclusive and a shared lock.

15.25 Define *serializability.*

15.26 What is a two-phase locking, and how can it be used to prevent the lost update problem?

15.27 What is a deadly embrace?

15.28 Describe two ways in which a DBMS can handle a deadly embrace.

15.29 Explain how a database can be recovered by reprocessing. Why is database recovery by reprocessing usually not feasible?

15.30 Define *rollback* and *rollforward.*

15.31 Why is it important to write to the log before changing the database?

15.32 Describe the rollback process. Under what conditions is rollback more advantageous than rollforward?

15.33 Describe the rollforward process. Under what conditions is rollforward more advantageous than rollback?

15.34 Why is it usually advantageous to take frequent checkpoints of a database?

15.35 Define *subject, object, action,* and *authorization constraint* as they apply to database security.

15.36 How does a DBMS implement subject-oriented security?

15.37 How does a DBMS implement object-oriented security?

15.38 Explain the use of programmable exits for security.

GROUP II QUESTIONS

15.39 Interview the DBA of a local company, and determine whether it uses a data dictionary system. Is it integrated with the DBMS? If so, what are the advantages and disadvantages? If not, ask why the company chose that type of data dictionary. Find out whether the dictionary system is active or passive.

15.40 Interview the manager of a local small business that uses a microcomputer DBMS. Is there a DBA? If not, determine who in the company performs each of the DBA's functions. Also find out whether any of the DBA's functions are not being performed. Why not? Find out what support the DBA (or people performing the DBA's functions) receives from the DBMS (for example, run-time statistics or a data dictionary).

15.41 Our discussion of database administration in this chapter assumed an organizational database. Explain how you think the tasks of database administration would change for a work-group database like the one used by SeaView Yachts in Chapter 1. How would the scope of the functions change? Would any of the functions described in this chapter be unnecessary? Would any new functions be required?

Distributed Processing

Part VII, the last part of this text, considers distributed processing. Chapter 16 introduces the subject and then focuses on *distributed applications processing*. With it, applications are moved from the central computer to distributed computers, but the database is processed on a central node, usually called a *server*. There are two approaches, resource sharing systems and client server systems.

Chapter 17 then considers *distributed database processing*, in which the database and the applications are moved from the central computer to distributed computers. This chapter describes the characteristics and components of distributed database systems and presents four processing goals for the distributed DBMS (DDBMS). Chapter 17 specifically addresses two difficult issues in distributed processing—concurrency control and failure recovery.

Chapter 16 presents distributed processing as it is done today, and Chapter 17 looks at the hopes and difficulties concerning the implementation of distributed processing as many would like it in the future. Today, the leading edge of the commercial application of distributed processing lies in between the discussions in these two chapters.

CLIENT SERVER
AND RELATED
APPLICATIONS

This chapter introduces the subject of distributed processing. The first section describes a number of multiuser processing alternatives and introduces client server, resource-sharing, and distributed database systems. Then the resource sharing and client server architectures are described in more detail. Distributed databases are addressed in the next chapter.

Both the resource sharing and client server architectures have increased in popularity as more organizations have installed local area networks. For database application processing, the client server architecture has important advantages over the resource sharing architecture and is preferred for such applications.

MULTIUSER DATABASE-PROCESSING ALTERNATIVES

Multiuser database systems are supported by a number of different system architectures. In the past, teleprocessing systems were the most common. But as the price of CPUs has fallen, it has become economically feasible to use more than one computer, resulting in new multiuser database alternatives. In this section, we introduce client server, resource sharing, and distributed databases alternatives.

■ Teleprocessing Systems

The classic method of supporting a multiuser database system is teleprocessing, which uses one computer and one CPU. All processing is done by this single computer.[1]

Figure 16-1 shows a typical teleprocessing system. Users operate dumb terminals (or microcomputers that emulate dumb terminals) that transmit transaction messages and data to the centralized computer. The communications control portion of the operating system receives the messages and data and sends them to the appropriate application program. The program then calls on the DBMS for services, and the DBMS uses the data management portion of the operating system to process the database. When a transaction is completed, the results are returned to the users at the dumb terminals via the communications control portion of the operating system.

Figure 16-1 shows n users submitting transactions processed by three different application programs. Since there is little intelligence at the users' end (that is, the *terminals* are dumb), all commands for formatting the screen must be generated by the CPU and transmitted over the communication lines. This means the users' interface is generally character oriented and primitive. Systems like this are called teleprocessing systems, since all inputs and outputs are communicated over a distance (*tele-* means "distance") to the centralized computer for processing.

Historically, teleprocessing systems have been the most common alternative for multiuser database systems. But as the price–performance ratio of computers has

FIGURE 16-1

Relationships of Programs in a Teleprocessing System

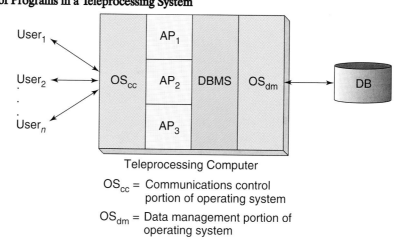

Teleprocessing Computer

OS_{cc} = Communications control portion of operating system

OS_{dm} = Data management portion of operating system

---

[1] In some teleprocessing systems, special-purpose computers are used as communications front ends and concentrators. In a strict sense, these are computers, but they are used only to process the communications control portion of the operating system. Because they have no direct role in applications or database processing, we ignore them in this disucssion.

fallen and, in particular, with the advent of the microcomputer, other alternatives that require multiple computers have begun to be used.

Client Server Systems

Figure 16-2 is a schematic of one of these alternatives, called a **client server system**. Unlike teleprocessing, which involves a single computer, client server computing involves multiple computers connected in a network. Some of the computers process application programs and are designated as *clients*. Another computer processes the database and is designated as the *server*.

Figure 16-2 shows an example in which each of *n* users has his or her own application processing computer: User$_1$ processes AP$_1$ and AP$_2$ on Computer 1. User$_2$ processes AP$_2$ on Computer 2, and User$_n$ processes AP$_2$ and AP$_3$ on Computer *N*. Another computer is used as the database server.

There are many options regarding computer type. Theoretically, the client computers can be mainframes, minis, or microcomputers. Because of cost, however, in almost all cases the client computers are microcomputers. Similarly, any type of computer can be the server, but again, because of cost, the server is most often a microcomputer. The clients and server are generally connected together using a local area network (LAN).

Although it is rare for client computers to be anything other than micros, sometimes the server is a mini or mainframe, especially when considerable power is required from the server or, for political or organizational reasons, it is inappropriate to locate the database on a microcomputer.

FIGURE 16-2

Client Server Architecture

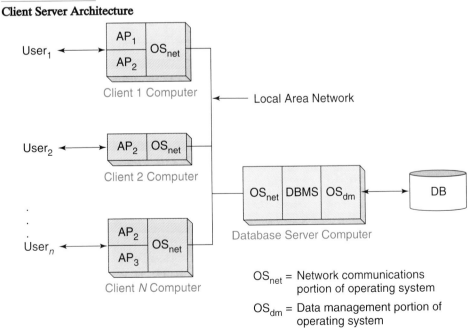

OS$_{net}$ = Network communications portion of operating system

OS$_{dm}$ = Data management portion of operating system

The system in Figure 16-2 has a single server, although this need not always be the case. Multiple servers may process different databases or provide other services on behalf of the clients. For example, in an engineering consulting firm, one server might process the database while a second server supports computer-assisted design graphics.

If there are multiple database processing servers, each one must process a different database in order for the system to be considered a client server system. When two servers process the same database, the system is no longer called a client server system; rather, it is termed a distributed database system.

Figure 16-3 summarizes the roles of the client and the server. The client computer manages the user interface, accepting data from the user, processing application logic, and generating requests for database services. The clients then transmit those requests to the server and receive results, which are then formatted for the user.

The server accepts the clients' requests, processes them, and returns a response. While doing this, the server performs database integrity checking, maintains the database overhead data, and provides concurrent access control. The server also performs recovery and optimizes query/update processing.

A client server system places the application processing closer to the user. One advantage of this is better performance, because several CPUs are processing applications in parallel. In addition, communications costs are reduced. Only the requests for DBMS processing and the responses to those requests need to be sent over the communications network, which means less communications traffic than in teleprocessing.

Because multiple computers process applications and because those computers utilize the server for database processing, CPU power is available to make the users' interface much more elaborate. Sophisticated menus and forms are possible, with

FIGURE 16-3

Roles of the Client and Server
Computers

Client Roles	Server Roles
Manage the user interface.	Accept database request from clients.
Accept data from the user.	Process database requests.
Process application logic.	Format results and transmit to client.
Generate database requests.	Perform integrity checking.
Transmit database requests to server.	Maintain database overhead data.
	Provide concurrent access control.
Receive results from server.	Perform recovery.
Format results.	Optimize query/update processing.

different colors, type fonts, and type sizes. Indeed, graphical user interfaces are becoming common for client server applications.

One disadvantage of client server systems concerns control. The client computers operate simultaneously and hence process applications in parallel. And this introduces the possibility of the lost update and other multiuser control problems. Such problems are worse than in teleprocessing systems because the computers process in parallel. Multiple operating systems that direct multiple CPUs must coordinate their processing over communications media, and this differs from teleprocessing in which all activity is governed by a single, local operating system.

■ Resource Sharing Systems

A second multicomputer architecture is shown in Figure 16-4. This architecture, called **resource sharing,** distributes to the processing computers not only the application programs but also the DBMS. In this case, the *server* is a file server and not a database server. If you compare Figures 16-1, 16-2, and 16-4, you will see that in each step, more software is moved to the users' computers. Almost all resource sharing systems employ local area networks of microcomputers.

The resource sharing architecture was developed before the client server architecture, and in many ways, it is more primitive than the client server. With resource sharing, the DBMS on each user's computer sends requests to the data management portion of the operating system on the file server for file-level processing. This means that considerably more traffic crosses the LAN than with the client server architecture.

FIGURE 16-4

Resource Sharing Architecture

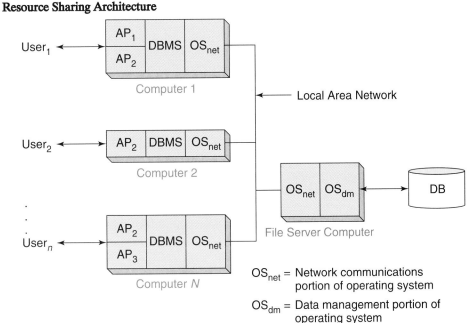

Consider the processing of a query to obtain the Name and Address of all rows in the CUSTOMER table where Zip equals 98033. In a client server system, the application program would send the following SQL command:

```
SELECT      NAME, ADDRESS
FROM        CUSTOMER
WHERE       ZIP = 98033
```

The server would respond with all qualifying Names and Addresses.

In a resource sharing system, the DBMS is on the local computer, and therefore no program on the file server is capable of processing SQL or any similar language. All such processing must be done on the user computer, and so the DBMS must ask the file server to transmit the entire CUSTOMER table. And if that table has indexes or other overhead associated with it, the overhead structures must be transmitted as well. Clearly, with resource sharing, much more data needs to be transmitted across the LAN. Furthermore, while one user computer is processing a request, it locks large portions of the database. Put differently, with resource sharing, a very high level of lock granularity is required, and as a consequence, throughput is reduced.

Because of these problems, resource sharing systems are seldom used for transaction-oriented multiuser database processing. Too much data needs to be locked and transmitted for each transaction, and so trying to use this architecture for transaction processing would result in very slow performance. There is, however, one database application for which this architecture makes sense: the query processing of downloaded, extracted data. If one or more users need access to large portions of the database in order to produce reports or answer queries, it can make sense to have a server that downloads large sections of data. In this case, the downloaded data is not updated and not returned to the database. We show examples of processing extracted data later in this chapter.

Resource sharing systems are also used for nondatabase applications. Resource sharing LANs are frequently used for applications that require large, fast disks to store large single-user files, large spreadsheets, and the like. They also are used to share expensive printers, plotters, and other peripheral equipment.

■ Distributed Database Systems

A fourth alternative, shown in Figure 16-5, is a distributed database system, in which the database itself is distributed. In Figure 16-5, the database (or a portion of it) is stored on all N computers. As shown, Computers 1, 2, and N process both the applications and the database, and Computer 3 processes only the database.

In Figure 16-5, the dashed line around the files indicates that the database is composed of all the segments of the database on all N computers. These computers may be physically located in the same facility, on different sides of the world, or somewhere in between.

DISTRIBUTED PROCESSING VERSUS DISTRIBUTED DATABASE PROCESSING

Consider Figures 16-1, 16-2, 16-4, and 16-5 again. The resource sharing, client server, and distributed database alternatives all differ from teleprocessing in an

FIGURE 16-5

Distributed Database Architecture

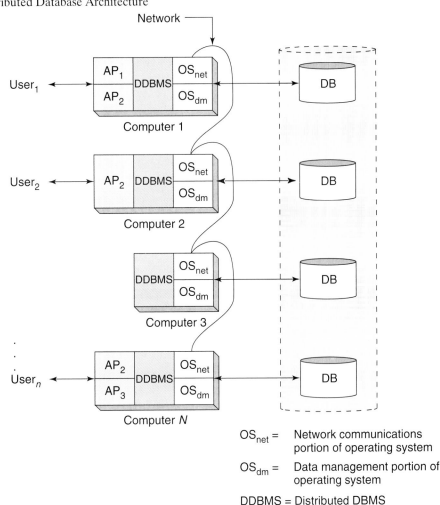

OS_{net} = Network communications portion of operating system

OS_{dm} = Data management portion of operating system

DDBMS = Distributed DBMS

important way: They all use multiple computers for applications or DBMS processing. Accordingly, most people would say that all three of these architectures are examples of **distributed systems**, because applications processing has been distributed among several computers.

Observe, however, that the database itself is distributed only in the architecture shown in Figure 16-5. Neither the client server nor the resource sharing architectures distribute the database to multiple computers. Consequently, most people would not refer to the resource sharing or client server architectures as **distributed database systems.**

When resource sharing systems are used to process downloaded, extracted data, they fall into a gray area. Strictly speaking, because the data is downloaded, it is distributed, and so such a system should be called a distributed database system. On the other hand, downloaded data is seldom updated. Since that is the case, the data is not distributed for all functions; that is, it is not fully distributed.

TYPES OF DISTRIBUTED DATABASES

There are a number of types of distributed database systems. First look at Figure 16-6(a), which shows a nondistributed database with four pieces, W, X, Y, and Z. All four pieces of these segments are located on a single database, and there is no data duplication.

Now consider the distributed alternatives in Figures 16-6(b) through (d). Figure 16-6(b) shows the first distributed alternative, in which the database has been partitioned into two pieces, W and X are stored on Computer 1, and Y and Z are stored on Computer 2. In Figure 16-6(c), the entire database has been replicated on two computers. Finally, in Figure 16-6(d), the database has been partitioned, and a portion (Y) has been replicated.

Two terms are sometimes used with regard to partitioning of databases. A **vertical partition** or **vertical fragment** refers to a table that is broken into two or more sets of columns. Thus a table R(C1, C2, C3, C4) could be broken into two vertical partitions of P1(C1, C2) and P2(C3, C4). Depending on the application and the reason for creating the partitions, the key of R would most likely also be placed into P2 to form P2(C1, C3, C4). A **horizontal partition** or **horizontal fragment** refers to the rows of a table when they are divided into pieces. Thus in the relation R, if the first 1000 rows are placed into R1(C1, C2, C3, C4) and the remaining rows are placed into R2(C1, C2, C3, C4), two horizontal partitions will result. Sometimes a database is broken into both horizontal and vertical partitions, and the result is sometimes called a **mixed partition**.

COMPARISON OF DISTRIBUTED DATABASE ALTERNATIVES

These alternatives are summarized on a continuum in Figure 16-7, arranged in increasing degree of distribution, from left to right. The nondistributed database is on the leftmost point of the continuum, and the partitioned, replicated database is on the rightmost point. In between these extremes is a partitioned database. The partitions are allocated to two or more computers and a database that is not partitioned, but each entire database is replicated on two or more computers.

The characteristics of the alternatives on this continuum are listed in Figure 16-7. The alternatives toward the right increase parallelism, independence, flexibility, and availability, but they also mean greater expense, complexity, difficulty of control, and risk to security.

One of these advantages is particularly significant to future business professionals. The alternatives on the right of Figure 16-7 provide greater flexibility and hence can be better tailored to the organizational structure and the organizational process. A highly decentralized manufacturing company, for example, in which plant managers have wide latitude in their planning, will never be satisfied with an organizational information system with the structure of Figure 16-6(a) because the structure of the information system architecture and the structure of the company fight with each other. Thus the alternatives on the right-hand side provide a better and more appropriate fit to that organization than do those on the left.

FIGURE 16-6

Types of Distributed Databases: (a) Nonpartitioned, Nonreplicated Alternative; (b) Partitioned, Nonreplicated Alternative; (c) Nonpartitioned, Replicated Alternative; (d) Partitioned, Replicated Alternative

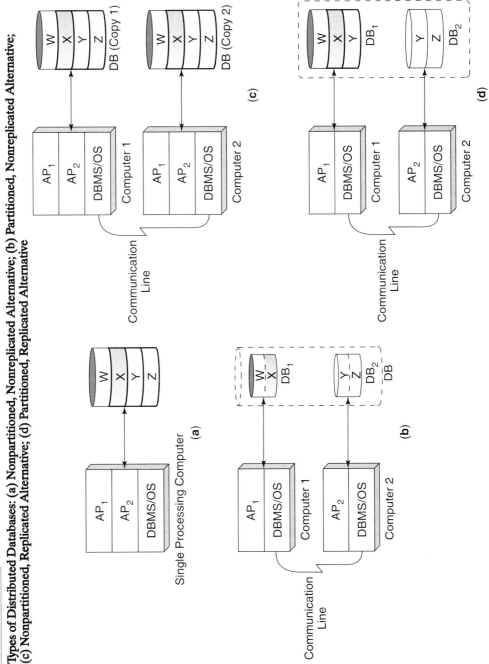

FIGURE 16-7

Continuum of Database Distribution Alternatives

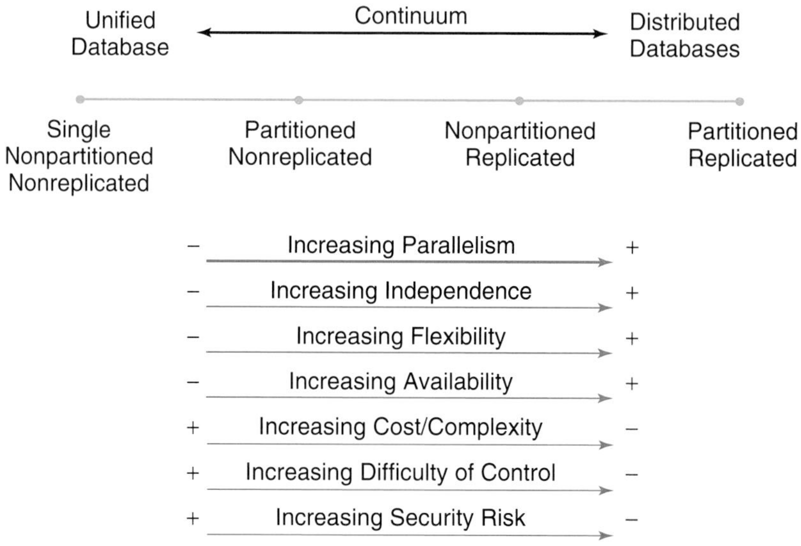

The greatest disadvantage is the difficulty of control and the resulting potential loss of data integrity. Consider the database architecture in Figure 16-6(d). A user connected to Computer 1 can read and update a data item in Partition Y on Computer 1 at the very same time that a different user connected to Computer 2 can read and update that data item in Partition Y on Computer 2.

For reasons explained in the next chapter, the strategies used to control concurrent processing for a database on one computer generally do not work for those on multiple computers. As you read this, new algorithms and technology are being developed, but as of this writing (December 1993), it is not possible to allow unrestricted concurrent processing of a partitioned, replicated database. Instead, if this architecture is to be used, restrictions must be placed on the processing.

In the remainder of this chapter, we discuss resource sharing and client server architectures.

RESOURCE SHARING

The number of applications using downloaded data has increased dramatically in recent years as the processing power of microcomputers has expanded. At first, bulk data was shared among computers by transferring it on magnetic media such as a diskette. But this approach was slow and cumbersome, since it required handling physical media. This style of sharing changed as microcomputers became integrated into the corporate communications network, and today, many organizations process downloaded data using resource sharing LAN-based systems.

When data is transferred in bulk from one computer to another, database administration tasks change significantly in character and complexity, and developers and users should be aware of this.

■ The Role of Resource Sharing

The resource sharing architecture is not suited for the transaction processing of multiuser databases, because too much of the database must be locked and transmitted for such an application to make sense. Resource sharing can be effective, however, for queries and reporting from downloaded data.

FIGURE 16-8

Resource Sharing of Downloaded Data with the Mainframe as the File Server

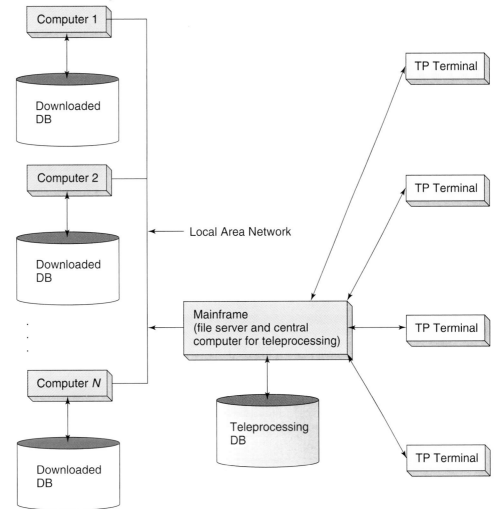

Figures 16-8 and 16-9 show two different alternatives that illustrate the use of resource sharing for processing downloaded data. In Figure 16-8, a local area network connects microcomputers with a file server. In this example, the file server role is fulfilled by a mainframe computer that is itself the center of a teleprocessing system that supports a multiuser, transaction-oriented database application. The users at the teleprocessing terminals (TP terminals) process transactions that reference the database stored on the mainframe.

Periodically—say, once a week—decision support users turn to their microcomputers to obtain an **extract** of the transaction processing database. This extract is taken from the mainframe with the understanding that the data will never be returned. In addition, if changes are made in the local data, the understanding is

FIGURE 16-9

Resource Sharing of Downloaded Data with a Gateway Micro as the File Server

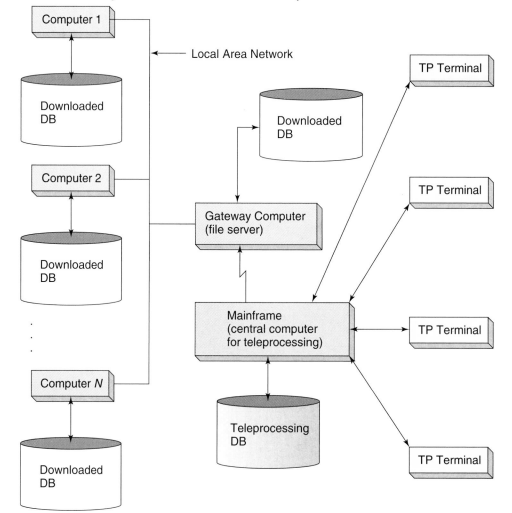

that such changes are not official, because official changes must be submitted for processing by users connected to the transaction-processing application.

Figure 16-9 shows an alternative resource sharing architecture, in which the decision support users also employ microcomputers on a LAN, but the LAN's file server is changed from the mainframe to another micro. In this case, the micro serves as a gateway to the teleprocessing system on the mainframe. The file server in Figure 16-9 periodically obtains a copy of all the data of interest to any of the decision support users that it supports on the LAN. When one of them requests data, the file server transmits it to the user from its own files. In this way, the workload on the mainframe computer is reduced because the mainframe is required to deal only with the LAN file server and not individually with each micro on the LAN.

These architectures make sense only if the decision support users do not have to make official changes in the data and can live with data that is not up-to-date. This structure can probably be justified only if the decision support users extensively use the data they obtain. And this happens if the users require sophisticated reports that are time-consuming to prepare or if they need the data for extensive ad hoc query processing.

■ Updating Downloaded Data

In some rare situations, the applications processing the downloaded data are allowed to update and return the data to the source database. When this is done, manual procedures must ensure that lost update and inconsistent read problems are not introduced when the data is returned. Either of these can happen if the applications on the source database and the distributed application are allowed to update the same data. Manual procedures must control the processing so that this cannot occur, but such processing is risky and consequently is seldom undertaken.

■ Example: Universal Equipment

The Universal Equipment Company manufactures and sells heavy equipment for the construction industry. Its products include bulldozers, graders, loaders, and drilling rigs. Every product is assigned to a product manager in the marketing department who is responsible for product planning, advertising, marketing support, development of sales support material, and so forth. Each product manager is assigned a group of two or three related products.

Advertising is the product managers' largest budget item, and so they want to be able to measure the effectiveness of the ads they run. Universal's ads always contain a mail-in card to request information. The cards have a preprinted number unique to each ad appearance so that this number can be used to identify the ad that generated a particular lead. To facilitate lead tracking, the marketing department has developed a microcomputer database application that the product managers can use.

Figure 16-10(a) shows the objects processed by this application. AD represents an advertisement; AD-APPEARANCE is the occurrence of a particular ad in a par-

FIGURE 16-10

Objects and Relations Supporting Universal's Product-marketing Database: (a) Objects Processed by the Universal Product Managers and (b) Relational Structure Supporting These Objects

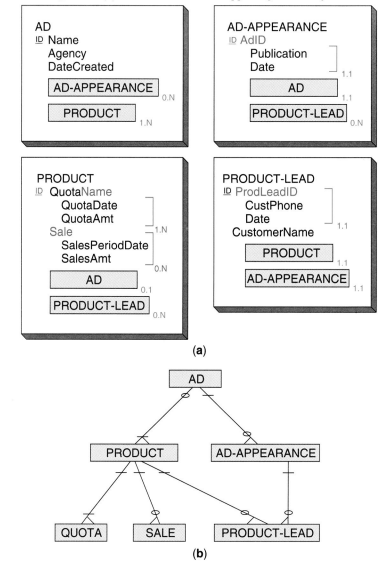

ticular publication; PRODUCT represents a particular product such as a bulldozer; and PRODUCT contains two repeating groups, one on quotas and one on sales. The groups are multivalued because sales quotas are assigned for each quarter and product sales are recorded on a weekly basis.

The view of PRODUCT is quite simple. The complete PRODUCT object actually contains more attributes, such as AD. But because the other relationships are not needed for the product managers' application, we have omitted them. The database structure that supports these objects is shown in Figure 16-10(b).

DOWNLOAD PROCESS

The product managers are assigned a microcomputer connected to other micros through a local area network in Universal's marketing department. To obtain sales and product-lead data, the micros call on a file server that serves as a gateway to Universal's mainframe (transaction-processing computer). The architecture is similar to that shown in Figure 16-9.

Every Monday, a key user in the marketing department runs a program developed by Universal's MIS department that updates the SALES, QUOTA, and PRODUCT-LEAD tables on the file server's database with data from the corporation's mainframe database. This program adds to the database the data from the previous week and also makes corrections. Product and sales data are imported for all related products to enable product managers to do comparative studies. Once the data has been downloaded to the file server, each product manager can obtain the data of interest to him or her from that server. Controls ensure that the product managers do not obtain data for which they are not authorized access.

■ Potential Problems in Processing Downloaded Databases

Importing data may cause problems, including coordination, consistency, access control, and computer crime.

COORDINATION

First consider **coordination**, using the PRODUCT-LEAD and AD-APPEARANCE tables for illustration. The PRODUCT-LEAD table is updated from data on the mainframe (leads are handled by sales personnel and are recorded on the mainframe). But the AD-APPEARANCE table is updated "locally" by the key user in the marketing department, who gets the data from reports prepared by the advertising manager and the advertising agency.

FIGURE 16-11

Issues and Potential Problems Regarding Downloaded Data Applications

Coordination
- Downloaded data must conform to database constraints.
- Local updates must be coordinated with downloads.

Consistency
- In general, downloaded data should not be updated.
- Applications need features to prevent updating.
- Users should be made aware of possible problems.

More Difficult Access Control
- Data may be replicated on many computers.
- Procedures to control data access are more complicated.

Increased Potential for Computer Crime
- Illegal copying is difficult to prevent.
- Diskettes and access via modem are easy to conceal.
- Risk may prevent the development of downloaded data applications.

This situation could cause problems when an ad is run for the first time in a new issue or publication. For example, the ad could generate leads that are recorded on the mainframe database before the AD-APPEARANCE data is stored on the file server. Then when those leads are downloaded, the program importing the data will have to reject the lead data, because such data violates the constraint that a PRODUCT-LEAD must have an AD-APPEARANCE parent. Thus the activities of local updating and downloading must be carefully coordinated: The key user needs to insert AD-APPEARANCE data before importing data from the mainframe. Similar coordination problems can occur when updating SALES and QUOTA data.

CONSISTENCY

The second problem with downloaded data concerns **consistency.** Each of the product managers receives downloaded SALES and QUOTA data that they are not supposed to change. But what would happen if a product manager did change the data? In this case, the data in that product manager's database might not match the data in the corporate database, the data in the file server, and possibly the data in other product managers' databases. The reports produced by that product manager could therefore disagree with other reports. And if several product managers update data, much inconsistent data could be generated.

Clearly this situation calls for strict control by the DBA. The database should be designed so that data cannot be updated. If this is not possible—say, the microcomputer database product will not enforce such a restriction, and the costs of writing programs to enforce it are prohibitively high—the solution to this problem is education. Product managers should be aware of the problems that will ensue if they change data, and they should be directed not to do so.

ACCESS CONTROL

A third problem is more difficult **access control.** When data is transferred to several computer systems, access control becomes more difficult. At Universal, for example, SALES and QUOTA data may be sensitive. For example, the vice-president of sales may not want the sales personnel to learn about upcoming sales quotas until the annual sales meeting. But if fifteen product managers have copies of this data in their databases, it can be difficult to ensure that it will be kept confidential until the appropriate time.

Furthermore, the file server receives all SALES and QUOTA data, which is supposed to be downloaded in such a way that a product manager receives only the SALES and QUOTA data for the products that he or she manages. Product managers can be quite competitive, however, and they may want to find the data for one another's products. Making this data accessible on the file server in the marketing department may thus create management problems.

COMPUTER CRIME

The fourth problem, a greater possibility of **computer crime,** is closely allied to that of access control. Whereas access control concerns inappropriate but legal activity, crime concerns illegal actions. Data on the corporate mainframe can be very valuable. Universal Equipment's sales and quota data, for example, is of great interest to its competitors.

When data is downloaded in bulk to the file server and then to one or many micro-computers, illegal copying becomes difficult to prevent. A diskette is easily concealed, and employees sometimes have modems with which they access work computers from off-site locations. In these situations, copying data over the telephone is nearly impossi-ble to detect or prevent. The greater risk of computer crime is an important problem of downloaded databases. In fact, it alone might prohibit such a system from being devel-oped, even though it would otherwise be an excellent solution. The potential problems of downloaded databases are summarized in Figure 16-11.

CLIENT SERVER SYSTEMS

As we stated, with client server database systems, application programs are distrib-uted to the client computers, and the database is processed by the server computer, as shown in Figure 16-2. Unlike resource sharing, the DBMS program resides on the database server and is not distributed to client computers. To illustrate characteris-tics of client server systems, we will use the following example.

▨ Example: Legacy Systems

Legacy Systems is a microcomputer software publisher with more than thirty prod-ucts and an installed base of over 100,000 customers. In addition to its software products, Legacy also sells extended customer support. The customer support department uses a client server system to keep track of customers and their queries.

The customer support department operates as follows: When customers call for service, the customer support personnel first ask for the customer's contract num-ber, which consists of two parts, the customer number and the license number for a particular product. These numbers are then verified against Legacy's records before service is provided.

Customer support personnel create a record of each call so that when the cus-tomer calls again, the Legacy personnel have a record of what has transpired (the customer may be assigned a different support representative each time he or she calls). In addition, while assisting a customer, the support representatives often gen-erate action items for departments within Legacy. For example, the representatives sometimes direct sales personnel to ship a replacement copy of a software product to a customer.

LEGACY CLIENT SERVER NETWORK

Legacy has installed a local area network of twenty-one microcomputers in the cus-tomer support department. One micro is the database server, and the other twenty process client application programs. The two types of programs are the Customer Support application and the Customer Processing application. The Customer Sup-port application is used by customer support representatives while they are serving customers, and the Customer Processing application is used to record new licenses, to produce mailing labels for newsletters and license renewal requests, and to update customer and other data. Each of the twenty application micros can process either application.

DATABASE STRUCTURE

Figure 16-12(a) shows the five objects that need to be processed to support these applications. The CUSTOMER object contains multiple occurrences of the CALL and LICENSE objects; CALL contains CUSTOMER and multiple occurrences of the object ACTION-ITEM; ACTION-ITEM contains CALL and DEPARTMENT as well as data about the action to be taken; and DEPARTMENT contains data about Legacy's departments as well as multiple occurrences of ACTION-ITEM. ACTION-ITEM is an association object establishing the relationship between

FIGURE 16-12

Database Structure for Legacy Systems' Application: (a) Objects Processed by Legacy Systems' Customer Support and (b) Relational Structure Supporting These Objects

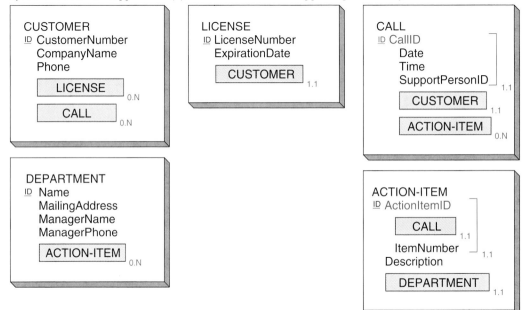

(a)

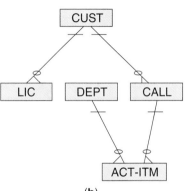

(b)

CALL and DEPARTMENT. The structure of the database supporting these objects is shown in Figure 16-12(b). Legacy defines a customer as any entity having a license for one of its products, and so a customer may be a person, a corporation, or some other organization. As shown in Figure 16-12(a), each CUSTOMER object may have many LICENSEs and many CALLs.

Parallel Application Processing

Unlike teleprocessing, in which the DBMS and all applications are processed on one machine, with client server applications, the multiple computers operate in parallel. For Legacy Systems, each of the twenty client computers can be processing applications in parallel while the server processes database requests, also in parallel. Thus a client server system can have greater throughput than can a teleprocessing system.

Figure 16-13 shows the processing of four transactions on two client computers and one server. Note that although the client computers must wait for data to be processed by the server, they do not need to wait for one another. For all but database activity, the two computers operate in parallel.

There is one restriction, however. Since there is only one database server, application programs cannot process an action against the database simultaneously. Rather, the database actions are serialized on the database server. Also, because a CUSTOMER can be an organization, it is possible that two customer support representatives may be dealing with the same CUSTOMER object at the same time. Two people who work for the same company, for example, may call about two different licenses on two different products. This means that client server systems must provide for some type of locking and must allow for deadlock and other problems.

Database Integrity

With the client server architecture, all database processing is consolidated on a single computer, and such consolidation enables a high degree of data integrity. Since every database request is processed by the server, if database constraints are defined to the server, it can consistently apply them. To understand the desirability of this, consider Figure 16-14. In Part (a), integrity checking is not performed by the server.

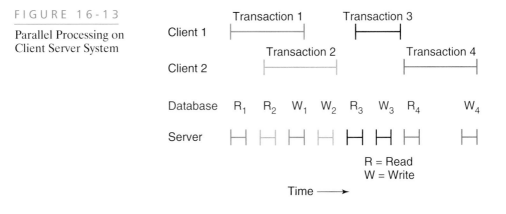

FIGURE 16-13

Parallel Processing on Client Server System

FIGURE 16-14

Client Server Integrity Checking: (a) Application Integrity Checking and (b) Centralized Integrity Checking

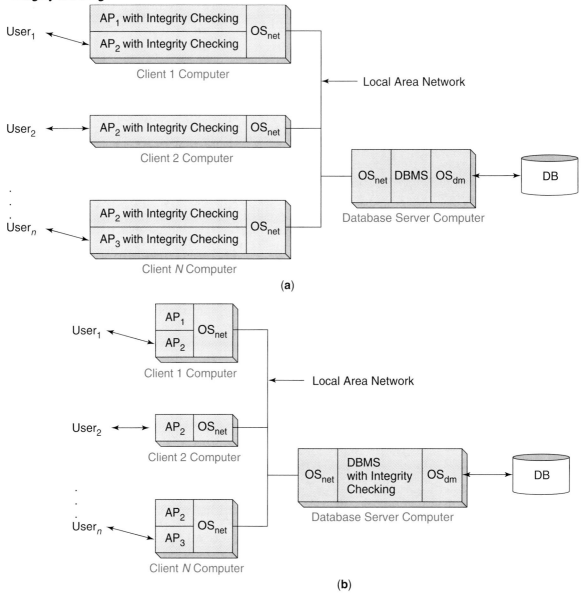

Instead, application programs on the client computers are required to check constraints during processing. In Part (b), integrity checking is performed by the DBMS on the server.

If you compare these two figures, you will see why server constraint checking is preferable. If the clients check constraints, the checking logic must be included in every application program, which is not only wasteful and inefficient but also susceptible to errors. That is, application programmers may understand the constraints differently and may make errors when programming them. Moreover, whenever a new application is developed, all of the constraint checking must be duplicated.

Not all data changes are made via application programs. That is, users can make changes through a query/update language, and data can be imported en masse. Unfortunately, in too many applications the constraints are not checked when importing data from these sources.

If the server performs constraint checking, the constraints need only be defined, verified, and validated once. Furthermore, the data changes from all sources will be checked for integrity. It will not matter whether a change is submitted by an application program or a query/update process or is imported. Regardless of the source, the DBMS will ensure that the constraints are not violated.

■ Triggers

A **trigger** is an application procedure automatically invoked by the DBMS when some event occurs. For example, in an inventory application, a trigger can be written to generate an order whenever the quantity of an item on hand falls below a certain threshold value.

To implement a trigger, the developer writes the trigger code and informs the DBMS of its existence and the conditions under which the trigger should be invoked. Later, when those conditions are realized, the DBMS calls the trigger. In a client server system, the triggers reside on and are invoked by the server.

Although they are very useful, triggers can also be a problem. In the presence of triggers, a user can cause activity on the database that he or she does not expect or even know about. A telemarketing person in order entry, for example, might want to reserve stock for a hot prospect. If he is not aware of the existence of the trigger, he may generate a dummy order to hold the stock. Later, if the prospect decides not to buy the stock, the user may return the stock to inventory. Meanwhile, unbeknownst to him, the trigger has generated orders for more of the product, orders that are unnecessary and that the user would not have generated had he been aware of them.

In a multiuser environment, trigger procedures sometimes need to invoke locks. The transaction that causes the event that invokes the trigger may have already obtained locks that conflict with the trigger. In this situation, a transaction can unknowingly come into deadlock with itself.

Finally, triggers can cascade and even form a closed loop. They cascade when one trigger creates a condition that causes another trigger to be invoked that creates a condition that causes a third trigger to be invoked, and so on. Triggers form loops when they cascade back to themselves. If this occurs, the DBMS must have some means of preventing an infinite loop.

As an aside, both DBMS-enforced constraint checking and triggers can be carried out by DBMS products in teleprocessing systems. There is no special characteristic of client server systems requiring that only they have centralized constraint checking and triggers. In practice, however, these capabilities are more common on client server DBMS products, because such products are newer than teleprocessing-oriented DBMS products and centralized constraint checking and triggers are relatively new ideas.

Concurrent Processing Control

One of the challenges in the development of client server applications is to gain the most parallelism on the client computers while protecting against problems such as lost updates and inconsistent reads.

To illustrate concurrent processing control for client server applications, consider the transaction logic shown in Figure 16-15, a transaction processed by customer support representatives at Legacy Systems. The support representative gets the customer and license data from the customer and uses it to read the appropriate row in CUST. Then the representative answers the customer's questions, updates the CUST data, and stores a new row in CALL. Finally, if the call results in an action item for one of Legacy's departments, a new row in ACT-ITM will be stored.

Since several representatives could process the same customer data, it is necessary to protect against the lost update and inconsistent read problems. There are two ways in which this can be done.

CONTROL BY MEANS OF PESSIMISTIC LOCKING

The first strategy, sometimes called *pessimistic locking* (because the locks are placed in anticipation of a conflict), is the same as that used in traditional teleprocessing systems such as DB2 (see Chapter 12). To implement this strategy, the DBMS places implicit locks on each DBMS command executed after the START TRANSACTION. These locks are then held until either a COMMIT or a ROLLBACK command is issued.

For the logic in Figure 16-15, an implicit lock is placed on CUST data when it is read at the start of the transaction. The lock is held until either a COMMIT or a ROLLBACK is issued. If the CUST data is valid, the customer's questions will be answered, and a new CALL record will be stored. The CUST data is also updated. Finally, if necessary, a new ACT-ITM row is created, and both the new CALL and the new ACT-ITM records are locked until the COMMIT command is issued.

Figure 16-16 shows the time required for processing two CALL transactions. In Part (a), the transactions process different CUST data, so there is no data conflict.

FIGURE 16-15

Logic of the CALL
Transaction

```
START TRANSACTION
READ CUST DATA
IF VALID
      THEN ANSWER CUSTOMER'S QUESTIONS
            UPDATE CUST DATA
            STORE CALL DATA
            IF NEED LEGACY ACTION
                  THEN ACT-ITM DATA
            END-IF
            COMMIT TRANSACTION
      ELSE ROLLBACK TRANSACTION
END-IF
```

Client 2 waits while the server processes Client 1's CUST data request, but after that, both clients process in parallel to the end of the transactions.

Figure 16-16(b) shows two transactions trying to process the same row in CUST. In this case, Client 2 waits for data until Client 1 has finished processing its CALL transaction. Such waiting may be a problem. If the customer talking to the support representative on Client 1 has many questions, the CUST data will be locked for a long time—several minutes or more. Also, if the user has much data to enter regarding the call or an action item, this, too, will extend Client 2's wait. Perhaps the user at Client 2 can process his or her CALL transaction much faster than the user at Client 1 can. If so, the user on Client 2 may be able to read the data, change it, and replace it while the user on Client 1 is talking to the customer.

These problems will become even worse if the DBMS does not support row-level locking. Some DBMS products, for example, lock a page (a block of rows) rather than a row, and some even lock the entire table. If locking is performed at such large levels of granularity, implicit locks can result in appreciable and unnecessary delays.

FIGURE 16-16

Locking on a Client Server System

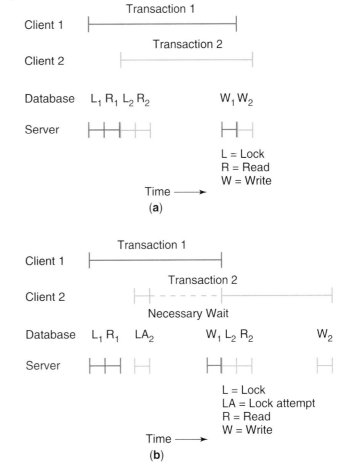

FIGURE 16-17

Page-Level Processing of Nonconflicting Data Requests on the Same Page

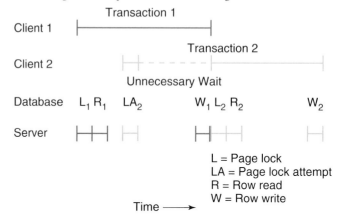

L = Page lock
LA = Page lock attempt
R = Row read
W = Row write

The situation depicted in Figure 16-17 assumes page-level locking. Two transactions are processing two different CUST rows that happen to be on the same page. In this case, Client 2 must wait for Client 1 to finish, even though the two transactions are processing different rows. Again, the delay may be substantial, and in this case, it is also unnecessary.

CONTROL BY MEANS OF OPTIMISTIC LOCKING

A second strategy, sometimes called *optimistic locking* (because no conflict is anticipated, but if there is one, one of the users must redo his or her work), is to defer the locking until the last possible moment and hope that there is no conflict. With this style, as much of the transaction is processed as possible before any locks are placed. Then the locks are obtained and held very briefly. To use this strategy, the DBMS must not apply any locks implicitly; instead, the application program must place the locks.

Figure 16-18 shows the CALL transaction logic using optimistic locking. The CUST data is read without any lock and without starting any transaction. A copy of the data, as read, is stored as OLD-CUST. Then the customer is serviced and the CUST data is modified in memory. CALL data is created in memory, as is ACT-ITM data, if appropriate.

At this point all of the time-consuming aspects of the transaction have been completed, and the user has keyed in all of the data, so the transaction is started and a lock is obtained on the CUST data. The CUST data is reread. If the data just read is the same as OLD-CUST, then no other user has changed the data since the customer service call was started. In this case, the data is updated and stored; the locks are released; and the transaction is committed.

If CUST data does not equal OLD-CUST, then someone has changed CUST while the call was in process. In this case, the user is informed that the CUST data has been changed by another user, and the user again makes the changes in CUST. This latter actions requires the user to repeat some work, but this should not be too much of a problem, since it should occur infrequently.

With delayed locks, the locks are held for very short periods of time, thus reducing the required waiting. Also, if two transactions are processing the same data in parallel,

FIGURE 16-18

Logic of the CALL Transaction Using Delayed Locks

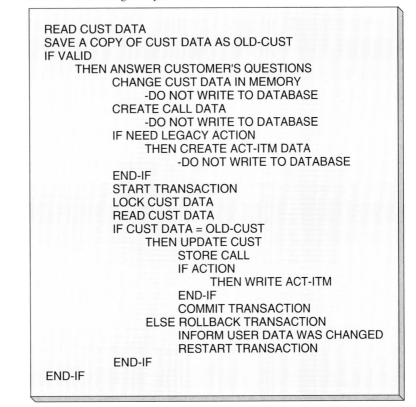

```
READ CUST DATA
SAVE A COPY OF CUST DATA AS OLD-CUST
IF VALID
        THEN ANSWER CUSTOMER'S QUESTIONS
                CHANGE CUST DATA IN MEMORY
                        -DO NOT WRITE TO DATABASE
                CREATE CALL DATA
                        -DO NOT WRITE TO DATABASE
                IF NEED LEGACY ACTION
                        THEN CREATE ACT-ITM DATA
                                -DO NOT WRITE TO DATABASE
                END-IF
                START TRANSACTION
                LOCK CUST DATA
                READ CUST DATA
                IF CUST DATA = OLD-CUST
                        THEN UPDATE CUST
                                STORE CALL
                                IF ACTION
                                        THEN WRITE ACT-ITM
                                END-IF
                                COMMIT TRANSACTION
                        ELSE ROLLBACK TRANSACTION
                                INFORM USER DATA WAS CHANGED
                                RESTART TRANSACTION
                END-IF
END-IF
```

the one that finishes first will be the one whose changes are committed to the database. The faster transaction will not need to wait for the slower transaction to finish.

Finally, the delayed locking strategy is particularly useful if the DBMS locks at a level higher than the row. Two users processing different rows in the same page or table, for example, can process nearly in parallel. Since the locks are held for such a short period of time, the users minimize their interference. Figure 16-19 shows the two transactions in Figure 16-17. Unlike implicit locking, there is almost no delay.

The problem with delayed locking is that transactions may need to be processed twice or even several times. Furthermore, the logic is more complicated, and so this scheme places a greater burden on the application programmer or client portion of the DBMS, or both.

■ Recovery

Recovery in client server systems can be carried out in the same way that it is in teleprocessing. The server computer keeps a log of changes in the database, and the database is periodically backed up to tape or another medium. When failures occur, the server DBMS can perform both rollback and rollforward. These statements

FIGURE 16-19

Delayed Lock Processing of Nonconflicting Data Requests on a Single Page

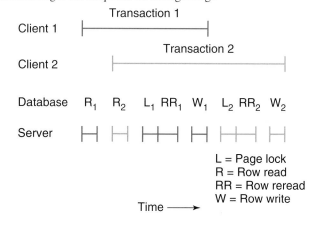

assume, however, a complete server DBMS. Unfortunately, not all products that are advertised as server DBMS products can support locking, constraint checking, backup, and recovery, as described here. As with any other product, the buyer should check for the features and functions he or she needs.

THE EMERGENCE OF TWO TYPES OF DBMS

As client server systems evolve, they are tending to split the DBMS products into two separate categories. The first category is server DBMS products. They offer a complete set of features for multiuser database processing including concurrency control and backup and recovery. The capabilities of a server DBMS are similar to those of a mainframe DBMS. Some popular server DBMS products are SYBASE SQL developed by the SYBASE Corporation, SQL Server (same as SYBASE SQL but licensed by Microsoft), Oracle, and INFORMIX.

The second category of products grew out of personal computer DBMS products. Although they are advertised as DBMS products, in the context of a client server system, they are actually application generators. In Figure 16-2, such a product would operate on client computers. Popular products in this category are Microsoft Access, Paradox for Windows, Paradox, and DataEase.

DBMS products that operate on the client side tend to focus on providing features and functions that ease application development and provide an easy-to-use front end to applications. DBMS products that operate on the server side tend to focus on providing features and functions for fast performance, concurrency control, integrity, and the like. This product differentiation will probably continue in the future.

SUMMARY

The classic method of supporting a multiuser database system is teleprocessing. But as computers have become less expensive, other architectures have been developed, among which are client server systems, resource sharing systems, and distributed database systems.

With teleprocessing, users operate dumb terminals or micros that emulate dumb terminals. The communications control program, application programs, DBMS, and operating system all are processed by a single, centralized computer. Because all processing is done by a single computer, the user interface of a teleprocessing system is usually simple and primitive.

A client server system consists of a network of computers, most often connected via a local area network. In nearly all cases, the user computers, called clients, are microcomputers, and in most cases, the server computer is also a micro, although minis and mainframes can be used. Application programs are processed on the client computer; the DBMS and the data management portion of the operating system reside on a server. A client server system can have multiple servers. If it does, each server will process a different database. Those systems in which two or more servers process the same database are called distributed database systems.

Client computers manage the user interface; they accept data from the user, process application logic, generate requests for database services, and process the data received. Server computers process the database, and while doing so, the server performs database integrity checking, maintains overhead data, and provides concurrent access control and related functions.

Client server systems place the application closer to the user, resulting in better performance and more sophisticated interfaces for the users. One disadvantage of client server systems is control; because of parallel processing, conflicts caused by concurrency are more difficult to manage.

Resource sharing systems also involve networks of computers, and like client server architectures, they usually consist of micros connected via local area networks. The chief difference between resource sharing systems and client server systems is that the server computer provides fewer services for the user computers. The server, which is called a *file* server and not a *database* server, provides access to files and other resources. Consequently, both the DBMS and the application programs must be distributed to the users' computers.

Resource sharing systems transmit considerably more data than do client server systems, and they require that locks be obtained on large groups of data and held for long periods of time. Thus resource sharing typically provides less throughput than do client server applications.

With a distributed database system, multiple computers process the same database. There are several types of distributed databases: partitioned, nonreplicated; nonpartitioned, replicated; and partitioned, replicated. In general, the greater the degree of partitioning and replication is, the greater the flexibility, independence, and reliability will be. At the same time, expense, control difficulty, and security problems increase. Distributed databases are discussed in the next chapter.

Resource sharing is used infrequently for multiuser, transaction-processing systems, but it can be used for the query and reporting of downloaded data. In this case, the data is extracted from an operational database and placed on the file server. Microcomputers on the resource sharing network then get copies of the data for query and report processing. Such downloaded data is almost never changed and is returned to the original data source. Problems with processing downloaded data are coordination, consistency, access control, and a greater likelihood of computer crime.

Client server systems are often used for multiuser transaction-processing applications. Such systems can provide high performance because of the parallel processing among client and server computers. In addition, integrity can be improved by placing integrity and constraint checking on the server. Triggers can be used for this purpose.

Concurrent-processing control is as important to client server systems as it is to other types of multiuser systems. Two styles are possible. Pessimistic locking requires implicit locks similar to the locks employed with traditional database applications. The data must be locked before it can be read for updating. With optimistic locking, the second style, as much of the transaction as possible is processed before obtaining a lock. Then the locks are obtained and the data is reread. If there has been no change, the transaction is committed to the database as processed. If there has been a change, the transaction is reprocessed as necessary. Optimistic locking is especially useful when locking is done at a level of granularity larger than a row at a time and when the transactions are likely to be lengthy because of slow human processing. Recovery in client server systems is similar to recovery in teleprocessing database systems.

As client server systems evolve, they are forcing the definition of two categories of DBMS. Server DBMS products are much like the mainframe and minicomputer DBMS products that have been used for years. They provide DBMS services on the operating system and file management interfaces. Client DBMS products are extensions of the personal DBMS products used on microcomputers. They provide an easy-to-use user interface that is also simple to develop. Client DBMS products are, in many ways, application development systems.

GROUP I QUESTIONS

16.1   Sketch the essential architecture of a teleprocessing system. Name and identify the computer(s) and programs involved, and explain which computer processes which programs.

16.2   Why is the users' interface on teleprocessing applications generally character oriented and primitive?

16.3   Sketch the essential architecture of a client server system. Name and identify the computer(s) and programs involved, and explain which computer processes which programs.

16.4   What types of processing hardware are used with client server systems?

16.5   How many servers can a client server system have? What restrictions apply to the servers?

16.6   Explain why client server systems can have fast performance.

16.7   How do typical user interfaces on client server systems differ from user interfaces on teleprocessing systems?

16.8   Describe an important disadvantage of client server systems.

16.9   Sketch the essential architecture of a resource sharing system. Name and identify the computer(s) and programs involved, and explain which computer processes which programs.

16.10 Explain how the processing of the following SQL query would differ between a client server system and a resource sharing system:

SELECT   StudentName, ClassName
FROM   STUDENT, GRADE
WHERE   STUDENT.StudentNumber = GRADE.StudentNumber
AND   GRADE.Grade = 'A'

Assume that the database contains two tables:

STUDENT (StudentNumber, StudenName, StudentPhone)
GRADE (ClassNumber, StudentNumber, Grade)

Also assume that the primary and foreign keys have indexes.

16.11 Explain why resource sharing systems are seldom used for multiuser transaction-processing applications.

16.12 Sketch the essential architecture of a distributed database system. Name and identify the computer(s) and programs involved, and explain which computer processes which programs.

16.13 Explain how distributed database systems differ from client server systems.

16.14 Describe three types of distributed database systems, and describe how they differ in terms of flexibility and control.

16.15 Sketch two alternative systems that could be used to facilitate the processing of downloaded data.

16.16 Why is it generally unwise to allow the updating of downloaded data? If such updating is allowed, what precautions must be taken?

16.17 Describe the possible coordination problems of processing downloaded data.

16.18 Describe the possible consistency problems of processing downloaded data.

16.19 Describe the possible access control problems of processing downloaded data.

16.20 Describe the possible problems of computer crime when processing downloaded data.

16.21 Explain why it is desirable to place integrity and constraint checking on the server in a client server system. What efficiencies result?

16.22 What is a trigger and what is its purpose? What problems can occur when using triggers?

16.23 Describe how to control concurrency in a client server system using pessimistic locking. First define the logic of a transaction, and then show how that logic would apply to a client server system that has three clients and a single database server.

16.24 Describe how to control concurrency in a client server system using optimistic locking. Use the same transaction logic and system as in your answer to Question 16.23.

16.25 How does recovery differ in a client server system from that in a teleprocessing system?

16.26 Describe two categories of DBMS products that are emerging from client server systems.

GROUP II QUESTIONS

Questions 16.27 through 16.29 concern the following example: Consider a database having the following five tables:

SP (<u>SPNumber</u>, SPName, Region, TotalSalesMade)

CUST (<u>CustNumber</u>, CustName, CustPhone, Balance)

ORDER (<u>OrderNumber</u>, OrderDate, *SPNumber*, *CustNumber*, Amount)

LINE-ITEM (<u>OrderNumber</u>, <u>LineItemNumber</u>, *ItemNumber*, Qty, Extended-Price)

INVENTORY (<u>ItemNumber</u>, Description, UnitPrice, QuantityOnHand)

Assume that the following transactions exist:

T_1 Add/change/delete a row in CUST

T_2 Add/change/delete a row in INVENTORY

T_3 Add a new order by creating a new row in ORDER, new rows in LINE-ITEM, decrementing QuantityOnHand in INVENTORY, adding Amount of ORDER to Balance in CUST, and adding Amount of ORDER to TotalSales-Made in SP. Ensure that sufficient stock is in inventory for each item ordered. Do not allow any backorders.

Further assume that the organization has three users in the order-processing department. Each of these three users is authorized to process transactions of type T_1. Only one of them is authorized to process transactions of type T_2, and the other two users are authorized to process transactions of type T_3.

16.27 Sketch the architecture of a teleprocessing system to process these three transactions against this database. Describe the programs that would be required. Develop pseudocode or a flowchart of the logic to process transaction T_3. Also give an example of a concurrent-processing problem that could occur in this system, and explain how to prevent it.

16.28 Sketch the architecture of a client server system to process these three transactions against this database. Explain the programs that would be required, and show where they would reside. Develop pseudocode or a flowchart of the logic to process transaction T_3. Explain what data would need to be transmitted across the LAN to process this transaction. Also give an example of a concurrent-processing problem that could occur in this system, and explain how it could be prevented using the delayed-locking strategy. Discuss the advantages and disadvantages of this system compared with the teleprocessing system described in your answer to Question 16.27.

16.29 Sketch the architecture of a resource sharing system to process these three transactions against this database. Explain the programs that would be required, and show where they would reside. Develop pseudocode or a flow-chart of the logic to process transaction T_3. Explain what data would need to be transmitted across the LAN to process transactions of this type. Also give an example of a concurrent-processing problem that could occur in this system, and explain how that problem could be prevented using locks. What level of granularity of lock would be required? Discuss the advantages and disadvantages of this system compared with the client server solution in Question 16.28.

CHAPTER

DISTRIBUTED

DATABASE PROCESSING

This chapter concludes this textbook with a discussion of distributed database processing. We describe the characteristics and components of distributed database systems and present four processing goals for a distributed DBMS (DDBMS). Finally, we consider two difficult issues in distributed processing, concurrency and failure/recovery.

You should be aware that distributed database processing continues to evolve and by no means are we dealing with a mature discipline. As Bernstein and Goodman wrote about one aspect of distributed processing, "Distributed concurrency control, by contrast [with nondistributed], is in a state of extreme turbulence. More than 20 concurrency control algorithms have been proposed for DDBMSs, and several have been, or are being, implemented. These algorithms are usually complex, hard to understand, and difficult to prove correct (indeed, many are incorrect)."[1] Although this quotation from two of the pioneering researchers in this discipline was published in 1981, it continues to be true today.

In short, many of the problems have been identified, but few *robust* solutions are known. Moreover, the subject is exceedingly complex, and research is divided among different facets of the problems. In addition, much of the work has been theoretical, and so important practical issues have been ignored.

---

[1] Philip A. Bernstein and Nathan Goodman, "Concurrency Control in Distributed Database Systems," *Computing Surveys*, June 1981, p. 185.

At the same time, end users equipped with microcomputers and local databases are increasing the pressure on the MIS department to provide some form of distributed processing. The resource sharing and client server systems described in Chapter 16 are the first indications of this pressure. In response, vendors of DBMS products have begun to announce so-called DDBMS products, most of which fail to resolve many of the distributed database–processing problems. But these products will improve, and over time, true distributed DDBMS products will be developed.

Your goal in reading this chapter should be to understand the nature of distributed database processing, its advantages and disadvantages, design considerations for distributed database systems, and the problems that need to be overcome. Such knowledge will provide a foundation for this complicated subject that is likely to grow and evolve during your career.

OVERVIEW

Distributed database processing is database processing in which the execution of transactions and the retrieval and updating of data occur across two or more independent and usually geographically separated computers. Figure 17-1 shows a distributed database system involving four computers.

FIGURE 17-1

Distributed Database Architecture

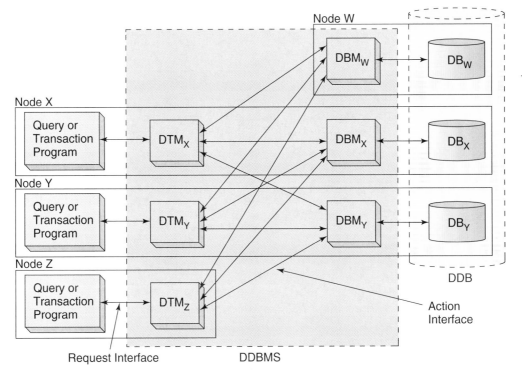

The **distributed database management system** (DDBMS) consists of the distributed transaction and database managers on all computers. As shown, this DDBMS is a generic schematic representing a collection of programs that operate on different computers. All these programs may be subsystems of a single DDBMS product licensed from a single vendor, or they may be a collection of programs from disparate sources: Some may be licensed from vendors, and some may be written in-house. The point of this figure is to illustrate the functions that must be served in distributed database processing.

A **distributed transaction manager** (DTM) is a program that receives processing requests from query or transaction programs and translates them into actions for the database managers. An important function of the DTM is to coordinate and control these actions. Depending on the nature of the application and the DDBMS, the DTM may be provided as part of the DDBMS, or it may be developed in-house by the organization that implements the distributed system. In less sophisticated applications, some of its functions may even be performed by people following manual procedures.

A **database manager** (DBM) is a program that processes some portion of the distributed database, such as retrieving and updating user and overhead data in accordance with action commands received from the DTMs. The DBM may be a subset of a DDBMS product, or it may be a commercial nondistributed DBMS. In some cases, the DDBMS may contain different DBMS products.

A **node** is a computer that executes a DTM, a DBM, or both. A **transaction node** processes a DTM, and a **database node** processes a DBM and its database. In Figure 17-1, Node W is a database node running DBM_W and storing DB_W. Node X is both a transaction and database node with DTM_X, DBM_X, and DB_X. Similarly, Node Y is both a transaction and database node, but Node Z is a transaction node only.

Query or transaction programs communicate with DTMs by means of requests similar to the requests for DBMS action. Examples are SELECT EMPLOYEE WHERE E# EQ 123 or STORE DUE-DATE. Such requests operate on logical constructs; the query or application program is not referring to any particular physical instance of the construct.

DTMs communicate with DBMs by means of actions to be executed on specific data instances. Thus if the new occurrence of DUE-DATE is to be stored in DB_X and DB_Y, the DTM will translate the *request* STORE DUE-DATE into two *actions*. One will direct DBM_X to store the new data, and the second will direct DBM_Y to store this data. In principle, requests and actions can also differ in terms of their level of abstraction. For example, a request can be expressed in terms of an object and be translated into actions expressed in terms of the distributed composite relations or files. To date, however, no such DDBMS exists.

■ Advantages of Distributed Processing

There are four advantages of distributed database processing. First, it can result in better performance than that obtained by centralized processing. Data can be located close to the point of use so that communication time is shorter. Also, several computers operating simultaneously can yield more processing throughput than a single computer can.

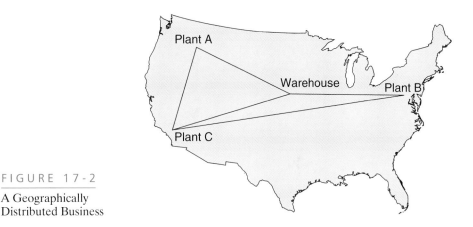

FIGURE 17-2

A Geographically
Distributed Business

Second, replicated data increases reliability. When a computer fails, replicated data can be obtained from other computers. Users are not dependent on the availability of a sole source for their data. A third advantage is that distributed systems are more easily scaled in size. Additional computers can be added to the network as the number of users or their processing workload expands. Adding a new, smaller computer is often easier and cheaper than upgrading a single, centralized computer. Then if the workload decreases, the size of the network can also be readily reduced.

Finally, distributed systems are more readily tailored to the structure of the users' organization. Figure 17-2 shows the organization of a geographically distributed manufacturer. The general managers of each plant have considerable authority and latitude in the operation of their facilities. If these plants were dependent on a single, centralized computer, the system architecture would conflict with the company's operational philosophy and policy. Even in more centralized organizations, distributed processing offers greater flexibility to fit organizational structure than does centralized processing.

■ Disadvantages of Distributed Processing

The first two disadvantages of distributed databases are the same as the first two advantages. First, performance can be worse for distributed processing than for centralized processing. Depending on the nature of the workload, the network, the DDBMS, and the concurrency and failure strategies used, the advantages of local data access and multiple processors can be overwhelmed by the coordination and control tasks required. This situation is especially likely when the workload calls for a large number of concurrent updates on replicated data that must be widely distributed.

Second, distributed database processing can be less reliable than centralized processing. Again, depending on the reliability of processing computers, the network, the DDBMS, the transactions, and error rates in the workload, a distributed system can be less readily available than a centralized one. Both of these disadvantages indicate that distributed processing is no panacea. Although it holds the promise of better performance and greater reliability, this promise is not guaranteed.

FIGURE 17-3

Advantages and Disadvantages
of Distributed Database
Processing

Advantages	Disadvantages
Better performance	Worse performance
Increased reliability	Decreased reliability
Easily scaled in size	Increased complexity
Readily tailored to organization structure	Higher costs
	Difficult to control

A third disadvantage is increased complexity, which often translates into high construction and maintenance expenses. Since there are more hardware components, there is more to learn about and more interfaces that can fail. Concurrency control and failure recovery can be exceedingly complicated and difficult to implement, often leading to a greater burden on programmers and on operations personnel and perhaps meaning that more experienced (and expensive) personnel are required.

Finally, distributed database processing is difficult to control. A centralized computer resides in a controlled environment with closely supervised operations personnel, and the processing activities can be monitored (though with difficulty). In a distributed system, processing computers often reside in the users' work areas. Physical access is frequently uncontrolled, and operations procedures are sometimes lax and performed by people who have little appreciation or understanding of their importance. Finally, in the event of a disaster or catastrophe, recovery can be far more difficult to synchronize than with a centralized system. The advantages and disadvantages of distributed database processing are summarized in Figure 17-3.

COMPONENTS OF DISTRIBUTED DATABASE SYSTEMS

The components of distributed database systems often are confusing because so many different types of processing fall under the term *distributed database processing* and can fit into the general architecture of Figure 17-1. For example, consider the system in Figure 17-4(a). It conforms to the architecture shown in Figure 17-1 in which the nodes are specified to be mainframe computers. For this system, the processing is most likely based on the equality of cooperating colleagues. Each database node (W, X, and Y) has the authority to insert, modify, delete, and read any data throughout the network. The data also is coordinated among the computers in as close to real time as possible.

Now consider Figure 17-4(b), in which Node W is a mainframe, Nodes X and Y are minicomputers, and Node Z is a microcomputer. In this instance, the processing rules could be the following: Only Node W can modify the database; Nodes X and Y, which have copies of data on Node W, are authorized for read-only access, and

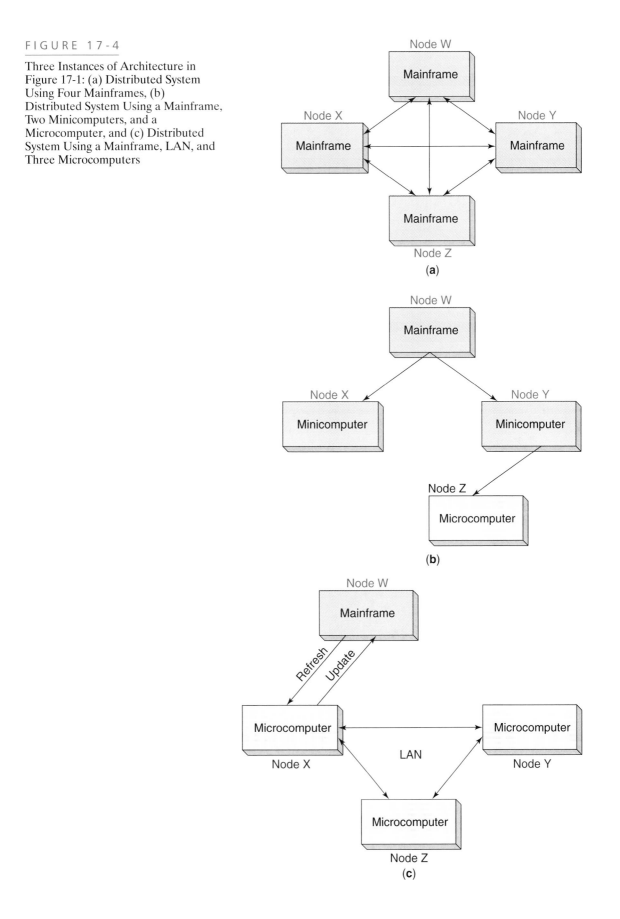

Three Instances of Architecture in
Figure 17-1: (a) Distributed System
Using Four Mainframes, (b)
Distributed System Using a Mainframe,
Two Minicomputers, and a
Microcomputer, and (c) Distributed
System Using a Mainframe, LAN, and
Three Microcomputers

Node Z may obtain data only from Node Y. No attempt is made to keep the data current in real time. Instead, once each day, Nodes X and Y are refreshed by Node W, and once each week, Node Z is refreshed by Node Y.

Figure 17-4(c) shows a third instance of the architecture in Figure 17-1, in which Node W is a mainframe, and Nodes X, Y, and Z are microcomputers attached to a local area network. Node X is a gateway to the mainframe; it obtains all of the database data that X, Y, and Z need from W and stores it on its own database. Suppose that Node Y needs frequent access to some of the data but processes it on a read-only basis. When either Node X or Node Z make changes in the data, they do it on the copy on W. Periodically, W refreshes X's database with data that has been changed.

These three examples all conform to the general architecture in Figure 17-1, but they are entirely different. They each have their own set of capabilities and their own set of problems. To bring order to this complexity, we consider the following five components of a distributed database system: hardware, programs, data, procedures, and personnel.

■ Hardware

As shown in Figure 17-4, processing nodes can consist of many different types of hardware. In some distributed systems, such as Figure 17-4(a), all of the nodes are homogeneous. In others, such as Figure 17-4(b) and (c), they are heterogeneous. Differences in processing speeds and storage capacities should be considered when determining the nodes' processing authorities.

■ Programs

The principal program that we need to consider in a distributed database system is the DDBMS. The DDBMS architecture shown in Figure 17-1 is generic. The DTMs and DBMs can be subsystems of a single DDBMS product that is licensed from one vendor. Alternatively and, at present, more commonly, the DDBMS is an amalgam of programs developed in-house and products obtained from various software vendors. In many cases, the DTMs are written in-house, and the DBMs are commercial DBMS products.

Consider the examples in Figure 17-4. In the first, all of the computers are the same class of machine (mainframe), and the company with this system could elect to license a DDBMS that is a single product. If it did, the DTMs and DBMs would be provided by the vendor as subsystems of the DDBMS. Each DTM would expect to be communicating with only the DBM provided by the vendor. R*, a prototype DDBMS developed by IBM, is an example of such a product. In reality, however, such DDBMS products are rare.

Now look at Figure 17-4(b). This system involves a mixture of hardware types, and it is unlikely that any commercial DDBMS product would work across all of them. The DBMs could be versions of a single commercial DBMS product, however, as long as that product runs on all classes of hardware. Oracle, for example, runs on mainframes, minicomputers, and microcomputers. The DTMs, however, are not part of the commercial product. Instead, they would be application programs written in-house that access the product on a foreign computer and download the data. Or several DBMS products could be used as DBMs, as described next.

Figure 17-4(c) shows a mainframe communicating with a local area network of microcomputers. In this case, the DBM could be a single product, as in the preceding case, or it could be a mixture of products. If it were a mixture, the DBM on Node W might be a mainframe DBMS product like DB2, and the DBMs on Nodes X, Y, and Z could be multiuser LAN versions of a microcomputer DBMS such as SQL Server or Informix. It is possible that an extract program, which obtains data from the database on Node X, would be provided by the microcomputer DBMS vendor. Thus the DDBMS can be a single product or an amalgam of different programs and products.

Data

One of the key characteristics of a distributed database system is whether or not the data is **replicated.** A distributed database can be nonreplicated, partially replicated, or fully replicated. If it is nonreplicated, one, and only one, copy of each data item exists. Data items are assigned to particular nodes, and they may reside only at their assigned node. Any application needing access to the data item must obtain it from the officially designated node.

A partially replicated database contains some data items that are duplicated and some that are not. A system directory indicates whether a data item is replicated and where it is stored. A fully replicated distributed database is one in which the entire database is duplicated on two or more nodes. A node contains either all of the database or none of it.

Procedures

Distributed database systems contain a multitude of procedural components. The first group pertains to **processing rights.** Which nodes can do what to which data? In the simplest distributed systems, data is nonreplicated, and only the node that stores the data can update it. (Actually, in the very simplest system, no data is updated at all but is obtained from a foreign source and processed as read-only data. Such a situation is rare, however.) In more complicated situations, any node can issue an update request for any data item on its own or any other node. If the data item is replicated, all copies are changed. When designing a distributed system, the developers must determine the processing rights, the requirements, the capabilities of the hardware and programs, the control of concurrency, and other factors.

Another component of procedures is **data currency.** How up-to-date must the data be? Does every node need the most current value of all of the data items it accesses? Can some databases be allowed to become out-of-date? In Figure 17-4(a), all nodes have access to the most current data. In Figure 17-4(b) and (c), some of the nodes are processing historical data. In general, the more current the replicated data is, the more expensive the system will be. Enormous numbers of processing cycles must be devoted to controlling and coordinating the system in Figure 17-4(a), and powerful and expensive CPUs are required to process this network.

Closely related to the issues of processing rights and currency is the issue of **data flow.** Who updates whom? In Figure 17-4(b), Node W updates the data on Nodes X and Y, whereas in Figure 17-4(c), Node X updates the data on Node W. Such flows are determined by the requirements and the processing rights of the nodes.

Another procedural component is **control.** In regard to conflicting processing requests, which node resolves the conflict? In general, authoritarian control—usually implemented in systems like those in Figures 17-4(b) and (c)—is easier to implement than are schemes based on equality—usually implemented in systems like that in Figure 17-4(a).

In fact, for distributed systems like the one in Figure 17-4(a), control can be distributed and diffused throughout the network. No single node need be in charge. Control decisions can be made by any of the nodes, depending on the control issue and the state of the system. This situation allows for greater flexibility, but it is far more complex.

■ Personnel

Distributed systems vary considerably in the demands they place on people. Systems with a sophisticated and powerful DDBMS place few special demands on users. In fact, the users do not know they are processing distributed data. They simply access their applications, and all the distributed processing is done for them by the DDBMS. In less sophisticated systems, the users must become involved.

Consider the system in Figure 17-4(b). The users at Nodes X and Y may need to invoke one or more programs to cause data to be downloaded from the mainframe. Similarly, the users at Node Z may need to manually start programs in order to bring data down from Node Y. Depending on the system's design, the users may also be responsible for inspecting processing reports to determine that the data was received without error and that the correct data was transmitted.

In very primitive distributed systems, the users may even bear some of the responsibilities of the DTM. For example, in some systems the users make data changes on the local database and then manually cause these changes to be made for replicated data on other nodes. In the most primitive systems, users employ the NIKE method (they put on their sneakers and run down the hall carrying diskettes of data changes from computer to computer).

FOUR GOALS FOR A DISTRIBUTED DBMS

Traiger and his colleagues defined four goals for a distributed DBMS, which provide an excellent framework for a survey of the issues, problems, and solutions proposed for distributed databases.[2] Each of the goals involves an aspect of **transparency**.

In a distributed database system, transparency means that query facilities and transaction programs are isolated from the management of the distributed database so that they can realize the advantages of distributed processing without having to become involved in the particulars of the database distribution. Programmers and users can then focus on the nature and logic of the information problem they need to solve and not be forced to deal with matters that more properly belong to the

---

[2] Irving L. Traiger, Jim Gray, Cesare A. Galtieri, and Bruce G. Lindsay, "Transactions and Consistency in Distributed Database Systems," *Transactions on Database Systems*, September 1982, pp. 323–342.

DDBMS. (To simplify this discussion, for the balance of this chapter, we will refer to query users and transaction programs simply as *transactions.*)

Specifically, transactions need access to the database via a DDBMS that provides the following four types of transparency: **data location, data replication, concurrency,** and **failure.** This means that ideally, the transaction is not even aware that the data is distributed. All four of these distribution issues are handled behind the scenes.

■ Location Transparency

Transactions need to be independent of the location of a particular data item. If they are not, then location issues will greatly complicate the transaction logic. Consider the manufacturing company used in Figure 17-2. If the inventory manager wants to move three refrigerators from Plant A to Plant B, two inventory records must be modified. Suppose the data involved is not replicated, but it may be stored on a computer at either facility. If the program that processes this transaction is not transparent to the location of the data, it will have to consider four cases: both records at A, one at A and one at B, one at B and one at A, and both at B. Obviously, the logic of the transaction is confounded by the need to consider the data's location. The logic would be much more complicated for a more sophisticated example, and in any case, such considerations are unnecessary and inappropriate for an *application* program.

Location transparency can be provided if the distributed transaction managers (DTMs in Figure 17-1) are responsible for determining the location of data and issuing actions on the appropriate DBMs. This can be done if the DTMs have access to directories of data locations. In this way, if the data is moved, only the DTM need be involved. All transactions are isolated from the change in location.

■ Replication Transparency

Transactions are transparent to replication if they can process without knowing how many times or even if the data is replicated. The transaction can act as if all data is stored only once on a single node. With replication transparency, new duplicates can be created, or existing duplicates can be eliminated, without any effect on the end user's transaction or query processing.

To provide replication transparency, the transaction managers must translate transaction-processing requests into actions for the database managers. Reads are straightforward. The DTM selects one of the nodes that stores the data and issues an action to read it. To facilitate the selection, the DTM may keep statistics about the time required to read data from various nodes, and then it can select the node with the best performance. Writing replicated data is more complicated, because the DTM must issue a write action for every DBM that stores a copy of that data.

This discussion assumes that every DTM has an accurate and up-to-date copy of a directory that indicates data locations. Interesting problems arise, however, when we consider what happens when the directory must be changed to account for new data copies or their elimination. Clearly, coordination is critical. All directories must be installed in such a manner that no DTM thinks that the data is available before it is (in the case of reads) and that every DTM knows that data is available when it is (in the case of writes). Otherwise, a DTM may request data that is not yet available or fail to issue a write on a DBM when data has become available (see Bernstein and Goodman for more information about directory processing[3]).

Concurrency Transparency

Although many transactions involving the distributed database can be executed at the same time, the results of the transactions must not be affected. The DDBMS provides concurrency transparency if the results of all concurrent transactions are logically consistent with the results that would have been obtained if the transactions had been executed one at a time, in some arbitrary serial order. Stated in another way, the logic of transactions processed concurrently with other transactions must be the same as it would have been if the transaction had been processed alone.

Two strategies have been developed to provide concurrency control. One, called **distributed two-phase locking,** is an extension of the concurrency control mechanism we discussed in Chapters 15 and 16. A second method is called **timestamp ordering.** Both have been implemented in DDBMS products. Distributed two-phase locking is more common, and we discuss it further in the next section.

Failure Transparency

The fourth goal for the DDBMS is to provide failure transparency, which means that transactions are correctly processed despite transaction, DDBMS, network, and computer failures. Stated in the terms of Chapter 15, in the face of failure, transactions will be **atomic**; that is, either all of a transaction will be processed, or none of it will be. Moreover, once the results of transactions have been committed, they will be permanent.

Failure transparency is the most difficult of the four goals. Part of the problem is that there are so many types of failure. On one end of the spectrum is a node that never fails, sometimes called a **perfect node.** On the other end is a node that fails in a totally unknown manner. Such a node may communicate garbage over the network or, because of its failure, may send validly formatted but inappropriate actions over the network. Such a node is called an **insane node.**

Another type of failure pertains to nodes that become malevolent, meaning that the node has the express purpose of performing an unauthorized activity or of intentionally causing harm. It is even possible to consider failures in which nodes conspire with one another to subvert the distributed system. Such failures are sometimes called **Byzantine failures.**

Between the extremes of perfect nodes and insane nodes are **sane nodes.** A sane node is a node that can fail, but only in a defined and known way. The simplest example of a sane node is one that either is perfect or fails to respond at all.[4]

Another reason that failure transparency is so difficult is that concurrency control is so complicated. In a sense, concurrency control problems are solved at the

[3] Philip A. Bernstein and Nathan Goodman, "An Algorithm for Concurrency Control and Recovery in Replicated Distributed Databases," *Transactions on Database Systems*, December 1984, pp. 696–615.

[4] Hector Garcia-Molina, Frank Pittelli, and Susan Davidson, "Applications of Byzantine Agreement in Database Systems," *Transactions in Database Systems*, March 1986, pp. 27–47.

expense of failure recovery. It is as if a bubble of air under the carpet is pushed from one corner only to reappear in another. The concurrency-control mechanisms work as long as no failure occurs at certain times or in certain states of the distributed database (or as long as recovery can be guaranteed to proceed in a certain manner, and so forth). In the general case of partitioned, replicated databases, many theoretical and practical implementation problems still remain to be solved. We discuss failure transparency in more detail later in this chapter.

DISTRIBUTED CONCURRENCY CONTROL

In this and the next section, we examine some of the technical issues in developing DDBMS products that provide concurrency and failure transparency. These two sections contain the most technical discussions in this text.

Distributed databases face the same concurrency problems as do centralized databases. Although the problems and their solutions are more complicated, because several independent computers and potentially replicated data exist. We begin with a discussion of the anomalies that can occur if processing is not controlled appropriately. These anomalies are similar to those described in Chapter 15 for centralized processing. We approach them somewhat more formally, however, in order to establish the terminology needed to address this more difficult problem.

■ Concurrent-processing Anomalies

Figure 17-5(a) illustrates the first anomaly, sometimes called the **lost update anomaly.** Suppose the transactions in this example are in the business of the distributed manufacturer in Figure 17-2. Assume that the transactions process the same non-replicated data item stored on a computer at Plant A. The transactions could arise from the same DTM or from different DTMs. Each transaction is reducing the quantity on hand for some item in inventory. (In these examples, we need not consider the identity of the item.)

The nomenclature, $r_1(N_A)$, refers to a read by transaction 1 of the value of N that is stored at Plant A. The arrow and value indicate the value read. Similarly, $w_1(N_A)$ means a write from transaction 1 of a value of N to the computer at Plant A. The arrow and value indicate the value written. As you can see from this example, w_1 is lost, because the write from transaction 2 overlays it. We described this problem for nondistributed systems in Chapter 15.

A second anomaly is shown in Figure 17-5(b), sometimes called the **inconsistent read anomaly**, which occurs when one transaction reads a data item while another one writes it. In this example, one transaction (T_3) is moving four units from the warehouse to Plant B while another transaction (T_4) is counting the total number of units at Plants A and B and the warehouse. Although there are a total of ten units in the three locations, T_4 concludes that there are only six, because T_4 reads N_W after T_3 decrements the units but reads N_B before T_3 adds them.

■ Serial and Serial-equivalent Executions

The situations illustrated in Figure 17-5 are judged to be anomalies because they generate results that the users do not expect. More specifically, they generate results

FIGURE 17-5

Examples of Anomalies Caused by Concurrency: (a) Lost Update Anomaly and (b) Inconsistent Read Anomaly

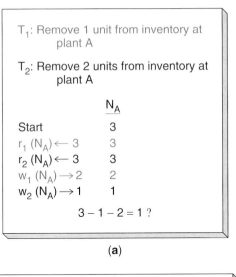

T_1: Remove 1 unit from inventory at plant A

T_2: Remove 2 units from inventory at plant A

	N_A
Start	3
$r_1 (N_A) \leftarrow 3$	3
$r_2 (N_A) \leftarrow 3$	3
$w_1 (N_A) \rightarrow 2$	2
$w_2 (N_A) \rightarrow 1$	1

$$3 - 1 - 2 = 1 \text{ ?}$$

(a)

T_3: Move 4 units from warehouse (W) to plant B

T_4: Count number of units at A, B, and W

	N_A	N_B	N_W
Start	3	1	6
$r_3 (N_W) \leftarrow 6$	3	1	6
$w_3 (N_W) \rightarrow 2$	3	1	2
$r_4 (N_W) \leftarrow 2$	3	1	2
$r_3 (N_B) \leftarrow 1$	3	1	2
$r_4 (N_A) \leftarrow 3$	3	1	2
$r_4 (N_B) \leftarrow 1$	3	1	2
$w_3 (N_B) \rightarrow 5$	3	5	2

(b)

that are logically inconsistent with the results that would have been produced if the transactions had been executed one at a time, or serially. Figure 17-6 shows two serial executions: one of T_1 followed by T_2 and a second of T_3 followed by T_4. In both cases the results are logically consistent with what the users would expect.

Even though they generate consistent results, serial executions prohibit concurrency and result in poor performance. Thus a goal of concurrency control is to allow concurrency but in such a way that the results of the concurrent execution are logically consistent with those of a serial execution.

EQUIVALENT EXECUTIONS

An execution of transactions that is not serial but that generates the same results as a particular serial execution does is said to be *equivalent to the serial execution*. Fig-

FIGURE 17-6

FIGURE 17-6

Examples of Serial Executions

Serial Execution of $T_1 T_2$	Serial Execution of $T_3 T_4$
$r_1 (N_A) \leftarrow 3$	$r_3 (N_W) \leftarrow 6$
$w_1 (N_A) \rightarrow 2$	$w_3 (N_W) \rightarrow 2$
$r_2 (N_A) \leftarrow 2$	$r_3 (N_B) \leftarrow 1$
$w_2 (N_A) \rightarrow 0$	$w_3 (N_B) \rightarrow 5$
	$r_4 (N_A) \leftarrow 3$
	$r_4 (N_W) \leftarrow 2$
	$r_4 (N_B) \leftarrow 5$

ure 17-7 shows an execution of T_3 and T_4 that is equivalent to a serial execution of T_3 followed by T_4.

More formally, two executions of a series of transactions are said to be **equivalent** if two conditions are met: (1) Each read in the two executions reads data item values produced by the same write in both executions, and (2) the final write of a data item is the same in both executions.[5] If you examine Figure 17-7, you will find that both of these conditions are met. These conditions make sense intuitively because they imply that the transactions receive the same inputs in both executions and that the final data item values are the same.

DEFINITIONS

Before proceeding, we need to define a number of terms. Two operations **conflict** if they operate on the same data item and at least one of the operations is a write. From this it follows that there are two types of conflict. A **read–write conflict** occurs when one operation is a read and the other is a write. A **write–write conflict** occurs when both operations are writes.

Figure 17-8 shows the intertransaction conflicts in the transactions T_1 through T_4. For example, $r_1(N_A)$ has a read–write conflict with $w_2(N_A)$, and $w_1(N_A)$ has a

FIGURE 17-7

Nonserial Execution of T_3, T_4 That Is
Equivalent to a Serial Execution of T_3, T_4

$r_3 (N_W) \leftarrow 6$
$r_3 (N_B) \leftarrow 1$
$r_4 (N_A) \leftarrow 3$
$w_3 (N_W) \rightarrow 2$
$r_4 (N_W) \leftarrow 2$
$w_3 (N_B) \rightarrow 5$
$r_4 (N_B) \leftarrow 5$

5   Bernstein and Goodman, "Concurrency Control in Distributed Database Systems," pp. 185–221.

FIGURE 17-8

Intertransaction Conflicts in T_1, T_2, T_3, and T_4

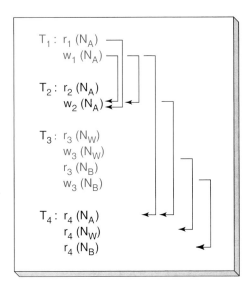

write–write conflict with $w_2(N_A)$. Other conflicts are shown by the arrows. Notice that in addition to these conflicts, there are conflicts within transactions. Such conflicts are assumed to be managed by the logic within the transaction program and need not concern the DDBMS.

Figure 17-8 shows a particular **execution** of the transactions T_1 through T_4. This execution is an ordered sequence of requests to DTMs, or a **schedule.** The schedule in Figure 17-8 is one of many possible ones. Schedules that are equivalent to serial schedules are called **consistent schedules.** For example, consider the serial execution T_1 followed by T_2 followed by T_3 followed by T_4. Any schedule that is equivalent to this serial execution is said to be a consistent schedule of that execution. We label the requests according to the transaction that generates them, and thus REQ_i refers to a generic request (either a read or a write) that arises in the processing of T_i.

SERIALIZATION

The following is a paraphrase of a fundamental theorem of serialization: Suppose we have a serial list of ordered transactions, T_1, T_2,. . .,T_n. Call this ordered list **T**. A particular schedule, **S,** is a consistent schedule of **T** if for any two conflicting requests, say REQ_i and REQ_j arising from distinct transactions T_i and T_j, respectively, REQ_i precedes REQ_j in **S** if, and only if, T_i precedes T_j in **T**.[6]

To understand this theorem, first realize that it is concerned only with the order of *conflicting* requests. That is, for the schedule to be consistent with **T,** the order of conflicting requests must mirror the order of the transactions that spawn them. By implication, we need not be concerned with the order of nonconflicting requests.

Figure 17-9 shows a consistent but nonserial execution of the serial execution T_1 followed by T_2 followed by T_3 followed by T_4. Observe that the order of conflicting requests does, in fact, mirror the order of the transactions.

---

[6] Ibid.

FIGURE 17-9

Consistent and Nonserial Schedule of T_1, T_2, T_3, and T_4

$$r_3 (N_W)$$
$$r_1 (N_A)$$
$$r_3 (N_B)$$
$$w_3 (N_W)$$
$$r_4 (N_W)$$
$$w_1 (N_A)$$
$$w_3 (N_B)$$
$$r_2 (N_A)$$
$$r_4 (N_B)$$
$$w_2 (N_A)$$
$$r_4 (N_A)$$

SERIALIZATION IN DISTRIBUTED SYSTEMS

So far, this discussion has concerned centralized teleprocessing as much as it has distributed processing. We can focus on distributed processing in the following way: The order of conflicting requests must mirror the order of the transactions no matter where they are processed and no matter how many times they are processed. Figure 17-10(a) shows a consistent and concurrent schedule of the transactions from Figure 17-8. These transactions are processed on two nodes without replication. Figure 17-10(b) shows a consistent and concurrent schedule of those transactions in which the Node B data is replicated.

This discussion implies that all nodes agree on a single order for the transactions, but in fact, they may not. Two nodes may each determine that its transactions should be next, a situation that creates other problems. To solve them, at times it may be necessary to abort a transaction in progress and back out its changes.

The fundamental theorem formalizes the objectives of concurrency control mechanisms. Somehow these mechanisms must ensure that conflicting requests are processed in the order of the transactions that generated them. There are many ways in which the requirements of this fundamental theorem could be met.

■ Concurrency Control Using Distributed Two-Phase Locking

The most common method of enforcing the constraints of the fundamental theorem of serialization is called **distributed two-phase locking.** Using this method, DTMs are required to hold locks before reading and writing data. Specifically, before reading a data item, the DTM must have been granted a read lock by the DBM from which the data is read, and before updating a data item, a DTM must have been granted a write lock from every DBM that stores this data item.

GROWING AND SHRINKING PHASES

Locks are granted with the following restrictions: A read lock may be granted as long as no other transaction holds a write lock on the data item, and a write lock may be granted as long as no other transaction has a lock, of either type, on the data

FIGURE 17-10

Examples of Distributed Consistent Schedules: (a) Consistent Concurrent Schedule of T_1, T_2, T_3, and T_4 on Two Nodes and (b) Consistent Schedule with Replicated Data

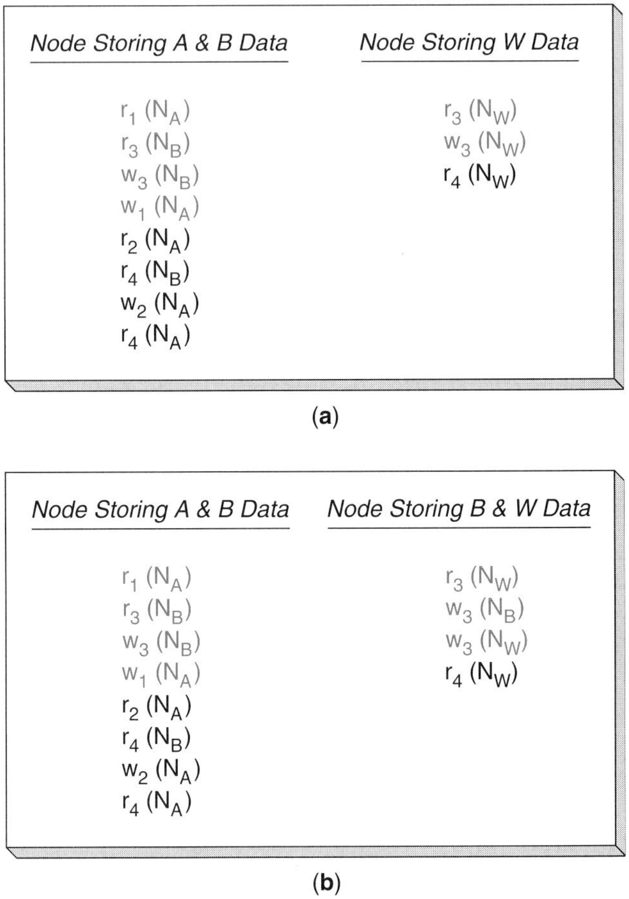

Node Storing A & B Data	Node Storing W Data
$r_1 (N_A)$	$r_3 (N_W)$
$r_3 (N_B)$	$w_3 (N_W)$
$w_3 (N_B)$	$r_4 (N_W)$
$w_1 (N_A)$	
$r_2 (N_A)$	
$r_4 (N_B)$	
$w_2 (N_A)$	
$r_4 (N_A)$	

(a)

Node Storing A & B Data	Node Storing B & W Data
$r_1 (N_A)$	$r_3 (N_W)$
$r_3 (N_B)$	$w_3 (N_B)$
$w_3 (N_B)$	$w_3 (N_W)$
$w_1 (N_A)$	$r_4 (N_W)$
$r_2 (N_A)$	
$r_4 (N_B)$	
$w_2 (N_A)$	
$r_4 (N_A)$	

(b)

item. Thus, read locks may be shared with reads but not writes, and write locks may not be shared at all. (If a lock cannot be granted, the transaction will be placed into a wait state until either the lock is granted or the transaction is aborted.) Finally, once a DTM releases a lock, it may never be granted another lock. It can only release locks from that point on.

The term *two-phase* arises from this last restriction. Eswaran and his associates proved that the read and write locks described will generate consistent schedules if, and only if, transactions process in two phases.[7] During the first phase, they are allowed to acquire locks but may not release any. This is called the growing phase. As soon as a transaction releases a lock, at a point called the **locked point,** transactions enter the shrinking phase. During this second phase, transactions may release locks but may not acquire them.

---

[7] K. P. Eswaran, J. N. Gray, R. A. Lorie, and I. L. Traiger, "The Notion of Consistency and Predicate Locks in a Database System," *Communications of the ACM*, November 1976, pp. 624–633.

If locks are held until the transaction issues an END or similar request, the growing phase will be the entire length of the transaction. The shrinking phase comes after the END is issued. This processing method, described for DB2 in Chapter 12, meets the two-phase restriction, and in fact, it is more restrictive than necessary. According to Eswaran and his associates' proof, the processing can continue after the locked point; the only restriction is that no more locks can be granted. Holding all locks until the commit point and then releasing them is thus sufficient but not necessary to produce consistent schedules.

DISTRIBUTED LOCKING

For distributed databases, each DBM must include a subsystem that grants and releases locks. Furthermore, the DTMs must be programmed to incorporate the rules we described. The DTM can issue a read request as soon as it obtains a single read lock. It must, however, obtain write locks from all nodes that store the data item before it issues the write commands.

To understand distributed locking, consider the cases of read–write conflict, write–read conflict, and write–write conflict. For read–write conflict, suppose a data item, A, resides on Nodes X, Y, and Z and that transaction T_5 holds a read lock for A on X. If another transaction, say T_6, wants to update A, it must obtain a write lock for A on X, Y, and Z. The DBMs on Y and Z will issue the lock without delay, but the DBM on X will not grant the lock until T_5 finishes. In this way, read–write conflicts are avoided.

Now consider write–read. Suppose that T_6 holds a write lock for A on X, Y, and Z. If T_7 wants to read A, it will need to obtain a read lock on one of X, Y, or Z. None of the DBMs on these nodes will grant the lock, however, until T_6 releases the locks. In this way, write–read conflicts are avoided.

Finally, consider write–write conflicts. Suppose that T_8 holds a write lock for A on X, Y, and Z and that T_9 wants to update A. T_9 must wait until all of the write locks have been released and it obtains a write lock for A on X, Y, and Z. In this way, write–write conflicts are avoided.

To show that this strategy generates consistent schedules, it is also necessary to show that the order of locks remains the same as for a serial schedule. This is done in the Eswaran proof, and it is what produces the need for the growing and shrinking phases.

▪ Distributed Deadlock Processing

The disadvantage of controlling concurrency with locking is that deadlock can result. Figure 17-11 shows a deadlock situation among three transactions running on three different nodes, A, B, and W. Each node holds a data item, N, which is a count of the number of units of something in inventory at that site. T_1 is attempting to transfer units from A to B; T_2 is attempting to transfer units from B to W; and T_3 is attempting to transfer units from W to A.

To make the transfer, each transaction first reads the data at the two sites involved. T_1, for example, reads both N_A and N_B. Before reading, it obtains a read lock on these two items. When T_1 attempts to write N_A, it must obtain a write lock on it, but it must wait because T_3 holds a read lock on that data item.

FIGURE 17-11

Example of Distributed
Deadlock

Node A	Node B	Node W
$r_1 (N_A)$	$r_2 (N_B)$	$r_3 (N_W)$
$r_1 (N_B)$	$r_2 (N_W)$	$r_3 (N_A)$
$w_1 (N_A)$–Wait	$w_2 (N_B)$–Wait	$w_3 (N_W)$–Wait

If you examine the locks, you will find that T_1 is waiting for T_3, T_3 is waiting for T_2, and T_2 is waiting for T_1. This situation is diagrammed in the wait–for graph in Figure 17-12. In this graph, the nodes (circles) represent transactions, and the edges (the lines connecting the circles) represent waits. A **deadlock** situation exists whenever there is a cycle or path from a node back to itself.

As with centralized processing, there are two strategies for dealing with deadlock. One method is to be careful in the placement of locks and not allow waiting that can lead to a deadlock situation. This strategy is called **deadlock prevention.** The second strategy is to place locks without restriction but then to detect deadlock when it occurs. This is called **deadlock detection.**

DEADLOCK PREVENTION

With deadlock prevention schemes, the lock managers in the DBMs are careful in allowing waiting to occur. When a transaction, T_i, attempts to place a lock that conflicts with a lock held by a second transaction, T_j, the lock manager evaluates the situation and does not allow waiting if there is a possibility of deadlock. If there is such a possibility, the lock manager can either deny T_i's request or abort T_j and approve the request. If the request is denied, the strategy is called **nonpreemptive.** In this case, T_i must be aborted and restarted. If T_j is aborted, the strategy is called **preemptive.** In this case, T_j is restarted.

There are several varieties of both strategies. The simplest nonpreemptive strategy is not to allow waiting at all. If a transaction, T_i, requests a lock that conflicts with a lock held by another transaction, it will automatically be aborted and restarted. This strategy simplifies lock processing but causes many restarts.

FIGURE 17-12

Example of Wait–For
Graph

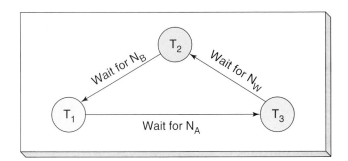

Another strategy is to assign priorities to the transactions and to allow the transaction with the higher priority to have precedence. Thus when T_i requests a lock on a resource held by T_j, the response will be nonpreemptive if the priority of T_i is less than or equal to T_j; it will be preemptive otherwise. As with all types of priority scheduling, there is the danger that low-priority transactions will never be allowed to complete.

A third strategy considers the age of the transactions. Each transaction is assigned a unique birth time. When a lock conflict arises, the relative ages are considered. In a **wait–die** strategy, when T_i requests a lock on data held by T_j, T_i is allowed to wait if it is younger than T_j. Otherwise it is aborted. This is a nonpreemptive strategy.

Wound–wait is a preemptive strategy, in which when T_i requests a lock on data held by T_j, if T_i is older than T_j, T_i is allowed to wait. Otherwise T_j is preempted and restarted. In both cases, it is important that the transactions keep their original birth time when they are restarted.

As with centralized database processing, it is also possible to prevent deadlock by having the transactions request all locks in an agreed-on order. But this restriction violates concurrency transparency because it forces application programmers to consider concurrency issues when developing programs.

DEADLOCK DETECTION

With deadlock detection strategies, waiting is allowed without restriction. All lock requests are accepted; if the locks conflict, the transactions are allowed to wait. There are two ways in which deadlock is detected. One involves time-outs. That is, transactions are allowed to wait a certain period of time for a resource to be freed. When the waiting time exceeds this amount, a deadlock is presumed to exist, and one of the transactions involved in the lock is aborted and restarted. One problem with this strategy is that waits can result from causes other than deadlock, especially in a distributed system, and so transactions may be aborted and restarted unnecessarily.

The second method of detecting deadlock is more precise. With it, wait–for graphs like the one in Figure 17-12 are constructed, and the graphs are searched for cycles. If cycles are found, a deadlock exists, and so one or more transactions are aborted and restarted. The data structures for representing graphs and algorithms for identifying cycles are well known.[8]

The problem with identifying cycles in a distributed database is that wait–for graphs require knowledge of all locks in the distributed system. Although no single lock manager possesses all of this information, there are several methods of providing it. In one method, a particular node is identified as the global deadlock detector, to which all lock managers periodically send their lock data. This node constructs the global wait–for graph and determines whether deadlocks exist. If they do, it will cause the appropriate transactions to be terminated and restarted (see Bernstein and Goodman for a summary of other deadlock detection schemes[9]).

[8]   A. V. Aho, E. Hopcroft, and J. D. Ullman, *The Design and Analysis of Computer Programs* (Reading, MA: Addison-Wesley, 1975).

[9]   Bernstein and Goodman, "Concurrency Control in Distributed Database Systems," pp. 185–221.

■ An Example of Concurrency Control

One of the earliest and best-known distributed DBMSs is R*, an operational, proto-type implementation developed by the IBM Almaden Research Center. It supports distributed partitioned databases but no redundancy. Concurrency is controlled by distributed two-phase locking. No attempt is made to prevent deadlock; instead, deadlock is detected by algorithms on the distributed nodes.

In R*, each node is responsible for determining its own local deadlocks. There is no global deadlock detector, and so deadlock detection is shared among the nodes. The nodes are programmed to detect the possibility of a global deadlock and to send lock information to nodes that are managing transactions that may be blocked. Also, each node is responsible for processing potential global lock data that is sent to it. Proponents of R* assert that the algorithm is such that only a single node can detect a particular global deadlock and that when detected, only local transactions are aborted.

FAILURE TRANSPARENCY

The fourth goal for a DDBMS is to provide transparency to failure. As we have seen, failures arise from a variety of sources. Sane nodes fail predictably. Insane nodes fail unpredictably and can broadcast validly formatted but inappropriate actions. Malicious, Byzantine-type failures are caused by nodes that intend to deceive.

In this discussion we assume the easiest type of failure. In particular, we assume that nodes are not only sane but also that when they fail, they do nothing at all. Insane nodes and Byzantine-type failure are beyond the scope of this discussion. We also assume that the distributed system is partitioned cleanly. If Node A is unable to communicate with Node B, we assume that Node B is unable to communicate with Node A as well.

As we stated earlier, failure transparency should provide atomic transactions; that is, either all of a transaction should be processed, or none of it should. More-over, once committed, the effects of a transaction should be permanent.

In reality, such atomicity cannot be achieved in all cases, even for sane failures. If too much of the network fails or if critical portions fail at critical times, recovery with guaranteed atomicity may not be possible. The recovery manager of SDD-1, a prototype DDBMS, recognizes this fact with the definition of system **catastrophes**.[10] Catastrophes result when too many components fail. Recovery from a catastrophe requires manual intervention and may result in a database containing fragments of transactions.

The discussion in this section assumes that a log is kept of transaction activities so that it is possible to back out of a transaction any time before the commit point.

---

[10] M. Hammer and D. Shipman, "Reliability Mechanisms for SDD-1: A System for Distributed Databases," *Transactions on Database Systems*, December 1980, pp. 431–466.

Also, at times it is important that the DDBMS be guaranteed that a log record will survive a failure. In these cases, we use the term *force-write*, meaning that the DDBMS issues a write command and, before continuing, waits for the operating system to confirm that the record has been written to nonvolatile storage.

◼ Need for Directory Management

In a distributed database, each DTM maintains a directory of the location(s) of data items. The processing of these directories is crucial, particularly in a system with replication. To understand why, consider the situation shown in Figure 17-13.

This distributed replicated database has four nodes, labeled A through D. Data item X is stored on Nodes A and B, and Item Y is stored on Nodes C and D. Transaction 1 reads the copy of X on A (first obtaining a read lock), and transaction 2 reads the copy of Y on D (also with a read lock). Then Node A fails, followed by Node D. Next, transaction 1 writes Y on all nodes that contain Y. To do so, it must first obtain a write lock on those nodes. The only such node is C, since Node D has failed. Consequently, transaction 1 is able to write Y, even though transaction 2 has a read lock on it. Similarly, transaction 2 writes X on all nodes that contain X. The only such node is B, since Node A has failed. Hence transaction 2 obtains a write lock on B and writes X on B, even though transaction 1 has a write lock on it.

When Nodes A and D subsequently recover, the database is in an inconsistent state. The values of X differ on Nodes A and B, and the values of Y differ on Nodes C and D. The inconsistency is caused by the transaction managers that were unable to detect locks held by failed nodes. The situation can be correctly processed if the directories are themselves subject to careful locking procedures. Such procedures are presented in a discussion of the **available copies algorithm.**[11] (This reference is also the source of this example.) Although a discussion of this algorithm is beyond

FIGURE 17-13

Inconsistency Generated by
Inopportune Node Failure

$r_1 (X_A)$ - with read lock on X_A
$r_2 (Y_D)$ - with read lock on Y_D
A fails
D fails
$W_1 (Y_C)$ - with write lock on
　　　　　available copies of Y
$W_2 (X_B)$ - with write lock on
　　　　　available copies of X
A recovers
D recovers
Database is now inconsistent

[11] Bernstein and Goodman, "An Algorithm for Concurrency Control and Recovery," pp. 596–615.

the scope of this text, you should be aware of this type of anomaly when you review DDBMS products.

◼ Commitment in Distributed Database Systems

In nondistributed systems, transaction atomicity is accomplished by delaying changes in the database until the transaction is committed or aborted. For distributed systems, committing data changes is more complicated.

Consider the following generic summary of the distributed commitment process: Every transaction is allocated a private work space during its processing. As the transaction progresses, updates are made in the private work space, but they are not committed to the database. When the transaction finishes, if all nodes requiring updates for the transaction are able to commit them to their respective databases, the changes are made. Otherwise the transaction and all of its changes are aborted.

Consider a distributed system like that shown in Figure 17-1. When a DTM issues an update request to a DBM, the DBM places the updated data in a private work space that it maintains for that transaction. (For the first such update action, it creates the private work space.) The DBM does not write the update in the database, however. If a DTM issues a read request for a data item that the transaction has changed, the DBM provides the updated value from the private work space. This much is straightforward. When, however, the transaction finishes and the DTM sends out commit actions, a complication arises.

Suppose that three DBMs hold changes in behalf of a particular transaction. In the process of committing, what if one of them discovers that it cannot commit its changes? Unless something is done, only two of three of the DBMs will update their databases. Clearly, this result is unacceptable.

TWO-PHASE COMMITMENT

To solve this problem, distributed commitment is broken into a two-stage process called **two-phase commitment**.[12] With this method, the DTM that is processing a transaction first sends out a precommit action to all DBMs holding updated data for that transaction. This precommit action informs the DBMs that the transaction is finished, and it asks the DBMs to respond YES or NO, according to whether or not they can commit the changes on data they store. If all DBMs respond YES, the DTM will send out a commit action; otherwise the DBM will issue an abort action to all DBMs and restart the transaction.

When a DBM receives the precommit action, it ensures that it can make the changes (depending on the form of concurrency control involved, the DBM may be unable to make the changes—resolution of deadlock is a case in point). If the DBM can make the changes, it will force-write log records stating that it can commit the changes, although these changes are not written to the database. Next, the node

---

[12] Observe that the standard vocabulary of database technology includes both the terms *two-phase commitment* and *two-phase locking*. Do not confuse them. Two-phase commitment pertains only to distributed database processing, whereas two-phase locking pertains to both distributed and non-distributed database processing.

responds YES to the DTM. Finally, when the DTM issues the commit action, the DBM updates the database.

This discussion does not consider cases in which either the DTM or the DBMs fail after the precommit action is accepted by the DBM. To understand what happens in this case, we need to be more specific. To do this, consider the example situation in Figure 17-14 (adapted from an article by Mohan, Lindsay, and Obermarck[13]). When studying this example, recall that a transaction can be committed only if all the DBMs involved are able to commit. A NO vote by any DBM is a veto.

TWO-PHASE COMMIT PROCESSING WITHOUT FAILURE

When the DBM receives the precommit action, it determines whether it can commit the transaction. If it can, it force-writes a PRE-COMMIT record on the log and sends a YES message back to the DTM. If the DBM is unable to commit the transaction, it force-writes an ABORT record on the log and sends a NO message. If it sends a NO, the DBM is guaranteed that the transaction will be aborted, and it can therefore forget about it.

When the DTM has received responses from all DBMs, it examines the votes. If any node responded NO, the DTM force-writes an ABORT record in its log, aborts the transaction, and sends ABORT actions to all DBMs that voted YES (it need not send actions to those that voted NO because they have already decided that the transaction will fail). If all DBMs voted YES, the DTM force-writes a COMMIT record to its log and sends COMMIT actions to all the DBMs.

FIGURE 17-14

Summary of a Two-Phase Commit

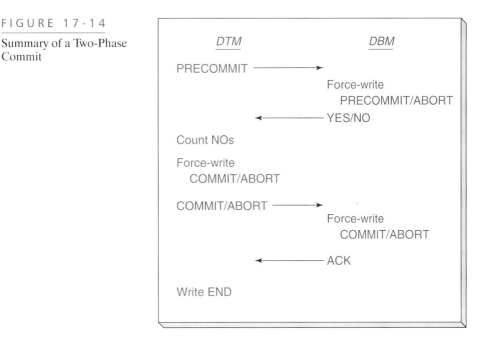

[13] C. Mohan, B. Lindsay, and R. Obermarck, "Transaction Management in the R* Distributed Database Management System," *Transactions on Database Systems*, December 1986, pp. 378–396.

If the DBMs receive an ABORT action, they force-write ABORT records on their logs and abort the transaction. If the DBMs receive a COMMIT action, they force-write COMMIT records on their logs and commit the transaction. In either case, the DBMs send an acknowledgment to the ABORT or COMMIT action sent by the DTM. Once the DTM receives ACKs from all DBMs, it writes an END record in its log and forgets the transaction.

TWO-PHASE COMMIT PROCESSING UNDER FAILURE

Now consider what happens when either the DTM or a DBM fails at various points in this process. If a DBM fails and, during recovery, finds part of a transaction in its log, with neither a PRECOMMIT nor an ABORT record, it can ignore that transaction. The node failed in the middle of the transaction, and therefore the DTM cannot have received a YES from this node. The transaction will have been aborted. But if it finds an ABORT record in its log, it can ignore the transaction, for similar reasons.

If the DBM finds a PRECOMMIT record without a COMMIT, it will not know what to do. It knows that it voted YES, but it does not know the outcome of the vote by other DBMs. Therefore, in this case, the DBM must ask the DTM for information about this transaction. Once it receives a response (whether an ABORT or COMMIT) from the DTM, it can process as under normal conditions. Finally, if the DBM finds both PRECOMMIT and COMMIT records in the log, it will know that the transaction should have been committed, and it will ensure that it was by applying after-images, as described in Chapter 15.

Now consider DTM failures. If the DTM fails before sending any PRECOMMIT actions, it will abort the transaction. Because it knows that all DBMs will (eventually) abort it as well, it need take no other action. (Here, by the way, is a case of something falling through the crack between failure/recovery issues and concurrency control issues. There may be locks on data items on the DBMs. Those locks will stay in place until a deadlock situation forces the DBM to abort the transaction, until the DBM fails and its recovery processor notices the incompleted transaction or until a utility program cleans up the log. It would be better for the DTM to send ABORT actions for such a transaction during recovery so that the DBMs can release their locks. There is nothing in the *failure processing* algorithm, however, that necessitates this.)

If the DTM finds a COMMIT record in its log with no corresponding END, it failed before all of the acknowledgments were received, and it periodically sends COMMIT actions to the DBMs that did not acknowledge them. Once it receives all such acknowledgments, it writes the END to the log. If the DTM finds an ABORT record in its log with no corresponding END, it will send ABORT actions to all DBMs that have not acknowledged them and will write an END to the log.

Review Figure 17-14 and make sure that you understand how this algorithm provides transaction atomicity with regard to these types of failure. In reality, the situation is somewhat more complicated than that described here, but this discussion should give you the gist of two-phased commitment. If you consider that failures can occur in the middle of failure recovery and that, especially for replicated data, directory processing needs to be considered as well, you can begin to sense how difficult failure transparency can be. (See Mohan, Lindsay, and Obermarck for more information about two-phased commitment.[14])

---

[14] Ibid.

■ Consistency in Partitioned Networks

The final failure issue we will consider concerns distributed database processing in partitioned networks. A **partition** is a subnetwork created when nodes become disconnected because of node or communication line failure. Figure 17-15(a) shows a distributed network, and Figure 17-15(b) shows a network that is broken into two partitions because of a failure of Node E.

When there is a partition, if the data is not replicated, the consequences, though undesired, are straightforward. A transaction can operate if all of the data it reads and writes is located on nodes in the partition in which the transaction is initiated. Otherwise, the transaction must wait until the network is recovered. For the example in Figure 17-15(b), the transactions initiated in Partition I can run if the data they read and write is located on Node A, B, C, or D. The transactions initiated in Partition II can run if the data they read and write is located on Node F, G, or H.

FIGURE 17-15

Sample Partitions: (a) Sample Distributed Network and (b) Partitions Caused by Node E's Failure

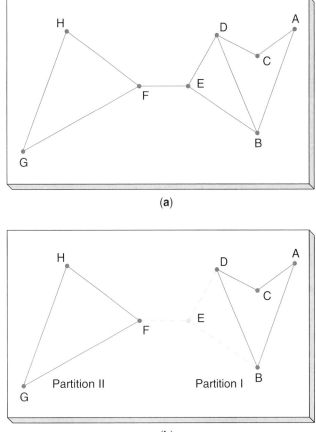

As we stated earlier, organizations often choose to replicate data in order to increase reliability and performance. When data is replicated, processing during a partition must be carefully controlled, and recovery is considerably more difficult. If the network in Figure 17-15 supports order entry and if inventory data is stored in both partitions, it would be possible to sell the same last item to two different customers. Furthermore, once the network has recovered, the two separately processed collections of inventory data must be combined to produce a single, consistent collection.

Correctness Versus Availability in Partitioned Networks

A wide variety of anomalies can occur when processing replicated data in a partitioned network. Figure 17-16 illustrates two of them. In the first example, both Nodes A and H, in two different partitions, sell diamond necklaces. They begin with

FIGURE 17-16

Anomalies Caused by Partitions: (a) Update Anomaly Caused by Partition and (b) Constraint Violation Caused by Partition

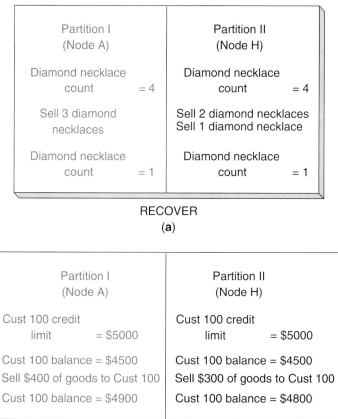

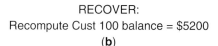

the same count of four. Node A sells three necklaces, and Node H sells two to one customer and one to a second customer. At the point of recovery, the records in both nodes indicate that there is one necklace remaining. In fact, a total of six necklaces were sold when only four were available. At recovery, Nodes A and H have the same item count. This example shows the recovery process must do more than ensure that data items from separate partitions have the same value.

In the second example, processing in two partitions violates a constraint. A customer's credit limit is $5000, and her starting balance is $4500. Node A sells the customer $400 worth of goods, and Node H sells the customer $300. After recovery, the customer's balance is $5200, $200 in excess of the credit limit.

As Davidson, Garcia-Molina, and Skeen point out, processing in partitioned networks requires a trade-off between the poles of correctness and availability.[15] Absolute correctness is the easiest to provide if no processing of replicated data is allowed during a partition. One could argue, however, that in that case, why bother to replicate the data at all? Improved performance during nonpartitions would be the only reason.

On the other extreme, availability is the greatest if no restrictions are placed on the processing of replicated data during partitions. For some applications, this is feasible. Since airlines overbook flights, what difference would it make if occasionally, during partitions, the same seat were sold to different customers? Both the airlines and the passengers prefer a high availability of reservations data to absolute correctness. The world's banking system takes a different attitude toward this matter, however. Once again we come back to the need for an understanding of system requirements.

■ Strategies for Processing Partitioned Replicated Data

Many different strategies have been proposed for processing replicated data in partitioned networks. The article just cited (by Davidson, Garcia-Molina, and Skeen) provides an excellent survey of many. Here we discuss one of the leading strategies, called the **optimistic protocol.**

This strategy uses graphs (like the wait–for graphs in Figure 17-12) to keep track of dependencies among data changes. While the network is partitioned, changes are allowed without restriction (hence the name *optimistic*), and precedence graphs are kept, indicating which transactions have read and written which data. During recovery, the graphs of all partitions are combined and analyzed. If inconsistencies have developed, some transactions are rolled back and their changes eliminated.

Figure 17-17 shows an example of a combined precedence graph involving two partitions (this figure is adapted from Figure 5 in another Davidson article[16]). The meaning of this figure is as follows: T_{ij} is transaction number j running in partition

[15] S. B. Davidson, H. Garcia-Molina, and D. Skeen, "Consistency in Partitioned Networks," *Computing Surveys*, September 1985, pp. 341–370.

[16] S. B. Davidson, "Optimism and Consistency in Partitioned Distributed Database Systems," *Transactions on Database Systems*, September 1984, pp. 456–482.

number i. The dotted arrows indicate that a transaction wrote a data item that was read by a subsequent transaction. A solid arrow indicates that a transaction read a data item that was later changed by another transaction. The data items read by a transaction are above the line next to the transaction, and the items written are shown below that line. Thus, T_{11} read items f and g and wrote item f.

Davidson proved that the database is consistent if, and only if, there are no cycles in the precedence graph. The graph in Figure 17-17 contains cycles (arrows that come back to a node), and therefore this database is inconsistent. There are actually several inconsistencies here. For one, T_{11} reads an old value of data item f. Although the item had been changed by T_{23}, T_{11} was unaware of the change because of the partition in the network.

The strength of this strategy is its robustness. It can detect all inconsistencies, and there is sufficient data available to be able to correct the database by means of rollback. There are two important disadvantages, however. First, logs must be kept of all read and write activity. Although Davidson does not say so, it would appear that many, if not all, of these log writes must be forced, and this will generate a significant performance problem.

Second, rolling back completed, committed transactions violates transaction atomicity. With this strategy, committed changes are not necessarily permanent. For the data in Figure 17-17, T_{22} may need to be rolled back after real outputs have been generated by the transaction. That is, customers may have been promised diamond necklaces that cannot be delivered. The fact that they will later receive an apology and explanation that the necklace did not exist at the time of the sale may not be much consolation. These disadvantages notwithstanding, however, the optimistic protocol strategy shows promise for networks that require consistent and correct processing despite the partitions in the network.

FIGURE 17-17

Precedence Graph Combined for Two Partitions

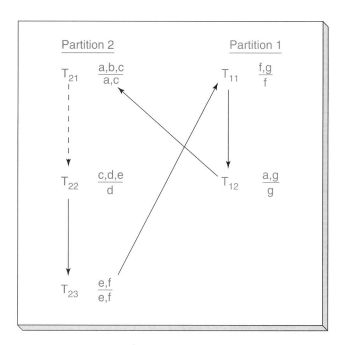

SUMMARY

Distributed database processing is database processing in which the execution of transactions and the retrieval and updating of data occur across two or more independent and usually geographically separated computers. The distributed DBMS (DDBMS) consists of the distributed transaction managers (DTMs) and database managers (DBMs) on all computers. The DTMs receive processing requests and translate them into actions for the DBMs. Coordination and control are important DTM functions. The DBMs process some portion of the distributed database in accordance with action requests from the DTMs.

The advantages of distributed database processing are better performance, increased reliability, and more readily adaptable requirements and matching with organization structures. The disadvantages are worse performance, reduced reliability, increased complexity, high construction and maintenance costs, and difficulty of control. The character, capabilities, and performance of distributed systems depend on the hardware used, the functionality of the DDBMS, the degree of data replication, the types of procedures, and the tasks required of the system's users.

The four goals for a DDBMS are location, replication, concurrency, and failure transparency. In theory, location and replication transparency are not too difficult to provide. The problems of concurrency and failure transparency are more difficult, and robust solutions are only beginning to be found, even in theory. Robust practical solutions do not yet exist.

The control of concurrent processing for distributed database systems is difficult. If processing is not controlled, problems such as the lost update and inconsistent read anomalies can occur. Distributed-processing transactions should be processed in such a manner that nonserial, concurrent executions of transactions have the same impact on the database as serial, nonconcurrent executions would have.

For both distributed and nondistributed processing, transactions must lock resources in a two-phased process. During the first phase, the growing phase, the locks are acquired. As soon as the first lock is released, the growing phase is terminated, and no more locks can be acquired. Releasing all locks at the end of a transaction meets this criterion but is more restrictive than necessary.

Distributed systems perform locking using a distributed two-phase locking strategy. Distributed deadlock can occur, and it must either be prevented or resolved by aborting one of the transactions. R* is a prototype DDBMS developed by IBM that implements distributed two-phase locking.

Failure transparency is difficult to provide because there are too many types of failure. Limited transparency can be provided for sane node failures. Data directories must be part of the locking and recovery mechanisms for distributed failure/recovery.

Update commitment is more complicated for distributed than for nondistributed processing. The commit process must be broken into two phases. During the first phase, the nodes declare their ability to commit. During the second phase, they perform actions to commit. Two-phased commit processing must include forced writes and acknowledgment among nodes.

A network is partitioned if it is broken into two or more pieces by a failure of some type. Processing in partitioned networks can create integrity problems. Correctness and availability are trade-offs in a partitioned network. One strategy for providing integrity in partitioned networks uses precedence graphs. This strategy may at times require that committed transactions be de-committed, which is undesirable but at present is unavoidable, at least for this type of processing.

GROUP I QUESTIONS

17.1   Define *distributed database processing*.

17.2   Describe the difference between a DBMS and a DDBMS. Explain how it is possible for a DDBMS to contain DBMS products.

17.3   What is the function of a distributed transaction manager?

17.4   What is the function of a database manager?

17.5   Define *node, transaction node,* and *database node*.

17.6   Explain the difference between a request and an action.

17.7   Summarize the advantages of distributed database processing.

17.8   Summarize the disadvantages of distributed database processing.

17.9   Explain how the choice of node hardware affects the character of the distributed system. Show two alternative systems that conform to the design in Figure 17-1, using Figure 17-4 as an example.

17.10   Explain the difference between a DTM that is provided as part of a DDBMS and a DTM that is developed in-house.

17.11   Define the terms *nonreplicated, partially replicated,* and *fully replicated* databases.

17.12   Explain how processing rights can vary from one distributed system to another.

17.13   How does the degree of data currency affect the design of a distributed database system?

17.14   Discuss the difference of control philosophies for the systems in Figure 17-4(a) and (b).

17.15   Explain this statement: "The less sophisticated the DDBMS is, the greater the role that people must take."

17.16   Define and describe *location transparency*.

17.17   Define and describe *replication transparency*.

17.18   Define and describe *concurrency transparency*.

17.19   Define and describe *failure transparency*.

17.20   What is a sane node?

17.21   Define and give an example of the *lost update anomaly*.

17.22   Define and give an example of the *inconsistent read anomaly*.

17.23   What is a serial execution? What is an execution of transactions that is equivalent to a serial execution?

17.24   Describe and explain the two conditions required for two executions to be equivalent.

17.25 Define *read–write, write–read,* and *write–write* conflict.

17.26 Define *schedule, serial schedule,* and *consistent schedule.*

17.27 Summarize the processing of two-phase locking.

17.28 Give an example of a distributed deadlock.

17.29 What are the two primary means of dealing with distributed deadlock?

17.30 Explain the meaning of the wait–for graph in Figure 17-12.

17.31 Explain the processing problem depicted in Figure 17-13.

17.32 Why is it necessary to break distributed commitment into two phases?

17.33 Explain the commit processing illustrated in Figure 17-14.

17.34 Define *partitioned network.*

17.35 Explain the problems illustrated in Figure 17-17.

17.36 Why does processing in partitioned networks require a trade-off between correctness and availability?

17.37 How can a precedence graph be used to determine whether the processing of a partitioned database is consistent?

GROUP II QUESTIONS

17.38 Contact a corporation that has installed a distributed database system. Interview the developers and users, and map the system components into the architecture of Figure 17-1. Did the company obtain a DDBMS, or did it assemble the equivalent of a DDBMS from other software components? What software serves the role of the DTMs? Of the DBMs? Identify the components of the distributed system. What has been the company's experience? What problems and pitfalls has it encountered? What were important factors that led to successes?

17.39 Contact a vendor of a commercial DDBMS. What hardware does the system use? Map the architecture of the DDBMS into the scheme in Figure 17-1. What components belong to the DTMs? What components belong to the DBMs? What claims does the vendor make regarding location, replication, concurrency, and failure transparency? How does the product control concurrent processing? Is two-phase locking used? If not, what technique is employed? What failure/recovery mechanisms are used? Is two-phase commit employed? What happens when the network is partitioned? Determine the number of installations of the product, and, if possible, the number of actual systems in use. What factors does the vendor believe lead to success? What problems and pitfalls are the most serious?

Appendix

DATA STRUCTURES FOR DATABASE PROCESSING

All operating systems provide data management services. These services, however, are generally not sufficient for the specialized needs of a DBMS. Therefore, to enhance performance, DBMS products build and maintain specialized data structures, which are the topic of this appendix.

We begin by discussing flat files and some of the problems that can occur when such files need to be processed in different orders. Then we turn to three specialized data structures: sequential lists, linked lists, and indexes (or inverted lists). Next we illustrate how each of three special structures discussed in Chapter 6—trees, simple networks, and complex networks—are represented using various data structures. Finally, we explore how to represent and process multiple keys.

Although a thorough knowledge of data structures is not required to use most DBMS products, this background is essential to database administrators and systems programmers working with a DBMS. Being familiar with the data structures will also help you evaluate and compare database products.

FLAT FILES

A *flat file* is a file that has no repeating groups. In Figure A-1, (a) shows a flat file, and (b) shows a file that is not flat because of the repeating field, Item. A flat file can be stored in any common file organization such as sequential, indexed sequential, or direct. Flat files have been used for many years in commercial processing. They are usually processed in some predetermined order, say in an ascending sequence on a key field.

Processing Flat Files in Multiple Orders

Sometimes users want to process flat files in ways that are not readily supported by the file organization. Consider, for example, the ENROLLMENT records in Figure A-1(a). To produce student schedules, they must be processed in StudentNumber sequence. But to produce class rosters, the records need to be processed in Class-Number sequence. The records, of course, can be stored in only one physical sequence. For example, they can be in order on StudentNumber or on ClassNumber, but not on both at the same time. The traditional solution to the problem of processing records in different orders is to sort them in student order, process the student schedules, then sort the records in class order, and produce class rosters.

For some applications, such as a batch-mode system, this solution, while cumbersome, is effective. But suppose that both orders need to exist simultaneously because two concurrent users have different views of the ENROLLMENT records. What do we do then?

One solution is to create two copies of the ENROLLMENT file and sort them as shown in Figure A-2. Since the data is listed in sequential order, this data structure is sometimes called a *sequential list.* Sequential lists can be readily stored as sequential files. This, however, is not generally done by DBMS products because sequentially reading a file is a slow process. Further, sequential files cannot be updated in the middle without rewriting the entire file. Also, maintaining several orders by keeping multiple copies of the same sequential list is usually not effective because the duplicated sequential list can create data integrity problems. Fortunately, other data structures allow us to process records in different orders and do not require the duplication of data. These include *linked lists* and *indexes.*

FIGURE A-1

Examples of (a) a Flat and (b) a Nonflat File

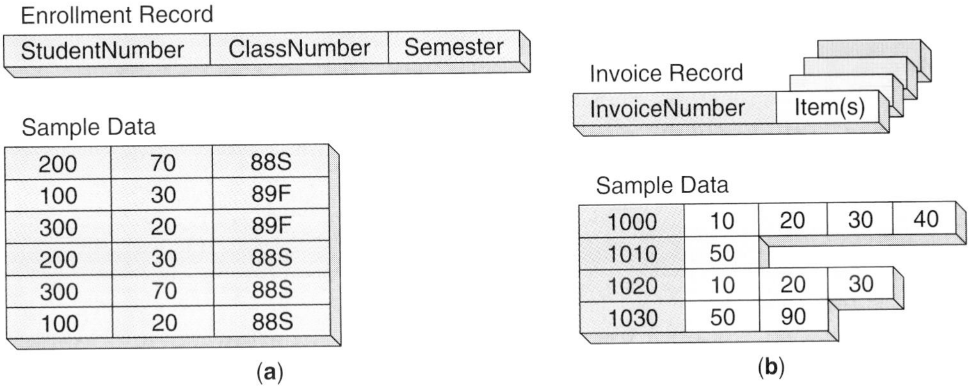

Enrollment Record

StudentNumber	ClassNumber	Semester

Sample Data

200	70	88S
100	30	89F
300	20	89F
200	30	88S
300	70	88S
100	20	88S

(a)

Invoice Record

InvoiceNumber	Item(s)

Sample Data

1000	10	20	30	40
1010	50			
1020	10	20	30	
1030	50	90		

(b)

FIGURE A-2

ENROLLMENT Data Stored as Sequential Lists: (a) Sorted by StudentNumber and (b) Sorted by ClassNumber

Student-Number	Class-Number	Semester
100	30	89F
100	20	88S
200	70	88S
200	30	88S
300	20	89F
300	70	88S

(a)

Student-Number	Class-Number	Semester
300	20	89F
100	20	88S
100	30	89F
200	30	88S
200	70	88S
300	70	88S

(b)

A Note on Record Addressing

Usually the DBMS creates large physical records, or blocks, on its direct access files. These are used as containers for logical records. Typically, there are many logical records per physical record. Here we assume that each physical record is addressed by its relative record number (RRN). Thus a logical record might be assigned to physical record number 7 or 77 or 10,000. The relative record number is thus the logical record's physical address. If there is more than one logical record per physical record, the address must also specify where the logical record is within the physical record. Thus the complete address for a logical record might be relative record number 77, byte location 100. This means the record begins in byte 100 of physical record 77.

To simplify the illustrations in this text, we assume that there is only one logical record per physical record, so that we need not be concerned with byte offsets within physical records. Although this is unrealistic, it simplifies our discussion to the essential points.

Maintaining Order with Linked Lists

Linked lists can be used to keep records in logical order that are not necessarily in physical order. To create a linked list, we add a field to each data record. The *link*

FIGURE A-3

ENROLLMENT Data in StudentNumber Order Using a Linked List

Relative Record Number	Student-Number	Class-Number	Semester	Link
1	200	70	88S	4
2	100	30	89F	6
3	300	20	89F	5
4	200	30	88S	3
5	300	70	88S	0
6	100	20	88S	1

Start of list = 2

Relative Record Number	Student-Number	Class-Number	Semester	Student Link	Class Link
1	200	70	88S	4	5
2	100	30	89F	6	1
3	300	20	89F	5	4
4	200	30	88S	3	2
5	300	70	88S	0	0
6	100	20	88S	1	3

Start of student list = 2
Start of class list = 6

field holds the address (in our illustrations, the relative record number) of the *next* record in logical sequence. For example, Figure A-3 shows the ENROLLMENT records expanded to include a linked list; this list maintains the records in Student-Number order. Notice that the link for the numerically last student in the list is zero.

Figure A-4 shows ENROLLMENT records with two linked lists: One list maintains the StudentNumber order, and the other list maintains the ClassNumber order. Two link fields have been added to the records, one for each list.

When insertions and deletions are made, linked lists have a great advantage over sequential lists. For example, to insert the ENROLLMENT record for Student 200 and Class 45, both of the lists in Figure A-2 would need to be rewritten. For the linked lists in Figure A-4, however, the new record could be added to the physical end of the list, and only the values of two link fields would need to be changed to place the new record in the correct sequences. These changes are shown in Figure A-5.

When a record is deleted from a sequential list, a gap is created. But in a linked list, a record can be deleted simply by changing the values of the link, or the *pointer* fields. In Figure A-6, the ENROLLMENT record for Student 200, Class 30, has been logically deleted. No other record points to its address, so it has been effectively removed from the chain, even though it still exists physically.

Relative Record Number	Student-Number	Class-Number	Semester	Student Link	Class Link
1	200	70	88S	4	5
2	100	30	89F	6	7
3	300	20	89F	5	4
4	200	30	88S	7	2
5	300	70	88S	0	0
6	100	20	88S	1	3
7	200	45	88S	3	1

Start of student list = 2
Start of class list = 6

FIGURE A-6

ENROLLMENT Data
After Deleting Student
200, Class 30 (in Two
Orders Using Linked Lists)

Relative Record Number	Student-Number	Class-Number	Semester	Student Link	Class Link
1	200	70	88S	7	5
2	100	30	89F	6	7
3	300	20	89F	5	2
4	200	30	88S	7	2
5	300	70	88S	0	0
6	100	20	88S	1	3
7	200	45	88S	3	1

Start of student list = 2
Start of class list = 6

There are many variations of linked lists. We can make the list into a *circular list*, or *ring*, by changing the link of the last record from zero to the address of the first record in the list. Now we can reach every item in the list starting at any item in the list. Figure A-7(a) shows a circular list for the StudentNumber order. A *two-way linked list* has links in both directions. In Figure A-7(b), a two-way linked list has been created for both ascending and descending student orders.

FIGURE A-7

ENROLLMENT
Data Sorted by
StudentNumber Using
(a) a Circular and (b) a
Two-Way Linked List

Relative Record Number	Student-Number	Class-Number	Semester	Link
1	200	70	88S	4
2	100	30	89F	6
3	300	20	89F	5
4	200	30	88S	3
5	300	70	88S	2
6	100	20	88S	1

Start of list = 2

(a) Circular linked list

Relative Record Number	Student-Number	Class-Number	Semester	Ascending Link	Descending Link
1	200	70	88S	4	6
2	100	30	89F	6	0
3	300	20	89F	5	4
4	200	30	88S	3	1
5	300	70	88S	0	3
6	100	20	88S	1	2

Start of ascending list = 2
Start of descending list = 5

(b) Two-way linked list

Records ordered using linked lists cannot be stored on a sequential file because some type of direct access file organization is needed in order to use the link values. Thus either indexed sequential or direct file organization is required for linked-list processing.

■ Maintaining Order with Indexes

A logical record order can also be maintained using *indexes* or, as they are sometimes called, *inverted lists*. An index is simply a table that cross-references record addresses with some field value. For example, Figure A-8, (a) shows the ENROLLMENT records stored in no particular order, and (b) shows an index on StudentNumber. In this index the StudentNumbers are arranged in sequence, with each entry in the list pointing to a corresponding record in the original data.

As you can see, the index is simply a sorted list of StudentNumbers. To process ENROLLMENT sequentially on StudentNumber, we simply process the index sequentially, obtaining ENROLLMENT data by reading the records indicated by the pointers. Figure A-8(c) shows another index for ENROLLMENT, one that maintains ClassNumber order.

To use an index, the data to be ordered (here, ENROLLMENT) must reside on an indexed sequential or direct file, although the indexes can reside on any type of file. In practice, almost all DBMS products keep both the data and the indexes on direct files.

FIGURE A-8

ENROLLMENT Data and Corresponding Indexes: (a) ENROLLMENT Data, (b) Index on StudentNumber, and (c) Index on ClassNumber

Relative Record Number	Student-Number	Class-Number	Semester
1	200	70	88S
2	100	30	89F
3	300	20	89F
4	200	30	88S
5	300	70	88S
6	100	20	88S

(a)

Student-Number	Relative Record Number
100	2
100	6
200	1
200	4
300	3
300	5

(b)

Class-Number	Relative Record Number
20	3
20	6
30	2
30	4
70	1
70	5

(c)

If you compare the linked list with the index, you will notice the essential difference between them. In a linked list, the pointers are stored along with the data. Each record contains a link field containing a pointer to the address of the next related record. But in an index, the pointers are stored in indexes, separate from the data. Thus the data records themselves contain no pointers. Both techniques are used by commercial DBMS products.

■ B-Trees

A special application of the concept of indexes, or inverted lists, is a *B-tree*, a multilevel index that allows both sequential and direct processing of data records. It also ensures a certain level of efficiency in processing, because of the way that the indexes are structured.

A B-tree is an index that is made up of two parts, the sequence set and the index set (these terms are used by IBM's VSAM file organization documentation. You may encounter other, synonymous, terms). The *sequence set* is an index containing an entry for every record in the file. This index is in physical sequence, usually by primary key value. This arrangement allows sequential access to the data records as follows: process the sequence set in order, read the address of each record, and then read the record.

The *index set* is an index pointing to groups of entries in the sequence set index. This arrangement provides rapid direct access to records in the file, and it is the index set that makes B-trees unique.

An example of a B-tree appears in Figure A-9, and an occurrence of this structure can be seen in Figure A-10. Notice that the bottom row in Figure A-9, the sequence set, is simply an index. It contains an entry for every record in the file (although for brevity, both the data records and their addresses have been omitted). Also notice that the sequence set entries are in groups of three. The entries in each group are physically in sequence, and each group is chained to the next one by means of a linked list, as can be seen in Figure A-10.

Examine the index set in Figure A-9. The top entry contains two values, 45 and 77. By following the leftmost link (to RRN2), we can access all the records whose key field values are less than or equal to 45; by following the middle pointer (to RRN3), we can access all the records whose key field values are greater than 45 and less than or equal to 77; and by following the rightmost pointer (to RRN4), we can access all the records whose key field values are greater than 77.

Similarly, at the next level there are two values and three pointers in each index entry. Each time we drop to another level, we narrow our search for a particular record. For example, if we continue to follow the leftmost pointer from the top entry and then follow the rightmost pointer from there, we can access all the records whose key field value is greater than 27 and less than or equal to 45. We have eliminated all that were greater than 45 at the first level.

B-trees are, by definition, balanced. That is, all the data records are exactly the same distance from the top entry in the index set. This aspect of B-trees ensures performance efficiency, although the algorithms for inserting and deleting records are more complex than those for ordinary trees (which can be unbalanced), because several index entries may need to be modified when records are added or deleted to keep all records the same distance from the top index entry.

General Structure of a Simple B-Tree

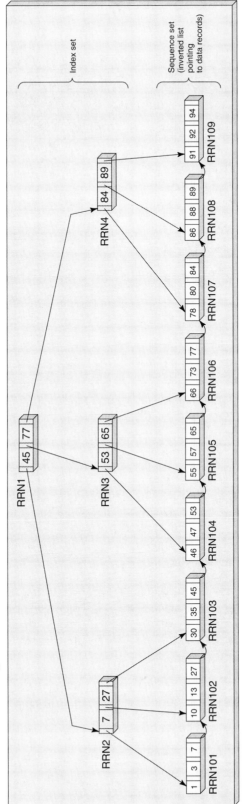

Occurrence of the B-Tree in Figure A-9

RRN	Link1	Value1	Link2	Value2	Link3	
1	2	45	3	77	4	
2	101	7	102	27	103	Index Set
3	104	53	105	65	106	
4	107	84	108	89	109	

.
.
.

	R1	Addr1	R2	Addr2	R3	Addr3	Link	
101	1	Pointer to 6	3	Pointer to 8	7	Pointer to 12	102	
102	10	· · ·	13	· · ·	27	· · ·	103	
103	30	· · ·	35	· · ·	45	· · ·	104	Sequence Set
104	46	· · ·	47	· · ·	53	· · ·	105	(Addresses of
105	55	· · ·	57	· · ·	65	· · ·	106	data records
106	66	· · ·	73	· · ·	77	· · ·	107	are omitted)
107	78	· · ·	80	· · ·	84	· · ·	108	
108	86	· · ·	88	· · ·	89	· · ·	109	
109	91	· · ·	92	· · ·	94	· · ·	0	

Summary of Data Structures and
Data Organizations Used for
Ordered Flat Files

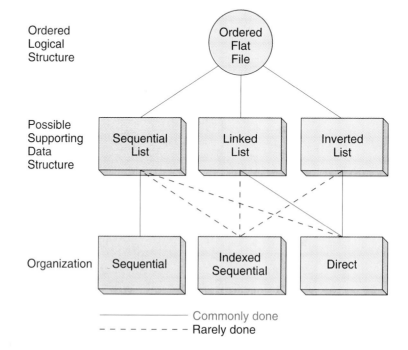

▦ Summary of Data Structures

Figure A-11 summarizes the techniques for maintaining ordered flat files. Three supporting data structures are possible. Sequential lists can be used, but the data must be duplicated in order to maintain several orders. Because sequential lists are not used in database processing, we will not consider them further. Both linked lists and indexes can be used without data duplication. B-trees are special applications of indexes.

As shown in Figure A-11, sequential lists can be stored using any of three file organizations. In practice, however, they are usually kept on sequential files. In addition, although both linked lists and indexes can be stored using either indexed sequential or direct files, DBMS products almost always store them on direct files.

REPRESENTING BINARY RELATIONSHIPS

In this section we examine how each of the specialized record relationships discussed in Chapter 6—trees, simple networks, and complex networks—can be represented using linked lists and indexes.

▦ Review of Record Relationships

Records can be related in three ways. A *tree* relationship has one or more one-to-many relationships, but each child record has at most one parent. The occurrence of faculty data shown in Figure A-12 illustrates a tree. There are several 1:N relationships, but any child record has only one parent, as shown in Figure A-13.

A *simple network* is a collection of records and the 1:N relationships among them. What distinguishes a simple network from a tree is the fact that in a simple network a child can have more than one parent as long as the parents are different

FIGURE A-12

Occurrence of a Faculty Member Record

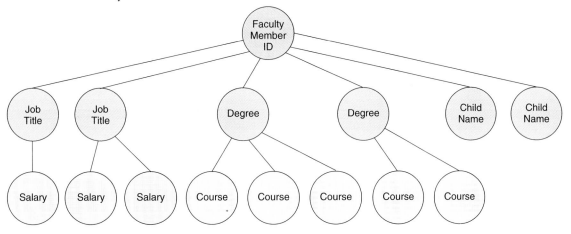

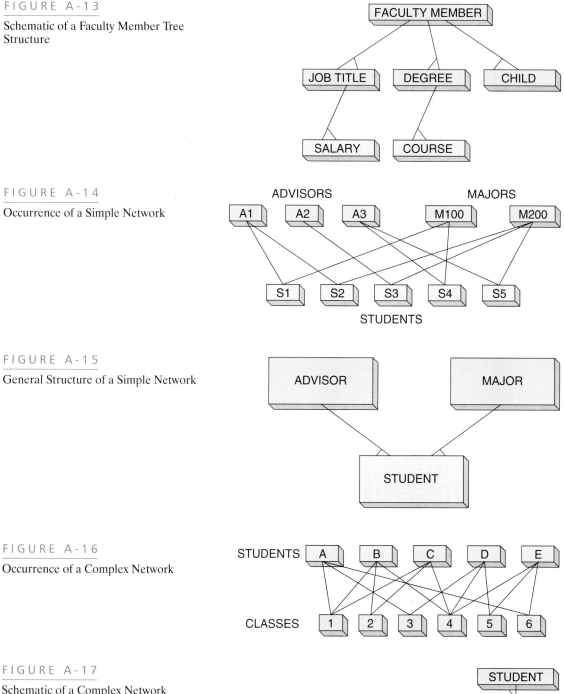

FIGURE A-13

Schematic of a Faculty Member Tree Structure

FIGURE A-14

Occurrence of a Simple Network

FIGURE A-15

General Structure of a Simple Network

FIGURE A-16

Occurrence of a Complex Network

FIGURE A-17

Schematic of a Complex Network

record types. The occurrence of a simple network of students, advisers, and major fields of study in Figure A-14 is represented schematically in Figure A-15.

A *complex network* is also a collection of records and relationships, but the relationships are many to many instead of one to many. The relationship between students and classes is a complex network. An occurrence of this relationship can be seen in Figure A-16, and the general schematic is in Figure A-17.

We saw earlier that we can use linked lists and indexes to process records in orders different from the one in which they are physically stored. We can also use those same data structures to store and process the relationships among records.

■ Representing Trees

We can use sequential lists, linked lists, and indexes to represent trees. When using sequential lists, we duplicate much data, and furthermore, sequential lists are not used by DBMS products to represent trees. Therefore we describe only linked lists and indexes.

LINKED-LIST REPRESENTATION OF TREES

Figure A-18 shows a tree structure in which the VENDOR records are parents and the INVOICE records are children. Figure A-19 shows two occurrences of this structure, and in Figure A-20, all of the VENDOR and INVOICE records have been written to a direct access file. VENDOR AA is in relative record number 1 (RRN1), and VENDOR BB is in relative record number 2. The INVOICE records have been stored in subsequent records, as illustrated. Note that these records are not stored in any particular order and that they do not need to be.

Our problem is that we cannot tell from this file which invoices belong to which vendors. To solve this problem with a linked list, we add a pointer field to every record. In this field we store the address of some other related record. For example, we place in VENDOR AA's link field the address of the first invoice belonging to it. This is RRN7, which is Invoice 110. Then we make Invoice 110 point to the next invoice belonging to VENDOR AA, in this case RRN3. This slot holds Invoice 118. To indicate that there are no more children in the chain, we insert a 0 in the link field for RRN3.

This technique is shown in Figure A-21. If you examine the figure, you will see that a similar set of links has been used to represent the relationship between VENDOR BB and its invoices.

The structure in Figure A-21 is much easier to modify than is a sequential list of the records. For example, suppose we add a new invoice, say number 111, to VENDOR AA. To do this, we just add the record to the file and insert it into the linked

FIGURE A-18
_____

Sample Tree Relating VENDOR and
INVOICE Records

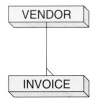

FIGURE A-19

Two Occurrences of VENDOR–INVOICE Tree

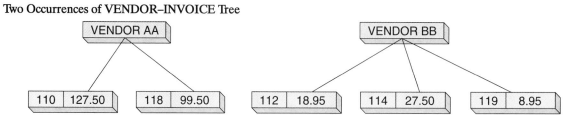

FIGURE A-20

File Representation of the Trees
in Figure A-19

Record Number	Record Contents	
1	VENDOR AA	
2	VENDOR BB	
3	118	99.50
4	119	8.95
5	112	18.95
6	114	27.50
7	110	127.50

FIGURE A-21

Tree Occurrences Represented
by Linked Lists

Relative Record Number	Record Contents		Link Field
1	VENDOR AA		7
2	VENDOR BB		5
3	118	99.50	0
4	119	8.95	0
5	112	18.95	6
6	114	27.50	4
7	110	127.50	3

FIGURE A-22

Inserting Invoice 111 into File
in Figure A-21

Relative Record Number	Record Contents		Link Field	
1	VENDOR AA		7	
2	VENDOR BB		5	
3	118	99.50	0	
4	119	8.95	0	
5	112	18.95	6	
6	114	27.50	4	
7	110	127.50	8	
8	111	19.95	3	← Inserted Record

FIGURE A-23

Deleting Invoice 114 from
File in Figure A-22

Relative Record Number	Record Contents		Link Field
1	VENDOR AA		7
2	VENDOR BB		5
3	118	99.50	0
4	119	8.95	0
5	112	18.95	4
6	114	27.50	4
7	110	127.50	8
8	111	19.95	3

← Deleted Record (pointing to RRN 6)

list. Physically, the record can be placed anywhere. But where should it be placed logically? Usually the application will have a requirement like children are to be kept in ascending order on invoice number. If so, we need to make Invoice 110 point to Invoice 111 (at RRN8), and we need to make Invoice 111, the new invoice, point to Invoice 118 (at RRN3). This modification is shown in Figure A-22.

Similarly, deleting an invoice is easy. If Invoice 114 is deleted, we simply modify the pointer in the invoice that is now pointing to Invoice 114. In this case, it is Invoice 112 at RRN5. We give Invoice 112 the pointer that Invoice 114 had before deletion. In this way, Invoice 112 points to Invoice 119 (see Figure A-23). We have effectively cut one link out of the chain and welded together the ones it once connected.

INDEX REPRESENTATION OF TREES

A tree structure can readily be represented using indexes. The technique is to store each one-to-many relationship as an index. These lists are then used to match parents and children.

Using the VENDOR and INVOICE records in Figure A-21, we see that VENDOR AA (in RRN1) owns INVOICEs 110 (RRN7) and 118 (RRN3). Thus RRN1 is the parent of RRN7 and RRN3. We can represent this fact with the index in Figure A-24. The list simply associates a parent's address with the addresses of each of its children.

If the tree has several 1:N relationships, then several indexes will be required, one for each relationship. For the structure in Figure A-13, five indexes are needed.

FIGURE A-24

Index Representation of
VENDOR–INVOICE Relationship

Parent Record	Child Record
1	7
1	3
2	5
2	6
2	4

FIGURE A-25

Simple Network Structure

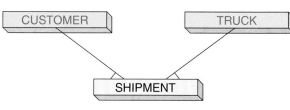

FIGURE A-26

Occurrence of the Simple Network in
Figure A-25

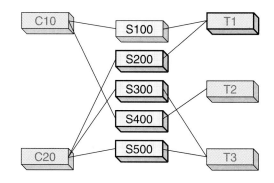

FIGURE A-27

Representation of a Simple Network with
Linked Lists

Relative Record Number	Record Contents	Link Fields	
1	C10	6	
2	C20	7	
3	T1		6
4	T2		9
5	T3		8
6	S100	9	7
7	S200	8	0
8	S300	10	10
9	S400	0	0
10	S500	0	0

CUSTOMER   TRUCK
Links   Links

FIGURE A-28

Representation of Simple Network with
Index

Customer Record	Shipment Record
1	6
1	9
2	7
2	8
2	10

Truck Record	Shipment Record
3	6
3	7
4	9
5	8
5	10

Representing Simple Networks

As with trees, simple networks can also be represented using linked lists and indexes.

LINKED-LIST REPRESENTATION OF SIMPLE NETWORKS

Consider the simple network in Figure A-25. It is a simple network because all the relationships are 1:N, and the SHIPMENT records have two parents of different types. Each SHIPMENT has a CUSTOMER parent and a TRUCK parent. The relationship between CUSTOMER and SHIPMENT is 1:N because a customer can have several shipments, and the relationship from TRUCK to SHIPMENT is 1:N because one truck can hold many shipments (assuming that the shipments are small enough to fit in one truck or less). An occurrence of this network is shown in Figure A-26.

In order to represent this simple network with linked lists, we need to establish one set of pointers for each 1:N relationship. In this example, that means one set of pointers to connect CUSTOMERs with their SHIPMENTs and another set of pointers to connect TRUCKs with their SHIPMENTs. Thus a CUSTOMER record will contain one pointer (to the first SHIPMENT it owns); a TRUCK record will contain one pointer (to the first SHIPMENT it owns); and a SHIPMENT record will have two pointers, one for the next SHIPMENT owned by the same CUSTOMER and one for the next SHIPMENT owned by the same TRUCK. This scheme is illustrated in Figure A-27.

A simple network has at least two 1:N relationships, each of which can be represented using an index, as we explained in our discussion of trees. For example, consider the simple network shown in Figure A-25. It has two 1:N relationships, one between TRUCK and SHIPMENT and one between CUSTOMER and SHIPMENT. We can store each of these relationships in an index. Figure A-28 shows the two indexes needed to represent the example in Figure A-26. Assume the records are located in the same positions as in Figure A-27.

Representing Complex Networks

Complex networks can be physically represented in a variety of ways. They can be decomposed into trees or simple networks, and these simpler structures can then be represented using one of the techniques we just described. Alternatively, they

FIGURE A-29

Decomposition of Complex
Network into Simple Network

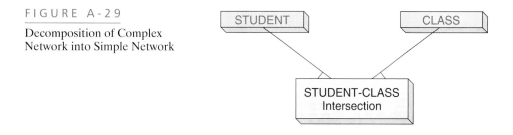

Instance of STUDENT–CLASS
Relationship Showing Intersection Records

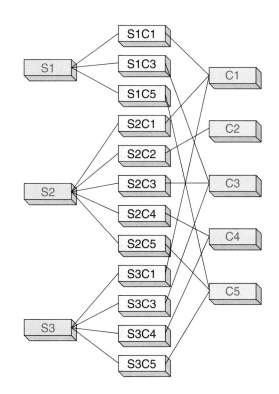

Occurrence of Network in Figure A-30

Relative Record Number	Record Contents	Link Fields	
1	S1	9	
2	S2	12	
3	S3	17	
4	C1		9
5	C2		13
6	C3		10
7	C4		15
8	C5		11
9	S1C1	10	12
10	S1C3	11	14
11	S1C5	0	16
12	S2C1	13	17
13	S2C2	14	0
14	S2C3	15	18
15	S2C4	16	19
16	S2C5	0	20
17	S3C1	18	0
18	S3C3	19	0
19	S3C4	20	0
20	S3C5	0	0

STUDENT Links   CLASS Links

can be represented directly using indexes. Linked lists are not used by any DBMS product to represent complex networks directly. In practice, complex networks are nearly always decomposed into simpler structures, and so we consider only those representations using decomposition.

A common approach to representing complex networks is to reduce them to simple networks and then to represent the simple networks with linked lists or indexes. Note, however, that a complex network involves a relationship between two records, whereas a simple network involves relationships among three records. Thus in order to decompose a complex network into a simple one, we need to create a third record type.

The record that is created when a complex network is decomposed into a simple one is called an *intersection record.* Consider the StudentClass complex network. An intersection record will contain a unique key from a STUDENT record and a unique key from a corresponding CLASS record. It will contain no other application data, although it might contain link fields. The general structure of this relationship is shown in Figure A-29. Assuming that the record names are unique (such as S1, S2,

FIGURE A-32

Record Relationships, Data Structures, and File Organizations

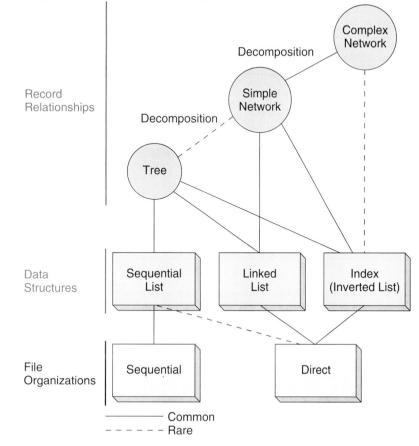

and C1), an instance of the STUDENT-CLASS relationship is illustrated in Figure A-30.

Notice that the relationship between STUDENT and the intersection record and that between CLASS and the intersection record both are 1:N. Thus we have created a simple network that can now be represented with the linked-list or index techniques shown earlier. A file of this occurrence using the linked-list technique is shown in Figure A-31.

■ Summary of Relationship Representations

Figure A-32 summarizes the representations of record relationships. Trees can be represented using sequential lists (although we did not discuss this approach), linked lists, or indexes. Sequential lists are not used in DBMS products. A simple network can be decomposed into trees and then represented, or it can be represented directly using either linked lists or indexes. Finally, a complex network can be decomposed into a tree or a simple network (using intersection records), or it can be represented directly using indexes.

SECONDARY-KEY REPRESENTATIONS

In many cases the word *key* indicates a field (or fields) whose value uniquely identifies a record. This is usually called the *primary key*. Sometimes, however, applications need to access and process records by means of a *secondary key*, one that is different from the primary key. Secondary keys may be unique (such as a professor's name) or nonunique (such as a customer's zip code). In this section we use the term *set* to refer to all records having the same value of a nonunique secondary key, for example, a set of records having ZIP Code 98040.

Both linked lists and indexes are used to represent secondary keys, but linked lists are practical only for nonunique keys. Indexes, however, can be used for both unique and nonunique key representations.

■ Linked List Representation of Secondary Keys

Consider the example of CUSTOMER records shown in Figure A-33. The primary key is AccountNumber, and there is a secondary key on CreditLimit. Possible CreditLimit values are 500, 700, and 1000. Thus there will be a set of records for the limit of 500, a set for 700, and a set for 1000.

To represent this key using linked lists, we add a link field to the CUSTOMER records. Inside this link field we create a linked list for each set of records. Figure A-34 shows a database of eleven customers, but for brevity, only AccountNumber

FIGURE A-33

CUSTOMER Record

FIGURE A-34

Representing CreditLimit Secondary Key Using Linked List

Relative Record Number	Link	Account-Number	Credit-Limit	Other Data
1	2	101	500	
2	7	301	500	
3	5	203	700	
4	6	004	1000	
5	10	204	700	
6	8	905	1000	
7	0	705	500	
8	9	207	1000	
9	11	309	1000	
10	0	409	700	
11	0	210	1000	

HEAD-500 = 1
HEAD-700 = 3
HEAD-1000 = 4

and CreditLimit are shown. A link field has been attached to the records. Assume that one database record occupies one physical record on a direct file using relative record addressing.

Three pointers need to be established so we know where to begin each linked list. These are called *heads* and are stored separate from the data. The head of the $500 linked list is RRN1. Record 1 links to record 2, which in turn links to record 7. Record 7 has a zero in the link position, indicating that it is the end of the list. Consequently, the $500 credit limit set consists of records 1, 2, and 7. Similarly, the $700 set contains records 3, 5, and 10, and the $1000 set contains relative records 4, 6, 8, 9, and 11.

To answer a query like, How many accounts in the $1000 set have a balance in excess of $900? the $1000 set linked list can be used. In this way, only those records in the $1000 set need to be read from the file and examined. Although the advantage of this approach is not readily apparent in this small example, suppose there are 100,000 CUSTOMER records and only 100 of them are in the $1000 set. If there is no linked list, all 100,000 records must be examined, but with the linked list, only 100 records need to be examined, namely, the ones in the $1000 set. Using the linked list therefore saves 99,900 reads.

Linked lists are not an effective technique for every secondary-key application. In particular, if the records are processed nonsequentially in a set, linked lists are inefficient. For example, if it often is necessary to find the 10th or 120th or nth record in the $500 CreditLimit set, processing will be slow. Linked lists are inefficient for direct access.

In addition, if the application requires that secondary keys be created or destroyed dynamically, the linked-list approach is undesirable. Whenever a new key is created, a link field must be added to every record, which often requires reorganizing the database, a time-consuming and expensive process.

Finally, if the secondary keys are unique, each list will have a length of 1, and a separate linked list will exist for every record in the database. Since this situation is unworkable, linked lists cannot be used for unique keys. For example, suppose that the CUSTOMER records contain another unique field, say Social Security Number. If we attempt to represent this unique secondary key using a linked list, every Social Security Number will be a separate linked list. Furthermore, each linked list will have just one item in it, the single record having the indicated Social Security Number.

Index Representation of Secondary Keys

A second technique for representing secondary keys uses an index; one is established for each secondary key. The approach varies depending on whether the key values are unique or nonunique.

UNIQUE SECONDARY KEYS

Suppose the CUSTOMER records in Figure A-33 contain Social Security Number (SSN) as well as the fields shown. To provide key access to the CUSTOMER records using SSN, we simply build an index on the SSN field. Sample CUSTOMER data is shown in Figure A-35(a), and a corresponding index is illustrated in Figure A-35(b). This index uses relative record numbers as addresses. It would be possible to use AccountNumbers instead, in which case the DBMS would locate the desired SSN in the index, obtain the matching AccountNumber, and then convert the AccountNumber to a relative record address.

NONUNIQUE SECONDARY KEYS

Indexes can also be used to represent nonunique secondary keys, but because each set of related records can contain an unknown number of members, the entries in the index are of variable length. For example, Figure A-36 shows the index for the

FIGURE A-35

Representing a Unique Secondary Key with Indexes: (a) Sample CUSTOMER Data (with SSN) and (b) Index for SSN Secondary Key

Relative Record Number	Account-Number	Credit-Limit	Social Security Number (SSN)
1	101	500	000-01-0001
2	301	500	000-01-0005
3	203	700	000-01-0009
4	004	1000	000-01-0003

(a)

SSN	Relative Record Number
000-01-0001	1
000-01-0003	4
000-01-0005	2
000-01-0009	3

(b)

FIGURE A-36

Index for CreditNumber Key in
Figure A-33

AccountNumber

CreditLimit					
500	101	301	705		
700	203	204	409		
1000	004	905	207	309	210

CreditLimit sets for the CUSTOMER data. The $500 set and the $700 set each have three members, so there are three account numbers in each entry. The $1000 set has five members, so there are five account numbers in that entry.

In reality, representing and processing nonunique secondary keys are complex tasks. Several different schemes are used by commercial DBMS products. One common method uses a values table and an occurrence table. Each values table entry consists of two fields, the first of which has a key value. For the CUSTOMER credit-limit key, the values are 500, 700, and 1000. The second field of the values table entry is a pointer into the occurrence table. The occurrence table contains record addresses, and those having a common value in the secondary-key field appear together in the table. Figure A-37 shows the values and occurrence tables for the Credit-limit key.

To locate records having a given value of the secondary key, the values table is searched for the desired value. Once the given key value is located in the values table, the pointer is followed to the occurrence table to obtain the addresses of those records having that key value. These addresses are then used to obtain the desired records.

When a new record is inserted into the file, the DBMS must modify the indexes for each secondary-key field. For nonunique keys, it must make sure that the new record key value is in the values table; if it is, it will add the new record address to the appropriate entry in the occurrences table. If it is not, it must insert new entries in the values and occurrence tables.

When a record is deleted, its address must be removed from the occurrence table. If no addresses remain in the occurrence table entry, the corresponding values table entry must also be deleted.

When the secondary-key field of a record is modified, the record address must be removed from one occurrence table entry and inserted into another. If the modification is a new value for the key, an entry must be added to the values table.

FIGURE A-37

Values and Occurrence Tables
for CreditLimit Key in Figure A-33

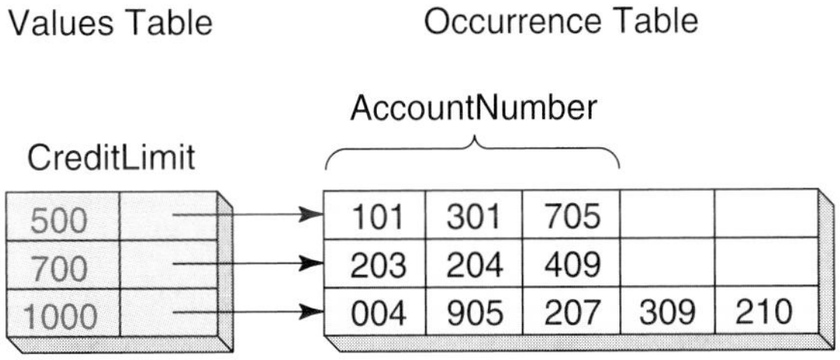

Values Table   Occurrence Table

AccountNumber

CreditLimit						
500	→	101	301	705		
700	→	203	204	409		
1000	→	004	905	207	309	210

The index approach to representing secondary keys overcomes the objections to the linked-list approach. Direct processing of sets is possible. For example, the third record in a set can be retrieved without processing the first or second ones. Also, it is possible to dynamically create and delete secondary keys. No changes are made in the records themselves; the DBMS merely creates additional values and occurrence tables. Finally, unique keys can be processed efficiently.

The disadvantages of the index approach are that it requires more file space (the tables use more overhead than the pointers do) and that the DBMS programming task is more complex. Note that the *application programming* task is not necessarily any more or less difficult—but it is more complex to write DBMS software that processes indexes than it is to write software that processes linked lists. Finally, modifications are usually processed more slowly because of the reading and writing actions required to access and maintain the values in the occurrence tables.

SUMMARY

In this appendix we surveyed data structures used for database processing. A flat file is a file that contains no repeating groups. Flat files can be ordered using sequential lists (physically placing the records in the sequence in which they will be processed), linked lists (attaching to each data record a pointer to another logically related record), and indexes (building a table, separate from the data records, containing pointers to related records). B-trees are special applications of indexes.

Sequential lists, linked lists, and indexes (or inverted lists) are fundamental data structures. (Sequential lists, however, are seldom used in database processing.) These data structures can be used to represent record relationships as well as secondary keys.

The three basic record structures—trees, simple networks, and complex networks—can be represented using linked lists and indexes. Simple networks can be decomposed into trees and then represented; complex networks can be decomposed into simple networks containing an intersection record and then represented.

Secondary keys are used to access the data on some field besides the primary key. Secondary keys can be unique or nonunique. Nonunique secondary keys can be represented with both linked lists and indexes. Unique secondary keys can be represented only with indexes.

GROUP I QUESTIONS

A.1 Define a flat file. Give an example (other than one in this text) of a flat file and an example of a file that is not flat.

A.2 Show how sequential lists can be used to maintain the file in Question A.1 in two different orders simultaneously.

A.3 Show how linked lists can be used to maintain the file in Question A.1 in two different orders simultaneously.

A.4 Show how inverted lists can be used to maintain the file in Question A.1 in two different orders simultaneously.

A.5   Define a tree and give an example structure.

A.6   Give an occurrence of the tree in Question A.5.

A.7   Represent the occurrence in Question A.6 using linked lists.

A.8   Represent the occurrence in Question A.6 using indexes.

A.9   Define a simple network and give an example structure.

A.10 Give an occurrence of the simple network in Question A.9.

A.11 Represent the occurrence in Question A.10 using linked lists.

A.12 Represent the occurrence in Question A.10 using indexes.

A.13 Define complex network and give an example structure.

A.14 Give an occurrence of the complex network in Question A.13.

A.15 Decompose the complex network in Question A.14 into a simple network, and represent an occurrence of it using indexes.

A.16 Explain the difference between primary and secondary keys.

A.17 Explain the difference between unique and nonunique keys.

A.18 Define a file containing a unique secondary key. Represent an occurrence of that file using an index on the secondary key.

A.19 Define a nonunique secondary key for the file in Question A.18. Represent an occurrence of that file using a linked list on the secondary key.

A.20 Perform the same task as in Question A.19, but using an index to represent the secondary key.

GROUP II QUESTIONS

A.21 Develop an algorithm to produce a report listing the IDs of students enrolled in each class, using the linked-list structure in Figure A-4.

A.22 Develop an algorithm to insert records into the structure in Figure A-4. The resulting structure should resemble the one in Figure A-5.

A.23 Develop an algorithm to produce a report listing the IDs of students enrolled in each class, using the index structure shown in Figures A-8(a), (b), and (c).

A.24 Develop an algorithm to insert a record into the structure in Figure A-8(a), being sure to modify both of the associated indexes in Figures A-8(b) and (c).

A.25 Develop an algorithm to delete a record from the structure in Figure A-34, which shows a secondary key represented with a linked list. If all records for one of the Credit-limit categories (say $1000) is deleted, should the associated head pointer also be deleted? Why or why not?

A.26 Develop an algorithm to insert a record into the structure shown in Figure A-34. Suppose the new record has a credit-limit value different from those already established. Should the record be inserted and a new linked list established? Or should the record be rejected? Who should make that decision?

Glossary

Action/object menu: A system of menus in which the top menu refers to actions and the lowest menus refer to the objects on which those actions are taken.

After image: A record of a database entity (normally a row or a page) after a change. It is used in recovery to perform rollforward.

AI: Artificial intelligence. A group of related disciplines providing capabilities that in the past were attributed only to humans. Vision, robotics, and expert systems are branches of artificial intelligence. Sometimes a vague term, artificial intelligence is used in marketing literature to mean new and exciting.

Anomaly: An undesirable consequence of a data modification used primarily in discussions of normalization. With an insertion anomaly, facts about two or more different themes must be added to a single row of a relation. With a deletion anomaly, facts about two or more themes are lost when a single row is deleted.

Application: A business computer system that processes a portion of a database to meet a user's information needs. It consists of menus, forms, reports, and application programs.

Application design: The process of creating the structure of programs and data to meet the application's requirements. Also the structure of the users' interface.

Application metadata: Data dictionary data concerning the structure and contents of application menus, forms, and reports.

Application plan: In DB2, a set of access paths for each SQL statement in an application program. It includes information about database tables' structures, available indexes, and data storage structures.

Application program: A custom-developed program for processing a database. It can be written in a standard procedural language such as COBOL, C, or BASIC or in a language unique to the DBMS.

Application view: That portion of a database processed by a particular application program.

Archetype/version object: A structure of two objects that represents multiple versions of a standardized item. For example, a SOFT-PRODUCT (the archetype) and PRODUCT-RELEASE (the version of the archetype). The identifier of the version always includes the archetype object.

Association object: An object that represents the combination of at least two other objects and that contains data about that combination. It is often used in contracting and assignment applications.

Atomic: A set of actions that is completed as a unit. Either all actions are completed or none is.

Atomic transaction: A group of logically related database operations that are performed as a unit. Either all of the operations are performed, or none of them is.

Attribute: (1) A column of a relation; also called a column, field, or data-item. (2) A property in an entity or semantic object.

Authorization rules: A set of processing permissions that describes which users or user groups can take particular actions against particular portions of the database.

Band: The section of a report definition that contains the format of a report section. There normally are bands for the report heading and footing, page heading and footing, and the detail line of the report. There are also bands for group or break points within the report.

Banded report writer: A report writer in which the sections of the reports are defined by bands. (See Band.)

Base table: In relational implementations, the table from which relational views are defined.

Before image: A record of a database entity (normally a row or a page) before a change. It is used in recovery to perform rollback.

Bill of materials: A recursive data structure in which a part (or, in general, any element) can be both an assembly of other parts and a component of other assemblies.

Binary relationship: A relationship between exactly two entities or tables.

Bind: A verb meaning to connect a program variable or a GUI control to a column of a table or query.

Bottom-up database design: The design of a database that works from the detailed and specific to the general. Although this sort of design takes little time, it may result in a database that is too narrow in scope.

Boyce–Codd normal form: A relation in third normal form in which every determinant is a candidate key.

Branch: A subelement of a tree that may consist of one or many nodes.

Buffer: An area of memory used to hold data. For a read, data is read from a storage device into a buffer; for a write, data is written from the buffer to storage.

Built-in function: In SQL, any of the functions COUNT, SUM, AVG, MAX, or MIN.

Byzantine failure: Intentional node or network failure caused by malevolent nodes, perhaps acting in a conspiracy.

Call: A programming-language statement that passes control to an external subroutine for a service. The expectation is that control will be passed back. Examples are CALL, GOSUB, and BAL.

Candidate key: An attribute or group of attributes that identifies a unique row in a relation. One of the candidate keys is chosen to be the primary key.

Cardinality: In a binary relationship, the maximum or minimum number of elements allowed on each side of the relationship. The maximum cardinality can be 1:1, 1:N, N:1, or N:M. The minimum cardinality can be optional–optional, optional–mandatory, mandatory–optional, or mandatory–mandatory.

Cartesian product: A relational operation on two relations, A and B, producing a third relation, C, with C containing the concatenation of every row in A with every row in B.

Catastrophe: A failure in a network that can be recovered only by manual intervention.

CCP: Communications control program. A program that controls and administers transactions requests and responses in a teleprocessing system. The CCP routes transactions to the correct application programs and returns responses to the correct user terminal.

Check box: In a GUI environment, an element of the user interface in which a user can select one or more items from a list. Items are selected by clicking on them.

Checkpoint: The point of synchronization between a database and a transaction log. All buffers are force-written to external storage. This is the standard definition of checkpoint, but this term is sometimes used in other ways by DBMS vendors.

Child: A row, record, or node on the many side of a one-to-many relationship.

Child and twin pointer scheme: In DL/I, a technique used to represent segment relationships of a data base record in storage.

Child pointer: In the child and twin pointer scheme, the address of a child node.

Client computer: A microcomputer on a local area network with client–server architecture. In a database application, the client computer processes database application programs. Requests for actions on the database are sent to the database computer.

Client–server database architecture: The structure of a networked computing system in which one computer (usually a microcomputer) performs services on behalf of other computers (usually a microcomputer). For a database system, the server computer, which is called a database server, processes the DBMS, and client computers process the application programs. All database activities are carried out by the database server.

Client server system: A system of two or more computers in which at least one computer provides services for one or more other computers. The services can be database services, communication services, printer services, or some other function.

COBOL: Common Business Oriented Language. The most widely used third-generation language for business applications.

CODASYL: Conference on Data Systems Languages. A nonprofit committee of vendor, user, and academic personnel who established and now maintain the conventions for COBOL. The DBTG, or DataBase task group, developed a network model that was popular in the 1970s and early 1980s but is now being phased out.

Column: A logical group of bytes in a row of a relation or a table. The meaning of a column is the same for every row of the relation.

Command: A statement input to a database application by which users specify the activity to be performed. Contrast this with Menu.

Commit: A command issued to the DBMS to make database modifications permanent. Once the command has been processed, the changes are written to the database and to a log in such a way that they will survive system crashes and other failures. A commit is usually used at the end of an atomic transaction. Contrast this with Rollback.

Communications control program: See CCP.

Complex network: A collection of entities, objects, or relations and their relationships, of which at least one of the relationships is complex (many to many).

Composite group: A group of attributes in a semantic object that is multivalued and contains no other object attributes.

Composite key: A key with more than one attribute.

Composite object: An object with at least one multivalued attribute or attribute group. It is called a composite object because the key of the relation that represents the multivalued attribute or group is a composite key.

Compound object: An object that contains at least one other object.

Computed value: A column of a table that is computed from other column values. Values are not stored but are computed when they are to be displayed.

Concurrency: A condition in which two or more transactions are processed against the database at the same time. In a single CPU system, the changes are interleaved; in a multi-CPU system, the transactions may be processed simultaneously, and the changes on the database server are interleaved.

Concurrency transparency: In a distributed database system, the condition in which application programs do not know and do not need to know whether data is being concurrently processed. The DDBMS organizes update activities so that the results produced when concurrent processing is under way are consistent with the results that would occur if there were no concurrent processing.

Concurrent processing: In teleprocessing applications, the sharing of the CPU among several transactions. The CPU is allocated to each transaction in a round robin or in some other fashion for a certain period of time. Operations are performed so quickly that they appear to users to be simultaneous. In local area networks and other distributed applications, concurrent processing is used to refer to the (possibly simultaneous) processing of applications on multiple computers.

Concurrent update problem: An error condition in which one user's data changes are overwritten by another user's data changes. Same as Lost update problem or Lost update anomaly.

Conflict: Two operations conflict if they operate on the same data item and at least one of the operations is a write.

Consistency: Two or more concurrent transactions are consistent if the result of their processing is the same as it would have been if they had been processed in some serial order.

Consistent schedule: An ordered list of transaction operations against a database in which the result of the processing is consistent.

Constraint: A rule concerning the allowed values of attributes whose truth can be evaluated. A constraint usually does not include dynamic rules such as "SalesPersonPay can never decrease" or "Salary now must be greater than Salary last quarter."

CPU: Central processing unit. The portion of the computer hardware that processes arithmetic and logic instructions. The term CPU usually includes main memory as well.

Currency indicator: In the CODASYL DBTG model, a variable that identifies the most recently accessed record or set. There are currency indicators for run-unit, record type, and set.

Cursor: An indicator of the current position or focus. (1) On a computer screen, a blinking box or underscore that indicates the position into which the next entry will be made. (2) In a file or embedded SQL SELECT, the identity of the next record or row to be processed.

Data access language: See Data sublanguage.

Data administration: The enterprisewide function that concerns the effective use and control of the organization's data assets. It can be a person but more often is a group. Specific functions include setting data standards and data policies and providing a forum for conflict resolution. Also see Database administrator.

Data base: In DL/I, a collection of data base records.

Database: A self-describing collection of integrated records.

Database administration: The function that concerns the effective use and control of a particular database and its related applications.

Database administrator: The person or group responsible for establishing policies and procedures to control and protect a database. He (she or it) works within guidelines set by data administration to control the database structure, manage data changes, and maintain DBMS programs.

Database data: The portion of a database that contains data of interest and use to the application end users.

Data base description: In DL/I, a data structure that describes the structure of a data base record.

Database machine: A special-purpose CPU designed specifically for processing a database. It is sometimes called a backend machine because it resides between the operating system and the data. The database machine has not been commercially successful, however, and is seldom used today.

Database manager (DBM): A program that processes some portion of a distributed database.

Database node: A computer that processes a database manager and its related database(s).

Data base record: In DL /I, a hierarchical arrangement of data segments. See Logical data base record and Physical data base record.

Data base request module: In DB2, a data structure that describes the SQL statements that need to be executed.

Database save: A copy of database files that can be used to restore the database to some previous, consistent state.

Database server: On a local area network with client–server database architecture, the microcomputer that runs the DBMS and processes actions against the database on behalf of its client computers.

Data definition language (DDL): A language used to describe the structure of a database.

Data dictionary: A user-accessible catalog of both database and application metadata. An active data dictionary is a dictionary whose contents are automatically updated by the DBMS whenever changes are made in the database or application structure. A passive data dictionary is one whose contents must be updated manually when changes are made.

Data dictionary and database administration subsystem: A collection of programs in the DBMS used to access the data dictionary and to perform database administration functions such as maintaining passwords and performing backup and recovery.

Dataflow diagram: A graphical display by system developers that illustrates business processes and the data interfaces. It also shows the flow of the system from the perspective of the data.

Data integrity: The state of a database in which all constraints are fulfilled. Usually refers to intertable constraints in which the value of a foreign key is required to be present in the table having that foreign key as its primary key.

Data-item: (1) A logical group of bytes in a record, usually used with file processing. (2) In the context of the relational model, a synonym for attribute.

Data Language I: See DL/I.

Data manipulation language (DML): A language used to describe the processing of a database.

Data model: (1) A model of the users' data requirements expressed in terms of either the entity-relationship model or the semantic-object model. It is sometimes called a users' data model. (2) A language for describing the structure and processing of a database. See Hierarchical data model, Network data model, and Relational data model.

Data owner: Same as Data proponent.

Data proponent: In data administration, a department or other organizational unit in charge of managing a particular data item.

Data replication: A term that indicates whether any portion (or all) of a database resides on more than one computer. If so, the data is said to be replicated.

Data structure diagram: A graphical display of tables (files) and their relationships. The tables are shown in rectangles, and the relationships are shown by lines. A many relationship is shown with a fork on the end of the line; an optional relationship is depicted by an oval; and a mandatory relationship is shown with hash marks.

Data sublanguage: A language for defining and processing a database intended to be embedded in programs written in another language—in most cases, a procedural language such as COBOL, C, or BASIC. A data sublanguage is an incomplete programming language, as it contains only constructs for data access.

DBA: See Database administrator.

DBM: Database manager. In a DDBMS, software that processes some portion of a distributed database in accordance with action requests received from distributed transactions managers (DTMs).

DBMS: Database management system. A set of programs used to define, administer, and process the database and its applications.

DBMS engine: A DBMS subsystem that processes logical I/O requests from other DBMS subsystems and submits physical I/O requests to the operating system.

DBTG: (1) A subcommittee of CODASYL that developed the DBTG network data model. (2) A network data model that models data as records and record relationships as sets. Only simple networks can be directly represented. Although the DBTG network data model is fading in popularity, it still is in use on mainframe computers.

DB2: Data base 2. A relational DBMS developed and licensed by IBM for use on mainframe computers.

DDBMS: Distributed database management system. (1) The collection of DTMs and DBMs on all computers that processes a distributed database (see Chapter 16). (2) A commercial DBMS product that has been modified to allow processing a distributed database.

DDL: Data definition language. The portion of a data model used to define the structure of the database, views, and subschemas.

Deadlock: A condition that can occur during concurrent processing in which each of two (or more) transactions is waiting to access data that the other transaction has locked. It is also called a deadly embrace.

Deadlock detection: The process of determining whether two or more transactions are in a state of deadlock.

Deadlock prevention: A way of managing transactions so that a deadlock cannot occur.

Deadly embrace: See Deadlock.

Definition tools subsystem: The portion of the DBMS program used to define and change the database structure.

Degree: For relationships in the entity-relationship model, the number of entities participating in the relationship. In almost all cases, such relationships are of degree 2.

Deletion anomaly: In a relation, the situation in which the removal of one row of a table deletes facts about two or more themes.

Determinant: One or more attributes that functionally determine another attribute or attributes. In the functional dependency (A, B) → C, the attributes (A, B) are the determinant.

Difference: A relational algebra operation performed on two union-compatible relations, A and B, that produces a third relation, C. Each row in C is present in A but not in B.

Distributed database: A database stored on two or more computers. Distributed data can be partitioned or not partitioned, replicated, or not replicated.

Distributed database application: A business computer system in which the execution of transactions and the retrieval and updating of data occur across two or more independent and usually geographically distributed computers.

Distributed database management system (DDBMS): In a distributed database, the collection of distributed transaction and database managers on all computers.

Distributed database processing: Database processing in which transactions are executed and data is retrieved and updated across two or more independent and usually geographically separated computers.

Distributed database system: A distributed system in which a database or portions of a database are distributed across two or more computers.

Distributed system: A system in which the application programs of a database are processed on two or more computers.

Distributed two-phase locking: Two-phase locking in a distributed environment, in which locks are obtained and released across all nodes on the network. See Two-phase locking.

DL/I: Data Language I. A data model developed by IBM in the late 1960s to define and process hierarchical databases. The IBM DBMS product IMS is based on DL/I. Although IMS is still in widespread use on mainframes, such databases are being replaced by relational databases.

DML: Data manipulation language. The portion of a data model used to describe the processing of a database.

Domain: (1) The set of all possible values an attribute can have. (2) A description of the format (data type, length) and the semantics (meaning) of an attribute.

Domain/key normal form (DK/NF): A relation in which all constraints are logical consequences of domains and keys.

Download: Copying database data from one computer to another, usually from a mainframe or mini to a microcomputer or LAN.

DSD: See Data structure diagram.

DSS: Decision support system. An interactive, computer-based facility for assisting decision making, especially for semistructured and unstructured problems. Such a system often includes a database and a query/update facility for processing ad hoc requests.

DTM: Distributed transaction manager. In a DDBMS, software that receives processing requests from users or application programs and translates them into DBM requests for actions. A DTM can send requests to DBMs on nodes different from its own.

Encapsulated data: Data contained in a program or object not visible or accessible to other programs or objects.

Encapsulated structure: A portion of an object that is not visible to other objects.

Entity: (1) Something of importance to a user that needs to be represented in a database. (2) In an entity-relationship model, entities are restricted to things that can be represented by a single table. Also see Existence-dependent entity, Strong entity, and Weak entity.

Entity class: A set of entities of the same type, for example, EMPLOYEE and DEPARTMENT.

Entity instance: A particular occurrence of an entity, for example, Employee 100 and the Accounting Department.

Entity-relationship diagram: A graphic used to represent entities and their relationships. Entities are normally shown in squares or rectangles, and relationships are shown in diamonds. The cardinality of the relationship is shown inside the diamond.

Entity-relationship model: The constructs and conventions used to create a model of the users' data (see Data model). The things in the users' world are represented by entities, and the associations among those things are represented by relationships. The results are usually documented in an entity-relationship diagram.

Entry-point relation: Used with regard to the relations representing an object. The entry-point relation is the relation whose key is the same as the key of the object it represents. The entry-point relation is normally the first relation processed. Also, the name of the entry-point relation is normally the same as the name of the object.

Enumerated list: A list of allowed values for a domain, attribute, or column.

Equijoin: The process of joining relation A containing attribute A1 with B containing attribute B1 to form relation C, so that for each row in C, A1 = B1. Both A1 and B1 are represented in C.

E-R diagram: See Entity-relationship diagram.

Exclusive lock: A lock on a data resource that no other transaction can either read or update.

Existence-dependent entity: Same as a weak entity. An entity that cannot appear in the database unless an instance of one or more other entities also appears in the database. A subclass of existence-dependent entities are ID-dependent entities.

Explicit lock: A lock requested by a command from an application program.

Export: A function of the DBMS, to write a file of data in bulk. The file is intended to be read by another DBMS or program.

Extract: A portion of an operational database downloaded to a local area network or microcomputer for local processing. Extracts are created to reduce communications cost and time when querying and creating reports from data created by transaction processing.

Failure transparency: In a distributed database system, the condition in which application programs are isolated from failure.

Field: (1) A logical group of bytes in a record; used with file processing. (2) In the context of a relational model, a synonym for attribute.

File-processing system: An information system in which data is stored in separate files. There is no integrated data dictionary. The format of the files is usually stored in application programs.

File server: In a local area network, a microcomputer containing a file that it processes on behalf of other microcomputers on the network. The term file server is normally used for the resource-sharing architecture. See Client computer, Client–server database architecture, Database server, and Resource-sharing architecture.

First normal form: Any table that fits the definition of a relation.

Flat file: A file that has only a single value in each field. The meaning of the columns is the same in every row.

Force-write: A write of database data in which the DBMS waits for acknowledgment from the operating system that the afterimage of the write has been successfully written to the log.

Foreign key: An attribute that is a key of one or more relations other than the one in which it appears.

Form: (1) A display on a computer screen used to present, enter, and modify data. A form is also called a data entry form or panel. (2) A paper document used in a business system to record data, usually concerning a transaction. Forms are analyzed in the process of building a data model.

Forms generator: A portion of the application development subsystem used to create a data entry form without having to write any application program code.

Formula domain: A domain whose values are computed by an expression containing arguments that are themselves domains.

Fourth normal form: A relation in third Boyce–Codd normal form in which every multivalued dependency is a functional dependency.

Fragment: A row in a table (or record in a file) in which a required parent or child is not present. For example, a row in a LINE-ITEM table for which no ORDER row exists.

Fully concatenated key: In DL/I, a composite of the sequence fields of a segment and the sequence fields of all its parents. The root occupies the leftmost position in the concatenated key, and the segment occupies the rightmost position.

Functional dependency: A relationship between attributes in which one attribute or group of attributes determines the value of another. The expressions $X \rightarrow Y$, "X determines Y," and "Y is functionally dependent on X" mean that given a value of X, we can determine the value of Y.

Generalization hierarchy: A set of objects or entities of the same logical type that are arranged in a hierarchy of logical subtypes. For example, EMPLOYEE has the subtypes ENGINEER and ACCOUNTANT, and ENGINEER has the subtypes ELECTRICAL ENGINEER and MECHANICAL ENGINEER. Subtypes inherit characteristics of their supertypes.

Generalization object: An object that contains subtype objects. The generalization object and its subtypes all have the same key. Subtype objects inherit attributes from the generalization object. A generalization object is also called a supertype object.

Granularity: The size of database resource that can be locked. Locking the entire database is large granularity; locking a column of a particular row is small granularity.

Graphical user interface: An interface having windows, graphical symbols, pop-down menus, and other structures that are often manipulated with a mouse pointer. Popular graphical user interface products are Windows from Microsoft and the Macintosh System Software from Apple.

Group identifier: An attribute that identifies a unique instance of a group within a semantic object or another group.

Growing phase: The first stage in two-phase locking in which locks are acquired but not released.

GUI: See Graphical user interface.

HAS-A relationship: A relationship between two entities or objects that are of different logical types, for example, EMPLOYEE HAS-A(n) AUTO. Contrast this with an IS-A relationship.

Hierarchical data model: A data model that represents all relationships using hierarchies or trees. Network structures must be decomposed into trees before they can be represented by a hierarchial data model. DL/I is the only surviving hierarchical data model.

Hierarchy: See Tree.

Horizontal partition: A subset of a table consisting of complete rows of the table. For example, in a table with ten rows, the first five rows.

Host variable: A variable in an application program into which a DBMS places a value from the database.

Hybrid object: An object containing a multivalued group that contains at least one object attribute.

ID-dependent entity: An entity that cannot logically exist without the existence of another entity. An APPOINTMENT, for example, cannot exist without a CLIENT to make the appointment. The ID-dependent entity always contains the key of the entity on which it depends. Such entities are a subset of a weak entity. See also Strong entity and Weak entity.

Implicit lock: A lock that is automatically placed by the DBMS.

Implied object: An object that exists in the user's mind when he or she requests a report "sorted by x" or "grouped by x." For example, when the user requests all ORDERs sorted by OrderDate, the implied object is the set of all ORDER objects.

Import: A function of the DBMS, to read an entire file of data in bulk.

IMS: Information management system: A transaction-processing system developed and licensed by IBM. It includes IMS/DC, a communications control program, and IMS/DB, a DBMS that implements the DL/I data model.

Inconsistent read problem: An anomaly that occurs in concurrent processing, in which transactions execute a series of reads inconsistent with one another. It can be prevented by two-phase locking and other strategies.

Index: Overhead data used to improve access and sorting performance. Indexes can be constructed for a single column or for groups of columns. They are especially useful for columns used for control breaks in reports and for columns used to specify conditions in joins.

Index space: An area of disk storage in which DB2 stores an index.

Information-bearing set: In the CODASYL DBTG data model, a set in which the relationship between records is not represented in the data values. The relationship, though not visible in the data, is recorded in overhead data created and processed by the DBMS. Contrast this with Non-information-bearing set.

Inheritance: A characteristic of objected-oriented systems whose attributes are obtained from parent objects.

Insane node: A node that fails in an unexpected manner. Such a node may transmit garbage across the network or accidentally transmit invalid transactions that appear valid. Contrast with Byzantine failure and Sane node.

Insertion anomaly: In a relation, the condition that exists when, to add a complete row to a table, one must add facts about two or more logically different themes.

Insertion status: In the CODASYL DBTG model, a rule that determines how records are to be placed into sets. Records can be placed automatically by the DBMS or manually by the application program.

Interrelation constraint: A restriction that requires the value of an attribute in a row of one relation to match the value of an attribute found in another relation. For example, CustNumber in ORDER must equal CustNumber in CUSTOMER.

Intersection: A relational algebra operation performed on two union-compatible relations, A and B, forming a third relation, C, so that C contains only rows that appear in both A and B.

Intersection relation: A relation used to represent a many-to-many relationship. It contains the keys of the relations in the relationship. When used to represent many-to-many compound objects, it has no nonkey data. When used to represent entities having a many-to-many relationship, it may have nonkey data if the relationship contains data.

Intrarelation constraint: A restriction on data values in a relation. For example, in PART (Part , P-name, Units), the rule is that if Part starts with a 1, then Units must equal Pounds.

I/O: Input/output. The process in the operating system that reads and writes data from and to peripheral storage devices.

IS-A relationship: A relationship between two entities or objects of the same logical type. In reference to ENGINEER IS-A(n) EMPLOYEE, both of these entities are employees and are of the same logical type. Contrast this with a HAS-A relationship.

Join: A relational algebra operation on two relations, A and B, that produces a third relation, C. A row of A is concatenated with a row of B to form a new row in C if the rows in A and B meet restrictions concerning their values. For example, A1 is an attribute in A, and B1 is an attribute in B. The join of A with B in which A1 < B1 will result in a relation, C, having the concatenation of rows in A and B in which the value of A1 is less than the value of B1. See Equijoin and Natural join.

Key: (1) A group of one or more attributes identifying a unique row in a relation. Since relations may not have duplicate rows, every relation must have at least one key, which is the composite of all of the attributes in the relation. A key is sometimes called a logical key. (2) With some relational DBMS products, an index on a column used to improve access and sorting speed. It is sometimes called a physical key.

LAN: Local area network. A group of microcomputers connected to one another by means of communications lines in close proximity, usually less than a mile. See Client–server database architecture and Resource-sharing architecture.

LDBR: See Logical data base record.

List box: In a GUI environment, an element of the user interface in which a list of choices is presented in a rectangle. The user moves the cursor to shade the item to be selected from the list.

Location transparency: In a distributed database system, the condition in which application programs do not know and do not need to know where data is located. The DDBMS finds data, wherever it is located, without the involvement of the application program.

Lock: The process of allocating a database resource to a particular transaction in a concurrent-processing system. The size of the resource locked is known as the lock granularity. With an exclusive lock, no other transaction may read or write the resource. With a shared lock, other transactions may read the resource, but no other transaction may write it.

Lock granularity: The size of a locked data element. The lock of a column value of a particular row is a small granularity lock, and the lock of an entire table is a large granularity lock.

Log: A file containing a record of database changes. The log contains before-images and afterimages.

Logical data base (LDB): In DL/I, the collection of all the logical data base records in the data base.

Logical data base record (LDBR): In DL/I, a hierarchy of segments as perceived by an application program. Such a structure may or may not exist physically; it may be taken from other structures using pointers and other overhead data.

Logical key: One or more columns that uniquely determine the row of a table or a record of a file. A synonym for a key. Contrast this with a physical key, which is a synonym for an index.

Logical unit of work: A group of logically related database operations that are performed as a unit. Either all of the operations are performed, or none of them is. A logical unit of work is the same as an atomic transaction. It is a term used with the DBMS DB2.

Look up: The process of obtaining related data by using the value of a foreign key, for example, when processing a row of ORDER (*OrderNumber*, Ord-Date, *CustNumber*, . . .), using the value of CustNumber to obtain the related value of CustName from CUSTOMER (*CustNumber*, CustName, . . .).

Lost update problem: Same as Concurrent update problem.

LUW: See Logical unit of work.

Mask: A format used when presenting data in a form or report.

Materialization: (1) The physical appearance of data in a form or report. (2) The appearance of a view of a semantic object in a form or report.

Maximum cardinality: (a) The maximum number of values that an attribute may have within a semantic object. (b) In a relationship between tables, the maximum number of rows to which a row of one table may relate in the other table.

Member: In the CODASYL DBTG model, a record type that is on the many side of a one-to-many or set relationship.

Menu: A list of options presented to the user of a database (or other) application. The user selects the next action or activity from a list. Actions are restricted to those in the list. Contrast this with Command.

Metadata: Data concerning the structure of data in a database stored in the data dictionary. Metadata is used to describe tables, columns, constraints, indexes, and so forth. Compare this with Application metadata.

Method: A program attached to an object-oriented programming (OOP) object. A method can be inherited by lower-level OOP objects.

Minimum cardinality: (a) The minimum number of values that an attribute may have within a semantic object. (b) In a relationship between tables, the number of rows to which a row of one table may relate in the other table.

Mixed partition: A combination of a horizontal and a vertical partition. For example, in a table with five columns and five rows, the first three columns of the first three rows.

Modeless processing: In a database application, the characteristic of inferring the mode of the user's processing from the user's actions, for example, on entering a key field, if the value exists in the database, inferring that an update is to occur; if the value does not exist in the database, inferring that an insert is to occur.

Modem: Modulator-demodulator. A device used to convert digital signals to analog signals and the reverse. It is most often used to communicate over telephone lines.

Modification anomaly: The situation existing when the storing of one row in a table records two separate facts or when the deletion of one row of a table eliminates two separate facts.

Multivalued attribute: The attribute of a semantic object that has a maximum cardinality greater than one.

Multivalued dependency: A condition in a relation with three or more attributes in which independent attributes appear to have relationships they do not have. Formally, in a relation R (A, B, C), having key (A, B, C) where A is matched with multiple values of B (or of C or both), B does not determine C, and C does not determine B. An example is the relation EMPLOYEE (EmpNumber, Emp-skill, Dependent-name), where an employee can have multiple values of Emp-skill and Dependent-name. Emp-skill and Dependent-name do not have any relationship, but they do appear to in the relation.

Natural join: A join of a relation A having attribute A1 with relation B having attribute B1 where A1 equals B1. The joined relation, C, contains either column A1 or B1 but not both. Contrast this with Equijoin.

Natural language interface: An interface to an application program or DBMS by which users can enter requests in the form of standard English or another human language.

Network data model: A data model supporting at least simple network relationships. The CODASYL DBTG, which supports simple network relationships but not complex relationships, is the most important network data model.

N.M.: An abbreviation for a many-to-many relationship between the rows of two tables.

Node: (1) An entity in a tree. (2) A computer in a distributed processing system.

Non-information-bearing set: In the CODAYSL DBTG model, a set in which the child record type contains the key of the parent record type. The set ownership is implied by the value of the key in the child record instances.

Nonobject attribute: An attribute of a semantic object that is not an object.

Normal form: A rule or set of rules governing the allowed structure of relations. The rules apply to attributes, functional dependencies, multivalued dependencies, domains, and constraints. The most important normal forms are 1NF, 2NF, 3NF, Boyce–Codd NF, 4NF, 5NF, and domain/key normal form.

Normalization: The process of evaluating a relation to determine whether it is in a specified normal form and, if necessary, of converting it to relations in that specified normal form.

Null value: A value that is either unknown or not applicable. A null value is not the same as a zero or blank, although in most commercial DBMS products, null values are represented by zeros or blanks.

Object: (1) A semantic object. (2) A structure in an object-oriented program that contains an encapsulated data structure and data methods. Such objects are arranged in a hierarchy so that objects can inherit methods from their parents. (3) In DB2, a term used to refer to data bases, tables, views, indexes, and other structures. (4) In security systems, a unit of data protected by a password or other means.

Object attribute: An attribute of a semantic object that is itself an object.

Object class: In object-oriented programming, a set of objects with a common structure.

Object class library: In object-oriented programming, a collection of object classes, usually a collection that serves a particular purpose.

Object constructor: In object-oriented programming, a function that creates an object.

Object destructor: In object-oriented programming, a function that destroys an object.

Object diagram: A portrait-oriented rectangle that represents the structure of a semantic object.

Object identifier: An attribute that is used to specify an object instance. Object identifiers can be unique, meaning that they identify one (and only one) instance, or nonunique, meaning that they identify exactly one object instance.

Object instance: The occurrence of a particular semantic object, for example, the SALESPERSON semantic object having LastName equal to Jones.

Object persistence: In object-oriented programming, the characteristic that an object can be saved to nonvolatile memory, such as a disk. Persistent objects exist between executions of a program.

Object view: The portion of a semantic object that is visible to a particular application. A view consists of the name of the semantic object plus a list of the attributes visible in that view.

1:N: An abbreviation for a one-to-many relationship between the rows of two tables.

Option button: In a GUI environment, an element of the user interface in which the user can select an item from a list. Clicking on one button de-selects the button currently pressed (if any). It operates like the radio buttons on a car radio and in fact is the same as a radio button (see Radio button) but was introduced under a different name to avoid litigation among vendors.

Orphan: Any row (record) that is missing its parent in a mandatory one-to-many relationship.

Overhead data: Metadata created by the DBMS to improve performance, for example, indexes and linked lists.

Owner: (1) In the CODASYL DBTG model, a record type that is on the one side of a one-to-many or set relationship. (2) In data administration, the department or other organizational unit in charge of the management of a particular data item. An owner can also be called a data proponent.

Page: A unit of disk storage. In DB2, a 4K block of contiguous disk space used to hold the database, data dictionary, and overhead data.

Paired attribute: In a semantic object, object attributes are paired. If object A has an object attribute of object B, then object B will have an object attribute of object A; that is, the object attributes are paired with each other.

Panel: A display on a computer screen used to present, enter, and modify data. It is the same as a form.

Parent: A row, record, or node on the one side of a one-to-many relationship.

Partition: (1) A portion of a distributed database. (2) The portion of a network that is separated from the rest of the network during a network failure.

Partitioned table space: In DB2, a table space that holds data for exactly one table.

PDBR: See Physical data base record.

Perfect node: A node that never fails. Such nodes exist only theoretically and are used only in the study of failure/recovery techniques.

Pervasive key: In a database application, a key that performs the same function throughout the application. The meaning of the key always remains the same.

Physical data base record (PDBR): In DL/I, a hierarchy of segments stored in data base files.

Physical key: A column that has an index or other data structure created for it. A synonym for an index. Such structures are created to improve searching and sorting on the column values.

PL/I: Programming language I. A third-generation programming language marketed by IBM.

Pointer: An address to an instance of a data structure. The address of a record often is in a directly addressed file.

Polymorphism: The situation in which one name can be used to invoke different functionalities, depending on the object that invokes the name.

Pop-down list box: In a GUI environment, the list box that appears when the user selects an icon that represents that box.

Precompiler: A program that translates the database access commands of a particular DBMS product. Such commands are embedded in an application program normally written in a third-generation language. The commands are translated into data structures and calls to DBMS-processing routines in the syntax of the third-generation language.

Primary key: A candidate key selected to be the key of a relation.

Processing-interface subsystem: The portion of the DBMS routines that executes commands for processing the database. It accepts input from interactive query programs and from application programs written in standard languages or in DBMS-specific languages.

Processing rights and responsibilities: Organizational policies regarding which groups can take which actions on specified data-items or other collections of data.

Product: A relational operation on two relations, A and B, producing a third relation, C, with C containing the concatenation of every row in A with every row in B. It is the same as a Cartesian product.

Program/data independence: The condition existing when the structure of the data is not defined in application programs. Rather, it is defined in the database, and then the application programs obtain it from the DBMS. In this way, changes can be made in the data structures that may not necessarily be made in the application programs.

Projection: A relational algebra operation performed on a relation, A, that results in a relation, B, where B has a (possibly improper) subset of the attributes of A. Projection is used to form a new relation that reorders the attributes in the original relation or to form a new relation that has only some of the attributes from the original relation.

Property: Same as an Attribute.

Proponent: See Data proponent.

Prototype: A quickly developed demonstration of an application or portion of an application.

QBE: Query by example. A style of query interface, first developed by IBM but now used by other vendors, that allows users to express queries by providing examples of the results they seek.

Query/update language: A language that can be employed by end users to query the database and to make changes in the database data.

R*: An experimental distributed database management system developed by IBM. It allows the database to be partitioned but not replicated.

Radio button: In a GUI environment, an element of the user interface in which the user can select one item from a list. Clicking on one button de-selects the button currently pressed (if any). It operates like the radio buttons on a car radio.

Read–write conflict: The situation in which two actions operate on the same data item. One of the actions is a read, and the other is a write.

Real output: Output transmitted to the client of an information system, such as an order confirmation. When produced in error, such outputs cannot be changed by recovering the database. Instead, compensating transactions must be executed.

Record: (1) A group of fields pertaining to the same entity; used in file-processing systems. (2) In a relational model, a synonym for row and tuple.

Recursive relationship: A relationship among entities, objects, or rows of the same type. For example, if CUSTOMERs refer other CUSTOMERs, the relationship *refers* is recursive.

Referential integrity constraint: The condition in a database in which all interrelation constraints are satisfied.

Relation: Same as a table. A two-dimensional array containing single-valued entries and no duplicate rows. The meaning of the columns is the same in every row. The order of the rows and columns is immaterial.

Relational database: A database consisting of relations. Usually such a database is structured according to the principles of normalization, although in practice, relational databases contain relations with duplicate rows. Most DBMS products include a feature that removes duplicate rows when necessary and appropriate. Such a removal is not done as a matter of course because it can be time-consuming and expensive.

Relational data model: A data model in which data is stored in relations and relationships between rows are represented by data values.

Relational schema: A set of relations with interrelation constraints.

Relationship: An association between two entities, objects, or rows of relations.

Replicated data: In a distributed database, data that is stored on two or more computers.

Replication transparency: In a distributed database system, the condition in which application programs do not know and do not need to know whether data is replicated. If it is replicated, the DDBMS will ensure that all copies are updated consistently, without the involvement of the application program.

Report: An extraction of data from a database. Reports can be printed, displayed on a computer screen, or stored as a file. A report is part of a database application. Compare this with a Form.

Report band: See Band.

Resource locking: See Lock.

Resource-sharing architecture: The structure of a local area network in which one microcomputer performs file-processing services for other microcomputers. In a database application, each user computer contains a copy of the DBMS that forwards input/output requests to the file server. Only file I/O is processed by the file server; all database activities are processed by the DBMS on the user's computer.

Retention status: In the CODASYL DBTG model, a rule that states whether or not a record must exist in a set. If FIXED, a record may never be removed from its original set. If MANDATORY, a record must be a member of a set once it is placed into a set. If OPTIONAL, a record may or may not reside in a set.

Rollback: The process of recovering a database in which beforeimages are applied to the database to return to an earlier checkpoint or other point at which the database is logically consistent.

Rollforward: The process of recovering a database by applying afterimages to a saved copy of the database to bring it to a checkpoint or other point at which the database is logically consistent.

Root: The top record, row, or node in a tree. A root has no parent.

Row: A group of columns in a table. All the columns in a row pertain to the same entity. A row is the same as a tuple and a record.

Run-unit: In the CODASYL DBTG model, the execution of an application program by a user. Several run-units may use the same application program concurrently.

Sane node: A node that fails only in a known and anticipated fashion.

Schedule: In a distributed database system, an ordered sequence of data requests.

Schema: A complete logical view of the database.

Screen: See Form.

Second normal form: A relation in first normal form in which all nonkey attributes are dependent on all of the key.

Segment: In DL /I, a collection of fields that is a node in a data base record.

Segment search argument: An expression in a DL /I that indicates the segment or segments to which the command is to be applied.

Selection: A relational algebra operation performed on a relation, A, producing a relation, B, with B containing only the rows in A that meet the restrictions specified in the selection.

Semantic object diagram: Same as Object diagram.

Semantic object model: The constructs and conventions used to create a model of the users' data. The things in the users' world are represented by semantic objects (sometimes called objects). Relationships are modeled in the objects, and the results are usually documented in object diagrams.

Semantic object view: The portion of a semantic object that is visible in a form or report.

Sequence field: In DL/I, a field that is used to order logically the segments of a given type under a given parent. The order can be ascending or descending.

Serializable: A condition pertaining to two or more transactions in which the results of the processing are the same as they would have been if the transactions had been processed in some serial manner.

Set: In the CODASYL DBTG model, a structure that represents a one-to-many relationship among records. The parent record type is called the set owner, and the child record type(s) is called the set member.

Set membership: In the CODASYL DBTG model, the records that belong to a particular set instance.

Shared lock: A lock against a data resource in which only one transaction may update the data, but many transactions can concurrently read that data.

Shrinking phase: In two-phase locking, the stage at which locks are released but no lock is acquired.

Sibling: A record or node that has the same parent as does another record or node.

Simple network: (1) A set of three relations and two relationships in which one of the relations, R, has a many-to-one relationship with the other two relations. The rows in R have two parents, and the parents are of different types. (2) Any set of tables and relationships containing the structure defined in (1).

Simple object: An object that contains no repeating attributes and no object attributes.

Simple table space: In DB2, a table space that contains data from more than one table.

Single-valued attribute: In a semantic object, an attribute having a maximum cardinality of one.

Special register: In the CODASYL DBTG model, an indicator of some aspect of the status of the database.

SQL: Structured query language. A language for defining the structure and processing of a relational database. It is used as a stand-alone query language, or it may be embedded in application programs. SQL is accepted as a national standard by the American National Standards Institute. It was developed by IBM.

Storage group: In DB2, a group of disk volumes on which database data is stored.

Strong entity: In an entity-relationship model, any entity whose existence in the database does not depend on the existence of any other entity. See also ID-dependent entity and Weak entity.

Subschema: A subset of a database that is processed by one or more applications. A subschema may also be called an application view; it is used primarily with the CODASYL DBTG model.

Subtype: In generalization hierarchies, an entity or object that is a subspecies or subcategory of a higher-level type. For example, ENGINEER is a subtype of EMPLOYEE.

Supertype: In generalization hierarchies, an entity or object that logically contains subtypes. For example, EMPLOYEE is a supertype of ENGINEER, ACCOUNTANT, and MANAGER.

Surrogate Key: A column of unique values that is maintained by the application or the DBMS. This column is used as the primary key of the table.

System set: In the CODASYL DBTG model, a set that is owned by the DBMS. It is used for the sequential processing of all the records of a given type.

Table space: In DB2, a collection of one or more VSAM data sets, or files, used to store database data on magnetic disk.

Third normal form: A relation in second normal form that has no transitive dependencies.

Top-down database design: The design of a database that works from the general to the specific. The resulting database can serve an organization's overall needs; the danger is that it may never be completed. See Bottom-up database design.

Transaction: (1) An atomic transaction. (2) The record of an event in the business world.

Transaction node: In a distributed database system, a computer that processes a distributed transaction manager.

Transform-oriented language: A data sublanguage such as SQL that provides commands and capabilities to transform a set of relations into a new relation.

Transitive dependency: In a relation having at least three attributes, R (A, B, C), the situation in which A determines B, B determines C, but B does not determine A.

Transparency: The hiding, from a system user, of the existence of some problem or characteristic.

Tree: A collection of records, entities, or other data structures in which each element has at most one parent, except for the top element, which has no parent.

Trigger: A procedure invoked when a specified condition exists in the data of a database. For example, when Quantity-on-Hand of an item reaches zero (or some specified amount), a procedure can be triggered to order more of the item.

Tuple: Same as Row.

Twin: A record or node that has the same parent as does another record or node.

Two-phase commitment: In a distributed database system, a process of commitment among nodes in which the nodes first vote on whether they can commit a transaction. If all the nodes vote yes, the transaction is committed. If any node votes no, the transaction is aborted. A two-phase commitment is required to prevent inconsistent processing in distributed databases.

Two-phase locking: The procedure by which locks are obtained and released in two phases. During the growing phase, the locks are obtained, and during the shrinking phase, the locks are released. Once a lock is released, no other lock will be granted that transaction. Such a procedure ensures consistency in database updates in a concurrent-processing environment.

Union: A relational algebra operation performed on two union-compatible relations, say A and B, forming a third relation, say C, with C containing every row in both A and B, minus any duplicate rows.

Union compatible: The condition in which two tables have the same number of attributes and the attributes in corresponding columns arise from the same domain.

Union incompatible: The condition in which either two tables have a different number of attributes or the attributes in corresponding columns arise from different domains.

User view: A particular user's view of a database.

User working area (UWA): In the CODASYL DBTG model, the area of main memory that contains data values pertaining to a particular run-unit.

UWA: See User work area.

VAR: Value-added reseller. A person, company, or group that develops database applications and sells them to other companies. The VAR adds value to the DBMS product by building the application.

Vertical partition: A subset of the columns of a table. For example, in a table with ten columns, the first five columns.

View: (1) The subset of a database that can be processed by an application. (2) An object view.

Weak entity: In an entity-relationship model, an entity whose existence in the database depends on the existence of another entity. See also ID-dependent entity and Strong entity.

Write–write conflict: The situation in which two write actions operate on the same data item.

WYSIWIG: What you see is what you get. A term used with form and report generators, in which the DBMS recreates exactly what the developer types on the screen while developing forms and reports.

Bibliography

Agostic, M., & R. G. Johnson. "A Framework of Reference for Database Design." *ACM Data Base* 15 (Summer 1984): 3–9.

Aho, A. V., E. Hopcroft, & J. D. Ullman. *The Design and Analysis of Computer Programs.* Reading, MA: Addison-Wesley, 1975.

ANSI X3. *American National Standard for Information Systems—Database Language—SQL.* ANSI, 1992.

Astrahan, M. M., et al. "A History and Evaluation of System R." *IBM Research Report* RJ2843, June 1980.

Astrahan, M. M., et al. "System R: Relational Approach to Database Management." *Transactions on Database Systems* 1 (June 1976).

Astrahan, M. M., et al. "System R: A Relational Database Management System." *Computer* 12 (May 1979).

Atre, S. *Data Base: Structured Techniques for Design, Performance, and Management.* New York: Wiley, 1980.

Banerjee, J. "Data Model Issues for Object-oriented Applications." *ACM Transactions on Office Information Systems* 5 (January 1987).

Bernstein, P. A., & N. Goodman. "An Algorithm for Concurrency Control and Recovery in Replicated Distributed Databases." *Transactions on Database Systems* 9 (December 1984).

Bernstein, P. A., & N. Goodman. "Concurrency Control in Distributed Database Systems." *Computing Surveys* 13 (June 1981).

Bernstein, P. A., J. B. Rothnie, & D. W. Shipman. *Distributed Data Base Management.* IEEE Catalog no. EHO 141-2, 1978.

Blaha, M., W. J. Premerlani, & J. E. Rumbaugh. "Relational Database Design Using an Object-oriented Methodology." *Communications of the ACM* 31 (April 1988): 414–427.

Blasgen, M. W., et al. "System R: An Architectural Overview." *IBM Systems Journal* 20 (January 1981).

Boulanger, D., & S. T. March. "An Approach to Analyzing the Information Content of Existing Databases." *ACM Data Base* 20 (Summer 1989): 1–8.

Boyce, R. F., et al. "Specifying Queries as Relational Expressions: SQUARE." *Communications of the ACM* 18 (November 1975).

Bray, O. H. *Distributed Database Management Systems.* Lexington, MA: Lexington Books, 1982.

Browning, D. "Data Managers and LANs." *PC Tech Journal* 5 (May 1987).

Carlson, D. A., & S. Ram. "An Architecture for Distributed Knowledge Based Systems." *ACM Data Base* 22 (Winter–Spring 1991).

Cashing, D. L. *A Programmer's Guide to File Processing.* PWS-Kent, 1991.

Chamberlin, D. D., et al. "SEQUEL 2: A Unified Approach to Data Definition, Manipulation, and Control." *IBM Journal of Research and Development* 20 (November 1976).

Chen, P. *Entity-Relationship Approach to Information Modeling.* E-R Institute, 1981.

Chen, P. *The Entity-Relationship Approach to Logical Data Base Design.* QED Information Sciences, Data Base Monograph Series no. 6, 1977.

Chen, P. "The Entity-Relationship Model: Toward a Unified View of Data." *ACM Transactions on Database Systems* 1 (March 1976).

Chouinard, P. "Domains, Datatypes, and Documentation." *Database Programming and Design*, March 1993, pp. 62–66.

Chu, W. W., & P. P. Chen. *Centralized and Distributed Data Base Systems.* IEEE Catalog no. EHO 154-5, 1979.

CODASYL. *Data Base Task Group Report, 1971.* Association for Computing Machinery, 1975.

CODASYL COBOL Committee. *COBOL Journal of Development,* 1978.

CODASYL Data Description Language Committee. *DDL Journal of Development,* 1978.

Codd, E. F. "Extending the Relational Model to Capture More Meaning." *Transaction on Database Systems* 4 (December 1979).

Codd, E. F. "Relational Database: A Practical Foundation for Productivity." *Communications of the ACM* 25 (February 1982).

Codd, E. F. "A Relational Model of Data for Large Shared Databanks." *Communications of the ACM* 13 (June 1970).

Date, C. J. *An Introduction to Database Systems.* 5th ed. Reading, MA: Addison-Wesley, 1990.

Davidson, S. B. "Optimism and Consistency in Partitioned Distributed Database Systems." *Transactions on Database Systems* 9 (September 1984).

Davidson, S. B., H. Garcia-Molina, & D. Skeen. "Consistency in Partitioned Networks." *Computing Surveys* 17 (September 1985).

Embley, D. W. "NFQL: The Natural Forms Query Language." *ACM Transactions on Database Systems* 14 (June 1989): 168–211.

Eswaran, K. P., J. N. Gray, R. A. Lorie, & I. L. Traiger. "The Notion of Consistency and Predicate Locks in a Database System." *Communications of the ACM* 19 (November 1976).

Ewing, J. J. "An Object-oriented Operating System Interface." *Conference Proceedings from the Object-oriented Programming Systems, Languages and Applications, ACM SIGPLAN* 21 (November 1986).

Fagin, R. "Multivalued Dependencies and a New Normal Form for Relational Databases." *Transactions on Database Systems* 2 (September 1977).

Fagin, R. "A Normal Form for Relational Databases That Is Based on Domains and Keys." *Transactions on Database Systems* 6 (September 1981).

Fernandez, E. B., R. C. Summers, & C. Wood. *Database Security and Integrity.* Reading, MA: Addison-Wesley, 1981.

Flavin, M. *Fundamental Concepts of Information Modeling.* New York: Yourdon Press, 1981.

Freedman, D. P., & G. M. Weinberg. *Walkthroughs, Inspections, and Technical Reviews.* 3rd ed. Boston: Little, Brown, 1982.

Garcia-Molina, H., F. Pittelli, & S. Davidson. "Applications of Byzantine Agreement in Database Systems." *Transactions on Database Systems* 11 (March 1986).

Garnto, C., & H. J. Watson. "An Investigation of Database Requirements for Institutional and Ad Hoc DSS." *ACM Data Base* 16 (Summer 1985): 3–9.

Gray, J., et al. "The Recovery Manager of the System R Database Manager." *Computing Surveys* 13 (June 1981).

Hammer, M., & D. McLeod. "Database Description with SDM: A Semantic Database Model." *Transactions on Database Systems* 6 (September 1981).

Hammer, M., & D. Shipman. "Reliability Mechanisms for SDD-1: A System for Distributed Databases." *Transactions on Database Systems* 5 (December 1980).

Herlihy, M. "Dynamic Quorum Adjustment for Partitioned Data." *Transactions on Database Systems* 12 (June 1987).

Higa, K., & O. R. Liu Sheng. "An Object-oriented Methodology for Database/Knowledgebase Coupling: An Implementation of the Structured Entity Model in Nexpert System." *ACM Data Base* 20 (Spring 1989): 24–29.

Honkanen, P. "The Integrity Problem, and What Can Be Done About It Using Today's DBMSs." *ACM Data Base* 20 (Fall 1989): 21–27.

IBM Corporation. *IBM Database 2 Concepts and Facilities Guide.* IBM Document GG24-1582.

IBM Corporation. *IBM Database 2 Relational Concepts.* IBM Document GG24-1581.

IBM Corporation. *IBM Database 2 SQL Usage Guide.* IBM Document GG24-1583.

IBM Corporation. *SQL/Data System Application Programming.* IBM Document SH24-5018-1.

IBM Corporation. *SQL/Data System General Information.* IBM Document GH24-5012-0.

IBM Corporation. *SQL/Data System Planning and Administration.* IBM Document SH24-5014-1.

Iivari, J. "Object-oriented Information Systems Analysis." *Proceedings of the Twenty-fourth Annual Hawaii International Conference on Systems Sciences.* New York: IEEE Computer Society Press, 1990, vol. 2, pp. 205–218.

Jackson, M. A. *Principles of Program Design.* New York: Academic Press, 1975.

Kim, W. "On Optimizing an SQL-like Nested Query." *Transactions on Database Systems* 7 (September 1982).

Knuth, D. E. *The Art of Computer Programming: Fundamental Algorithms.* Reading, MA: Addison-Wesley, 1968.

Knuth, D. E. *The Art of Computer Programming: Sorting and Searching.* Reading, MA: Addison-Wesley, 1973.

Kulkarni, U. R., & H. K. Jain. "Using Semantic Knowledge in Partitioning and Allocation of Data in Distributed Databases." *Proceedings of the Twenty-fourth Annual Hawaii International Conference on Systems Sciences.* New York: IEEE Computer Society Press, 1990, vol. 2, pp. 146–154.

Kydd, C. T. "Understanding the Information Content of MIS Management Tools." *MIS Quarterly,* September 1989.

Lamport, L. "Time, Clocks, and the Ordering of Events in a Distributed System." *Communications of the ACM* 21 (July 1978).

Litwin, W., & A. Abdellatif. "Multidatabase Interoperability." *Computer* 19 (December 1986).

Lum, V. Y., P. S. T. Yuen, & M. Dodd. "Key to Address Transform Techniques: A Fundamental Performance Study on Large Existing Formatted Files." *Communications of the ACM* 14 (April 1971).

Lyon, J. K. *The Database Administrator.* New York: Wiley, 1976.

Maier, D., P. Nordquist, & M. Grossman. "Displaying Database Objects." *Proceedings of the 1st International Conference on Expert Database Systems.* Menlo Park, CA: Benjamin-Cummings, 1985.

Maier, D., J. Stein, A. Otis, & A. Purdy. "Development of an Object-oriented DBMS." *Conference Proceedings from the Object-oriented Programming Systems, Languages and Applications, ACM SIGPLAN* 21 (November 1986).

Mohan, C., B. Lindsay, & R. Obermarck. "Transaction Management in the R* Distributed Database Management System." *Transactions on Database Systems* 11 (December 1986).

Moriarty, T. "Business Rule Analysis." *Database Programming and Design,* April 1993, pp. 66–69.

Moriarty, T. "Losing the Business." *Database Programming and Design,* June 1993, pp. 66–69.

Nolan, R. L. *Managing the Data Resource Function.* St. Paul: West Publishing, 1974.

Oracle Corporation. *ORACLE.* Oracle Corporation, 1991.

Orenstein, J. A. "Spatial Query Processing in an Object-oriented Database System." *ACM SIGMOD International Conference on Management of Data, 1986* 15 (June 1986).

Orr, K. T. *Structured Requirements Definition.* Kansas City, MO: Ken Orr & Associates, 1981.

Orr, K. T. *Structured Systems Development.* New York: Yourdon Press, 1977.

Ozsu, M. T., & P. Valduriez. *Principles of Distributed Database Systems.* Englewood Cliffs, NJ: Prentice-Hall, 1990.

Page-Jones, M. *The Practical Guide to Structured Systems Design.* New York: Yourdon Press, 1980.

Potter, W. D., & R. P. Trueblood. "Traditional, Semantic, and Hyper-Semantic Approaches to Data Modeling." *IEEE Computer,* June 1988, pp. 53–63.

Rasmus, D. W., "Merging Objects and Knowledge Bases." *Object Magazine,* May–June 1993, pp. 36–37.

Reisner, P. "Human Factor Studies of Database Query Languages: A Survey and Assessment." *Computing Surveys* 13 (March 1981).

Schaeffer, H. *Data Center Operations.* Englewood Cliffs, NJ: Prentice-Hall, 1981.

Shipman, D. "The Functional Data Model and the Data Language DAPLEX." *ACM Transactions on Database Systems* 6 (January 1987).

Skarra, A. H., & S. B. Zdonik. "The Management of Changing Types in an Object-oriented Database." *Conference Proceedings from the Object-oriented Programming Systems, Languages and Applications, ACM SIGPLAN* 21 (November 1986).

Stonebraker, M., ed. *Readings in Database Systems.* San Francisco: Morgan Kaufmann, 1988.

Stonebraker, M. R., et al. "The Design and Implementation of INGRES." *Transactions on Database Systems* 1 (September 1976).

Sybase Corporation. *SYBASE SQL Server: Technical Overview.* Sybase Corporation, 1989.

Thomson, D., "Interfacing Objects with the Relational DBMS." *Database Programming and Design,* August 1993, pp. 33–41.

Traiger, I. L., J. Gray, C. A. Galtieri, & B. G. Lindsay. "Transactions and Consistency in Distributed Database Systems." *Transactions on Database Systems* 7 (September 1982).

Tsichritzis, D. C., & F. H. Lochovsky. *Data Models.* Englewood Cliffs, NJ: Prentice-Hall, 1982.

Ullman, J. D. *Principles of Database Systems.* New York: IEEE Computer Science Press, 1980.

Vetter, M., & R. N. Maddison. *Database Design Methodology.* Englewood Cliffs, NJ: Prentice-Hall International, 1981.

Warnier, J. D. *Logical Construction of Systems.* New York: Van Nostrand Reinhold, 1981.

Weinberg, V. *Structured Analysis.* New York: Yourdon Press, 1978.

Wellesley Software. *Learning SQL.* Englewood Cliffs, NJ: Prentice-Hall, 1991.

Welty, C., & D. W. Stemple. "Human Factors Comparison of a Procedural and a Nonprocedural Query Language." *Transactions on Database Systems* 6 (December 1981).

Wiederhold, G. "Views, Objects, and Databases." *Computer* 19 (December 1986).

Woelk, D., W. Kim, & W. Luther. "An Object-oriented Approach to Multi-Media Databases." *ACM SIGMOD International Conference on Management of Data, 1986* 15 (June 1986).

Yourdon, E., & L. L. Constantine. *Structured Design.* Englewood Cliffs, NJ: Prentice-Hall, 1979.

Zaniolo, C., & M. A. Melkanoff. "A Formal Approach to the Definition and the Design of Conceptual Schemata for Database Systems." *Transactions on Database Systems* 7 (March 1982).

Zdonik, S. B., & D. Maier, eds. *Reading in Object-oriented Database Systems.* San Francisco: Morgan Kaufmann, 1990.

Zhao, L., & S. A. Robers. "An Object-oriented Data Model for Database Modeling, Implementation and Access." *Computer Journal* 31 (February 1988): 116–124.

Zloof, M. M. "Query by Example." *Proceedings of the National Computer Conference, AFIPS* 44 (May 1975).

INDEX